Hardening
Linux

JAMES TURNBULL

Hardening Linux

Copyright © 2005 by James Turnbull

ISBN (pbk): 1-59059-444-4

Printed and bound in the United States of America 9 8 7 6 5 4 3 2 1

Lead Editor: Jim Sumser

Technical Reviewer: Judith Myerson

Editorial Board: Steve Anglin, Dan Appleman, Ewan Buckingham, Gary Cornell, Tony Davis, Jason Gilmore, Chris Mills, Dominic Shakeshaft, Jim Sumser

Project Manager: Kylie Johnston

Copy Edit Manager: Nicole LeClerc

Copy Editor: Kim Wimpsett

Production Manager: Kari Brooks-Copony

Production Editor: Kelly Winquist

Compositor: Linda Weidemann

Proofreader: Lori Bring

Indexer: Kevin Broccoli

Artist: Kinetic Publishing Services, LLC

Cover Designer: Kurt Krames

Manufacturing Manager: Tom Debolski

Distributed to the book trade in the United States by Springer-Verlag New York, Inc., 233 Spring Street, 6th Floor, New York, NY 10013, and outside the United States by Springer-Verlag GmbH & Co. KG, Tiergartenstr. 17, 69112 Heidelberg, Germany.

In the United States: phone 1-800-SPRINGER, fax 201-348-4505, e-mail orders@springer-ny.com, or visit http://www.springer-ny.com. Outside the United States: fax +49 6221 345229, e-mail orders@springer.de, or visit http://www.springer.de.

For information on translations, please contact Apress directly at 2560 Ninth Street, Suite 219, Berkeley, CA 94710. Phone 510-549-5930, fax 510-549-5939, e-mail info@apress.com, or visit http://www.apress.com.

The source code for this book is available to readers at http://www.apress.com in the Downloads section.

For Lucinda, who put up with having an absentee husband
for many months and without whose love and support
I would not have been able to write this book.

For my grandparents, Alice and Jim Turnbull,
whose love and support is greatly missed.

Contents at a Glance

Contents

About the Author

JAMES TURNBULL is an IT&T security consultant at the Commonwealth Bank of Australia. He is an experienced infrastructure architect with a background in Linux/Unix, AS/400, Windows, and storage systems. He has been involved in security consulting, infrastructure security design, SLA and support services design, and business application support.

About the Technical Reviewer

JUDITH MYERSON is a systems architect and engineer. Areas of interest include middleware technologies, enterprise-wide systems, database technologies, application development, server/network management, security, firewall technologies, and project management.

Acknowledgments

Mark Chandler, for his friendship and technical assistance during the writing of this book. Nate Campi, for providing syslog-NG, SEC, and logging information.

Introduction

This book is a technical guide to hardening and securing Linux hosts and some of the common applications used on Linux hosts. It provides information on how to harden the base Linux operating system, including firewalling and securing connections to your hosts. It also looks at hardening and securing some of the applications commonly run on Linux hosts, such as e-mail, IMAP/POP, FTP, and DNS.

No single book on security, even a book on the security of a single operating system, will ever answer all the security questions or address all the possible threats. This book is about providing risk mitigation and minimization. I have set out to identify risks associated with running Linux and some of the applications that run on Linux hosts. I have then provided technical solutions—backed by frequent examples, code, and commands—that minimize, mitigate, or in some circumstances negate those risks. The configurations and examples I provide are designed to ensure your Linux hosts are hardened against attack while not limiting the functionality available to your users.

So why should you care about security? The answer to this is simple—because a significant portion of businesses today rely heavily on the security of their IT assets. To use a metaphor: running a computer host is like owning a house. When Unix-flavored operating systems and TCP/IP networking were in their infancy, it was like owning a house in a small country town. The emphasis was on making it easy for people to cooperate and communicate. People left their doors open and did not mind other people exploring their houses or borrowing a cup of sugar. You probably did not really keep anything too valuable in your house, and if you did, people respected it. Your neighborhood was friendly, everyone knew everyone else, and you trusted your neighbors. Your local neighborhood "hacker" was someone who showed expertise with programming, systems, or telecommunications. Security was a secondary consideration, if it was considered at all.

Times have changed. Now the little country town has a big interstate running right through it. You need to lock up your house, install a burglar alarm, and put up a big fence. Your neighbors have become considerably unfriendlier, and instead of borrowing a cup of sugar, they are more interested in stealing your DVD player or burning your house down. Additionally, the items you store in your house now have considerably more value to you, in terms of both their financial cost and their importance to you. Worse, your local neighborhood "hacker" has morphed into a variety of bad guys with skills ranging from the base to the brilliant.

Note I do not like the term *hacker* to describe the people who attack your hosts. The term still has ambiguities associated with it, and its usage to describe attackers is not 100 percent accurate. Throughout this book I use the term *attacker* to describe the people who threaten your hosts and applications.

Many people scoff at IT security. They claim IT security professionals are paranoid and are overstating the threat. Are we paranoid? Yes, probably we are. Is this paranoia justified? We believe so; in fact, a common refrain in the IT security industry is "Are we being paranoid enough?" IT assets have become absolutely critical to the functioning of most businesses, both large and small. They have also become the repositories of highly valuable commercial, research, customer, and financial information. The guys in the white hats are not the only ones who have noticed the increase in importance of IT assets and the increase in value of the information they contain. The guys in the black hats know exactly how important IT assets are. They know how much damage they can do and how much they can gain from attacking, penetrating, and compromising those assets.

The IT security skeptics claim that the threat of these attackers is overstated. They state that the vast majority of attackers are unskilled, use collections of prepackaged tools that exploit known vulnerabilities, and are no threat to most of your assets. That these make up a significant portion of attacks is indeed true. Take a look at your Internet-facing firewall or IDS logs, and you will see a considerable volume of attacks on your hosts with the patterns or signatures of automated attack tools. Does this lessen the threat to your hosts? Yes, sometimes. It can be easier to defend against the less-skilled attacker using a prepackaged tool. The vulnerabilities exploited by these tools and how to fix them are usually well-documented or can be easily patched. But if you do not know about the vulnerability or have not applied the patch, then an attacker using an automated or prepackaged attack tool becomes the same level of threat as a brilliant attacker with a hand-coded attack tool.

The danger posed by these unskilled attackers has also increased. New vulnerabilities are discovered daily. Exploits are frequently built on these vulnerabilities within hours of them being discovered. Some vulnerabilities are not even discovered until someone uses them to exploit a host. This means pre-packaged attack tools are often available to exploit a vulnerability before the application developer or vendor has even released a patch. The combination of the speed with which new methods of attack spread and the diminishing gap between the discovery of a vulnerability and the development of an exploit means the risk that one of these attacks gets through is significantly increased if you are not being vigilant. You must take serious, consistent, and systematic precautions to secure your hosts.

In addition to the vast majority of unskilled attackers, a smaller group of skilled attackers exists. These are either intelligent and cunning outsiders or internal staff with in-house knowledge. These attackers also pose a serious threat to your hosts, and you need to ensure that your hosts are protected from them, too. This requires that your hosts be hardened and locked down to ensure that only activities that you have authorized using functionality you have approved and installed are conducted.

To return to the metaphor of an IT asset as a house, securing your host is a bit like having home insurance. You hope you do not need it, but you would be foolish not to have it. Do not underestimate the potential damage an attacker can cause or envisage these threats as being somehow hypothetical. For example, imagine the response if you asked the staff of your organization to go without e-mail for a week? This happened to many organizations during the Netsky, Sobig, and Mimail virus attacks. Or imagine if your customers were denied access to your e-commerce site as happened to Amazon, eBay, and Yahoo as the result of Distributed Denial of Service (DDoS) attacks in 1999, 2000, and 2001. Or imagine if an attacker penetrated your hosts and stole your organization's bank account detail, the numbers of its corporate credit cards, or, worse, the credit card numbers of your customers.

You can see that the potential cost of attacks on IT assets is high. There is a potential monetary cost to your organization from theft, loss of revenue, or productivity. There is also a potential public relations cost through loss of customer or industry confidence. You need to understand how to simply, consistently, and practically secure your IT environment. For your Linux hosts and applications, this book provides this practical understanding.

▓**Note** In a later section of this introduction, "Basic Security Tenets," I talk broadly about some basic security tenets and theory. This should provide a basic understanding of IT security theory. I recommend you read more widely in this area.

Who Should Read This Book?

This book is aimed at people who are new to security but who are not entirely new to Linux. This includes system administrators and engineers, security administrators, and IT managers. This is not a book for absolute beginners. I provide real-world examples of configurations, commands, and scenarios that will help you harden and secure your Linux hosts. While doing this, I try to explain in as much detail as possible to accommodate systems administrators of varying skills. But I do expect that readers are at least familiar with basic to intermediate Linux operations and systems administration.

I recommend you understand the following:

- Basic file manipulation (editors, grep, and so on)

- Basic file permissions and ownership

- Basic user administration

- Package management including some knowledge of compiling source packages

- Basic understanding of init and init scripts

- Basic networking including IP addressing, subnets, and administering network resources using the command line

- Basic storage management: partitions, mounting and unmounting, and devices

The book is also designed to be used by those setting up new hosts in addition to people seeking to harden and existing hosts. Thus, it covers addressing security vulnerabilities from scratch, but you can also take the instructions and examples provided in this book and apply them selectively to harden portions of your existing hosts and applications.

■**Note** One of the topics I do not cover in this book is Web serving, specifically Apache. For this I recommend another book in this series, *Hardening Apache* (Apress, 2004) by Tony Mobily, for the complete picture on installing, configuring, and running secure Apache servers.[1] In the limited space available in this book, I could not do this complicated and extensive topic justice.

How This Book Is Structured

This book covers the following topics:

Chapter 1, "Hardening the Basics," covers the basics of hardening your Linux hosts. It introduces the core security features of the Linux operating system and kernel and provides information and examples on how to harden them. It also covers patching and updating your hosts and how to keep up-to-date with the latest security-related information for Linux.

Chapter 2, "Firewalling Your Hosts," addresses securing your Linux hosts with the iptables firewall. It covers setting up a basic firewall and configuring and managing iptables and then moves onto advanced topics such as firewall logging, protecting from Denial of Service (DoS) attacks and other network-based attacks. (Appendix A contains firewall scripts for securing a bastion host based on the contents of this chapter.)

Chapter 3, "Securing Connections and Remote Administration," examines securing connections on your hosts. This includes providing secure connections for the administration of your systems using tools such as OpenSSH. I address using OpenSSL and Stunnel to encapsulate connections, and I show how to set up VPN connections.

Chapter 4, "Securing Files and File Systems," looks at securing your files and file systems. I cover file permissions, file attributes, and symmetric file encryption. I also explain securely mounting your disks and removable file systems, encrypting entire file systems, and using the Tripwire tool to monitor the integrity and status of your files and directories.

Chapter 5, "Understanding Logging and Log Monitoring," covers logging and monitoring and filtering your logs. I cover the syslog and syslog-ng tools for gathering your log messages. I also show you how to use the SEC tool to correlate log messages and demonstrate how to manage and rotate your log files.

Chapter 6, "Using Tools for Security Testing," provides information on the tools available to you for testing the security of your hosts. I address testing the security of your passwords and scanning for root kits. I cover scanning your hosts for vulnerabilities and open ports with tools such as nmap and Nessus. I also demonstrate how to use the Bastille hardening script to harden your host.

---

1. http://www.apress.com/book/bookDisplay.html?bID=320

Chapter 7, "Securing Your Mail Server," looks at securing and hardening two of the most commonly used e-mail servers, Sendmail and Postfix. I examine running these e-mail servers in a chroot jail as well as other methods of limiting their exposure to attack. I also explain how to protect your users from spam and viruses.

Chapter 8, "Authenticating and Securing Your Mail," addresses securing the transmission of your e-mail and the authentication of your clients to your e-mail servers. I examine using Cyrus SASL and SMTP AUTH to ensure only authenticated clients can use your e-mail servers and demonstrate how to use TLS to provide encryption of the transmission of your e-mail.

Chapter 9, "Hardening Remote Access to E-mail," addresses securing your user's remote access to their e-mail via IMAP and POP and using tools such as Fetchmail. I cover providing secure IMAP and POP using SSL and how to build a "black box" secure IMAP server using Cyrus IMAP.

Chapter 10, "Securing an FTP Server," covers the FTP server and file transfers. I demonstrate how to run secure local and anonymous FTP servers, including how to integrate it with SSL/TLS and authenticate your users with PAM.

Chapter 11, "Hardening DNS and BIND," looks at running DNS services. I cover DNS-related threats and attacks, how to choose your DNS server, and the basics of secure DNS design. I also cover installing and hardening a BIND DNS server and take you through the security-related configurations options of BIND. Finally, I cover some BIND security features such as TSIG. (Appendix B contains a number of secure BIND configuration files based on the contents of this chapter.)

Basic Security Tenets

The practical examples I demonstrate in this book are built on some underlying tenets that are crucial to maintaining your security.

- Be minimalist and minimize the risk.

- Defense in depth

- Vigilance

An understanding of these tenets, in combination with the examples and a little common sense, can help you mitigate the risk of an attack on your hosts. In the following sections I briefly articulate the IT security tenets on which I have based this book.

Be Minimalist, and Minimize the Risk

The first principle, that of minimalism, can also be expressed with the acronym KISS, or Keep It Simple Stupid. The safest way to reduce the risks to your hosts is to not introduce risks in the first place. For example, many distributions install services, tools, applications, and functionality that could pose risks to your host. In some cases, they even start services. They also create users for these services and applications that are often not needed or could be used by an attacker to compromise your host. The first step in minimizing the risk to your hosts is to remove this excess and unnecessary material. The second step is ensuring that you tightly control what is installed on your hosts. Do not install more than you need to, do not run services or functionality you do not need, and do not have users you do not need.

This is something you need to do from scratch with the installation of a new hardened host or if hardening an existing host. Obviously, minimizing the functionality of an existing host is harder. You need to make sure you are fully aware of all the functions that host performs and ensure you do not switch off or remove something that is required for that host to provide the required functionality. Hardening a production host requires extensive testing, and I recommend you proceed only if you have the ability to back out any changes and revert to your original configuration in the event a security change has an adverse effect.

Tip I recommend you use a change control system to ensure all changes are managed and planned rather than simply implemented. At the least you should keep a journal of the activities you conduct on a particular host. Every time you make a configuration change, you should detail the old and new settings and the change performed in a logbook.

Defense in Depth

The second tenet of good security is defense in depth. At its most basic, defense in depth means taking a layered approach to defending your hosts. The defense in depth concept proposes using layers of technology, policies, and processes to protect your systems. This means that, wherever possible in your environment, you do not rely on a single layer for defense of your hosts.

As an example you can look at your connectivity to the Internet. Just installing a firewall between your internal network and the Internet is not enough. In addition to a firewall between your network and the Internet, you should firewall your individual internal hosts, install an IDS system of some kind, and conduct regular penetration testing and vulnerability scanning of your hosts. You should apply this principle to all the components of your host security.

Vigilance

One of the biggest threats to your security is simply doing nothing. No matter how secure your hosts are at this point in time, they will, at varying rates, become less secure as time goes by. This is a consequence of simple entropy, as changes to your applications, environment, and requirements alter the configuration and potentially purpose of your systems. It is also a consequence of the changing nature of the threats against you. What you have protected yourself against now may not be what you need to protect yourself against in the future. This is most obviously manifested as new vulnerabilities and exploits of those vulnerabilities are discovered in the operating systems, applications, and tools you have running.

You need to ensure you include security administration and monitoring as part of your regular system administration activities. Check your logs, audit your users and groups, and monitor your files and objects for suspicious activity. Know the routines and configuration of your hosts; the more you understand about the normal rhythms of your hosts, the easier it is to spot anomalies that could indicate you are under attack or have been penetrated.

You also need to ensure you keep up-to-date with vulnerabilities, threats, and exploits. In Chapter 1 I talk about some of the sources of information you can utilize to do this. You should subscribe to or review the security-related information your vendors distribute as well as those available from third-party sources such as SANS or CIS.

Finally, the truly vigilant test. And test again. Perform regular security assessments of your hosts and environment. Scan for vulnerabilities using tools such as Nessus or commercial tools such as ISS Security Scanner. Consider using independent third parties to perform penetration testing of your environment and hosts. Ongoing security assurance is vital to make sure you stay protected and hardened from attack.

Downloading the Code and Examples

Some of the lengthier configurations and examples from this book are also available in a zip file from the Downloads section of the Apress Web site (http://www.apress.com). These include the iptables firewall script from Chapter 2, the BIND named.conf configuration files from Chapter 11, and a variety of other configuration files and scripts.

Contacting the Author

You can reach James Turnbull at james@hardening-linux.com.

CHAPTER 1

■ ■ ■

Hardening the Basics

At the heart of your Linux system is the Linux kernel and operating system. Combined, these form the base level of your system on which all your applications run. Comparatively speaking, the Linux operating system and kernel are actually reasonably secure. A large number of security features are built in the kernel, and a variety of security-related tools and features come with most distributions or are available in open-source form. Additionally, Linux offers exceptional control over whom, how, and what resources and applications users can access. So, where are the risks?

Well, as the old saying goes, "The devil is in the details." The security of your system depends on a wide variety of configuration elements both at the operating system level and the application level. Additionally, the Linux operating system and kernel are complex and not always easy to configure. In fact, Linux systems are nearly infinitely configurable, and subtle configuration changes can have significant security implications. Thus, some security exposures and vulnerabilities are not always immediately obvious, and a lack of understanding about the global impact of changing configuration elements can lead to inadvertent exposures.

Furthermore, security on Linux systems never stays static. Once secured, your system does not perpetually stay secure. Indeed, the longer you use your system, the less secure it becomes. This can happen through operational or functional changes exposing you to threats or through new exploits being discovered in packages and applications. Securing your system is an ongoing and living process. Many of the steps and concepts in this chapter you will apply more than once (for example, after you make an operational change to reaffirm the required level of security), or you will apply on a regular basis to keep your security level consistent.

Finally, many distributions come prepackaged or preconfigured for you with a recommended default set of packages, applications, and settings. Usually this configuration is based on the author or vendor understanding what their end user requires of the distribution. Generally speaking, a lot of this preconfiguration is useful and enhances the potential security of your system; for example, Red Hat comes preconfigured to use Pluggable Authentication Modules (or PAM) for a variety of authentication processes. But sometimes this preconfiguration opens security holes or is poorly designed from a security perspective. For example, as a result of the vendor's desire to make it easy for you to set your system up, they may install, configure, and start applications or services for you. Red Hat automatically configures and starts Sendmail when you take the default installation options, for example.

To be able to address these issues, you need to have a solid understanding of the underlying basic security requirements of your system—those of your operating system and kernel. This chapter is entitled "Hardening the Basics" because it is aimed at exploring and explaining the key areas of security and security configuration at that operating system and kernel level. Additionally, I try to address some of the key weaknesses of a freshly installed Linux distribution or an existing unhardened Linux system and provide quick and practical fixes to them. I will start with some guidelines for installing a Linux distribution and then address boot security, user and password security, PAM, updates and package upgrades, and your kernel, and I will finish up with some information that should help you keep up-to-date with the latest vulnerabilities and security exposures.

Installing Your Distribution Securely

This book does not specifically cover a single distribution but rather tries to offer practical examples that you can use on the majority of Linux distributions (though I most keenly focus on Red Hat and Debian when offering examples of commands and application configuration). As a result, I am not going to take you through the process of installing a particular distribution but rather offer some recommendations about how you should install your Linux distribution. As I articulated in the chapter's introduction, one of the key tenets of information technology (IT) security is minimizing your risks. The default installation process for most Linux distributions does the opposite. Extraneous and inappropriate applications are installed, unnecessary users are created, and some potentially highly insecure configuration decisions are made.

Let's look at some ways to reduce the risks and the issues created during your distribution's installation process.

Some Answers to Common Installation Questions

Almost all Linux distributions installations ask you a series of questions about your system's proposed configuration during the installation process. They are usually some important security-related questions that you should take care answering. Obviously, whilst I cannot run through what every distribution is going to ask, some questions remain similar across many distributions.

If prompted, enable MD5 and shadow passwording. This will make your passwords significantly more secure.

When prompted to input a root password, always chose a secure password. I will briefly talk about choosing suitable passwords in the "Users and Groups" section of this chapter.

Create a user other than root if prompted, ensuring you choose a suitable password for this user also, so you have a user other than root to log onto the system.

If prompted during installation, enable any proposed firewall. If options to control the configuration of the firewall are offered, select the bare minimum of allowed connections. Only explicitly enable connections when you absolutely require them. Remember any firewall you configure during installation will generally not be suitable for production purposes, and you should see Chapter 2 for further information on firewalls.

Install Only What You Need

As I have stated, minimalism is important. If your distribution offers a Minimal or Custom option when selecting packages that will allow you install a minimal numbers of packages or allow you to deselect packages for installation, then you should use that option. In fact, on a Red Hat system I recommend you deselect every possible package option and then install the base system.

I cannot provide you with a definitive list of packages not to install. But a lot of this is common sense. Do you really need NetHack on your production Apache server? I can identify some of the types of packages that are installed by default that you should be able to remove. This also applies to hardening existing systems. You should review all installed packages and remove those not required or those that present significant risks.

Some of the areas I recommend you remove packages from are as follows:

- Games

- Network servers

- Daemons and services

- Databases

- Web tools

- Editors

- Media-related (CD and MP3 players, CD burners)

- Development tools and compilers

- Printing and printing tools

- Office-style applications and tools

- Document management and manipulation

- X-Windows (including Gnome and KDE)

One of my most important recommendations when choosing not to install packages involves X-Windows. Most, if not all, production Linux systems do not need X-Windows to perform their functions. An e-mail server, for example, should have no requirement for X-Windows. So *do not* install it. X-Windows is a huge package with numerous components and a history of numerous security vulnerabilities that make it a potentially dangerous package to install. Additionally, on a Linux system, unlike Windows systems, nothing requires the use of a graphical user interface (GUI) to configure that you cannot configure from the command line.

Caution Do not install your distribution whilst connected to the Internet or to a network that is connected to the Internet.

It may seem like a good idea to be connected to the Internet when you install your distribution to get patches and updates or register your system. But is it? Often the media used to install a distribution could be quite old. A number of vulnerabilities could and probably will have been discovered since the media was constructed. This means your system could be vulnerable to any number of potential attacks. Until you have downloaded the updates that fix these vulnerabilities, then your system is vulnerable. While you are busy waiting to download the required patches, then an attacker has the potential to identify your unprotected system and penetrate it using an as yet unfixed vulnerability.

To mitigate the risks of connecting an unpatched system to the Internet, I recommend you stay offline until you have updated your system with all the required patches. To do this, I recommend you download all the updates and patches required for your system onto another system first and check the MD5 checksums of the updates against those published by the vendor and their GNU Privacy Guard (GPG) public key. For Red Hat updates the checksums and public key are published on the Red Hat Network site, and for Debian they are contained in the .dsc file, which describes each dpkg package. I go into more detail about how to do this in the "Package Management, File Integrity, and Updating" section later in this chapter.

I recommend setting up a central "updates and patches" machine and download and verify all updates and patches on that system. You can also use this system to perform testing of new releases or updates before migrating them to your production systems. For a new installation you can package and burn the updates onto a CD and load them from the media directly onto the system to be patched.

Secure Booting, Boot Loaders, and Boot-Time Services

An attacker who has physical access to your system can easily bypass a great deal of your system's inherent security (especially controls such as users and passwords) and can reboot it or change the configuration of your boot loader or your init process—including what services are run at boot and what sequence they are run in. You need to secure the boot process and ensure you fully understand what happens during your boot process so that your system is secure from this sort of attack.

Attackers who are able to reboot your system can create two major problems. The first is that Linux systems allow a great deal of access to someone who can control how they boot into your system. The second is that taking your system offline is an excellent Denial of Service attack. Thus, control over who is allowed to reboot your system, how they interact with your boot loader, and what kernel they boot into is something you need to tightly restrict.

Additionally, what services you start and the order you start them in can expose your system to further risks. Indeed, after a default installation or on an unhardened system, many services that are started at boot are not required. Some of the running services even expose you to vulnerabilities because of their particular functionality. In the next section, I will cover some good rules you should follow for securing and organizing your boot process and sequence, including what you allow to start up when your system boots.

■**Note** I have described the items that start at boot time as services, but of course not all of them are. Some are daemons, one-off commands, or configuration tools. I will use the generic term *services* for simplicity's sake.

Securing Your Boat Loader

Most Linux systems use one of two boot loaders, the Linux Loader (LILO) or Grub. These boot loaders control your boot images and determine what kernel is booted when the system is started or rebooted. They are loaded after your Basic Input/Output System (BIOS) has initialized your system and generally wait a set period of time (generally between 10 and 30 seconds, but you can override this) for you to select a kernel to boot into; if you have not intervened, then they default to a specified kernel and boot into that.

I recommend you do not have too many kernel versions available to boot into, especially older versions of kernels. Many people leave older kernels on their systems and in their boot loader menus. The risk exists that you, or an attacker, could boot into an older kernel with a security vulnerability that could allow an attacker to compromise your system. Clean up when you perform kernel upgrades. I recommend leaving the current and previous versions of the kernel on the system (unless, of course, you have upgraded from the previous kernel to correct a security vulnerability).

Both boot loaders, LILO and Grub, are inherently insecure if your attacker has physical access to your system. For example, by default both LILO and Grub will allow you to boot into single-user mode. In single-user mode you have root privileges without having to enter the root password. Additionally, you can enter a variety of other parameters on both the boot loader's command lines that can provide an attacker with opportunities to compromise your system.

But both LILO and Grub have the option of being secured with passwords to prevent this, and I will show how to address this for both boat loaders.

▓**Tip** You should do this in addition to securing your BIOS. Set a BIOS password for your system, and disable booting from a floppy drive or CD/DVD drive.

Securing LILO with a Password

To prevent LILO from allowing unrestricted booting, you can specify a password in the `lilo.conf` file that must be entered if you want to pick a nondefault boot item, add options to the boot items, or boot into single-user mode. Listing 1-1 shows a sample `lilo.conf` file.

Listing 1-1. *Sample* `lilo.conf` *File*

```
prompt
timeout=50
default=linux
boot=/dev/hda
map=/boot/map
install=/boot/boot.b
message=/boot/message
linear
password=secretpassword
restricted
```

```
image=/boot/vmlinuz-2.4.18-14
      label=linux
      initrd=/boot/initrd-2.4.18-14.img
      read-only
      append="root=LABEL=/"
```

The two important lines to note are the restricted and password options. These do not appear in your lilo.conf file by default; I have added them to Listing 1-1.

The password option allows you to specify a password that must be entered before you are allowed to boot when the system is first started. In Listing 1-1 you would replace the phrase *secretpassword* with a suitably secure password.[1] Unfortunately, this password is added into the lilo.conf file in clear text, which means anyone with access to this file (though it should be those only with root privileges) can see the password.

The restricted option changes the behavior of the password option. With restricted specified, LILO will prompt for a password only if you specify parameters on the boot loader command line. For example, it would prompt you for a password if you tried to enter the parameter single (to enter single-user mode) on the boot loader command line.

You can also specify the password and restricted options with a particular kernel image statement. This way you can protect a particular kernel image or provide separate passwords for each kernel image. In the following example I have omitted the restricted option, which means a password will always be prompted for when trying to boot this kernel image:

```
image=/boot/vmlinuz-2.4.18-14
      password=secretpassword
      label=linux
      initrd=/boot/initrd-2.4.18-14.img
      read-only
      append="root=LABEL=/"
```

Anytime you change your lilo.conf file, you need to run the lilo command to update your LILO configuration.

```
puppy# /sbin/lilo
```

Finally, you need to ensure the lilo.conf file has the correct ownerships and permissions to ensure only those authorized can see the password in the file.

```
puppy# chown root:root /etc/lilo.conf
puppy# chmod 0600 /etc/lilo.conf
```

Securing Grub with a Password

Like LILO, Grub suffers from security issues and allows anybody with access at boot time to boot into single-user mode or change the boot parameters. The available Grub password security to address these issues is somewhat more advanced than LILO's and relies on generating an MD5-encrypted password to secure the boot menu and boot entries. This MD5-encrypted

---

1.   See the "Passwords" section for a definition of a suitably secure password.

password means that the password cannot be extracted by simply reading the Grub configuration file, /etc/grub.conf.

Let's first generate a Grub password. Listing 1-2 shows how to do this.

Listing 1-2. *Generating a Grub Password*

```
puppy# grub
grub> md5crypt
Password: ********
Encrypted: $1$2FXKzQO$I6k7iy22wB27CrkzdVPe70
grub> quit
```

You enter the Grub shell, execute the md5crpyt option, and are prompted for a password. The password is then encrypted and output on the screen in the form of an MD5 hash. Copy the MD5-encrypted password. Now you need to add the password to your grub.conf configuration file.

■Tip Red Hat has an unusual location for its grub.conf file. The grub.conf file in /etc is symlinked to /boot/grub/grub.conf, which in turn is symlinked to /boot/grub/menu.lst. I recommend for simplicity's sake you edit /etc/grub.conf.

Listing 1-3 shows a sample grub.conf file.

Listing 1-3. *Sample* grub.conf *File*

```
default=1
timeout=10
splashimage=(hd0,0)/grub/splash.xpm.gz
password --md5 $1$2FXKzQO$I6k7iy22wB27CrkzdVPe70
title Red Hat Linux (2.6.7)
        root (hd0,0)
        kernel /vmlinuz-2.6.7 ro root=LABEL=/
        initrd /initrd-2.6.7.img
```

I have added the option password --md5 to the file and specified the generated MD5 password. Now when you reboot you will not be allowed to interact with the Grub boot menu unless you type **p** and enter the required password.

■Tip You could also specify a plain-text password by excluding the --md5 from the password option, but I recommend for security that you stick with the MD5 password.

You can also add another parameter to the password option to launch a particular menu file when you have entered the password. To do this, change your password option to the following:

```
password --md5 $1$2FXKzQO$I6k7iy22wB27CrkzdVPe70 /boot/grub/administrator-menu.lst
```

When you enter the correct password, Grub will launch the specified menu file. This allows you, for example, to create an additional menu of other kernels or boot options available only to those users who provide the required password.

Like LILO, Grub allows you to protect a specific boot entry. It offers two ways of protecting a particular entry. If you specify the option lock directly after the title entry, then you will not be able to run that boot entry without entering a password previously specified by the password option. I have modified Listing 1-3 to add the lock option to the following configuration file:

```
default=1
timeout=10
splashimage=(hd0,0)/grub/splash.xpm.gz
password --md5 $1$2FXKzQO$I6k7iy22wB27CrkzdVPe70
title Red Hat Linux (2.6.7)
        lock
        root (hd0,0)
        kernel /vmlinuz-2.6.7 ro root=LABEL=/
        initrd /initrd-2.6.7.img
```

Now unless you specified the password defined by the password option, you would not be able to boot the Red Hat Linux (2.6.7) kernel image.

You can also use the password option within a boot entry to allow you to specify a particular password for each boot entry; Listing 1-4 shows you how to do it.

Listing 1-4. *Protecting a Boot Entry with Grub*

```
title Red Hat Linux (2.6.7)
        password --md5 $1$2QO$I6k7iy22wB27CrkzdVPe70
        root (hd0,0)
        kernel /vmlinuz-2.6.7 ro root=LABEL=/
        initrd /initrd-2.6.7.img
```

Here I have placed the password option directly after the title option. Now before you can boot this entry you will need to specify the correct password.

Finally, you need to ensure the grub.conf file has suitable ownership and permissions to ensure only those authorized can work with the file. Enter the following:

```
puppy# chown root:root /etc/grub.conf
puppy# chmod 0600 /etc/grub.conf
```

Init, Starting Services, and Boot Sequencing

Most systems come with a large number of services that start at boot. Obviously, some of these are actually important to the functioning of your system, and others are designed to start applications such as Sendmail or Apache that run on your system. But many of the others are not necessary or start services that potentially pose security risks to your system.

Table 1-1 shows some of the typical services that are generally started on both Red Hat and Debian systems, describes what they do, and tells whether I recommend removing them from your startup.

Note I am referring to the releases Red Hat 9, Red Hat Fedora Core, Red Hat Enterprise Linux 3, and Debian Woody 3 here, but generally speaking most distributions start similar services.

Table 1-1. *Starting Services for Red Hat and Debian*

Service	Description	Remove?
anacron	A variation on the cron tool	Yes
apmd	Advanced Power Management	Yes
atd	Daemon to the at scheduling tool	Yes
autofs	Automount	Yes
crond	The cron daemon	No
cups	Printing functions	Yes
functions	Shell-script functions for init scripts	No
gpm	Mouse support for text applications	Yes
irda	IrDA support	Yes (unless you have IrDA devices)
isdn	ISDN support	Yes (unless you use ISDN)
keytable	Keyboard mapping	No
kudzu	Hardware probing	Yes
lpd	Printing daemon	Yes
netfs	Mounts network file systems	Yes
nfs	NFS services	Yes
nfslock	NFS locking services	Yes
ntpd	Network Time Protocol daemon	No
pcmcia	PCMCIA support	Yes
portmap	RPC connection support	Yes
random	Snapshots the random state	No
rawdevices	Assigns raw devices to block devices	Yes
rhnsd	Red Hat Network daemon	Yes
snmpd	Simple Network Management Protocol (SNMP) support	Yes
snmtptrap	SNMP Trap daemon	Yes
sshd	Secure Shell (SSH) daemon	No
winbind	Samba support	Yes
xfs	X Font Server	Yes
ypbind	NIS/YP client support	Yes

■**Tip** I will talk about `inetd` and `xinetd` in Chapter 3.

A lot of the services listed in Table 1-1 you can apply common sense when deciding whether to start them. The `pcmcia` script, for example, is required only if you have PCMCIA devices or the `winbind` service if you are using Samba. If you are not doing any printing, then do not start the `lpd` and `cups` daemons. My recommendations to disable particular services listed in Table 1-1 are based on my experience that these services are not required on a secured production server. For example, you would rarely find the `apmd` daemon running on a production server, but it is commonly used on laptops to provide the appropriate power management functionality.

■**Tip** The other area of security vulnerability during startup is the potential for your daemons to create files that are too permissive. You set this using the `umask` function; I will cover `umask` in Chapter 4.

You can stop these services from starting via a number of methods depending on your distribution. I will focus on the Red Hat and Debian distributions' methods for handling `init` scripts. After stopping services, I recommend also removing the related package to stop someone restarting it.

■**Tip** If you use SuSE, then the `yast` central configuration tool will provide much the same functionality as `chkconfig` or `update-rc.d`.

Working with Red Hat init Scripts

To help handle your `init` scripts, Red Hat comes with the command `chkconfig`. The `chkconfig` command works by reading two commented lines near the top of each of your `init` scripts. (Your `init` scripts should be located in the `/etc/rc.d/init.d` directory.) Listing 1-5 shows the top two lines of a typical Red Hat `network init` script.

Listing 1-5. *Sample* `chkconfig` *Line in an* `init` *Script*

```
# chkconfig: 2345 10 90
# description: Activates/Deactivates all network interfaces configured to \
#              start at boot time.
```

You can see the first line in the script starts with `chkconfig:`, followed by three components. The first component comprises the run levels at which a service should start. The second component consists of the starting sequence number of the service, and the third component contains the stopping sequence number of the service. This means at run levels 2, 3, 4, and 5, the network begins the service at sequence number 10, and, in turn, each higher sequence number (in ascending order) until it stops when the sequence number reaches 90. The description line details the purpose of the service.

You need to add both these lines into any init script you want to manipulate using the chkconfig command.

To use this embedded information, you have to use some command-line options. The first --list shows the current status of all init scripts and what run levels they will start. Listing 1-6 shows this functionality.

Listing 1-6. *Listing* init *Scripts Using the* chkconfig *Command*

```
puppy# chkconfig --list
kdcrotate      0:off   1:off   2:off   3:off   4:off   5:off   6:off
ntpd           0:off   1:off   2:off   3:on    4:off   5:on    6:off
courier-imap   0:off   1:off   2:on    3:on    4:on    5:on    6:off
```

You can see from Listing 1-6 that each init script is listed together with the available run levels. An on after the run level indicates the service will be started at that run level, and an off indicates that it will not be started.

To stop a service from starting, you can use the --del option.

```
puppy# chkconfig --del name
```

In this syntax, you should replace the *name* variable with the name of a script to remove. That script must exist and must contain the two commented chkconfig lines in the top of the script. To add the service back to the boot sequence, you can use the --add option.

```
puppy# chkconfig --add name
```

Again, you should replace the *name* variable with the name of the appropriate init script to be added. If you do not intend to add the script to the init sequence again, then I recommend you delete the script from the /etc/rc.d/init.d/ directory.

Red Hat also comes with the useful ntsysv command-line graphical interface that can be used to configure what services will start in the current or specified run level. See the ntsysv man page for further details.

After removing scripts from your /etc/rc.d/init.d directory, I recommend you further secure the contents of this directory.

```
puppy# chown root:root /etc/rc.d/init.d/*
puppy# chmod -R 700 /etc/rc.d/init.d/*
```

Working with Debian init Scripts

Debian stores its init scripts in a slightly different location than Red Hat does. The base init scripts are located in /etc/init.d. Debian also uses different commands for managing init scripts. The update.rc-d command is the Debian equivalent of the chkconfig command and works in a similar manner. To add or change an init script, first you must have a copy of the script stored in /etc/init.d. Without the script being installed in this directory, update-rc.d has nothing to use. Listing 1-7 shows how you can add a new init script with update-rc.d.

Listing 1-7. *Adding a Debian* init *Script*

```
kitten# update-rc.d network defaults
```

The defaults option is useful for adding a typical init script. The defaults tells Debian to start the service at run levels 2, 3, 4, and 5 and to stop the service at run levels 0, 1, and 6 with a default sequence number of 20. You can also specify the sequence numbers with the default option by adding the required sequence numbers after the defaults option as a suffix.

```
kitten# update-rc.d network defaults 20 80
```

The first number indicates the starting sequence number, and the second number indicates the stopping sequence number for the service. You can also more explicitly control when an init script is started and stopped. Listing 1-8 shows how you can specify this control.

Listing 1-8. *Explicitly Controlling a Debian* init *Script*

```
kitten# update-rc.d network start 20 2 3 4 5 . stop 20 0 1 6 .
```

The command in Listing 1-8 provides the same configuration as the defaults option but using the full command-line options. You should be able to customize any start and stop combinations required by modifying the command in Listing 1-8.

If you want to remove an init script, update-rc.d also provides an option to do this. In the opposite manner of adding an init script, you must first delete the required init script from the /etc/init.d directory before removing the associated start and stop scripts from the various run levels. Listing 1-9 shows how to do this.

Listing 1-9. *Removing a Debian* init *Script*

```
kitten# rm -f /etc/init.d/network
kitten# update-rc.d network remove
```

The update-rc.d command also comes with two command-line flags you can use. The first option, -n, makes no actual change to the system and merely shows the proposed changes.

```
kitten# update-rc.d -n network defaults
 Adding system startup for /etc/init.d/network ...
    /etc/rc0.d/K20network -> ../init.d/network
    /etc/rc1-d/K20network -> ../init.d/network
    /etc/rc6.d/K20network -> ../init.d/network
    /etc/rc2.d/S20network -> ../init.d/network
    /etc/rc3.d/S20network -> ../init.d/network
    /etc/rc4.d/S20network -> ../init.d/network
    /etc/rc5.d/S20network -> ../init.d/network
```

The other command-line option, -f, is used in conjunction with the remove option to specify that the update-rc.d command should remove all links even if the original init script still exists in the /etc/init.d directory.

After removing scripts from your /etc/init.d directory, I recommend you further secure the contents of this directory. Enter the following:

```
kitten# chown root:root /etc/init.d/*
kitten# chmod -R 700 /etc/init.d/*
```

Tip If you want, you can also download and install chkconfig on a Debian system. You can find a source version that will compile on Debian at http://www.fastcoder.net/~thumper/software/sysadmin/ chkconfig/.

The inittab File

Your init scripts are not the only place where services are started. You should also review the contents of the inittab file in the /etc directory. Though its use to start services is rarer these days, some items still end up in this file. Red Hat systems, for example, place several services in this file, including a trap for the Control+Alt+Delete key combination. Additionally, tty terminals are often started in this file. Listing 1-10 shows some service lines in the inittab file.

Listing 1-10. inittab *Service*

```
sysacc:235:acct:/usr/sbin/acct -q -d
~~:S:wait:/sbin/sulogin
ca::ctrlaltdel:/sbin/shutdown -t3 -r now
```

The first line shows starting a service called sysacc. The line is broken down into the name of the service being started, the run levels the service will start at, a label for the service, and the command and any options to run separated by colons.

```
servicename:runlevels:label:command -option -option
```

You should review all commands being started in this file and determine if they are all needed. If you want to remove a service, simply comment out or delete that line.

Tip For consistency I recommend not starting services in inittab but using init scripts.

The second line in Listing 1-10 shows a trap I have added specifically for Red Hat systems. Red Hat allows booting into single-user mode by typing linux single on the LILO command line or the Grub boot-editing menus. This line forces the execution of the command /sbin/sulogin if single-user mode is started (run level S). The /sbin/sulogin requires the root password be to be entered before single-user mode will be started. See the sulogin man page for more information.

The third line in Listing 1-10 shows a trap for the Control+Alt+Delete key combination commonly used to reboot systems.

■Tip Linux pays attention only to the Control+Alt+Delete key combination when used from the console or virtual consoles. For users who are logged into the system via other means—for example, a terminal session—pressing these keys will do nothing.

By default most Linux kernels trap this key combination when pressed and pass it to the init system for processing. This allows you to specify the action taken when the Control+Alt+Delete key combination is pressed. The default action is usually to run the shutdown command. I recommend securing this a bit further by adding the -a option to the trap in Listing 1-10.

```
ca::ctrlaltdel:/sbin/shutdown -a -t3 -r now
```

The -a option enables the use of the shutdown.allowed file. Create a file called shutdown.allowed in the /etc directory. Add the users you want to be authorized to use the shutdown command to the file, one username per line. You can also have comments and empty lines in this file. Listing 1-11 shows what is inside the sample shutdown.allowed file.

Listing 1-11. *Sample* shutdown.allowed *File*

```
root
bob
sarah
```

If someone other than these users tries to issue a Control+Alt+Delete from the console, they will get an error message.

```
shutdown: no authorized users logged in
```

On some systems you may not want anybody to be able to use Control+Alt+Delete. To do this, change the trap line to the following:

```
ca::ctrlaltdel:
```

Your /etc/inittab file also contains the definitions for the virtual terminals available to you on the console using the Alt+*number* key combination. You can define them using the following lines in inittab:

```
1:2345:respawn:/sbin/mingetty tty1
2:2345:respawn:/sbin/mingetty tty2
```

Generally most distributions define six or so virtual terminals. You can reduce the number of virtual terminals started by commenting out some of the ttys in the /etc/inittab file.

After making any changes to the inittab file, you need to tell the init process to review the file. Use the following command:

```
puppy# telinit q
```

Then you need to ensure the inittab file has the correct ownerships and permissions to ensure only those authorized can work with the file.

```
puppy# chown root:root /etc/inittab
puppy# chmod 0644 /etc/inittab
```

Boot Sequencing

The order in which you start and stop services on your system is also important. This is mainly for controlling when your firewall and logging services start and stop. Ensure you start your firewall, (iptables, for example) and your syslog daemon before you bring up your network. This ensures your system will not be connected to any external systems or networks without the protection of your firewall or without any logging of your system occurring. Then during the shutdown of your system, ensure you stop your networking services before you stop your firewall and syslog services.

On most systems init scripts are started and stopped according to the sequence number given to them; sequence 20 will start before 30, and so on. I briefly covered sequence numbers in the previous "Working with Debian init Scripts" and "Working with Red Hat init Scripts" sections. You should ensure the start sequence numbers for your firewall and your syslog daemons are lower than the sequence number for your system's networking service, in other words, the daemons start before your network. Your networking services are usually started by an init script called network on a Red Hat system and a script called networking on a Debian system. Then confirm that your system's networking service stops before your firewall and logging.

Tip I will talk further about booting and some additional security features related to securing file systems in Chapter 4.

Consoles, Virtual Terminals, and Login Screens

The next area I will cover is the security of your console, your terminals, and the login screens presented to your users when they log into the system. The console of your system is usually physically attached to your system. (It is usually from the console you will have installed your distribution.) In the Linux world, logging onto the console often allows you to perform activities, commands, or functions that you would not be able to do from other locations, such as via a secure shell (SSH) login. You need to understand what the capabilities of a user logged into the console are and how to secure them further. Additionally, your console also has a number of virtual terminals defined that you can access. I talked about defining these virtual terminals in the earlier "The inittab File" section. These also need to be secured, and I will cover in the "Securing Virtual Terminals" section a method of locking these virtual terminals from unauthorized use.

Lastly, when users connect to your systems, they are presented with a login screen. The information presented on most default login screens can offer attackers information about your system you do not want to share. Additionally, these login screens are a good method of communicating warnings and notices to the user logging into your system.

Tip In addition to securing your console and terminals, do not neglect your physical security. Ensure your systems are stored somewhere that makes access to the console difficult to all those bar authorized people. Ensure the access is logged of any authorized people who can enter the area in which the console and system are stored. Additionally, if you have a case lock or similar physical security devices on your system, then use it to secure access to the interior of your system.

Securing the Console

I will first talk about where root can log on. In Chapter 3 I will talk about restricting root logons over SSH to your system. You can further limit where root can log on by restricting it to a specific set of terminals. To do this, edit the contents of the /etc/securetty file. The login program refers to this file to determine whether the root user can log into a particular device. Listing 1-12 shows a sample of a typical securetty file.

Listing 1-12. *A Sample* securetty *File*

```
tty1
#tty2
#tty3
#tty4
```

All devices you want to allow root to log in from should be listed in the file (without the /dev/ prefix). I recommend allowing root login only on one terminal and forcing all other logins to be a non-root user and if required use su to gain root privileges. In Listing 1-12 you can see that only device tty1 allows a root login. All other devices have been commented out of the file, disabling root login on those devices. You also need to secure the securetty file to ensure it is modifiable only by root. Enter the following:

```
puppy# chown root:root /etc/securetty
puppy# chmod 0600 /etc/securetty
```

■**Tip** You can also achieve similar results using the PAM module, pam_access.so. See its configuration file in /etc/security/access.conf.

The Red Hat Console

On Red Hat systems[2] when non-root users log into the console, they are granted access to some additional programs that they would otherwise not be able to run. Additionally, they are given permissions to certain files they would not have as normal users solely because they are logged onto the console. To achieve this, Red Hat uses a PAM module called pam_console.so, which is defined in the PAM login service. See the "Pluggable Authentication Modules (PAM)" section.

■**Tip** If more than one non-root user is logged onto console, the first user to log in gets the right to run these programs and the additional permissions.

---

2. Red Hat 8, Red Hat 9, and Red Hat Enterprise Linux 3

The configuration files contained in the /etc/security/console.apps/ directory define the additional programs that users logged onto the console can run. This directory contains a collection of files, and each file corresponds to a command that users, after logging onto the console, can run as if they were root.

```
puppy# ls -l /etc/security/console.apps/
-rw-r--r--    1 root      root        10 Aug 22   2003 authconfig
-rw-r--r--    1 root      root        87 Aug 22   2003 authconfig-gtk
-rw-r--r--    1 root      root        83 Sep 20   2003 dateconfig
-rw-r--r--    1 root      root        64 May 29  01:31 ethereal
-rw-r--r--    1 root      root        66 Apr 15  00:33 gdmsetup
-rw-r--r--    1 root      root        14 Sep 26   2003 halt
```

Whilst perhaps this model of granting extra privileges to console users makes administration for your system easier, I do not think this is a good idea from a security perspective. Most, if not all of these programs, should be run only by root, and the risk posed by this access being granted to a non-root user just because the user is able to login to the console is not acceptable on a production system. So, I recommend you disable this functionality. You can do this by removing the contents of the /etc/security/console.apps directory. Enter the following:

```
puppy# rm -f /etc/security/console.apps/*
```

The file /etc/security/console.perms contains the additional permissions provided. I also recommend you go through the permissions granted to users in the console.perms file and confirm you are comfortable granting all of them to non-root users who are logged into the console.

■**Tip** You will also find sample configuration files for other PAM modules in the /etc/security directory. I will talk about some of them in the Pluggable Authentication Modules (PAM)" section later in this chapter.

Securing Virtual Terminals

Your virtual terminals are useful to allow you to log into multiple sessions on your console. But they can be dangerous if you leave sessions logged on unattended. I will show you a way to lock them against unauthorized use with a password. This is especially useful when you need to leave a process running interactively on the console. You start your process, change to another virtual terminal, and lock all the other virtual terminals. Then, unless someone has the root password, they cannot unlock the terminals and interfere with your running process.

You will learn how to do this using a tool called Vlock. The Vlock tool comes with some Linux distributions but may need to be installed on others. Checking for the presence of the vlock binary on your system will tell you if you have it installed. Otherwise you can install packages for Red Hat, Mandrake, Debian, and other distributions at http://linux.maruhn.com/sec/ vlock.html. If not already installed, then add Vlock to your system, such as a Red Hat system.

```
puppy# rpm -Uvh vlock-1-3-13.i386.rpm
```

With Vlock you can lock a single virtual terminal and allow people to change to another virtual terminal or lock all virtual terminals and disable changing between virtual terminals. You can lock your current virtual terminal with the command in Listing 1-13.

Listing 1-13. *Locking Your Current Virtual Terminal*

```
puppy# vlock -c
This TTY is now locked.
Please enter the password to unlock.
root's Password:
```

To now unlock this virtual terminal, you need to enter the root password.

To disable all virtual terminals and prevent switching between virtual terminals, use the -a option.

```
puppy# vlock -a
The entire console display is now locked.
You will not be able to switch to another virtual console.
Please enter the password to unlock:
root's Password:
```

Again, to now unlock the virtual terminals, you need to enter the root password. If you are not able to enter the root password, the only way to disable the lock is to hard reset the system.

Securing Login Screens

Your login screen is the first thing users (and attackers) see when they connect to your system. As a result, it is a good idea if it abides by some guidelines.

- It should warn against unauthorized use.

- It should never reveal the operating system and version of the system you are signing onto or indeed any more information than absolutely required. I call this defense through obscurity; the less information attackers have, the harder it is for them to penetrate your system.

- It should ensure the screen is clear from previous sessions.

To do this, you need to edit the contents of the /etc/issue and /etc/issue.net files. The issue file is displayed when you log in via a terminal session and the issue.net file when you login via a telnet session. Most distributions use these files for this purpose, including both Red Hat and Debian. These files can contain a combination of plain text and escape characters. I usually start my files by forcing it to clear the screen; I achieve this by redirecting the output of the clear command to the /etc/issue and issue.net files. Enter the following:

```
puppy# clear > /etc/issue
puppy# clear > /etc/issue.net
```

This will clear the screen of anything that was on it prior to displaying the login prompt to ensure when a user signs off no information will be left on the screen that could be used by an attacker to gain some advantage.

You should also include a warning message stating that unauthorized access to the system is prohibited and will be prosecuted. You can also use one of a series of escape characters in the files to populate the login screen with data from your system. I usually use a login screen such as the screen in Listing 1-14.

Listing 1-14. *Sample Login Screen*

```
^[c
\d at \t
Access to this system is for authorized persons only.
Unauthorized use or access is regarded as a criminal act
and is subject to civil and criminal prosecution. User
activities on this system may be monitored without prior notice.
```

The \d and \t escape characters would display the current date and time on the system, respectively. Other escape characters are available to you if you check the issue, issue.net, and getty man pages.

Tip If you find your changes in the /etc/issue and /etc/issue.net files are being overwritten every time you reboot, you may find that your distribution resets the content of these files automatically as part of your boot process to content such as the output of the uname -a command. If this is happening, it is usually handled by an entry in the rc.local file in the last stage of the boot process. You need to comment out or remove this entry to ensure your issue and issue.net files keep the content you require.

Also, the /etc/motd file's contents display directly after login, and you may want to adjust them to include an Acceptable Use Policy or similar information.

You need to secure all these files to stop other people from editing them. Enter the following:

```
puppy# chown root:root /etc/issue /etc/issue.net /etc/motd
puppy# chmod 0600 /etc/issue /etc/issue.net /etc/motd
```

Users and Groups

One of the key facets of your system security is user and password security. Ensure that only legitimate users can log in and that attackers will not be able to penetrate your system via a weak or easily determined login. Additionally, once logged on it is important to understand how users gain access to resources and to protect your system from improper and unauthorized use of those resources by controlling them by managing user accounts and groups.

What is a user account? User accounts provide the ability for a system to verify the identity of a particular user, to control the access of that user to the system, and to determine what resources that user is able to access. Groups are used for collecting like types of common users for the purpose of providing them access to resources. This could both include groups of users from a particular department who all need access to particular shared files or a group of users who all need access to a particular resource such as a connection, piece of hardware such as a scanner or printer, or an application.

Linux stores details of users, groups, and other information in three files: /etc/passwd, /etc/shadow, and /etc/group. The first file, /etc/passwd, contains a list of all users and their details. Listing 1-15 shows an example of some passwd entries.

Listing 1-15. *Some Sample* passwd *Entries*

```
root:x:0:0:root:/root:/bin/bash
daemon:x:2:2:daemon:/sbin:/sbin/nologin
```

The entries can be broken into their component pieces, each separated by a colon.

```
username:password:UID:GID:GECOS:Home Directory:Shell
```

The username is up to eight characters long and is case sensitive (though usually all in lowercase). As you can see in Listing 1-15, the x in the next field is a marker for the password. The actual password is stored in the /etc/shadow file, which I will discuss in the "Shadow Passwording" section.

■**Tip** Systems often have usernames that are constructed from a combination of a user's first and last names. Introducing random usernames instead is often a good idea. Random usernames do not link users to personal information. Even if a user has a password that is related to personal information, an attacker will be less likely to be able to make the connection to a random username.

Next is the User ID (or UID) and the Group ID (GID). On a Linux system each user account and group is assigned a numeric ID. Users are assigned a UID and groups a GID. Depending on the distribution, lower-numbered UIDs and GIDs indicate system accounts and groups such as root or daemon. On Red Hat systems UIDs and GIDs are those IDs lower than 500, and on Debian those IDs are lower than 100.

■**Note** The root user has a UID and GID of 0. This should be the only user on the system with a UID and GID of 0.

In many cases the UID and GID for a user will be identical.

■**Tip** You can specify the range of the UIDs and GIDs for users in the /etc/login.defs file using the UID_MIN and UID_MAX range for UIDs and the GID_MIN and GID_MAX range for GIDs.

The next item is the GECOS[3] information that has been previously used to store `finger` daemon information and can contain data such as the name of the user, office locations, and phone numbers. If you have more than one item of data in the GECOS field, then a comma separates each data item.

The next item is the user's home directory. This is usually located for most users in the `/home` partition.

The last item is the user's default shell. If the default shell points to a nonexistent file, then the user will be unable to log in. The second line in Listing 1-15 uses the shell `/sbin/nologin`, which not only stops the user from logging it but logs the login attempt to `syslog`. This is commonly used on Red Hat systems to indicate that this user cannot log on. On Debian systems the shell `/bin/false` is used. On more recent versions of distributions these login shells have been binaries with the sole function of logging error messages to `syslog` and exiting without allowing a login to the system.

On older Linux systems, these shells, `/sbin/nologin` and `/bin/false`, are in fact shell scripts. This is dangerous, because there have been instances where a shell script used here has been subverted. You should replace these shell scripts with binaries or replace them entirely with an alternative shell.

Unfortunately, whilst a user may not be able to log in with these shells defined, this is not always a guarantee that this user cannot be utilized for other purposes. Some versions of Samba and File Transfer Protocol (FTP) assume that if a shell is listed in the `/etc/shells` file,[4] then it is acceptable to use this user for Samba and FTP purposes. This is a big risk, and I recommend setting the shell of those users you do not want to log in to `/dev/null` or using the `noshell` binary that comes with the Titan hardening application.[5] This will prevent the login and use of this account for any other purposes.

Using `/dev/null` as a shell has a weakness, however. If a login attempt is made, then no `syslog` entry is generated that records a disabled user tried to log in. The `noshell` binary from the Titan hardening application is useful for this purpose. You can download the source code and compile it on your system. Listing 1-16 shows you the commands to download and verify the source code.

Listing 1-16. *Downloading* `noshell.c`

```
puppy# wget http://www.fish.com/titan/src1/noshell.c
puppy# md5sum noshell.c
d4909448e968e60091e0b28c149dc712 noshell.c
```

The current MD5 checksum for the `noshell.c` file is `d4909448e968e60091e0b28c149dc712`.

Now you need to compile `noshell`. You should compile the `noshell` command using static libraries, and you can use the `Makefile` in Listing 1-17 to do this on both Red Hat and Debian systems.

---

3. From the General Electric Comprehensive Operating System and also called the *comment* field

4. This contains a list of all the shells you can use on this system; see `man shells`.

5. `http://www.fish.com/titan/`

Listing 1-17. Makefile *for* noshell

```
CC = gcc
CPPFLAGS =
CFLAGS    = -static
LDFLAGS   = -dn
LIBS      = -static /usr/lib/libc.a -static /usr/lib/libnsl.a
noshell: noshell.o
        $(CC) $(CFLAGS) -o noshell $(LIBS) $(LDFLAGS) noshell.o
```

Create the Makefile from Listing 1-17 and you can now compile noshell. Enter the following:

```
puppy# make noshell
```

Then copy the resulting noshell binary to /sbin and delete the downloaded source code, the output, and the newly compiled binary.

```
puppy# cp noshell /sbin
puppy# rm -f noshell.c noshell.o noshell
```

Now you can use /sbin/noshell as the shell for those users for which you do not want a shell login.

```
daemon:x:2:2:daemon:/sbin:/sbin/noshell
```

When a user with their shell set to noshell attempts a log into the system, the following log entry will be generated to the auth facility with a log level of warning, and you can monitor for this.

```
Jul 25 14:51:47 puppy -noshell[20081]: Titan warning: user bob login from a ➥
disabled shell
```

■**Caution** Just remember to ensure the noshell binary is *not* added to your /etc/shells file.

Shadow Passwording

You may have noted that no password appears in /etc/passwd but rather the letter x. This is because most (if not all) modern distributions use shadow passwording now to handle password management. Previously passwords were stored as one-way hashes in /etc/passwd, which provided limited security and exposed your usernames and passwords to brute-force cracking methods (especially as the passwd file needs to be world readable). This was especially dangerous when a copy of your passwd file could be stolen from your system and brute force cracked offline. Given the weak security of this type of password when stored in the passwd file, it can take only a matter of minutes on a modern computer to crack simple passwords or only days to crack harder passwords.

■**Tip** If prompted when installing your distribution, you should always install shadow and MD5 passwords to ensure maximum potential security.

Shadow passwording helps reduce this risk by separating the users and passwords and storing the passwords as MD5 hashes in the /etc/shadow file. The /etc/shadow file is owned by the root user, and root is the only user that has access to the file. Additionally, implementing shadow passwording includes the ability to add password-aging features to your user accounts and provides the login.defs file that allows you to enforce a system-wide security policy related to your users and passwords. Listing 1-18 shows a sample of the /etc/shadow file.

Listing 1-18. *Some Sample Shadow Entries*

```
root:$1$5SszKz9V$vDvPkkazUPIZdCheEGOuX/:12541:0:99999:7:::
daemon:!*:12109:0:99999:7:::
```

You can also break down the shadow file into components, and like the passwd file, these components are separated by colons. The components of the shadow file are as follows:

- Username
- Password
- Date password last changed
- Minimum days between password changes
- Password expiry time in days
- Password expiry warning period in days
- Number of days after password expiry account is disabled
- Date since account has been disabled

The username matches the username in the passwd file. The password itself is encrypted, and two types of special characters can tell you about the status of the user account with which the password field can be prefixed. If the password field is prefixed with ! or *, then the account is locked and the user will be allowed to log in. If the password field is prefixed with !!, then a password has never been set and the user cannot log into the system. The remaining entries refer to password aging, and I will cover those in the "Password Aging" section.

Groups

On Linux systems, groups are stored in the /etc/groups file. Listing 1-19 shows a sample of this file.

Listing 1-19. *Sample of the /etc/groups File*

```
root:x:0:root
mail:x:12:mail,amavis
```

The group file is structured much like the `passwd` file with the data entries separated by a colon. The file is broken into a group name, a password, the GID number, and a comma-separated list of the members of that group.

```
groupname:password:GID:member,member
```

The password in the group file allows a user to log into that group using the `newgrp` command. If shadow passwording is enabled, then like the `passwd` file the passwords in the group file are replaced with an x and the real passwords stored in the `/etc/gshadow` file. I will talk about passwords for groups in the "Adding Groups" section.

■**Note** I will cover permissions and file security and how they interact with users and groups in Chapter 4.

Adding Users

To add a user to the system, you use the `useradd` command. Listing 1-20 shows a basic user being created.

Listing 1-20. *Creating a User*

```
puppy# useradd bob
```

This will create the user bob (and on Red Hat systems a corresponding private group called bob) with a home directory of /home/bob and a shell of whatever the system's default shell is, often /bin/bash. You can see the results of this in the passwd, shadow, and group files.

```
bob:x:506:506::/home/bob:/bin/bash
bob:!!:12608:0:99999:7:::
bob:x:506:
```

All the home directory and shell information in the previous lines are the default settings for the `useradd` command. So where does the `useradd` command get these defaults from? Your distribution should contain the `/etc/default/useradd` file. Listing 1-21 shows a sample of a typical Red Hat file.

Listing 1-21. *The* /etc/default/useradd *File*

```
puppy# cat /etc/default/useradd
# useradd defaults file
GROUP=100
HOME=/home
INACTIVE=-1
EXPIRE=
SHELL=/bin/bash
SKEL=/etc/skel
```

This file is sometimes populated by default at system installation, but you can also create the file yourself and use your own settings. Table 1-2 shows the possible options you can include in the useradd file.

Table 1-2. *The* /etc/default/useradd *File*

Option	Description
SHELL	The full path to the default shell
HOME	The full path to the user's home directory
SKEL	The directory to use to provide the default contents of a user's new home directory
GROUP	The default GID
INACTIVE	Maximum number of days after password expiry that a password can be changed
EXPIRE	Default expiration date of user accounts

Additionally, you can change most of the options running the useradd command with the -D option. Listing 1-22 shows you how to change the default shell for your new users, and Table 1-3 shows the additional options available for use with the -D option.

Listing 1-22. *Changing* useradd *Defaults with the* -D *Option*

```
puppy# useradd -D -s /bin/bash
```

■**Tip** You can also change your default shell with the chsh command. Use chsh -l to see a list of all the available shells (which are specified in the /etc/shells file).

Table 1-3. *The* useradd -D *Defaults*

Option	Description
-b *path/to/default/home*	Specifies the initial path prefix of a new user's home directory
-e *date*	Specifies the default expiry date
-f *days*	Specifies the number of days after a password has expired before the account will be disabled
-g *group*	Specifies the default group
-s *shell*	Specifies the default shell

As I have shown in Table 1-2 another option in the /etc/defaults/useradd file, the SKEL option, specifies a location under which you can create the required default directory and file structure for all of your users. For example, I use Maildir-format mailboxes so I usually create a Maildir mailbox under /etc/skel that will get copied into the new home directory of any new user.

As you can see in Table 1-4 all these defaults can also be overridden on the useradd command.

Table 1-4. *Some* useradd *Command-Line Options*

Option	Description
-c comment	The new user's password file comment field.
-d homedir	The user's home directory.
-g initial group	The group name or number of the user's initial login group.
-G group1,group2	A list of additional groups of which the user is to be a member.
-m	Create the user's home directory if it does not exist.
-M	Do not create the user's home directory.
-n	Red Hat creates a group with the same name as the user automatically when the user is created. This option disables that behavior.
-r	You can create a system account (with a UID in the range of system accounts).
-p password	Specifies the user's password.
-s shell	Specifies the shell the user will use.

Listing 1-23 shows a user addition command using some of these command-line options.

Listing 1-23. *Creating a User with* useradd

```
puppy# useradd -s /sbin/noshell -G mail,clam -d /var/spool/amavis amavis
```

In Listing 1-23 I am creating a user called amavis who cannot login (the shell is set to /sbin/noshell), belongs to the additional groups mail and clam, and whose home directory is /var/spool/amavis.

Adding Groups

To add a group to your system, you need to use the groupadd command. Listing 1-24 shows you how to use this command.

Listing 1-24. *The* groupadd *Command*

```
puppy# groupadd sales
```

This will create the resulting group in the /etc/group file.

```
sales:x:508:
```

As shown in Table 1-5 command-line options are available with the groupadd command.

Table 1-5. *The* groupadd *Command-Line Options*

Option	Description
-g GID	Set the GID for the group. This must be a unique number.
-r	Creates a system group (with a GID inside the system GID range).
-f	Exits if the group already exists.

Once you have created groups, you need to assign users to these groups. You can do this one of two ways. First, you can edit the /etc/groups file itself and add the specific user to a group; second, you can use the gpasswd command. The gpasswd command provides a way to add users to groups via the command line and can also assign passwords to a particular group (storing these in the /etc/gshadow file).

To add users to a group, you would use the gpasswd command with the -a option.

```
puppy$ gpasswd -a bob sales
```

In the previous command the user bob is added to the group sales. To remove a user from a group, you would use the -d option.

```
puppy$ gpasswd -d jane sales
```

In the previous command the user jane is removed from the group sales using the -d option.

You can also define one or more users as administrators of a particular group and allow them to use the -a and the -d options to add and remove users to that particular group. To add a group administrator to a group, use the following command:

```
puppy# gpasswd -A bob sales
```

This adds the user bob as an administrator of the group sales. Now bob can use the gpasswd command to add users (jane, chris, and david) to the sales group. Or you can add both an administrator and users at the same time to a group using this command:

```
puppy# gpasswd -A bob -M jane chris david sales
```

The -A option adds the group administer, bob, and the -M option specifies a list of users.

You can also add a password to a group. The password will be stored in the /etc/gshadow file.

```
puppy# gpasswd sales
Changing the password for group sales
New Password:
Re-enter new password:
```

This password will allow users to use the newgrp command to temporarily add themselves to the sales group if they know the required password.

```
puppy# newgrp sales
Password:
```

This gives them the access rights of the users of this group. The group access is removed when the user logs off. You can use gpasswd -r to remove the password from a particular group.

Another option you can use with the gpasswd command is the -R option, which stops from anyone adding themselves to the group using the newgrp command.

```
puppy# gpasswd -R sales
```

Tip You can use another command, grpck, to check the integrity of your /etc/group and /etc/gshadow files. See its man page for further information.

Other tools are available for manipulating users and groups. First, if you want to delete a user, then you can use the userdel command; for groups, you can use the groupdel command. Second, you can modify existing users and groups with the usermod and groupmod commands, respectively. You will look at deleting some users and groups next.

Deleting Unnecessary Users and Groups

Most distributions create a variety of default user accounts and groups. Many of these are not required, and to enhance the security of your system you should remove them. Like with removing packages or services from your system, I recommend using common sense when removing users and groups. For example, if you do not use Network File System (NFS), then you have no requirement for the nfsnobody user; if you have not installed X Windows, then the gdm and xfs users will not be required. Table 1-6 lists users, describes their purposes, and includes my recommendations regarding removing them. I have also provided a list of groups that can generally be removed. Again, consider carefully the packages your system contains and the functions your system will perform before removing any groups.

■**Tip** I recommend making copies of your passwd and group files before performing multiple edits of them to ensure you can recover if you delete a user or group that is fundamental to your system or an application.

Table 1-6. *Default Users*

User	Purpose	Remove?
adm	Owns diagnostic and accounting tools	Yes
backup	Used by packing for backing up critical files	No
bin	Owns executables for user commands	No
daemon	Owns and runs system processes	No
desktop	KDE user	Yes
ftp	Default FTP user	Yes
games	Games user	Yes
gdm	GDM user	Yes
gnats	GNATS (bug tracking) user	Yes
gopher	Gopher user	Yes
halt	/sbin/halt user	No
identd	User for identd daemon	Yes
irc	Internet relay chat (IRC) user	Yes
list	Mailman user	Yes (if not using mailman)
lp	Printing user	Yes (if no printing)
lpd	Printing user	Yes (if no printing)
mail	Default user for Mail Transfer Agent (MTA)	Maybe
mailnull	Sendmail user	Yes (if no Sendmail)

Table 1-6.

User	Purpose	Remove?
man	Man-db user	No
news	Default news user	Yes
nfsnobody	NFS User	Yes
nobody	Default user for Apache or NFS	Maybe
nscd	Name Service Cache Daemon user	Yes (if not using nscd)
ntp	Network Time Protocol user	No
operator	Ops user	Yes
postgres	Postgres default user	Yes (if no Postgres)
proxy	Default proxy user	Yes
root	Root user	No
rpc	RPC user	Yes
rpcuser	Default RPC user	Yes
rpm	RPM user	No
shutdown	Shutdown user	No
sshd	Privilege split sshd user	No
sync	Sync user	Yes
sys	Default mounting user	No
telnetd	Telnetd default user	Yes
uucp	Default uucp user	Yes
vcsa	Virtual console memory	No
www-data	Owns www data	Yes (if not Web server)
xfs	X Font Server	Yes

Table 1-6 contains a combined list of the typical users created when a fresh Red Hat or Debian system is installed; thus, not all users in the table may be present on your system, as some are specific to one distribution or the other. This is also dependent on the packages you have installed on your system, so others may be present on your installation.

I labeled two users as Maybe, meaning that they are optionally removable from your system. These were the mail and nobody users. Several packages utilize these users to run processes after the package has dropped privileges. For example, some e-mail servers, such as Sendmail, use the mail user for this purpose, and it is common for Apache to use the nobody user. You should check to see if any processes or packages are utilizing these users before you delete them. You can do this by using the ps command.

```
puppy# ps -U mail -u mail
PID TTY          TIME CMD
809 ?        00:00:03 fetchmail
```

Replace mail with the username of each user you want to check.

To remove a user from your system, you can use the userdel command. If you use the userdel command in conjunction with the -r option, you will also remove users' home directories, any files in their home directories, and their mail spools. Be sure to check you are removing material that should be deleted. Additional files or directories belonging to that user outside their home directory will not be removed, and you will need to optionally find these files and directories and remove them if required.

These are the groups that can generally be removed:

- lp
- news
- uucp
- proxy
- postgres
- www-data
- backup
- operator
- list
- irc
- src
- gnats
- staff
- games
- users
- gdm
- telnetd
- gopher
- ftp
- nscd
- rpc
- rpcuser
- nfsnobody
- xfs
- desktop

To remove a group from the system, you can use the groupdel command. This command has no options.

```
puppy# groupdel sales
```

Passwords

As part of the user and group creation process, you need to ensure your users choose suitable and secure passwords for their accounts and that those passwords are managed and changed on a regular basis. I mentioned earlier in this chapter shadow passwords and using the /etc/shadow file. Additionally, most distributions also come with support for MD5 passwords. Without MD5 your passwords are encrypted via DES (the Data Encryption Standard), which is significantly more vulnerable to cracking attempts than MD5 passwords. You should enable both shadow passwording and MD5 passwords as part of your install process.

Your users' ability to choose their own passwords is one of the most frustrating and dangerous parts of user administration. Almost all your users have one objective when choosing a password: choosing one that is easy for them to remember. Security is simply not a consideration. Changing their password on a regular basis for them is an inconvenience and a chore. But it is an essential activity for the ongoing security of your system. A lot of people in the security world believe this sort of attitude is able to be changed with education about the risks of poor password security. I believe this is only partially true. To an extent no matter how often most of your users are told to treat their password like the personal identification number (PIN) to their cash card, they simply do not attach the same importance to it as they would something valuable to them personally. This is not to say you should not attempt to educate them, but do not count on it changing their attitudes. I recommend taking a consultative but ultimately dictatorial approach to determining the characteristics of your password variables and regime. Explain the security requirements of your environment to your end users, but do not compromise that security by making exceptions to your overall password rules.

I recommend you set your password rules, taking into consideration the following points:

- Do not allow passwords with dictionary words, such as *dog, cat,* or *elephant.* The same applies for non-English-language words.

- Do not allow passwords with only letters or numbers, such as *12345678* or *abcdefghi.*

- Ensure users do not use personal information such as dates of birth, pet names, names of family members, phone numbers, or post and zip codes.

- Set a minimum password length of ten. Longer is better.

- Force users to mix case; in other words, use both uppercase and lowercase letters in the password.

- Force users to mix letters, numbers, and punctuation in the password.

- Ensure your users change their passwords regularly; and if the password expires without being changed, then set a time limit after which that user account should be disabled.

- Ensure the new password is not the same as a number of previous passwords.

You can control the characteristics of your users' passwords in Linux via PAM. I talk about PAM in more detail in the "Pluggable Authentication Modules (PAM)" section later in this chapter, but I will cover the PAM modules specifically designed to handle the passwd application here.

The PAM modules are defined in individual files located in the /etc/pam.d directory. The file you want to look at in this directory is passwd and contains all the relevant PAM modules used by the passwd command. Listing 1-25 shows the contents of the default Debian /etc/pam.d/passwd file.

Listing 1-25. *Debian* default *File*

```
password  required  pam_unix.so nullok obscure min=4 max=8 md5
```

The entry in the line, password, indicates the module interface type of this line. In this case, it includes password-related functions for manipulating authentication tokens. The next entry, required, is the control flag that determines what PAM will do if the authentication succeeds or fails. The required entry indicates the authentication module must succeed for the password to be set or changed. The next entry, pam_unix.so, is the PAM module to be used. By default this is located in the /lib/security directory. The pam_unix.so module is designed to handle Unix password authentication using the /etc/passwd and /etc/shadow files.

The last entries are arguments to be passed to the pam_unix.so module, and these arguments also allow you to control the characteristics of your passwords and tell your system whether a password is suitable for use. The first argument, nullok, allows you to change an empty password. Without this option if the current password is blank or empty, then the account is considered locked, and you will not be able to change the password. The next option, obscure, performs some basic checks on the password.

Note The obscure option is the same as the OBSCURE_CHECKS_ENAB option that used to be defined in the login.defs file.

The min=4 argument sets the minimum password length to four characters, and the max=8 argument sets the maximum password length to four characters. The last argument tells PAM to use MD5 password encryption.

So, for the Debian distribution, the default PAM setup for passwords essentially addresses only one of the proposed password rules, that of password length. I do not recommend this as an acceptable password policy. But by adding additional PAM modules to the mix, you can control additional passwords characteristics. Both Debian and Red Hat have an additional PAM module, pam_cracklib.so, that you can use to address some of your other requirements. You can also use the existing pam_unix.so module in another module; type account to check that the user password has not expired or whether the account has been disabled. You first comment out the line in Listing 1-25 in the /etc/pam.d/passwd file and instead use the lines in Listing 1-26.

Note You may need to install the pam_cracklib.so module on your system. On Debian this is a package called libpam-cracklib. On Red Hat the pam_cracklib.so module comes with the pam RPM.

Listing 1-26. *Using Additional PAM Modules in* /etc/pam.d/passwd

```
account required pam_unix.so
password required pam_cracklib.so retry=3 minlen=10 dcredit=-1 ucredit=-1 ➥
ocredit=-1 lcredit=0 difok=3
password required pam_unix.so use_authtok remember=5 nullok md5
```

The construction of the PAM module declaration line in Listing 1-26 is essentially the same as that of Listing 1-25 except you are now using what is called *module stacking.* With module stacking you can combine modules together, so the results of their checks become cumulative. The account interface of pam_unix.so is checked, and then the password interfaces of the pam_cracklib.so and pam_unix.so modules are checked. As I have used the control flag required for all modules, all these checks need to be successful for the password to successfully set.

The first line shows how to use the pam_unix.so module, but I have specified an interface type of account that checks the age, expiry, and lock status of the user account before allowing a user to change a password. On the next line I have specified the pam_cracklib.so module with some new arguments. The first of these arguments is retry, which specifies the number of tries the passwd program will give the user to choose a suitable password. I have specified three attempts here. If the user has not provided a password by this point, then the password change will fail. The next option, minlen, specifies the proposed minimum length of the new password, which I have set to ten characters.

The next options control what sort of characters need to be present in the password. They work on a system of credits toward the minimum length of the password. For example, specifying dcredit=1 means each digit in your password will count as one character for the purposes of determining the minimum password length. If you specify dcredit=2, then each digit you use in your password counts as two characters for the purposes of meeting the minimum password length. This is generally relevant only for longer passwords. With a minimum password length of ten, you can make better use of "negative" credits. To do this, you would specify dcredit=-1. This tells PAM that the new password must have a minimum of one digit character in it to be a successful password. You can specify dcredit=-2, and so on, to insist on more characters of a particular type. The four credit options available to you are dcredit for digits, ucredit for uppercase characters, lcredit for lowercase characters, and ocredit for other characters, such as punctuation. So in Listing 1-26 you see a password with a minimum of ten characters that must have one digit, one uppercase character, one other character, and one lowercase character.

The final option in Listing 1-26 is difok. This controls how many characters have to be different in the new password from the old password. As I have specified difok=3 in Listing 1-26, then if at least three characters in the old password do not appear in the new password, the new password is acceptable. Be careful using this option. If you specify that a large number of characters in the old password cannot appear in the new password, you can make it hard for a user to choose a new password.

You should be able to use a combination of these settings to implement a password policy that suits your environment. In addition to these checks, the pam_cracklib.so module performs some other checks that do not require arguments.

- It checks whether the password is a palindrome[6] of the previous password.

- It checks the password against a list of dictionary words contained in /usr/lib/ cracklib_dict.pwd on Red Hat systems and /var/cache/cracklib_dict.pwd on Debian.

- It checks whether the password is only a case change from the previous password (in other words, from uppercase to lowercase, and vice versa).

After processing the pam_cracklib.so module, PAM moves onto the pam_unix.so module. I used some new arguments for this module when I used it in Listing 1-26. In this case I am specifying the pam_unix.so module with a special argument, use_authtok. This tells the pam_unix.so module not to prompt the user for a password but rather use the password that has already been checked by the pam_cracklib.so module as the password to be processed. I have also specified the remember option on this line. This enables a password history function. I have specified that PAM should check that the new password is different from the last five passwords, but you can specify a number suitable for your environment. To enable password history, you must first create a file to hold your old passwords.

```
puppy# touch /etc/security/opasswd
puppy# chown root:root /etc/security/opasswd
puppy# chmod 0644 /etc/security/opasswd
```

Now the last five passwords for all users will be held in the file /etc/security/opasswd in MD5-encrypted format, and the user will not be able to use them as a new password.

Tip Other PAM modules are available for password authentication. One of the best is pam_passwdqc, available from http://www.openwall.com/passwdqc/. It contains some additional characteristics you can configure, including support for randomly generated passwords.

On Red Hat systems the PAM authentication works the same way but is configured differently. Listing 1-27 shows the content of the default /etc/pam.d/passwd file.

Listing 1-27. *Default Red Hat File*

```
auth       required    pam_stack.so service=system-auth
account    required    pam_stack.so service=system-auth
password   required    pam_stack.so service=system-auth
```

The /etc/pam.d/passwd file here calls the special module pam_stack.so that tells passwd to check another file, system-auth in the /etc/pam.d directory for the required PAM modules and authentication rules required for a password change. Listing 1-28 shows the contents of the default system-auth file.

---

6.   A word or phrase that reads the same backward as forward

Listing 1-28. *The Red Hat* system-auth *File*

```
#%PAM-1.0
# This file is autogenerated.
# User changes will be destroyed the next time authconfig is run.
auth        required     /lib/security/pam_env.so
auth        sufficient   /lib/security/pam_unix.so likeauth nullok
auth        required     /lib/security/pam_deny.so
account     required     /lib/security/pam_unix.so
password    required     /lib/security/pam_cracklib.so retry=3 type=
password    sufficient   /lib/security/pam_unix.so nullok use_authtok md5 shadow
password    required     /lib/security/pam_deny.so
session     required     /lib/security/pam_limits.so
session     required     /lib/security/pam_unix.so
```

The important lines you need to change to add your password policy here are as follows:

```
password    required     /lib/security/pam_cracklib.so retry=3 type=
password    sufficient   /lib/security/pam_unix.so nullok use_authtok md5 shadow
```

You should change these lines to match the requirements of your password policy.

■**Tip** The message in the second two comment lines in Listing 1-28 indicates that this file is auto-generated by running the `authconfig` tool and your changes will be lost. I recommend not running this tool if you are going to manually change this file.

Password Aging

Password aging allows you to specify a time period for which a password is valid. After the time period has expired, so will the password forcing the user to enter a new password. This has the benefit of ensuring passwords are changed regularly and that a password that is stolen, cracked, or known by a former employee will have a time-limited value. Unfortunately for many users, the need to regularly change their passwords increases their desire to write down the passwords. You need to mitigate this risk with user education about the dangers of writing down passwords. I often use the metaphor of a cash card PIN. Writing down your password at your desk is the same as putting your cash card PIN on a sticky note attached to your card. You need to regularly enforce this sort of education with users; I recommend any acceptable use policies within your organization also cite the users' responsibilities for ensuring they do not reveal their passwords to anyone else either through carelessness or deliberately.

■**Tip** I recommend you use a password age between 30–60 days for most passwords depending on the nature of the system.

Two ways exist to handle password aging. The first uses the command-line tool chage to set or change the password expiry of a user account individually. Listing 1-29 shows this command working.

Listing 1-29. *The* chage *Command*

```
puppy# chage -M 30 bob
```

Listing 1-29 uses the -M option to set the password expiry period for the user bob to 30 days. Table 1-7 shows several other variables you can set.

Table 1-7. *Command-Line Options for the* chage *Command*

Option	Description
-m *days*	Sets the minimum number of days between password changes. Zero allows the user to change it at any time.
-M	Sets the maximum number of days for which a password stays valid.
-E	Sets a date on which the user account will expire and automatically be deactivated.
-W *days*	Sets the number of days before the password expires that the user will be warned to change it.
-d *days*	Sets the number of days since Jan. 1, 1970, that the password was last changed.
-I *days*	Sets the number of days after password expiry that the account is locked.

First, the -m option allows you to specify the minimum amount of time between password changes. A setting of 0 allows the user to change the password at any time. Second, the next option, -W, specifies the number of days before a user's password expires that they will get a warning that their password is about to expire. The -d option is principally useful to immediately expire a password. By setting the -d option to 0, the user's last password change date becomes Jan. 1, 1970, and if the -M option is greater than 0, then the user must change their password at the next login. The last option, -I, provides a time frame in days after which user accounts with expired and unchanged passwords are locked and thus unable to be used to log in. If you run chage without any options and specify only the user, then it will launch an interactive series of prompts to set the required values. Listing 1-30 shows this. The values between the [ ] brackets indicate the current values to which this user's password aging is set.

Listing 1-30. *Running* chage *Without Options*

```
puppy# chage bob
Changing the aging information for bob
Enter the new value, or press return for the default
Minimum Password Age [0]:
Maximum Password Age [30]:
Last Password Change (YYYY-MM-DD) [2004-06-27]:
Password Expiration Warning [7]:
Password Inactive [-1]:
Account Expiration Date (YYYY-MM-DD) [2004-07-28]:
```

Users can also utilize the `chage` command with the `-l` option to show when a password is due to expire.

```
puppy# chage -l bob
```

The other method to handle password aging is to set defaults for all users in the `/etc/login.defs` file.

■**Tip** The `/etc/login.defs` file is used to also control password lengths. On both Debian and Red Hat (and other distributions), PAM has taken over this function.

Listing 1-31 shows the controls available for password aging in `/etc/login.defs`.

Listing 1-31. *The* `login.defs` *Password-Aging Controls*

```
PASS_MAX_DAYS    60
PASS_MIN_DAYS    0
PASS_WARN_AGE    7
```

As you can see, you can set the core password-aging controls here, and I have set the maximum password age to 60 days, allowing users to change their passwords at any time and providing a warning to users that their passwords will expire seven days before password expiry.

sudo

One of the first things most system administrators are told is not to use the root user to perform activities that do not require it. This is inconvenient for administration purposes but greatly enhances the security of the system. This enhancement reduces the risk of the root user being compromised or used by unauthorized people and the risk of accidental misuse of the root user privileges.

One of the ways you can reduce the inconvenience this causes whilst not increasing the security exposure is to use the `sudo` function, which is a variation on the `su` function. I will cover securing this in the "Pluggable Authentication Modules (PAM)" section. The `sudo` function allows selected non-root users to execute particular commands as if they were root. The `sudo` command is a `setuid` binary that is owned by root to which all users have execute permissions. If you are authorized to do so, you can run `sudo` and effectively become the root user. `sudo` is a complicated package, and I will take you through the basics of configuring it.

■**Note** Most distributions come with `sudo` installed, but you may need to install it. On both Debian and Red Hat, the package is called `sudo`.

The sudo command checks the /etc/sudoers file for the authorization to run commands. You can configure the sudoers file to restrict access to particular users, to certain commands, and on particular hosts.

Let's look at Listing 1-32 to see how to use sudo. I am logged onto the system as the user bob.

Listing 1-32. *Using* sudo

```
puppy$ cat /var/log/secure
cat: /var/log/secure: Permission denied
puppy$ sudo cat /var/log/secure
Password:
```

In the first command in Listing 1-32, I try to cat the /var/log/secure, which would normally be accessible only by root. As you can see, I get a permission-denied error, which is the result I expect. Then I try again, prefixing the command with the sudo command. You will be prompted for your password (not the root password). If you have been authorized to use sudo and authorized to use the cat command as root on this system, then you would be able to view the file.

■**Note** You can also run sudo using a time limit. You can specify that for a defined time period after executing the sudo command the user can act as root. I do not recommend configuring sudo this way because it creates similar issues to simply using the root user for administration. But if you want to configure it like this, you can see how to do it in the sudo man page.

Let's look at what you need to add to the /etc/sudoers file to get Listing 1-32 to work. You need to use the command visudo to edit the /etc/sudoers file. The visudo command is the safest way to edit the sudoers file. The command locks the file against multiple simultaneous edits, provides basic sanity checks, and checks for any parse errors. If the file is currently being edited, you will receive a message to try again later. I have added the content of Listing 1-33 to the sudoers file.

Listing 1-33. *Sample* sudoers *Line*

```
bob ALL=/bin/cat
```

We can break this line down into its component parts.

```
username host = command
```

Listing 1-33 shows the user bob is allowed to, on all hosts (using the variable ALL), use the command /bin/cat as if he were root. Any command you specify in the command option must be defined with its full path. You can also specify more than one command, each separated by commas, to be authorized for use, as you can see on the next line:

```
bob ALL=/bin/cat,/sbin/shutdown,/sbin/poweroff
```

In the previous line bob is now authorized to use the cat, shutdown, and poweroff commands as if he were the root user. All configuration lines in the sudoers file must be on one line only, and you can use the \ to indicate the configuration continues on the next line.

A single sudoers file is designed to be used on multiple systems. Thus, it allows host specific access controls. You would change your sudoers file on a central system and distribute the updated file to all your systems. With host access controls you can define different authorizations for different systems, as you can see in Listing 1-34.

Listing 1-34. *Different* sudo *Authorization on Multiple Systems*

```
bob puppy=/bin/cat,/sbin/shutdown
bob kitten=ALL
```

In Listing 1-34 the user bob is allowed to use only the cat and shutdown commands on the system puppy, but on the system kitten he is allowed to use ALL possible commands. You should be careful when using the ALL variable to define access to all commands on a system. The ALL variable allows no granularity of authorization configuration. You can be somewhat more selective with your authorization by granting access to the commands in a particular directory, as you can see on the next line:

```
bob puppy=/bin/*
```

This applies only to the directory defined and not to any subdirectories. For example, if you authorized to the /bin/* directory, then you will not be able to run any commands in the /bin/extra/ directory unless you explicitly define access to that directory like the configuration on the next line:

```
bob puppy=/bin/*,/bin/extra/*
```

Sometimes you want to grant access to a particular command to a user, but you want that command to be run as another user. For example, you need to start and stop some daemons as specific users, such as the MySQL or named daemon. You can specify the user you want the command to be started as by placing it in parentheses in front of the command, like so:

```
 bob puppy=(mysql) /usr/local/bin/mysqld,(named) /usr/local/sbin/named
```

As you can imagine, lists of authorized commands, users, and hosts can become quite long. The sudo command also comes with the option of defining aliases. Aliases are collections of like users, commands, and hosts. Generally you define aliases at the start of the sudoers file.

Let's look at some aliases. The first type of alias is User_Alias. A User_Alias groups like users.

```
User_Alias OPERATORS = bob,jane,paul,mary
```

You start an alias with the name of the alias type you are using, in this case User_Alias, and then the name of the particular alias you are defining, here OPERATORS. Then you specify a list of the users who belong to this alias. You can then refer to this alias in a configuration line.

```
OPERATORS ALL=/bin/mount,/sbin/raidstop,/sbin/raidstart, \
(named) /usr/local/sbin/named
```

In the previous line I have specified that the users in User_Alias OPERATORS (bob, jane, paul, and mary) are able to use the mount, raidstart, and raidstop commands and the named command.

The next type of alias you can define is a command alias, Cmnd_Alias, which groups collections of commands.

```
Cmnd_Alias DNS_COMMANDS = /usr/local/sbin/rndc,(named) /usr/local/sbin/named
```

You can use this alias in conjunction with the previous alias.

```
OPERATORS ALL=/bin/mount,DNS_COMMANDS
```

Now all users defined in the alias OPERATORS can use the commands /bin/mount and all those commands defined in the command alias DNS_COMMANDS on ALL hosts.

You can also specify an alias that groups a collection of hosts. The Host_Alias alias can specify lists of host names, IP addresses, and networks.

```
Host_Alias DNS_SERVERS = elephant,tiger,bear
```

You can combine this alias with the preceding ones you have defined.

```
OPERATORS DNS_SERVERS=DNS_COMMANDS
```

Now all users specified in the OPERATORS alias can run the commands specified in DNS_COMMANDS on the hosts defined in the DNS_SERVERS alias group.

You can also negate aliases by placing an exclamation (!) mark in front of them. Let's look at an example of this. First you define a command alias with some commands you do not want users to use, and then you can use that alias in conjunction with a sudo configuration line.

```
Cmnd_Alias DENIED_COMMANDS = /bin/su,/bin/mount,/bin/umount
bob puppy=/bin/*,!DENIED_COMMANDS
```

Here the user bob can use all the commands in the /bin directory on the puppy host except those defined in the DENIED_COMMANDS command alias.

■**Caution** This looks like a great method of securing commands via sudo, but unfortunately it is relatively easy to get around negating commands simply by copying or moving the denied command from the directory you have denied it in to another location. You should be aware of this risk when using negated aliases.

Let's look at one of the other ways you can authorize users to sudo. Inside the sudoers file you can define another type of alias based on the group information in your system by prefixing the group name with %.

```
%groupname ALL=(ALL) ALL
```

Replace *groupname* with the name of a group defined on your system. This means all members of the defined group are able to execute whatever commands you authorize for them, in this case ALL commands on ALL hosts. On Red Hat a group called wheel already exists for this purpose, and if you uncomment the following line on your Red Hat system, then any users added to the wheel group will have root privileges on your system.

```
%wheel ALL=(ALL) ALL
```

Additionally, the sudoers file itself also has a number of options and defaults you can define to change the behavior of the sudo command. For example, you can configure sudo to send e-mail when the sudo command is used. To define who to send that e-mail to, you can use the option on the following line:

```
mailto "admin@puppy.yourdomain.com"
```

You can then modify when sudo sends that e-mail using further options.

```
mail_always on
```

To give you an idea of the sort of defaults and options available to you, Table 1-8 defines a list of the e-mail–related options.

Table 1-8. *Send E-mail When* sudo *Runs*

Option	Description	Default
mail_always	Sends e-mail every time a user runs sudo. This flag is set off by default.	
mail_badpass	Sends e-mail if the user running sudo does not enter the correct password. This flag is set to off by default.	
mail_no_user	Sends e-mail if the user running sudo does not exist in the sudoers file. This flag is set to on by default.	
mail_no_host	Sends e-mail if the user running sudo exists in the sudoers file but is not authorized to run commands on this host. This flag is set to off by default.	
mail_no_perms	Sends e-mail if the user running sudo exists in the sudoers file but they do not have authority to the command they have tried to run. This flag is set to off by default.	

There are a number of other options and defaults you can see in the sudoers man page.

The sudo command itself can also have some command-line options you can issue with it. Table 1-9 shows some of the most useful options.

Table 1-9. sudo *Command-Line Options*

Option	Description
-l	Prints a list out the allowed (and forbidden) commands for the current user on the current host
-L	Lists any default options set in the sudoers file
-b	Runs the given command in the background
-u *user*	Runs the specified command as a user other than root

The -l option is particularly useful to allow you to determine what commands the current user on the current host is authorized and forbidden to run.

```
puppy# sudo -l
Password:
User bob may run the following commands on this host:
    (root) ALL
```

The sudo command is complicated and if improperly implemented can open your system to security exposures. I recommend you carefully test any sudo configuration before you implement it and you thoroughly explore the contents of the sudo and sudoers man pages.

User Accounting

Keeping track of what your users are doing is an important part of user management. In Chapter 5 I will talk about logging onto your system, and indeed one of the first resources you will use to keep track of the actions of your users is the content of your syslog log files. But also other commands and sources are useful for keeping track of your users and their activities.

■**Caution** The data used to populate the output of these commands is often one of the first targets of an attacker. You should secure the integrity of this data by ensuring only root can read the log files.

The first command I will cover is the who command. This command displays all those users logged onto the system currently, together with the terminal they are logged on to and if they have connected remotely then the IP address or hostname from which they have connected. Listing 1-35 shows the default output of the who command.

Listing 1-35. *The Output of the who Command*

```
puppy# who
root      tty1         Jul  3 12:32
bob       pts/0        Jul  8 11:39 (host002.yourdomain.com)
```

You can also modify the output of the who command. Table 1-10 shows the command-line options available to modify its output.

Table 1-10. *The who Command-Line Options*

Option	Description
-a	Displays all options in verbose mode
-b	Displays the time of the last system boot
-d	Displays any dead processes
-H	Prints a line of column headings
--login	Prints the system login processes
-p	Prints all active processes spawned by init
-q	Generates a count of all login names and number of users logged on
-r	Prints the current run level
-t	Prints the last system clock change

These options are mostly self-explanatory, but you should note the -a option that combines a variety of the command-line options to provide a detailed overview of who is logged into your system, the login processes, and the system reboot and run level details.

The next commands you will learn about are the last and lastb commands, which display a record of when users last logged into the system and a record of bad user logins, respectively. To start collecting the data required to populate the output of these commands, you need to create a couple of files to hold the data. Some distributions automatically create these files, but others require them to be created manually. Once they are created, you do not need to do anything else. The system will automatically detect the created files and begin logging the required information. The two files you will require are /var/log/wtmp and /var/log/btmp. If these files exist in the /var/log/ directory, then you can proceed to using the commands. If not, then you need to create them and secure them from non-root users.

```
puppy# touch /var/log/wtmp /var/log/btmp
puppy# chown root:root /var/log/wtmp /var/log/btmp
puppy# chmod 0644 /var/log/wtmp /var/log/btmp
```

The /var/log/wtmp file contains the data for the last command, and the /var/log/btmp file contains the data for the lastb command.

If you execute the last command without any options, it will print a report of the last logins to the system. Listing 1-36 shows the results of this command.

Listing 1-36. *Running the Last Command*

```
puppy# last
root     tty1                          Sat Jul  3 12:32   still logged in
bob      pts/0        192.168.0.23     Sat Jul  3 14:25 - 14:26  (00:01)
reboot   system boot  2.4.20-28.8      Sat Jul  3 12:31          (4+05:40)
```

As you can see, the last command tells you that root is logged into tty1 and is still logged in. The list also shows the user bob, who logged in from the IP address 192.168.0.23 and stayed logged on for one second. The last entry shows a reboot entry. Every time the system is rebooted, an entry is logged to the wtmp file, giving the time of the reboot and the version of the kernel into which the system was booted.

The lastb produces the same style of report but lists only those logins that were "bad." In other words, it lists those logins in which an incorrect password was entered, or some other error resulted in a failure to log in.

Both the last and lastb commands have some additional command-line options you can use. Table 1-11 shows these additional options.

Table 1-11. *Additional* last *and* lastb *Command-Line Options*

Option	Description
-n *num*	Lists *num* of lines in the output
-t *YYYYMMDDHHMMSS*	Displays the login status at the time specified
-x	Displays the shutdown and run level changes
-f *file*	Specifies another file to read for the last information

Related to the last and lastb commands is the lastlog command. The lastlog command displays a report that is based on information in the /var/log/lastlog file that shows the login status of all users on your system including those users who have never logged in. Like the wtmp and btmp files, you may need to create the lastlog file.

```
puppy# touch /var/log/lastlog
puppy# chown root:root /var/log/lastlog
puppy# chmod 0644 /var/log/lastlog
```

This displays a list of all users and their last login date and time. Or it displays a message indicating **Never Logged In** if that user has never logged in. You can also specify only the lastlog record for a particular user by using the -u command-line option. Or you can use the -t *days* option to specify only those logins more recent than *days* be displayed. Using the -t flag overrides the use of the -u flag.

```
puppy# lastlog -u bob
puppy# lastlog -t 30
```

■**Tip** Many systems also come with the ac command that provides statistics about the amount of time users have been connected to your system, which can often provide useful information. The ac command uses the contents of the /var/log/wtmp file to produce these reports; you can see its options in the sa man page.

Process Accounting

Another useful tool in tracking the activities on your system is *process accounting*. Process accounting is a method of tracking every command issued on your system, the process or user initiating that command, and the amount of processing time used, amongst other information. All modern distributions have process accounting enabled in their kernels, and you simply need to add some utilities for turning on and manipulating that data on your system.

If you have Red Hat, you can install the package psacct, which contains the required tools. For Debian systems you can use the acct package. If you cannot find a suitable process accounting package for your distribution, then you can also download and compile the Acct utilities from http://www.ibiblio.org/pub/linux/system/admin/accounts/acct-1-3.73.tar.gz. This is an old release of the tools and, although stable, does not have the full functionality of the utilities available in the Red Hat and Debian packages, so some of the functions I will describe may not work.

If you installed a package, then skip down until you reach the section on the discussion of starting process accounting. If you downloaded the utilities, then unpack the archive and change into the resulting directory. This directory contains some kernel patches (which you will not all need, as all modern kernels include process accounting code) and two directories, utils and scripts. Change into the utils directory, and compile the programs in this directory. Enter the following:

```
puppy# make
```

Then copy the compiled binaries to a program directory in your path; the recommended default path is /usr/local/sbin.

```
puppy# cp acctentries accton accttrim dumpact lastcomm /usr/local/sbin
```

You can also refer to the man pages for each of these commands in this directory you can install.

To get process accounting running, first create a file in /var/log to hold your process accounting information. I usually create a file called pacct.

```
puppy# touch /var/log/pacct
```

As this file is going to contain some sensitive data, you need to secure it, and you must ensure only root has privileges to it.

```
puppy# chown root:root /var/log/pacct
puppy# chmod 0644 /var/log/pacct
```

Now to turn on process accounting, you need to run the accton command and provide it with the name of the file you have nominated to hold your process accounting information.

```
puppy# /usr/local/sbin/accton /var/log/pacct
```

If you want run process accounting all the time, you need to add this into the startup process of your system also to ensure process accounting is started every time you reboot. You also need to tell process accounting to stop when the system is shut down. If you execute the accton command without any options, this will turn off process accounting.

```
puppy# /usr/local/sbin/accton
```

Now you have process accounting collecting information. You can query this information and find out who has been running what on your system. The easiest and fastest way to do this is to use the lastcomm command, which summarizes the last commands used on the system in reverse order. To run lastcomm and display all the commands run on the system in the current process accounting file, you simply need to specify the file to be read.

```
puppy# lastcomm -f /var/log/pacct
ls                      root    stdout    0.01 secs Wed Jul  7 17:49
accton           S      root    stdout    0.01 secs Wed Jul  7 17:49
```

This shows the root user has started the accton command and also has performed the ls command. Each entry contains the command name of the process that has been run, some flags (for example, in the previous accton entry the flag S indicates that the command was executed by a superuser, and other flags are documented in the lastcomm man page), the name of the user who ran the process, where the output of the process was directed, and the time the process ended. You can also filter the information by telling lastcomm to specify only some commands executed or only those commands executed by a specific user or from a specific device.

```
puppy# lastcomm -f /var/log/pacct --user bob
```

The previous line tells lastcomm to display only those commands issued by the user bob. You can also specify the option --command *commandname* to list all occurrences of that specific command or the --tty *ttyname* option to specify only those commands issued on the specified TTY. You can also specify a combination of these options to further narrow your search.

The Red Hat and Debian packages also include the sa tool. The sa tool is capable of producing detailed reports and summaries of your process accounting information. This includes generating output reports of all processes and commands sorted by user or by command. You can get more information about sa from its man page.

Process accounting can accumulate a lot of data quickly, especially on big systems with a large number of users. To keep this manageable, you should trim down the size of your process accounting file. In the Acct utilities, which are available to download, the scripts directory contains a script called handleacct.sh, which is an automated shell script for trimming the size of your pacct file. You could easily modify this and run it regularly through cron to do this trimming of files.

Pluggable Authentication Modules (PAM)

Sun Microsystems designed PAM to provide a plug-in authentication framework. It is heavily used and developed in the Linux world, and a large number of PAM modules exist to perform a variety of authentication functions. PAM is designed to integrate authentication into services without changing those services. It means developers merely need to make applications PAM aware without having to develop a custom authentication module or scheme for that application. A suitable PAM module can be integrated and used to provide the authentication.

On most Linux distributions you have two possible locations to look for PAM configuration. The legacy file /etc/pam.conf used to hold PAM configuration information on Linux distributions but now is generally deprecated and has been replaced by the /etc/pam.d directory. This directory holds a collection of configuration file for PAM-aware services. The service shares the same name as the application it is designed to authenticate; for example, the PAM configuration for the passwd command is contained in a file called /etc/pam.d/passwd. I call these files *service configuration files*.

The service configuration files themselves have four major directives, and Listing 1-37 shows a sample of a PAM service configuration file from the system-auth service on a Red Hat system.

Note The system-auth service provides a default authentication process for a variety of system functions such as logins or changing passwords. I talk about it further in the "PAM Module Stacking" section.

Listing 1-37. *Sample Red Hat* system-auth *Line*

```
auth        required      pam_unix.so nullok
```

The first of the four directives is the interface type. In Listing 1-37 you can see the interface type is auth. There are four major interface types available in PAM.

- auth: These modules perform user authentication using permissions, for example, and can also set credentials such as group assignments or Kerberos tickets.

- account: These modules confirm access is available by checking the user's account, for example, confirming that the user account is unlocked or if only a root user can perform an action.

- `password`: These modules verify and test passwords and can update authentication tokens such as passwords.

- `session`: These modules check, manage, and configure user sessions.

You can use some modules for more than one interface type. For example, you can use the pam_unix.so module to authenticate `password`, `auth`, `account`, and `session` interface types.

```
auth        sufficient    /lib/security/pam_unix.so likeauth nullok
account     required      /lib/security/pam_unix.so
password    sufficient    /lib/security/pam_unix.so nullok use_authtok md5 shadow
session     required      /lib/security/pam_unix.so
```

It is also possible to stack modules of the same interface type together to allow more than one form of authentication for that interface type. For example, on the next line I have stacked together the pam_cracklib.so and pam_unix.so modules to perform `password` interface type authentication.

```
password    required      /lib/security/pam_cracklib.so retry=3 type=
password    sufficient    /lib/security/pam_unix.so nullok use_authtok md5 shadow
```

This is described as a *stack*, and I talk about module stacking in the "PAM Module Stacking" section.

The next directive, `required` in Listing 1-37, is a control flag that tells PAM what to do with the module's results. Processing a PAM module ends in either a success or a failure result. The controls flags tell PAM what to do with the success or failure results and how that result impacts the overall authentication process. The `required` flag means the module result must be a success in order for the authentication process to succeed. If the result of this module is a failure, then the overall authentication is also a failure. If more than one module is stacked together, the other modules in the stack will also be processed but the overall authentication will still fail.

Three other possible control flags exist. The `requisite` flag indicates that the module result must be successful for authentication to be successful. Additionally, unlike the `required` flag, the success or failure of this module will be immediately notified to the service requesting authentication, and the authentication process will complete. This means that if any modules are stacked together and a module with a `requisite` control flag fails, then the modules remaining to be processed will not be executed. But with the `required` control flag, the remaining modules in the stack would continue to be processed.

The next control flag is `sufficient`. The `sufficient` flag means that the success of this module is sufficient for the authentication process to be successful or if modules are stacked for the stack to succeed. This is dependent on no other `required` modules, processed prior to this module, failing. If a `sufficient` module fails, then the overall stack does not fail.

The last control flag is `optional`. An `optional` module is not critical to the overall success and failure of the authentication process or the module stack. Its success or failure will not determine the success or failure of the overall authentication process.

The next directive from Listing 1-37, pam_unix.so, indicates what PAM module will be used and its location. If you specify a PAM module without a path such as shown in Listing 1-37, then the module is assumed to be located in the /lib/security directory. You can also specify a module from another location here by providing the path to it, as you can see in the following line:

```
auth        required      /usr/local/pamlib/pam_local.so id=-1 root=1
```

The last directive from Listing 1-37, nullok, is an argument to be passed to the PAM module. In the previous line, for example, you can see two arguments, id=-1 and root=1, being passed to the module pam_local.so. Most modules will ignore invalid or incorrect arguments passed to them, and the module will continue to be processed though some modules do generate an error message or fail.

■Tip You can find documentation on your Red Hat system for PAM and all the PAM modules supplied with the pam RPM at /usr/share/doc/pam-*version*/txts, replacing *version* with the version number of your pam RPM, or at http://www.kernel.org/pub/linux/libs/pam/.

PAM Module Stacking

As I mentioned earlier, you can stack modules for processing, with multiple modules being used to authenticate each interface type of a particular service. If modules are stacked, then they are processed in the order they appear in the PAM service configuration file. As you can specify a variety of control flags when stacking modules, it is important to carefully consider how to stack your modules and what dependencies to configure. In Listing 1-38, you will see the Debian login PAM configuration file.

Listing 1-38. *The Debian Login* /etc/pam.d *Configuration File*

```
password required       pam_cracklib.so retry=3 minlen=6 difok=3
password required       pam_unix.so use_authtok nullok md5
```

Here I am first running the pam_cracklib.so module to check the strength of a new or changed password and then the pam_unix.so module. Both are using a control flag of required, which means both modules need to succeed for the password to be successfully changed and both modules would be tested. If you changed the pam_cracklib.so control flag to requisite and the pam_cracklib.so module failed, then the password change process would immediately fail and the pam_unix.so module would not be checked at all.

Additionally, if you specified a module as sufficient that was not adequately secure, then if this module check is successful the entire module stack is considered successful and you have authenticated something without adequate authentication. For example:

```
auth sufficient pam_notsosecure.so
auth required pam_secure.so
```

In this case, if the check of pamnotsosecure.so was successful, then the authentication process would be halted and authentication would be successful. If this module does not in reality provide a sufficient security check for authentication, then this is a serious security risk. Thus, it is important to ensure you order your modules and control flags in your PAM configuration files.

Additionally on Red Hat systems, you can use a special module called pam_stack.so. This module allows you to include another list of modules contained in an external file into a service configuration file. For example, Red Hat systems use a special service called system-auth to perform the default authentication for most services. In Listing 1-39 you will see the Red Hat service configuration file for the passwd function.

Listing 1-39. *The Red Hat* passwd *Function Service Configuration File*

```
auth       required     /lib/security/pam_stack.so service=system-auth
account    required     /lib/security/pam_stack.so service=system-auth
password   required     /lib/security/pam_warn.so
password   required     /lib/security/pam_stack.so service=system-auth
```

Instead of defining the particular PAM modules to be used for authentication, the service configuration file defines the pam_stack.so module with an option of service=system-auth. This tells PAM to use the service configuration file called system-auth and the modules defined in it for the authentication process. This is especially useful for maintaining a single, centralized authentication method that you refer to in a number of services. If you want to change the authentication process, you have to change it in only one place—not in all the service configuration files.

Finally, you should check the contents of all your PAM module stacks and configuration to ensure you fully understand the sequence in which authentication occurs. Additionally, you should check for the presence of the pam_rhosts_auth.so module. This module is designed to allow access using .rhosts files, which are used by the so-called r-tools, rlogin, rsh, and so on. These tools and this authentication model are not secure, and I strongly recommend you remove all references to this module from your PAM configuration. I will talk about the r-tools and their security weaknesses further in Chapter 3.

The PAM "Other" Service

One of the advantages of implementing PAM on your system is that it comes with a catchall authentication service that handles the authentication for any PAM-aware service that does not have a specific service configuration file. The PAM configuration for this is located in the /etc/pam.d/other file, and in Listing 1-40 you can see the default Red Hat other file.

Listing 1-40. *Default Red Hat* /etc/pam.d/other *File*

```
#%PAM-1-0
auth       required     /lib/security/pam_deny.so
account    required     /lib/security/pam_deny.so
password   required     /lib/security/pam_deny.so
session    required     /lib/security/pam_deny.so
```

Listing 1-40 shows a very strong other file. Each of the possible interface types is represented here with a control flag of required, which means each authentication request must succeed for the service to authenticate and that all interface types will be checked. The specified module, pam_deny.so, does exactly what the name suggests and denies any request made to it. So this is a good configuration for security purposes because the authentication in Listing 1-40 will *never* succeed, thus stopping any PAM-aware service from being inadvertently authenticated.

This configuration does pose a risk, though, if you or someone else accidentally deletes one of the service configuration files from the /etc/pam.d directory, for example, the login file.

Then the login command will default to using the other configuration and deny all logins to the system. The other risk is that when the pam_unix.so module denies a request, it does not log any record of that denial. This can sometimes make it hard to both spot any intrusion attempts or to determine for diagnostic purposes where an authentication attempt is failing. Listing 1-41 shows a way around this by using the additional PAM module, pam_warn.so.

Listing 1-41. *Updated Red Hat* /etc/pam.d/other *File*

```
#%PAM-1-0
auth      required      /lib/security/pam_warn.so
auth      required      /lib/security/pam_deny.so
account   required      /lib/security/pam_warn.so
account   required      /lib/security/pam_deny.so
password  required      /lib/security/pam_warn.so
password  required      /lib/security/pam_deny.so
session   required      /lib/security/pam_warn.so
session   required      /lib/security/pam_deny.so
```

The pam_warn.so module will log a warning message to syslog every time an authentication request is made using the syslog facility of auth and a log level of warning.

Tip On Red Hat system this usually logs to the /var/log/secure file with a program ID of PAM-warn if you want to use your log filtering tools to highlight these messages as I will describe in Chapter 5.

I recommend reviewing the current contents of your /etc/pam.d/other file to see if it meets your security requirements. I strongly recommend that the default PAM authentication response be to deny any request from a service that is not explicitly configured with its own PAM service configuration file.

Restricting su Using PAM

The su command allows you to log into a new shell as another user.

```
puppy$ su jane
Password:
```

This would log into a new shell as the user jane with the privileges of that user (if you entered that user's correct password). If you use the su command without specifying a user, then the system will attempt to log in as the root user. For example, you can also use the su command to log in as the root user if you know the root password.

```
puppy$ su
Password:
```

Tip You can find more about su using man su.

As you can imagine, this is a powerful tool but also a dangerous one to which you should restrict access. PAM offers a way to easily secure access to this tool to only those users you want. To configure for access restriction, review the contents of the `su` PAM service configuration files inside your `/etc/pam.d` directory. On both Debian and Red Hat systems, you should find the following line:

```
auth       required      /lib/security/pam_wheel.so use_uid
```

Uncomment this line, so PAM will allow `su` to be used only by members of the `wheel` group.

■Note The `wheel` group may exist on your system already, or you may need to create it and add the required members to it.

The `use_uid` option tells PAM to check the `UID` of the current user trying to use `su` to log in. You can also specify the `group=` option to indicate that a group other than `wheel` is allowed to use `su` to log in. See the following line:

```
auth       required      /lib/security/pam_wheel.so use_uid group=allowsu
```

Now only those users belonging to the `allowsu` group will be able to use the `su` command.

■Tip Some other useful configuration models for `su` are documented in the `/etc/pam.d/su` service and are worth examining. These may also give you ideas for some other uses of PAM.

Setting Limits with PAM

The PAM module `pam_limits.so` is designed to prevent internal- and some external-style Denial of Service attacks. An internal Denial of Service attack can occur when internal users either deliberately or inadvertently cause a system or application outage by consuming too many resources such as memory, disk space, or CPU. External Denial of Service attacks occur in the same manner but originate from outside the host.

To enable limits on functionality, you need to add or enable the `pam_limits.so` module in the services for which you require limiting to operate. On a Debian system, for example, an entry exists for the `pam_limits.so` functionality in the `login` service configuration file in `/etc/pam.d`.

```
session    required      pam_limits.so
```

By default on Debian, this entry is commented out. Uncomment it to enable limits. As you can see, the `pam_limits.so` module is used for the `session` interface type.

■Note On the Red Hat system the default `system-auth` service contains an entry for the `pam_limits.so` module.

You can also add it to other services, for example, adding it to the `imap` service to provide limits to users accessing IMAP resources.

The `pam_limits.so` module is controlled by a configuration file called `limits.conf` that is located in `/etc/security`. Listing 1-42 shows an example of this file.

Listing 1-42. *Sample* `limits.conf` *File*

```
# domain type item value
* soft core 0
* hard core 0
```

Here the `limits.conf` file is controlling the size of any core dumps generated. This is one of the most common uses of the `pam_limits.so` module. Let's examine the structure of the file. It is broken into four elements: domain, type, item, and value.

The domain is the scope of the limit and who it effects, for example, a particular user, group of users, or a wildcard entry (*), which indicates all users. The type is either `soft` or `hard`. A `soft` limit is a warning point and can be exceeded but will trigger a warning `syslog` entry. A `hard` limit is the maximum possible limit. A resource cannot exceed this `hard` limit. Thus, you should set your `soft` limits as a smaller size or number than your `hard` limits.

The type of limit describes what is being limited, and the value is the size of that limit. Table 1-12 lists all the possible types of resources you can limit with the `pam_limits.so` module.

Table 1-12. *Limits You Can Impose*

Limit	Description	Value
core	Limits the core file size	Kilobytes
data	Limits the maximum data size	Kilobytes
fsize	Limits the maximum file size	Kilobytes
memlock	Defines the maximum locked-in-memory address space	Kilobytes
nofile	Limits the number of open files	Number
rss	Limits the maximum resident set size	Kilobytes
stack	Limits the maximum stack size	Kilobytes
cpu	Limits the maximum CPU time	Minutes
nproc	Limits the maximum number of processes	Number
as	Specifies the address space limit	Number
maxlogins	Limits the maximum number of logins for a user	Number
priority	Limits the priority with which to run a user's process	Number

I also show the type of value you can use for a resource limit. For example, the `maxlogins` limit type is expressed as number that indicates the maximum number of times a user or users can simultaneously log in. `cpu` is expressed as the maximum number of minutes of CPU time that a user can consume.

Where the value is set to 0, this indicates the specified user or users (or all users) are unable to use any of that resource. For example, setting the `core` limit to 0 will result in no core dump files being created.

```
bob soft core 0
bob hard core 0
```

So, in the previous two lines, the user bob is prevented from creating any core dump files.

■**Tip** Even if you do not use any other type of limit, you should set the core dump size limit to 0 to prevent the creation of core dump files. Core dump files often contain valuable or dangerous information, and unless you have a requirement for them (for example developers need them), then I recommend you limit their creation.

You can also restrict this to a particular group by prefixing the group name with an at (@) character

```
@sales soft core 0
@sales hard core 0
```

or to everyone on the system using the * wildcard, as you saw in Listing 1-42.

■**Note** You can also control the limits being set with the ulimit command.

Restricting Users to Specific Login Times with PAM

Most distributions come with the pam_time.so module. This allows you to control when and where from users can log onto the system. It is defined as an account interface type. You can add it to the login service in the so file like this:

```
account required /lib/security/pam_time.so
```

If you have more than one module stacked, then you should add the pam_time.so module before all the other account interface type modules. In the previous line, I added it as a required module, which means the check must be successful for authentication to succeed.

The pam_time.so module is configured using the file time.conf, which is stored in the /etc/security directory. Listing 1-43 shows a line from this file.

Listing 1-43. *The* time.conf *File*

```
login;*;bob|jane;!Al2100-0600
```

I will break this rather confusing piece of configuration down and explain its component elements. Each element is separated by a semicolon. Each of these elements is a logic list, and you can use logical operators and tokens to control it further.

```
service;terminal;users;times
```

So the first element is service. In Listing 1-43 you can see that login is the service. If you specify a line in this file that refers to a service, you must also define the pam_time.so module in that service's configuration file in /etc/pam.d. You can add the pam_time.so module to almost any one of the services defined in the /etc/pam.d directory.

The next element is the terminal to which this time restriction applies. Here I have specified the wildcard operator * for all terminals. You can use a wildcard in any element except service but only once per element. You could also specify a list of terminals separated by a |, tty1|tty2|tty3, or a type of terminal suffixed with a * wildcard such as ttyp*.

In the next element I specify which users this time restriction applies to, and I have used a logical operator here. The first user is bob. I have then used the logical or separator, |, to specify a second user, jane. In this example this means the time restrictions apply to either bob or jane. You could also use the logical operator & here to represent and. For example, time restrictions apply to both bob and jane as in bob&jane.

The last element is the time restriction itself. The time here is prefixed with !. This means "anything but." The next two letters Al is short for "all," which indicates all days of the week. The next eight digits are start and finish times in 24-hour time format separated by a hyphen (-). In Listing 1-43, you saw that the start and finish times are 21:00 (or 9 p.m.) and 06:00 (or 6 a.m.), respectively. If the finish time is lower than the start time (as is the case in Listing 1-43), then the finish time is deemed to be during the next day. So, putting this all together means that bob and jane can log onto any terminal at any time except between 9 p.m. and 6 a.m.

Let's look at another example.

```
login;ttyp*;!root;!Wd0000-2400
```

Here I block logins from all pseudo-terminals on the weekends for all users except root. In the time element I have used the Wd entry, which indicates weekends. You can also use Wk, which stands for weekdays, or the entries for the individual days of the week, which are Mo, Tu, We, Th, Fr, Sa, Su.

Logging an Alert on User Login with PAM

The next PAM module is called pam_login_alert.so and alerts via e-mail or syslog when a particular user (or users) logs onto the system. You can download the module at http://www.kernel.org/pub/linux/libs/pam/pre/modules/pam_login_alert-0.10.tar.gz.

■**Tip** A variety of other PAM modules are also available at this site that you may find useful.

Create a temporary directory, and unpack the tar file into it. The package contains a number of files, including the source for the module. To create the module, you need to make and install it.

```
puppy$ make
puppy# make install
```

This will results in a file called pam_login_alert.so, which is installed by default to the /lib/security directory. Also, two configuration files are created and copied to /etc. They are login_alert.conf and login.alert.users.

Let's have a look at these configuration files first. Listing 1-44 shows the `login_alert.conf` file.

Listing 1-44. *The* `login_alert.conf` *File*

```
# PAM_login_alert configuration file
# Specify e-mail support
mail on
# Specify the user to e-mail the alert
email admin@puppy.yourdomain.com
# Specify syslog support
syslog off
# Specify the syslog facility
syslog_facility LOG_AUTHPRIV
# Specify the syslog priority
syslog_priority LOG_INFO
# Specify the user list
user_list /etc/login_alert.users
```

Its contents are fairly self-explanatory. You can send an alert either by e-mail or by syslog (with e-mail being the default). The e-mail is sent by default to `root`. You specify the list of users to alert on in the `/etc/login_alert.users` file. Let's add some users to this file.

```
puppy# echo 'bob' >> /etc/login_alert.users
puppy# echo 'jane' >> /etc/login_alert.users
```

I have added the users `bob` and `jane` to the file. Now I need to define the new module to the PAM configuration. As I am sending an alert on the login of a user, I need to add the module to the `login` service in the `/etc/pam.d` directory. Currently on my Red Hat system, the `login` service looks like this:

```
auth       required      pam_securetty.so
auth       required      pam_stack.so service=system-auth
auth       required      pam_nologin.so
account    required      pam_stack.so service=system-auth
password   required      pam_stack.so service=system-auth
session    required      pam_stack.so service=system-auth
session    optional      pam_console.so
```

The `pam_login_alert.so` module is available with the `account` and `session` interface types. I will add it as a `session` interface with a control flag of `optional`. I will also add the module at the end of the stack of modules using the `session` interface type. I use the end of the `session` modules because I am interested in when the user logs on, the time of which can take place only after the `auth` and `account` modules were successfully processed. I use `optional` because I am considering logging not critical to the authentication process. My `login` service would now look like this:

```
auth       required      pam_securetty.so
auth       required      pam_stack.so service=system-auth
auth       required      pam_nologin.so
```

```
account    required    pam_stack.so service=system-auth
password   required    pam_stack.so service=system-auth
session    required    pam_stack.so service=system-auth
session    optional    pam_console.so
session    optional    pam_login_alert.so
```

Now when bob or jane logs in, an e-mail will be generated and a message will be sent to root notifying of the new login. You could also enable the `syslog` function to send a log entry when either of these users log in.

Some Other Pam Modules

I recommend you investigate some other PAM modules and potentially configure them to aid in securing your system.

pam_access.so: The `pam_access.so` module controls login access and is configured using the `/etc/security/access.conf` file. For example, it controls who can log in and where they can log in from. It can include restrictions based on group membership as well.

pam_group.so: The `pam_group.so` module works with group membership and PAM. This is a slightly more dangerous module, as it is able to grant temporary group membership to users; you should use it with caution. See the `/etc/security/group.conf` file for configuration details.

pam_env.so: This module allows you to set your environment variables using PAM. See the `/etc/security/pam_env.conf` file for configuration details.

Package Management, File Integrity, and Updating

One of the great advantages attackers have when attempting to penetrate systems is some system administrators' inertia about updating software packages and applications. A large number of systems have software installed that is one or more versions behind the current release. Or the software is the original version installed when the system was installed. These older versions of software frequently have exploits and vulnerabilities that expose your system to attack. It is critical you update your software on a regular basis to ensure your system has the most recent and secure version of packages and applications.

■**Note** I talk about how to find out when a security vulnerability is discovered in the "Keeping Informed About Security" section.

The package management and update tools on the various distributions are powerful and perform a variety of functions that do not have any security implications. I will focus on those aspects of updating and package management on your system that do have security implications, such as verifying the integrity of a package or securely downloading an update.

Ensuring File Integrity

When you download packages and files from the Internet or install from CD/DVDs, a risk exists that you are getting more than you bargained for. You have no guarantee that the file you have downloaded contains the contents it claims to hold. The file or some of its contents could have been replaced, altered, or intercepted and modified during transmission. You can mitigate the risk of this by using integrity checking to validate the contents and the file. You will learn about three methods of determining the integrity of packages you have downloaded from the Internet. The first and second methods use the md5sum and sha1sum commands to validate a checksum to confirm the integrity of a package. The third uses the gpg application, part of the GPG package, to verify a digital signature file that you would also download with the package you want to verify.[7]

MD5 and SHA1 Checksums

Let's look at MD5 hash checksums first. The MD5 checksum is a digital "fingerprint" of a file that is frequently used by open-source software vendors and authors to prove the integrity of files, ISO images, and the like that are available for download. MD5 is a message digest algorithm. It takes a data string (in the case of a checksum, the data string is the file), and it produces a hash of that data string. The hash is unique for each data string. Listing 1-45 shows what an MD5 hash checksum looks like.

Listing 1-45. *A Sample MD5 Checksum*

```
0a5f5f226e41ce408a895bec995e8c05
```

So how do you use this checksum? Let's assume you have downloaded a file from a Web site, `iptables-1-2.11-tar.bz2`. On the Web site next to the download link to this file is the following MD5 checksum `0a5f5f226e41ce408a895bec995e8c05`. You use the md5sum command to check the file to confirm this is the checksum of the file.

```
puppy# md5sum iptables-1-2.11-tar.bz2
0a5f5f226e41ce408a895bec995e8c05 iptables-1-2.11-tar.bz2
```

If the checksum matches the one displayed on the site, then the integrity of the file has been confirmed to the extent possible using this sort of method. I say *extent possible* because file checksums predispose that the site you are downloading the file from is secure and that the file you have downloaded has not been replaced with another file entirely and the checksum generated from this replacement file.

Additionally, recent developments have suggested that there is a possibility that MD5 checksums are not always unique.[8] With this potential insecurity in mind, you will also learn about the similar checksum SHA1, or Secure Hash Algorithm. SHA1 is also a message digest algorithm. It was designed by the National Security Agency (NSA) and uses a more secure digest based on 160-bit digests. The SHA1 algorithm works on similar principles to MD5. When downloading a file, you make a note of the SHA1 checksum. Then using the sha1sum command, check the file against the SHA1 checksum.

---

7. http://www.gnupg.org/
8. http://www.md5crk.com/

```
puppy# sha1sum image.iso
1929b791088db2338c535e4850d49f491b3c7b53 image.iso
```

So where you have the option of using a SHA1 checksum, I recommend using these over MD5 checksums.

The SHA1 checksums of course still does not address the issue of a total replacement of the file and substitution of a new checksum based on the substituted file. The only way to address this is via using a digital signature.

Digital Signatures and GNU Privacy Guard

Digital signatures rely on the principles of public-key encryption, which I will discuss in more detail in Chapter 3. Public-key encryption depends on two keys: a public key and a private key. You publish your public key to anyone who wants to exchange encrypted information with you and keep your private key secret. You encrypt the information with the recipient's public key, and the recipient of that information uses their private key to decrypt the information. You can also do this encryption in reverse and encrypt the information with your private key and have your public key able to decrypt it. It is this second model that digital signatures use to ensure file integrity.

Digital signatures are created by combining hashes and public-key encryption. A hash is generated of the information (in this case, a package or file) that an author wants to confirm as valid. Like the checksum hashes I have just discussed, this hash is unique to the file; if the contents of the file change, then so does the hash. This hash is then encrypted, or *signed*, with the package author's private key. This creates the digital signature.

Now the author of the package distributes the file with its digital signature and also makes available their public key. When you download the package, you also download the signature and the author's public key. You import this public key into your *keyring*. Your keyring is a collection of the public keys that your system knows about, which is managed by whatever tool you are using for public-key encryption, in this case gpg. You can then verify the file with the digital signature by using the author's public key to decrypt the checksum hash and then verify that the hash matches the hash of the downloaded file. You now know the file is valid because you know the author must have used their private key to encrypt the digital signature; otherwise you would not have been able to use their public key to decrypt it.

Let's look at an example of this at work. Download the GPG package, its digital signature, and the public key of the author and use them to verify the integrity of the package. First, download the package and its signature.

```
puppy# wget ftp://ftp.gnupg.org/gcrypt/gnupg/gnupg-1.2.4.tar.bz2
puppy# wget ftp://ftp.gnupg.org/gcrypt/gnupg/gnupg-1.2.4.tar.bz2.sig
```

Second, download and import the GPG group's public key into your public keyring.

```
puppy# wget ftp://ftp.gnupg.org/gcrypt/gnupg/gnupg.asc
puppy# gpg --import gnupg.asc
gpg: key 57548DCD: public key imported
gpg: Total number processed: 1
gpg:              imported: 1
```

To do the import, you use the gpg --import option.

Now that you have imported the public key, you can use the same gpg command to validate the file you have downloaded. To do this, you use the gpg option --verify and provide the name of the signature you have downloaded; it is gnupg-1-2.4.tar.bz2.sig, as you can see in Listing 1-46.

Listing 1-46. *Verifying a File Using* gpg

```
puppy# gpg --verify gnupg-1.2.4.tar.bz2.sig
gpg: Signature made Wed 24 Dec 2003 07:24:58 EST using DSA key ID 57548DCD
gpg: Good signature from "Werner Koch (gnupg sig) <dd9jn@gnu.org>"
gpg: checking the trustdb
gpg: no ultimately trusted keys found
gpg: WARNING: This key is not certified with a trusted signature!
gpg:          There is no indication that the signature belongs to the owner.
Fingerprint: 6BD9 050F D8FC 941B 4341  2DCC 68B7 AB89 5754 8DCD
```

The gpg command will take the contents of this digital signature and look for the contents of a file of the same name with the suffix of .sig removed from the filename. Thus, in this example, the gpg command will be looking for a file called gnupg-1.2.4.tar.bz2. If the filename is different from the signature file; you can specify the file you want to verify after the signature file on the command line.

```
puppy# gpg --verify gnupg-1.2.4.tar.bz2.sig gnupg.tar.gz
```

As you can see from Listing 1-46, the file was signed with the author's private key and the signature is valid. The warning message that appears tells you that this validation is not 100 percent complete, though, because the trust ends with the key used to sign the signature. This means the gpg has no way of confirming that the author is the actual owner of the key used to sign the signature. I will talk about this concept of trusted relationship further in Chapter 3. For the purposes of verifying the integrity of the package you have downloaded, I suggest this level of validation is suitable for most instances.

Tip Though I do not show the process every time you download a file or package during the chapters of this book, I strongly urge you to verify all files you download using whatever means are available to you. Be extremely wary of files that offer no means of verifying their integrity.

RPM and Digital Signatures

Most recent releases of the RPM package (including those with recent versions of Red Hat and Mandrake) handle digital signature checking internally and transparently to you with some initial setup. The RPM file itself holds the digital signature and a variety of checksums. You then verify those checksums and digital signatures using the rpm command. To do this, you need to import the RPM provider or vendor's public key into your RPM public keyring.

Your RPM public keyring is different from your GPG public keyring. If you have imported a public key into your GPG keyring, this does not mean you can use that public key with RPM. For example, Red Hat provides its public key in a variety of locations for you to add to your

RPM public keyring. You can find it at the Red Hat site at http://www.redhat.com/security/ db42a60e.txt. It is also located on your system when your distribution is installed at /usr/share/ rhn/RPM-GPG-KEY.

To add a public key the RPM keyring, you use the rpm --import command. So, to add the Red Hat public key, enter the following:

```
puppy# rpm --import /usr/share/rhn/RPM-GPG-KEY
```

You can also download the public key from a keyserver using the gpg command and then place it in the RPM keyring. To do this, you first need to use the gpg command to get the key, specifying a keyserver and a key ID. The default keyserver for the Red Hat public key is pgp.mit.edu, and the key ID is DB42A60E.[9] Listing 1-47 retrieves the Red Hat public key from a keyserver using the gpg command.

Listing 1-47. *Using the* gpg *Command to Download a Key from a Keyserver*

```
puppy# gpg --keyserver pgp.mit.edu --recv-keys DB42A60E
gpg: requesting key DB42A60E from HKP keyserver pgp.mit.edu
gpg: key DB42A60E: public key imported
gpg: Total number processed: 1
gpg:              imported: 1
```

As you can see from Listing 1-47, you have successfully downloaded the Red Hat public key from the key server and imported it into the GPG keyring. Now you need to add it to the RPM keyring. You can enter the following:

```
puppy# gpg -a --export DB42A60E > redhat.asc; rpm --import redhat.asc; \
rm -f redhat.asc
```

In the previous line you have exported the key you just downloaded into the GPG keyring by selecting it via its key ID and using the -a option to create ASCII armored output. You then imported the resulting file into the RPM keyring and finally deleted the file you just used for the import.

You can see all the public keys stored in your RPM public keyring using the following command:

```
puppy# rpm -qa gpg-pubkey\* --qf "%{version}-%{release} %{summary}\n"
db42a60e-37ea5438 gpg(Red Hat, Inc <security@redhat.com>)
```

As you can see, the only key you have is the Red Hat security key.

■**Tip** You can find the Mandrake GPG key at http://www.mandrakesoft.com/security/RPM-GPG-KEYS, on the Mandrake CD/DVD or via the pgp.mit.edu using key ID 22458A98. Debian public keys are available on the Debian release media or via the Debian FTP sites and mirrors.

---

9. This is the current Red Hat key ID, but you can check for a new or updated key ID at http://www.redhat.com/security/team/key.html.

With the `rpm` command and the public key, you can now validate the digital signature. Now if you download an RPM produced by Red Hat, you are now able to verify it. To do this, you use the `rpm` command with the `--checksig` option (or the `-K` option, which performs the same function).

```
puppy# rpm --checksig kernel-2.4.21-15.0.2.EL.src.rpm
kernel-2.4.21-15.0.2.EL.src.rpm: (sha1) dsa sha1 md5 gpg OK
```

You can see the results of the `--checksig` option on the previous line. First the name of the RPM being checked is displayed, and then the successful checks are displayed. The line before the results shows that the RPM has valid `dsa`, `sha1`, and `md5` checksums and is signed with a valid gpg signature. The final `OK` confirms the validity of the RPM file. If you want to display more detail of the validation, you can add the `-v` option to the `rpm` command.

```
puppy# rpm --checksig -v kernel-2.4.21-15.0.2.EL.src.rpm
kernel-2.4.21-15.0.2.EL.src.rpm:
    Header V3 DSA signature: OK, key ID db42a60e
    Header SHA1 digest: OK (a0c3ab5a36016f398e0882a54164796f2ae9044f)
    MD5 digest: OK (ef590ee95255210aca8e2631ebaaa019)
    V3 DSA signature: OK, key ID db42a60e
```

You can display even more information by using the `-vv` option.

If the RPM fails to validate, then the `rpm --checksig` command will return different results. Any checks that have failed will be displayed in uppercase, and the results will end with `NOT OK`.

```
puppy# rpm --checksig kernel-2.4.21-15.0.2.EL.src.rpm
kernel-2.4.21-15.0.2.EL.src.rpm: size gpg MD5 NOT OK
```

You can see in the previous line that the `size` check has validated, but the MD5 checksum has failed and the results display `NOT OK`. If the GPG digital signature fails to validate, then you will see output similar to the following line. In this instance the GPG key is missing.

```
puppy# rpm --checksig kernel-2.4.21-15.0.2.EL.src.rpm
kernel-2.4.21-15.0.2.EL.src.rpm: (SHA1) DSA sha1 md5 (GPG) NOT OK ➡
(MISSING KEYS: GPG#db42a60e)
```

You should verify all RPMs using the `--checksig` option before installing them, and do not install an RPM package if any of these checks fail.

Downloading Updates and Patches

You can use a variety of automated tools for updating your system via the Internet. I will briefly cover three of them: `up2date`, `apt-get`, and `yum`. Of the three, the only one that offers real security is the `up2date` command, which uses SSL certificates to confirm you are downloading from a valid and verifiable update source in addition to verifying the file integrity of the files downloaded. Unfortunately, `up2date` is a Red Hat–only solution. The remaining tools, `apt-get` and `yum`, are capable only of verifying the file integrity of downloads using MD5, SHA1, and GPG checks.

up2date

The up2date tool comes with Red Hat systems and allows you to retrieve updates from the Red Hat Network. As mentioned, it uses SSL to verify it is connecting to a valid update source. The up2date command does this SSL authentication transparently for you. For any Red Hat releases with a purchase price (for example, Red Hat Enterprise Linux), you need to pay for an entitlement to download updated patches. For the Fedora Core releases, you can download the updates for free. The up2date client is a propriety Red Hat tool and does not work with any other distributions.

Tip An open-source variation of up2date, called NRH-up2date, is available at http://www.nrh-up2date.org/. This tool also allows you to run a centralized Red Hat update server.

The up2date tool downloads RPMs from the Red Hat network and then passes them to the rpm command to be processed and installed transparently to the user. As part of this transfer to the rpm command, the standard rpm --checksig processing is performed on the RPM(s) to be installed. This means the size, MD5, and SHA1 checksums as well as the GPG key are all checked before installing the RPM(s). If any of these fail to validate, then the respective RPM will not be installed.

You would usually configure up2date and the Red Hat Network when you first install your Red Hat distribution. But you can reregister your system to the Red Hat Network using the following command:

```
puppy# rhn_register
```

If your system is registered, you can use the up2date command to retrieve RPMs from Red Hat. To list all the available packages, enter the following:

```
puppy# up2date -l
Fetching package list for channel: rhel-i386-as-3...
```

And if you want to fetch and download the available updates, you can enter the following:

```
puppy# up2date -u
```

Finally, the up2date man page contains further information on how to use the up2date command.

apt-get

The APT package-handling application is a front-end interface for the Debian dpkg command. A version also exists that can act as a front-end to RPM.[10] It fetches deb or RPM files from remote repositories and uses either dpkg or rpm to install them. It is extremely easy to use. Each command consists of the apt-get command followed by the required function to be performed and potentially a package name.

```
puppy# apt-get update
```

---

10. http://freshrpms.net/apt/

For example, the command on the previous line updates the list of packages that are available for download. The configuration for the apt-get command is held in the /etc/apt directory. For Debian, review the contents of the apt.conf.d directory in /etc/apt; for the Red Hat variation, review the apt.conf file to see how apt-get is configured to function. Both versions use a file called sources.list in the /etc/apt directory to store the list of repositories. The repositories are generally HTTP or FTP sites that store the available updates.

To install a particular package using apt-get, use the install option, as follows, replacing the *packagename* variable with the name of the particular package to be installed:

```
puppy# apt-get install packagename
```

To install all available updates, use the upgrade option. Enter the following:

```
puppy# apt-get upgrade
```

■**Caution** Some older versions of apt-get continue to install packages even if the checksums or keys have failed. I recommend upgrading to the latest version of apt-get.

Yum

Yum (Yellow dog Updater, Modified) is another update and patch tool that works with RPM packages. It functions much like the apt-get and up2date tools. Like these tools, Yum fetches RPMs from remote repositories and uses the rpm command to check checksums and to perform the installation. You can download Yum from http://linux.duke.edu/projects/yum/download.ptml. It comes in different versions depending on the version of RPM you have installed. Check your RPM version before you choose a version of Yum to install. Enter the following:

```
puppy# rpm --version
RPM version 4.2.2
```

Yum performs much the same functions as the other tools you have seen in this chapter. For example, to view a list of all the packages available to download, you would use the list option, as follows:

```
puppy# yum list
```

You can configure Yum using the file yum.conf located in the /etc directory. In Listing 1-48 you can see a sample of this file.

Listing 1-48. *Sample* yum.conf *File*

```
[main]
cachedir=/var/cache/yum
logfile=/var/log/yum.log
distroverpkg=redhat-release
```

```
[base]
name=Red Hat Linux $releasever - $basearch - Base
baseurl=
http://mirror.dulug.duke.edu/pub/yum-repository/redhat/$releasever/$basearch/
gpgcheck=1
```

The [main] configuration block shown in Listing 1-48 contains the global variables used by Yum. You can read about those in the yum.conf man page. The [base] configuration defines a repository to check for updated packages. I have added the option gpgcheck=1 to this repository to make Yum check for valid GPG signatures. You need to add this option to the definitions of all repositories defined to Yum if you want them to use GPG signature checking.

To install a package with Yum, use the install option, as follows, replacing the *packagename* variable with the name of the particular package to be installed:

```
puppy# yum install packagename
```

To upgrade all available packages with Yum, use the upgrade option.

```
puppy# yum upgrade
```

You can see the additional options available with Yum in its man page.

Compilers and Development Tools

Compilers and associated development tools are incredibly useful to have on your system—that is, they are handy for you and any potential attackers. If an attacker has access to development tools, it makes the process of penetrating your system easier. An attacker can write their own penetration programs on your system and then use your compilers and development tools to compile them. Additionally, some root kits require the attacker compile them on your system. Removing the compilers and development tools makes it that much harder for an attacker.

I recommend that on your production systems you remove the compiler packages and associated development tools or at least restrict access to them to selected users or groups. The easiest way to restrict access to them is to create a new group and restrict execute access on all the compiler and development tool binaries to this group.

Removing the Compilers and Development Tools

Let's now take you through an example of removing the compilers and development tools on a Red Hat system. Listing 1-49 shows you how you can identify the packages you should remove or restrict on Red Hat system using the rpm command.

Listing 1-49. *Identifying the Compilers and Development Tools*

```
puppy# rpm -qg Development/Languages Development/Tools
cpp-3.2-7
dev86-0.16.3-4
gcc-3.2-7
gcc-g77-3.2-7
...
```

> **■Tip** On SuSE you can use the `yast` tool to do this or on Debian the `dselect` tool.

Using `rpm` with the `-qg` will query on a group of packages. In Listing 1-49 this will list all the packages that are in the package groups Development/Languages and Development/Tools. These groups contain the compilers and associated tools. On a Debian system this package group is called `devel`. If you want to remove the individual packages, you can do this using `rpm`. Enter the following:

```
puppy# rpm -e gcc
```

You may run into troubles with dependencies, as many of the compilers and development tools are dependencies for other packages installed of their type. The easiest way to do this is to remove the packages with the `--nodeps` option.

```
puppy# rpm -e --nodeps gcc
```

> **■Caution** One of the packages in the Development/Languages group is Perl. A lot of applications use Perl, and you would probably be safer not removing this and looking at options for restricting access to the Perl interpreter.

Restricting the Compilers and Development Tools

If you do not want to remove the packages and want to restrict access to them via permissions, you can also do this. First you need to query individual packages to see what binaries are contained in them. Then you need to restrict the permissions of these binaries.

```
puppy# rpm -q --filesbypkg gcc | grep 'bin'
gcc                     /usr/bin/c89
gcc                     /usr/bin/c99
gcc                     /usr/bin/cc
gcc                     /usr/bin/gcc
gcc                     /usr/bin/gcov
...
```

Here I have used `rpm` to show you the files provided by the `gcc` package. I have also used `grep` to only select those files that are contained in binaries directories, `/bin`, `/usr/bin`, `/usr/sbin`, and so on.

Now you need to create a group that will have access to the compiler binaries.

```
puppy# groupadd compiler
```

Then change the ownership of the binary you want to restrict. I have changed the binaries group to `compiler`. Enter the following:

```
puppy# chown root:compiler /usr/bin/gcc
```

And finally you change its permissions to be executable only by the `root` user and members of the `compiler` group. Enter the following:

```
puppy# chmod 0750 /usr/bin/gcc
```

Now unless the user running the `gcc` command belongs to the group `compiler`, they will get a permission-denied message when they try to run the `gcc` compiler.

```
puppy$ gcc
bash: /usr/bin/gcc: Permission denied
```

Hardening and Securing Your Kernel

The Linux kernel is the core of your operating system. It provides the coordinating engine for the rest of the operating system and organizes and manages the processes of your system. It is unfortunately also subject to some weaknesses through which attackers can gain control of system resources or your system itself. These weaknesses can allow attackers to run attack tools such as root kits.

■Note See Chapter 6 for more details on root kits and detecting them.

To combat these weaknesses and prevent their exploitation, you need to harden the kernel. You do this by applying one or more of a series of available patches that address some of these weaknesses. These patches are not perfect, though, but they will significantly reduce the risk to your system from these exploits. I will cover one of the major kernel hardening patches: Openwall. I will show you how you can apply this patch to your system, and I will explain the various benefits, risks, and limitations created by using the patch. I will discuss the particular features and fixes the Openwall patch offers in the section "The Openwall Project."

Securing your kernel and hardening using available patches is not an easy process. Fundamentally perhaps one of the hardest Linux operating system activities that a system administrator can undertake is patching and rebuilding a kernel. This is not a reason not to do this! I will take you through the steps you need to follow and the outputs you should expect to see when doing this. At the end of this, you should be comfortable with doing this whenever you need.

Getting Your Kernel Source

If you patch and harden your kernel for security purposes, then you need to work from a fresh copy of the kernel, not the kernel that came with your distribution. You can download the latest version of the Linux kernel from `http://www.kernel.org`. Most distributions currently come with a version 2.4 kernel; for example, the currently supported kernel for Red Hat 3AS is 2.4.26. Run the `uname -a` command to find out what kernel is running on your system.

```
puppy# uname -a
Linux puppy.yourdomain.com 2.4.26-EL #2 Mon Jul 19 18:00:36 EST 2004 i686 i686 ➡
i386 GNU/Linux
```

You can see in the previous line the current kernel is version 2.4.26-EL. (The EL indicates a Red Hat–specific designation meaning Enterprise Linux.)

At the time of writing, the most recently released version of the kernel was 2.6.7. But at this stage most distributions are supporting 2.4 release kernels, so I will base my explanation of how to install them on this release of the kernel. Nothing, though, should fundamentally differ between the installation process for version 2.4.*x* kernels and version 2.6.*x* kernels.

Download kernel version 2.4.26. You should download the most up-to-date version at the time you are reading this. Replace the 2.4.26 version in the next few examples with the version of the kernel you are downloading. So Listing 1-50 shows how to download the kernel.

Listing 1-50. *Downloading the Kernel Source*

```
puppy$ cd /usr/src
puppy$ wget ftp://ftp.kernel.org/pub/linux/kernel/v2.4/linux-2.4.26.tar.gz
puppy$ wget ftp://ftp.kernel.org/pub/linux/kernel/v2.4/linux-2.4.26.tar.gz.sign
puppy$ gpg --keyserver wwwkeys.pgp.net --recv-keys 0x517D0F0E
gpg: key 517D0F0E: public key "Linux Kernel Archives Verification Key ➥
<ftpadmin@kernel.org>" imported
gpg: Total number processed: 1
gpg:               imported: 1
```

Let's look at Listing 1-50. The Linux kernel sources are generally stored in the /usr/src directory on your system. You have downloaded the most recent version of kernel source and the signature file for this release of the kernel source to this directory. You have also downloaded from the pgp.net key server the gpg public key for http://www.kernel.org and imported it into your gpg keyring.

■**Note** You should check for the current key at http://www.kernel.org/signature.html.

Listing 1-51 shows how to use this public key and the signature file to verify the integrity of the kernel source.

Listing 1-51. *Verifying the Kernel Source*

```
puppy$ gpg --verify linux-2.4.26.tar.gz.sign linux-2.4.26.tar.gz
gpg: Signature made Wed 14 Apr 2004 23:23:32 EST using DSA key ID 517D0F0E
gpg: Good signature from "Linux Kernel Archives Verification Key ➥
<ftpadmin@kernel.org>"
gpg:                 aka "Linux Kernel Archives Verification Key ➥
<ftpadmin@kernel.org>"
gpg: checking the trustdb
gpg: no ultimately trusted keys found
gpg: WARNING: This key is not certified with a trusted signature!
gpg:           There is no indication that the signature belongs to the owner.
Primary key fingerprint: C75D C40A 11D7 AF88 9981  ED5B C86B A06A 517D 0F0E
```

You have used the gpg command to verify the signature of the file and the downloaded file together with the PGP public key downloaded in Listing 1-50. The response in Listing 1-51 shows this is a good signature. Do not worry about the last lines claiming the key is not certified with a trusted signature. This merely means you do not have the full trust chain for this signature.

Now that you have verified the integrity of the file, you can unpack it. A lot of patches and other related items look for the source in the directory /usr/src/linux, so you will create a symbolic link to this directory using the unpacked source directory as the source of the link. You can see this Listing 1-52.

Listing 1-52. *Unpacking and Creating the Linux Symbolic Link*

```
puppy$ tar -zxf linux-2.4.26.tar.gz
puppy$ ln -s linux-2.4.26.tar.gz linux
```

You now have a fresh copy of kernel source available to work with and on which to apply the hardening patches.

The Openwall Project

The Openwall Project is a collection of security features, patches, and fixes designed to harden and secure your kernel. You can configure the individual security features during the kernel complication process after patching your kernel source; I will take you through doing that in the following sections. So, what security features does Openwall introduce?

Provides a nonexecutable user stack area: The nonexecutable user stack area is designed to reduce the risk of buffer overflows. Most buffer overflows are based on overwriting a function's return address on the stack to point to some malicious code. This code is put on the stack and executed. By making the stack nonexecutable, the code is prevented from functioning and your system is protected. This is not a perfect solution to the threat of buffer overflows, but it does reduce the risk that a major group of exploits that function in this way can take advantage of the weaknesses in your system.

Restrict links in /tmp: The /tmp directory (or other +t directories) are popular spots for exploits to be executed in and from because of the openness of the directory. Several of these types of exploit methods involve using hard links. For example, one form of hard link attack is based on hard linking setuid or setgid binaries to a directory such as /tmp. An exploit is discovered in one of these binaries. You update or patch the binary, but a hard linked version still exists in another directory that the attacker can use to compromise your system. Other forms of hard link attack include using hard links to cause Denial of Service attacks by overwriting critical files or by overflowing disk space or quotas using hard links of temporary files.

The Openwall patch stops hard links being created by users to files they do not own unless they have read or write permissions to the file (usually permissions provided through group membership). This may potentially impact some poorly designed applications and stop them from functioning. I recommend you test this option after implementation with any applications that utilize hard links in temporary directories.

Restrict FIFOs in /tmp: This restricts writes to first in/first out (FIFO) named pipes in +t directories such as /tmp. This disallows writing to named pipes that are not owned by the user unless the owner of the pipe is the same as the owner of the directory. This prevents the use of untrusted named pipes to conduct attacks or for other malicious purposes. Like the previous feature, this can also cause issues with applications. I recommend you test this with any applications that create named pipes in temporary directories.

Restrict /proc: This function restricts the permission on the /proc directory so that users can see only those processes they have initiated or that belong to their session. This adds a layer of privacy and security to your system that stops potential attackers from seeing other processes that could provide exploitable insights into your system.

Destroy shared memory segments not in use: This stops shared memory existing without belonging to a process and destroys any shared memory segments after a process terminates. Unfortunately, this breaks a lot of applications, including many databases (for example, Oracle). I recommend not implementing this feature unless you understand the implications of it.

Enforce RLIMIT_NPROC on execve(2): This allows you to control how many processes the user can have with the RLIMIT_NPROC setting when executing programs using the execve(2) function.

Installing Openwall

You first need to download the Openwall patch and a signature to verify the contents of the patch. Each version of the patch is designed to match a kernel release version. You need to get the Openwall patch that matches the kernel version you propose hardening and compiling. Listing 1-53 shows you how to download the Openwall patch for kernel 2.4.26. Let's download the files to the /usr/src directory.

Listing 1-53. *Getting the Openwall Patch*

```
puppy$ cd /usr/src
puppy$ wget http://www.openwall.com/linux/linux-2.4.26-ow2.tar.gz
puppy$ wget http://www.openwall.com/linux/linux-2.4.26-ow2.tar.gz.sign
```

Once you have the Openwall patch, you need to verify the patch is authentic and the integrity of the patch is maintained. This is similar to the process used with the kernel source itself; you start by downloading and importing the Openwall gpg public key. Then you use the signature you downloaded in Listing 1-53 to verify the patch file you downloaded. See Listing 1-54 for the commands you need to achieve this.

Listing 1-54. *Verifying the Openwall Signature*

```
puppy$ wget http://www.openwall.com/signatures/openwall-signatures.asc
puppy$ gpg --import openwall-signatures.asc
puppy$ gpg --verify linux-2.4.26-ow2.tar.gz.sign linux-2.4.26-ow2.tar.gz
```

```
gpg: Signature made Sun 06 Jul 2003 13:54:56 EST using RSA key ID 295029F1
gpg: Good signature from "Openwall Project <signatures@openwall.com>"
gpg: checking the trustdb
gpg: no ultimately trusted keys found
gpg: WARNING: This key is not certified with a trusted signature!
gpg:           There is no indication that the signature belongs to the owner.
Primary key fingerprint: 0C 29 43 AE 1E CD 24 EA  6E 0C B6 EE F5 84 25 69
```

If your patch has a good signature (and again ignore the last four lines about trusted signatures as you did when downloading the kernel source), then you can unpack it and patch your kernel source with it. Listing 1-55 takes you through the process of doing this.

Listing 1-55. *Patching the Kernel Source*

```
puppy$ cd /usr/src
puppy$ tar -zxf linux-2.4.26-ow2.tar.gz
puppy$ cp linux-2.4.26-ow2/linux-2.4.26-ow2.diff .
puppy$ patch -p0 < linux-2.4.26-ow2.diff
patching file linux/Documentation/Configure.help
patching file linux/Makefile
patching file linux/arch/alpha/config.in
patching file linux/arch/alpha/defconfig
patching file linux/arch/alpha/kernel/osf_sys.c
...
```

First, you change to the /usr/src directory. It is easiest to place your patch here for continuity's sake for your kernel source. Then unpack the patch to create a directory linux-*version-owpatchnumber*, in this case linux-2.4.26-ow2, where *version* is the version of the kernel to be patched and *patchnumber* is the version of the Openwall patch for this kernel release.

Next copy the .diff file (which contains the instructions telling the patch command which source files and lines to change in order to implement the patch) to the /usr/src directory. Now from the /usr/src directory run the patch command, inputting the contents of the .diff file with the < operator. This patches your kernel source using the .diff file to tell the patch which source files and lines need to be changed.

You should see similar output to the patching lines in Listing 1-55, and if the patch is successful, then you should be returned to the command line without any reports of FAIL'ed patch lines or prompts. If the patch does fail, then check you have the right version of the patch for your kernel and that you copied the .diff file into the right location, /usr/src.

Now you have patched your kernel source, and you can start by compiling your new hardened kernel. You need to make sure you are starting from a clean compile. Change to the /usr/src/linux directory, and run the following command to confirm your kernel source compile is going to be from a clean start.

```
puppy$ make mrproper
```

The make mrproper function clears out any leftover files from previous compilations and old configuration files. When the process completes, then you can continue onto configuring your kernel.

Next you would normally be using the make config command (or its menu-based variation make menuconfig) to configure the features of your new kernel. Kernel configuration involves choosing the features, modules, and drivers your kernel will support. It can be a tricky and painful process to conduct from scratch, with multiple recompilations potentially required to ensure all your requirements are addressed.

But you have a simpler way to configure your kernel. You already have a kernel that was been compiled as part of the installation process of your distribution. This is the kernel you use every day to run your system, so you know it works. When this kernel was created, a configuration file was produced that contains all the information about the kernel and the hardware, drivers, modules, and features enabled. This configuration file is usually stored on Red Hat and Debian systems in the /boot directory and called by config-*version*, where *version* is the version of the kernel currently running. You can short-circuit the configuration process by copying this config to /usr/src/linux as the file .config. The .config file would normally be created by running the make config or make menuconfig commands. See Listing 1-56 for the process of copying this file.

Listing 1-56. *Copying the Old Kernel Configuration*

```
puppy$ cp /boot/config-2.4.26-EL /usr/src/linux/.config
```

You can then use a different command, make oldconfig, to pick up your old configuration from the .config file rather than going through and selecting an entirely new configuration.

Now you can run the command in Listing 1-57 to configure your kernel.

Listing 1-57. *Configuring the Kernel*

```
puppy$ cd /usr/src/linux
puppy$ make oldconfig
```

You will find that instead of being prompted for the majority of kernel configuration options, you will be prompted only for a few. These few will consist of any new features added to your kernel (if upgrading to a more recent kernel version) and the Openwall configuration options. If you are prompted for new features and options, they will appear similar to the option on the next line.

```
Atmel at76c502/at76c504 PCMCIA cards (CONFIG_PCMCIA_ATMEL) [N/y/m/?] (NEW)
```

This example prompts you to compile support for some new hardware. You could also be prompted to install new modules or software features. I recommend that unless you require any of these features or functions for which you have been prompted, select N for No. This is usually the default. If you require more information on the new item, then you can use the ? option to get more information about the item.

■**Note** If you really insist on totally reconfiguring your kernel (and I recommend against it unless you know what you are doing), then you would run the make config command (for command-line-based configuration of your kernel) or the make menuconfig (for a menu-based version of the kernel configuration) instead of the make oldconfig command. I recommend the make menuconfig variation.

Let's now look at the Openwall configuration options. Listing 1-58 shows the prompts you will be asked to answer as part of the Openwall configuration. The Openwall configuration options should appear at the end of the make oldconfig (or whatever variation of the kernel configuration process you have chosen to use) process. In Listing 1-58 I have configured these in line with the recommendations I made when discussing the various features of Openwall previously. For these options by answering y, you enable a feature. Use N to disable a feature.

Listing 1-58. *Openwall Configuration Prompts*

```
*
* Security options
*
Non-executable user stack area (CONFIG_HARDEN_STACK) [N/y/?] (NEW) y
  Autodetect and emulate GCC trampolines (CONFIG_HARDEN_STACK_SMART) [N/y/?] (NEW) N
Restricted links in /tmp (CONFIG_HARDEN_LINK) [N/y/?] (NEW) y
Restricted FIFOs in /tmp (CONFIG_HARDEN_FIFO) [N/y/?] (NEW) y
Restricted /proc (CONFIG_HARDEN_PROC) [N/y/?] (NEW) y
Enforce RLIMIT_NPROC on execve(2) (CONFIG_HARDEN_RLIMIT_NPROC) [N/y/?] (NEW) y
Destroy shared memory segments not in use (CONFIG_HARDEN_SHM) [N/y/?] (NEW) N
```

The only option from Listing 1-58 I have not discussed is the Autodetect and emulate GCC trampolines option, which is an extension of the nonexecutable user stack area feature. This allows the use of a nonexecutable user stack area with the glibc version 2.0 nested function extensions and predominantly with version 2.0 kernels. To check your version of glibc, enter the command in Listing 1-59.

Listing 1-59. *Checking the glibc Command*

```
puppy# /lib/libc.so.6
\GNU C Library stable release version 2.3.2, by Roland McGrath et al.
```

On most recent distributions it should be at least version 2.3. If it is more recent than version 2.0, then enter n to not install this option.

Now that you have configured your Openwall patch, you need to compile your kernel. The commands in Listing 1-60 will do this for you.

Listing 1-60. *Compiling the Kernel*

```
puppy# cd /usr/src/linux
puppy# make dep bzImage modules modules_install
puppy# make install
```

The first make line combines a number of compilation steps. First it makes all the required dependencies using the dep option. Then it makes a new boot image using the bzImage option. Then it compiles any modules required using the modules option. Finally it installs any modules using the modules_install option. At the end of this first make line you should have a fully compiled kernel and new boot image. The next line, make install installs that new boot image in your boot loader ready for you to reboot and use that new kernel.

Let's just confirm the boot loader configuration has been suitably updated. Listing 1-61 shows what your `lilo.conf` entry for the new kernel should look like after being updated by the `make install` action. You have added the `password` option to the `lilo.conf` file to secure your new kernel, too. Remember to run the `lilo` command after adding the password to update your boot loader configuration.

Listing 1-61. *Confirming Your* `lilo.conf` *Configuration*

```
image=/boot/vmlinuz-2.4.26-ow2
        password=secretpassword
        label=linux 2.4.26 (Owl)
        initrd=/boot/initrd-2.4.26-ow2.img
        read-only
        append="root=LABEL=/"
```

If you use Grub, you can see the updated entry for the `grub.conf` configuration file in Listing 1-62. I have also added a password here, too.

Listing 1-62. *Confirming your* `grub.conf` *Configuration*

```
title Red Hat Enterprise Linux AS (2.4.26-ow2)
    password --md5 $1$2Q0$I6k7iy22wB27CrkzdVPe70
        root (hd0,0)
        kernel /vmlinuz-2.4.26-ow2 ro root=LABEL=/
    initrd /initrd-2.4.26-ow2.img
```

After rebooting your system, selecting the new kernel, and booting it, you should be running with your new kernel. To confirm this, run the `uname -a` command after you have rebooted.

```
puppy# uname -a
Linux puppy.yourdomain.com 2.4.26-ow2 #2 Mon Jul 19 18:00:36 EST 2004 i686 i686 ➡
i386 GNU/Linux
```

You can now see that the puppy system is running a new kernel, `2.4.26-ow2`, which is the Openwall patched kernel.

Testing Openwall

So you installed your Openwall patch and now you want to know if it does anything? Well, the patch does come with some code you can use to test some functions. Inside the directory you unpacked you will find the Openwall, which is a C program called `stacktest.c`. You will compile this program and run some tests. Listing 1-63 shows how to compile the program.

Listing 1-63. *Compiling the* `stacktest.c` *Program*

```
puppy$ cd /usr/src/linux-.2.4.26-ow2/optional
puppy$ gcc -o stacktest stacktest.c
```

This compile uses gcc to produce a binary called stacktest in the /usr/src/linux-2.4.26-ow2 directory. You can run stacktest to simulate a buffer overflow by running the following command:

```
puppy# ./stacktest -e
Attempting to simulate a buffer overflow exploit...
Segmentation fault
```

If the command execution ends in a Segmentation fault, then the buffer overflow attempt has failed and the patch is functioning as intended.

If you have enabled the /tmp restrictions, you should also be able to test these by trying to create hard links in /tmp to files that you do not own or trying to write to named pipes you do not own. Do these tests as a normal user, *not* as the root user. Doing the tests as the root user proves nothing.

Other Kernel-Hardening Options

Other "hardened" kernels and kernel-hardening patches are available, and I will briefly cover some other available options. Many of the patches offer similar functionality, and I recommend you carefully read the documentation that accompanies them to find the one that suits you best.

grsecurity

The grsecurity package available at http://www.grsecurity.net/ provides a collection of detection, prevention, and containment modifications to the kernel. These include a role-based access control system that allows you to add a finer granularity of access controls to users, applications, and processes based on defining roles. Amongst other features it also adds security to the chroot application, increases protection against buffer overflows, and provides a security infrastructure to the kernel. This package takes a considerable effort to configure and implement, and you need to design the role-based controls to suit your environment.

LIDS

The Linux Intrusion Defense System (LIDS) is another patch that offers access controls such as SELinux and grsecurity. It also comes with a port scanner detector built into the kernel and provides some further file system–hardening and network-hardening modifications that are related to security. LIDS is available from http://www.lids.org/, currently supports version 2.6 kernels, and is regularly updated.

RSBAC

The Rule Set Based Access Controls (RSBAC) project is one of the more fully featured kernel security packages. It offers a number of different access control models that you can use separately or together. It also offers process jails (a kernel-based version of the chroot command), resource controls, and support for the PaX project[11] (designed to reduce the risk of buffer overflow and similar style of attacks). It is available at http://www.rsbac.org/, and it supports version 2.4 and 2.6 kernels.

---

11. http://pax.grsecurity.net/

SELinux

The SELinux package is an initiative of the NSA and is available at `http://www.nsa.gov/selinux/`. Similar in style to the grsecurity package, it provides role-based access control lists (ACLs) that control what resources applications and processes are able to use. These ACLs are governed by a central security policy. The package comes with a kernel patch, some patches to system tools, and some administration tools. Like grsecurity this package also takes a considerable effort to configure and implement. You also need to design the role-based controls to suit your environment though the SELinux package does come with a sample security policy that you can modify for your purposes. SELinux also supports 2.6 kernels, and in the case of Red Hat Enterprise Linux it is integrated into version 3 of this distribution.

Keeping Informed About Security

In the "Package Management, File Integrity, and Updating" section I talked about older releases of packages and applications having exploits and vulnerabilities and the need to keep them up-to-date. In the following sections I will cover some of the ways to find out about these exploits and vulnerabilities and how to keep up-to-date with security issues in general. This allows you to ensure you know what to update and upgrade your packages in a timely manner when exploits are discovered. Doing so denies any potential attackers the opportunity to use those exploits on your system.

Security Sites and Mailing Lists

The following are sites that contain information relevant to Linux security and security in general:

CERT: CERT (`http://www.cert.org/`) is a coordination center and clearinghouse for reporting incidents and vulnerabilities. It also runs the CERT advisory mailing list, which consists of announcements of major vulnerabilities across a variety of operating systems and applications as well as notifications of major virus attacks or notable security incidents. You can subscribe at `http://www.cert.org/contact_cert/certmaillist.html`.

LinuxSecurity.com: The Linuxsecurity.com site (`http://www.linuxsecurity.com/`) contains a variety of documents and resources that focus on Linux Security–related issues including HOWTOs, FAQs, articles, and interviews. It also has a variety of mailing lists you can subscribe to at `http://www.linuxsecurity.com/general/mailinglists.html`.

SANS: The SANS Institute (`http://www.sans.org/`) largely runs information security training and oversees a variety of security certification programs. The site also contains a large collection of documents regarding all aspects of information security. It has a number of newsletters you can subscribe to at `http://www.sans.org/sansnews`. It also runs its own early warning site called the Internet Storm Center, which you can access at `http://isc.sans.org/`.

Security Focus: The Security Focus site[12] (`http://www.securityfocus.com`) is a vendor-neutral site containing a collection of security resources. These include the BugTraq mailing list, which is probably the most comprehensive mailing list of security vulnerabilities. You can subscribe to the mailing list at `http://www.securityfocus.com/archive`. The site also contains the Security Focus Vulnerability Database. The database should be one of your first ports of call when checking for vulnerabilities in an application, distribution, or tool. You can find it at `http://www.securityfocus.com/bid`.

Vendor and Distribution Security Sites

These are sites maintained by the authors and vendors of a variety of Linux distributions that focus on security and security-related announcements specific to that distribution. Many of them also contain links to distribution specific mailing lists, such as Red Hat's Watch-List Advisories, which provide notifications of security-related material.

- **Debian**: `http://www.debian.org/security/`

- **Gentoo**: `http://www.gentoo.org/security/en/glsa/`

- **Mandrake**: `http://www.mandrakesoft.com/security/`

- **Red Hat**: `http://www.redhat.com/support/errata/`

- **SuSE**: `http://www.suse.com/us/support/security/index.html`

- **Yellow Dog**: `http://www.yellowdoglinux.com/resources/updates.shtml`

Resources

The following are some resources for you to use.

Mailing Lists

- **PAM mailing list**: `https://listman.redhat.com/mailman/listinfo/pam-list`

- **Kernel traffic mailing list**: `http://zork.net/mailman/listinfo/ktdistrib`

- **grsecurity** mailing list: `http://grsecurity.net/cgi-bin/mailman/listinfo/grsecurity`

- **LIDS mailing list**: `http://www.lids.org/maillist.html`

- **RSBAC mailing list**: `http://www.rsbac.org/mailman/listinfo/rsbac/`

- **SELinux mailing list**: `http://www.nsa.gov/selinux/info/subscribe.cfm`

- **GNU Privacy Guard mailing list**: `http://lists.gnupg.org/pipermail/gnupg-users/`

---

12. Symantec acquired the Security Focus site in 2002, but part of the sale agreement states the site must remain vendor neutral.

Sites

- **Chkconfig**: http://www.fastcoder.net/~thumper/software/sysadmin/chkconfig/

- **Vlock**: http://linux.maruhn.com/sec/vlock.html or
  http://freshmeat.net/projects/vlock/

- **Titan hardening script**: http://www.fish.com/titan/

- **PAM**_passwdqc: http://www.openwall.com/passwdqc/

- **Acct tools**: http://www.ibiblio.org/pub/linux/system/admin/accounts/
  acct-1.3.73.tar.gz

- **General PAM**: http://www.kernel.org/pub/linux/libs/pam/

- **PAM modules**: http://www.kernel.org/pub/linux/libs/pam/pre/modules/

- **Openwall**: http://www.openwall.com/linux/

- **Grsecurity**: http://www.grsecurity.net/

- **LIDS**: http://www.lids.org/

- **RSBAC**: http://www.rsbac.org/

- **SELinux**: http://www.nsa.gov/selinux/

- **PaX**: http://pax.grsecurity.net/

- **MD5 Crack**: http://www.md5crk.com/

- **GPG**: http://www.gnupg.org/

- **NRH-up2date**: http://www.nrh-up2date.org/

- **APT for RPM**: http://freshrpms.net/apt/

- **Yum**: http://linux.duke.edu/projects/yum/

CHAPTER 2

■■■

Firewalling Your Hosts

Perhaps the most important element of your host's defenses against attack is the firewall. In many cases, the firewall is the first line of defense against attacks on your hosts. A firewall can help you defend your hosts in three principal ways: dealing with unwanted incoming traffic, dealing with unwanted outgoing traffic, and handling the logging of suspicious traffic or traffic known to be of malicious intent. A firewall functions as both a defensive measure and an early warning system.

So what is this firewall thing I am talking about? Well, a variety of firewalls are designed to be deployed in different locations on your network. For example, most networks have a firewall installed at the perimeter of the network to protect your entire network. These are often hardware-based firewalls such as Cisco PIX devices, software-based firewalls such as Check Point Firewall-1,[1] or Linux-based solutions such as SmoothWall.[2] Other firewalls, such as `iptables` or Zone Alarm, are designed to protect individual hosts.

In this chapter, I focus on protecting individual hosts with Netfilter through its user space interface `iptables`. I thus will not cover Netfilter's capabilities as a dedicated firewall-router, which includes functions such as packet forwarding and Network Address Translation (NAT). The emphasis in this chapter is on building secure firewalls for stand-alone and bastion hosts while not limiting the capabilities of your applications and services. This means I will not cover every single feature of `iptables` and Netfilter; instead, I recommend some books and sites in the "Resources" section that offer further information on the areas I have not covered in this chapter.

The doctrine for setting up the securest possible host-based firewall reflects some of the concepts I discussed in the book's introduction: minimalism and vigilance. Your firewall should be minimalist in design and managed by exception. The simplest, securest, and most minimally configured possible firewall is one that denies everything: from everywhere and to everywhere. I recommend this should be your default firewall design. Any access to your host should be the exception, not the rule—you create a wall and then carefully remove only those bricks that are required for access.

This applies to network traffic in two ways: when you assess what a single host is expected to receive and transmit on your local network and when you decide what traffic you want to enter your bastion host from foreign networks. In the second case, I am deliberately not saying the "Internet," because the principle applies to *all* internetworking. You should be thinking about protecting and monitoring all your network borders whether they are shared with

---

1. http://www.checkpoint.com/products/firewall-1/
2. http://www.smoothwall.org/

subsidiaries, clients, service providers, and so on. This makes sense because you may not be able to control the security policies of those connected networks, and therefore you may not be able to trust them.

Vigilance also comes into your firewall design and management as it is going to be a key aspect of firewall construction. They allow you to both see where you are going wrong and when your rules are being effective in addition to providing information on what traffic is being generated on a host and who is generating it. I recommend getting a laptop and small hub that you can use to connect to any host on your network to see what traffic it creates and consumes. Using this combination, you can quickly see over which ports and to what networks a host communicates and then adjust your firewall rules accordingly. Tools such as Ethereal and tcpdump are great for snooping on network conversations (and I will show you how to use tcpdump in the "Testing and Troubleshooting" section). Do not forget the ethical implications this has. You may need sign-off from your organization's management before you can legitimately monitor traffic on some or all of your network.

I will show you how iptables-based firewalls work on a Linux host, how to construct a firewalls for stand-alone and bastion hosts, and cover additional Netfilter modules and kernel-tuning parameters, testing and troubleshooting your firewalling, and some tools you can use with your firewalls and firewalling. In Appendix A, I provide you with a script for a bastion host–based on the information in this chapter; you can edit and configure it to provide a suitable firewall for your own hosts.

I will not explain basic networking to you. To understand this chapter, you should have an understanding of IP addressing, subnetting, and the basic operation of TCP/IP traffic. You should also be able to control the networking configuration of your host using the basic configuration tools available such as ifconfig. Also, I will not cover network design in any great detail because this book is aimed at host-level security, not network security in a broader context. I will not examine NAT and routing using iptables. Books are available that better cover those issues aimed at using Linux and iptables for firewalling and routing, and I list some of them in the "Resources" section at the end of this chapter.

Note This chapter focuses on IPv4 networking. At this point, industry-spread acceptance of IPv6 networking is not sufficient to merit its coverage.

So, How Does a Linux Firewall Work?

The tools I will be using to provide firewall functions are built on the Netfilter framework that exists in the Linux kernel. Netfilter was written by Rusty Russell[3] and has been in Linux since version 1.0 although at that stage it was a rewrite of pf from NetBSD. It allows the operating system to perform packet filtering and shaping at a kernel level, and this allows it to be under fewer restrictions than user space programs. This is especially useful for dedicated firewall and router hosts.

---

3. http://ozlabs.org/~rusty/

Netfilter is a stateful packet-filtering firewall. Two types of packet-filtering firewalls exist: stateful and stateless. A stateless packet-filtering firewall examines only the header of a packet for filtering information. It sees each packet in isolation and thus has no way to determine if a packet is part of an existing connection or an isolated malicious packet. A stateful firewall maintains information about the status of the connections passing through it. This allows the firewall to filter on the state of the connection, which offers considerably finer-grained control over your traffic.

Netfilter is controlled and configured in user space by the `iptables` command. In previous versions of the Linux kernel, other commands provided this functionality. In kernel version 2.2 it was `ipchains`, and in version 2.0 it was `ipfwadm`. I cover the `iptables` command in this chapter, and I will frequently use this name to refer to the firewall technology in general. Most Linux-based distributions will have an `iptables` package, but they may also have their own tool for configuring the rules. Some of these may be worth looking into, but they may not be easy to use for more complicated configurations or may make dangerous configuration assumptions.

■Note This chapter was written using `iptables` version 1.2.11, which was the most recent at the time of writing. You can use the command, `iptables -V`, to find the version of the `iptables` command on your host.

Netfilter works by referring to a set of tables. These tables contain chains, which in turn contain individual rules. Chains hold groups of like rules; for example, a group of rules governing incoming traffic could be held in a chain. Rules are the basic Netfilter configuration items that contain criteria to match particular traffic and perform an action on the matched traffic.

Traffic that is currently being processed by the host is compared against these rules, and if the current packet being processed satisfies the selection criteria of a rule, then the action specified by that rule is carried out. These actions, amongst others, can be to ignore the packet, accept the packet, reject the packet, or pass the packet onto other rules for more refined processing. Let's look at an example; say the Ethernet interface on your Web server has just received a packet from the Internet. This packet is checked against your rules and compared to their selection criteria. The selection criteria include such items as the destination IP address and the destination port. For example, you want incoming Web traffic on the HTTP port 80 to go to the IP address of your Web server. If your incoming traffic matches these criteria, then you specify and action to let it through. This is a simple example that shows how an `iptables` rule could work.

Each `iptables` rule relies on specifying a set of network parameters as selection criteria to select the packets and traffic for each rule. You can use a number of network parameters to build each `iptables` rule. For example, a network connection between two hosts is referred to as a *socket*. This is the combination of a source IP address, source port, destination IP address, and destination port. All four of these parameters must exist for the connection to be established, and `iptables` can use these values to filter traffic coming in and out of hosts. Additionally, if you look at how communication is performed on a TCP/IP-based network, you will see that three protocols are used frequently: Internet Control Message Protocol (ICMP), Transmission Control Protocol (TCP), and User Datagram Protocol (UDP). The `iptables` firewall can easily distinguish between these different types of protocols and others.

With just these five parameters (the source and destination IP addresses, the source and destination ports and the protocol type), you can now start building some useful filtering rules. But before you start building these rules, you need to understand how iptables rules are structured and interact. And to gain this understanding, you need to understand further some initial iptables concepts such as tables, chains, and policies.

Tables

I talked about Netfilter having tables of rules that traffic can be compared against and some action taken. Netfilter has three built-in tables that can hold rules for processing traffic. The first is the filter table, which is the default table used for all rules related to the filtering of your traffic. The second is nat, which handles NAT rules, and the last is the mangle table, which covers a variety of packet alteration functions. When constructing the iptables rules in this chapter, I will focus on the filter table.

Chains

The iptables rules are broken down within the tables I have described into groupings called *chains*. Each table contains default chains that are built into the table. You can also create chains of your own in each table to hold additional rules. Let's focus on the built-in chains in the filter table. These are FORWARD, INPUT, and OUTPUT. Each chain correlates to the basic paths that packets can take through a host. When the Netfilter logic encounters a packet, the first evaluation it makes is to which chain the packet is destined. If a packet is coming into the host through a network interface, it needs to be evaluated by the rules in the INPUT chain. If the packet is generated by this host and going out onto the network via a network interface, then it needs to be evaluated by the rules in the OUTPUT chain. The FORWARD chain is used for packets that have entered the host but are destined for some other host (for example, on hosts that act as routers or software-based firewalls at the perimeter of your network or between your network and the Internet).

Policies

Each chain defined in the filter table also can have a policy. A policy is the default action a chain takes on a packet to determine if a packet makes it all the way through the rules in a chain without matching any of them. The policies you can use for packets are DROP, REJECT, and ACCEPT. When the iptables commands is first run, it sets some default policies for built-in chains. The INPUT and OUTPUT chains will have a policy of ACCEPT, and the FORWARD chain will have a policy of DROP.

The DROP policy discards a packet without notifying the sender. The REJECT policy also discards the packet, but it sends an ICMP packet to the sender to tell it the rejection has occurred. The REJECT policy means that a device will know that its packets are not getting to their destination and will report the error quickly instead of waiting to be timed out, as is the case with the DROP policy. The DROP policy is contrary to TCP RFCs and can be a little harsh on network devices; specifically, they can sit waiting for a response from their dropped packet(s) for a long time. But for security purposes it is generally considered better to use the DROP policy rather than the REJECT policy, as it provides less information to the outside world.

The ACCEPT policy accepts the traffic and allows it to pass through the firewall. Naturally from a security perspective this renders your firewall ineffective if it is used as the default policy. By default iptables configures all chains with a policy of ACCEPT, but changing this to a policy of

DROP for all chains is recommended. This falls in line with the basic doctrine of a default stance of denial for the firewall. You should deny all traffic by default and open the host to only the traffic to which you have explicitly granted access. This denial can be problematic, because setting a default policy of DROP for the INPUT and OUTPUT chains means incoming and outgoing traffic are not allowed unless you explicitly add rules to allow traffic to come into and out of the host. This will cause all services and tools that connect from your host that are not explicitly allowed to enter or leave that host to fail.

Adding Your First Rules

The majority of our work will be on the INPUT and OUTPUT chains of the filter table, as I will be defending hosts from the outside world by attempting to narrow down the incoming traffic to only the bare minimum required for the host to perform its designated function. So I will create some rules for the INPUT and the OUTPUT chains to demonstrate how iptables works. To create a new rule, you can simply add one to a chain with the iptables command. Let's add the rule to deal with HTTP traffic on port 80 that I described earlier.

```
puppy# iptables -A INPUT -i eth0 -p tcp --dport 80 -d 192.168.0.1 -j ACCEPT
```

Note The iptables function is interactive. The rule will take effect immediately upon being added. All rules exist in memory and will be lost when the system is rebooted. I will cover methods of saving rule sets and starting and stopping iptables in the "Managing iptables and Your Rules" section.

So what does this command do? Well, in the next few paragraphs let's break it down into its component pieces. The first flag, -A, tells iptables that this is an addition and specifies to which chain the new rule should be added.

Note By default, unless overridden, all new rules are added to the filter table, so you do not need to define to which table you are adding it.

The -i flag specifies which device the traffic will use to enter the host. I have indicated eth0, which would be the first Ethernet device on your host. If you do not specify a device then iptables assumes the rule applies to all incoming network traffic from all devices.

The next flag, -p, specifies the protocol of the packets you are filtering, in this case tcp. As HTTP is a TCP protocol, I have told iptables to select only TCP packets. If you were selecting a protocol that used UDP or ICMP traffic, you would specify udp here for UDP traffic or icmp for ICMP traffic, respectively. You could also select a particular protocol by number; for example, you could use -p 50, which is the Authentication Header that is used for IPSec connections.[4]

---

4. You can see a list of all the protocol numbers at http://www.iana.org/assignments/protocol-numbers.

The following flags are related to the destination of the packets that `iptables` is filtering. The `--dport` flag tells `iptables` to select only packets destined for port 80, the standard port for HTTP traffic. The `-d` selects only those packets destined for the specified IP address, `192.168.0.1`. If you do not specify a destination IP address, then `iptables` would apply this rule to all incoming HTTP traffic on eth0.

The last flag in the rule, `-j`, specifies the ultimate action or target of the rule. In this case I am using the ACCEPT target, which accepts the packets. The ACCEPT target also indicates that if the packet being filtered matches this rule, then no other rule matches are performed and the packet can pass through the firewall. Several other targets exist. For example, you could change the proposed target to DROP, as shown in the next line:

```
puppy# iptables -A INPUT -i eth0 -p tcp --dport 80 -d 192.168.0.1 -j DROP
```

Then if the incoming packet matched this rule, it would be dropped and no other rules would be checked. Targets offer similar functionality to the policies I have described. Indeed, ACCEPT, DROP, and REJECT targets perform the same function as their policy namesakes. But there are also more targets available to you than their policy counterparts, and I will describe some of these targets in the coming sections.

Let's say this is the first rule for a Web server. The example Web server also runs a secure site using HTTPS, so you decide to add a rule to handle this traffic, too.

```
puppy# iptables -A INPUT -i eth0 -p tcp --dport 443 -d 192.168.0.1 -j ACCEPT
```

Here I have created an almost identical rule to the previous one except I have specified that the rule will filter on the destination HTTPS port 443.

So now both HTTP and HTTPS traffic are allowed into the host and will be passed to the Web server. But what happens if you want HTTP and HTTPS traffic to get back out of the host, which would be required to allow the Web server to correctly function? All outgoing traffic is handled by rules defined in the OUTPUT chain. So you need to add rules to handle the outgoing traffic from the Web server to the OUTPUT chain.

```
puppy# iptables -A OUTPUT -o eth0 -p tcp --sport http -j ACCEPT
puppy# iptables -A OUTPUT -o eth0 -p tcp --sport https -j ACCEPT
```

While these new rules are similar to the rules you have already defined, they have some important differences. The first is that the `-A` flag is now adding these rules to the OUTPUT chain rather than the INPUT chain. I have also specified the device eth0 again, but I have specified it using the `-o` flag. The `-o` flag indicates traffic outgoing on the specified device as opposed to the `-i` flag, which indicates incoming traffic on the specified device.

Like the previous rules, you are still specifying the TCP protocol using the `-p` flag but instead of the destination port as indicated by the `--dport` flag, you are now using the `--sport` flag, which defines the source port from which the HTTP or HTTPS traffic comes. You can also specify both the `--sport` and `--dport` options in a rule to allow you dictate the ports at both end of the connection, as you can see in the next line. Enter the following:

```
puppy# iptables -A INPUT -i eth0 -p tcp --sport imap --dport imaps -j ACCEPT
```

In the rule on the previous line all incoming TCP traffic from the `imap` port is allowed to go through to the `imaps` port.[5]

---

5. Ports 143 and 993, respectively

In the last three rules you have also replaced the references to the numeric p
with the name of the services being filtered, http and https and imap and imaps. The
are defined in the file /etc/services. Listing 2-1 shows the service definitions for these p
cols from this file.

Listing 2-1. *Service Definitions in the /etc/services File*

```
http       80/tcp      www www-http    # WorldWideWeb HTTP
imap       143/tcp     imap            # IMAP
https      443/tcp                     # MCom
imaps      993/tcp     imaps           # IMAPS
```

I recommend using the service name rather than the port for your source and destination ports, as it makes your rules easier to read and understand.

Finally, you have again used the target of ACCEPT as defined by the -j flag to indicate that this traffic is allowed to leave the host.

In combination, the four rules you have defined allow a Web server to receive and send HTTP and HTTPS traffic from a host. While not an ideal (or complete) configuration, this represents a limited-functioning iptables firewall. From this you will build more complicated firewall configurations, but first you will examine how to identify what to filter on and look at the iptables command and some of its options.

THE /etc/services FILE

It is important to secure the /etc/services file. It contains a list of network services and matching ports. Listing 2-2 shows a sample of this file.

Listing 2-2. *Sample /etc/services File*

```
ftp        21/tcp
ftp        21/udp      fsp fspd
ssh        22/tcp                          # SSH Remote Login Protocol
ssh        22/udp                          # SSH Remote Login Protocol
telnet     23/tcp
telnet     23/udp
```

Although actually disabling services you do not use in this file can inconvenience attackers, it will not actively stop them using the service you have disabled. But I recommend not allowing anyone to edit this file and potentially add any services to your host. Use the following commands to secure the file:

```
puppy# chown root:root /etc/services
puppy# chmod 0644 /etc/services
puppy# chattr +i /etc/services
```

The chattr +i command makes the /etc/services immutable: it cannot be deleted, it cannot be renamed, and no link can be created to this file.

...g Criteria

...rule is going to filter on is an important part of the configura-
...understand the basic structure of a TCP/IP transaction. As I have
...source and destination IP addresses, source and destination ports,
...other options. The best method of choosing how to filter your traffic
...incoming and outgoing traffic. Table 2-1 provides an example of how

Table 2-1. *Hi...* *Incoming*

Interface	Source Au... s	Source Port	Protocol	Destination Address	Destination Port
eth0	Any	32768 to 61000	TCP	192.168.0.1	80

For the example in Table 2-1. I have used incoming HTTP traffic and laid out all the information I know about the incoming traffic. First I have highlighted the incoming interface, eth0,
that will be handling the traffic. Then I have identified the potential source addresses that will
be the clients querying the Web server. The first question is now whether you can determine
who the client is. Most Web servers will be open to traffic from all source addresses, but in some
cases—for example, for an Intranet Web server used only in a local network—you may be able
to use the local network source address as a filtering criteria. In the example in Table 2-1. I will
be allowing traffic from any source address.

The next item is the source port of the incoming traffic. The source and destination ports
of a TCP connection are determined in one of two ways: the server end of a connection is generally assigned a predetermined port number for that particular service; for example, by default
DNS servers use port 53 and SMTP server use port 25. The Internet Assigned Numbers Authority (IANA) assigns these numbers, and you can see the definitive list at http://www.iana.org/
assignments/port-numbers. At the client end, incoming requests from remote clients can come
in from a range of random source ports called *ephemeral ports*. The remote client assigns each
outgoing connection a port from this range. The exact range varies from operating system to
operating system. On Linux systems to see what the range of your ephemeral ports is, you can
review the contents of the file /proc/sys/net/ipv4/ip_local_port_range. For Red Hat Linux
systems this range is generally 32768 to 61000. For Debian systems the range is 1024 to 4099.
Unless you know the range of ephemeral ports being used by all your client systems I recommend not using this as a filter for rules.

Next I have identified the protocol the traffic will be using, tcp, which is a filtering criteria
you should be able use in most rules to filter traffic. Finally, I have identified the destination
address and destination port; in this case for the incoming HTTP, traffic is the IP address of the
local Web server and the HTTP port 80. Again, for incoming traffic, these are going to be commonly used to filter your traffic.

You can list all your proposed incoming traffic this way (see Table 2-2).

Table 2-2. *Incoming Traffic Flow*

Interface	Source Address	Source Port	Protocol	Destination Address	Destination Port
eth0	Any	32768 to 61000	TCP	192.168.0.1	80
eth0	Any	Any	TCP	192.168.0.1	25
eth0	Any	Any	TCP	192.168.0.1	22
eth1	192.168.0.0/24	Any	TCP	192.168.0.1	53

Of course, you can also conduct this same exercise for the outgoing traffic (see Table 2-3).

Table 2-3. *Outgoing Traffic Flow*

Interface	Source Address	Source Port	Protocol	Destination Address	Destination Port
eth0	192.168.0.1	80	TCP	Any	32768 to 61000
eth0	192.168.0.1	25	TCP	Any	Any
eth0	192.168.0.1	22	TCP	Any	Any
eth1	192.168.0.1	25	TCP	192.168.0.0/24	Any

You can model all the connections on your host this way to allow you to apply suitable iptables rules to your incoming and outgoing connections. You can then combine these lists of traffic into an overall test plan for your firewall rules. Then using a tool such as tcpdump, you can identify whether your rules cover all the incoming and outgoing traffic on your host.

The iptables Command

The iptables command principally controls adding and removing rules to your chains. You have already seen the -A flag, which adds rules to your firewall. When you use the -A flag to add a rule, it is appended to the end of the current rules in a chain. You can also add rules using the -I flag, which adds rules to the top of the chain of current rules. So why do you need the different types of flags to add rules to your firewall? Well, the sequence of your rules is important. The rules in a chain are checked in sequence, in the order they are added, with the first rule added to the chain being checked first and the last rule added to the chain being checked last.

With the -I flag you can also add a rule into a chain using a line number, which you can specify to place that rule exactly where you require in the chain. Let's look at the line numbers of rules. Line numbers are important because, as I have described, your rules are checked in a sequence in each chain. If you have a rule specifying all traffic is accepted into your host at line number 1 of the rules in a chain, then all traffic will be accepted by this rule and any following rules that may restrict traffic will be ignored. For example, let's look at the following two rules:

```
puppy# iptables -I INPUT 1 -i eth0 -p tcp -j ACCEPT
puppy# iptables -I INPUT 2 -i eth0 -p tcp --dport 143 -j DROP
```

The first rule ACCEPTs all TCP traffic that enters the host from device eth0, and the number 1 after the chain indicates it is the first rule in the INPUT chain. The second rule DROPs all traffic that enters the host from device eth0 bound for port 143, or IMAP, and the number 2 after the chain indicates it is the second rule in the INPUT chain. As the rules are checked in sequence, the second rule would be totally ignored because the first rule indicates all TCP traffic is to be accepted. So you should ensure your rules make logical sense and do not contradict each other.

Each of your rules is assigned a line number in the chain to which they are assigned. You can see this line number and the details of the rules in a chain by using the -L flag to list your rules (see Listing 2-3).

Listing 2-3. *Listing Your Rules*

```
puppy# iptables -L INPUT -n --line-numbers
Chain INPUT (policy DROP)
num  target     prot opt source            destination
1    ACCEPT     tcp  --  0.0.0.0/0         192.168.0.1          tcp dpt:80
2    ACCEPT     tcp  --  0.0.0.0/0         192.168.0.1          tcp dpt:443
```

In Listing 2-3 I have listed all the rules in the INPUT chain. I have used two flags; the first -n tells iptables not to look up any IP addresses via DNS or port numbers via the /etc/services file but rather display the raw numerics. This makes the listing faster as it stops iptables waiting for DNS resolution and service lookups before displaying the rules. I have also specified the --line-numbers flag, which will show the rules with their line numbers.

If I had omitted the chain name from the -L flag, it would have displayed all the rules from all chains.

```
puppy# iptables -L -n --line-numbers
Chain INPUT (policy DROP)
num  target     prot opt source            destination
1    ACCEPT     tcp  --  0.0.0.0/0         192.168.0.1          tcp dpt:80
2    ACCEPT     tcp  --  0.0.0.0/0         192.168.0.1          tcp dpt:443
Chain FORWARD (policy DROP)
target       prot opt source              destination
Chain OUTPUT (policy DROP)
num  target     prot opt source            destination
1    ACCEPT      tcp  --  0.0.0.0/0         0.0.0.0/0          tcp spt:80
2    ACCEPT      tcp  --  0.0.0.0/0         0.0.0.0/0          tcp spt:443
```

So now you want to add a rule in the INPUT chain at line 3. To do this you must use the -I flag with which you can specify the line number. The -A flag does not allow you to specify a line number.

```
puppy# iptables -I INPUT 3 -i eth0 -p tcp --dport 22 -d 192.168.0.1 -j ACCEPT
```

You can see, you have specified the required line number after the name of the chain in the -I flag. Now if you list the rules in the INPUT chain, you will see the new rule at line number 3 in Listing 2-4.

Listing 2-4. *Listing After Inserting the New Rule*

```
puppy# iptables -L INPUT -n --line-numbers
Chain INPUT (policy DROP)
num  target     prot opt source              destination
1    ACCEPT     tcp  --  0.0.0.0/0           192.168.0.1          tcp dpt:80
2    ACCEPT     tcp  --  0.0.0.0/0           192.168.0.1          tcp dpt:443
3    ACCEPT     tcp  --  0.0.0.0/0           192.168.0.1          tcp dpt:22
```

If you add a rule to the chain using a line number that already exists in the sequence, the rule is inserted ahead of the existing line. So if you added another rule using the line number 3 into the INPUT chain, it would be inserted into the chain ahead of the existing line number 3 in Listing 2-4.

If you have added a rule that you no longer want, you can delete rules from your chains using the -D flag. You can see the -D flag in Listing 2-5.

Listing 2-5. *Removing a Rule*

```
puppy# iptables -D INPUT -i eth0 -p tcp --dport https -d 192.168.0.1 -j ACCEPT
```

The command in Listing 2-5 would delete the HTTPS rule you specified earlier. The -D flag deletes rules by matching the filtering specifications of that rule. You must match the exact specifications of the rule to be deleted. If you do not specify the rule adequately, then the deletion will fail.

```
puppy# iptables -D INPUT -p tcp --dport https -d 192.168.0.1 -j ACCEPT
iptables: Bad rule (does a matching rule exist in that chain?)
```

In the previous line you have tried to delete the HTTPS rule in the INPUT chain with the command in Listing 2-5. This time, though, you have omitted the -i eth0 from the iptables command. Hence, iptables has failed to match it with the existing rule; thus, the deletion has failed.

You can also delete rules via their line number. In Listing 2-6 you can see the deletion of the third rule in the INPUT chain.

Listing 2-6. *Removing Rules Using Sequence Numbers*

```
puppy# iptables -D INPUT 3
```

You can also delete all the rules in a chain or all chains by using the -F flag. This is often described as *flushing*.

```
puppy# iptables -F INPUT
```

If you omit the name of the chain, then all the rules in all chains will be flushed, as you can see in the next line. Enter iptables -F to flush the rules and then iptables -L to list the resultant empty chains.

```
puppy# iptables -F
puppy# iptables -L
Chain INPUT (policy DROP)
target     prot opt source            destination
Chain FORWARD (policy DROP)
target     prot opt source            destination
Chain OUTPUT (policy DROP)
target     prot opt source            destination
```

You can see that after flushing all the rules in all chains that the listing of the chains reveals they are all empty.

You can use some additional command-line flags with the `iptables` command. The most obvious you have yet to look at is the `-t` flag, which when specified at the start of the command indicates which table you are using. Listing 2-7 shows the rules contained in the nat table.

Listing 2-7. *Specifying a Particular Table*

```
puppy# iptables -t nat -L
Chain PREROUTING (policy DROP)
target     prot opt source            destination
Chain POSTROUTING (policy DROP)
target     prot opt source            destination
Chain OUTPUT (policy DROP)
target     prot opt source            destination
```

You can use the `-t` in front of all the possible command-line flags for `iptables`. As I mentioned earlier, by default if you do not specify a table, then the `iptables` command defaults to the `filter` table.

You can see the renaming command-line flags for `iptables` in Table 2-4.

Table 2-4. *Additional* iptables *Command-Line Flags*

Flag	Description
-P *policy*	Sets the default policy for a chain.
-R *chain seq# rule*	Replaces an existing rule based on the sequence number.
-Z *chain*	Zeros the byte and packet counts on a chains or chains.
-N *chain*	Creates a new chain. The chain name must be unique.
-E *oldchain newchain*	Renames a user-created chain. Built-in chains cannot be renamed.
-X *chain*	Deletes a user-created chain. The chain must be empty (in other words, have no rules) before it can be deleted. You cannot delete built-in chains.

The first flag ,`-P`, sets the default policy for built-in chains. I have described policies earlier in the chapter. The `-R` flag allows you to replace a rule in your chain based on its line number. The `-Z` flag relates to the handling of the `iptables` byte and packet counter. Each rule has an associated counter that tracks how many bytes and packets have been processed by that rule. You can see these counters and a total for each chain when you list all your rules by adding the `-v` flag to the `-L` flag (see Listing 2-8).

Listing 2-8. *Displaying Rules and Their Counters*

```
puppy# iptables -L -v
Chain INPUT (policy ACCEPT 25897 packets, 2300K bytes)
 pkts bytes target     prot opt in     out     source              destination
```

The -Z flag sets all counters back to zero.

The last flags from Table 2-4 relate to the creation of user chains. You can utilize user-created chains to better structure your rules. For example, creating a new chain to hold all the rules related to incoming ICMP traffic. You can then direct traffic to your user-created chains by using them as a target with the -j flag (see Listing 2-9).

Listing 2-9. *Redirecting Packets to a User-Created Chain*

```
puppy# iptables -A INPUT -p icmp -j NEW_CHAIN
```

In Listing 2-9 all incoming ICMP traffic is redirected to the user-created chain NEW_CHAIN. You can create this new chain using the -N flag (see Listing 2-10).

Listing 2-10. *Creating a User Chain*

```
puppy# iptables -N NEW_CHAIN
```

You can also rename your user-created chain using the -E flag.

```
puppy# iptables -E NEW_CHAIN OLD_CHAIN
```

And finally, you can delete a user-created chain (if it contains no rules and is not referenced as a target by any other rules) using the -X flag.

```
puppy# iptables -X OLD_CHAIN
```

If you do not specify a particular chain to be deleted, then the -X flag will delete all user-created chains. You cannot delete the built-in chains such as INPUT or OUTPUT.

Creating a Basic Firewall

One of the best ways to learn how to use iptables is to construct a basic firewall. I will do that for a stand-alone host, puppy. This is a host that is not directly connected to the Internet and lives in a local network. Then I will expand on this basic configuration to include securing a bastion host, which is frequently located in DMZs[6] and is directly connected to the Internet, to explain some of the more advanced features and functions of iptables. I will start by describing the stand-alone host I intend to firewall.

---

6. A demilitarized zone (DMZ) is an isolated segment of your network designed to hold hosts and services that are at greater risk than others, for example, bastion hosts. The DMZ is generally more secure than the other segments of your network.

- The host has one IP address: `192.168.0.1` that is bound to interface eth0. The host is in the `192.168.0.0/24` subnet.

- I want to allow HTTP traffic in and out because the host runs a Web server.

- I want to allow DNS traffic in and out to allow the host to query remote DNS servers.

- I want to allow outgoing SMTP traffic to allow the host to send e-mail.

- The host is administered using SSH, so I need to allow incoming SSH traffic.

I will start by flushing all the rules from the existing chains to get a fresh start.

```
puppy# iptables -F
```

Now I want to set the default policies of DROP I discussed earlier for each of the chains in the filter table. You use the iptables command with the -P flag for this, and you can see how to do it in Listing 2-11.

Listing 2-11. *Setting Default Policies for Chains*

```
puppy# iptables -P INPUT DROP
puppy# iptables -P OUTPUT DROP
puppy# iptables -P FORWARD DROP
```

■Caution If you are remotely connected to the host you are setting your rules on, and you set a policy of DROP for your INPUT chain while there are no other rules in your firewall, you will be disconnected from the host because the default policy is now to drop all traffic. I have assumed you are signed onto the console of your host to set your rules.

Do not worry too much about the FORWARD chain in the basic firewall, because for the most part you will not be forwarding any packets, as this is more the job of a router. You really should be interested only in conversations with the host itself. The forwarding policy will take care of any packets that are trying to be forwarded through the host by dropping them immediately.

Now you want to address traffic using the loopback host, lo. This is the internal `127.0.0.1` address of the host, and in order for the host to correctly function, you need to allow all traffic in and out on this interface. You can see the rules for this in Listing 2-12.

Listing 2-12. *Enabling Loopback Traffic*

```
puppy# iptables -A INPUT -i lo -j ACCEPT
puppy# iptables -A OUTPUT -o lo -j ACCEPT
```

Now add the rules to allow in and out HTTP traffic.

This will allow you to run a Web server on port 80 of the host. But I have also added a new flag -m to the rules in Listing 2-13. The -m option enables the match function. This allows you to load modules that can match a variety of additional packet characteristics and allows you to filter on them. In Listing 2-13 I have enabled the state module using the flag -m state. This allows you to perform state inspection and matching on the incoming packets, which is one of the key features of a stateful packet-filtering firewall such as iptables.

Listing 2-13. *Adding the HTTP Rules*

```
puppy# ipables -A INPUT -i eth0 -p tcp --dport http -d 192.168.0.1 -m state ➥
--state NEW,ESTABLISHED -j ACCEPT
puppy# iptables -A OUTPUT -o eth0 -p tcp --sport http -m state ➥
--state ESTABLISHED -j ACCEPT
```

■**Note** The state module is provided by the ipt_conntrack Netfilter kernel module, which should be loaded by default with most recent iptables releases. If it is not, you can load it with the insmod command, insmod ipt_conntack.

By enabling the state module, you can check if a packet is part of a connection that is in one of four possible states: NEW, ESTABLISHED, RELATED or INVALID.

The NEW connection state indicates a freshly initiated connection where data has not passed back and forth. You must allow the NEW connection state either incoming or outgoing if you want to allow new connections to a service. For example, if you do not specify that the NEW connection state is accepted for incoming SMTP traffic on a mail server, then remote clients will not be able use the mail server to send e-mail.

An ESTABLISHED connection state indicates an existing connection that is in the process of transferring data. You need to allow ESTABLISHED connections if you want a service to be able maintain a connection with a remote client or server. For example, if you want to allow ssh connections to your host, you must allow NEW and ESTABLISHED incoming traffic and ESTABLISHED outgoing traffic to ensure the connection is possible.

The RELATED state refers to a connection that is used to facilitate another connection. A common example is an FTP session where control data is passed to one connection and actual file data flows through another one.

The INVALID state is branded on a connection that has been seen to have problems in processing packets: they may have exceeded the processing ability of the firewall or be packets that are irrelevant to any current connection.

By specifying in your rules that traffic has to fit a certain state, you can eliminate potentially harmful packets getting to the services that you do need to keep open by only allowing traffic of a particular connection state. If you do not need to be able to make new connections using a service, you can simply specify that only established or related connections can use that service and preclude new connections from being made. By adding the connection state you further enhance the principle of allowing only the bare minimum of access to our host. The more closely you filter the traffic entering and leaving your host (by identifying it by as many possible characteristics as you can, including the protocol, port, interface, source or destination address, and now state), the more you reduce the risk that the incoming traffic is malicious and not intended for your host.

You can also add the connection state to the maps of the host's traffic flow I discussed in the "Choosing Filtering Criteria" section (see Table 2-5).

Table 2-5. *Traffic Flow Incoming Including Connection State*

Interface	Source Address	Source Port	Protocol	Destination Address	Destination Port	States
eth0	Any	32768 to 61000	TCP	192.168.0.1	80	NEW,ESTABLISHED

Another beneficial side effect is that the connection-tracking mechanism used for state inspection also defragments packets. One form of attack seen in the past is the practice of deliberately fragmenting communications so that a firewall may mistakenly allow it, but when it comes to being assembled on the target host, the resulting packets are malevolent in nature. I will further cover this sort of attack a little later in this chapter.

In Listing 2-13 you can see that I select the required states with the --state flag. I am allowing traffic that is in the NEW and ESTABLISHED connection state into the host. This means incoming new and already established HTTP connections are allowed to be made to the host, and I am allowing only traffic that is in the ESTABLISHED connection state out of the host. This means new outgoing HTTP connections are not allowed to be made. If you tried to connect to a remote Web site from this host, you would not be able to do so.

Now I will add in some rules to handle DNS traffic. The internal network has two DNS servers, 192.168.0.10 and 192.168.0.11. You want only the host to connect to these DNS servers and no others, and you can see the required INPUT rules to achieve this in Listing 2-14.

Listing 2-14. *Adding the DNS* INPUT *Rules*

```
puppy# iptables -A INPUT -i eth0 -p udp -s 192.168.0.10 --sport domain ➥
-m state --state ESTABLISHED -j ACCEPT
puppy# iptables -A INPUT -i eth0 -p udp -s 192.168.0.11 --sport domain ➥
-m state --state ESTABLISHED -j ACCEPT
```

To restrict which DNS servers the host can query I have specified them by IP addresses with the -s flag. The -s flag allows you to specify the source IP address of the incoming traffic. This flag is the opposite of the -d flag, which allows you to specify the destination IP address. Using the -s flag increases the security of your host by allowing only the traffic from the specific IP addresses of the DNS servers. You could also specify an entire subnet using CIDR notation with the -s flag.

```
puppy# iptables -A INPUT -i eth0 -p udp -s 192.168.0/24 --sport domain ➥
-m state --state ESTABLISHED -j ACCEPT
```

This would allow querying of any DNS server in the 192.168.0/24 subnet.

I have also enabled state inspection for these rules, and in Listing 2-14 I am allowing only traffic that is in the ESTABLISHED connection state. This is because no incoming traffic from the DNS servers should require establishing a new connection, and therefore you do not have to allow traffic in the NEW connection state. The only incoming traffic should be in response to a query from the host where traffic will be in the ESTABLISHED connection state. This prevents a potential attack initiated by sending malicious DNS packets to the host because incoming packets have to be part of an existing and established connection. Any traffic in a NEW connection state would be dropped.

■Note The DNS traffic is UDP based, and UDP is a stateless protocol. So how does iptables track the connection state? The iptables function records a connection pseudo-state for each connection that allows you to use state inspection on UDP traffic. This pseudo-state is recorded in the state table. You can see the state table at /proc/net/ip_conntrack.

Listing 2-15 shows the OUTPUT rules you need to add to allow the host to query the DNS servers.

Listing 2-15. *Adding the DNS* OUTPUT *Rules*

```
puppy# iptables -A OUTPUT -o eth0 -p udp -d 192.168.0.10 --dport domain ➡
-m state --state NEW,ESTABLISHED -j ACCEPT
puppy# iptables -A OUTPUT -o eth0 -p udp -d 192.168.0.11 --dport domain ➡
-m state --state NEW,ESTABLISHED -j ACCEPT
```

Because I know the IP addresses of the DNS servers the host will be connecting to, I have specified them with the -d flag. This limits the possible destinations of the DNS traffic, further tightening outgoing access from the host. Additionally, I have allowed traffic in both NEW and ESTABLISHED states to connect because the host will be querying the remote DNS servers, which requires a new connection.

The rules in Listing 2-16 allow incoming and outgoing SMTP connections from the host much like you have allowed DNS traffic. An SMTP server in the local network is called 192.168.0.20. I am allowing traffic in the NEW and ESTABLISHED connection state to connect from the host to the SMTP server. This means you can initiate new and maintain existing SMTP connections to the SMTP server from this host. The host will only accept incoming traffic in the ESTABLISHED connection state. This is because there is no requirement for new SMTP connections to be created by the host.

Listing 2-16. *Adding the SMTP Rules*

```
puppy# iptables -A INPUT  -i eth0 -p tcp -s 192.168.0.20 --sport smtp ➡
-m state --state ESTABLISHED -j ACCEPT
puppy# iptables -A OUTPUT -o eth0 -p tcp -d 192.168.0.20 --dport smtp ➡
-m state --state NEW,ESTABLISHED -j ACCEPT
```

Finally, you want to allow access via SSH to perform secure administration to the host. For this you add some rules allowing incoming SSH access only from the local network. Listing 2-17 shows these rules.

Listing 2-17. *Adding SSH Rules*

```
puppy# iptables -A INPUT -i eth0 -p tcp -s 192.168.0.0/24 --dport ssh ➥
-m state --state NEW,ESTABLISHED -j ACCEPT
puppy# iptables -A OUTPUT -o eth0 -p tcp -d 192.168.0.0/24 --sport ssh ➥
-m state --state ESTABLISHED -j ACCEPT
```

Here you have also enabled state inspection, and the SSH-related INPUT rule allows both NEW and ESTABLISHED connections because you want to be able to connect remotely to the host via SSH. This requires traffic in the NEW connection state to pass through the firewall. But you have restricted the outgoing SSH traffic in the OUTPUT rule to ESTABLISHED connections only. This means outgoing SSH connections from the host are not allowed.

Let's now look at the full set of rules for the basic firewall. Listing 2-18 shows the listing of the final firewall configuration.

Listing 2-18. *The Basic Firewall*

```
puppy# iptables -L --line-numbers
Chain INPUT (policy DROP)
num  target     prot opt source              destination
1    ACCEPT     tcp  --  anywhere            192.168.0.1         ➥
tcp dpt:http state NEW,ESTABLISHED
2    ACCEPT     udp  --  192.168.0.10        anywhere            ➥
udp spt:domain state ESTABLISHED
3    ACCEPT     udp  --  192.168.0.11        anywhere            ➥
udp spt:domain state ESTABLISHED
4    ACCEPT     tcp  --  192.168.0.20        anywhere            ➥
tcp spt:smtp state ESTABLISHED
5    ACCEPT     tcp  --  192.168.0.0/24      anywhere            ➥
tcp spt:ssh state NEW,ESTABLISHED

Chain FORWARD (policy DROP)
num  target     prot opt source              destination

Chain OUTPUT (policy DROP)
num  target     prot opt source              destination
1    ACCEPT     tcp  --  anywhere            anywhere            ➥
tcp spt:http state ESTABLISHED
2    ACCEPT     udp  --  anywhere            192.168.0.10        ➥
udp dpt:domain state NEW,ESTABLISHED
3    ACCEPT     udp  --  anywhere            192.168.0.11        ➥
udp dpt:domain state NEW,ESTABLISHED
4    ACCEPT     tcp  --  anywhere            192.168.0.20        ➥
tcp dpt:smtp state NEW,ESTABLISHED
5    ACCEPT     tcp  --  anywhere            192.168.0.0/24      ➥
tcp dpt:ssh state ESTABLISHED
```

This is a highly secure firewall from the point of view of securing your services and only allowing access, both incoming and outgoing, to those services you require. But it is also somewhat unwieldy from an operational perspective because of the default policies of the chains. This is because your input and output chains by default deny all incoming and outgoing traffic, which means processes and users on your local host cannot initiate any new connections that you have not allowed them to initiate. If you think this is going to be a problem on your host, you could, but I do not recommend doing this, use state inspection to do the following:

- Allow all traffic in the ESTABLISHED and RELATED connection states incoming access to your host.

- Allow all traffic in the NEW, ESTABLISHED, and RELATED connection states outgoing access from your host.

This means any connection incoming to your host that iptables think (using state inspection) is the result of a connection initiated on your host is allowed. Additionally, processes and users are allowed to initiate new connections out of your host. Listing 2-19 shows the rules you would need to add to achieve this.

Listing 2-19. *Relaxing Your Firewall Rules Using State Inspection*

```
puppy# iptables -A INPUT -i eth0 -m state --state ESTABLISHED,RELATED -j ACCEPT
puppy# iptables -A OUTPUT -i eth0 -m state --state NEW,ESTABLISHED,RELATED -j ACCEPT
```

This greatly reduces the overall security of your host, so I recommend you carefully consider this before making this change.

Creating a Firewall for a Bastion Host

Bastion hosts are usually the most at-risk hosts on your network. They can be a firewall-type host; for example, a Cisco PIX firewall operating between your network and an untrusted network such as the Internet is considered a bastion host. It can also be a Web, DNS, mail, or FTP server with an Internet-facing role. Much of the application-related configuration in this book is aimed at securing hosts such as these to be suitable as bastion hosts and the level of threat this entails. Thus, the focus in this section is on bastion hosts that perform an Internet-facing server role such as a mail, DNS, or Web server. In the course of explaining how to secure bastion hosts, I will also address some more advanced iptables functions such as logging. You will also look at ways to address some of the direct threats to your hosts such as Denial of Service, spoofing, and flood attacks in the course of securing the bastion host.

When you compare the design of the final firewall I have generated for the bastion host and the firewall I generated previously for the stand-alone host, you will see that the differences between them are not significant. Obviously, the bastion host firewall configuration has more security, and I have introduced some more advanced concepts, but essentially the basic premises of denial by default and accepting traffic by exception are maintained. Although the threat level is higher for bastion hosts, you should consider a firewall for your hosts inside your internal networks as being a critical component of your overall security. This is for two reasons. The first is that not all threats are external. Some of threats against your hosts will come from internal sources, and the securest Internet-facing firewall or packet-filtering regime will do nothing to safeguard your hosts from an internal attack. The second is that strong host-level security on the hosts in your internal network stops the bastion hosts or firewalls between the internal network and the Internet from becoming a security single point of failure.

I am now going to create an iptables configuration for a bastion host, kitten. I will start by describing the bastion host I intend to firewall.

- The host has two IP addresses: 220.240.52.228, which is bound to eth0 and is the link to the Internet, and 192.168.0.100, which is bound to interface eth1 and is a link to the internal network.

- I want to allow SMTP traffic in and out because the bastion host is a mail server, including relaying e-mail to the internal network SMTP server.

- I want to allow DNS traffic in and out because the bastion host is also a DNS server, including sending zone transfers to the internal DNS servers.

- I want to allow NTP traffic in and out, both over the Internet and into the internal network, as the bastion host will be the local NTP server and provide a time source for internal hosts.

- The host is administered using SSH, so I need to allow incoming SSH traffic from the internal network only.

First let's get a start by flushing the existing rules and setting the default policies. First flush the existing rules.

```
kitten# iptables -F
```

Then add the default policies. I will set all the chains to DROP all traffic by default.

```
kitten# iptables -P INPUT DROP
kitten# iptables -P OUTPUT DROP
kitten# iptables -P FORWARD DROP
```

Then you want to allow access to traffic on the loopback host, lo. This is the internal 127.0.0.1 address of the host, and in order for the host to correctly function, you need to allow all traffic in and out on this interface. You can see the rules for this in Listing 2-20.

Listing 2-20. *Enabling Loopback Traffic*

```
kitten# iptables -A INPUT -i lo -j ACCEPT
kitten# iptables -A OUTPUT -o lo -j ACCEPT
```

Securing the Bastion Services

I will first handle the traffic to the services running on the bastion host. Start with the SMTP traffic. You want incoming and outgoing new and established SMTP traffic to be allowed on the bastion host on the Internet interface, eth0. This allows remote SMTP servers to connect to the local SMTP server and allows the local server to connect to remote servers. You achieve this using the rules in Listing 2-21.

Listing 2-21. *The External SMTP Rules*

```
kitten# iptables -A INPUT -i eth0 -p tcp --dport smtp -m state ➥
--state NEW,ESTABLISHED - j ACCEPT
kitten# iptables -A OUTPUT -o eth0 -p tcp --sport smtp -m state ➥
--state NEW,ESTABLISHED -j ACCEPT
```

But you also want the internal SMTP server at 192.168.0.20 to be able to send mail to the bastion host and receive e-mail from it. So set up some SMTP rules for the internal 192.168.0.100 IP address, which is bound to interface eth1 to handle this incoming and outgoing SMTP traffic. These rules are in Listing 2-22.

Listing 2-22. *The Internal SMTP Rules*

```
kitten# iptables -A INPUT -i eth1 -p tcp -s 192.168.0.20 --sport smtp ➥
-m state --state NEW,ESTABLISHED -j ACCEPT
kitten# iptables -A OUTPUT -o eth1 -p tcp -d 192.168.0.20 --dport smtp ➥
-m state --state NEW,ESTABLISHED -j ACCEPT
```

Next you want to handle DNS traffic. You have two types of traffic, external traffic to and from the Internet and internal traffic including zone transfers to and from the internal DNS servers at 192.168.0.10 and 192.168.0.11. I have allowed new DNS queries into and out of the Internet-facing interface in Listing 2-23.

Listing 2-23. *The External DNS Rules*

```
kitten# iptables -A INPUT -i eth0 -p udp --dport domain -m state ➥
--state NEW,ESTABLISHED -j ACCEPT
kitten# iptables -A INPUT -i eth0 -p tcp --dport domain -m state ➥
--state NEW,ESTABLISHED -j ACCEPT
kitten# iptables -A OUTPUT -o eth0 -p udp --sport domain -m state ➥
--state NEW,ESTABLISHED -j ACCEPT
kitten# iptables -A OUTPUT -o eth0 -p tcp --sport domain -m state ➥
--state NEW,ESTABLISHED -j ACCEPT
```

The first two rules in Listing 2-23 allow NEW and ESTABLISHED incoming DNS traffic on the eth0 interface. The second two rules allow NEW and ESTABLISHED outgoing DNS traffic on the eth0 interface. This allows the bastion host to query remote DNS servers and receive queries from remote DNS servers.

For the internal traffic you need to allow more than just queries of the DNS servers. You also want to allow zone transfers, which use TCP traffic, but you want to restrict these zone transfers and the TCP traffic to only the internal DNS servers. Listing 2-24 shows the required INPUT chain rules.

Listing 2-24. *The internal* INPUT *DNS Rules*

```
kitten# iptables -A INPUT -i eth1 -p udp -s 192.168.0.10 --dport domain ➥
-m state --state NEW,ESTABLISHED -j ACCEPT
kitten# iptables -A INPUT -i eth1 -p udp -s 192.168.0.11 --dport domain ➥
-m state --state NEW,ESTABLISHED -j ACCEPT
kitten# iptables -A INPUT -i eth1 -p tcp -s 192.168.0.10 --dport domain ➥
-m state --state NEW,ESTABLISHED -j ACCEPT
kitten# iptables -A INPUT -i eth1 -p tcp -s 192.168.0.11 --dport domain ➥
-m state --state NEW,ESTABLISHED -j ACCEPT
```

The rules in Listing 2-24 allow incoming DNS queries and zone transfers between the bastion host and the two internal DNS servers. I have shown the outgoing DNS rules in Listing 2-25.

Listing 2-25. *The internal* OUTPUT *DNS Rules*

```
kitten# iptables -A OUTPUT -o eth1 -p udp -d 192.168.0.10 --sport domain ~CC
-m state --state NEW,ESTABLISHED -j ACCEPT
kitten# iptables -A OUTPUT -o eth1 -p udp -d 192.168.0.11 --sport domain ➥
-m state --state NEW,ESTABLISHED -j ACCEPT
kitten# iptables -A OUTPUT -o eth1 -p tcp -d 192.168.0.10 --sport domain ➥
-m state --state NEW,ESTABLISHED -j ACCEPT
kitten# iptables -A OUTPUT -o eth1 -p tcp -d 192.168.0.11 --sport domain ➥
-m state --state NEW,ESTABLISHED -j ACCEPT
```

The rules in Listing 2-25 allow outgoing DNS queries and zone transfers between the bastion host and the two internal DNS servers.

Now you want to add access for the Network Time Protocol (NTP), as the bastion host is going to be the local network's NTP server. NTP traffic uses UDP on port 123. First let's allow access to the Internet and to some selected remote NTP servers, clock3.redhat.com and ntp.public.otago.ac.nz. Listing 2-26 shows these rules.

■**Note** I randomly selected these NTP servers, but you can find a list of public NTP servers at http://www.eecis.udel.edu/~mills/ntp/servers.html.

Listing 2-26. *The External NTP Rules*

```
kitten# iptables -A INPUT -i eth0 -p udp -s clock3.redhat.com --dport ntp ➥
-m state --state ESTABLISHED -j ACCEPT
kitten# iptables -A OUTPUT -o eth0 -p udp -d clock3.redhat.com --sport ntp ➥
-m state --state NEW,ESTABLISHED -j ACCEPT
kitten# iptables -A INPUT -i eth0 -p udp -s ntp.public.otago.ac.nz ➥
--dport ntp -m state --state ESTABLISHED -j ACCEPT
kitten# iptables -A OUTPUT -o eth0 -p udp -d ntp.public.otago.ac.nz ➥
--sport ntp -m state --state NEW,ESTABLISHED -j ACCEPT
```

You have allowed only ESTABLISHED incoming connections from the two specified NTP servers' IP addresses with a destination of the NTP port 123. You have allowed outgoing traffic of NEW and ESTABLISHED connections to allow you to query remote NTP servers, but again I have limited the outgoing connections to the hostname of the selected NTP servers. Next you need to add some rules to handle the internal NTP traffic (see Listing 2-27).

Listing 2-27. *The Internal NTP Rules*

```
kitten# iptables -A INPUT -i eth1 -p udp -s 192.168.0.0/24 --dport ntp ➡
-m state --state NEW,ESTABLISHED -j ACCEPT
kitten# iptables -A OUTPUT -o eth1 -p udp -d 192.168.0.0/24 --sport ntp ➡
-m state --state ESTABLISHED -j ACCEPT
```

The rules in Listing 2-27 allow only hosts in the 192.168.0.0/24 subnet to connect to the NTP server and requests time updates. All outgoing traffic on this port on the eth1 interface is also limited to a destination of this subnet and to ESTABLISHED traffic only, as the bastion host has no requirement to initiate a connection to any system in the internal network.

Finally, you want to be able to administer the bastion host using ssh. You want to provide only ssh access to the bastion host from the internal network and not allow the bastion host to initiate ssh connections back to the internal network to help protect the internal systems in the event the bastion host is compromised. Listing 2-28 show the rules required to structure ssh access as required.

Listing 2-28. *The SSH Rules*

```
kitten# iptables -A INPUT -i eth1 -p tcp -s 192.168.0.0/24 --dport ssh ➡
-m state --state NEW,ESTABLISHED -j ACCEPT
kitten# iptables -A OUTPUT -o eth1 -p tcp -d 192.168.0.0/24 --sport ssh ➡
-m state --state ESTABLISHED -j ACCEPT
```

Firewall Logging

With iptables you can log the traffic processed by the firewall to syslog. This is extremely useful both for determining if your firewall is functioning and also to keep track of anomalous or malicious traffic. Logging with iptables requires directing the traffic you want logged to a new target I will introduce, the LOG target. You can see this target in Listing 2-29.

Listing 2-29. *Logging* iptables *Traffic*

```
kitten# iptables -A INPUT -p tcp --dport smtp -j LOG --log-prefix "IPT_INPUT "
```

In Listing 2-29 I am logging all incoming TCP traffic on port 25 to the LOG target, as indicated by the -j flag. The --log-prefix flag specifies a prefix you can place in front of the log message to help you identify the iptables traffic in your logs. This prefix can be up to 29 letters long.

■**Caution** Because of a bug in the Netfilter code, you should add a trailing space (as you can see in Listing 2-29) to stop the prefix field running into the next log field. This will make it easier to manipulate your `iptables` log traffic.

You can add other flags after the LOG target (see Table 2-6).

Table 2-6. LOG *Target Flags*

Option	Description
`--log-level` *level*	Log level (in other words, `info`).
`--log-tcp-sequence`	Logs the TCP sequence numbers. You should not log these unless you are sure your log files are secure.
`--log-tcp-options`	Logs TCP options from the IP packet header.
`--log-ip-options`	Logs IP options from the IP packet header.

The `--log-level` flag allows you to specify with which logging level your `iptables` logs will be generated. This defaults to `info`. The facility used by `iptables` logging is `kernel`. You can see Chapter 5 for more details of `syslog` logging and log levels.

The `--log-tcp-sequence` logs the sequence numbers of the packets being logged to `syslog` with the rest of the logging information. This can be dangerous if your logs are readable by non-`root` users (which they should not be!), as it may assist someone in a spoofing or hijacking attack to guess possible sequence numbers and insert malicious traffic. Unless you have a real use for this information, I recommend not logging it.

The `--log-tcp-options` and `--log-ip-options` flags add the contents of the OPTIONS section of the TCP and IP headers, respectively, to your logging output.

The LOG target is a nonterminating target, and any traffic passed to the LOG target will simply continue to the next rule after being logged. This means you need to specify any logging rules before any rules that may reject or drop traffic. In Listing 2-30 you can see `iptables` logging UDP DNS traffic from a host, `192.168.0.100`, in the first rule and then dropping this traffic after it has been logged. If these rules were reversed, then no log entries would be generated by this traffic.

Listing 2-30. *Logging and Dropping Traffic with the* LOG *Target*

```
kitten# iptables -A INPUT -p udp -s 192.168.0.111 --dport domain -j LOG ➥
--log-prefix "IPT_BAD_DNS"
kitten# iptables -A INPUT -p udp -s 192.168.0.111 --dport domain -j DROP
```

This is another instance where the sequence of your rules is important to ensure you actually log the required traffic before it is accepted, dropped, or rejected.

So what do you see in your log entries? Well, Listing 2-31 shows a typical log entry from the LOG rule in Listing 2-30.

Listing 2-31. *A Typical* iptables *Log Entry*

```
Aug  8 21:32:56 kitten kernel: IPT_INPUT IN=eth0 OUT=
MAC=00:01:02:89:ad:de:00:06:5b:cb:d8:b3:08:00 ➠
SRC=192.168.0.111 DST=192.168.0.1 LEN=92 TOS=0x00 ➠
PREC=0x00 TTL=128 ID=7301 DF PROTO=TCP SPT=3610 ➠
DPT=53 WINDOW=65535 RES=0x00 ACK PSH URGP=0
```

I have dissected each portion of the sample line from Listing 2-31 in Table 2-7.

Table 2-7. *Listing 2-31* iptables *Log Entry*

Field	Description
IPT_INPUT	The prefix specified by the --log-prefix flag.
IN=*interface*	The incoming interface on which the packet was received. Blank if the entry is for outgoing traffic.
OUT=*interface*	The outgoing interface the packet was received on. Blank if the entry is for incoming traffic.
MAC=*MAC* address	The MAC address of the interface the packet used.
SRC=*IP address*	The source IP address of the packet.
DST=*IP address*	The destination IP address of the packet.
LEN=*length*	The length of the packet in bytes.
TOS=*type*	The Type of Service Type field (deprecated usually).
PREC=*precedence*	The Type of Service Precedence field (deprecated usually).
TTL=*hops*	The Time to Live in hops.
ID=*id*	The unique ID number of this packet.
DF	The "Don't fragment" flag that tells the stack not to fragment the packet.
PROTO=*protocol*	The protocol of the packet.
SPT=*port*	The source port of the packet.
DPT=*port*	The destination port of the packet.
WINDOW=*size*	The TCP Receive Window size.
RES=*bits*	The reserved bits.
ACK	The ACK (or Acknowledgment) flag is set.
PSH	The PSH (or Push) flag is set.
URGP=0	The Urgent Pointer (rarely used).

Most of the items are self-explanatory and should be clear to you from the packet and filtering rules that have generated the log entry. Perhaps the most useful pieces of information provided by the logging process that would normally not be readily apparent about the packet being logged are the TCP flags, such as ACK or PSH, set for the packet. You can use this information, for example, to help determine the structure of attacks based on inappropriate or malicious combinations of TCP flags being set. You will examine attacks based on TCP flag combinations in the "iptables and TCP Flags" section.

The log entries generated by using the LOG target can be separated from your other log entries by controlling your syslog or syslog-ng configuration. Listing 2-32 shows two sample logging rules that would log all incoming and outgoing traffic.

Listing 2-32. *Sample Logging Rules*

```
kitten# iptables -A INPUT -i eth0 -j LOG --log-prefix "IPT_INPUT " ➡
--log-level warning
kitten# iptables -A OUTPUT -o eth0 -j LOG --log-prefix "IPT_OUTPUT " ➡
--log-level warning
```

Listing 2-33 shows the syslog.conf entry to trap these log entries into a separate file. This is not precise and you may end up with entries not related to your iptables traffic, as the basic syslog daemon does not have the full functionality to allow you to sort the iptables entries from other kernel facility messages.

Listing 2-33. syslog.conf *Entries for the Listing 2-32 Logging Entries*

```
kern.warn        /var/log/ipt_log
```

In Listing 2-34 I have provided the same configuration but for the syslog-NG daemon, which allows considerably greater flexibility in selecting only those log entries from your firewall logging.

Listing 2-34. Syslog-NG *Configuration for Logging* iptables *Traffic*

```
destination d_ipti { file("/var/log/ipt_input"); };
destination d_ipto { file("/var/log/ipt_output"); };
filter f_filter_in    { facility(kernel) and level(warning) ➡
and match(IPT_INPUT ); };
filter f_filter_out   { facility(kernel) and level(warning) ➡
and match(IPT_OUTPUT ); };
log { source(s_sys); filter(f_filter_in); destination(d_ipti); };
log { source(s_sys); filter(f_filter_out); destination(d_ipto); };
```

In Listing 2-34 I have separated the incoming log entries from the outgoing log entries and written them to two different files.

■**Tip** You can find further information on logging and using other tools such as SEC to process your firewall log files in Chapter 5.

I have not explicitly added any new rules to the bastion host firewall as a result of the information described in this section but I will incorporate rules with the LOG target into the overall bastion host firewall in the next few sections.

■**Caution** You should be aware that firewall logging on a busy system can generate a lot of data, and you should ensure you have sufficient disk space and a suitable log rotation regime to accommodate your required level of logging.

Handling ICMP Traffic

Together with TCP and UDP, one of the most commonly used protocols is ICMP.[7] ICMP provides error, control, and informational messages such as the messages used by the ping command. In the past, ICMP messages have formed an important component of network troubleshooting and diagnostics. Unfortunately in recent years, the widespread use and access granted to ICMP traffic has meant a variety of vulnerabilities and exploits, including some serious Denial of Service attacks related to ICMP traffic, have emerged. Bastion hosts are particular targets of these types of attacks. In the last five years more than 40 ICMP-related vulnerabilities and potential attacks have been discovered.[8] These have included attacks such as the following:

- ICMP flood attacks where a storm of pings overwhelm a system and consume available bandwidth resulting in a Denial of Service.

- ICMP "smurf" attacks where an attacker sends forged ICMP echo packets to network broadcast addresses allegedly from a particular targeted host. The broadcast addresses reply with ICMP echo reply packets, which are sent to the targeted host, consuming all available bandwidth and killing the host with a Denial of Service attack.

- The "ping of death" in which an attacker sends an ICMP echo packet larger than the maximum IP packet size. The packet is fragmented and because of bugs in the IP stack attempts to reassemble the packets crash the system.

- ICMP "nuke" attack in which the ICMP packet contains information that the receiving system cannot handle, which results in a system crash.

You can prevent all these attacks or mitigate the risk of attack using iptables by tightly controlling how your hosts handle ICMP traffic. But this traffic is also used by some important network diagnostic tools such as ping.

If you look at ICMP, you can see it consists of a whole series of message types with related message codes. For example, the ping command generates an echo-request or an ICMP Type 8 message. The response to a ping is an echo reply or an ICMP Type 0 message. Table 2-8 presents all the ICMP message types.

---

7. The RFC for ICMP is RFC 792; you can review it at http://www.ietf.org/rfc/rfc0792.txt?number=792.

8. http://icat.nist.gov/icat.cfm

Table 2-8. *ICMP Message Types*

Type	Description
0	Echo Reply
3	Destination Unreachable
4	Source Quench
5	Redirect
8	Echo Request
11	Time Exceeded
12	Parameter Problem
13	Timestamp
14	Timestamp Reply
15	Information Request
16	Information Reply

The most frequently used and seen ICMP message types are Type 0 and 8 for ping, Type 3 (which is frequently used to indicate hosts that are down or that decline to respond to queries), and Type 11 (Time Exceeded). For example, in addition to UDP packets, the `traceroute` command relies on ICMP Type 11 messages to map the route between the host and a remote host and relies on Type 3 messages to indicate if the host at the end of the route is unreachable.

So how should you handle ICMP traffic? Well, there are two schools of thought on this. The first suggests that ICMP traffic is acceptable if the source and destination of this traffic is controlled—for example, if you allow only traffic to and from authorized hosts. I think this is dangerous, because it assumes you can rely on the security of these authorized hosts. The second school of thought believes that all incoming ICMP traffic should be barred except responses to outgoing connections. For example, all incoming ping (`echo-request`) packets are dropped, but incoming ping reply (`echo reply`) packets that are in reply to pings generated on the local host are accepted. I believe this model of barring all but clearly excepted ICMP traffic is the most secure and suitable; I will show you how to configure this variation. I will now articulate a policy for ICMP traffic that fits this model.

- Allow outbound `echo` messages and inbound `echo reply` messages. This allows the use of `ping` from the host.

- Allow `time exceeded` and `destination unreachable` messages inbound, which allows the use of tools such as `traceroute`.

To implement this policy, you want to create some chains to hold the ICMP-related rules. I will create two chains. The first I have called `ICMP_IN` to handle incoming ICMP traffic. The second I have called `ICMP_OUT` to handle outgoing ICMP traffic. User-created chains allow you to better structure your rules and allow you to group related rules that handle specific traffic types, protocols, or responses to particular threats or vulnerabilities. When traffic is redirected to a user chain by a rule, it will be processed against all the rules in the new chain and then return to the chain that redirected it to be processed by the next rule in sequence. You use the `iptables` command-line option `-N` to create new chains. By default new chains are added to the filter table.

```
kitten# iptables -N ICMP_IN
kitten# iptables -N ICMP_OUT
```

Now let's create some rules in the INPUT and OUTPUT chains to refer the ICMP traffic to the newly created ICMP_IN and ICMP_OUT chains. You send traffic to the user-created chains by referring to them as a rule target using the -j flag. Listing 2-35 shows the two rules directing ICMP traffic to the user-created chains.

Listing 2-35. *Directing ICMP Traffic to the User-Created Chains*

```
kitten# iptables -A INPUT -p icmp -j ICMP_IN
kitten# iptables -A OUTPUT -p icmp -j ICMP_OUT
```

Now when ICMP traffic is received by the INPUT chain, it is directed to be filtered by the user-created chain ICMP_IN; and when it is received by the OUTPUT chain, it is handled by the ICMP_OUT chain.

The iptables rules can target individual ICMP messages types by selecting only ICMP traffic with the -p icmp flag in combination with the --icmp-type flag to select the particular ICMP message type. The next line shows this selection in the rule:

```
kitten# iptables -A ICMP_IN -p icmp --icmp-type echo-request -j DROP
```

I have added this rule to the ICMP_IN chain, which I have specified will handle incoming ICMP traffic. I have selected only ICMP traffic using the -p flag. Then I selected the type of ICMP traffic using the --icmp-type flag. Within the ICMP traffic I have selected the message type of echo-request, which indicates an incoming ping request, and I have opted to drop this traffic. You could have also indicated the echo-request traffic with the type number of the ICMP message type.

```
kitten# iptables -A ICMP_IN -p icmp --icmp-type 8 -j DROP
```

You can now create the rules you need to address the required policy. Allow inbound echo reply, time exceeded, and destination unreachable messages to the host (see Listing 2-36).

Listing 2-36. *Incoming ICMP Traffic*

```
kitten# iptables -A ICMP_IN -i eth0 -p icmp --icmp-type 0 -m state ➥
--state ESTABLISHED,RELATED -j ACCEPT
kitten# iptables -A ICMP_IN -i eth0 -p icmp --icmp-type 3 -m state ➥
--state ESTABLISHED,RELATED -j ACCEPT
kitten# iptables -A ICMP_IN -i eth0 -p icmp --icmp-type 11 -m state ➥
--state ESTABLISHED,RELATED -j ACCEPT
kitten# iptables -A ICMP_IN -i eth0 -p icmp -j LOG_DROP
```

I have added these rules to the ICMP_IN incoming ICMP traffic chain and selected ICMP Types 0, 3, and 11 that are in an ESTABLISHED or RELATED state, which indicates that this traffic is in reply to a request generated on the bastion host. It does not allow NEW connections using ICMP to be made. This means attempts to ping this host will result in an error.

Finally, I have added a last rule to ensure any other incoming ICMP traffic is logged and dropped. I have done this by specifying the target of the last rule as a user-created chain called

`LOG_DROP`. This chain is going to direct the ICMP traffic to a set of `iptables` rules that will log the packets to be dropped and then drop the packets. First, create the `LOG_DROP` chain.

```
kitten# iptables -N LOG_DROP
```

Second, create a rule to log the incoming ICMP traffic. You will log the ICMP traffic to `syslog` adding a prefix of `IPT_ICMP_IN` (with a trailing space) to the log entries to allow you to identify them.

```
kitten# iptables -A LOG_DROP -i eth0 -p icmp -j LOG --log-prefix "IPT_ICMP_IN "
kitten# iptables -A LOG_DROP -i eth0 -p icmp -j DROP
```

The last rule drops the traffic after it has been logged. This takes care of all the incoming ICMP traffic.

■Caution Be careful about logging your ICMP traffic. Large amounts of logging traffic can be generated by ICMP traffic. You should ensure you have sufficient disk space and a suitable log rotation regime.

Now you add the rules to take care of the outbound ICMP traffic. You can see these rules on the following lines:

```
kitten# iptables -A ICMP_OUT -o eth0 -p icmp --icmp-type 8 -m state ➥
--state NEW -j ACCEPT
kitten# iptables -A ICMP_OUT -o eth0 -p icmp -j LOG_DROP
```

I have allowed outgoing echo messages so that I can ping remote hosts; then you added a rule to log and drop all other outgoing ICMP traffic.

I will also add two more rules to the user-created chain `LOG_DROP` to handle logging and dropping the outgoing ICMP traffic.

```
kitten# iptables -A LOG_DROP -o eth0 -p icmp -j LOG --log-prefix "IPT_ICMP_OUT "
kitten# iptables -A LOG_DROP -o eth0 -p icmp -j DROP
```

From this information and these rules, you should now be able to design and implement some rules to handle incoming and outgoing ICMP traffic in your environment.

■Note Some kernel parameters relate to ICMP traffic; I will cover them in the "Kernel Modules and Parameters" section.

Spoofing, Hijacking, and Denial of Service Attacks

Attacks based on incoming traffic are not limited to ICMP-based traffic. Some of the other common forms of attack on hosts are spoofing, hijacking, and Denial of Service attacks. In this section I will provide some rules for defending against these types of attacks.

These sorts of attacks can take three major forms (though all these forms can be combined and used in conjunction with each other). In the first form, an attacker tries to subvert the traffic between two hosts from a third host by trying to fool one of the hosts into believing it is actually the other host in the conversation. The attacker can then connect to the targeted host or insert some malicious information into packets sent to the targeted system to compromise or penetrate it. This form of attack includes so-called man-in-the-middle attacks and blind spoofing attacks.

In the second form, an attacker redirects routing information by using methods such as ICMP `redirect` or by manipulating the host's ARP table. The routing changes redirect traffic from the original host to the attacker's host. This allows the attacker to receive all the traffic from the original host and potentially use this information to exploit the original host or another host with which the original host communicates.

■**Caution** Attacks based on manipulating or poisoning ARP tables are hard to defend against and hard to detect. I recommend looking at a tool such as ARPWatch to monitor incoming ARP traffic. You can find ARPWatch at `ftp://ftp.ee.lbl.gov/arpwatch.tar.gz`.

The third form of attack is similar in nature to the ICMP flood attack. An attacker spoofs the target's address and utilizes mechanisms such as network broadcasts to flood the target with incoming connections and consume all available connection resources. This results in a Denial of Service on the targeted host. This last form is often called *smurfing* or *fraggling*.

It can be hard to both detect and stop some of these sorts of attacks, but it is not impossible. One of the best ways to prevent these types of attacks is to explicitly deny traffic from hosts, networks, and sources you know traffic should not or cannot be coming from. This includes sources such as the following:

- Incoming traffic that has a source address of an IP address assigned to a local interface; for example, if eth0 is bound to 192.168.0.1, then incoming traffic cannot have a source address of 192.168.0.1, as the IP address should be unique in the subnet.

- Outgoing traffic that does not have a source address of an interface on your local host; for example, this includes a process trying to send traffic with a source address of 10.0.0.1 when you do not have this address bound to a local interface.

- Traffic coming from the Internet on RFC 1918's private IP address ranges. These are private address ranges and should not be routable on the Internet.

- The Zeroconf IP address range, 169.254.0.0/16.

- The TEST-NET address range of 192.0.2.0/24.

- The reserved IP address Class D and E (Broadcast) addresses 224.0.0.0/4 and 240.0.0.0/5 and the unallocated address range 248.0.0.0/5.

- Loopback addresses in the range 127.0.0.0/8 should also be nonroutable on the Internet and finally broadcast address range 255.255.255.255/32 and the older broadcast address range, 0.0.0.0/8.

So, I will show how to set some rules to reduce the risk that incoming traffic to your host is malicious, and then later in the "Kernel Parameters section" I will introduce some kernel parameters that will also help further reduce the risk of these sorts of attacks.

The first set of rules you will add handle traffic that allegedly comes from your own host. Incoming traffic with the source addresses of your system is going to be spoofed traffic because you know it cannot be generated by the host or it would be outgoing rather than incoming. You add a rule to handle packets allegedly from the internal LAN IP address and then a rule to handle packets allegedly to the external IP address.

```
kitten# iptables -A INPUT -i eth1 -s 192.168.0.100 -j DROP
kitten# iptables -A INPUT -i eth0 -s 220.240.52.228 -j DROP
```

You can also add a rule saying that any outgoing traffic that is not from your source IP address is incorrect. This is both useful to stop your host sending bad packets and also polite as your host should not be generating packets that do not come from your IP address.

```
kitten# iptables -A OUTPUT -o eth1 -s ! 192.168.0.100 -j DROP
kitten# iptables -A OUTPUT -o eth0 -s ! 220.240.52.228 -j DROP
```

These rule uses the negate symbol (!) together with the source address to indicate all outgoing traffic *not* from the specified IP address. For example, in the first rule, all traffic that is not from IP address192.168.0.100 is dropped. This is because only traffic from the IP address 192.168.0.100 should be outgoing from this interface.

You can also use the negate symbol on most other iptables flags; for example, to select all traffic except ICMP, you could use the following rule:

```
kitten# iptables -A INPUT -p ! imcp -J ACCEPT
```

As you were using iptables on a bastion host between your network and the Internet, you will block the RFC 1918 private address space ranges.[9] These address ranges, 10.0.0.0/8, 172.16.0.0/12, and 192.168.0.0/16, are reserved for private IP networks and should be used only as internal IP addresses ranges. These addresses are not routable on the Internet. You should block these address ranges on any Internet-facing interfaces.

```
kitten# iptables -A INPUT -i eth0 -s 10.0.0.0/8 -j DROP
kitten# iptables -A INPUT -i eth0 -s 172.16.0.0/12 -j DROP
kitten# iptables -A INPUT -i eth0 -s 192.168.0.0/16 -j DROP
```

You do not need to block this traffic on the internal network because these address ranges are frequently used, including by the internal network you have specified, as internal address ranges.

Next you want to block incoming traffic from the Internet that is from the Zeroconf address range.[10] The Zeroconf address range is used primarily by hosts that use DHCP to acquire their IP address. An address from this range is assigned when these hosts are unable to find a DHCP server to provide them with an address. It is also being proposed to use this address range to provide addressing when connecting two devices together with a crossover cable. Add a rule to prevent any traffic on the Internet and the internal LAN interfaces.

```
kitten# iptables -A INPUT -s 168.254.0.0/16 -j DROP
```

---

9. http://www.faqs.org/rfcs/rfc1918.html

10. http://www.zeroconf.org/

Now you will restrict the TEST-NET 192.0.2.0/24 address range, which is used for test purposes and, like the private address ranges of RFC 1918, should not be routable on the Internet.

```
kitten# iptables -A INPUT -i eth0 -s 192.0.2.0/24 -j DROP
```

Next you want to restrict any incoming traffic coming from the reserved Class D and E IP address ranges and the unallocated address range, 248.0.0.0/5. These are designed for broadcast and experimental purposes only and should not be routed on the Internet.

```
kitten# iptables -A INPUT -i eth0 -s 224.0.0.0/4 -j DROP
kitten# iptables -A INPUT -i eth0 -s 240.0.0.0/5 -j DROP
kitten# iptables -A INPUT -i eth0 -s 248.0.0.0/5 -j DROP
```

Additionally, restrict the loopback and zero addresses, which also should not be routable on the Internet.

```
kitten# iptables -A INPUT -i eth0 -s 127.0.0.0/8 -j DROP
kitten# iptables -A INPUT -i eth0 -s 255.255.255.255/32  -j DROP
kitten# iptables -A INPUT -i eth0 -s 0.0.0.0/8 -j DROP
```

Adding these rules to the overall `iptables` configuration should help keep the bastion host somewhat secure from spoofing, hijacking, and a variety of Denial of Service attacks.

iptables and TCP Flags

Another series of attacks on your hosts that you will add `iptables` rules to address use either malicious combinations of TCP flags or inappropriate volumes of packets with particular TCP flags. Each TCP header has a TCP flag or flag set. These flags tell the receiving host what sort of packets it is receiving. For example, when a new TCP is created, a process that is commonly referred to as the *three-way handshake* occurs. Figure 2-1 shows Host A sending a packet to Host B. If this is the initiation of the connection, then the first TCP package has the SYN flag set. This is the first step of the three-way handshake. Host B responds with a packet of its own with the SYN and ACK flags set. This is the second step. Lastly Host B should respond with a packet with the ACK flag set as the third step of the handshake and completes the handshake.

■**Note** All of these packets are assigned sequence numbers so that the hosts know which order they should be processed in and to provide some security that this is the same connection.

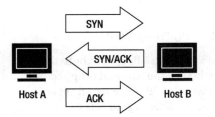

Figure 2-1. *An example of a TCP connection*

Table 2-9 describes all the TCP flags.

Table 2-9. *TCP Flags*

Flag	Description
ACK	This flag informs the receiving host that the field ACK number has a valid ACK number. This helps the host trust the packet.
RST	This flag asks the receiving host to recover (reset) the connection. Packets with RST flags are generally sent when a problem occurs with a connection.
SYN	This flag instructs the receiving host to synchronize sequence numbers. This flag indicates the start of a new connection.
FIN	This flag lets the receiving host know that the sender is finished sending data. The receiving host should respond with a FIN flagged packet to complete and close the connection.
URG	This flag lets the receiving host know that the field of the Urgent Pointer points to urgent data.
PSH	This flag calls a PUSH. If this flag is set to on, then data in a packet is sent directly to the target application. Normally incoming data would be stored in a buffer and then passed to the target application. This flag is used for interactive services such as SSH or Telnet to see responses without lag.

The SYN to SYN/ACK to ACK flag combination in your packets is something you will commonly see in your firewall logs, but many other TCP flag are not only illegal and invalid but have the potential to compromise your system or assist a remote attacker in determining information about your system. For example, tools such as nmap often use unusual TCP flag combinations to aid in the process of scanning and operating system fingerprinting.

You can use iptables to select packets with particular TCP flags using the --tcp-flags flag. The --tcp-flags flag has two parts to its selection of TCP flags. The first part selects which TCP flags are to be examined in the packet, and the second part selects the flags that need to be set on the packet for the rule to match. You can see this in Listing 2-37.

Listing 2-37. *Selecting Packets with Particular TCP Flags*

```
kitten# iptables -A INPUT -p tcp --tcp-flags ALL SYN -j DROP
```

In Listing 2-37 you are using the --tcp-flags flag with the first selector of ALL. The ALL setting tells iptables to examine all possible flags (this is the same as saying SYN,ACK,FIN,RST,URG,PSH), and the second selector is SYN flag, which indicates the SYN flag must be set for this rule to match a packet. So Listing 2-37 would match packets containing ANY flag but with only the SYN flag set and DROP them. You can also specify only a particular subset of flags, as you can see in the following line:

```
kitten# iptables -A INPUT -p tcp --tcp-flags SYN,RST SYN,RST -j DROP
```

The rule in the previous line checks packets with the SYN and RST flags, and both these flags have to be set in the packet for the packet to be matched by the rule and dropped. You separate multiple flags in each option with commas, and you should not leave any spaces between the specified flags. You can also use the special option NONE in your rules.

```
kitten# iptables -A INPUT -p tcp --tcp-flags ALL NONE -j DROP
```

The rule in the previous line tests packets with any of the TCP flags and selects those packets with no flags set at all and DROPs them.

Blocking Bad Flag Combinations

Now you will look at some combinations of flags that you want to block with your iptables rules. Most of these are not actually attacks but rather more likely to be attempts by attackers to determine more information about the host with tools such as nmap.

■**Tip** You can see a fairly complete list of nmap scan forms at http://security.rbaumann.net/ scans.php?sel=1. Most other scanners use variations on this, and these rules should address most of these scan forms.

For example, probably the best-known combination of illegal flags is SYN/FIN, which is used by a variety of network scanners to perform operating system detection. The SYN flag opens a connection, and the FIN flag closes a connection. In combination these flags make no sense in a single packet. Thus, any occurrence of this combination of flags will be malicious traffic, and you will start the TCP flag rules by blocking this traffic. But first I will start by adding a chain to hold the bad TCP flag rules.

```
kitten# iptables -N BAD_FLAGS
```

Then you place a rule toward the start of the bastion host rules to redirect all TCP traffic to the bad TCP flags rules to be processed. The traffic that does not match these rules and is not dropped will then proceed to be processed by the other rules.

```
kitten# iptables -A INPUT -p tcp -j BAD_FLAGS
```

Here you are putting all incoming TCP traffic through the BAD_FLAGS chain. As explained earlier, when traffic is redirected to a user chain by a rule, it will be processed against all the rules in the new chain and then return to the chain that redirected it to be processed by the next rule in sequence. Thus, all the TCP traffic will pass through the rules in the BAD_FLAGS user chain and then return to the INPUT chain.

You can now add the first rules to handle bad flags. I have added a rule that logs and drops the SYN/FIN TCP flag combination, which you can see in Listing 2-38.

Listing 2-38. *Blocking SYN/FIN packets*

```
kitten# iptables -A BAD_FLAGS -p tcp --tcp-flags SYN,FIN SYN,FIN -j LOG ➥
--log-prefix "IPT: Bad SF Flag "
kitten# iptables -A BAD_FLAGS -p tcp --tcp-flags SYN,FIN SYN,FIN -j DROP
```

You start with a logging statement, which logs all packets with this combination of TCP flags to your log file. Unlike the ICMP traffic where you specified a single logging rule for the traffic, in this instance you will log each type of TCP flag combination with its own log prefix. This will aid you in determining from where particular types of attacks have originated. To further aid in this, you have added a log prefix that specifies exactly what sort of illegal packet you are seeing, with SF indicating SYN/FIN. Then after logging the packets, you have dropped them.

Other variations on the SYN/FIN flag combination are used for similar purposes: SYN/RST, SYN/FIN/PSH, SYN/FIN/RST, and SYN/FIN/RST/PSH. Let's add some additional rules in Listing 2-39 to handle these variants.

Listing 2-39. *Rules for* SYN/FIN *Variations*

```
kitten# iptables -A BAD_FLAGS -p tcp --tcp-flags SYN,RST SYN,RST -j LOG ➥
--log-prefix "IPT: Bad SR Flag "
kitten# iptables -A BAD_FLAGS -p tcp --tcp-flags SYN,RST SYN,RST -j DROP
kitten# iptables -A BAD_FLAGS -p tcp --tcp-flags SYN,FIN,PSH SYN,FIN,PSH ➥
-j LOG --log-prefix "IPT: Bad SFP Flag "
kitten# iptables -A BAD_FLAGS -p tcp --tcp-flags SYN,FIN,PSH SYN,FIN,PSH -j DROP
kitten# iptables -A BAD_FLAGS -p tcp --tcp-flags SYN,FIN,RST SYN,FIN,RST ➥
-j LOG --log-prefix "IPT: Bad SFR Flag "
kitten# iptables -A BAD_FLAGS -p tcp --tcp-flags SYN,FIN,RST SYN,FIN,RST -j DROP
kitten# iptables -A BAD_FLAGS -p tcp ➥
--tcp-flags SYN,FIN,RST,PSH SYN,FIN,RST,PSH -j LOG --log-prefix "IPT: Bad SFRP Flag "
kitten# iptables -A BAD_FLAGS -p tcp --tcp-flags SYN,FIN,RST,PSH SYN,FIN,RST,PSH ➥
-j DROP
```

Next in Listing 2-40 you add a rule to address single FIN flag packets. You will never find a packet that has only a FIN flag in normal TCP/IP connections; thus, any you do find are generally being used for port scans and network probing.

Listing 2-40. *Rules for* FIN-*Only Flag Packets*

```
kitten# iptables -A BAD_FLAGS -p tcp --tcp-flags FIN FIN -j LOG ➥
--log-prefix "IPT: Bad F Flag "
kitten# iptables -A BAD_FLAGS -p tcp --tcp-flags FIN FIN -j DROP
```

These rules in Listing 2-40 select only those packets with a FIN flag, and only those packets with a FIN flag set then log and drop them.

Lastly you want to block so-called null packets, which have all flags present and set, and any other related Xmas-style scanning packets. These are generally used for other forms of network probing used by scanning tools such as nmap. Listing 2-41 shows how you can block these using the ALL and NONE special flag selectors.

Listing 2-41. *Rules for Null and Xmas Flag Packets*

```
kitten# iptables -A BAD_FLAGS -p tcp --tcp-flags ALL NONE -j LOG ➥
--log-prefix "IPT: Null Flag "
kitten# iptables -A BAD_FLAGS -p tcp --tcp-flags ALL NONE -j DROP
kitten# iptables -A BAD_FLAGS -p tcp --tcp-flags ALL ALL -j LOG ➥
--log-prefix "IPT: All Flags "
```

```
kitten# iptables -A BAD_FLAGS -p tcp --tcp-flags ALL ALL -j DROP
kitten# iptables -A BAD_FLAGS -p tcp --tcp-flags ALL FIN,URG,PSH
 -j LOG --log-prefix "IPT: Nmap:Xmas Flags "
kitten# iptables -A BAD_FLAGS -p tcp --tcp-flags ALL FIN,URG,PSH
 -j DROP
kitten# iptables -A BAD_FLAGS -p tcp --tcp-flags ALL SYN,RST,ACK,FIN,URG ➥
-j LOG --log-prefix "IPT: Merry Xmas Flags "
kitten# iptables -A BAD_FLAGS -p tcp --tcp-flags ALL SYN,RST,ACK,FIN,URG -j DROP
```

SYN Flooding

Another use of malicious TCP flags is the SYN flood attack. This Denial of Service attack is usually aimed at e-mail or Web servers and relies on subverting the three-way handshake connection process discussed earlier in this chapter. The attacker sends a packet with the SYN flag set to the receiving host. The source address of this packet is a nonexistent or uncontactable machine. The receiving host replies with a packet with the SYN/ACK flags set. As the source address of the packet cannot be replied to, the send fails and no ACK packet is received to fully open the connection. Eventually the connection timeout is reached, and the connection closes. This seems harmless enough, but on the receiving host each new connection adds connection information to a data structure in system memory. This data structure has a finite size. Normally failed connections would time out, and the data structure would be purged of the connection information. But in the SYN flood attack, the attacker continues to send connection requests from nonexistent hosts until the data structure in memory overflows and no new connections are possible. Generally, until the incoming SYN flood ceases, no new connections to the host are possible. In some cases, the system may even halt entirely.

You can reduce the risk of this sort of attack using another iptables match module. I discussed the state module earlier in this chapter, and now you will look at the limit module. The limit module limits the rate and volume at which packets are matched to rules. It is commonly used to limit traffic such as ICMP and to limit logging. For example, you can limit the rate at which packets are logged (see Listing 2-42).

Listing 2-42. *Limiting Logging with the* limit *Module*

```
kitten# iptables -A INPUT -p tcp -m limit --limit 10/second -j LOG
```

Listing 2-42 shows all incoming TCP packets being logged, but the addition of the limit module limits the logging to ten entries per second. All other packets are discarded until the average rate decreases to below the limit. You can also limit packets being processed to minute, hour, and day intervals in addition to second intervals. The limit module also has a burst function.

```
 kitten# iptables -A INPUT -p tcp -m limit --limit-burst 100 ➥
--limit 10/minute -j LOG
```

The --limit-burst option in the preceding line tells iptables to log 100 matching packets; then if this number of packets is exceeded, apply the rate limit of ten packets per minute. The burst limit is enforced until the number of packets being received has decreased below the rate limit. The burst limit then recharges one packet for each time period specified in the limit option where the packet rate is maintained below the limit. So, in the preceding example, the burst limit is recharged one packet for every minute where the rate of received packets is less than ten per minute.

Let's look at restricting SYN flooding now. You can use the rule in Listing 2-43 to limit the number of incoming SYN packets on your Internet-facing port.

Listing 2-43. *Limiting Incoming SYN Packets*

```
kitten# iptables -A INPUT -i eth0 -p tcp --syn -m limit --limit 5/second -j ACCEPT
```

In Listing 2-43 you have used the special TCP option --syn, which matches all packets with the ACK and RST bits cleared and SYN flag set. It is the equivalent of setting the TCP flags option to --tcp-flags SYN,RST,ACK SYN. You have limited the number of incoming SYN packets to five per second. This would limit the number of incoming connections to five per second and should (you hope) prevent an attacker from using a SYN flood attack on the bastion host. I recommend you test a suitable connection rate for your system taking into consideration the volume of incoming connections to your host and its size and performance when setting the limit.

Limiting the number of SYN packets connections to your host is not, however, an ideal solution to SYN flood attacks because it does limit the number of potential incoming connections and does not do any checking of the connections it is dropping to ensure they are actually malicious connections. On a busy system this can cause bottlenecking and the dropping of legitimate connections. A possible solution to this is the introduction of SYN cookies; I will cover them in the "Kernel Parameters" section.

Some Final Bastion Host Rules

Now you will look at some final rules to catch some remaining potentially bad packets. The first rule goes back to the state module introduced earlier. You will remember that one of the potential states that is tracked by Netfilter is the INVALID state. Packets in the INVALID state are not associated with any known connection. This means any incoming packets in the INVALID state are not from connections on the host and should be dropped. On the bastion host you will log and discard all incoming packets in this state (see Listing 2-44).

Listing 2-44. *Logging and Discarding Packets in the* INVALID *State*

```
kitten# iptables -A INPUT -m state --state INVALID -j LOG ➥
--log-prefix "IPT INV_STATE "
kitten# iptables -A INPUT -m state --state INVALID -j DROP
```

Like you did with the BAD_FLAGS chain, you specify this rule to cover all incoming packets on all interfaces and log and drop them.

Lastly, you have added a rule to deal with packet fragments. Packet fragments occur when a packet is too large to be sent in one piece. The packet is broken up into fragments that are then reassembled on the receiving host. Fragments have some issues, though. Only the first fragment contains the full header fields of the packet. The subsequent packets have only a subset of the packet headers and contain only the IP information without any protocol information. This means most packet filtering based on this information fails. Not only this, but packet fragments have not only been responsible for a number of bugs in network servers and services but can also be used in attacks designed to crash servers and services.

This is mitigated if you are using connection tracking (using -m state), or NAT, as the packets are reassembled before being received by the filtering rules. Most modern Netfilter implementations should have connection tracking enabled by default, so fragments should not appear. But you should add rules that log and block fragments in Listing 2-45 both as a precaution and for completeness sake.

Listing 2-45. *Fragmented Packets*

```
kitten# iptables -A INPUT -f -j LOG --log-prefix "IPT Frag "
kitten# iptables -A INPUT -f -j DROP
```

The -f flag in Listing 2-45 tells iptables to select all fragments, and you have then logged and dropped them.

With these rules you have completed the iptables rules section of the bastion hosts firewall. You can see all these rules together with additional features such as kernel parameters in a script in Appendix A that you can modify for your own purposes.

Kernel Modules and Parameters

Netfilter is constructed of two components: the Netfilter kernel code and the userland tools, of which iptables is the principal tool. In addition to providing the standard packet-filtering rules, Netfilter also has a series of patches you can apply to the kernel code, as well as additional modules that you can load to provide additional functionality. Furthermore, you can set a variety of kernel parameters that allow you to tune and further configure iptables.

Patch-o-Matic

In the more recent releases of Netfilter, all the available patches and modules for Netfilter have been bundled into a tool called Patch-o-Matic (Next Gen), or POM. POM is designed to simplify the occasionally complicated process of applying patches to your kernel. The POM tool is available to download from the Netfilter site; Listing 2-46 goes through the download and verification process.

Listing 2-46. *Downloading and Verifying the POM Archive*

```
kitten# wget http://www.netfilter.org/files/patch-o-matic-ng-20040621.tar.bz2
kitten# wget http://www.netfilter.org/files/coreteam-gpg-key.txt
kitten# gpg --import coreteam-gpg-key.txt
gpg: key CA9A8D5B: public key "Netfilter Core Team <coreteam@netfilter.org>"
imported
gpg: Total number processed: 1
gpg:                imported: 1
kitten# wget http://www.netfilter.org/files/patch-o-matic-ng-20040621.tar.bz2.sig
kitten# gpg --verify patch-o-matic-ng-20040621.tar.bz2.sig
gpg: Signature made Tue 22 Jun 2004 08:06:15 EST using DSA key ID CA9A8D5B
gpg: Good signature from "Netfilter Core Team <coreteam@netfilter.org>"
gpg: checking the trustdb
gpg: no ultimately trusted keys found
```

```
gpg: WARNING: This key is not certified with a trusted signature!
gpg:          There is no indication that the signature belongs to the owner.
Primary key fingerprint: 02AC E2A4 74DD 09D7 FD45 2E2E 35FA 89CC CA9A 8D5B
```

In Listing 2-46 I have downloaded the POM source, the GPG key of the Netfilter team, and the signature of the POM source. I downloaded the version of POM (20040621) at the time of writing, but you should check the Netfilter site for the most recent version. I then imported the Netfilter GPG key and verified the source archive against it with the signature I downloaded.

You will also need a copy of your current kernel source and the source of the `iptables` tool. See Chapter 1 for instructions on how to get the source of your current kernel. I will assume you have followed the instructions in Chapter 1 and stored your kernel source in `/usr/src/linux`. To get the source of `iptables`, you can download it from Netfilter. To check the current version of `iptables` on your system, use the following command:

```
kitten# iptables -V
iptables v1.2.11
```

If you have not got the latest version of the `iptables` userland tools, I recommend upgrading to the latest version. Download the source for your version of `iptables` or the latest version if you have chosen to upgrade. You can see this process in Listing 2-47.

Listing 2-47. *Downloading and Verifying the POM Archive*

```
kitten# wget http://www.netfilter.org/files/iptables-1.2.11.tar.bz2
kitten# wget http://www.netfilter.org/files/iptables-1.2.11.tar.bz2.sig
kitten# gpg --verify iptables-1.2.11.tar.bz2.sig gpg: ➥
Signature made Tue 22 Jun 2004 07:48:54 EST using DSA key ID CA9A8D5B
gpg: Good signature from "Netfilter Core Team <coreteam@netfilter.org>"
gpg: WARNING: This key is not certified with a trusted signature!
gpg:          There is no indication that the signature belongs to the owner.
Primary key fingerprint: 02AC E2A4 74DD 09D7 FD45  2E2E 35FA 89CC CA9A 8D5B
```

In Listing 2-47 I have downloaded the `iptables` userland source archive and verified it with its signature. As I have already downloaded the Netfilter GPG key, I do not need to download it again and import it. Unpack the `iptables` source archive, and make a note of the location, as you will need it later when you use the POM tool.

▓**Tip** I recommend installing your `iptables` source in the `/usr/src` directory.

Now that you have the POM, the kernel source, and the `iptables` source code, the prerequisites for POM are complete. Unpack the POM archive, and change into the resulting directory.

The POM tool contains two types of patches are. The first are patches fixing or adjusting `iptables` functionality. The second are patches and modules adding functionality to `iptables`. In both cases, you will generally need to recompile your kernel and the userland tools. With both types of patch or functionality, you are required to choose from a list of possible patches and modules to install. This is much like the process of kernel configuration. The POM tool has some built-in checking and does not let you install patches or modules that are already compiled into your kernel.

■ **Caution** The patches and modules contained within the Patch-o-Matic tool are new features that could potentially seriously impact how Netfilter and `iptables` function. The Netfilter team considers many of the patches and modules not stable enough to be included in the core Netfilter release. Install them with caution, and test the functionality carefully.

If you want to just see the first type of patches for Netfilter, you can run POM using the commands in Listing 2-48.

Listing 2-48. *Applying the Latest patches for Netfilter with POM*

```
kitten# cd patch-o-matic-ng-20040621
kitten# export KERNEL_DIR=/path/to/kernel/source
kitten# export IPTABLES_DIR=/path/to/iptables/source
kitten# ./runme
```

In Listing 2-48 replace the KERNEL_DIR path with the path to your kernel source and the IPTABLES_DIR path with the path to your `iptables` source. The runme script calls the POM configuration script in the patching mode.

In you want to see the second type of patches and additional functionality for Netfilter, you can access them by adding the extra variable to the runme script (see Listing 2-49).

Listing 2-49. *Applying the Extra Functionality for Netfilter with POM*

```
kitten# cd patch-o-matic-ng-20040621
kitten# export KERNEL_DIR=/path/to/kernel/source
kitten# export IPTABLES_DIR=/path/to/iptables/source
kitten# ./runme extra
```

Again in Listing 2-49, replace the KERNEL_DIR path with the path to your kernel source and the IPTABLES_DIR path with the path to your `iptables` source.

When you run the runme script, it displays a list of the available patches and/or modules for Netfilter. Figure 2-2 shows the POM patching script.

As you can see in Figure 2-2, the patch script screen has four sections. The first at the top of the screen displays your kernel and `iptables` versions and the location of your source files. The second section displays all the patches and modules that have either been already installed in the kernel or are not appropriate to your kernel version.

In the third section, the proposed patch or module to apply to your kernel appears with a description, and in the last section you can select a series of actions to perform on the patch that is being displayed. Table 2-10 describes the most useful actions available to you.

```
Welcome to Patch-o-matic (1.17)!

Kernel:   2.4.26, /usr/src/linux-2.4.26
Iptables: 1.2.11, /usr/src/iptables-1.2.11
Each patch is a new feature: many have minimal impact, some do not.
Almost every one has bugs, so don't apply what you don't need!
-------------------------------------------------------------
expect-slab-cache does not match your source trees, skipping...
Already applied: 01_iptables-1.2.10.patch 01_linux-2.4.23.patch 02_linux-2.4.24.
patch 03_linux-2.4.25.patch 04_linux-2.4.26-helper_reassign.patch 05_linux-2.4.2
6-orphaned_expect.patch

Testing init_conntrack-optimize... not applied
The init_conntrack-optimize patch:
   Author: Pablo Neira <pablo@eurodev.net>
   Status: Pending for kernel inclusion


-------------------------------------------------------------
Do you want to apply this patch [N/y/t/f/a/r/b/w/q/?]  █
```

Figure 2-2. *The POM patching script*

Table 2-10. *POM Patching Options*

Option	Description
t	Tests that the patch will apply cleanly
t	Applies the patch
N	Skips a patch
f	Applies patch even if the T option fails
q	Quits
?	Displays help

Let's apply a patch now. The patch in Figure 2-2 has the following description:

`This patch fixes an oops while listing /proc/net/ip_conntrack.`

It also contains some further information on the patch. Read this carefully to determine the potential impact of the patch.

If you decide to apply the patch, you first want to test that you can apply the patch cleanly to the kernel source. You use the t option to do this, as you can see in the following line:

```
Do you want to apply this patch [N/y/t/f/a/r/b/w/q/?] t
Patch 04_linux-2.4.26-helper_reassign.patch applies cleanly
```

Then you want to set the patch to be applied using the y option:

```
Do you want to apply this patch [N/y/t/f/a/r/b/w/q/?] y
```

This marks the patch to be added to your kernel source and proceeds to display the next available patch. If you do not want to apply the displayed patch, you can continue to the next patch using the n option.

```
Do you want to apply this patch [N/y/t/f/a/r/b/w/q/?] N
```

The POM tool will proceed to the next patch to be applied and display its description. When you have selected all patches and modules you want, you can quit the POM tool using the q option.

After you have quit from the POM tool, you should see lines similar to Listing 2-50.

Listing 2-50. *Patching the Kernel with POM*

```
Do you want to apply this patch [N/y/t/f/a/r/b/w/q/?] q
Excellent! Source trees are ready for compilation.
Recompile the kernel image.
Recompile the netfilter kernel modules.
Recompile the iptables binaries.
```

The list in Listing 2-50 may be different pending on the compilation requirements of the patches or modules you have selected. You may not need to recompile all the items listed in Listing 2-50 in all circumstances.

Now you need to recompile the kernel and the Netfilter kernel modules. The commands in Listing 2-51 will do this for you. I have assumed you have followed the instructions in Chapter 1 and stored your kernel source in /usr/src/linux. I have also assumed you have copied and used your old .config file to run the make oldconfig process also as described in Chapter 1.

Listing 2-51. *Compiling the Kernel*

```
puppy# cd /usr/src/linux
puppy# make dep bzImage modules modules_install
puppy# make install
```

The first make line combines a number of compilation steps. First, it makes all the required dependencies, dep. Second, it makes a new boot image, bzImage. Then it compiles any modules required, modules, and finally it installs those modules, modules_install. The modules and modules_install commands will recompile all your Netfilter modules. At the end of this first make line you should have a fully compiled kernel and a new boot image. The next line, make install, installs that new boot image in your boot loader ready for you to reboot and use that new kernel together with the new patches or modules.

Next make the iptables binaries; to do this, use the commands in Listing 2-52.

Listing 2-52. *Recompiling the* iptables *Binaries*

```
kitten# cd /usr/src/iptables-1.2.11
kitten# make KERNEL_DIR=/path/to/kernel/source
kitten# make install KERNEL_DIR=/path/to/kernel/source
```

Replace the */path/to/kernel/source* part with the location of your kernel source.

When you have recompiled your kernel and the iptables userland tools, you need to reboot your system into the new kernel.

Now let's look at some of the additional modules available in the POM tool. You will look at three modules: the iprange module, the mport module, and the comment module.

The iprange Module

The iprange module allows you to specify inclusive source and destination IP address ranges. This means instead of only being able to specify a particular host or subnet as a source or destination address, you can now specify a range of hosts inside a subnet or a range of subnets.

Before you can use the module, you need to load it using the insmod command exactly as you would load any other kernel module. The names of Netfilter modules are usually prefixed with ipt_ so that iprange becomes ipt_range. To load the module, enter the following:

```
kitten# insmod ipt_iprange
Using /lib/modules/2.4.26/kernel/net/ipv4/netfilter/ipt_iprange.o
```

Now that you have loaded the module, you can add the module to rules using the -m flag. Let's start with a rule that allows you to use a range of hosts like the rule in Listing 2-53.

Listing 2-53. *Using a Range of Source Hosts with the* iprange *Module*

```
kitten# iptables -A INPUT -p tcp -m iprange ➡
--src-range 192.168.0.1-192.168.0.20 -j ACCEPT
```

The rule in Listing 2-53 accepts all incoming TCP traffic from the source IP address range 192.168.0.1 to 192.168.0.20. You can also specify a destination range of IP addresses or subnets as I have done in Listing 2-54.

Listing 2-54. *Using a Range of Destination Subnets with the* iprange *Module*

```
kitten# iptables -A FORWARD -p tcp -m iprange ➡
--dst-range 192.168.0.0-192.168.255.255 -j ACCEPT
```

■**Tip** You can also negate the --dst-range or --src-range flag using the ! option.

You can see the help text for the iprange module using the command in Listing 2-55.

Listing 2-55. iptables *Module Help*

```
kitten# iptables -m iprange -h
irange match v1.2.11 options:
[!] --src-range ip-ip        Match source IP in the specified range
[!] --dst-range ip-ip        Match destination IP in the specified range
```

You can also substitute the iprange module in Listing 2-55 for the name of any other modules for which you want to see help text or syntax.

The mport Module

The mport module provides an enhancement of the multiport module, which allows you to specify multiple ports using the --sport and --dport flags. The multiport module allows only comma-separated lists of individual ports and no ranges. The rule on the next line, for example, shows the use of the multiport module:

```
kitten# iptables -A INPUT -i eth0 -p tcp -m multiport --dport 80,443 -j ACCEPT
```

The rule in the previous line selects all incoming TCP traffic on both port 80 and port 443. This is pretty much the extent of the module's functionality. The mport module takes this further by allowing byte ranges as well as lists of single ports. To use the module, you first need to load it using the insmod command, as shown on the next line:

```
kitten# insmod ipt_mport
Using /lib/modules/2.4.26/kernel/net/ipv4/netfilter/ipt_mport.o
```

Once you have the module loaded, you can add it to rules. You can see an example rule on the next line that uses the module:

```
kitten# iptables -A INPUT -p tcp -m mport --dport 80:85,8080 -j ACCEPT
```

This rule allows incoming TCP traffic and invokes the mport module using the -m flag to allow traffic into the destination port range 80 to 85 and the individual port 8080. You can specify up to 15 ports or port ranges. A port range takes up two port slots.

The comment Module

POM also has a comment module that provides the ability to add comments to individual rules explaining their purpose. You can add comments of up to 256 characters in length to a rule. Like the other modules, first you need to confirm it is loaded; you use the insmod command again to do this (see Listing 2-56).

Listing 2-56. *Loading the* comment *Module*

```
kitten# insmod ipt_comment
Using /lib/modules/2.4.26/kernel/net/ipv4/netfilter/ipt_comment.o
insmod: a module named ipt_comment already exists
```

In Listing 2-56 I have shown the result that would occur if the comment module were already loaded.

Now you want to add comments to your rules. Listing 2-57 shows a comment added to one of the bastion host rules.

Listing 2-57. *Using the* comment *Module*

```
kitten# iptables -A INPUT -i eth1 -p udp -s 192.168.0.10 --dport domain ➡
-m state --state NEW,ESTABLISHED -m comment --comment "Allows incoming DNS ➡
traffic" -j ACCEPT
```

Using the -m flag you add the comment module to the rule; then using the only argument for the comment module, --comment, you provide a comment for the rule. Let's take a look at how the comment appears in the rule when you display your rules. Enter the following:

```
kitten# iptables -L INPUT
Chain INPUT (policy DROP)
target     prot opt source              destination
ACCEPT     udp  --  192.168.0.10        anywhere            ➥
udp dpt:domain state NEW,ESTABLISHED /* Allows incoming DNS traffic */
```

Kernel Parameters

Netfilter comes with a variety of kernel parameters that can be used to change its behavior, performance, and other features. You will examine some of these parameters to further enhance the security of your iptables firewall.

■Note All changes you make to your kernel parameters are lost when you reboot your system. To mitigate this, most distributions have a file located in /etc, called sysctl.conf, in which you can set those kernel parameters that you want automatically set at the bootup of the system. I recommend setting any iptables-related kernel parameters in this file to ensure they are set at system startup.

The parameters you will be manipulating are stored in the /proc directory structure. The /proc directory is a virtual file system that exists in memory and is created when the system boots (and is why the settings are reset when you reboot). It contains a variety of data structures and files that contain information gathered from the kernel and other sources. Generally each parameter correlates to a file in the /proc directory structure. These data structures and files can be changed and manipulated like any other file on your system. I will focus on the parameters contained in /proc/sys/net, which contains all the Netfilter-related settings.

■Tip The /proc/net directory contains a variety of files that include information about your iptables environment, including information such as the current connections and connection states being tracked.

You will use the sysctl command to manipulate these kernel parameters. The sysctl command comes with all distributions. Let's use it to view all your kernel parameters. Listing 2-58 shows an abbreviated listing of all the available kernel parameters.

Listing 2-58. *Display All Parameters*

```
kitten# sysctl -a
abi/fake_utsname = 0
abi/trace = 0
abi/defhandler_libcso = 68157441
abi/defhandler_lcall7 = 68157441
...
```

You can also selectively list the setting of a particular parameter by specifying that parameter on the sysctl command line, as in Listing 2-59.

Listing 2-59. *Display an Individual Parameter*

```
kitten# sysctl net/ipv4/ip_forward
```

As mentioned, each parameter correlates to a file in the /proc directory structure. This net.ipv4.ip_forward parameter correlates to a file called /proc/sys/net/ipv4/ip_forward. The sysctl command automatically prefixes /proc/sys/ to the parameter location, so you need to specify only its location from the net directory onward.

You can see all the sysctl command-line options in Table 2-11.

Table 2-11. *The* sysctl *Command-Line Options*

Option	Description
-a	Displays all kernel parameters.
-p *file*	Loads the parameters from a file. If no file is specified, it defaults to /etc/sysctl.conf.
-n	Disables printing the parameter name when displaying the parameter value.
-w *parameter=value*	Sets a parameter to the specified value.

If you want to change a kernel parameter using sysctl, you can do it using the -w option. Most kernel parameters are either numeric or Boolean values: with 0 indicating off and 1 indicating on. Let's change the ip_forward option you looked at in Listing 2-59 to demonstrate this parameter change. Listing 2-60 demonstrates this change.

■**Note** You need to be root or equivalent to change these parameters.

Listing 2-60. *Changing a Kernel Parameters Using* -w

```
kitten# sysctl -w net/ipv4/ip_forward="1"
```

By default the ip_forward option is set off, or 0. In Listing 2-60 I have set it to on, or 1. You can also change parameters by echoing values to them. For example, to change the ip_forward value back to off, you would use the following command:

```
kitten# /bin/echo "0" > /proc/sys/net/ipv4/ip_forward
```

Let's now look at some of the relevant kernel parameters for iptables that can enhance the security of your host.

■**Caution** Be sure you totally understand what each parameter does before you change it. Changing a parameter without a full understanding of its purpose can have unexpected results.

/proc/sys/net/ipv4/conf/all/accept_redirects

The accept_redirects parameter determines whether your system accepts ICMP redirects. ICMP redirects are used to tell routers or hosts that there is a faster or less congested way to send the packets to specific hosts or networks. Generally your hosts will not require this, especially stand-alone and bastion hosts. Even firewalls using iptables should only rarely have a use for redirects. Accepting redirects is also a security risk, because ICMP redirects can be easily forged and can potentially redirect your traffic somewhere malicious. I recommend you turn accept_redirects off, as in Listing 2-61.

Listing 2-61. *Turning Off the* accept_redirects *Parameter*

```
kitten# sysctl -w net/ipv4/conf/all/accept_redirects="0"
```

/proc/sys/net/ipv4/conf/all/accept_source_route

This parameter tells Netfilter if it should allow source-routed packets. Source-routed packets have their paths between two hosts exactly defined, including through which interfaces those packets are routed. In some instances this source routing can be subverted, which can allow attackers to route packets through an untrusted or insecure interface. I recommend you turn this parameter off, as in Listing 2-62.

Listing 2-62. *Turning Off the* accept_source_route *Parameter*

```
kitten# sysctl -w net/ipv4/conf/all/accept_source_route="0"
```

/proc/sys/net/ipv4/conf/all/log_martians

The log_martians parameter logs all packets from "impossible" addresses to the kernel. This includes bad IP addresses (similar to what I described when I discussed IP spoofing attacks), bad source routing, and the like. Many of these types of packets could indicate an IP address spoofing attack on your host. With this enabled, you will have entries appear in your logs similar to Listing 2-63.

Listing 2-63. `log_martians` syslog *Entry*

```
Aug  3 00:11:41 kitten kernel: martian source 255.255.255.255 from ➥
192.168.0.150, on dev eth0
```

I recommend you turn this on to keep track of these packets, which could potentially indicate an attack on your host. You can see the `log_martians` parameter turned on in Listing 2-64.

Listing 2-64. *Turning On the* `log_martians` *Parameter*

```
kitten# sysctl -w net/ipv4/conf/all/log_martians="1"
```

/proc/sys/net/ipv4/conf/all/rp_filter

This parameter controls reverse path filtering, which tries to ensure packets use legitimate source addresses. When it is turned on, then incoming packets whose routing table entry for their source address does not match the interface they are coming in on are rejected. This can prevent some IP spoofing attacks. If you have some unusual routing arrangements, such as asymmetric routing where packets take a different route from your host to another host than they take from that host to you, or if you have interfaces bound to more than one IP addresses, then you should test this parameter carefully to ensure you are not going to reject legitimate traffic.

You can set this parameter for each interface on your host individually. Each of your interfaces has a file called `rp_filter` that controls this parameter in the `/proc/sys/net/ipv4/conf/` directory, as you can see in Listing 2-65.

Listing 2-65. *Listing of the* `/proc/sys/net/ipv4/conf` *Directory*

```
kitten# ls -l
total 0
dr-xr-xr-x    2 root     root            0 Aug 23 01:39 all
dr-xr-xr-x    2 root     root            0 Aug 23 01:39 default
dr-xr-xr-x    2 root     root            0 Aug 23 01:39 eth0
dr-xr-xr-x    2 root     root            0 Aug 23 01:39 eth1
dr-xr-xr-x    2 root     root            0 Aug 23 01:39 lo
```

An `rp_filter` file exists in each of the directories in Listing 2-65, and you can change each of them to enable this function for individual interfaces. Or you could change all of them with a simple script like Listing 2-66.

Listing 2-66. *Enabling* `rp_filter` *for All Interfaces*

```
kitten# for interface in /proc/sys/net/ipv4/conf/*/rp_filter; do
   /bin/echo "1" > ${interface}
done
```

You can also set this parameter for all interfaces by changing the setting of the rp_filter file in the /proc/sys/net/ipv4/conf/all directory. This file controls this setting for all your interfaces.

Tip This is true of all the parameters that are interface specific. Changing the file located in the /proc/sys/net/ipv4/conf/all directory will change that setting for all interfaces.

/proc/sys/net/ipv4/icmp_echo_ignore_all

If this parameter is turned on, then Netfilter will ignore all ICMP echo requests. This will ignore all rules set to handle ICMP echo traffic. This is another method of handling ICMP echo traffic. I personally prefer to have a finer granularity of control over the handling of ICMP echo traffic and set up particular rules to address a variety of potential situations, for example, denying ICMP echo traffic incoming on an Internet-facing interface whilst allowing it on an internal network interface. You should consider what option best suits your environment. In Listing 2-67 I turn the parameter off.

Listing 2-67. *Setting* icmp_echo_ignore_all *Off*

```
kitten# sysctl -w net/ipv4/icmp_echo_ignore_all="0"
```

/proc/sys/net/ipv4/icmp_echo_ignore_broadcasts

This parameter works in the same manner as the icmp_echo_ignore_all parameter except that it ignores only ICMP messages sent to broadcast or multicast addresses. This significantly reduces the risk of a host being targeted by a smurf attack; I recommend you set it on, as in Listing 2-68.

Listing 2-68. *Setting* icmp_echo_ignore_broadcasts *On*

```
kitten# sysctl -w net/ipv4/icmp_echo_ignore_broadcasts ="1"
```

/proc/sys/net/ipv4/icmp_ignore_bogus_error_responses

Some routers, switches, and firewalls do not behave in accordance with the standards set out in RFC 1122[11] and send out incorrect responses to broadcasts. These incorrect responses are logged via the kern logging facility. If you do not want to see these log entries, you can set this parameter on. I recommend leaving this option on (as in Listing 2-69), because what may appear to be a bogus error response may in fact be a sign of an attack or probe of your system.

Listing 2-69. *Setting* icmp_ignore_bogus_error_responses *Off*

```
kitten# sysctl -w net/ipv4/icmp_ignore_bogus_error_responses="0"
```

---

11. You can find requirements for Internet Hosts—Communication Layers at http://www.faqs.org/rfcs/rfc1122.html.

/proc/sys/net/ipv4/ip_forward

The `ip_forward` parameter turns IP forwarding on or off. With this off (which it generally is by default), then packets will not be forwarded between interfaces. The `ip_forward` parameter is generally needed only if `iptables` is being used for routing, for NAT, as a network firewall, or for masquerading. For a bastion or stand-alone host, this should be set off, as you can see in Listing 2-70.

Listing 2-70. *Setting* `ip_forward` *Off*

```
kitten# sysctl -w net/ipv4/ip_forward="0"
```

/proc/sys/net/ipv4/tcp_syncookies

In response to the `SYN` flooding attacks described earlier, a kernel method was developed to mitigate the risk. When a host has `SYN` cookies enabled, it sends back encoded `SYN/ACK` packets. These encoded `SYN/ACK` packets have information about the connection state encoded into the sequence number of the reply to the initial `SYN` packet. If a reply is received to one of these packets, then its acknowledgement number will be one more than the sequence number sent. Netfilter then subtracts one from this number and decodes it to return and verify the original connection information. Any nonencoded or packets without do not verify are discarded. This process is conducted without consuming memory or connection resources. The kernel is now insulated from a Denial of Service attack using a `SYN` flood. I recommend turning it on, as I have in Listing 2-71.

Listing 2-71. *Setting* `tcp_syncookies` *On*

```
kitten# sysctl -w net/ipv4/tcp_syncookies="1"
```

Managing iptables and Your Rules

Many distributions come with tools to help you create your firewall. Gnome Lokkit on Red Hat or Debian and third-party tools such as Firestarter,[12] MonMotha,[13] and GuardDog[14] are all examples of these. These tools allow you to input configuration settings and variables, and they output `iptables` rules. I will not cover any of these tools because they are dangerous and encourage poor security. Gnome Lokkit is a good example of this. Its default policy is to ACCEPT traffic by default and not by exception. This violates what I think is good firewall design and leaves your system exposed whilst giving you the impression it is secure because you have used Red Hat's recommended tool.

Additionally, these tools often set extra configuration and firewall settings without consulting you. This assumption that this default configuration will suit your host and environment is a dangerous risk. It is a much better approach to configure your own rules and have a full understanding of how the various rules interact than to assume that a third-party tool

---

12. http://firestarter.sourceforge.net/
13. http://monmotha.mplug.org/firewall/index.php
14. http://www.simonzone.com/software/guarddog/

will provide a suitable configuration. This chapter should have shown you that the configuration of host firewalls with iptables is easy to master and that you do not require a third-party tool to achieve secure and hardened firewalls.

iptables-save and iptables-restore

Even if I do not recommend using a tool to construct iptables firewalls, a large number of rules and settings are still involved in the average iptables firewall. These can become cumbersome to manage and maintain and can be time consuming to reenter if you accidentally flush your rules or if you need to duplicate firewall settings on multiple hosts. The iptables package comes with some tools to assist in the process of managing your rules. These are iptables-save and iptables-restore. The iptables-save command saves the iptables rules currently in memory to STDOUT or to a file. The iptables-restore command allows you to restore rules from a file or STDIN.

Start by saving some of your rules using iptables-save. The iptables-save command without options outputs all current rules to STDOUT. You can see a sample of the output from the command in Listing 2-72.

Listing 2-72. *Sample* iptables-*save Output*

```
kitten# iptables-save
*filter
:INPUT ACCEPT [2:184]
:FORWARD ACCEPT [0:0]
:OUTPUT ACCEPT [9:904]
:BAD_FLAGS - [0:0]
...
...
-A INPUT -i lo -j ACCEPT
-A ICMP_OUT -o eth0 -p icmp -j LOG --log-prefix "IPT: ICMP_OUT "
-A ICMP_OUT -o eth0 -p icmp -j DROP
COMMIT
```

The format of the file is not critical, as I recommend you do not change your rules and configuration in the outputted file but rather use iptables to edit your rules as it was designed to do. But to give you some brief information on the structure of the file, you can see that the start of each table described in the iptables-save output is prefixed by the asterisk symbol (*) and the end of the iptables-save output is indicated by the line COMMIT.

The iptables-save command had two flags; the first flag -t allows you to specify only those rules from a particular table. To save only the filter table rules, enter the following:

```
kitten# iptables-save -t filter
```

If you omit the -t flag, the table selection defaults to the filter table.

The second flag, -c, saves your rules together with the values of the packet and byte counters for each chain and rule.

The best approach to storing your iptables configuration is to redirect the output of the iptables-save command to a file, as shown in Listing 2-73.

Listing 2-73. *Redirecting the* iptables-save *Output*

```
kitten# iptables-save > kitten-iptables-rules-20040803
```

Once you have your saved rules and configuration, you can restore them using the iptables-restore command. Listing 2-74 shows the restoration of the rules you saved in Listing 2-74.

Listing 2-74. *Restoring* iptables *Rules*

```
kitten# iptables-restore < kitten-iptables-rules-20040803
```

In Listing 2-74 your existing rules will be flushed from the system and replaced with the rules contained in the kitten-iptables-rules-20040803 file.

The iptables-restore has two flags; the first -c restores the values of your byte and packet counters (if they were saved with your rules using the iptables-save -c command). The second flag, -n, restores your rules without flushing the existing rules from your system. This adds any restored rules to your current rules.

iptables init Scripts

The iptables firewall is not a daemon. Rules changes happen interactively. When you add a rule to a chain, that rule is immediately active and no service or daemon needs to be restarted or refreshed. When iptables is started and stopped using an init script, your script generally relies on the iptables-save and iptables-restore commands to set up and take down your firewall. You should examine the contents of your iptables init script, /etc/rc.d/init.d/iptables on Red Hat and /etc/init.d/iptables on Debian, to see how this is done.

On Red Hat to start and stop your iptables, enter the following:

```
puppy# /etc/rc.d/init.d/iptables stop
puppy# /etc/rc.d/init.d/iptables start
```

Or you can use iptables restart to restart the firewall. You can use the same options on Debian with the iptables init script in /etc/init.d.

On Red Hat and Debian systems the iptables init script also acts as an interface to the iptables-save and iptables-restore commands, allowing you to save and restore your rules. On Red Hat systems to save your rules, enter the following:

```
puppy# /etc/rc.d/init.d/iptables save
```

The rules are saved to the file /etc/sysconfig/iptables. The Red Hat init script reloads these rules from this file when you restart the system.

On Debian systems you can use the init script to both load and save your rules. To save your rules, enter the following:

```
kitten# /etc/init.d/iptables save ruleset
```

Replace ruleset with the name of a file to hold the saved rules. To load the saved rules, enter the following:

```
kitten# /etc/init.d/iptables load ruleset
```

Replace *ruleset* with the name of a rule set you previously saved that you now want to load.

The Red Hat init script also has another option, panic, which stops your firewall by flushing all your rules and setting your default policies to DROP. This is useful in an emergency to terminate access to your host, for example, if your host was under attack. To do this, enter the following:

```
puppy# /etc/rc.d/init.d/iptables panic
```

Like Red Hat, Debian also has an emergency halt function, which you can use by entering the following:

```
kitten# /etc/init.d/iptables halt
```

Note As mentioned in Chapter 1, you should start your iptables firewall before you activate the interfaces and networking, and you should stop the firewall after you deactivate your interfaces and networking.

Testing and Troubleshooting

One of the greatest difficulties with managing iptables firewalls is testing that your firewall is allowing and blocking the traffic you want. In Chapter 6 I will talk about using nmap to scan your system, and this is one way to ensure the correct ports are open and closed on your host. But this does not tell you enough information about the specifics of your rules and their interactions, for example, whether the controls are working correctly on which hosts or networks may connect to and from your host. To do this, you need to monitor the traffic coming in and out of your host, including the most detail possible about individual packets. You can do this using the tcpdump command.

The tcpdump command prints the headers of packets being transmitted on your network interfaces. It can display these headers on the screen in a terminal session or save them to a file for later review or analysis using a variety of tools. You can also load and replay these saved capture files. Most important, you can use tcpdump to select only those headers you want to see using selection criteria, including selecting only traffic from particular hosts or traffic on particular ports.

MAKING REMOTE iptables CHANGES

If you are changing configurations over a network, you may want to test them using a series of commands such as the following:

```
kitten# iptables restart; sleep 10; iptables stop &
```

This will allow your changes to take effect for a short while and then completely turn off. Your session should be able to recover in that time, and if it does not, you will still be able to login again. A better approach may be to save the current configuration using iptables-save, load the new configuration, wait, and then load the saved configuration. This way, you can still have a protected host as you test new configurations. Ideally, though, you can do your testing in a nonproduction environment and will not have to resort to these types of measures.

> **■Note** The `tcpdump` command in the process of gathering these packet headers will place the interface it is capturing packets from into promiscuous mode unless you specifically specify otherwise.

Most distributions come with the `tcpdump` package installed; if not, it is usually available on your distribution's installation media, or you can download and install it from the `tcpdump` home page at `http://www.tcpdump.org/`.

If you run `tcpdump` on the command line without any options, as you can see in Listing 2-75, it will print all packet headers from all interfaces on your host to the screen until stopped with a `SIGINT` signal such as Control+C.

Listing 2-75. *Basic* `tcpdump`

```
kitten# tcpdump
tcpdump: verbose output suppressed, use -v or -vv for full protocol decode
listening on eth0, link-type EN10MB (Ethernet), capture size 96 bytes
00:18:39.980445 IP puppy.yourdomain.com.ssh > kitten.yourdomain.com.3717: ➥
P 900077725:900077841(116) ack 260615777 win 9648
1 packets captured
1 packets received by filter
0 packets dropped by kernel
```

You can also display more information on the packet using the `-v` and `-vv` flags, which increase the verbosity of the capture. You can also limit the number of packet headers captured using the `-c` flag and specifying the number of packet headers you would like to capture. You can see both these flags in operation in Listing 2-76.

Listing 2-76. *Verbose* `tcpdump` *with Packet Count*

```
kitten# tcpdump -v -c 1
tcpdump: listening on eth0, link-type EN10MB (Ethernet), capture size 96 bytes
00:28:09.202191 IP (tos 0x10, ttl  64, id 41395, offset 0, flags [DF], proto 6,
length: 92) puppy.yourdomain.com.ssh > kitten.yourdomain.com.3717: ➥
P 900095437:900095489(52) ack 260624565 win 9648
1 packets captured
1 packets received by filter
0 packets dropped by kernel
```

In Listing 2-76 I have captured another packet showing a `ssh` connection from host `puppy` to host `kitten` but with the verbose flag enabled and additional information contained in the capture, including the TOS, TTL, and the packet's flags.

Other flags are available to you on the `tcpdump` command line, and Table 2-12 describes some of the more useful flags.

Table 2-12. `tcpdump` *Command-Line Flags*

Option	Description
`-i interface`	Listen on a particular interface. Use any to listen on all interfaces.
`-N`	Do not print domain information (`puppy` instead of `puppy.yourdomain.com`).
`-p`	Do not put the interface in promiscuous mode.
`-q`	Quiet mode that prints less protocol information.
`-r file`	Read in packets from a file.
`-t`	Do not print a time stamp.
`-vv ｜ -vvv`	More verbose and even more verbose. Prints increasing amounts of information.
`-w file`	Write the packets to a file; use - for writing to standard out.

With testing `iptables` using `tcpdump`, the objective is to monitor the incoming and outgoing traffic on your host to ensure traffic is correctly being allowed and denied using your rules. Obviously, most interfaces generate a huge volume of traffic, so `tcpdump` offers the capability to filter that traffic and display only those packets you want to monitor. The `tcpdump` command offers three key filtering selection criteria: types, directions, and protocols. For example, Table 2-13 shows the list of possible type-filtering criteria.

Table 2-13. `tcpdump` *Type Selectors*

Selector	Description
`host`	Selects only traffic from a particular host
`net`	Selects only traffic from a particular network
`port`	Selects only traffic on a particular port

I discuss some of the other filtering criteria shortly, or you can refer to the `tcpdump` man page for more information.

Listing 2-77 shows `tcpdump` selection at its most basic—selecting only traffic from a particular host using the Type selector, `host`.

Listing 2-77. *Basic* `tcpdump` *Selection*

```
kitten# tcpdump -v -c 1 host puppy
```

In Listing 2-77 the `tcpdump` command selects only packets that contain a reference to the host puppy. This will include both packets to and from the host puppy. In addition to single hosts, you can also capture only that traffic from a particular network using the `net` selector. Enter the following to capture traffic only from the 192.168.0.0/24 network:

```
kitten# tcpdump net 192.168.0.0 mask 255.255.255.0
```

The `tcpdump` command also allows Boolean operators to be used with its selectors. In Listing 2-78 I am selecting all traffic between the host puppy and either the host `kitten` or the host `duckling` using the and / or Boolean operators.

Listing 2-78. *Boolean Selectors*

```
kitten# tcpdump host puppy and kitten or duckling
```

Notice that I have not prefixed the kitten or duckling hosts with the host selector. If you omit the selector, the tcpdump command will assume you meant to use the last selector utilized. This means Listing 2-78 is equivalent to the filter on the next line:

```
kitten# tcpdump host puppy and host kitten or host duckling
```

In addition to and/or Boolean operators, you can also use the not operator. Enter the following, which captures traffic from any host except puppy:

```
kitten# tcpdump not host puppy
```

With the tcpdump filtering selectors, you can also restrict the filtering to specific ports. To select all ssh traffic from host puppy, enter the following:

```
kitten# tcpdump host puppy and port ssh
```

You can also further restrict Listing 2-78 to a traffic direction using the src and dst direction selectors, as you can see in Listing 2-79.

Listing 2-79. *Specifying Traffic Direction*

```
kitten# tcpdump src host puppy and dst host kitten or duckling
```

In Listing 2-79 you are now selecting only traffic outgoing from the host puppy with a destination of the hosts kitten or duckling.

In Listing 2-80 you can use the protocol selectors to select only that traffic from a particular protocol type.

Listing 2-80. *Selecting Traffic via Protocol*

```
kitten# tcpdump tcp host puppy and port domain
```

In Listing 2-80 tcpdump selects only TCP traffic to and from the host puppy on port 53. You can also use the ip selector to capture IP traffic, udp to select UDP traffic, and icmp to capture ICMP traffic.

This was a brief introduction to tcpdump; you can do a lot more with the command. I recommend you read the tcpdump man page, which contains detailed and useful documentation for the command.

■**Tip** You should also look at some of the tools discussed at the end of Chapter 6, which should also prove useful in troubleshooting, testing, and dissecting your network traffic.

Resources

The following are some resources for you to use.

Mailing Lists

- **Netfilter mailing lists**: http://lists.netfilter.org/mailman/listinfo

- **tcpdump** mailing list: http://www.tcpdump.org/#lists

Sites

- **Netfilter**: http://www.netfilter.org/

- **Netfilter Packet Filtering HOWTO**:
  http://www.netfilter.org/documentation/HOWTO//packet-filtering-HOWTO.html

- **Netfilter NAT HOWTO**: http://www.netfilter.org/documentation/HOWTO//
  NAT-HOWTO.html

- **Shorewall**: http://www.shorewall.net/

- **Firestarter**: http://firestarter.sourceforge.net/

- **MonMotha**: http://monmotha.mplug.org/firewall/index.php

- **GuardDog**: http://www.simonzone.com/software/guarddog/

- **tcpdump**: http://www.tcpdump.org

Books

- McCarty, Bill. *Red Hat Linux Firewalls*. Indianapolis, IN: Red Hat, 2002.

- Zeigler, Robert. *Linux Firewalls, Second Edition*. Indianapolis, IN: Sams, 2001.

■ ■ ■

## CHAPTER 3

Securing Connections and Remote Administration

In Chapter 2 I talked about using firewalls, specifically `iptables`, to secure your system from network threats. This principally allows you to block all connections to the system except those you explicitly want to allow through your firewall. But what about those allowed connections? Can you be sure they are going to be secure? They need to be secure from the perspective of preventing penetrations of your system using those connections, and they also need to be secure from the traffic itself running over those connections from attackers using tools such as sniffers that try to obtain information from your systems, including passwords and other potentially valuable data.

Additionally, many of the nonapplication connections to your system are going to be administration related. It is unfortunate that securing your system from intrusion often makes the job of administering your system more difficult. While it is not only harder for an attacker to penetrate your system, it is also harder for you or another systems administrator to access the system for legitimate purposes—especially if those administrative purposes require a higher level of access (for example, `root` access) to the system than a normal user.

In this chapter, I will cover some methods of securing the incoming and outgoing connections to and from your systems, including both the connection and the traffic running across that connection. I will also cover the basics of virtual private networks (VPNs) using IPSec and provide you with a practical example of joining two subnets via a VPN tunnel over the Internet. In addition, I will cover some methods of securely administering your system. My aim is to show some practical examples of using particular applications securely and effectively while ensuring they do not put your system at risk of attack. Some of the tools and applications I will cover in this chapter you will put to further practical use elsewhere in this book. As a result of the practical focus on this chapter, I will not delve into a great deal of the theory behind some of the tools covered, with the exception of a brief discussion on public-key encryption that is important for everyone to understand because of its widespread use in the Unix and networking security arena.

Public-Key Encryption

Any connections using TCP/IP you have open from your system are at risk from a variety of attacks. Often, your connections pass through many different networking devices and systems before reaching their final destination, which further increases the risk that someone may be able to use the connection to gain access to or disrupt your systems or use the information flowing over that connection for nefarious purposes, such as acquiring credit card details from an e-commerce site or banking details from an e-mail. The risks associated with running these types of connections are as follows:

- **Eavesdropping**: Your information is monitored or intercepted.

- **Tampering**: Your information is changed or replaced.

- **Spoofing or impersonation**: Someone pretends to be the recipient of your information or sends false or substituted information back to you.

However, a well-established methodology exists for securing connections against the risks I have articulated; it is called *public-key cryptography*.[1] Public-key cryptography (in conjunction with the use of digital signatures) provides a variety of functions, including the encryption and decryption of information being transmitted, authentication of the information's sender, detection of tampering, and an audit trail that allows both parties to see the information has been sent. In combination, these can mitigate the risks I detailed previously. What follows is a highly simplified description of public-key cryptography. I aim to give you a clear understanding of the concepts involved without covering a great deal of theoretical information. For example, I will not discuss widely the various ciphers you could use but instead focus on the well-known and default RSA cipher, which should provide more than adequate security for most purposes. My focus is on getting you running secured connections quickly. If you want more information, I recommend Netscape's "Introduction to Public-Key Cryptography."[2]

In public-key cryptography you have two keys: a public key and a private key. The public key is published (often in conjunction with a certificate), and the private key is kept secret. The public key can be as widely distributed as you like without comprising security, but your private key must be kept secure. The sender will encrypt the information they want to send with the recipient's public key. They then send the information. The recipient receives the information and uses their private key to decrypt the information. This ensures your information is protected from monitoring or eavesdropping.

Added to the public-key encryption is a digital signature that addresses the issues of tampering and spoofing. The signature itself is called a *one-way hash* or *message digest*. A one-way hash is a mathematical function that creates a number that is a unique representation of the information to be sent. If the information is changed in any way, then the hash is no longer a valid representation of the new information. When sent with the information, this allows the signing mechanism at the receiving end to ensure the information has not been changed during its transmission from the sender to the recipient. The one-way indicates that it is not possible to extrapolate the information being sent from the hash, thus preventing someone from using the hash to determine the information.

To generate a digital signature, the encryption approach is reversed from the original public-key encryption process. The signing mechanism generates the one-way hash, and you use your private key to encrypt it. The encrypted hash together with some additional

---

1. The entire components of a public-key encryption system (including CAs, policies, procedures, and protocols) are often referred to as *public-key infrastructure* (PKI).

2. http://developer.netscape.com/docs/manuals/security/pkin/index.html

information, most notably the hashing algorithm, is sent with the information to the recipient as the digital signature. The signing mechanism at the recipient end then uses your public key to decrypt the hash and uses it to verify the integrity of the information sent.

The final layer in the public-key encryption infrastructure I will cover is a *certificate*. A certificate is just like a passport. It binds certain identifying information, such as your name and location or the name of a server or Web site to a particular public key. It also usually has an expiry period and is valid only for that period. Most public certificates are valid for one year. Most of the certificates you will deal with follow the X.509 standard, which is an ITU recommendation[3] adopted by a variety of developers.

Certificates are generally issued by a certificate authority (CA). A CA is usually a privately run organization that guarantees to its customers and users it has verified the identity of the owner or purchaser of a certificate. Some organizations run their own internal CAs using products, such as Netscape Certificate Management System and Microsoft Certificate Server, or using open-source products such as EJBCA.[4]

So how does this work? Well, let's say you wanted to use public-key encryption using certificates to secure a Web site. You first create a signing request and a private key. A signing request is a type of certificate. The signing request is then sent to a CA to be signed and therefore become a fully fledged certificate. Your private key remains with you. The CA sends you a public certificate (which, as discussed previously, combines a public key and some associated identifying information, in this case probably the hostname of the Web site to be secured) and a copy of its public certificate, called a *CA certificate*. The CA certificate it has sent to you is like a receipt from the CA. Every time the authenticity and validity of your public certificate is checked, the signing mechanism checks your CA certificate to ensure your public certificate was signed by someone valid and trusted. Sometimes you may have a chain of CA certificates. For example, it could be that the CA certificate that signed your public certificate was in turn signed by another CA certificate. Each of these associated CA certificates would need to be verified in sequence to ensure your public certificate is valid. You then install your new public certificate into your Web site and server, and when users connect to your site, they will do so over an authenticated and encrypted connection.[5]

■**Tip** Of course, one of the great benefits of the open-source world is that you do not need to use commercial CAs to sign all your certificates. This can considerably save on costs because commercial CAs can sometimes charge steep fees for certificate signing. In the previous example, you are securing a Web site. So you would almost certainly need a commercial CA involved to sign your certificate to ensure third parties were comfortable and trusted your site. But for other sorts of connections (for example, a secure connection between two `syslog` systems), you could use a CA you have created locally. You will look at this in the "SSL, TLS, and OpenSSL" section.

---

3. `http://www.itu.int/rec/recommendation.asp?type=items&lang=e&parent=T-REC-X.509-200003-I`

4. You'll find links to these products in the "Resources" section.

5. Arguably, some risks are associated with PKI overall. An excellent document that details some of these risks is available at `http://www.schneier.com/paper-pki.html`.

SSL, TLS, and OpenSSL

One of the most well-known examples of the use of public-key encryption and digital signatures for securing connections are the Secure Sockets Layer (SSL) protocol and the Transport Layer Security (TLS) protocol. In the example in the previous section, in which I talked about securing a Web site using public-key encryption and certificates, the protocol securing your Web site would be SSL, and you would have connected to the site by using the https prefix instead of the standard http prefix.

Developed by Netscape, SSL is a protocol for handling the security of message transmission over networks and most specifically the Internet. SSL operates between the TCP/IP network layer and the application layer. When you connect to a device or service running SSL, a *handshake* takes places in which the device or service presents its public certificate to the connecting party to authenticate its identity. This is called *server authentication*. If the server and the connecting party authenticate, then all transmissions between the parties are now authenticated and encrypted using whatever encryption method you have selected, for example, RSA or DSA encryption. You can also configure SSL so that the connecting party must also prove their bona fides to the device or service; this is called *client authentication*.

Similar in operation to SSL is TLS. TLS was also developed by Netscape and was based on SSL version 3.0. It is detailed in RFC 2246.[6] It offers significant advantages over SSL version 2.0, and it is slightly more secure than SSL version 3.0. Thus, I recommend using it over either version of SSL if your application or service supports using TLS. In Chapters 8 and 9, when I discuss using SSL/TLS to secure SMTP and IMAP/POP, I focus on TLS. Unfortunately, few Web browsers support TLS; most of them still use SSL rather than TLS.

To use SSL/TLS (hereafter just referred to as TLS) on your Linux system, I will show how to implement the OpenSSL package. OpenSSL is an attempt to develop a secure and robust open-source implementation of SSL (versions 2.0 and 3.0) and TLS (version 1.0). You can find OpenSSL at http://www.openssl.org/. The implementation is well maintained and updated frequently, and I recommend you look at it before considering an investment in a commercial package that offers similar capabilities.

You can download OpenSSL from http://www.openssl.org/source/, and I will show you how to install it.

■Tip You should check the authenticity of the download using md5 or gpg[7] to ensure you have an authentic package. See Chapters 1 and 4 for details of how to do this.

Before you install OpenSSL, you should check whether you already have it installed and what version it is. More so than other applications, you need to keep applications such as OpenSSL up-to-date. It is a vital component of a large number of security-related solutions on Linux systems. Vulnerabilities in OpenSSL could have spillover effects on multiple other applications and create a series of vulnerabilities and exploitable weaknesses in those applications

---

6. http://www.ietf.org/rfc/rfc2246.txt

7. md5 is the Message Digest algorithm developed by Prof. Ronald Rivest, and gpg is the GNU Privacy Guard utility that you can see at http:// www.gnupg.org.

that rely on the functionality of OpenSSL to secure them. To check what version of OpenSSL you have, run the following:

```
puppy$ openssl version
```

You will get these results:

```
OpenSSL 0.9.7a Feb 19 2003
```

Then check the OpenSSL site to confirm the current version. If the version you have has been superseded, I strongly recommend you download and install the latest version either from the source package or via your package management tool if your vendor has a more up-to-date package.

If you have downloaded OpenSSL in the form of a source package, then unpack it and change into the resulting directory. OpenSSL relies on the `config` script to configure the basic settings for OpenSSL. The major option of the `config` script is the specification of the location in which to install OpenSSL. By default when installed from the source package, OpenSSL is installed with a prefix of `/usr/local` and an OpenSSL directory of `/usr/local/ssl`. If you are replacing an existing OpenSSL installation, you need to confirm where your current version is installed and make sure you specify that location to the `config` script. Listing 3-1 shows how to replace the existing OpenSSL installation on a Red Hat system.

Listing 3-1. *Replacing OpenSSL on a Red Hat System*

```
puppy$ ./config --prefix=/usr --openssldir=/usr/share/ssl shared
```

■**Tip** The last option `shared` tells OpenSSL to create shared libraries as well as the static libraries. This is not strictly necessary, and the shared libraries function is considered experimental until the version 1 release of OpenSSL. However, on most Linux systems it is stable enough and may offer some performance enhancements and better use of memory.

Then you need to `make`, `make test` to ensure all of OpenSSL's cryptographical functions are working, and then finally `make install` to install OpenSSL onto your system.

```
puppy$ make && make test
puppy# make install
```

You saw the `openssl` command previously when you used it to check the version of your OpenSSL installation. It also has a number of other functions that are useful to you such as creating keys and certificates, testing SSL connections, and encrypting and decrypting items. Table 3-1 details the features and functions you are most likely to use. These functions are specified directly after the `openssl` command, as you can see in Listing 3-2 in which I generate a new RSA private key.

Listing 3-2. *Generating a New RSA Private Key Using* openssl

```
puppy# openssl genrsa -out puppy_key.pem -des3 1024
Generating RSA private key, 1024 bit long modulus
.................................................++++++
....................++++++
e is 65537 (0x10001)
Enter pass phrase for puppy_key.pem:
Verifying - Enter pass phrase for puppy_key.pem:
```

This command uses the genrsa option to specify a new private key identified by the -out option as puppy_key.pem. You also specify the -des3 option to encrypt the key and prompt for a passphrase to secure it. The last option on the line, 1024, is the number of bits in length of the key to generated. I recommend a minimum of 1024 for most keys and 2048 for your CA keys.

Table 3-1. *The* openssl *Command-Line Functions*

ca	Performs CA functions.
gendsa	All creation of DSA-based certificates. Same options as the genrsa option.
req	Performs X.509 certificate-signing request (CSR) functions.
rsa	Process RSA keys and allows conversion of them to different formats.
rsautl	An RSA utility for signing, verification, encryption, and decryption.
s_client	Tests SSL/TLS client connections to remote servers.
s_server	Tests SSL/TLS server connections from remote clients and servers.
smime	S/MIME utility that can encrypt, decrypt, sign, and verify S/MIME messages
verify	Performs X.509 certificate verification functions.
x509	Performs X.509 certificate data management functions.

■**Tip** All of the openssl options have their own man pages. You can access them via man and the name of the option. For example, for the openssl req options, use the command man req.

Creating a Certificate Authority and Signing Certificates

For the purposes of this explanation, I will cover only one type of certificate model. In this model you are running your own CA and signing certificates with that CA. The reason I have chosen to cover this model is because it is financially cost free and does not require you to purchase certificates. But there are some risks with having your own CA and signing your own certificates, and you need to weigh those risks before proceeding and consult with any partners with which you intend to authenticate.

The major risk for running your own CA is that you have to secure it. If you issue a large volume of certificates, you need to ensure there is absolutely no possibility that your CA can be compromised. If your CA is compromised, your entire certificate and key infrastructure is

CIPHERS, KEYS, AND KEY LENGTH

As I mentioned, I will not cover a lot of detail on cipher systems, as I recommend you use the default RSA cryptosystem. To use RSA, though, it is important to have at least a limited understanding of the mechanics of the cryptosystem. RSA is a public-key encryption system that provides encryption, decryption, and digital signature functionality for authentication purposes. Ronald Rivest, Adi Shamir, and Leonard Adleman developed it in 1977, and the RSA acronym was taken from the first letters of the last names of its developers. The RSA algorithm relies on prime-number factoring to provide security. Two large primes are taken, and their product computed to produce a third number, the *modulus*. Two more numbers are chosen that are less than the modulus and relatively prime to the original large primes. The combination of the modulus and one of the relative primes make up the private and public keys, respectively.[8] The two biggest threats to the RSA cryptosystem and to your PKI environment are if someone discovers a way to shortcut factoring or, far more likely, if your PKI environment is not secure and an attacker manages to acquire your private key.

Your public-key encryption system is only as secure as your private keys. You must ensure that your private keys are protected at all costs. Some basic rules should help with this.

- Ensure you set suitable ownership and set your permissions on the keys as tightly as possible.

- Use only secure mediums to transmit your private keys, especially any CA keys.

- I recommend you consider expiring your keys after a suitable period of use. This gives you the opportunity to also review your key length, as I talk about shortly.

Five years ago RSA Laboratories issued a challenge to crack a 140-bit RSA encryption key. It took one month for someone to crack the key.[9] More recently in December 2003, a team in Germany successfully cracked a 576-bit RSA encryption key in three months.[10] Admittedly, the team used a significant amount of processing power (more than 100 workstations), but this emphasizes that any keys you create need to be of a suitable length. Additionally, as hardware performance increases, the time needed to crack short key lengths will obviously decrease. So at this stage I recommend you use keys 1024 bits in length or longer as a minimum. The RSA Laboratories claim these keys will be secure up until at least 2010. As you can see in Listing 3-2, I have specified a minimum key length using the `openssl` command of 1024-bits, and you can also specify a default in your `openssl.cnf` file.

But having longer key lengths has issues also. The major issue with having longer keys is the risk that performance will suffer and that the time taken to encrypt and decrypt information will make encryption detrimental to productive operations. Of course, the risk that increased hardware performance will allow keys to be cracked faster also means improved performance for your cryptosystem, which means longer key lengths are more feasible and will have less impact on the speed of operations. You will need to assess and test the performance of your applications using the required key sizes.

---

8. If you are interested in the mathematics involved, see the RSA Laboratories site at http://www.rsasecurity.com/rsalabs/node.asp?id=2214.

9. http://www.rsasecurity.com/rsalabs/node.asp?id=2099

10. http://www.rsasecurity.com/rsalabs/node.asp?id=2096

at risk. If you are serious about becoming your own CA on a large scale, I recommend setting up an isolated system that is not connected to your network and is physically secured. Also, I recommend Tempest-shielding technology to prevent electronic monitoring.[11] Obviously, the associated cost of this probably will mean that a commercial CA is a cheaper option. Further details on how to secure your CA are outside the scope of this book.

Lastly, using your own CA is generally not trusted by third parties and applications. Users may not accept your certificates, and applications may generate error messages. For example, if a Web browser or mail program encounters a certificate that is signed by a CA that it believes it is not a recognized CA (many browsers and e-mail clients come with a collection of "trusted" commercial CA root certificates), then it will prompt the user with an error message or series of error messages. However, if you were doing mail server authentication—for example, as opposed to a Web page—I usually assume that you have a limited number of partners you are going to authenticate with certificates (almost certainly all clients and systems you administer), which means it is more likely those partners will accept a private CA rather than a commercial CA.

■**Caution** By detailing this model I am not recommending it as the preferred option. If you operate production systems, especially e-commerce–related systems that use SSL, I recommend you use a commercial CA.

I will now quickly walk you through creating a new CA for your system. This walk-through assumes you are going to create the CA on the local system on which you will use the certificates. You do not have to do it this way, but for the purposes of this explanation it is the easiest approach. First, choose somewhere to store your certificates. I often use /etc/ssl/certs as the location. For the purposes of the following examples, I will use /etc/ssl/certs.

Next, initialize your CA. The OpenSSL distribution comes with a script called CA, which has a number of options, including creating a new CA. Listing 3-3 shows the commands and process for creating a new CA.

Listing 3-3. *Creating a New CA*

```
puppy$ cd /etc/ssl/certs
puppy# /usr/share/ssl/misc/CA -newca
CA certificate filename (or enter to create)
Making CA certificate ...
Generating a 1024 bit RSA private key
....++++++
.......................++++++
writing new private key to './demoCA/private/./cakey.pem'
Enter PEM pass phrase:
Verifying - Enter PEM pass phrase:
-----
```

---

11. See information on TEMPEST at http://searchwebservices.techtarget.com/sDefinition/ 0,,sid26_gci522583,00.html.

```
You are about to be asked to enter information that will be incorporated
into your certificate request.
What you are about to enter is what is called a Distinguished Name or a DN.
There are quite a few fields but you can leave some blank
For some fields there will be a default value,
If you enter '.', the field will be left blank.
-----
Country Name (2 letter code) [GB]:AU
State or Province Name (full name) [Berkshire]:New South Wales
Locality Name (eg, city) [Newbury]:Sydney
Organization Name (eg, company) [My Company Ltd]:yourdomain.com
Organizational Unit Name (eg, section) []:
Common Name (eg, your name or your server's hostname) []:puppy
E-mail Address []:admin@puppy.yourdomain.com
```

In Listing 3-3 I have changed into the directory where I want to put the CA, /etc/ssl/
certs, and then run the CA script with the option -newca. This creates a new CA. Press Enter
to create a new CA and then fill in the required details for your new CA, including a passphrase and details of your location, organization, and the system on which the CA is running.
Replace the information in Listing 3-3 with the information for your environment, for example, replacing *yourdomain.com* and *puppy* with the domain name and hostname of the system
on which you are creating the CA.

■**Tip** You should treat any CA or certificate passphrases with the same respect as you treat your other system passwords—carefully and securely.

The CA script creates a directory called demoCA. Change this directory to something more
explanatory. I often use *hostname*CA, replacing *hostname* with the name of the host on which
you are creating the CA.

```
puppy# mv demoCA puppyCA
```

Now you need to create a SSL .cnf file for your new CA. Copy the example, which is usually in /usr/share/ssl/openssl.cnf to a new file. Enter the following:

```
puppy# cp /usr/share/ssl/openssl.cnf /etc/ssl/certs/puppyCA/openssl.cnf
```

Then change the following line:

```
dir             = ./demoCA              # Where everything is kept
```

to the name and location of your new CA. In this case, enter the following:

```
dir             = /etc/ssl/certs/puppyCA     # Where everything is kept
```

Inside your new openssl.cnf you may want to adjust the defaults for your location. You may
also want to change the default_bits option in this file from 1028 to 2048 to increase the level of
encryption of your certificates, keeping in mind what I discussed earlier about key lengths.

Also inside your new puppyCA directory will be the CA's certificate file, in this case called cacert.pem. This is a particularly important file, and you need to do a couple of things to it. Copy the CA's certificate file to /etc/ssl/certs (or wherever you have placed your certificates). You will need to define the CA's certificate file to most of the applications you intend to enable TLS for, so this is a good place to put it. You will also need to create a *hash* of the CA's certificate file in your certs directory. A *hash* is used by OpenSSL to form an index of certificates in a directory and allows it to look up certificates. Use the command in Listing 3-4, replacing the cacert.pem filename with the name of your CA cert file.

Listing 3-4. *Hashing Your CA Cert*

```
puppy# ln -s cacert.pem `openssl x509 -noout -hash < cacert.pem`.0
```

■**Tip** If you have more than one CA certificate (for example, a self-created CA and one from a commercial CA), you need to have hashes of each certificate.

After creating your new CA, you can start to create and sign your own certificates.

To create your first certificate, you need to create a certificate request that will then be signed by the new CA. You will not create a certificate that is unencrypted and valid for one year and a private key.

The certificate you create consists of several items, but the most important for the purposes of using TLS is the *distinguished name*. This consists of a series of pieces of information you provide during the certificate creation process, including your geographical location, the hostname of the system, and an e-mail address. This information, in conjunction with the validity of the certificate, identifies a valid certificate.

One of the most important pieces of information you need to provide for the certificate's distinguished name is the common name, which for the purposes of TLS is generally the hostname of your system or, for example, the hostname of a Web site to secured with the certificate. If you want this to work with your Mail Transfer Agent (MTA), for example, then this needs to be the fully qualified domain name of the system for which the certificate is being created. In Listing 3-5, the common name will be puppy.yourdomain.com. So to create your first certificate, go to your certs directory and run the command in Listing 3-5.

Listing 3-5. *Creating a Certificate Request*

```
puppy# openssl req -config /etc/ssl/certs/puppyCA/openssl.cnf -new ➥
-keyout puppy.yourdomain.com.key.pem -out puppy.yourdomain.com.csr
Generating a 1024 bit RSA private key
..........++++++
.........++++++
writing new private key to 'puppy.yourdomain.com.key.pem'
Enter PEM pass phrase:
Verifying - Enter PEM pass phrase:
-----
```

```
You are about to be asked to enter information that will be incorporated
into your certificate request.
What you are about to enter is what is called a Distinguished Name or a DN.
There are quite a few fields but you can leave some blank
For some fields there will be a default value,
If you enter '.', the field will be left blank.
-----
Country Name (2 letter code) [AU]:
State or Province Name (full name) [New South Wales]:
Locality Name (eg, city) [Sydney]:
Organization Name (eg, company) [puppy.yourdomain.com]:
Organizational Unit Name (eg, section) []:
Common Name (eg, your name or your server's hostname) []:puppy.yourdomain.com
Email Address []:admin@puppy.yourdomain.com

Please enter the following 'extra' attributes
to be sent with your certificate request
A challenge password []:
An optional company name []:
```

The last two prompts are for extra information. The first is the provision of a challenge password. The challenge password is optionally used to authenticate the process of certificate revocation. Certificate revocation allows you to revoke the validity of a particular certificate, and I will cover that briefly shortly. In most cases you can simply leave this blank by hitting Enter. You can also leave the second optional company name blank.

In Listing 3-5 you could also have used the -nodes option to create the certificate and private key. This tells OpenSSL not to secure the certificate with a passphrase. This allows you to use the certificate for authenticating services such as the Simple Mail Transfer Protocol (SMTP), which have no scope to enter a passphrase, and a connection would simply hang waiting for the passphrase to be entered.

Listing 3-5 will create two files, puppy.yourdomain.com.key.pem and puppy.yourdomain.com.csr. These files consist of a key file for your system and a certificate request for your system. With these files, now the final stage of your certificate creation is to sign the certificate request using your new CA. In the event you used a commercial CA, this is the point at which you would submit the puppy.yourdomain.com.csr certificate request to the commercial CA for signing. Since you are using your own CA, you continue onto the signing stage on your local system. You can see this stage in Listing 3-6.

Listing 3-6. *Signing Your Certificate Request*

```
puppy# openssl ca -config /etc/ssl/certs/puppyCA/openssl.cnf ➡
-policy policy_anything -out puppy.yourdomain.com.cert.pem -infiles ➡
puppy.yourdomain.com.csr
Using configuration from /etc/ssl/certs/puppyCA/openssl.cnf
Enter pass phrase for /etc/ssl/certs/puppyCA/private/cakey.pem:
Check that the request matches the signature
Signature ok
```

```
Certificate Details:
        Serial Number: 1 (0x1)
        Validity
                Not Before: Jun 19 02:35:17 2004 GMT
                Not After : Jun 19 02:35:17 2005 GMT
        Subject:
                countryName             = AU
                stateOrProvinceName     = New South Wales
                localityName            = Sydney
                organizationName        = puppy.yourdomain.com
                commonName              = puppy.yourdomain.com
                emailAddress            = admin@puppy.yourdomain.com
        X509v3 extensions:
                X509v3 Basic Constraints:
                    CA:FALSE
                Netscape Comment:
                    OpenSSL Generated Certificate
        X509v3 Subject Key Identifier:
            7A:D2:26:2C:D2:19:79:F9:5E:51:53:2C:9E:89:1E:94:48:F5:DA:A2
        X509v3 Authority Key Identifier:
            keyid:50:27:56:92:74:26:FC:F1:3D:18:75:8D:49:D2:85:06:EA:15:C2:4E
            DirName:/C=AU/ST=New South Wales/L=Sydney/O=ABC Enterprises Pty
            Ltd/CN=James Turnbull/emailAddress=root@puppy.yourdomain.com
                    serial:00
Certificate is to be certified until Jun 19 02:35:17 2005 GMT (365 days)
Sign the certificate? [y/n]:y
1 out of 1 certificate requests certified, commit? [y/n]y
Write out database with 1 new entries
Data Base Updated
```

This will output a final file called puppy.yourdomain.com.cert.pem, which is your certificate file. You can now delete the certificate request file, puppy.yourdomain.com.csr.

■**Note** You can use whatever naming convention you like for your certificates, keys, and requests. I just use the previous convention because it represents a simple way to identify all of your SSL components and to what system they belong.

Finally, change the permissions of the puppyCA directory and of the files in the directory to ensure they are more secure.

```
puppy# cd /etc/ssl
puppy# chmod 0755 certs
puppy# cd certs
puppy# chmod -R 0400 *
```

Now you have your first set of keys and certificates and can use them to secure your TLS connections.

Revoking a Certificate

In the event a certificate is compromised, you need to be able to stop people using it for encryption and authentication. Or you may want to schedule a particular certificate to expire on a particular date. In either case, one of the ways of doing that is to revoke the certificate. You can tell your internal CA about certificate revocation by adding the revoked certificates to a special file called a *certificate revocation list* (CRL). Listing 3-7 shows how to generate an empty CRL using the openssl command. You will store your CRL file in the CA itself (in this case in the directory /etc/ssl/certs/puppyCA). The openssl.cnf file specifies the default CRL as crl.pem in the directory containing the CA. When prompted, enter the passphrase for the CA's key.

Listing 3-7. *Creating a CRL*

```
puppy# cd /etc/ssl/certs/puppyCA/
puppy# openssl ca -gencrl -out crl.pem -config /etc/ssl/certs/puppyCA/openssl.cnf
Using configuration from /etc/ssl/puppyCA/openssl.cnf
Enter pass phrase for /etc/ssl/puppyCA/private/cakey.pem:
```

CRLs are generally valid for one month only. If you want to create one for a longer period, use the option -crldays to specify the number of days for which you want the CRL to be valid.

Once you have your CRL file, you can revoke a certificate using the command in Listing 3-8.

Listing 3-8. *Revoking a Certificate*

```
puppy# openssl ca -revoke puppy.yourdomain.com.cert.pem \
-config /etc/ssl/puppyCA/openssl.cnf
Using configuration from /etc/ssl/puppyCA/openssl.cnf
Enter pass phrase for /etc/ssl/puppyCA/private/cakey.pem:
Revoking Certificate 01.
Data Base Updated
```

If you have specified a challenge password in your certificate when you created it, you will be prompted for that password before you are allowed to revoke the certificate. If you do not have the password, you cannot revoke the certificate.

After you have revoked a certificate, you should re-create the CRL from Listing 3-7. Now if you attempt to use the certificate you have just revoked, the connection will fail and you will get an error message indicating the certificate is revoked.

■**Caution** If you have something (an e-mail, for example) encrypted with that certificate and you revoke the certificate, you will not be unable to decrypt that information.

You also need to let your users and applications know that a certificate has been revoked. In the openssl.cnf file, it references the location of your CRL files and the default directory for them. By default this is the crl directory underneath the root directory of your CA and the file crl.pem. Place your CRL in this directory. All users should have read permissions to this area, but no users should have write permissions. You also need to create hashes of your CRLs as you have with your CA certificates. You can use the command in Listing 3-9 to do this replacing *yourcrl.pem* with the name of your CRL file.

Listing 3-9. *Creating a Hash of Your CRL File*

```
puppy# ln -s yourcrl.pem `openssl crl -hash -noout -in yourcrl.pem`.r0
```

Store your CRL hash in the `crl` directory also.

Testing Connections Using the openssl Command

The `openssl` command also allows you to test both client- and server-style connections using the `s_client` and `s_server` functions. The `s_client` function allows you to test connecting to a remote SSL-enabled service or daemon. This is useful for testing connections and diagnosing problems. Listing 3-10 shows an example of testing an MTA running SSL.

Listing 3-10. *Testing an MTA Using* `openssl s_client`

```
puppy$ openssl s_client -connect puppy.yourdomain.com:25 -starttls smtp
```

The `openssl s_client` command in Listing 3-10 will connect to port 25 and try to start TLS using the `-starttls` option. The `smtp` parameter tells OpenSSL that the target system being connected to is a SMTP server. At this stage the only other option available to use with the `-starttls` command is `pop3`, which you can use to connect to a POP3 server and do similar tests. The command will return the details of the connection, any certificates being used and attempt to ensure all certificates and CA root certificates are verified.

You can also connect to a non-MTA client such as an IMAP server. Enter the following:

```
puppy$ openssl s_client -connect puppy.yourdomain.com:993
```

You can provide some other options to the `openssl s_client` function. Table 3-2 shows the most useful of these options.

Table 3-2. `openssl s_client` *Options*

Option	Description
`-cert certname`	If you need to provide a certificate to the server, you can define it here. By default one is not provided.
`-key keyfile`	Provides a private key to use.
`-verify depth`	Specifies the verify depth to use that indicates the depth to which OpenSSL will check the certificate chain.
`-reconnect`	Performs five reconnects using the same session ID to ensure session caching is working.
`-showcerts`	Displays the entire certificate chain not just the server certificate.
`-state`	Prints the SSL session states.
`-debug`	Provides extra debugging information including a hex dump of all the SSL traffic.
`-msg`	Shows all the protocol messages if you are performing the debug hex dump.
`-ssl2, -ssl3, -tls1, -no_ssl2, -no_ssl3, -no_tls1`	Enables and disables the available SSL and TLS protocols.

The last option is extremely useful when diagnosing issues. Some older versions of SSL implemented with applications will not function when connected to with newer versions of the SSL/TLS protocols. For example, some servers require TLS to be disabled. Alternatively, others servers require that you connect to a remote server that allows only one type of SSL protocol.

The openssl s_server function allows you to set up a functioning SSL server that you can connect to and test certificates and keys. Listing 3-11 shows how to start a test SSL server.

Listing 3-11. *Starting a Test SSL Server Using the* openssl s_server *Function*

```
puppy$ openssl s_server -key puppy.yourdomain.com.key.pem \
-cert puppy.yourdomain.com.cert.pem
Using default temp DH parameters
Enter PEM pass phrase:
ACCEPT
```

The command in Listing 3-11 will start a server and bind it onto port 4433 and await input from a remote application. The choice of port 4433 is the default, and you can override that by specifying the -accept option and telling s_server to bind to another port. As you can see from Listing 3-11, I have specified a key and certificate for the function to use. If you specify a certificate or key that has a passphrase, you will be prompted to enter the required password. You can also define the location of the CA certificate file and a path to the CA files using the -CAfile option and the -CApath option, respectively.

You can also emulate a typical SSL Web server. To emulate a simple Web server, specify the -WWW option on the command line. Any HTML files requested will be sourced relative to the directory from which the openssl s_client function was started; in other words, a request for index.html will assume the file is located at ./index.html. You can also add the -www option to the command line to have the openssl command send back detailed status and response information in the form of a HTML document to the requesting Web server.

While in the session, if it was not been initiated with the -www or -WWW option, you can send commands to the client from within the server session. Table 3-3 details the commands available to you.

Table 3-3. *SSL Commands Within an* openssl s_server *Session*

Command	Description
P	Sends some plain text to the client. This should disconnect the client by causing a protocol violation.
q	Ends the current SSL connection but still accepts new connections.
Q	Ends the current SSL connection and ends the server.
r	Renegotiates the current SSL session.
R	Renegotiates the current SSL session and requests a client certificate from the client.
S	Prints the session cache status information.

■**Tip** A useful tool called SSLdump is available from `http://www.rtfm.com/ssldump/` and is designed to function like `tcpdump` except it focuses on SSL/TLS traffic. This is a good tool for diagnosing connection with SSL/TLS. If provided with keys and passwords, it can also decrypt the monitored traffic.

Stunnel

Stunnel provides an excellent example of how you can use OpenSSL to secure connections. Many daemons that rely on connections for their functionality, such as a `sendmail` daemon or the Apache Web server, either have built-in access controls and have encryption mechanisms such as OpenSSL or have the ability to be integrated with an access control or encryption mechanism. Using Sendmail as an example, I will show in Chapter 8 how to incorporate OpenSSL and Cyrus SASL to provide authenticated and encrypted message transfer using TLS and a variety of potential authentication mechanisms. These types of connections generally do not require any special additional security other than what is incorporated or integrated with them. The connections from applications and daemons do not offer any or not enough access controls or encryption that you need to consider securing them further. These types of connections (for example, a network-enabled `syslog` daemon like in Chapter 5) require some kind of wrapper to provide that access control and encryption. The ideal wrapper for those connections is provided with the combination of OpenSSL and Stunnel.

■**Note** Stunnel tunnels only TCP packets, not UDP packets. It also works only on connections that use single connections. A service such as FTP requires two connections (a control channel and a data connection) and therefore cannot be tunneled with Stunnel. If you do need to secure FTP, I will talk about that in Chapter 10. Otherwise, if you want to transfer files, you can use secure tools such as `sftp` or `scp`, which I talk about in the "scp and sftp" section later in this chapter.

Obviously, Stunnel relies on OpenSSL, and it needs to be installed before you install Stunnel. You may also have an existing installation of Stunnel of your system. Run the Stunnel command to check for its presence and version.

```
puppy# stunnel -version
stunnel 4.04 on i386-redhat-linux-gnu PTHREAD+LIBWRAP with ➥
OpenSSL 0.9.7a Feb 19 2003
```

If installed by your distribution, the Stunnel binary is usually located in `/usr/sbin` with its configuration located in the `/etc/stunnel` directory. Like OpenSSL, Stunnel is a package you should ensure is kept as up-to-date as possible either through your distribution's package management system or via upgrading a source package.

■**Tip** If you install Stunnel on Debian using `apt-get`, you should check the `README.Debian` file in the directory `/usr/share/doc/stunnel/` for further instructions on configuring Stunnel on Debian.

You can download Stunnel from `http://www.stunnel.org/download/stunnel/src/`. Unpack the source package, and change into the resulting directory. You need to `configure` Stunnel. Listing 3-12 shows a basic `configure`.

Listing 3-12. *Using the* `configure` *Script for Stunnel*

```
puppy$ ./configure --with-tcp-wrappers --prefix=/usr \
--sysconfdir=/etc --localstatedir=/
```

This `configure` script specifies Stunnel should enable support for TCP Wrappers and use an installation prefix of `/usr`, which would generally overwrite an existing installation of Stunnel if it has been installed as part of your base distribution. I have also specified the locations of the Stunnel configuration files as `/etc/` using the `--sysconfdir` option (with the install process creating a subdirectory called `stunnel`) and the state files to be located in `/var` using the `--localstatedir` option. Some other configuration options are available. Probably the most commonly used is the `--with-ssl` option, which allows you to specify the exact location of your SSL libraries if they are installed in a nonstandard location.

```
puppy$ ./configure --with-tcp-wrappers --prefix=/usr \
--sysconfdir=/etc   --localstatedir=/ --with-ssl=/usr/local/ssl
```

You can see any additional options available by running the `configure` script with the `--help` option.

Once you have configured Stunnel, you need to `make` and `make install` it. When you make Stunnel, you will be prompted to create a server certificate for the system on which you are installing it. Stunnel uses the standard OpenSSL `openssl` command to do this, and you should be able to easily follow the prompts to create the certificate.

The `stunnel` binary is designed to start Stunnel and by default looks for a file called `stunnel.conf` in `/etc/stunnel` to find its configuration information. Enter the following:

```
puppy# stunnel
```

You can override this by specifying a different filename on the command line. This can allow you to launch a number of individual Stunnel sessions using different configuration files (for example, if you want to use different certificates and keys for different connections), or you can place all your connections in one configuration file using the same certificate and key for all of them. Enter the following:

```
puppy# stunnel /etc/stunnel/another_config.conf
```

You can also use a couple of other options; `-sockets` prints the socket option defaults and `-help` prints the Stunnel help screen. By default running the `stunnel` binary will start Stunnel in daemon mode. Generally I recommend starting Stunnel via an `init` script. Stunnel includes a sample `init` script in the `tools` subdirectory in the source package. You can modify and copy it to use it for your system. I recommend at least adjusting the location of the default process identifier (PID) file in the top of the script, which generally points to an unsuitable location.

▓**Tip** Stunnel used to have command-line options available to it. This was changed in version 4 of Stunnel, and now all configuration is handled via the configuration file. Command-line options will no longer work!

The stunnel.conf file controls Stunnel. The source package comes with a sample configuration file called stunnel-sample.conf, which provides examples of a few options. It is installed into the directory you have specified as the configuration directory using the --sysconfdir option. The configuration file is divided into two types of options: global options and service options. The global options specify settings and parameters that affect how Stunnel runs. The service options allow you to define particular services, tunnels, and connections to Stunnel, which are the core functionality of the application. Listing 3-13 shows a simple stunnel.conf file.

Listing 3-13. *Sample* stunnel.conf *File*

```
cert = /etc/stunnel/stunnel.pem
pid = /var/run/stunnel/stunnel.pid
setuid = stunnel
setgid = stunnel

[imaps]
accept  = 993
connect = 143
```

The first two options specify the location of the default server certificate to use and the PID file for the Stunnel process. By default Stunnel starts in server mode and requires you specify a certificate to be used. You have already specified the certificate that was created by default when you installed Stunnel (as shown in Listing 3-13). The next two options specify the user and group that Stunnel will run as.

I recommend creating a user and group specifically for Stunnel. Enter the following:

```
puppy# groupadd stunnel
puppy# useradd -g stunnel -s /sbin/nologin -d /dev/null stunnel
```

You should also create the directory for the PID file and change its ownership and permissions to accommodate the new user and group. Enter the following:

```
puppy# mkdir /var/run/stunnel
puppy# chown stunnel:stunnel /var/run/stunnel
puppy# chmod 0755 /var/run/stunnel
```

In Listing 3-13 the third line shows a service option defined to Stunnel. This is a simple wrapper for IMAPS. First, you see the name of the service defined in brackets, [ ], in this case imaps. This is useful because Stunnel logs to syslog each service by this name, so you should define it here. Also, if you are using TCP Wrappers, this identifies the service for it.

Second, the next two lines specify what Stunnel is listening for and where it is going to send that connection. In this case, it is listening on port 993 (the accept statement) for an SSL-enabled client to try to connect to the IMAP server. It then diverts all traffic from that port to port 143 (the connect statement). As you have not included a hostname, Stunnel assumes you are listening on the local host and connecting to the local host. This is the simplest form of tunnel you can create, and now all traffic between port 993 and port 143 will be encrypted using SSL/TLS.

■**Note** A small note about firewalls and Stunnel. In Listing 3-13 I show Stunnel listening for connections on port 993 and redirecting all those connections to port 143 all on the local host. It is not necessary to have both ports open to the network in the `iptables` configuration. I would configure `iptables` so that it would allow connections to port 993 from whatever local and/or remote sources I required and restrict port 143 to connections only from local host or the local network depending on your requirements.

Let's look at some other types of service connections. Stunnel is also capable of listening on a local port and forwarding that port to another port on a remote system. Enter the following:

```
[rsmtp]
accept  = 1025
connect = kitten.yourdomain.com:25
```

In the service defined previously, `rsmtp`, Stunnel is listening on port 1025 on the local host and forwarding all traffic on that port with SSL/TLS enabled to port 25 on the remote system `kitten.yourdomain.com`. You can also do the reverse and listen to a port on a remote system and forward that encrypted to a port on the local host. Enter the following:

```
[rsmtp2]
accept = kitten.yourdomain.com:25
connect = 1025
```

This listens to any traffic emerging from port 25 on the remote system `kitten` and forwards it to the local port of 1025.

You can define some other global options to Stunnel (see Table 3-4).

Table 3-4. *Stunnel Configuration Global Options*

Option	Description
key = *file*	Specifies the certificate private key.
CApath = *path*	Defines the CA certificate directory.
CAfile = *file*	Defines the CA certificate file.
CRLpath = *path*	Defines the directory for CRLs.
CRLfile = *file*	Defines the CRL file.
verify = *level*	Specifies the level of certificate verification.
debug = *facility*.level	Specifies the logging facility and level. The level 7 or debug will produce the most logging output.
foreground = *yes* | *no*	Stays in the foreground and does not daemonize.
output = *file*	Specifies output logging to a file instead of `syslog`.
chroot = *directory*	Specifies the directory to which to `chroot` the stunnel process.
client = *yes* | *no*	Specifies enabling client mode.

The first five options allow you to specify the location of a variety of SSL infrastructure items, including a private key you can use (the default key created during the Stunnel installation contains the private key and public certificate concatenated in the stunnel.pem file) and the location of your CA and CRL paths and files.

■**Tip** Remember for Stunnel to properly use your CA and CRL files, they need to be hashed, and the hashes are located in the paths defined in the CApath and CRLpath options.

The verify option has three levels of peer certificate verification: Level 1, Level 2, and Level 3. Peer certificate verification indicates Stunnel will attempt to verify any certificates presented by remote connections to the local Stunnel daemon. Level 1 tells Stunnel to connect if no certificate is present; but if a certificate is presented, then verify it, and if a verified certificate does not exist, drop the connection. Level 2 requires a certificate be presented and verifies that certificate. The connection is again dropped if the verification fails. Level 3 also requires a certificate to be presented and verified, but additionally the presented certificate is verified against a store of local certificates to confirm the remote system is authorized to connect. By default Stunnel does not perform certificate verification.

By specifying the chroot option, you can run Stunnel inside a chroot jail. Listing 3-14 shows a portion of a stunnel.conf file with chroot enabled.

Listing 3-14. *Stunnel with* chroot *Enabled*

```
cert = /etc/stunnel/stunnel.pem
setuid = stunnel
setgid = stunnel
chroot = /var/run/stunnel
pid = /stunnel.pid
```

You leave the cert option alone because Stunnel loads any certificates or keys before starting the chroot jail. So, the location of any of your SSL infrastructure would remain relative to the normal root of the system. Stunnel will also start running as the defined user and group before "chrooting" itself. The chroot option itself specifies the new root of the chroot jail, in this case /var/run/stunnel. The next option, the location of the PID file, is specified relative to the chroot jail. So in Listing 3-13 previously, the PID is located in /var/run/stunnel.

The last option of Table 3-4. client, allows Stunnel to function as a client of a server. You can see how this works in Chapter 5 where I show how to use this function to secure a syslog-ng logging connections to allow using a central log server.

Finally for Stunnel configuration, the service functions can have some additional options defined (see Table 3-5).

Table 3-5. *Service-Level Options*

Option	Description
delay = yes | no	Delays the DNS lookup for connects.
local = IP Address	IP address to be used as source for remote connections.
protocol = protocol	A protocol to negotiate before SSL initialization, which includes cifs, nntp, pop3, and smtp.
TIMEOUTbusy = seconds	Number of seconds to wait for expected data.
TIMEOUTclose = seconds	Number of seconds to wait for close_notify.
TIMEOUTidle = seconds	Number of seconds to keep idle connection open.

The delay option tells Stunnel to delay any DNS lookups until a connection is made if it is set to yes. The protocol option allows Stunnel to negotiate a particular protocol before the SSL session is initialized. This is particularly useful with SMTP services where they are expecting some negotiation before initializing SSL. To provide negotiation for an SMTP service, set the protocol option to smtp like this:

```
protocol = smtp
```

The last options offer timeout values to help manage your connections. The TIMEOUTbusy option provides a timeout for a response from a remote connection, the TIMEOUTclose waits for a busy connection close notification, and the TIMEOUTidle provides a length in seconds for Stunnel to keep alive an idle connection. You will need to experiment with these values to determine what best suits the type and purpose of your connections.

Let's look at an example of how to use Stunnel. I will encapsulate a virtual network computing (VNC) session in a secure tunnel. VNC is remote-access software incorporating remote control, a screen viewer, and a Java-based viewer that can allow remote control from within a browser window. It is a popular tool for systems administrators and remote user access. Unfortunately, it is not very secure. Most of the information transmitted via VNC can be sniffed from the network, including usernames and passwords. It is especially dangerous to use VNC across an Internet connection. You will now look at securing VNC using Stunnel.

VNC comes in two portions: a client and a server. The server portion runs on the machine you want to connect to and the client portion on your local machine. For the purposes of this explanation, I will assume your server system is a Linux system and you are connecting to it using a desktop system running Linux. So, set up the server end of Stunnel and VNC. Listing 3-15 shows the server-side stunnel.conf file.

Listing 3-15. *Server-Side* stunnel.conf *Configuration for the VNC Tunnel*

```
cert = /etc/stunnel/stunnel.pem
chroot = /var/run/stunnel
pid = /stunnel.pid
setuid = stunnel
setgid = stunnel

[vnc]
accept  = puppy.yourdomain.net:5999
connect = 5901
```

I have already explained the first five options in Listing 3-15 in the previous section, but note that I have enabled the chroot function so that any connections to the system will be to the chroot jail. This may not be ideal if you are using the VNC connection for remote administration. The service function defines a service called vnc, which accepts connections on host puppy.yourdomain.com on port 5999 and then forwards those connections to the port 5901 on the local host. Now start Stunnel to continue. Enter the following:

```
puppy# stunnel
```

The port 5901 is where the VNC is going to be listening for connections. Let's start it now. Enter the following:

```
puppy# vncserver :1
```

If this is the first time you have started the VNC server, you will be prompted for a password that will be required by any clients to be able to connect to your system. The :1 part indicates the VNC server should start allocating displays to incoming clients from Display #1. Display #1 equates to port 5901, Display #2 equates to port 5902, and so on.

On the client the configuration is similar, as you can see from Listing 3-16.

Listing 3-16. *Client-Side* stunnel.conf *Configuration for the VNC Tunnel*

```
cert = /etc/stunnel/stunnel.pem
chroot = /var/run/stunnel
pid = /stunnel.pid
setuid = stunnel
setgid = stunnel

[vnc]
accept  = 5901
connect = puppy:yourdomain.com:5999
```

In this case, the defined service vnc is listening on the local host port 5901 for any connections and is configured to forward those connections onto the host puppy.yourdomain.com on port 5999. You also need to start Stunnel on your client system.

With Stunnel and VNC running on the server system, and Stunnel running on the client system, you can now try to connect to the server system securely using VNC over Stunnel. Enter the following:

```
kitten# vncviewer localhost:1
```

On the sample client system, kitten, you launch the vncviewer binary and request a connection to localhost:1, which means Display #1 on the local system. This display equates to the port 5901, which Stunnel is listening on and forwarding to port 5999 on the puppy.yourdomain.com system. From there the Stunnel daemon forwards the connection to port 5901 on puppy where the VNC server is waiting for connections. You will be prompted for a password, and then, if authenticated, you will then be connected to the puppy system via VNC.

You could also update this configuration as I will do with the syslog-ng secure connection demonstrated in Chapter 5. This allows connections from specific systems and from systems with valid certificates when you use the verify option in your stunnel.conf configuration file.

IPSec, VPNs, and Openswan

IPSec is short for *IP security* and represents a collection of extension standards and protocols for the original Internet protocol related to the secure exchange of IP packets. It was first developed for IPv6 and then made backward compatible for IPv4. At the core of this collection of standards is RFC2401.[12] A variety of products and tools use IPSec to secure connections between systems. IPSec works at a lower level than the SSL/TLS protocols. Whereas SSL operates between the network and application layers, IPSec encrypts traffic at the IP level and is capable of encapsulating the entire IP datagram (tunnel mode) or just the data portion of the IP datagram (transport mode). The tunnel mode allows the encapsulation of the entire original IP datagram with a new encrypted datagram. While the transport mode encrypts only the payload of the IP datagram, leaving the IP header unencrypted. With IPSec you could even layer a protocol like SSL/TLS over the top of a connection, further enhancing your security.

You will now look at the S/WAN[13] implementation of IPSec. S/WAN can be best described as a virtual private network (VPN) solution. S/WAN stands for *secure wide area network* and was an initiative by RSA Security both to develop a standard for the use of IPSec to build VPNs and to promote the deployment of Internet-based VPNs using IPSec. While S/WAN is no longer being actively developed, a number of open-source packages have developed out of the S/WAN project. One example of this is Openswan. Openswan is an open-source S/WAN IPSec implementation principally for Linux and other *nix operating systems (though it also supports Windows to some degree). It is available at `http://www.openswan.org/`. I will show you how to install Openswan and create a VPN tunnel between two subnets over the Internet using RSA encryption.[14] You can perform other tasks with Openswan, including a variety of functions aimed at providing remote VPN connectivity for roving users. See the Openswan wiki for further details.[15]

■**Tip** Additionally, you do not have to only connect two systems. You could also connect a system to a firewall or router. For example, instructions are available at `http://www.johnleach.co.uk/documents/freeswan-pix/freeswan-pix.html` that should provide a starting point for connections between a system and a Cisco PIX firewall using Openswan.

Openswan has a couple of prerequisites for installation. These are the GMP (GNU Multi-Precision) libraries from `http://swox.com/gmp/`. These should probably be installed by default on your distribution, but an up-to-date version is the safest. Openswan itself is available in two branches of code, which you can download from `http://www.openswan.org/code/`. The first, version 2, supports all current kernels up to version 2.6 and is the current path of development of the Openswan package. The second, version 1, supports only kernel versions 2.0, 2.2, and 2.4. It contains a fixed feature set that is somewhat limited compared to the version 2

---

12. `http://www.faqs.org/rfcs/rfc2401.html`

13. Pronounced "swan"

14. You can also use shared secrets and X.509 certificate authentication with Openswan.

15. `http://wiki.openswan.org/`

branch. Openswan version 1 is well tested and stable, but given the lack of support for 2.6 kernels it may have a limited life span as more people upgrade to more recent kernel versions. I recommend going with the version 2 branch for this reason to avoid a potentially complicated upgrade path as more distributions default to a version 2.6 kernel. For the purposes of this explanation, I will assume you are going to download the version 2 branch of Openswan.

■**Caution** Openswan works best with 2.4.*x* and 2.6.*x* kernels, and I recommend that all your systems run at least version 2.4. Indeed, not only is support unpredictable for older versions of 2.0 and 2.2 kernels (2.0 earlier than release 2.0.39 and 2.2 earlier than release 2.2.20), but these versions of the kernel also suffer from a variety of security issues.

Installing Openswan on kernel version 2.4 is not an easy task for a beginner because it involves working with your kernel. If this worries you or you are not comfortable with activities such as working with your kernel or recompiling your kernel, I recommend you avoid Openswan.

■**Tip** Red Hat Enterprise Linux 3-0 (AS, WS, and ES) and Red Hat Fedora Core 2 do not require a kernel recompilation; although they have version 2.4 kernels, they also have the IPSec modules from the version 2.6 kernel that is backward compatible.

Download Openswan from the Web site. If you are running Red Hat Enterprise 3 or Fedora Core 2–based systems, you are able to install Openswan via RPM. If you have downloaded the RPM, then install it using the following command and move onto the section talking about Openswan configuration. Enter the following:

```
puppy# rpm -Uvh openswan-version.as3.i386.rpm
```

If you have downloaded the source package, then unpack the package and change to the resulting directory.

For kernel version 2.4 systems, you need a clean copy of your kernel source either from your distribution or downloaded via http://www.kernel.org. The best method to ensure your installation goes smoothly is to compile your kernel from source prior to installing Openswan. Once you have done this, make a note of the location of your kernel source package and you can begin to install Openswan. If you require Network Address Translation Traversal (NAT-T) support, you need to patch the kernel source. NAT-T allows IPSec traffic to work with NAT devices such as routers and firewalls. From inside the Openswan source directory, run the following command replacing the */path/to/kernel/source* with the location of your kernel source, as follows. The last command make bzImage will make a new boot image for your system. You will need to install this new boot image; I recommend you reboot after this to test the new boot image.

```
puppy$ make nattpatch | (cd /path/to/kernel/source && patch -p1 && make bzImage)
```

Now you need to build the userland tools and the `ipsec.o` module. Listing 3-17 shows the required command.

Listing 3-17. *Building the Openswan Userland and the IPSec module for Kernel Version 2.4*

```
puppy$ make KERNELSRC=/path/to/kernel/source programs module
```

Again, replace */path/to/kernel/source* with the location of your kernel source. Once this is compiled, the last step is to install the tools and your new IPSec module. Use the command in Listing 3-18 for this.

Listing 3-18. *Building the Userland Tools and IPSec Module*

```
puppy# make KERNELSRC=/path/to/kernel/source install minstall
```

Remember to replace */path/to/kernel/source* with the location of your kernel source.

With version 2.6 kernels, Openswan relies on the built-in IPSec support and does not need to compile a module.

■**Note** This implies you have enabled the IPSec support in your 2.6 kernel. You also should be using at least version 2.6.4 of the kernel because earlier versions have IPSec bugs that can result in system crashes.

From inside the Openswan source directory, use the commands in Listing 3-19 to compile and install Openswan for version 2.6 kernels.

Listing 3-19. *Compiling and Installing Openswan for Version 2.6 kernels*

```
puppy$ make programs
puppy# make install
```

Once you have installed Openswan, you need to start it. Openswan comes with an `init` script called `ipsec` that is installed with your other `init` scripts when you run the `make install` process. I will start this script first (see Listing 3-20).

Listing 3-20. *Starting the `ipsec` Script*

```
puppy$ /etc/rc.d/init.d/ipsec start
ipsec_setup: Starting Openswan IPSec 2.1.3...
```

Next you should verify that all the required components for Openswan are available using the `verify` function, which is run using the `ipsec` command. The `ipsec` command provides an interface to Openswan and allows you to control it. Listing 3-21 shows the `ipsec` `verify` function.

Listing 3-21. *The* ipsec verify *Command*

```
puppy$ ipsec verify
Checking your system to see if IPSec got installed and started correctly:
Version check and ipsec on-path                              [OK]
Linux Openswan U2.1.3/K2.4.21-4.EL (native) (native)
Checking for IPSec support in kernel                         [OK]
Checking for RSA private key (/etc/ipsec.secrets)            [OK]
Checking that pluto is running                               [OK]
Checking for 'ip' command                                    [OK]
Checking for 'iptables' command                              [OK]
Checking for 'setkey' command for native IPSec stack support [OK]
Opportunistic Encryption DNS checks:
    Looking for TXT in forward dns zone: puppy.yourdomain.net  [MISSING]
    Does the machine have at least one non-private address?    [FAILED]
```

The results of the command in Listing 3-21 show that all Openswan and IPSec options are installed and started correctly. The last two options relate to using the Opportunistic Encryption (OE) DNS checks that rely on DNS TXT records to authenticate VPN connections. I will not cover this, but if you are interested in looking at OE, then see this quick start guide at http://www.freeswan.org/freeswan_snaps/CURRENT-SNAP/doc/quickstart.html. The guide is for Openswan's predecessor, FreeSWAN, but because Openswan is drawn from the FreeSWAN code base, configuration is nearly identical.

The ipsec.conf File

Openswan connections are controlled via the ipsec.conf file. You will need to have a copy of this file on both systems you want to connect with Openswan. Listing 3-22 shows an example of an ipsec.conf file.

Listing 3-22. *A Sample* ipsec.conf *File*

```
version 2.0

config setup
interfaces="ipsec0=eth0"
klipsdebug=none
plutodebug=all

conn puppy_to_kitten
auth=rsasig
left=203.28.11.1
leftsubnet=192.168.0.0/24
leftid=@puppy.yourdomain.net
leftrsasigkey=key
leftnexthop=%defaultroute
```

```
right=203.28.12.1
rightsubnet=192.168.1.0/24
rightid=@kitten.anotherdomain.com
rightrsasigkey=key
rightnexthop=%defaultroute

#Disable Opportunistic Encryption
include /etc/ipsec.d/examples/no_oe.conf
```

■**Tip** The `ipsec.conf` file is occasionally highly temperamental when parsed. If you have issues with the `ipsec init` script failing to start or connections failing to start because of parse errors in your configuration file, then make sure you have the file properly indented, no extra spaces or special characters are present, and all your sections starts in the first column. If all else fails, try to remove all comments and empty lines in your `ipsec.conf` file.

Let's go through the file line by line. The first option specifies the use of version 2.0 of Openswan. The rest of the `ipsec.conf` file is divided into sections. The sections currently available for Openswan are the `config` and `conn` sections. The `config` section handles the general configuration of Openswan, and the `conn` sections describe connections. You need to indent the parameters under each section with a tab; otherwise the configuration file will not be parsed correctly.

The section `config setup` refers to configuration options related to the startup of Openswan. I have used three options on this section. The first specifies a matched pair of virtual and physical interfaces to be used by Openswan for IPSec connections, in this case the virtual interface `ipsec0` matched with the physical interface `eth0`. You can specify more than one interface here. You can also use the variable `%defaultroute`, which finds the default route and uses the interface associated with that. Enter the following:

```
interfaces=%defaultroute
```

You will need at least two interfaces in both your systems for most VPN configurations. This is because you need one interface for each end of the VPN tunnel in addition to an interface or interfaces on each system for non-VPN tunnel traffic to use. For example, the simple system-to-system tunnel you are creating here requires two interfaces on each system: one to connect to the local internal network and the other to provide the interface for the VPN tunnel.

The last two options are both related to the output of debugging data. The `klipsdebug` option handles the debugging output from the IPSec module of the kernel, which can be outputted to `syslog` as part of Openswan's operation. I have set it to `none`, which will produce no debug output. The `plutodebug` option handles the output from the Pluto IKE daemon, which is started when you run the `ipsec init` script. The Pluto IKE (or IPSec Key Exchange) daemon handles the low-level key negotiation daemon. You can read more about Pluto (and its related control interface `whack`) via `man ipsec pluto`. Table 3-6 describes some other useful options.

Table 3-6. *Useful Configuration Options for* `ipsec.conf`

Option	Description
syslog=*facility*.*priority*	Specifies the facility and priority of syslog output.
dumpdir=*dir*	A directory for core dumps. Specifies an empty value to disallow core dumps.
plutoload=*conn*	Specifies connections to load into Pluto's internal database at startup. You can specify the %search variable that loads all connections with auto=route or route=add.
plutostart=*conn*	Specifies connections to be started by Pluto at startup. You can specify the %search variable that starts all connections with auto=route, route=add, and auto=start.
nat_traversal=*yes* | *no*	Allows or disallows NAT traversal.

The next section in Listing 3-22 is the conn section. Your VPN connections are defined in this section. I show a simple subnet-to-subnet connection that is the most basic form of VPN that Openswan is capable of generating. Specify the name of the connection puppy_to_kitten. The first option, auth, specifies how the connection will be authenticated. I have specified authentication using RSA encryption. The VPN connection you are creating has two sides, the left and right sides, with each side representing a system you want to connect. You will define the left side first. The first thing you define is the public IP address of the left system you are connecting from using the left parameter, in this case 203.28.11.1. You then specify the subnet of the left-side network using the leftsubnet parameter. This is the internal private subnet of the left-side network you are connecting to, which is 192.168.0.0/24. Next you define how the left-side connection is identified for authentication by specifying @puppy.yourdomain.com. This should generally be set to @*domain*.*name*.

Next you need to define your RSA signatures. You can do this using the ipsec newhostkey command. On each system you want to connect run the following command:

```
puppy# ipsec newhostkey --bits 2192 --hostname puppy.yourdomain.com
kittten# ipsec newhostkey --bits 2192 --hostname kitten.anotherdomain.com
```

This will create a file /etc/ipsec.secrets on each system, which contains a public and private host key for each system. I have specified a bit size of 2192 and the hostname of the system for which you are generating the key.

Once you have the keys, you need to add the public portion of the keys to the leftrsasigkey and rightrsasigkey parameters on your ipsec.conf file. You can display the public portion of the host key using the command in Listing 3-23.

Listing 3-23. *Display the Public-Key Portion using the IPSec* showhostkey *Command*

```
puppy# ipsec --showhostkey --left
# RSA 2192 bits    puppy.yourdomain.com    Thu Jun 24 23:53:33 2004
leftrsasigkey=0sAQNkjDGFsIH6Kx1EhOE79BFxXwJtZiSJFOohvZvhiPtNaWobvSbSmhqKAd+fYCInEbrp
zkOs+qop7vtQB/JpwxHF52UwdUQL92OEaMOPbM4dJAqaf/KkXxMaWmrwWforIx3WcppBwX7nuHfCx6f5FKdn
2FcD92yF9XarlbET726WHJnZ1RidwNq8WtA7Wu84YSmH59OL4v+bMWgO1R5nM4COtN4SU/NcRIrB5OaWEPsc
nbSjNuchogYNwTvj7jGmQSnnb/DC7Ay4rpaZY8/HCeaiHKCTa+ZGsXEem6/7TSZmpkkx2sE4DxeshaPWHTDr
VHh3mMkGqLnAXev5JgJpkyanKifvPHa73jZ3rHauCpgm/Eh
```

Lastly you need to specify a next hop for the VPN connection. This can be the IP address of the next hop of that system, or you can use the variable %defaultroute to specify the next hop using the default route of the system.

You then need to setup the right-side connection. Repeat the process of configuring the right side using the appropriate IP addresses, subnets, next hop, and the correct public key (obtained on the remote system with the ipsec showhostkey --right command).

Some other options are available in your conn sections, which can be useful (see Table 3-7).

Table 3-7. *Additional* ipsec.conf conn *Options*

Option	Description
type=*type*	The type of connection to be made, which defaults to tunnel but can also include transport, passthrough, drop, and reject. See the man page for more details.
auto=*option*	This option governs behavior of the connection at startup. For example, use add to add the connection to the Pluto database at startup and start to add and start the connection
authby=*auth_mech*	The authentication method that can include secret for shared secrets and rsasig for RSA.

The last line of the ipsec.conf file in Listing 3-22 shows an include statement that allows additional files to be included into the ipsec.conf file. In this case I have included an additional file no_oe.conf that disables using OE. But you can also include other files containing any other Openswan configuration items or connections.

Now I have configured the ipsec.conf file I need to ensure it is present on both systems. I recommend using the scp command to copy the configuration files. Listing 3-24 shows how to do this.

Listing 3-24. *Copying the* ipsec.conf *File to Another System*

```
puppy# scp ipsec.conf root@kitten.anotherdomain.com:/etc/ipsec.conf
```

Firewalling for Openswan and IPSec

After configuring IPSec with Openswan, you need to ensure the firewall configuration allows connections to pass through. To do this, you need to enable TCP protocol 50, the Encapsulating Security Payload (which authenticates and encrypts VPN traffic), to and from the systems you want to connect in your firewall configuration. You need to do this on both of the systems you are connecting, as well as on any network devices such as firewalls or routers between the two systems. The emphasis on the word *protocol* is important. You are not enabling a port here. You are enabling the ESP encryption and authentication protocol that is not bound to a particular port (using the iptables option -p).[16] You also need to enable UDP port 500 between the systems and other devices for the Internet Key Exchange (IKE), which handles connection and key negotiation. Listing 3-25 shows some simple iptables rules for this.

---

16. For more information, see Chapter 2.

Listing 3-25. `iptables` *Rules for Openswan and IPSec*

```
iptables -A INPUT  -p 50 -j ACCEPT
iptables -A OUTPUT -p 50 -j ACCEPT
iptables -A INPUT  -p udp --sport 500 --dport 500 -j ACCEPT
iptables -A OUTPUT -p udp --sport 500 --dport 500 -j ACCEPT
```

I recommend you further adjust these rules to allow only protocol 50 and UDP port 500 traffic from specific gateways (in other words, only from those systems to which you want to connect). This is the basic configuration required for almost all Openswan configurations. Some additional configurations also require the Authentication Header (AH) protocol, which handles packet authentication. If you do need the AH protocol, then you will need to also enable protocol 51. The Openswan and IPSec documentation clearly indicates in what circumstances this protocol is also required. Enter the following:

```
iptables -A INPUT  -p 51 -j ACCEPT
iptables -A OUTPUT -p 51 -j ACCEPT
```

The ipsec Command

With copies of the `ipsec.conf` file on both systems, you want to connect, and with the firewalls rules right, you can now attempt to start the VPN tunnel. You use the `ipsec auto` command to start a VPN tunnel. Enter the following:

```
puppy# ipsec auto --up puppy_to_kitten
102 "puppy_to_kitten" #1: STATE_MAIN_I1: initiate
104 "puppy_to_kitten" #1: STATE_MAIN_I2: from STATE_MAIN_I1; sent MI2, expecting MR2
106 "puppy_to_kitten" #1: STATE_MAIN_I3: from STATE_MAIN_I2; sent MI3, expecting MR3
004 "puppy_to_kitten" #1: STATE_MAIN_I4: ISAKMP SA established
110 "puppy_to_kitten" #2: STATE_QUICK_I1: initiate
004 "puppy_to_kitten" #2: STATE_QUICK_I2: sent QI2, IPSec SA established
```

You only need to start the connection from one system. Once you have run this command, your IPSec tunnel should be up and connected. You can also use the `ipsec auto` command to shut down the connection. Enter the following:

```
puppy# ipsec auto --down puppy_to_kitten
```

The `ipsec` command comes with a variety of other useful functions. One of which is `barf`, which outputs a considerable quantity of debugging and logging data that is often useful for assisting in resolving issues and problems with Openswan. Listing 3-26 shows how to run `barf`.

Listing 3-26. *Debugging Openswan*

```
puppy# ipsec barf > barf.log
```

Here I have directed the `barf` output to a file. Another useful command if you have changed your IPSec configuration is the `ipsec setup` command, which you can use to stop and restart IPSec. Enter the following:

```
puppy# ipsec setup --stop
puppy# ipsec setup --start
```

You can see details of the other ipsec commands by entering the following:

```
puppy$ ipsec --help
```

inetd and xinetd-Based Connections

In the previous section you looked at securing persistent connections in the form of always active applications such as a mail server or a network-enabled syslog daemon. But other types of connections exist also, most notably on-demand connections such as those initiated and controlled by the inetd or xinetd daemons (sometimes called *master* daemons). As a result of the number of systems that use inetd and xinetd, it is worth taking a brief look at these daemons and decide whether you need to run them. These daemons monitor the ports defined to them, and if they receive a connection on that port, then the daemons start the required application. The inetd/xinetd daemons can also provide access control (including using TCP Wrappers) and additional logging while they manage the applications and connections. In contrast, most persistent connections are started using init scripts and consist of running a program and placing it in the background or in daemon mode. The daemon handles binding itself to required ports and generally handles its own access controls and logging. The Sendmail daemon, for example, binds itself to port 25, has the ability to control who connects to it, and logs to the maillog log file.

The original daemon used on a lot of Linux systems was called inetd. These days many Linux distributions—Red Hat, for example—use a more secure and advanced version called xinetd[17] that added better access controls, some protection from Denial of Service attacks, and considerable further sophistication of potential configuration. Debian, though, still uses inetd. The origin of inetd/xinetd-style functionality comes from a requirement to have a central server to manage and control a variety of independent networked services. Some of the services that inetd/xinetd traditionally handle are functions such as echo, chargen, and finger. Debian also uses inetd by default to start telnet, smtp, and ftp. I recommend you disable whichever of these your system uses and instead rely on individual init scripts to start those services, daemons, and applications you require.

I recommend you do this for two reasons. The first is that most of the services that inetd/xinetd controls are often unnecessary for many systems and can even pose a security risk to your system. Review all the services started by inetd/xinetd carefully, but I suggest that most of them are either not required or could be started equally securely using an init script. One of the elements of good security is operating with the principle of minimalism in mind. So stop and disable any service or application that is not 100 percent required for the function of your secured system.

The second reason I recommend you disable inetd/xinetd is because both of these daemons pose a security risk to your system in their own rights. This risk is both in the many security vulnerabilities discovered in both daemons but also because it adds another potential point of security failure. Indeed, many attackers can often use your inetd/xinetd daemon to install or prime a backdoor on your system by penetrating the daemon. Any potential security

---

17. http://www.xinetd.org/

value-add or enhancement offered by either inetd or xinetd is outweighed by the additional exposure created by using these daemons on your system.

To remove initd or xinetd, you need to first check whether init or xinetd is running on your system and, if so, which of the daemons you are using. Listing 3-27 shows an easy way of doing this.

Listing 3-27. *Finding Out if Either* inetd *or* xinetd *Are Running*

```
puppy$ ps -A | grep 'xinetd\|inetd'
2106 ?        00:00:00 xinetd
```

The inetd/xinetd daemon is usually started by an init script when your system starts. The inetd daemon is controlled by the inetd.conf file and xinetd by the xinetd.conf file, both located in /etc. With the inetd daemon, all the services and the programs initiated by it are defined solely in the inetd.conf file, and the xinetd.conf file references a further directory, xinetd.d, which contains a collection of files, each of which contains configuration controlling a particular service or application.

■**Tip** Make sure you have added a means of starting any applications that inetd or xinetd currently handle that you continue to want to run on your system before proceeding.

Once you know which daemon is running, then stop that daemon. To stop either inetd or xinetd, the easiest way is to run the init script that starts the daemon and instruct it to stop the daemon instead. You could also simply kill the process. Remember that this will generally also kill any services that the daemons are running. Enter the following:

```
puppy$ /etc/rc.d/init.d/xinetd stop
```

On a Debian system you can use the invoke-rc.d command. Enter the following:

```
kitten$ invoke-rc.d inetd stop
```

Now you need to stop inetd/xinetd from starting when your system runs. On a Red Hat system, simply use the chkconfig command.

```
puppy$ chkconfig --del xinetd
```

And on a Debian system, use the update-rc.d command. Enter the following:

```
kitten$ update-rc.d -f inetd remove
```

With the service stopped, you should neaten your system by deleting the associated inetd/xinetd files. Listing 3-28 shows the files you need to remove for inetd, assuming a Debian-style system.

Listing 3-28. *Removing the* inetd *Files*

```
kitten# rm -f /etc/init.d/inetd
kitten# rm -f /etc/inetd.conf
```

And for `xinetd`, Listing 3-29 shows the files you need to remove assuming a Red Hat–style or Mandrake-style system.

Listing 3-29. *Removing the* `xinetd` *Files*

```
puppy# rm -f /etc/rc.d/init.d/xinetd
puppy# rm -f /etc/xinetd/conf
puppy# rm -fr /etc/xinetd.d
```

It is probably a good idea at this point to restart your system and test what connections are open using the `ps -A` and `netstat -a` commands to confirm all the services have been stopped.

You can also remove the `inetd` and `xinetd` packages from your system using your chosen package management tool. This will guarantee the daemons cannot be used to penetrate or compromise your system.

■**Note** As I have recommended removing `inet.d` and `xinet.d` from your system, this chapter will not cover the use of TCP Wrappers.

Remote Administration

Most system administrators manage systems to which they need to remotely connect. Sometimes these connections are made over the Internet to a remote location. In the past, the only tools available to administer your systems were `telnet`, `ftp` and the so-called r-tools, `rcp`, `rlogin`, and `rsh`. These tools are highly insecure. If you are still using any of these tools to administer your systems—STOP NOW. These tools transmit all their information, including any passwords you input, in clear text with no encryption. Anybody sniffing on your network or monitoring devices your traffic passes through on the Internet can grab this information and use it to penetrate your systems. The r-tools would appear to offer marginal improvement on straight `telnet` by using the `rhosts` file to check that the user and source machine for the connection is valid and able to sign on. In reality this provides little or no comfort these days because it is incredibly simple to "spoof" a system to believe a connection is coming from a valid system.

I will cover `SSH`, as implemented in the `OpenSSH` package, to replace these clear-text tools and additionally secure some of the other tools you can use for remote administration such as remote X-Windows, Webmin, and VNC. `SSH` stands for *Secure Shell* and is a command interface and protocol for establishing secure connections between systems. I will cover the free implementation called OpenSSH.

■**Tip** If you want to purchase a solution or feel more comfortable with a commercial product, I recommend SSH Tectia from `http://www.ssh.com/`.

OpenSSH is not a single tool but rather a suite of tools including ssh, which replaces telnet and rlogin; scp, which replaces rcp; and sftp, a secure replacement for ftp. It also contains sshd, which is a SSH server, and ssh-agent, ssh-keygen, and ssh-add, which handle key generation and management for OpenSSH. It is also capable of performing a variety of secure tunneling functions, has a number of different forms of encryption, and uses a number of authentication methods.

You can find OpenSSH at http://www.openssh.com/, and you can download it from a number of FTP and HTTP mirrors listed at http://www.openssh.com/portable.html. Most Linux distributions come with OpenSSH installed already, though, often an older version is present; you should consider upgrading to the most recent version to ensure you are protected against any vulnerabilities that have been discovered in OpenSSH. You can check if your system has OpenSSH installed on Red Hat or Mandrake by running the following command:

```
puppy# rpm -q openssh
openssh-3-6.1p2-18
```

On Debian, run the following:

```
kitten$ dpkg --list openssh*
```

You can check the version of OpenSSH installed by entering the following command:

```
puppy$ ssh -V
```

This will show you the version, as follows:

```
OpenSSH_3-6.1p2, SSH protocols 1.5/2.0, OpenSSL 0x0090701f
```

I recommend downloading the latest version of OpenSSH and compiling it from source. You will need a couple of prerequisites before installing OpenSSH. You will need Zlib at least version 1.1.4 and OpenSSL version 0.9.6 or greater. Unpack the source package of OpenSSH, and change into the resulting directory. You need to configure the package first; I list some of the possible configure options in Table 3-8.

Table 3-8. *OpenSSH* configure *Options*

Option	Description
--prefix=*prefix*	Sets the prefix for the OpenSSH binaries and files
--with-pam	Enables PAM
--with-ssl-dir=*path*	Sets the location of the OpenSSL files
--with-kerberos5=*path*	Enables Kerberos 5 support
--with-md5-passwords	Enables MD5 passwords

The options in Table 3-8 are mostly self-explanatory. Listing 3-30 shows my configure statement that uses the prefix of /usr, which will override your existing OpenSSH installation. This way you do not need to remove any RPMs or packages and worry about any complex dependency chains if OpenSSH is already installed. I have also enabled PAM.

Listing 3-30. *OpenSSH* configure *Statement*

```
puppy$ ./configure --prefix=/usr --with-pam
```

You now need to make and install the OpenSSH package. Enter the following:

```
puppy# make && make install
```

ssh

Now that you have installed OpenSSH, you will learn about the functionality of the ssh command, which is the core of the OpenSSH suite. At its base level, the ssh command acts as a replacement for telnet and rlogin, but it is capable of much more than just that. The first and probably most useful task you can perform with ssh is connect to another system. Listing 3-31 shows the ssh command at work.

■Note The remote system needs to have sshd running and have TCP port 22 open.

Listing 3-31. *Connecting to Another System Using* ssh

```
puppy$ ssh -l bob kitten
bob@kitten's password:
```

The command in Listing 3-31 shows the simplest use of ssh by connecting the user bob (as indicated by the use of the -l option to specify a particular user, or you can use the structure *user@remote.host*) to the remote server kitten via the default SSH port of 22. If you do not specify a user, then it will try to use the same username you are currently signed onto as on the local system. Once connected, ssh then prompts the connecting user for the shell password of the user bob on the server kitten. If the correct password is inputted, then you will have an active shell session on that remote system. Mostly important, the password you have sent to the remote system will be encrypted and therefore considerably harder for an attacker to sniff off your network and use to aid an attack.

You can use some additional command-line parameters with ssh (see Table 3-9).

Table 3-9. *Additional* ssh *Command-Line Options*

Option	Description
-a	Disables forwarding of the authentication agent connection.
-A	Enables forwarding of the authentication agent connection.
-i *identity*	Selects a file with a particular private key.
-F *configfile*	Specifies an alternative configuration file.
-o *option*	Gives options in the format used in the configuration file.
-p *port*	Port to connect to on the remote host.
-C	Requests compression of all data.

(Continues)

Table 3-9. *Continued*

Option	Description
-L *port:host:hostport*	Specifies that the given port on the local (client) host is to be forwarded to the given host and port on the remote side.
-R *port:host:hostport*	Specifies that the given port on the remote (server) host is to be forwarded to the given host and port on the local side.
-2	Forces ssh to try protocol version 2 only.
-4	Forces ssh to use IPv4 addresses only.
-6	Forces ssh to use IPv6 addresses only.
-x	Disables X11 Forwarding.
-X	Enables X11 Forwarding.
-q	Quiet mode.
-v	Verbose mode.

The -a and -A options control the use of Agent Forwarding, which I will talk about shortly when I discuss ssh-agent. The -i option allows you specify a particular private key to use with this connection, and the -F option allows you to specify an alternative configuration file from the default .ssh/ssh_config. The -o option allows you to specify options that do not have a command-line equivalent from the configuration file on the command line (for example, -o 'ForwardAgent no'). You can override the port you want to connect to on the remote system (defaults to port 22) with the -p option. The -C option enables ssh compression, which can greatly enhance performance on your connection.

The -L and -R options allow you to perform port forwarding or tunneling over SSH. I talk about port forwarding in the "Port Forwarding with OpenSSH" section.

The -2 option forces ssh to use only version 2 of the SSH protocol. The -4 and -6 options force ssh to use either IP version 4 or IP version 6. The -x and -X option either disables or enables X11 Forwarding. I talk about X11 Forwarding in the "Forwarding X with OpenSSH" section. The last two options control the verbosity of the ssh program.

Listing 3-31 showed a simple connection to a remote system, but there is more to this process that is immediately apparent here. First, the connection to the remote system can rely on more than just authentication via password. ssh is capable of three types of authentication. The first will be familiar to most people who have used the r-tools and is a form of host-based authentication. This is disabled by default because it suffers from the same security issues I discussed with the use of telnet and the like. Second, you have public-key authentication, which utilizes RSA or DSA encryption to verify authenticity. The last form of authentication is what you saw previously, an encrypted password sent to the remote system. The authentication methods are tried in this sequence, and ssh makes the connection with the first authentication method that is successful. You can also require more than one form of authentication (in other words, public-key authentication and password authentication).

■**Note** OpenSSH has two versions of the SSH protocol it can use, 1 and 2. I will focus on using version 2 of the SSH protocol because it is considerably more secure and reliable than version 1. In the "Configuring ssh and sshd" section, I will show you how to disable version 1 entirely. In the last paragraph where I discussed different authentication methods, these were the methods that work with version 2 only.

Let's look at each form of authentication. You will ignore the first simple host-based authentication as insecure (and thus disabled), and I have pretty much covered the details of the encrypted password-based authentication. The authentication based on public-key encryption requires some more explanation, though. The authentication can be based on RSA or DSA encryption. When you first install OpenSSH, it will create a set of public and private keys for each of the available sets of encryption types: RSA1, RSA, and DSA. These keys are usually stored in /etc/ssh. These are called *host keys* and do not have a passphrase.

But let's look at creating your own public-private key combination. OpenSSH comes with a command to assist in doing this called ssh-keygen. Listing 3-32 shows this command.

Listing 3-32. *Running* ssh-keygen

```
puppy# ssh-keygen -t rsa
Generating public/private dsa key pair.
Enter file in which to save the key (/root/.ssh/id_dsa):
Enter passphrase (empty for no passphrase):
Enter same passphrase again:
Your identification has been saved in /root/.ssh/id_dsa.
Your public key has been saved in /root/.ssh/id_dsa.pub.
The key fingerprint is:
be:0f:b9:41:37:ad:19:24:e9:6a:cc:61:ca:36:86:23 root@puppy
```

Listing 3-32 shows the creation of a RSA public and private key. The public key is stored in /root/.ssh/id_dsa.pub, and the private key is stored in /root/.ssh/id_dsa. The keys are normally stored in a directory called .ssh underneath the home directory of the user creating the keys; but for this example, you created these keys as the root user, so they have been created underneath the root directory. You indicated to ssh-keygen what type of key you would like to generate using the -t option. You should add a good passphrase to the key utilizing the same standards you would use to set your system passwords. You can also create a public-key pair without a password by hitting Enter on the passphrase prompt. This is obviously less secure than having a passphrase, but it allows you to use OpenSSH commands in cron jobs and scripts without needing interactive intervention.

A few other useful options are available to the ssh-keygen command (see Table 3-10).

Table 3-10. *Additional* ssh-keygen *Command-Line Options*

Option	Description
-b *bits*	Number of bits in the key that defaults to 1024.
-f *keyfile*	Specifies a particular key file.
-e	Exports a specified keyfile (using the -f option) in SECSH format to stdout.
-i	Imports a SECSH or SSH2 key file and outputs an OpenSSH-compatible file to stdout.
-l	Shows the fingerprint of a specified keyfile.
-t *type*	Specifies the type of key generated, which can include rsa1, rsa, and dsa.
-y	Reads in a specified private key file and outputs an OpenSSH public-key file to stdout.

The -b option allows you specify the number of bits. It defaults to 1024, and I recommend not using a size smaller than that. The -f option is designed to be used in conjunction with other options such as -y, -e, or -i to specify a particular key file. The -e and -i options allow the export and import of keys into OpenSSH, respectively. The imported keys need to be in SSH2 or SECSH format.[18] The -l option displays the fingerprint of a particular key specified by the -f option. You can use the -t option to specify what type of encryption to use to create the key. By default ssh-keygen uses RSA encryption, but you can specify DSA encryption using the option dsa. I recommend you use RSA. Using the last option, -y, you can input an OpenSSH private key and output the equivalent public key. You can use other options, which you can find in the ssh-keygen man page.

■**Note** In the last paragraph I recommend using RSA encryption over DSA encryption. This is a somewhat subjective judgment; considerably debate takes place in cryptography circles about which is more secure.[19] That debate falls out of the scope of this book, but at this point until more information is available I recommend going with the better-documented and better-researched cipher system, RSA. But as previously mentioned, you should be using SSH version 2 only.

So, you have keys on your local system, either created when you installed OpenSSH or created using the ssh-keygen tool. Next you need to add your public key to the remote systems lists of suitable keys. OpenSSH maintains a register of the public keys it will accept connections from in two places. The first is on a per-user basis in the file *homedirectory*/.ssh/authorized_keys. The second is a centralized register in the file /etc/ssh/authorized_keys. In either of these files, each key should be on a single line in the file. When a user logs into the server, the remote ssh command tells the local sshd server what key pair it will use; this key is checked against the central authorized_keys file and then the user's authorized_keys file to see if the key is permitted. It then sends the user a challenge, encrypted with the specified

---

18. http://www.openssh.org/txt/draft-ietf-secsh-publickeyfile-02.txt

19. If you are interested in the debate, see http://www.rsasecurity.com/rsalabs/node.asp?id=2240.

public key, which can be decrypted only by the proper private key. If the ssh command is able to decrypt it, then the decrypted challenge is sent back to the remote sshd server and the connection is authenticated. This happens all without the private key being disclosed across the network or to the remote server.

Once you have authenticated to a remote system, you have both the option of signing onto a shell session on the remote system, but you can also replicate the functionality of the rsh, or remote shell command shell, which allows you to remotely execute commands on another system. Listing 3-33 shows a remote command execution using ssh.

Listing 3-33. *Remote Command Execution Using* ssh

```
puppy$ ssh bob@kittten.yourdomain.com "ls -l /etc/ssh"
bob@kitten's password:
total 124
-rw-------    1 root     root        88039 Sep 18  2003 moduli
-rw-r--r--    1 root     root         1163 Jun  6 02:56 ssh_config
```

scp and sftp

As mentioned earlier, OpenSSH is also capable of replicating the functionality of rcp and ftp. The rcp command allows you to copy a file to a remote system from the command line. The OpenSSH equivalent of rcp is called scp, and Listing 3-34 shows scp working.

Listing 3-34. *Using* scp *for Remote Copy*

```
puppy$ scp /root/example.txt bob@kitten:/root
root@kitten's password:
example.txt      100% |*****************************|  4711        00:00
```

Listing 3-34 shows sending via scp the file example.txt from the directory /root on the local host to the /root directory on the remote system kitten. To do this, I signed on as the user bob at kitten. You can send one file to multiple hosts as well by adding additional user@remote.host:*/path/to/destination* statements to the scp command. You can use a few additional options with the scp command (see Table 3-11).

Table 3-11. scp *Command-Line Options*

Option	Description
-p	Preserves modification times, access times, and modes from the original file
-r	Recursively copies entire directories
-v	Enables verbose mode
-B	Enables batch mod
-i	Specifies a particular private key
-q	Disables the progress meter
-C	Enables ssh compression

The first option, -p, tells scp to preserve the details including the modification time and permissions of the original file and give those details to the copied file. If you specify the -r option with a directory when using the scp command, then scp will recursively copy the entire directory. The -v option enables verbose logging.

The -B option allows you to send files in batch mode, which is designed to allow you send files without scp needing to prompt for passwords. You achieve this by using public-key encryption with public keys that do not have a passphrase, as discussed in the "ssh-agent and Agent Forwarding" section. So you need to ensure the public key of the sending system is added to the authorized_keys file on the target system. Then when you use scp in batch mode (for example, in a cron job), you are not prompted for a password and the cron job requires no interactive input. Listing 3-35 shows this at work in a cron entry.

Listing 3-35. *Using* scp *in Batch Mode in a* crontab *Entry*

```
15 * * * * /usr/bin/scp -q -i /root/.ssh/nopasskitten_id ➥
-B /home/bob/example.txt bob@kitten:/home/bob/recvfile.txt
```

Listing 3-35 shows a crontab entry sending a file every hour to a remote server in batch mode. I have also used the -i option to specify a particular private key to use. This allows you to have a separate set of keys for your batch transactions without a passphrase and another key for purposes such as shell access.

Of the last two options, -q disables the progress meter that you can see in Listing 3-34, and -C enables ssh compression.

The sftp command provides a secure version of the ftp command. It works in nearly identical format to a standard FTP session. You enable the sftp server in the sshd_config file, and it is started as a subsystem of the sshd daemon. You will see the configuration for this in the "Configuring ssh and sshd" section a little later. Listing 3-36 shows starting an sftp connection to a remote system.

Listing 3-36. *Initiating an* sftp *Connection and an* sftp *Session*

```
puppy$ sftp -C bob@kitten
Connecting to kitten...
bob@kitten's password:
sftp> cd /root
sftp> put example.txt
Uploading example.txt to /root/example.txt
sftp> exit
```

As you can see from Listing 3-36 you can also use the -C option to enable ssh compression. You can also see that you can use the standard FTP commands to perform functions within the sftp connection. Additionally, you can use the -b option to specify a file containing a series of commands that you can input in batch mode and the -v option to increase the logging level.

ssh-agent and Agent Forwarding

OpenSSH also comes with a set of tools for managing and caching keys. The primary tool I will use in this example is called `ssh-agent`. It runs as a daemon and allows you to cache keys in RAM so that you can use the keys for a variety of purposes, such as in a script or in an automated process, and have to enter only the passphrase for the key once. You first need to start the `ssh-agent` daemon and then add keys to it using an additional tool called `ssh-add`.

This may seem insecure to you. What is to stop the user `bob` from using a key the `root` user has added to the `ssh-agent` daemon? Well, the `ssh-agent` daemon runs on a per-user basis. Thus, if the `root` user started an `ssh-agent` and added keys to it, and then user `bob` started another `ssh-agent` and added keys to it, these would be separate processes and the keys in one process are not accessible in the other. Additionally, the `ssh-agent` is accessible only locally—through a local socket. It is not directly connected to your network (though you can read about authentication agent forwarding next). Listing 3-37 shows you how to start `ssh-agent`.

Listing 3-37. *Starting the* `ssh-agent` *Process*

```
puppy$ ssh-agent
SSH_AUTH_SOCK=/tmp/ssh-UITsiD7123/agent.7123; export SSH_AUTH_SOCK;
SSH_AGENT_PID=7124; export SSH_AGENT_PID;
echo Agent pid 7124;
```

This starts the `ssh-agent` daemon and forks it into the background. You will note it sends an output of some commands to `stdout`. These are environment variables that need to be set in order for you to use `ssh-agent`. The first, `SSH_AUTH_SOCK`, indicates the location of the local socket `ssh-agent` uses. The second is `SSH_AGENT_PID`, which indicates the process ID of `ssh-agent` that is being started. The process of the commands being written out to `stdout` does not mean the environment variables are being set. You need to cut and paste the commands into the shell, or you can run the `ssh-agent` encapsulated in the `eval` function, which will set all of the environment variables. Enter the following:

```
puppy$ eval `ssh-agent`
Agent pid 7183
puppy$ env | grep 'SSH'
SSH_AGENT_PID=7183
SSH_AUTH_SOCK=/tmp/ssh-SKxNXX7249/agent.7183
```

The `ssh-agent` binary also has a few additional command-line options (see Table 3-12).

Table 3-12. `ssh-agent` *Command-Line Options*

Option	Description
`-c`	Generates C-shell commands on `stdout`.
`-s`	Generates Bourne shell commands on `stdout`.
`-k`	Kills the current agent (which needs the `SSH_AGENT_PID` environment variable set).
`-t` *life*	Sets a default value for the maximum lifetime of keys added to the agent in seconds. Defaults to forever.
`-d`	Debug mode.

The first two options, -c and -s, will output the commands for setting the environmental variables in the form of csh and Bourne shell commands. The next option, -k, will kill the running ssh-agent daemon based on the process ID contained in the SSH_AGENT_PID environmental variable. Enter the following:

```
puppy$ ssh-agent -k
```

The -t option allows you to set a lifetime for the keys you add to ssh-agent in seconds. After that period the key will expire and be removed from RAM. You can override this using the ssh-add command. The last option, -d, is debug mode that will start the ssh-agent but not fork it to the background.

Now that you have ssh-agent running, you need to add keys to it. You do this using the ssh-add command. Listing 3-38 shows the ssh-add command.

Listing 3-38. *Adding Keys to* ssh-agent *Using the* ssh-add *Command*

```
puppy$ ssh-add
```

If you run ssh-add without specifying a particular key file to load, the command will load id_rsa, id_dsa, and identity from the .ssh directory of the current user. If these keys require a passphrase, then you will be prompted to enter that phrase to successfully add that key to the cache. You can use additional command-line options with ssh-add (see Table 3-13).

Table 3-13. ssh-add *Command-Line Options*

Option	Description
-l	Lists fingerprints of all keys currently stored by the agent.
-L	Lists public-key parameters of all keys stored by the agent.
-d	Instead of adding the key, removes the key from the agent.
-D	Deletes all keys from the agent.
-x	Locks the agent with a password.
-X	Unlocks the agent.
-t *life*	Sets a default value for the maximum lifetime of keys added to the agent in seconds. This defaults to forever.

The first options, -l and -L, list the fingerprints and the public-key parameters of the keys stored in the agent, respectively. The -d option allows you to remove a key you previously added to the ssh-agent. Enter the following:

```
puppy$ ssh-add -d /root/.ssh/id_rsa
```

You can also remove all keys from the agent by using the -D option. The next two options allow you to lock and unlock the agent with a password to prevent anybody from making any changes without the password. The -x option locks the agent, and the -X option unlocks the agent. You will be prompted for a password for both options. The last option, -t, is the same as the -t option for the ssh-agent command, which sets the life span of the keys in the agent in seconds.

The ssh-agent also allows *authentication-agent forwarding*. Authentication-agent forwarding means that remote systems can use a local trusted ssh-agent daemon to perform authentication. To do this, you need to ensure either the -A command line option is issued or the ForwardAgent option in the ssh_config configuration file is set to yes. Let's see an example.

1. You have a trusted secure system running ssh-agent on it called puppy.

2. You have two other systems, kitten and duckling. Both kitten and duckling have your public key in their authorized_keys file.

3. You have a terminal session on puppy, and you ssh to kitten. The ssh-agent takes care of the authentication, and you sign on. You do what you need to on the kitten system.

4. Now you want to do something on duckling, so you need to ssh over there. But your private key is stored on the ssh-agent on puppy, and the kitten system does not have a copy of your private key.

5. But you have AgentForward enabled on the kitten and duckling systems. Your ssh session has recognized this, and when you connect to duckling it connects to the ssh-agent on puppy and passes your private key through to the duckling system. Thus, you are able to be authenticated to the duckling system.

■**Caution** This has risks, though. Never enable agent forwarding on a system where you do not control root or do not trust the system. This is because your private key and passphrase are now in memory of the systems you have agent forwarded to, and the root user can pluck them from the memory of the system.

The sshd Daemon

The last area of OpenSSH you will look at in this section is the sshd daemon itself. To allow remote connections via ssh to your system, you need to have the sshd daemon running and by default the TCP port 22 open (you can override this port in the sshd_config file, which I will discuss shortly). The sshd daemon is usually started when your system is started through an init script.

■**Tip** You can find examples of init scripts for Red Hat (which will work for Mandrake, Yellow Dog, and similar) and SuSE in the contrib directory of the OpenSSH source package.

You can also start it from the command line; Listing 3-39 shows this.

Listing 3-39. *Starting the* sshd *Daemon*

```
puppy$ sshd -p 22
```

Listing 3-39 starts the sshd daemon, and the -p option tells the daemon to bind itself on TCP port 22. You can also specify multiple ports after the -p option to have sshd listen on more than one port. Table 3-14 describes some of the other command-line options available for sshd.

Table 3-14. sshd *Command-Line Options*

Option	Description
-d	Debug mode. Can be used more than once to increase verbosity.
-D	Do not detach and become a daemon.
-t	Test mode.
-e	When this option is specified, sshd will send the output to the standard error instead of the system log.
-f *configuration_file*	Specifies the name of the configuration file. The default is /etc/ssh/sshd_config.
-g *grace time*	Gives the grace time for clients to authenticate themselves. Defaults to 120 seconds.
-h *key file*	Specifies a file from which a host key is read.
-o *option*	Can be used to give options in the format used in the configuration file. This is useful for specifying options for which there is no separate command-line flag.
-q	Quiet mode.

The first four options are useful for testing. The first -d enables debug output. You can specify it up to three times in the command line to get more verbosity. The second -D tells sshd not to detach and become a daemon, and the last, -t, tells sshd to test its configuration and return any errors without starting. The -e option redirects output from sshd to standard error and not to the syslog.

You can specify the location of a configuration file using the -f option; if this option is not specified, then sshd defaults to using /etc/ssh/sshd_config. You can also specify the grace time allowed for clients to authenticate themselves using the -g option. A setting of 0 means sshd will wait forever. You can also specify a particular host key for the sshd daemon using the -h option. The next option allows you to specify any of the configuration file options from the sshd_config file that do not have a command-line equivalent. Enter the following:

```
puppy# sshd -p 22 -o 'PasswordAuthentication no'
```

The last option, -q, suppresses all sshd output and runs the daemon in quiet mode.

Configuring ssh and sshd

You can customize all the commands you have seen so far by configuring the OpenSSH environment. The majority of this client-side configuration is controlled by the ssh_config file, and the server-side configuration of the daemon is controlled by the sshd_config file. You will look at the ssh_config file first. Usually two versions of this file exist: a local version that is located in the .ssh directories of local users and a global version that is overridden by the contents of the local ssh_config. The local ssh_config file is in turn overridden by any command-line option with which you start ssh. Listing 3-40 shows a sample ssh_config file.

Listing 3-40. *A Sample* ssh_config *File*

```
Host *
BatchMode no
Compression yes
CheckHostIP yes
StrictHostKeyChecking ask
ForwardAgent no
ForwardX11 no
```

The configuration file is easy to understand. The first entry, Host, defines the scope of the configuration items beneath it. In Listing 3-40 the Host statement is followed by an asterisk (*), which indicates all hosts. If you define a particular hostname with the Host statement, the configuration items following it will apply to connecting to that host only. You can have multiple Host statements defined in the file.

■**Tip** The hostname after the Host statement refers to the argument entered on the command line— not a resolved or canonical hostname. If you use a complete hostname on the command line, puppy.yourdomain.com, and have Host puppy in your ssh_config file, then it will not recognize that you are referring to the same system.

The next option, Batchmode, enables or disables the use of ssh in batch mode (equivalent to using the -b option on the command line). The Compression option enables OpenSSH compression if set to yes. The CheckHostIP option tells ssh to check the IP address of the target system for DNS spoofing. I recommend you always have this on. If set to yes, the StrictHostKeyChecking never prompts you to add the host key of a new system to the known_hosts file when you first connect. It also will not allow connections to systems if their host key has changed from the key contained in the known_hosts file.

I have discussed the ForwardAgent option previously. Unless you are totally sure of what systems you intend to allow agent forwarding on, and are aware of the risk involved, then keep this off by setting it to no. The ForwardX11 option allows you to use ssh to forward X-Windows sessions over SSH. I will cover this in the "Forwarding X with OpenSSH" section, but if you do not intend to use SSH to forward X11 connections, I recommend setting this to no as it can pose a security risk. The next two options control which port to connect to on the remote system and the protocol you intend to use to connect. Port 22 is the default, and as I have previously discussed I recommend using version only 2 of the SSH protocol. Quite a few other options are available to you in the ssh_config file; you can see them in the ssh_config man file. Enter the following:

```
puppy$ man ssh_config
```

Listing 3-41 shows a sample of the sshd daemon configuration file, sshd_config, which is normally stored in /etc/ssh. Many of the options from ssh_config are identical in the sshd_config file; where I have previously defined them, I have not redefined them in this section.

Listing 3-41. *A sample* sshd_config *File*

```
Port 22
Protocol 2
SyslogFacility AUTH
LogLevel INFO
PermitRootLogin no
StrictModes yes
UsePrivilegeSeparation yes
PasswordAuthentication yes
RSAAuthentication yes
Compression yes
X11Forwarding no
Subsystem        sftp     /usr/libexec/openssh/sftp-server
```

Unlike the ssh_config file, no Host entry exists. The settings here apply to the sshd server overall, not to a specific client connection. The first entries Port and Protocol explicitly specify the port sshd will bind to and the version of the SSH protocol to use. In this case, I am binding to the default TCP port of 22 and using only the SSH Version 2 protocol. The next two options control how sshd logs to the syslog daemon; the SyslogFacility option allowing you to specify the facility you want to log to, and LogLevel controls the verbosity of the output of the sshd daemon.

The next options deal with the security of sshd. The first option, PermitRootLogin, is particularly important and something I recommend you always set to no. This prevents the root user from logging into the system via ssh. With this set to no, you prevent an attacker from even attempting connections to root using ssh. The next option, StrictModes, checks if the files and directories in a user's home directory are world-writable. If this option is set to yes and any of the files or directories in a user's home directory are world-writable, then the user will not be allowed to log on. The final of these three options is UsePriviledgeSeparation. If set to yes, the sshd process is divided into two processes, one of them a child process that is unprivileged and that handles all incoming network traffic. Only when the incoming user has been authenticated does the child process pass the user to a process with the authority of a privileged user. This helps reduce the risk of a compromise of the sshd daemon allowing root access to the system. The PasswordAuthentication and RSAAuthentication options, if set to yes, tell sshd to allow these authentications mechanisms.

The last option enables the use of the sftp-server, which allows a remote user to connect to the system using the sftp. The subsystem option spawns the additional command sftp-server when sshd detects an incoming sftp request. You can also run other subsystems if you want.

You can add some additional options to the sshd_config file (see Table 3-15).

Table 3-15. `sshd_config` *Options*

Option	Description
AllowGroups	Allows only those groups listed to connect to the system.
AllowUsers	Allows only those users listed to connect to the system.
DenyGroups	Denies connections from the listed groups to the system.
DenyUsers	Denies connections from the listed users to the system.
LoginGraceTime	The server disconnects after this time if the user has not successfully logged in.
VerifyReverseMapping	Specifies whether sshd should try to verify the remote hostname.

The first four options simply control who can sign into the system. This allows you to be selective about what users and groups have permission to connect via ssh. The LoginGraceTime option allows you to specify a time limit for users to log in. The default is 120 seconds after which the session is disconnected. The VerifyReverseMapping option tells sshd to confirm that the resolved remote hostname for the remote IP address maps back to the IP address from which the connection has been initiated. The default is no.

Port Forwarding with OpenSSH

The OpenSSH package also has the capability to forward ports much like Stunnel does. You can forward any TCP traffic such as POP3, SMTP, or HTTP traffic through the SSH tunnel. However, any ports below 1024 are considered privileged; if you want to forward one of these, the user creating the tunnel must have root privileges. You will also need to have sshd running on the remote system to make the initial connection and create the tunnel. You will also need to ensure you are able to authenticate to the system you are creating the tunnel to and that you have sufficient privileges for the tunnel to be created.

OpenSSH is capable of two types of forwarding—local and remote. Local-port forwarding forwards any traffic coming into a specific local port to a specific remote port. Remote-forwarding monitors a specific remote port and forwards the traffic from that port to a specific local port. Listing 3-42 shows OpenSSH local-port forwarding of traffic from port 25 on the local system to port 1025 on the remote system, 192.168.0.1.

Listing 3-42. *Local Port Forwarding Using* ssh

```
puppy# ssh -fN -L 25:192.168.0.1:1025 bob@192.168.0.1
bob@192.168.0.1's password:
```

The -L option is structured as `localport:remotehost:remoteport`, or in this example 25:192.1658.0.1:1025. I have also added the -fN options to the command to tell ssh to go into the background after establishing the port forwarding. The connection will then exist as an ssh process and forward the ports until the process is killed or the system restarted. Remote-port forwarding works in a similar way. Listing 3-43 shows a remote-port forward.

Listing 3-43. *Remote Port Forwarding Using* ssh

```
puppy# ssh -fN -R 995:localhost:110 jim@kitten.yourdomain.com
jim@localhost's password:
```

The -R option is structured as remoteport:localhost:localport, so in Listing 3-43 you are listening to remote port 995 on kitten.yourdomain.com and forwarding it to port 110 on localhost. You have also added the -fN options again to have the ssh command go into the background.

With the port forwarding I have demonstrated here, the user is prompted for a password based on the user specified on the command line. You could also use a system that has been authenticated via RSA key exchange or generate a key specifically for this connection. You can specify the use of a particular private key using the -i option. The matching public key obviously needs to be in the authorized_keys file on the remote system. Enter the following:

```
puppy# ssh -fN -i /home/jim/.ssh/kitten_key -R 995:localhost:110
jim@kitten.yourdomain.com
```

This could potentially also allow you to incorporate the command into a script because it does not require prompting for a password.

Another option you can add to the ssh port-forwarding command is the -g option. By default OpenSSH does not allow remote hosts to connect to local forwarded ports. When you add the -g option, remote hosts are able to connect to those local forwarded ports.

Forwarding X with OpenSSH

The last use of OpenSSH you will look at is the forwarding of X11 traffic over SSH. This allows you to execute X applications on a remote system via a secure SSH tunnel. Normal X traffic is unencrypted and easily sniffed across a network. But there are still risks with doing this, and you should never enable X11 Forwarding on systems where you do not explicitly trust the remote system. Also, X offers too many potential threats, even with an SSH tunnel, to forward X11 traffic over the Internet. In fact, as I have mentioned elsewhere in this book, I recommend not running X on a system that provides a server function because of the risks that X poses.

But if you do want to use remote X sessions, I will show you how to tunnel those X sessions through an SSH tunnel. First, you need sshd running on the remote machine on which you want to run X applications. Your sshd_config file on that remote machine needs to have the option on the next line enabled:

```
X11Forwarding yes
```

Second, change your ssh_config file to add the option on the following line:

```
ForwardX11 yes
```

You could also enable X11 Forwarding on your ssh command by using the -X command-line option.

> **■Caution** From OpenSSH version 3.8 onward, ssh will use untrusted X11 Forwarding by default. This more secure untrusted forwarding will limit what you can change and control using a remote X11 connection. This will be the default behavior when using the X11Forward, ForwardX11, and -X options with OpenSSH. If you want to revert to the previous X11 Forwarding behavior, you can set the option ForwardX11Trusted to yes in your ssh_config file or use the command-line option -Y.

Once you have configured this, then you can connect to the remote system and run an X application; in this case, I have chosen to run xterm. Enter the following:

```
puppy# ssh -X bob@kitten
bob@kitten's password:
kitten# xterm
```

The X11 Forwarding option of OpenSSH will automatically define and assign a $DISPLAY variable to your forwarded X connection.

Resources

The following are some resources for you to use.

Mailing Lists

- **Openswan mailing lists**: http://lists.openswan.org/mailman/listinfo/

- **OpenSSH mailing lists**: http://www.openssh.org/list.html

- **Stunnel mailing lists**: http://www.stunnel.org/support/

Sites

- **Certificate Service Provider**: http://devel.it.su.se/projects/CSP/

- **EJBCA**: http://ejbca.sourceforge.net/

- **IPSec HOWTO for Linux**: http://www.ipsec-howto.org/

- **Netscape Certificate Management System**: http://wp.netscape.com/cms/v4.0/index.html

- **Openswan**: http://www.openswan.org/

- **Openswan wiki**: http://wiki.openswan.org/

- **OpenSSH**: http://www.openssh.org/

- **RSA Laboratories**: http://www.rsasecurity.com/

- **Stunnel**: http://www.stunnel.org/

- **VNC**: http://www.realvnc.com/

CHAPTER 4

■■■

Securing Files and File Systems

In the past few chapters I have covered basic operating system security, firewalls, and the security of your connections. In this chapter I will cover the security of your data itself—the files and file systems that hold both user data and the files and objects used by the kernel, your operating systems, and your applications. Your file systems and the files and objects stored on them are your system's assets. The data contained on these assets is often the ultimate target of attackers who have the intention of stealing, tampering with, or destroying them.

Attacks on your files and file systems come in a number of forms. They can take the form of vulnerabilities and exploits of applications, tools, or the kernel. These vulnerabilities and exploits take advantage of security weaknesses or idiosyncrasies in Linux's implementation of files and file systems. Or they can take advantage of the functionality of your file attributes, for example, through the malicious exploitation of `setuid` or `setgid` binaries. They can also occur because attackers are able to circumvent your system security through inappropriately set permissions or poorly managed or administered files and file systems.

I will take you through a series of explanations of various facets of file and file system security. First, I will run through some basic permission and file attributes concepts. This will include looking at some file attributes such as object ownership, `setuid`, and world-writable permissions that could potentially offer attackers opportunities or leverage on your system. Second, I will cover setting a secure `umask` for your system. Additionally, I will cover some ways of protecting the files on your system, including making them immutable and encrypting them. I take the same approach to addressing file systems by covering individual security-related items such as securely mounting file systems, encrypting file systems, and using tools such as Tripwire.

This chapter is not a detailed examination of how Linux and other Unix dialects files and file systems work but rather covers security-related features, highlights areas of potential security risk that result from certain types of file attributes, and covers some file and file-specific security enhancements, tools, and functions that can assist you in securing your files.

> **Note** One significant area I have not covered is access control lists (ACLs). ACLs allow more advanced file permissions to be applied to your files and objects. ACL access frameworks provide more granular permissions to objects, for example, granting multiple users and groups varying permission to a particular object. I have not discussed ACLs because at this stage of their development, there are too many varying approaches for different types of file systems and for different distributions to provide a simple and accurate explanation of ACLs. I have included some URLs in the "Resources" section that will provide more information on ACLs.

Basic File Permissions and File Attributes

Each file or object on a Linux system has a number of attributes including the type of object, its ownership, the permissions users and groups have been granted to it, its size, and so on. If you list the contents of a directory using the ls command, you can see all of these attributes. In Listing 4-1 I have used the ls command with the options l and a to display in a *long* listing format *all* file attributes.

Listing 4-1. *Listing a File*

```
puppy$ ls -la *
-rwxr-xr-x   2   bob sales   4096   Apr  2 01:14   test.sh
```

I will briefly touch on each of the attributes of objects on Linux systems. As you can see in Listing 4-1, the attributes are divided into seven columns. Listing 4-2 shows these seven columns.

Listing 4-2. *File Attributes*

```
     1              2            3        4       5        6           7
permissions   file entries   owner    group   size    date/time   object name
```

The first column indicates the permissions of the file or object. These are probably the most important attributes of a file or object. The second column indicates the number of file entries. This applies to directories and indicates how many files are contained in a directory. If the file is an ordinary file, then the file entry will be 1. The third and fourth columns indicate the owner and group to which the file or object is assigned. Of these remaining file attributes, you will most closely be examining the first column of permissions and the third and fourth columns on ownership. The fifth, sixth, and seventh columns, respectively, indicate the size of the object in bytes, the date and time of the last modification of the object, and the name of the object. These attributes are self-explanatory, so I will not cover them in any detail.

Access Permissions

Let's look at the permissions column. This column has ten flags. It starts with a single flag indicating the object type. In Listing 4-1 this is a hyphen, -, which indicates this is an ordinary file. Table 4-1 lists all the possible flags in this first flag. These represent all the types of files and objects available on a Linux system.

Table 4-1. *File and Object Types*

Flag	Description
-	Regular file
d	Directory
l	Link
c	Special file
s	Socket
p	Named pipe

The next nine flags indicate what the permissions of the object are. They are divided into three groups, or *triplets*, of three flags each. Each triplet of flags is the permission settings for a particular class of user. These classes of users are the owner of the object, the group assigned to the object, and everyone.[1] The individual flags within each triplet represent the three basic permissions used on Linux systems: read, write and execute. Let's look at what access each permission grants.

- **Read**: Allows you to read, view, and print a file

- **Write**: Allows you to write, edit, and delete a file

- **Execute**: Allows you to execute a file, such as a binary or script, and search a directory

So, if you look back at Listing 4-1, you can see the first triplet of flags is rwx. This indicates that the owner of the object has the read, write, and execute permissions to the test.sh object. The next group of flags indicates the permissions that the group the object is assigned to have been granted to the object. In this case, it is r-x or read and execute. The - indicates that write permissions have not been granted to the group of the object. The last group of flags indicates the permissions that everyone on the system has to this object, in this case r-x or read and execute. Again, the - indicates that the write permission is not granted to the world.

These groups of permissions can also be indicated numerically, and I have used this form of notation throughout this book. Listing 4-3 shows an example of this notation in conjunction with the chmod command.

Listing 4-3. *Numerical Permissions Notation*

```
puppy# chmod 0755 test.sh
```

The notation 0755 is a number in octal mode. This number is the same as setting the nine permission flags to rwxr-x-r-x. Or explained further, the owner has all three permissions to this object, and both the members of the group that this object belongs to and everyone on the system have been granted read and execute permissions for this same object. So where do these octal-mode numbers come from?

---

1. Also known as *world* or *other* permissions. I will use the term *world permissions* throughout this chapter.

Well, the first digit, 0, in the mode number is used with setuid, setgid, or sticky bit permissions. I will talk more about it in the "Sticky Bits" and "setuid and setgid Permissions" sections later in this chapter. For the remaining three digits, each of the digits in 755 corresponds to one of the triplets of permission flags: the owner, group, and world permissions, respectively. The digits themselves are created by assigning a value to the possible permission types: 4 for r, 2 for w, and 1 for x. These values are then added to create the permissions triplet. So the triplet rwx is equal to a value of 7, or 4 + 2 + 1. To represent the triplet r-x, you add 4 for r and 1 for x to get 5. If you want to represent ---, or no permissions to an object, you use the numeric notation of 0. Table 4-2 describes the possible mode numbers.

Table 4-2. *Mode Numbers*

Mode Number	Description
0400	Allows the owner to read
0200	Allows the owner to writ
0100	Allows the owner to execute files and search in the directory
0040	Allows group members to read
0020	Allows group members to write
0010	Allows group members to execute files and search in the directory
0004	Allows everyone or the world to read
0002	Allows everyone or the world to writ
0001	Allows everyone or the world to execute files and search in the directory
1000	Sets the sticky bit
2000	Sets the setgid bit
4000	Sets the setuid bit

You can add these mode numbers together to provide the correct permissions for your file. For example, 0600, commonly used for system files, allows the owner of the file write and read permissions (4 + 2 = 6) and no permissions to the group or world (the 00 portion of the mode number).

The chmod command can also use symbolic notation, and it can add permissions using a + sign and remove them using a - sign. Listing 4-4 shows how to grant the write permission to the owner of the object.

Listing 4-4. *Using* chmod *Symbolic Notation*

```
puppy# chmod u+w test.sh
```

The u flag indicates the owner of the object, and the w flag indicates the write permission. You can also do multiple operations using this form of notation. The next line grants the write permission to the owner of the object and the execute permission to the object's group.

```
puppy# chmod u+w,g+x test.sh
```

To grant world read permissions to the test.sh file, you would use the following:

```
puppy# chmod o+r test.sh
```

where o indicates world or everyone permissions and r indicates read.

You can get more information on this style of notation in the chmod man page.

umask

By default on Linux systems, each file or object is created with default file permissions. You need to ensure these default permissions are not overly generous and users and applications are granted an appropriate level of permissions to files and objects. To achieve this Linux comes with the umask command. This command adjusts how the file and object permissions will be set when a file or object is created and is intended to ensure any new files created by users, applications, or the system itself are not inadvertently granted excessive permissions. Listing 4-5 shows a typical umask setting.

Listing 4-5. umask *Settings*

```
puppy# umask 022
```

The umask command works by applying a umask value to a series of default permissions for different types of objects on your system. For example, the default file permissions for a new directory or binary executable file are 777, and for an ordinary file they are 666. In Listing 4-5 the umask is set to 022. If you create a new binary file, you take the default file permissions of 777 and subtract the 022 from them (777 – 022) to get the permissions of the new file, 755. If you were to create an ordinary file and umask was set to 022, you would subtract the 022 from 666 to get the new default permissions of 644.

You can set the umask on the command line, as demonstrated in Listing 4-5. The umask command also has a couple of command-line options. You can see the -S option on the next line:

```
puppy# umask -S
u=rwx,g=rx,o=rx
```

The -S option prints the current umask in symbolic notation. On the previous line you can see the symbolic notation for the octal-mode number, 755. The second option, -p, prints the current umask in a form that can be reused as an input in a script or the like. Entering the command umask without any options will print the umask of the current user.

The umask command can be set by default at a few different points on your system. The first, and most commonly utilized, is via the boot process in init scripts. For example, on Red Hat systems the umask is set in the /etc/rc.d/init.d/functions init script, which is referenced in most Red Hat init scripts. On Debian systems it is set in the /etc/rcS init script. Additionally, each user on your system generally has the umask command set for them in their profile. For example, if you use the bash shell, it is set in the .bash_profile file in the user's home directory or globally for all user profiles in the /etc/bashrc file. On some other distributions the umask is set in the /etc/profile file.

Typical umask settings include 022, 027, and the most restrictive setting 077. I recommend a default umask of at least 022, but you should look at increasing this to a setting such as 077 on systems that will not have users creating large numbers of files (such as a bastion host) and where the applications creating files are easily quantifiable. Like most permissions settings, this will require some testing with your applications, and you should note that some users (especially those that run processes to create files or objects) will require more lenient umask settings than other users.

■**Note** If you are using Red Hat, then the default umask for all users with a UID greater than 99 (in other words, nonsystem users) is 002 rather than 022. The default umask of 022 would normally prevent other users and members of the primary group to which a user belongs from modifying any files they create. But because most users on a Red Hat system are created together with a group of the same name that is their primary group (a convention generally called *user private groups*; see Chapter 1), they do not need this protection and a umask of 002 is adequate to protect their newly created files.

World-Readable, World-Writable, and World-Executable Files

As I have mentioned, the last triplet of access permissions is the access granted to everyone, or *world access*. World access includes all users on your system. This means that if an attacker were to compromise an ordinary user account on your system, they would have whatever world access is granted to all your files and objects. This poses three significant risks.

- The first is what world-readable files and directories are on your system, and how could their content benefit an attacker?

- The second is what world-executable files and directories exist on your system, and what could running them gain an attacker?

- The last and arguably most significant risk is what world-writable files and directories exist on your system, and how could changing, editing, or deleting them benefit or assist an attacker in penetrating your system?

I recommend you carefully audit the files and objects on your system for those with world-readable, world-executable, and world-writable permissions. Find all those files and directories on your system, and determine whether they require the world permissions; if not, remove those permissions. Some files on your system will require world access permissions such as some devices in the /dev and /proc directories or some files required for particular applications. I recommend you carefully conduct tests before you make changes to your permissions in a production environment. In Listing 4-6, you can see a command to find all files and objects with world access on your system.

Listing 4-6. *Finding World Permissions*

```
puppy# find / -perm -o=w ! -type l -ls
```

The find command is using the -perm option to search for files and objects with particular permissions set. The -o=w flag for the -perm option selects files with at least world-writable access (which includes lesser access such as readable and executable permissions). The ! -type l part selects all file and object types except links, and the last option, -ls, outputs the list of files in the same format as used when you execute the ls command with the -dla options specified.

■Tip The find command is a powerful tool for searching for particular files and objects on your system; you can find further information on how to use it in the find man page.

Sticky Bits

Linux security permissions can be highly inflexible. If a user has the write permissions, or a group they belong to has write permissions to a directory, the user will be able to delete the files in that directory even if they do not own those files. This has some serious implications for directories to which more than one user or application share write permissions. In Listing 4-7 user bob belonging to the group sales can create a file in the directory /usr/sharedfiles.

Listing 4-7. *Sticky Bits*

```
puppy$ su bob
puppy$ cd /usr/
puppy$ ls -l sharedfiles
drwxrwxr-x    2 root       sales          4096 Sep  8 19:13 sharedfiles
puppy$ cd sharedfiles
puppy$ vi bobsfile
puppy$ ls -l bobsfile
-rw-rw-r--    1 bob        bob               5 Sep  8 19:25 bobsfile
```

User jane also belongs to the group sales. As the group sales has write permission to the /usr/sharefiles directory, she can delete user bob's file.

```
puppy$ su jane
puppy$ cd /usr/sharedfiles
puppy$ rm bobsfile
rm: remove write-protected regular file `bobsfile'? y
```

Obviously, bob may not be so happy about jane deleting his file. *Sticky bits* help solve this issue. When the directory sticky bit is set, users will still be able to create and modify files within the directory, but they will be able to delete only files that they themselves have created. The sticky bit is set for a directory if a t or T is present in place of the x in the world permissions triplet, like this:

```
drwxrwxrwt
```

A lowercase t indicates that the world permission of execute is set together with the sticky bit. An uppercase T indicates that only the sticky bit is set and the world execute bit is not set. You can set the sticky bit using the chmod command.

```
puppy# chmod 1775 sharedfiles
puppy# ls -la sharedfiles
drwxrwxr-t    2 root       sales          4096 Sep  8 19:29 sharedfiles
```

■Note Only the `root` user can set the sticky bit.

Now with the sticky bit set for this directory, the user `jane` would not be able to delete the user `bob`'s file. To set the sticky bit without giving the world execute permission to the directory, you would use the `chmod` command on the next line. Enter the following:

```
puppy# chmod 1774 sharedfiles
puppy# ls -la sharedfiles
drwxrwxr-T    2 root      sales         4096 Sep  8 19:29 sharedfiles
```

Notice that the mode number is now 1774 rather than 1775, which indicates that the world execute permission has not been granted.

I recommend you examine the option of setting the sticky bit for all world-writable directories. This prevents users from either accidentally or maliciously deleting or overwriting each other's files and limits the use of world-writable directories by attackers who are trying to penetrate your system. Of course, like any permissions-related setting, you should carefully test permission changes with all your applications.

■Note Setting the sticky bit on files and symbolic links does not have a security impact but rather is related to local paging and transition links.

---

setuid and setgid Permissions

You can set the `setuid` and `setgid` permissions on a binary to allow it to run with the privileges of the owner or group of the binary rather than the user actually running the binary. You will look at how this works and then see why this is a risk and how to mitigate this risk. Probably the best example of `setuid` permissions is the `passwd` binary. Normally the access to the `passwd` file is limited to the `root` user and no other user. But all users on your system can use the `passwd` binary to change their passwords. The `setuid` permission makes this possible. The `passwd` binary is owned by the `root` user with `setuid` permissions set. When executed by a normal, unprivileged user on your system, the `passwd` binary does not run as this user, as a normal binary would, but rather adopts the privileges of its owner, the `root` user. In Listing 4-8 you can see the permissions of the `passwd` binary.

Listing 4-8. setuid *Permissions*

```
-r-s--x--x    1 root      root          16336 Feb 14  2003 passwd
```

The `s` specified in the `execute` flag of the owner permissions triplet indicates that this binary has `setuid` set. Like the sticky bit, the lowercase `s` indicates that the owner of the file also has `execute` permissions. If binary had an uppercase `S` instead of a lowercase `s`, then the owner of the binary would not have the `execute` permission to the file. You can set the `setuid` permission with the `chmod` command by prefixing the mode number with the digit 4.

```
puppy# chmod 4755 test.sh
puppy# ls -l test.sh
-rwsr-xr-x   1 root     root         992 Aug  4 15:49 test.sh
```

Thus, the digit 4 in the 4755 sets the lowercase s in the execute flag of the owner permission triplet. To set the S setuid permission, you enter the following:

```
puppy# chmod 4655 test.sh
puppy# ls -l test.sh
-rwSr-xr-x   1 root     root         992 Aug  4 15:50 test.sh
```

The setgid permission operates in a similar way to the setuid permission. But instead of allowing the binary to run with the permissions of the owner, it allows the binary to run with the permissions of the owning group. You can tell if the setgid permission is set if an s or S is set in the execute flag of the group permissions triplet. Like the setuid permissions, you set the setgid permissions with the chmod command. Instead of prefixing the mode number with a 4, you prefix it with a 2. In Listing 4-9 you can see how setgid is set.

Listing 4-9. setgid *Permissions*

```
puppy# chmod 2755 test.sh
puppy# ls -l test.sh
-rwxr-sr-x   1 root     root         992 Aug  4 15:50 test.sh
```

So why are setuid and setgid binaries a potential security risk on your system? Well, they have two problems. The first problem is that a user can use an existing setuid binary's greater privileges to perform actions that could be malicious on your system. Of course, some setuid and setgid files on your system actually require this functionality to operate, with the previously cited passwd command being one of these. The sendmail binary is another example.

The second problem is that setuid or setgid commands or binaries owned by privileged users such as the root user can be easily created on your system by an attacker. This binary can be used to run an attack or compromise your system. Indeed, many root kits (see Chapter 6) use setuid or setgid binaries to compromise systems. So, the two aspects of setuid and setgid permissions you need to monitor and manage are as follows:

- Limit the number of setuid and setgid binaries on your system to only those binaries that require it.

- Regular checks for new and existing binaries that may have had setuid and/or setgid permissions set without your approval or knowledge.

To do this, the first thing you need to do is identify all the setuid and setgid binaries on your system. Listing 4-10 provides a find command designed to locate setuid binaries.

Listing 4-10. *Finding* setuid *Files*

```
puppy# find / -perm -4000 -ls
```

And Listing 4-11 provides a variation of this command for locating setgid binaries.

Listing 4-11. *Finding* setgid *Files*

```
puppy# find / -perm -2000 -ls
```

■**Tip** You can also use a tool such as sXid (available from http://linux.cudeso.be/linuxdoc/ sxid.php) to automatically find setuid/setgid binaries. You could also look at the Debian command checksecurity.

After using the commands in Listings 4-10 and 4-11 you need to review all the files found and determine whether they all require setuid or setgid. If they can have the permissions removed, then use the chmod command to remove them.

■**Note** For a scanning tool that can scan for a variety of different file types, see the "Scanning for Files with Adeos" sidebar.

SCANNING FOR FILES WITH ADEOS

The Adeos[2] tool is designed to automatically scan your system for files and objects in a variety of potential states, such as world-writable or setuid files, and output a report that you can review. You can download Adeos from http://linux.wku.edu/~lamonml/software/adeos/. The tool has not been updated for some time, but its basic functionality remains suitable to use. Download the archive file containing the Adeos scanner, and unpack it.

```
puppy$ wget http://linux.wku.edu/~lamonml/software/adeos/adeos-1.0.tar.gz
puppy$ tar -zxf adeos-1.0.tar.gz
```

Change into the adeos-1.0 directory created when you unpack the archive. The configuration and installation process for Adeos is a simple configure and make process.

```
puppy$ ./configure && make
```

The compilation process will create a binary called adeos. You can copy the binary to a location of your choice or run it from the adeos-1.0 directory. The binary can be run from the command line or via a cron job. Table 4-3 lists the options it can use.

(Continues)

---

2.   Adeos is the Roman goddess of modesty.

SCANNING FOR FILES WITH ADEOS *(Continued)*

Table 4-3. *Adeos Command-Line Options*

Option	Description
-d	Includes dynamic directories such as /tmp or /proc in the scan
-h	Outputs the scan as a HTML file called results.html in the current working directory
-r	Formats the output as a collated report
--help	Displays the Adeos help and usage information

Adeos supports three scan modes: normal, verbose, and paranoid. The normal mode scans for setuid and setgid files, world-writable files, and directories. This is the default mode that Adeos will run in if you do not provide a mode on the command line. The next mode is verbose mode, which looks for all the file types in the normal scan mode plus files with the sticky bit set, unreadable directories, and inaccessible files. The last mode, paranoid, is the most detailed and scans for all the types in the normal and verbose modes and adds world-readable and world-executable objects.

Let's first run Adeos in the normal mode. Enter the following:

```
puppy$ ./adeos
World-writeable file: /var/lib/mysql/mysql.sock
World-writeable directory: /var/tmp
World-writeable directory: /var/spool/vbox
World-writeable directory: /var/spool/samba
World-writeable directory: /tmp
SUID file: /usr/X11R6/bin/XFree86
SUID file: /usr/sbin/usernetctl
...
```

The adeos command will output a list of files will be outputted. This list may be quite long, and I recommend you redirect the output of the command to a file. This will allow you to better use the results. You can also run Adeos with the -r option to output the results in a report format suitable for printing. Listing 4-12 runs Adeos in verbose mode with the report option enabled.

Listing 4-12. *Adeos in* verbose *Report Mode*

```
puppy$ ./adeos -r verbose
```

You can also output the results of the Adeos scan as a HTML document using the -h option. Listing 4-13 runs Adeos in paranoid mode with the HTML output option.

Listing 4-13. *Adeos in* paranoid *Mode*

```
puppy$ ./adeos -h paranoid
```

The -h option will create a HTML file called results.html in the current working directory.

■**Caution** Occasionally when running in paranoid mode with the -r option set, Adeos can consume large quantities of memory and significantly slow your system. You should be careful when running Adeos in this mode with this option.

Ownership

Now I will go back to Listing 4-2 and the seven columns of attributes for the objects. The third and fourth columns are the owner of the object and the group of the object, respectively. In Listing 4-1 the test.sh object is owned by the user bob and belongs to the group sales. The user bob, as the owner, is entitled to the first triplet of access permissions, rwx, as I have described in the previous section, and the group sales is entitled to the second triplet of permissions, r-x. As I stated earlier, everyone on the system has been granted the world permissions, r-x, to the test.sh object.

One of the important characteristics of ownership is that all files and objects on your system should have an owner. Unowned objects can often indicate that an attacker has penetrated your system. Listing 4-14 provides a find command that will return all files that do not have an owner or a group.

Listing 4-14. *Find Unowned Files and Objects*

```
puppy# find / -nouser -o -nogroup -ls
```

You should review any files and objects that are unowned by a user or do not belong to a group and either remove them or assign them to the appropriate owner or group.

Immutable Files

Immutable files are one of the most powerful security and system administration features available on Linux systems. Immutable files cannot be written to by any user, even by the root user, regardless of their file permissions. They cannot be deleted or renamed, and no hard link can be created from them. They are ideal for securing configuration files or other files to which you want to prevent changes and which you know will not or should not be changed.

■**Note** Immutable file functionality is available for ext2 and ext3 type file systems in kernel versions 2.4 and onward on most distributions. The chattr commands and associated functionality is provided by the e2fsprogs package, which is usually installed by default on most Linux systems.

You can add or remove the immutable attribute using the chattr command. Only the root user can use the chattr command to make files immutable. Listing 4-15 makes the /etc/passwd file immutable. This would prevent any new users being created on the system, because new users could not be written to the /etc/passwd file.

Listing 4-15. *Setting the Immutable Attribute*

```
puppy# chattr -V +i /etc/passwd
chattr 1.34 (25-Jul-2003)
Flags of /etc/passwd set as ----i--------
```

The chattr command is similar in function to the chmod command. Like the chmod command, you specify either a plus (+) sign or minus (-) sign and the required attribute. The plus sign adds the specified attribute, and the minus sign removes it. So, to make a file immutable, you use the option +i. To remove the immutable attribute, you use the -i option. Listing 4-15 also specifies the -V option to run the chattr command in the verbose mode and displays more information about the attribute change. If you run the chattr command without the -V option, it will complete without output, unless an error occurs.

■**Tip** The chattr command has another attribute you can potentially use: a. If this attribute is set, then a file can be opened only for append or update operations and cannot be deleted. This is useful for log files or for files you want to be able to write to but not to delete. Like the i attribute, it can be set or removed by the root user only.

Now the /etc/passwd file is immutable, you will not be able to delete or change it. Listing 4-16 tries to delete the file.

Listing 4-16. *Deleting an Immutable File*

```
puppy# rm /etc/passwd
rm: remove write-protected regular file `/etc/passwd'? y
rm: cannot remove `/etc/passwd': Operation not permitted
```

As you can see from the error message in Listing 4-16, the file cannot be deleted without removing the immutable attribute. In Listing 4-17 you can also see that you are unable to create a hard link to the file.

Listing 4-17. *Linking Immutable Files*

```
puppy# ln /etc/passwd /root/test
ln: creating hard link `/root/test' to `/etc/passwd': Operation not permitted
```

■**Tip** You can still create symbolic links to immutable files.

Immutable files are also useful for securing more than just individual configuration files. On many hardened systems, a number of binaries that are not likely to change can be made immutable. For example, the contents of the /sbin, /bin, /usr/sbin, and /usr/lib directories can be made immutable to prevent an attacker from replacing a critical binary or library file with an altered malicious version.

■**Caution** Obviously, upgrading applications and tools is not possible while the binaries or libraries you need to update are marked immutable. You need to remove the immutable attribute to perform updates or upgrades, such as installing a new version of Sendmail.

Capabilities and lcap

As I previously mentioned, only the root user can add and remove the immutable (or append-only) attribute to and from a file. This provides a certain degree of security to any files marked with these attributes. But under some circumstances you may want to prevent even the root user from removing these attributes. I will show you a way, using Linux kernel capabilities, of doing this. Kernel capabilities were introduced in version 2.1 of the Linux kernel to provide some granular control to the capabilities of the root user. Previously the authority granted to the root user was universal, and it could not be allocated into smaller portions of authority or capability, unlike the administrative accounts of other operating systems. The introduction of capabilities provides the ability to allow or disallow particular pieces of the root user's available authority and functionality.

■**Note** This includes more than just the ability to add or remove the immutable attribute.

To control these capabilities, you need to utilize a userland tool called lcap. You can download lcap in the form of an RPM, a source package, or a Debian package file. You can use the RPM file to install lcap. You can download the RPM from http://dag.wieers.com/packages/lcap/ and install it using the rpm command.[3]

```
puppy# wget http://dag.wieers.com/packages/lcap/lcap-0.0.6-6.1.el3.dag.i386.rpm
puppy# rpm -Uvh lcap-0.0.6-6.1.el3.dag.i386.rpm
```

When you have installed the RPM, you can use the lcap command to disable capabilities. Running the lcap command without options will list the capabilities that you can control and their current status.

```
puppy# lcap
Current capabilities: 0xFFFFFEFF
     0) *CAP_CHOWN                    1) *CAP_DAC_OVERRIDE
     2) *CAP_DAC_READ_SEARCH          3) *CAP_FOWNER
     4) *CAP_FSETID                   5) *CAP_KILL
     6) *CAP_SETGID                   7) *CAP_SETUID
     8)  CAP_SETPCAP                  9) *CAP_LINUX_IMMUTABLE
    10) *CAP_NET_BIND_SERVICE        11) *CAP_NET_BROADCAST
    12) *CAP_NET_ADMIN               13) *CAP_NET_RAW
    14) *CAP_IPC_LOCK                15) *CAP_IPC_OWNER
    16) *CAP_SYS_MODULE              17) *CAP_SYS_RAWIO
    18) *CAP_SYS_CHROOT              19) *CAP_SYS_PTRACE
    20) *CAP_SYS_PACCT               21) *CAP_SYS_ADMIN
    22) *CAP_SYS_BOOT                23) *CAP_SYS_NICE
    24) *CAP_SYS_RESOURCE            25) *CAP_SYS_TIME
    26) *CAP_SYS_TTY_CONFIG          27) *CAP_MKNOD
    28) *CAP_LEASE
     * = Capabilities currently allowed
```

---

3. The source package is available from http://packetstormsecurity.org/linux/admin/lcap-0.0.3.tar.bz2, and the Debian package is available from http://packages.debian.org/stable/admin/lcap.

Capabilities marked with an asterisk (*) are currently allowed, and those without this asterisk sign are disallowed. Disallowing a capability requires specifying it by name on the `lcap` command line. The following line disallows the `root` user's capability to add or remove the immutable attribute:

```
puppy# lcap CAP_LINUX_IMMUTABLE
```

■**Note** To remove a capability, you must be the `root` user.

Now not even the `root` user can add or remove the immutable attribute.

■**Caution** This means you or *any* user on your system will not be able to edit or delete any files marked immutable. And you will not be able to remove the immutable attribute until the capability is restored through a reboot of the system.

You can also use some other command-line options with `lcap`. The first is the `-v` option, which enables verbose mode and provides more information about what `lcap` is doing. If you rerun the previous command with the `-v` option, you can see a lot more detail about disallowing the capability.

```
puppy# lcap CAP_LINUX_IMMUTABLE
Current capabilities: 0xFFFFFEFF
  Removing capabilities:
     9) CAP_LINUX_IMMUTABLE    immutable and append file attributes
```

If you want to disallow all capabilities, run `lcap` with the `-z` option.

```
puppy# lcap -z
```

Be careful when you do this, as disallowing capabilities can cause your system to become unstable. The `lcap` command also comes with some built-in help, which you can access with the `-h` option.

Once you have disallowed a capability, it cannot be allowed again without rebooting your system. Only the `init` process resets the capabilities of your system. If you inadvertently disallowed a particular capability, you will have to reboot your system to allow it again. Additionally, if you want to ensure a capability is disallowed when you start your system, you should include the `lcap` command, disallowing that capability in your `rc.local` file for Red Hat and your `rcS` file for Debian.

■**Tip** To find out more about the other capabilities that can be controlled with the `lcap` command, see the contents of the `/usr/include/capabilities.h` file.

Encrypting Files

Elsewhere in this book I have discussed using public-key encryption to manage a variety of encryption tasks, such as encrypting your e-mail using TLS. But sometimes you may simply want to encrypt a single file. To do this you use a cryptographic algorithm secured with a pass-phrase. This is called *symmetrical encryption* and is not as strong or as flexible as asymmetrical (public-key encryption) encryption.[4] It is not as strong, as it solely relies on the strength of a single key used to encrypt the required data. It is not as flexible, as it makes the process of key management more difficult. With symmetrical encryption, the single private key must be totally protected. This limits the means by which the key can be communicated to any parties who need to decrypt the required data. But sometimes you may need to quickly and simply encrypt data on your systems where private-key encryption is the easiest choice or where key management and distribution is not a priority (for example, if you do not need to distribute the private key to many people).

To do this conventional symmetric encryption, you can use the gpg command discussed in Chapter 1. In the model I am describing, the private key will be a passphase you will specify when you encrypt the data. This private key will also be required when you decrypt the data. To encrypt a file, you run the gpg command with the -c option to enable symmetric encryption. Listing 4-18 shows the encryption of a simple text file.

Listing 4-18. *Symmetric Encryption with* gpg

```
puppy# cat test.txt
This is a test document - please encrypt me.
puppy# gpg -c test.txt
Enter passphrase:
Repeat passphrase:
```

When you enter the gpg -c command, you will be prompted to enter a passphrase, which will be the private key to protect your data. You will be prompted to enter it twice to ensure the passphrase recorded is correct. You should carefully select a passphrase using similar rules to how you would choose a suitable and secure password (see Chapter 1). In the case of private key passphrases, you should choose a longer than normal passphrase than your other pass-words. This will reduce the risk of subjecting your encrypted files to a brute-force attack. Do not reveal this pass phase to anyone who does not need to know it.

At the completion of the gpg -c command, an encrypted version of the test.txt file will be created called test.txt.gpg. If you no longer need or want the unencrypted version of your file, you should delete it to prevent it from becoming a very fast shortcut for an attacker to read your encrypted data.

In Table 4-4 you can see some options you can provide to gpg that you can use for symmetrical encryption.

---

4. Symmetric encryption is defined as encryption where the data is encrypted and decrypted with the same key. It is sometimes called *private-key encryption*.

Table 4-4. gpg *Symmetric Encryption Options*

Option	Description
-a	Creates ASCII armored output.
--cipher-algo *name*	Uses a particular cipher algorithm.
--version	Displays the list of available cipher algorithms.
-o *file*	Writes the output to the specified file.
-v	Enables the verbose mode. Uses twice to increase the verbosity.

The first option, -a, provides gpg with ASCII armored output. The current test.txt.gpg file is not very screen friendly and contains a number of characters that cannot be displayed on the screen. If you wanted to send this file via e-mail to someone else, you would need to send it in the form of a file attachment, as it could not be placed inline in the message body of an e-mail. If you had specified the -a option, then gpg would have produced a file called test.txt.asc, which would be the same encrypted data but in ASCII armored format. Listing 4-19 shows what this file looks like.

Listing 4-19. test.txt.asc

```
-----BEGIN PGP MESSAGE-----
Version: GnuPG v1.2.3 (GNU/Linux)

jAOEAwMCzuPpG+gDJnJgyUdnUU8TxWy4oAoS4dPErY+4jPt6YasKHUxkwOAoXNdH
G/yXyQOrqitmGXc3ojfbSLGGaUNOA6NPh/GOTXcJiIR5/v8WG+Bj9A===/keh
-----END PGP MESSAGE-----
```

This message can be pasted into the body of an e-mail and then cut out of it by the recipient and decrypted (or automatically decrypted if you had a GnuPG or PGP plug-in for your mail client). This is a much friendlier way of outputting encrypted data, and I recommend you use this.

The next option, --cipher-algo, allows you to specify the cryptographic algorithm to use for encrypting your data. Symmetrical encryption using gpg can be done with a variety of different cryptographic algorithms depending on which you have installed on your distribution. You can display all the available algorithms by running gpg with the --version option.

```
puppy# gpg --version
gpg (GnuPG) 1.2.3
Copyright (C) 2003 Free Software Foundation, Inc.
This program comes with ABSOLUTELY NO WARRANTY.
This is free software, and you are welcome to redistribute it
under certain conditions. See the file COPYING for details.

Home: ~/.gnupg
Supported algorithms:
Pubkey: RSA, RSA-E, RSA-S, ELG-E, DSA, ELG
Cipher: 3DES, CAST5, BLOWFISH, AES, AES192, AES256, TWOFISH
Hash: MD5, SHA1, RIPEMD160, SHA256
Compression: Uncompressed, ZIP, ZLIB
```

By default gpg installations will use 3DES as the cipher algorithm, but you can override this using the `--cipher-algo` option, like this:

```
puppy# gpg -c -a --cipher-algo BLOWFISH test.txt
```

The previous line encrypted the `test.txt` file with the Blowfish cipher. The file outputted by the command would remain `test.txt.asc` (`.asc` because you used the `-a` option).

The `-o` option allows you to specify the name of the file that will be outputted when the `gpg -c` command is run. For example:

```
puppy# gpg -c -a -o test2.encrypted test.txt
```

The previous line would output a file called `test2.encrypted` that contains the encrypted contents of the `test.txt` file.

The last option, `-v`, enables verbose output from the encryption process. You can enable it twice, `-vv`, to provide even more detail.

Securely Mounting File Systems

When your system starts, each of your file systems is mounted to allow you to access the data stored on your system. Your file systems can be mounted using different options: ranging from the ability to write to a file system to specifying what sort of files can be run on that file system. These options allow you to lock down the capabilities and functionality of each of your file systems. These options are controlled by the `/etc/fstab` file. This section is not going to be a definitive breakdown of every setting in the `fstab` file (the man page will give details of the settings I don't cover), but it will cover several settings you can use to ensure your file systems are mounted more securely.

In Listing 4-20 you can see a sample of the `/etc/fstab` file. The `/etc/fstab` file is generally similar across most distributions.

Listing 4-20. `/etc/fstab` *File*

```
LABEL=/              /              ext3    defaults          1 1
LABEL=/boot          /boot          ext3    defaults          1 2
none                 /dev/pts       devpts  gid=5,mode=620    0 0
none                 /dev/shm       tmpfs   defaults          0 0
none                 /proc          proc    defaults          0 0
none                 /sys           sysfs   defaults          0 0
/dev/hda3            swap           swap    defaults          0 0
/dev/cdrom           /mnt/cdrom     udf,iso9660 noauto,owner,kudzu,ro 0 0
```

Each line in the `/etc/fstab` file is an entry defining a file system that can be mounted. Each line consists of columns that define various facets of the file system. Let's quickly look at each column and what it does.

The first column is the name or label of the file system to be mounted. This is generally a device name, such as `/dev/cdrom`, or a volume label, such as `/` for the root volume or `/boot` for the boot volume. The second column is the mount point for the file system. This is the directory or location on your system where you want to mount the file system. The third column is the type of file system that you are mounting (for example, `ext3` or `swap`).

The fourth column allows you to specify options that define how your file systems are mounted. This fourth column contains the major options you will be using to secure your file systems. These options include how the file system is mounted (for example, being mounted read-only) and exactly how users can interact with the file system (for example, what types of files they can run or whether they can run files at all).

The fifth and sixth columns handle options for the dump and fsck commands, respectively. You can read about these in the fstab man page.

Table 4-5 describes some of the security-related mount options that can be placed in the fourth column of the /etc/fstab file.

Table 4-5. fstab *Mount Options*

Option	Description
auto	File system will be mounted automatically at boot time.
noauto	File system will *not* be mounted automatically at boot time.
dev	Allows interpretation of block or character special devices on this file system.
nodev	Does *not* interpret block or character special devices on this file system.
exec	Execution of binaries is allowed on this file system.
noexec	Execution of binaries is NOT allowed on this file system.
suid	setuid bits are allowed to take effect on this file system.
nosuid	setuid bits are *not* allowed to take effect on this file system.
user	Normal users can mount this device.
nouser	Only root users can mount this device.
owner	Allows the owner of the device to mount the file system.
ro	File system will be mounted read-only.
rw	File system will be mounted read-write.
defaults	Sets this file system's options as rw, suid, dev, exec, auto, nouser, and async.

■**Note** Other options not explained here are described in the fstab man page.

As you can see from Table 4-5 you can specify a variety of different ways to control how file systems are mounted. The first options in Table 4-5 are the auto and noauto options, which tell your system whether to load to load a particular file system at boot time. This can allow you to specify file systems that you want to mount in the event they are required, thus preventing casual discovery of them. The next two options, dev and nodev, control the functioning of character and block devices on your file systems. When the nodev option is specified, these devices will not be interpreted and thus will not function. You need to ensure that only file systems where you know you do not need these types of devices are mounted in this way—so check your file systems for the presence of device files first. You can do this using the find command on the next line:

```
puppy# find / -type b -or -type c
```

The exec and noexec options allow you to control whether binary execution is allowed on a particular file system. If you specify noexec on a file system, then no binaries or executable files will be allowed to run. Be careful setting this option on some file systems, especially operating system–focused file systems such as /boot or /, as the potential exists to prevent your system from operating because your operating system cannot execute a required binary.

I discussed setuid files earlier in this chapter and emphasized how important it is to limit their numbers and track their purposes. The suid and nosuid options control the functioning of binaries with the setuid or setgid bits set on your file systems. When binaries are executed on a file system with the nosuid option, their setuid and setgid bits will be ignored. With this setting being ignored, most setuid binaries will fail because they do not have the required level of permissions to function.

The user, nouser, and owner options are all interrelated and provide control over who is allowed to mount your file systems. By default only root users can mount file systems. If you have file systems with the user option specified, then any user can mount (or unmount) these file systems. If the owner option is specified, then the owner of the device can mount the device as well as the root user. I recommend you never allow non-root users to mount your file systems and that all your file system devices are owned by the root user.

The next mount options in Table 4-5 are ro and rw, read-only and read-write, respectively. These allow you to control whether your users and applications can write to a particular file system. When you specify the ro option, a file system's contents cannot be changed by any user, including the root user. This is useful for mounting file systems with static contents. Any applications requiring write access to objects on that read-only file system will not function.

The last option in Table 4-5 is defaults. You can see in Listing 4-20 that most of the file systems contain the option, defaults. The defaults option specifies that the rw, suid, dev, exec, auto, nouser, and async options should be applied to the file system being mounted. You will need to remove this and replace it with the mount options you require; otherwise, your selection of mount options will be overridden by the defaults option.

Let's look at some examples of how you could use these mount options. For example, many systems have a /home file system that contains the users' home directories. You know what you want to allow your users to be able to do in their home directories, so you can enforce some controls when you mount the file system using the mount options. You determine that you do not want your users to execute any binaries, that any device files should not be interpreted, and that any setuid files should have their bits ignored, thus preventing the binaries from executing with those permissions. In Listing 4-21 you can see a /etc/fstab line where I have added the mount options to achieve all this.

Listing 4-21. *Example of Mounting /home Securely*

```
/dev/hda8        /home    ext2    noexec,nodev,nosuid  0  2
```

You can now see in the fourth column that I have added the noexec, nodev, and nosuid options. Each option is listed in this column and separated by a comma. Now when this file system is next mounted, your policy for the /home file system will be enforced.

Another common method of securing your file systems is to mount all those file systems that do not require write access as read-only. This is commonly also used with network-mounted file systems to export read-only shares. To do this, you add the ro option to the mount options for the file systems you want to mount read-only.

In Listing 4-22 I have specified that the /usr file system will be mounted with ro, the read-only option, and nodev, the option to stop block or character devices being interpreted.

Listing 4-22. *Mounting a Read-Only File System*

```
/dev/hda7        /usr    ext2    ro,nodev  0  2
```

These are merely two examples of how you could combine the available options to manage your file system mounting and control how and what users can do in your file systems. I recommend you determine if you can restrict how your file systems are mounted using these options and ensure only the activities you want can be performed. Where you do not need particular functionality and can apply restrictions such as nodev and nosuid, you should apply these. But, like immutable files, the mount options should also be used with caution, as they can cause issues on your system if improperly used; for example, marking your /boot file system as noexec will result in your system being unable to boot.

Securing Removable Devices

One of the ways your system can be penetrated is through viruses or the introduction of compromised files onto your system through removable media such as floppy or CD drives. More recently, various other removable devices, such as memory cards and sticks or removable USB devices, have created alternative methods for attackers to introduce malicious files onto your system. I will show you two ways of reducing the risk of introducing malicious files through your removable devices.

The first way is to restrict who can mount removable devices. For most purposes on your systems there should be no reason for any users other than the root user to mount floppy disks or CDs. On most distributions this is the default setting and is achieved through the nouser option in the /etc/fstab file, as discussed in the previous section. You should confirm that all your removable devices in the /etc/fstab file have the nouser option set.

Additionally on Red Hat systems, non-root users can mount devices if they are signed onto the console. This is managed by the file console.perms located in the /etc/security directory (see Chapter 1). This file allows non-root users logged into the console to mount CDs or floppy disks (and a variety of other removable devices such as Jaz or Zip drives). Listing 4-23 shows a sample of the contents of the console.perms file that you can use to control the mounting of removable devices.

Listing 4-23. console.perms *Mounting Options*

```
<console>  0660  <floppy>      0660 root.floppy
<console>  0600  <cdrom>       0660 root.disk
<console>  0600  <jaz>         0660 root.disk
<console>  0600  <zip>         0660 root.disk
<console>  0600  <memstick>    0600 root
<console>  0600  <diskonkey>   0660 root.disk
<console>  0600  <rem_ide>     0660 root.disk
<console>  0600  <fb>          0600 root
```

You can restrict removable devices that non-root users can mount from the console by commenting out the lines in Listing 4-23 that refer to particular devices. Listing 4-24 disables the mounting of CD and floppy drives by non-root users. I recommend you disable the mounting of all removable devices by these users.

Listing 4-24. *Disabling Non-root Mounting*

```
#<console>  0660 <floppy>     0660 root.floppy
#<console>  0600 <cdrom>      0660 root.disk
```

The second way of reducing the risk of having your removable devices introduce malicious files is to limit what files you can utilize on removable devices using the nosuid and nodev options and potentially the noexec option in the /etc/fstab file. Listing 4-25 shows a CD drive with these mount options specified.

Listing 4-25. *Mounting Removable Devices*

```
/dev/cdrom       /mnt/cdrom        udf,iso9660   noauto,ro,nodev,nosuid,noexec   0 0
```

In Listing 4-25 the CD-ROM is mounted read-only, will not allow any binaries to run (including setuid binaries), and will not interpret block or character device files. This will prevent most potential infiltrations of malicious files from this removable device. Of course, it will also make it difficult for you to install software from a CD, and you would need to adjust the mounting options to do this.

Creating an Encrypted File System

I demonstrated earlier the capability to encrypt files on your system but, I can extend this principle to include the encryption of entire file systems. This allows you to encrypt and protect entire volumes of data (for example, backups), logging data, or private files. Encryption also means that even if an attacker has penetrated your system, the attacker is not able to read any file systems that you have encrypted. Many roving users with critical data on devices such as laptops also use file system encryption to further secure data that is physically insecure (for example, when the user is traveling).

File system encryption was not a feature that was available out of the box with most Linux distributions but rather was provided by a number of different third-party solutions such as CFS[5] or loop encryption file systems such as Loop-AES.[6] These third-party solutions required patching the kernel to support them. More recently with the version 2.6 kernel release, some progress has been made toward incorporating this functionality directly into the kernel, first with Cryptoloop and then with dm-crypt.[7] I will cover using dm-crypt to encrypt a file system. The dm-crypt functionality was incorporated into release 2.6.4 of the kernel, so you need at least this version of the 2.6 kernel. This minimum level of kernel release is provided by a number of current distributions: Red Hat Fedora Core 2, SUSE Linux 9.1, Mandrake 10, and Debian

---

5. http://www.crypto.com/software/

6. http://loop-aes.sourceforge.net/

7. http://www.saout.de/misc/dm-crypt/

Sarge. Most other distributions are also moving toward providing this level of kernel release. Or if you need this functionality, you can upgrade your kernel to the required version yourself. To do this, you can start with the instructions provided in Chapter 1.

I will cover using `dm_crypt` to create a loop encryption file system. A loop encryption file system allows you to create an encrypted file system from an image file. This allows you to store private files in a single encrypted file system rather than encrypting all the individual files. This is the simplest use of `dm_crypt`, and you can extend the principles demonstrated next to encrypt entire partitions or disks.

Installing the Userland Tools

First, though, you need to ensure you have all the tools required to perform the encryption. If you have confirmed you have the required kernel version, you need to install the userland tools that allow you to manipulate the `dm_crypt` functionality. These are provided by a package called `cryptsetup`, which is available for Red Hat and Debian via those distribution's update tools. In Listing 4-26 you use `yum` to install it.

Listing 4-26. *Installing* `cryptsetup`

```
puppy# yum install cryptsetup
```

This will also prompt you to install the additional required packages: `libgcrypt` and `libgpg-error`. Install all three packages.

■Tip These packages should also be on the distribution media for your distribution, but it is a good idea to ensure you have the latest versions.

Enabling the Functionality

Most distributions have provided the `dm_crypt` functionality in the form of loadable kernel modules. You will need to load these modules before being able to use `dm_crypt`. You can use the `modprobe` command to load the required modules like this:

```
puppy# modprobe aes dm_crypt dm_mod
```

The first module, `aes`, enables support for AES encryption, which is the default cipher used by `dm_crypt`.[8] I will show you how to use `dm_crypt` with this cipher, but you can also enable alternative ciphers, such as Blowfish, by ensuring they have been compiled into your kernel and then load them via modules.

You can check the contents of your kernel configuration file in `/boot` for which ciphers are available by using the following command:

```
puppy# cat /boot/config-version | grep 'CRYPT'
```

---

8. Read about AES at http://csrc.nist.gov/publications/fips/fips197/fips-197.pdf.

Replace *version* with the version of the kernel you are running. In Listing 4-27 you can see a partial list of the kernel options produced by the previous command. Those options prefixed by CONFIG_CRYPTO are the ciphers compiled into your kernel.

Listing 4-27. *Ciphers Available in Your Kernel*

```
CONFIG_CRYPTO_BLOWFISH=m
CONFIG_CRYPTO_TWOFISH=m
CONFIG_CRYPTO_SERPENT=m
CONFIG_CRYPTO_AES_586=m
CONFIG_CRYPTO_CAST5=m
CONFIG_CRYPTO_CAST6=m
CONFIG_CRYPTO_TEA=m
```

The =m suffix indicates that this kernel functionality is provided via a loadable module. As you did with the AES cipher, you can load these ciphers with the modprobe command.

```
puppy# modprobe blowfish
```

You can see what other ciphers are currently loaded and available on your system by looking at the contents of the /proc/crypto file. In Listing 4-28 you cat this file.

Listing 4-28. *Viewing Available Ciphers*

```
puppy# cat /proc/crypto
name        : md5
module      : kernel
type        : digest
blocksize   : 64
digestsize  : 16

name        : aes
module      : aes
type        : cipher
blocksize   : 16
min keysize : 16
max keysize : 32
```

Finally, the additional modules, dm_crypt and dm_mod, provide the file system encryption functionality itself.

If you want to automatically enable this functionality, you can add these modules (including any additional ciphers you would like to enable) to your /etc/modules.conf file. This will load these modules when your system is started.

Encrypting a Loop File System

Now that you have enabled all the required modules and have installed the userland tools, you can create your encrypted file system. You need to create an image file to hold your encrypted file system. Listing 4-29 uses the dd command to create an empty file of a suitable size.

Listing 4-29. *Creating an Empty Image File*

```
puppy# dd if=/dev/urandom of=/home/bob/safe.img bs=1k count=10024
```

The dd command converts and copies files, but here I am using it to populate an empty image file. The if option specifies the input file, dev/urandom. This device is a randomness source and allows you to populate the imagine file with random data. The of option specifies the output file; I have created a file called safe.img in the /home/bob directory. The next options control the size of the file to be created. The bs option indicates that the size of the file will be measured in kilobytes, 1k, and the count option tells dd how many kilobytes to add to the file. In this case I have created a 10 megabyte (MB) file to hold the encrypted file system.

Now that you have your image file, you need to create a loop device from it. Loop devices allow images files to be mounted as block devices as if they were a normal hard disk drive or floppy disk.[9] Listing 4-30 shows how you use the command to create the loop device.

Listing 4-30. *Creating a Loop Device*

```
puppy# losetup /dev/loop0 /home/bob/safe.img
```

The losetup command creates the loop device /dev/loop0 from the file safe.img.

Now you need to create the encrypted device on your loop device. Installing the cryptsetup package will have provided a command called cryptsetup that you will use to create that encrypted device. Listing 4-31 uses the cryptsetup command to create an encrypted device in your loop device.

Listing 4-31. *Creating Encrypted File System*

```
puppy# cryptsetup -y create safe /dev/loop0
Enter passphrase:
Verify passphrase:
```

Listing 4-31 maps the /dev/loop0 device to a special kind of encrypted block device, which I have called safe. This device is created in the /dev/mapper directory. You can now format a file system on this device and then mount it. If you list the contents of the /dev/mapper directory, you will see this newly created device.

```
puppy# ls -l /dev/mapper
total 0
crw-------  1 root root  10, 63 Sep  2 18:18 control
brw-r-----  1 root root 253,  0 Sep 19 13:17 safe
```

The cryptsetup command also prompts you to enter the passphrase that will secure your file system. Like when choosing other passphrases discussed in the "Encrypting Files" section earlier in this chapter (and in Chapter 1 when I discussed passwords), you should choose a secure and suitable passphrase. You will need to remember this passphrase. If you forget it, you will not be able to access your encrypted file system. The -y option in Listing 4-31 tells

---

9. You can read further about loop devices at http://people.debian.org/~psg/ddg/node159.html.

cryptsetup to prompt for the passphrase twice; the second time is to add some validity checking and ensure you enter the correct passphrase. After you have inputted the password, cryptsetup will hash the passphrase and use it as the key for the encrypted file system.[10] By default your passphrase will be hashed with the ripemd160 hashing algorithm.

Let's break the cryptsetup command down a bit further; I will show some details of each of the functions it can perform. The command is structured like this:

cryptsetup *options action name device*

I will now cover the combinations of options and actions you can perform with cryptsetup. Table 4-6 describes some of the more useful options of the cryptsetup command.

Table 4-6. cryptsetup *Options*

Option	Description
-c *cipher*	Cipher used to encrypt the disk. Defaults to aes.
-h *hash*	Hash used to create the encryption key from the passphrase. Defaults to ripemd160.
-s *keysize*	Specifies the key size in bits. Defaults to 256 bits.
-y	Verifies the passphrase by asking for it twice.
-v	Verbose mode.
-?	Shows the help and usage information.

■Note Currently cryptsetup does not have a man page.

The -c and -h options control how your file system is encrypted. The -c option specifies the cipher that will be used to encrypt the file system. As mentioned earlier, the default cipher for dm_crypt is AES, but you can specify any suitable cipher available on your system; for example, you earlier enabled Blowfish.

```
puppy# cryptsetup -c blowfish create safe /dev/loop0
```

The choice of cipher really depends on the required performance and cipher standards by which you want to abide. For some information about some of the available ciphers that can be used with dm_crypt, including their relative performance, see http://www.saout.de/tikiwiki/tiki-index.php?page=UserPageChonhulio.

■Caution I recommend you avoid using DES encryption, as it is not secure.

---

10. I will talk about hashing in Chapter 3.

The -h option specifies what form of hashing is used to create an encryption key from your passphase. By default dm_crypt uses the ripemd160 hash, but you can use any digest hash available on your system (for example, sha1).

```
puppy# cryptsetup -c blowfish -h sha1 create safe /dev/loop0
```

The -s option allows you to specify the size of the encryption key to be used. The size is expressed in bits. The default key size is 256 bits. The larger the key size you use, then generally the more secure your encrypted file system will be, but the larger key sizes can also have negative performance impacts on your system. I recommend that for most purposes 256 bits is suitable, but depending on the speed of your disk, memory, and CPU you may want to experiment with larger key sizes.

You can enable the -v option to provide more information when the cryptsetup command runs. Lastly, the -? option provides help, usage, and information.

Next are the actions that the cryptsetup command can perform. You have already seen the create option, which you have used to create an encrypted file system. Table 4-7 shows some of the other possible actions.

Table 4-7. cryptsetup *Actions*

Action	Description
create	Creates a device
remove	Removes a device
reload	Modifies an active device
resize	Resizes an active device
status	Shows the device status

The remove option you will look at when you examine unmounting an encrypted file system; it reverses the process of mapping the encrypted block device that the create option produces. The reload option allows you to reload the device mapping, and the resize option allows you to resize the device. The last option, status, provides you with useful status information on your mapped devices.

```
puppy# cryptsetup status safe
/dev/mapper/safe is active:
  cipher:  aes-plain
  keysize: 256 bits
  device:  /dev/loop0
  offset:  0 sectors
  size:    20048 sectors
```

After selecting options and associated actions, you need to specify the name of the encrypted file system for an action to be performed on. In the previous command you specified the name safe. This will be the name of the mapped device created in the /dev/mapper directory.

Then lastly on the cryptsetup command line you need to specify the actual device that will be used to create the file system. In this explanation I have used a loop device, /dev/loop0, but you could also use a normal block device such as a disk or another type of device such as memory stick or USB drive.

I have now created an image file, mounted that image file as a loop device, and created an encryption device using the `cryptsetup` command. Now you need to create a file system on that device to allow you to mount and write files to it. I have decided to create an ext3 type file system on the device I have created, `/dev/mapper/safe`, using the `mkfs.ext3` command.

```
puppy# mkfs.ext3 -j /dev/mapper/safe
```

This now gives you a disk space of 10MB for the ext3 file system on which to place the files you want to encrypt.

Now let's create a mount point (a directory) to mount your new file system. I have created the image file, `safe.img`, in `/home/bob`, so I will create a mount point off that directory for consistency. You could create the mount point anywhere.

```
puppy# mkdir /home/bob/safe
```

Finally, you mount the new file system using the `mount` command.

```
puppy# mount -t ext3 /dev/mapper/safe /home/bob/safe
```

I have mounted the file system, specifying its type, ext3, and the device to mount, `/dev/mapper/safe`, to the mount point I have just created, `/home/bob/safe`.

You can now add whatever files you want to this file system. But is this it? Not quite. You also need a process for unmounting and remounting your new encrypted file system.

Unmounting Your Encrypted File System

When you shut down your system or no longer require access to the encrypted file system, you need to unmount it. This process basically consists of a reversal of some of the steps you used to create the file system.

First you need to unmount your file system using the `umount` command.

```
puppy# umount /home/bob/safe
```

Then you need to unmap the device you created with the `cryptsetup` command.

```
puppy# cryptsetup remove safe
```

The command's `remove` action is used to unmap the `/dev/loop0` device. Do not panic, though; this has not deleted any of your data. It merely removes the mapping of the device. All your data is intact in the loop device and the associated image file. But to protect your data you must run the `cryptsetup remove` action; otherwise, anybody can remount your device without providing the passphrase.

Lastly you need to stop your loop device. You again use the `losetup` command but with the `-d` option that indicates you want to detach the `/dev/loop0` device.

```
puppy# losetup -d /dev/loop0
```

The encrypted data is now contained in the `safe.img` file you created at the start of the previous section.

Remounting

To remount, you follow an abbreviated version of the process you used to create the encrypted file system. You again need to create a loop device from your image file. You use the same image file, safe.img, and the same loop device, /dev/loop0.

```
puppy# losetup /dev/loop0 safe.img
```

Next you need to reestablish your encrypted file device map using the cryptsetup command. For this you will need the passphrase you used to create the original file system device mapping. If you do not have this passphrase, you will not be able to mount your encrypted file system. Listing 4-32 maps the device with the same name, safe, and from the same device, /dev/loop0, that you did previously.

Listing 4-32. *Remapping the Encrypted Device*

```
puppy# cryptsetup -y create safe /dev/loop0
Enter passphrase:
Verify passphrase:
```

Disconcertingly, if you put into the wrong passphrase when entering the cryptsetup command, then the command will not fail but rather will complete without error. You will not, however, be able to mount the encrypted file system, as I will demonstrate next.

Now that you have re-established the device mapping, you can mount your device. You again mount it to the /home/bob/safe mount point.

```
puppy# mount -t ext3 /dev/mapper/safe /home/bob/safe
```

If you had entered the incorrect pass in Listing 4-32, then your mount attempt would fail with the following error:

```
mount: wrong fs type, bad option, bad superblock on /dev/mapper/safe, ➥
or too many mounted file systems
```

Unfortunately, this error message is generic and can result from a number of error conditions. I recommend you carefully enter your passphrase. Use the cryptsetup -y option to be prompted for your passphrase twice to reduce the risk of entering the wrong passphrase.

■**Tip** As you can see, the creating, unmounting, and remounting process is quite complicated. I recommend you automate the process with a script. You can find some examples of this at the dm_crypt wiki at http://www.saout.de/tikiwiki/tiki-index.php.

Maintaining File Integrity with Tripwire

Once you have hardened and secured your files and file systems, you need to ensure they stay that way. One of the biggest threats to security hardening is entropy—over time changes are introduced to the environment that could expose you to risk of attack. The security and integrity of your files is no different. As things change on your systems, so can the permissions and content of your files and objects. Additionally, one of the key indicators of an attack or penetration of your system is unexpected changes in permissions, attributes, and the contents of files and objects.

To mitigate the risk of these sorts of changes and to detect any malicious changes to your files and objects, several checksum and integrity scanners exist. These scanners take a baseline of your system and then run regular, usually scheduled, scans of your system and compare the results against the baseline. I will cover the most well-known scanner, Tripwire.

Tripwire works on a policy-compliance model. You need to configure a policy covering all the objects you want to monitor and the changes to these objects in which you are interested. Taking this policy, Tripwire then initializes and generates a baseline database of all the file and objects covered by this policy. You next schedule a regular scan of the system, and if Tripwire detects a variation from the baseline, then it will be reported.

Tripwire is available in a number of different forms and variations. Many distributions have created their own branches of Tripwire. This is in addition to the open-source version available at `http://sourceforge.net/projects/tripwire/` and the commercial version available at the Tripwire site, `http://www.tripwire.com`. These branched versions of Tripwire tend to have subtle differences. Usually these differences are aimed at addressing the idiosyncrasies of a particular distribution; for example, the Tripwire version available for Red Hat moves and renames some commands to bring Tripwire in line with Red Hat's conventions. I recommend you look at the package available for your distribution first. This package is likely to be easier to configure for your system than other versions.

Tripwire is available via Apt for Debian, as an RPM for Red Hat Enterprise Linux and Mandrake on those distributions' media, and for Red Hat Fedora Core.[11] It is also available from SourceForge as a source tarball. The source tarball is often difficult to compile. I recommend installing Tripwire via an RPM; the following line installs the Fedora RPM.

```
puppy# rpm -Uvh tripwire-2.3.1-20.fdr.1.2.i386.rpm
```

■**Tip** So, when do you install and initialize Tripwire? Well, I recommend you install and initialize Tripwire after you have installed your operating system and applications and have applied any updates or patches but *before* you have connected your system to a production network. This ensures Tripwire can be configured with all the required files and binaries being monitored and reduces the risk that an attacker could penetrate your system before you enable Tripwire.

Configuring Tripwire

In this section, you will see the base Tripwire configuration, and then I will show you how to initialize and run Tripwire. As you are going to configure Tripwire using the Red Hat Fedora RPM, some of the configuration options, especially their naming conventions, may differ from other versions of Tripwire. This is especially true of the source tarball version where many configuration options differ. I will try to address this where I can.

---

11. Via `http://download.fedora.us/`

After installing Tripwire, the configuration for the tool will be installed into the /etc/tripwire directory in the form of two files: twcfg.txt and twpol.txt. The twcfg.txt file contains the default configuration for Tripwire, including the location of the Tripwire binaries and policies. The twpol.txt file contains the Tripwire policy that tells Tripwire what to monitor. I will talk about it in the "Explaining Tripwire Policy" section.

Listing 4-33 shows a sample of the twcfg.txt file.

Listing 4-33. *Tripwire* twcfg.txt

```
ROOT                    =/usr/sbin
POLFILE                 =/etc/tripwire/tw.pol
DBFILE                  =/var/lib/tripwire/$(HOSTNAME).twd
REPORTFILE              =/var/lib/tripwire/report/$(HOSTNAME)-$(DATE).twr
SITEKEYFILE             =/etc/tripwire/site.key
```

The file consists of directives and answers (for example, ROOT=/usr/sbin), which indicates where the Tripwire binaries are located. Most of the directives in twcfg.txt are self-explanatory. Table 4-8 describes some of the other directives and their functions.

Table 4-8. *Tripwire* twcfg.txt *Directives*

Directive	Description
LATEPROMPTING=*true* | *false*	Limits the time the Tripwire password is in memory by delaying prompting for it. Defaults to false.
LOOSEDIRECTORYCHECKING=*true* | *false*	If true, then report if files in a watched directory change but do not report on the directory itself. Defaults to false.
SYSLOGREPORTING=*true* | *false*	Specifies whether Tripwire logs to syslog.
EMAILREPORTLEVEL=*number*	Specifies the verbosity of Tripwire e-mail reports. Defaults to 3.
REPORTLEVEL=*number*	Specifies the verbosity of Tripwire printed reports. Defaults to 3.
MAILMETHOD=SENDMAIL | SMTP	Specifies how Tripwire sends e-mail. Defaults to SENDMAIL.
MAILPROGRAM=*program*	Specifies the Sendmail binary for Tripwire. Defaults to /usr/lib/sendmail -oi -t. Valid only if the mail method is SENDMAIL.
SMTPHOST=*SMTP Host*	Specifies the SMTP host to use. Valid only if the mail method is SMTP.
SMTPPORT=*port*	Specifies the SMTP port to use. Valid only if the mail method is SMTP.
MAILNOVIOLATIONS=*true* | *false*	Sends a notification when a Tripwire report is run even if no violations were found.

■**Note** Most of these variables are present in all versions of Tripwire, but in some versions, most notably the source tarball, these options are prefixed with the letters TW. So, MAILPRORAM becomes TWMAILPROGRAM.

The defaults in `twcfg.txt` should be suitable for most Tripwire installations, but some of the options in Table 4-8 may be useful to tweak. If the first option, `LATEPROMPTING`, is set to `true`, then Tripwire delays the prompting of the user for passwords as long as possible to limit the time the password spends in memory. If the second option, `LOOSEDIRECTORYCHECKING`, is set to `true`, then it reports on changed files and objects in a watched directory but does not report the directory change itself. This stops Tripwire from reporting two changes, one for file and one for the directory, which reduces redundant reporting. It defaults to `false`.

If you want Tripwire to log violations to `syslog`, then set the `SYSLOGREPORTING` directive to `true`. You can control the verbosity of Tripwire's reporting with the two report-level options, `REPORTLEVEL` and `EMAILREPORTLEVEL`. The verbosity ranges from 0 to 4, with 0 as minimal detail and 4 as the most verbose.

The last five options relate to how Tripwire notifies you via e-mail if it detects a violation. The first is the `MAILMETHOD`, which determines how Tripwire will send e-mails. Tripwire can send e-mail directly via the Sendmail binary or can connect to an SMTP host. Specify `SENDMAIL` to send via the binary and `SMTP` to send to an SMTP host. If you specified `SENDMAIL` as the mail method, then the location and options of the Sendmail binary are set with the `MAILPROGRAM` directive. If you specified `SMTP`, then you can designate the SMTP host and port you want to send e-mails to using the `SMTPHOST` and `SMTPPORT` directives, respectively.

If the last of these options, `MAILNOVIOLATIONS`, is set to `true`, then Tripwire generates an e-mail report when it is run, even if no violations are found. If you do not want to receive a report when Tripwire is run and does not find any violations, then set this option to `false`. The default is `true`.

Additionally, some variables are available to you in the `twcfg.txt` file, such as `$(HOSTNAME)` for hostname and `$(DATE)` for the current date.

Explaining Tripwire Policy

The `twpol.txt` file is the input file for the Tripwire policy for your host. This file will be used to create a proprietary file called a *policy file*. The policy determines what files and objects Tripwire will monitor for changes. It also specifies exactly what changes to those files and objects it will monitor. The RPM you have installed comes with a default policy. This policy is designed to monitor Red Hat Fedora systems. If you are running Tripwire on a different distribution, it may have come with a sample policy of its own. Either way you will need to change the policy to reflect exactly what objects you want to monitor on your system. I recommend you at least monitor important operating system files and directories, logging files, and the configuration files and binaries of your applications.

Let's look at the `twpol.txt` file. The file contains two types of items. It contains the directives and the rules that identify the individual files, and it contains the objects Tripwire is monitoring. I will break the sample `twpol.txt` file into these items to demonstrate its content and then show how to structure your Tripwire policy file.

Tripwire Policy Global Variables

The global Tripwire variables define the location of Tripwire-specific objects and directories and the hostname of the system on which Tripwire is running. These variables are contained in a special section of the policy file called a *directive*. This directive is entitled `@@section` `GLOBAL` and is located toward the start of the policy file. Listing 4-34 shows a sample of the global variables section of the default `twpol.txt` file created when I installed Tripwire.

Listing 4-34. *Tripwire Global Variables*

```
@@section GLOBAL
TWROOT=/usr/sbin;
TWBIN=/usr/sbin;
TWPOL="/etc/tripwire";
TWDB="/var/lib/tripwire";
TWSKEY="/etc/tripwire";
TWLKEY="/etc/tripwire";
TWREPORT="/var/lib/tripwire/report";
HOSTNAME=puppy.yourdomain.com;
```

Each variable is terminated by a semicolon. If the semicolon is missing, then the policy file will not parse correctly, so loading the policy into Tripwire (as I will demonstrate in the "Initializing and Running Tripwire" section) will fail. Most of the variables in Listing 4-34 are self-explanatory and specify the directories that Tripwire will use. The last variable is HOSTNAME. You need to set HOSTNAME to your system's fully qualified domain name (FQDN) to ensure Tripwire functions correctly. In this case, this is puppy.yourdomain.com.

■Note In the sample twpol.txt file installed by the RPM, you also have the FS directive section, which contains some predefined property summaries and other variables used by the example policy. I discuss these property summaries and variables briefly in the "Tripwire Rules" section.

Tripwire Rules

A Tripwire *rule* is defined as a file or directory name and a property mask separated by the symbols ->. Additionally, it can have some optional rule attributes. In Listing 4-35 you can see the structure of a Tripwire rule.

Listing 4-35. *Tripwire Rule Structure*

```
filename -> property mask (rule attribute = value);
```

Let's look at each part of the Tripwire rule. The first portion of the rule is the file or object you want to monitor. This could be a single file or an entire directory. If you specify a directory, then Tripwire will monitor the properties of that directory and the entire contents of that directory. You can have only one rule per object or file. If an object has more than one rule, Tripwire will fail with an error message and not conduct any scanning.

The file or object is then separated from the property mask by a space or tab and the -> symbols, followed by another space or tab. The property mask tells Tripwire exactly what change about the file or object you want to monitor. For example, you could monitor for a change to the user who owns the file, the size of the file, or the file's permissions. Each property is indicated by a letter prefixed with either a plus (+) sign or a minus (-) sign. For example, the following line monitors the ownership of the /etc/passwd file:

```
/etc/passwd -> +u;
```

The u is the Tripwire property for object ownership, and the plus (+) sign indicates you want to monitor this property. You can add further properties to be monitored by adding property letters to your Tripwire rule. On the next line you add the property, s, which indicates file size:

```
/etc/passwd -> +su;
```

Now Tripwire will monitor for any changes to the /etc/passwd file's ownership and its size.

■**Note** You must terminate all rules with a semicolon (;).

Table 4-9 lists all the properties you can monitor for in Tripwire.

Table 4-9. *Tripwire Property Masks*

Property	Description
a	Access time stamp.
b	Number of blocks.
c	Inode time stamp.
d	ID of the device on which the inode resides.
g	Owning group.
i	Inode number.
l	File increases in size.
m	Modification time stamp.
n	Number of links to the object.
p	Permissions.
r	ID of the device pointed to by inode. Valid only for device type objects.
s	File size.
t	File type.
u	Object owner.
C	CRC-32 hash value.
H	Haval hash value.
M	MD5 hash value.
S	SHA hash value.

These properties are generally fairly self-explanatory file system attributes. The only property that needs further explanation is l. The l property is designed for files that will only grow. Tripwire thus monitors to see if the file shrinks in size but ignores the file if it grows in size.

The minus (-) sign prefixing a property indicates that you do not want to monitor for that property. In the next line I am monitoring the /etc/passwd file for its ownership and size, but I have explicitly told Tripwire that I do not care about its last modification time stamp.

```
/etc/passwd -> +su-m;
```

In addition to the individual properties you can monitor for, you can also use property summaries. These property summaries are variables that represent particular combinations of properties. For example, Tripwire has a built-in property summary called $(Device), which contains the recommended properties for devices (or other types of files that Tripwire should not try to open). On the next line you can see the $(Device) property summary in a rule:

```
/dev/mapper/safe -> $(Device);
```

As I have described, each property summary represents different combinations of properties. The $(Device) property summary is equivalent to setting the properties in the following rule:

```
/dev/mapper/safe -> +pugsdr-intlbamcCMSH;
```

The previous line indicates that any rule that uses the $(Device) property summary will monitor files and objects for changes to their permissions, ownership, group owner, size and device, and inode ID monitored, but all other changes will be ignored. Table 4-10 lists all the default property summaries, the property mask value they are equivalent to, and what they are designed to monitor.

Table 4-10. *Property Summaries*

Summary	Mask Value	Description
$(Device)	+pugsdr-intlbamcCMSH	Devices or other files that Tripwire should not attempt to open
$(Dynamic)	+pinugtd-srlbamcCMSH	User directories and files that tend to be dynamic
$(Growing)	+pinugtdl-srbamcCMSH	Files that should only get larger
$(IgnoreAll)	-pinugtsdrlbamcCMSH	Checks for the file presence or absence but does not check any properties
$(IgnoreNone)	+pinugtsdrbamcCMSH-l	Turns on all properties
$(ReadOnly)	+pinugsmtdbCM	Files that are read-only

Two of the most useful of these property summaries are $(IgnoreAll) and $(IgnoreNone). The $(IgnoreAll) summary allows you to simply check if a file is present and report on that. The $(IgnoreNone) summary is a good starting point for custom property masks. By default it turns on all properties to be monitored. Using the - syntax you then deduct those properties you do not want to monitor.

```
/etc/hosts.conf -> $(IgnoreNone) - CHn;
```

This is a much neater syntax that using the full property mask +piugtsdrbamcMS-CHnl.

■**Note** The $(IgnoreNone) summary does not set the l property.

Because property summaries are simply preset variables, you can also declare your own. You can declare a variable using the following syntax:

```
variable = value;
```

Thus, you can declare a variable to create a property summary for objects whose ownership and permissions should never change.

```
STATIC_PO = +pug;
```

The `STATIC_PO` variable could then be used in a rule, like so:

```
/home/bob/safe -> $(STATIC_PO);
```

In the example `twpol.txt` file, some of these variables have already been declared. In Listing 4-36 you can see several of these predefined variables.

Listing 4-36. *Property Summary Variables in* `twpol.txt`

```
SEC_CRIT      = $(IgnoreNone)-SHa;  # Critical files that cannot change
SEC_SUID      = $(IgnoreNone)-SHa;  # Binaries with the SUID or SGID flags set
SEC_INVARIANT = +tpug;              # Directories that should never change ➥
permission or ownership
```

You can use variables for a variety of other purposes, too. You can substitute any text in the variable declaration. For example, you can declare an object name as a variable at the start of your policy file.

```
BOB_DIR = /home/bob;
```

Then you can refer to it using a variable when defining rules.

```
$(BOB_DIR); -> +p;
```

The last parts of Tripwire rules are rule attributes. These attributes work with your rules to modify their behaviors or provide additional information. One of the most commonly used attributes is `emailto`. The `emailto` attribute allows you to specify an e-mail address (or addresses) to be notified if a rule is triggered.

```
/etc/host.conf -> +p (emailto=tripwire@yourdomain.com);
```

In the previous line, if the permissions of the `/etc/host.conf` file changed, then an e-mail would be sent (using the mail method you specified in the `twcfg.txt` file) to the `tripwire@yourdomain.com` e-mail address. Listing 4-37 specifies multiple e-mail addresses by enclosing them in quotes.

Listing 4-37. *Multiple E-mail Addresses*

```
/etc/hosts.conf -> +p (emailto="tripwire@yourdomain.com admin@anotherdomain.com");
```

■**Tip** You can test your e-mail settings using the command `/usr/sbin/tripwire --test --email` `email@yourdomain.com`, replacing the `email@yourdomain.com` with the e-mail address to which you want the test message sent.

The other attributes available to Tripwire are `recurse`, `severity`, and `rulename`. The `recurse` attribute is specified for directories and specifies whether Tripwire should recursively scan a directory and its contents.

```
/etc -> +p (recurse=false);
```

Using the rule in the previous line Tripwire normally would scan the `/etc` directory and all its contents. With the `recurse` attribute set to `false`, Tripwire will now scan only the `/etc` directory itself for changes. You can also use the `recurse` setting to specify the depth to which Tripwire will recurse. A setting of `recurse=0` will scan only the contents of the directory and not recurse to any lower directories. On the other hand, a setting of `recurse=1` will scan the contents of the specified directory and recurse one directory level lower, and so on.

The `severity` and `rulename` attributes allow you to group files in the Tripwire report according to classification. The `severity` attribute allows you to define a severity to the file being monitored.

```
/etc/host.conf -> +p (severity=99);
```

In your Tripwire report, all the results from rules, which have been specified as `severity` 99 using this attribute, will be grouped, which allows you to better sort your results. The `rulename` attribute provides similar functionality by allowing you to describe a particular rule.

```
/etc/host.conf -> +p (rulename="Network Files");
```

You can also assign multiple attributes to a rule. Listing 4-38 adds both `severity` and `rulename` attributes to a rule.

Listing 4-38. *Multiple Attributes*

```
/etc/host.conf -> +p (severity=99, rulename="Network Files");
```

You can also specify rule attributes for a group of rules. Listing 4-39 demonstrates this.

Listing 4-39. *Attributes for Groups of Rules*

```
(rulename="Network files", severity=99, emailto=tripwire@yourdomain.com)
{
/etc/host.conf -> +p;
/etc/hosts -> +p;
/etc/nsswitch.conf -> +p;
/etc/resolv.conf -> +p;
}
```

You specify your attributes first. You enclose them in brackets, and then place your rules below them and enclose them in brackets, { }. This allows you to group similar rules for ease of update and reporting.

Finally, you can specify a special type of rule called a *stop rule*. This allows you to specify files within a directory that you want to exclude, which will stop Tripwire from scanning those files. Listing 4-40 specifies that you want to monitor the /etc directory for permissions changes but you specifically want to exclude the /etc/fstab and /etc/mstab files from being monitored.

Listing 4-40. *Stop Rules*

```
/etc/hosts -> +p;
! /etc/hosts;
! /etc/hosts;
```

The ! prefix indicates that the file should be excluded. Each stop rule must be terminated with a semicolon (;).

■**Tip** You can also add comments to your Tripwire policy file by prefixing lines with a pound sign (#).

Initializing and Running Tripwire

After you have configured Tripwire and created a suitable policy for your system, you need to set up and initialize Tripwire. Tripwire comes with a command, tripwire-setup-keyfiles, that you can use to perform this initial setup. The command is usually located in the directory /usr/sbin.

■**Tip** Running this command performs the same actions as running the script twinstall.sh that came with earlier releases of Tripwire.

This command will create two keyfiles: the site key that signs your configuration and policy and the local key that protects your database and reports. You will be prompted to enter passphrases for both. Listing 4-41 shows the results of this command.

Listing 4-41. *The* tripwire-setup-keyfiles *Command*

```
puppy# /usr/sbin/tripwire-setup-keyfiles
----------------------------------------------
The Tripwire site and local passphrases are used to sign a variety of
files, such as the configuration, policy, and database files.
Passphrases should be at least 8 characters in length and contain both
letters and numbers.
See the Tripwire manual for more information.
----------------------------------------------
```

```
Creating key files...
(When selecting a passphrase, keep in mind that good passphrases typically
have upper and lower case letters, digits and punctuation marks, and are
at least 8 characters in length.)
Enter the site keyfile passphrase:
Verify the site keyfile passphrase:
```

■**Caution** You need to take good care of these passphrases, as you will be forced to reinstall Tripwire if you lose one or both of them.

The `tripwire-setup-keyfiles` command will also create encrypted versions of your `twcfg.txt` and `twpol.txt` files, called `tw.cfg` and `tw.pol`, respectively. These files will be signed with your new site key and are located in the `/etc/tripwire` directory. Listing 4-42 shows the contents of the `/etc/tripwire` directory after you run the `tripwire-setup-keyfiles` command.

Listing 4-42. *The* /etc/tripwire *Directory*

```
puppy# ls -l
-rw-r-----  1 root root   931 Sep 26 17:03 puppy.yourdomain.com-local.key
-rw-r-----  1 root root   931 Sep 26 17:02 site.key
-rw-r-----  1 root root  4586 Sep 26 17:03 tw.cfg
-rw-r--r--  1 root root   603 Jun 16 11:31 twcfg.txt
-rw-r-----  1 root root 12415 Sep 26 17:03 tw.pol
-rw-r--r--  1 root root 46551 Sep 21 15:44 twpol.txt
```

You now need to either encrypt or delete the `twcfg.txt` and `twpol.txt` files to prevent an attacker from using them for information or using them to compromise Tripwire. Either use gpg to encrypt them and store them on removable media or delete them altogether. You can re-create your Tripwire policy and configuration using the `twadmin` command, as I will demonstrate in a moment.

Now that you have created your signed configuration and policy files, you need to create the baseline Tripwire will use to compare against. Listing 4-43 initializes the Tripwire database with the `tripwire` command.

Listing 4-43. *Initializing the Tripwire Database*

```
puppy# /usr/sbin/tripwire --init
Please enter your local passphrase:
Parsing policy file: /etc/tripwire/tw.pol
Generating the database...
*** Processing Unix File System ***
Wrote database file: /var/lib/tripwire/puppy.yourdomain.com.twd
The database was successfully generated.
```

The `--init` option initializes your Tripwire database, and you will be prompted to enter your local key passphrase to continue. The `tripwire` binary then parses the `/etc/tripwire/tw.pol` file and creates a baseline state for all the objects on your system you want to monitor. In Listing 4-43 this baseline is stored in the database file `/var/lib/tripwire/puppy.yourdomain.com.twd`. You can set the location of your Tripwire database in the Tripwire global variables, as shown in Listing 4-44.

Now that you have your database, you can run your first check using the `tripwire` binary.

Listing 4-44. *Tripwire Integrity Check*

```
puppy# /usr/sbin/tripwire --check
Parsing policy file: /etc/tripwire/tw.pol
*** Processing Unix File System ***
Performing integrity check...
...
Wrote report file: /var/lib/tripwire/report/puppy.yourdomain.com-20040926-172711.twr
```

The Tripwire integrity check will display the results of the check to the screen and save it as a Tripwire report file. In Listing 4-44 the report was saved as `/var/lib/tripwire/report/puppy.yourdomain.com-20040926-172711.twr`. Each report filename contains the date and time it was run. Like the Tripwire database location, you can override this location in the `twcfg.txt` file.

■**Tip** You should schedule Tripwire to run regularly using a `cron` job. If you have installed Tripwire from a Red Hat RPM, then it will also have installed a `cron` job to run a daily Tripwire check.

You can view the results of each Tripwire report using the `twprint` command. Listing 4-45 prints the report you generated.

Listing 4-45. *Printing Reports with* `twprint`

```
puppy# twprint --print-report --twrfile
/var/lib/tripwire/report/puppy.yourdomain.com20040926-172711.twr
Note: Report is not encrypted.
Tripwire(R) 2.3.0 Integrity Check Report

Report Summary:
Host name:                    puppy.yourdomain.com
Host IP address:              127.0.0.1
Host ID:                      None
Policy file used:             /etc/tripwire/tw.pol
Configuration file used:      /etc/tripwire/tw.cfg
Database file used:           /var/lib/tripwire/puppy.yourdomain.com.twd
Command line used:            /usr/sbin/tripwire --check
...
```

```
Total objects scanned:  45606
Total violations found:  1
...
Rule Name: Tripwire Data Files (/var/lib/tripwire)
Severity Level: 100
...
Modified Objects: 1
Modified object name:  /var/lib/tripwire/puppy.yourdomain.com.twd
Property:           Expected                Observed
* Mode              -rw-r--r--              -rwxr-xr-x
```

■Tip You may want to run the twprint command through the more or less commands to display it more effectively.

The --print-report option prints the report specified by the --twrfile option. In Listing 4-45 you can also see an abbreviated extract of the Tripwire report. I have removed some of the output of the Tripwire report but have kept the key sections: the summary of the parameters used, the total objects scanned, and the violations recorded. Only one violation is recorded, a modification of the puppy.yourdomain.com.twd file located in the /var/lib/tripwire directory. You can see that the permissions of this file have been modified from -rw-r--r-- to -rwxr-xr-x. The report displays the rule name, Tripwire Data Files, for the rule covering the /var/lib/tripwire directory and the severity level of 100.

You can also use the twprint command to display a Tripwire database entry for a file or object on your system. Listing 4-46 demonstrates this.

Listing 4-46. *Printing Tripwire Database Entry*

```
puppy# twprint --print-dbfile /etc/passwd
Object name:  /etc/passwd
Property:             Value:
------------          ----------
Object Type           Regular File
Device Number         770
Inode Number          607017
Mode                  -rw-r--r--
Num Links             1
UID                   root (0)
GID                   root (0)
```

I have displayed the database entry for the file /etc/passwd using the --print-dbfile option. If you use twprint --print-dbfile without an individual file specified, it will output the entire contents of the Tripwire database.

If you find violations in your report, you should first check if these are normal occurrences. During normal operations some files may change, be added to, or be removed from

your system. You can adjust your Tripwire policy to reflect these normal changes using the
tripwire command with the -update option. This option allows you to read in a report file,
indicate which violations are in fact normal operational changes, and update the Tripwire
policy to prevent it being triggered by these again. Listing 4-47 demonstrates this.

■Note Of course, some changes may not be normal operational changes; you should always investigate
any and all violations in your Tripwire reports.

Listing 4-47. *Updating Tripwire Policy*

```
puppy#  /usr/sbin/tripwire --update \
--twrfile /var/lib/tripwire/report/puppy.yourdomain.com20040926-172711.twr
```

Listing 4-47 will launch a special editor window that contains the Tripwire report file
specified by the --twrfile option. Inside the editor window you can use the standard vi commands to move around and edit. For each violation detailed in the report, you have the option
to either update the database with the new change or not update it. If you update the change
in the Tripwire database, then it will no longer register as a violation when you run integrity
checks. Listing 4-48 demonstrates this.

Listing 4-48. *Tripwire Database Updates*

```
Rule Name: Tripwire Data Files (/var/lib/tripwire)
Severity Level: 100
Remove the "x" from the adjacent box to prevent updating the database
with the new values for this object.
Modified:
[x] "/var/lib/tripwire/puppy.yourdomain.com.twd"
```

To update the Tripwire database with the new change, leave the x next to each violation.
If you do not want to update the database with the new change, delete the x from the brackets,
[ ]. As Tripwire will update the database by default with all the new changes, you should go
through each violation to make sure you actually want Tripwire to update the database with
the change. When you have updated the file with all the changes you want to make, use the vi
command, :wq, to exit the editor window. You will be prompted to enter the local site password.

```
Please enter your local passphrase:
Wrote database file: /var/lib/tripwire/puppy.yourdomain.com.twd
```

After entering the password, your database will be updated with the new changes.
You can also make changes to the policy file and update the Tripwire database with the new
policy. For this you need a copy of the current policy. You can output a copy of the current policy
file using the twadmin command.

```
puppy# twadmin --print-polfile > /etc/tripwire/twpol.txt
```

■**Tip** The `twadmin` command also has other options that can help you administer Tripwire. See the `twadmin` man file.

You can then edit your policy file to add or remove rules. Once you have finished your editing, you need to use the `tripwire` command with the `--update-policy` option to update your policy file.

```
puppy# /usr/sbin/tripwire --update-policy /etc/tripwire/twpol.txt
Please enter your local passphrase:
Please enter your site passphrase:
======== Policy Update: Processing section Unix File System.
======== Step 1: Gathering information for the new policy.
======== Step 2: Updating the database with new objects.
======== Step 3: Pruning unneeded objects from the database.
Wrote policy file: /etc/tripwire/tw.pol
Wrote database file: /var/lib/tripwire/puppy.yourdomain.com.twd
```

You will be prompted for your local and site passphrases; when the process is completed, your Tripwire database will be updated with your new policy. You then need to either encrypt or delete your plain-text `twpol.txt` file to protect it.

Network File System (NFS)

Sun designed the Network File System (NFS) protocol in the mid-1980s to provide remote network share functionality to Unix systems. Much like Microsoft Windows' file system sharing, it uses a client-server model, with a system hosting the shared data and "sharing" it with a series of clients who can connect to the shared file system. NFS describes this process as "exporting" a file system, and the remote clients connecting to the exported file system are "importing." The NFS protocol runs over either TCP or UDP and uses Sun's Remote Procedure Call (RPC) protocol to communicate with and authenticate clients.

NFS is vulnerable to three major forms of attack: eavesdropping, penetration, and substitution. The *eavesdropping* vulnerability appears because NFS broadcasts its information across the network, potentially allowing an attacker to listen in or sniff that data as it crosses the network. The *penetration* vulnerability appears because of the potential for an attacker to compromise and penetrate the NFS file system and thus gain unauthorized access to the data. A *substitution* attack occurs when an attacker intervenes in the NFS data transmission process to change or delete information traveling across the network.

My recommendation with NFS is simply to not use it. In the past, NFS has proven vulnerable to a variety of types of attack, its vulnerabilities are common, it is technically and operationally complicated to secure (or encrypt) NFS data, and the authentication of remote users to NFS file systems lacks the resiliency required to share files in a production environment.

■Note A new version of NFS has been proposed. NFS 4 proposes considerably stronger security, including strong authentication and encryption. You can read about it at `http://www.nfsv4.org/`. At this stage, though, it is still in RFC form and not ready for deployment.

If you decide to use NFS (and I really think you should not!), I recommend you mitigate the risk as much as possible by following these guidelines:

- Keep your version of NFS and its associated applications such as `portmap` or `rpcbind` up-to-date and ensure you install any NFS-related security patches.

- Export file systems only to those hosts you need. Restrict your file systems to only those hosts and users who need them. Do not publicly export file systems.

- Install NFS file systems on different hard disks or partitions other than your other file systems.

- If possible, export your file systems as read-only to help reduce the risk attackers could manipulate or delete your data.

- Disable `setuid` files on your NFS file systems using the `nosuid` option in the `/etc/fstab` file.

- If possible, use SSH to tunnel NFS traffic.

- Block the NFS TCP and UDP ports 2049 and 111 from any of your Internet-facing hosts or any hosts or networks that you do not trust or are unsure whether they are secure.

■Tip A couple of tools are available to you that can help monitor and secure NFS. The first is `nfsbug`,[12] which checks NFS installations for bugs and security holes. It is a little dated these days but still offers some insights. Also available is the `nfswatch`[13] command, which can be used to monitor NFS traffic on your network.

---

12. Available from `http://ftp.nluug.nl/security/coast/sysutils/nfsbug/`
13. Available from `http://ftp.rge.com/pub/networking/nfswatch/`

Resources

The following are some resources for you to use.

Mailing Lists

- **dm_crypt**: Send empty e-mail to: dm-crypt-subscribe@saout.de

- **Tripwire**: http://sourceforge.net/mail/?group_id=3130

Sites

- **Adeos**: http://linux.wku.edu/~lamonml/software/adeos/

- **dm_crypt**: http://www.saout.de/misc/dm-crypt/

- **dm_crypt wiki**: http://www.saout.de/tikiwiki/tiki-index.php

- **NFS**: http://nfs.sourceforge.net/

- **NFS 4**: http://www.nfsv4.org/

- **sXid**: http://linux.cudeso.be/linuxdoc/sxid.php

- **Tripwire**: http://www.tripwire.org/

Sites About ACLs

- **Red Hat Enterprise Linux and ACLs**: http://www.redhat.com/docs/manuals/enterprise/RHEL-3-Manual/sysadmin-guide/ch-acls.html

- **Linux ACLs**: http://www.vanemery.com/Linux/ACL/linux-acl.html

- **Debian ACLs**: http://acl.bestbits.at/

CHAPTER 5

■ ■ ■

Understanding Logging and Log Monitoring

One of the key facets of maintaining a secure and hardened environment is knowing what is going on in that environment. You can achieve this through your careful and systematic use of logs. Most systems and most applications, such as Apache or Postfix, come with default logging options. This is usually enough for you to diagnose problems or determine the ongoing operational status of your system and applications. When it comes to security, you need to delve a bit deeper into the logging world to gain a fuller and clearer understanding of what is going on with your systems and applications and thus identify potential threats and attacks.

Logs are also key targets for someone who wants to penetrate your system—for two reasons. The first reason is that your logs often contain vital clues about your systems and their security. Attackers often target your logs in an attempt to discover more about your systems. As a result, you need to ensure your log files and /var/log directory are secure from intruders and that log files are available only to authorized users. Additionally, if you transmit your logs over your network to a centralized log server, you need to ensure no one can intercept or divert your logs.

The second reason is that if attackers do penetrate your systems, the last thing they want to happen is that you detect them and shut them out of your system. One of the easiest ways to prevent you from seeing their activities is to whitewash your logs so that you see only what you expect to see. Early detection of intrusion using log monitoring and analysis allows you to spot them before they blind you.

I will cover a few topics in this chapter, including the basic syslog daemon and one of its successors, the considerably more powerful and more secure syslog-NG. I will also cover the Simple Event Correlation (SEC) tool, which can assist you in highlighting events in your logs. I will also discuss logging to databases and secure ways to deliver your logs to a centralized location for review and analysis.

Syslog

Syslog is the ubiquitous Unix tool for logging. It is present on all flavors of Linux and indeed on almost all flavors of Unix. You can add it using third-party tools to Windows systems, and most network devices such as firewalls, routers, and switches are capable of generating Syslog messages. This results in the Syslog format being the closest thing to a universal logging standard that exists.

Tip RFC 3164 documents the core Syslog functionality.[1]

I will cover the Syslog tool because not only is it present on all distributions of Linux, but it also lays down the groundwork for understanding how logging works on Linux systems. The syslog utility is designed to generate, process, and store meaningful event notification messages that provide the information required for administrators to manage their systems. Syslog is both a series of programs and libraries, including syslogd, the syslog daemon, and a communications protocol.

The most frequently used component of syslog is the syslogd daemon. This daemon runs on your system from startup and listens for messages from your operating system and applications. It is important to note that the syslogd daemon is a passive tool. It merely waits for input from devices or programs. It does not go out and actively gather messages.

Note Syslog also uses another daemon, klogd. The Kernel Log Daemon specifically collects messages from the kernel. This daemon is present on all Linux systems and starts by default when your system starts. I will talk about that in some more detail in the "syslog-NG" section.

The next major portion of the syslog tools is the syslog communications protocol. With this protocol it is possible to send your log data across a network to a remote system where another syslog daemon can collect and centralize your logs. As presented in Figure 5-1, you can see how this is done.

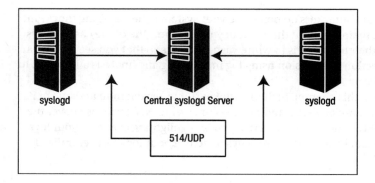

Figure 5-1. *Remote* syslogd *logging*

But my recommendation, though, is that if you have more than one system and either have or want to introduce a centralized logging regime, then do not use syslog. I make this

---

1. See http://www.faqs.org/rfcs/rfc3164.html. Also, some interesting work is happening on a new RFC for Syslog; you can find it at http://www.syslog.cc/ietf/protocol.html.

recommendation as a result of `syslog`'s reliance on the User Datagram Protocol (UDP) to transmit information. UDP has three major limitations.

- On a congested network, packets are frequently lost.

- The protocol is not fully secure.

- You are open to replay and Denial of Service (DoS) attacks.

If you are serious about secure logging, I recommend the syslog-NG package, which I will discuss later in the "syslog-NG" section.

The `syslog` communications protocol allows you to send `syslog` messages across your network via UDP to a centralized log server running `syslogd`. The `syslogd` daemon usually starts by default when your system boots. It is configured to collect a great deal of information about the ongoing activities of your system "out of the box."

Tip Syslog traffic is usually transmitted via UDP on port 514.

Configuring Syslog

The `syslog` daemon is controlled by a configuration file located in `/etc` called `syslog.conf`. This file contains the information about what devices and programs `syslogd` is listening for (filtered by facility and priority), where that information is to be stored, or what actions are to be taken when that information is received. You can see in Listing 5-1 that each line is structured into two fields, a selector field and an action field, which are separated by spaces or a tab.

Listing 5-1. `syslog.conf` *Syntax*

```
mail.info      /var/log/maillog
```

This example shows a facility and priority selector, `mail.info`, together with the action `/var/log/maillog`. The facility represented here is `mail`, and the priority is `info`. Overall the line in Listing 5-1 indicates that all messages generated by the `mail` facility with a priority of `info` or higher will be logged to the file `/var/log/maillog`. Let's examine now what facilities, priorities, and actions are available to you on a Linux system.

Facilities

The facility identifies the source of the `syslog` message. Some operating-system functions and daemons and other common application daemons have standard facilities attached to them. The `mail` and `kern` facilities are two good examples. The first example is the facility for all mail-related event notification messages. The second example is the facility for all kernel-related messages. Other processes and daemons that do not have a prespecified facility are able to log to the `local` facilities, ranging from `local0` to `local7`. For example, I use `local4` as the facility for all messages on my Cisco devices. Table 5-1 lists all Syslog facilities.

Table 5-1. *Syslog Facilities on Linux*

Facility	Purpose
auth	Security-related messages
auth-priv	Access control messages
cron	cron-related messages
daemon	System daemons and process messages
kern	Kernel messages
local0–local7	Reserved for locally defined messages
lpr	Spooling subsystem messages
mail	Mail-related messages
mark	Time-stamped messages generated by syslogd
news	Network News–related messages (for example, Usenet)
syslog	Syslog-related messages
user	The default facility when no facility is specified
uucp	UUCP-related messages

■**Tip** On Mandrake and Red Hat systems local7 points at /var/log/boot.log, which contains all the messages generated during the boot of your system.

The mark facility is a special case. It is used by the time-stamped messages that syslogd generates when you use the -m (minutes) flag. You can find more on this in the "Starting syslogd and Its Options" section.

You have two special facilities: *, which indicates all facilities, and none, which negates a facility selection. As shown in the following example, you can use these two facilities as wildcard selectors. See Listing 5-2.

Listing 5-2. syslog.conf * *Wildcard Selector*

```
*.emerg     /dev/console
```

This will send all messages of the emerg priority, regardless of facility, to the console. You can also use the none wildcard selector to not select messages from a particular facility.

```
kern.none    /var/log/messages
```

This will tell syslog to not log any kernel messages to the file /var/log/messages.

Priorities

Priorities are organized in an escalating scale of importance. They are debug, info, notice, warning, err, crit, alert, and emerg. Each priority selector applies to the priority stated and all higher priorities, so uucp.err indicates all uucp facility messages of err, crit, alert, and emerg priorities.

As with facilities, you can use the wildcard selectors * and none. Additionally, you can use two other modifiers: = and !. The = modifier indicates that only one priority is selected; for example, cron.=crit indicates that only cron facility messages of crit priority are to be selected. The ! modifier has a negative effect; for example, cron.!crit selects all cron facility messages except those of crit *or higher priority.* You can also combine the two modifiers to create the opposite effect of the = modifier so that cron.!=crit selects all cron facility messages except those of crit priority. Only one priority and one priority wildcard can be listed per selector.

Actions

Actions tell the syslogd what to do with the event notification messages it receives. Listing 5-3 lists the four actions syslogd can take, including logging to a file, device file, named pipes (fifos) and the console or a user's screen. In Listing 5-2 you saw device logging at work with all the emerg messages on the system being sent to the console.

Listing 5-3. *File, Device, and Named Pipe Actions*

```
cron.err        /var/log/cron
auth.!=emerg    /dev/lpr3
auth-priv       root,bob
news.=notice    |/var/log/newspipe
```

In the first line all cron messages of err priority and higher are logged to the file /var/log/cron. The second line has all auth messages except those of emerg priority being sent to a local printer lpr3. The third line sends all auth-priv messages to the users root and bob if they are logged in. The fourth sends all news messages of notice or greater priority to a named pipe called /var/log/newspipe (you would need to create this pipe yourself with the mkfifo command).

■**Caution** When logging to files, syslogd allows you to add a hyphen (-) to the front of the filename like this: -/var/log/auth. This tells syslog to not sync the file after writing to it. This is designed to speed up the process of writing to the log. But it can also mean that if your system crashes between write attempts, you will lose data. Unless your logging system is suffering from performance issues, I recommend you do not use this option.

You can also log to a remote system (see Listing 5-4).

Listing 5-4. *Logging to a Remote System*

```
mail      @puppy.yourdomain.com
```

In this example all mail messages are sent to the host puppy.yourdomain.com on UDP port 514. This requires that the syslogd daemon on puppy is started with the -r option; otherwise, the syslogd port will not be open.

■**Caution** Opening `syslogd` to your network is a dangerous thing. The `syslogd` daemon is not selective about where it receives messages from. There are no access controls, and any system on your network can log to the `syslogd` port. This opens your machine to the risk of a DoS attack or of a rogue program flooding your system with messages and using all the space in your log partition. I will briefly discuss some methods by which you can reduce the risk to your system, but if you are serious about remote logging I recommend you look at the "syslog-NG" section. I will also discuss secure logging using the syslog-NG tool in conjunction with Stunnel in the "Secure Logging with syslog-NG" section.

Combining Multiple Selectors

You can also combine multiple selectors in your `syslog.conf` file, allowing for more sophisticated selections and filtering. For example, you can list multiple facilities separated by commas in a selector. See Listing 5-5.

Listing 5-5. *Multiple Facilities*

```
auth,auth-priv.crit     /var/log/auth
```

This sends all `auth` messages and all `auth-priv` messages with a priority of `crit` or higher to the file `/var/log/auth`.

You cannot do this with priorities, though. If want to list multiple priorities, you need to list multiple selectors separated by semicolons, as shown in Listing 5-6.

Listing 5-6. *Multiple Priorities*

```
auth;auth-priv.debug;auth-priv.!=emerg    /var/log/auth
```

This example shows you how to send all `auth` messages and all `auth-priv` messages with a priority of `debug` or higher, excluding `auth-priv` messages of `emerg` priority to the file `/var/log/auth`.

■**Tip** Just remember with multiple selectors that filtering works from left to right; `syslogd` will process the line starting from the selectors on the left and moving to the right of each succeeding selector. With this in mind, place the broader filters at the left, and narrow the filtering criteria as you move to the right.

You can also use multiple lines to send messages to more than one location, as shown in Listing 5-7.

Listing 5-7. *Logging to Multiple Places*

```
auth            /var/log/auth
auth.crit       bob
auth.emerg      /dev/console
```

Here all auth messages are logged to /var/log/auth as previously, but auth messages of crit or higher priority are also sent to user bob, if he is logged in. Those of emerg priority are also sent to the console.

Starting syslogd and Its Options

The syslogd daemon and its sister process, the klogd daemon, are both started when your system boots up. This is usually in the form of an init script; for example, on Red Hat the syslog script in /etc/rc.d/init.d/ starts syslogd and klogd. You can pass a number of options to the syslogd program when it starts.

■**Tip** On most Red Hat and Mandrake systems the syslog file in /etc/sysconfig/ is referenced by the syslog init script and contains the options to be passed to syslogd and klogd when it starts.

The first option you will look at is the debug option (see Listing 5-8).

Listing 5-8. *Running* syslogd *with Debug*

```
puppy# syslogd -d
```

This will start syslogd and prevent it from forking to the background. It will display a large amount of debugging information to the current screen (you will probably want to pipe it into more to make it easier to read). A lot of the information the debug option displays is not useful to the everyday user, but it will tell you if your syslog.conf file has any syntax errors, which is something that becomes useful if your file grows considerably.

The next option you will look at tells syslogd where to find the syslog.conf file. By default syslogd will look for /etc/syslog.conf, but you can override this (see Listing 5-9).

Listing 5-9. *Starting* syslogd *with a Different Config File*

```
puppy# syslogd -f /etc/puppylog.conf
```

In this example syslogd would look for /etc/puppylog.conf. If this file does not exist, then syslogd will terminate. This is useful for testing a new syslog.conf file without overwriting the old one.

I discussed earlier mark facility messages. These are time stamps that are generated at specified intervals in your logs that look something like this:

```
Feb 24 21:46:05 puppy -- MARK -
```

They are useful, amongst other reasons, for acting as markers for programs parsing your log files. These time stamps are generated using the -m *mins* option when you start syslogd. To generate a mark message every ten minutes, you would start syslogd as shown in Listing 5-10.

Listing 5-10. *Generating* mark *Messages*

```
puppy# syslogd -m 10
```

Remember that mark is a facility in its own right, and you can direct its output to a particular file or destination (see Listing 5-11).

Listing 5-11. *Using the* mark *Facility*

```
mark     /var/log/messages
```

In Listing 5-11 all mark facility messages will be directed to /var/log/messages. By default most syslogd daemons start with the -m option set to 0.

Often when you set up a chroot environment, the application in the jail is unable to log to syslog because of the restrictive nature of the chroot jail. In this instance, you can create an additional log socket inside the chroot jail and use the -a option when you start syslogd to allow syslog to listen to it. You will see how this works in more detail in Chapter 11 when I show how to set up a BIND daemon in a chroot jail. See Listing 5-12.

Listing 5-12. *Listening to Additional Sockets*

```
puppy# syslogd -a /chroot/named/dev/log -a /chroot/apache/dev/log
```

Here the syslogd daemon is listening to two additional sockets: one in /chroot/named/dev/log and the other in /chroot/apache/dev/log.

Lastly you will look at the -r option, which allows syslogd to receive messages from external sources on UDP port 514. See Listing 5-13.

Listing 5-13. *Enabling Remote Logging*

```
puppy# syslogd -r
```

By default most syslogd daemons start without -r enabled, and you will have to specifically enable this option to get syslogd to listen.

▓Tip If you enable the -r option, you will need to punch a hole in your firewall to allow remote syslogd daemons to connect to your system.

If you are going to use syslogd for remote logging, then you have a couple of ways to make your installation more secure. The most obvious threat to syslogd daemons are DoS attacks in which your system is flooded with messages that could completely fill your disks. If your logs are located in the root partition, your system can potentially crash. To reduce the risk of this potential crash, I recommend you store your logs on a nonroot partition. This means that even if all the space on your disk is consumed, the system will not crash. The second way to secure your syslogd for remote logging is to ensure your firewall rules allow connections only from those systems that will be sending their logging data to you. Do not open your syslog daemon to all incoming traffic!

syslog-NG

Syslog and `syslogd` are useful tools; however, not only are they dated, but they also have limitations in the areas of reliability and security that do not make them the ideal tools to use in a hardened environment. A worthy successor to `syslog` is syslog-NG. Developed to overcome the limitations of `syslog`, it represents a "new-generation" look at logging with an emphasis on availability and flexibility and considerably more regard for security.

Additionally, syslog-NG allows for more sophisticated message filtering, manipulation, and interaction. syslog-NG is freeware developed by Balazs Scheidler and is available from `http://www.balabit.com/products/syslog_ng/`.

■**Note** syslog-NG goes through a lot of active development, and new features are added all the time. With the active development cycle of the product, sometimes the documentation becomes out-of-date. If you want to keep up with all the activity and need help for something that is not explained in the documentation, then I recommend you subscribe to the syslog-NG mailing list at `https://lists.balabit.hu/mailman/listinfo/syslog-ng`. syslog-NG's author, Balazs Scheidler, is a regular and helpful participant on the list. As a result of this busy development cycle, I also recommend you use the most recent stable release of `libol` and syslog-NG to get the most out of the package.

The following sections cover installing and compiling syslog-NG and then configuring it as a replacement for syslog. I will also cover configuring syslog-NG to allow you to store and query log messages in a database. Finally, I will cover secure syslog-NG logging in a distributed environment.

Installing and Configuring syslog-NG

Download syslog-NG and `libol` (an additional library required for installing syslog-NG) from `http://www.balabit.com/products/syslog_ng/upgrades.bbq`. You will need to build `libol` first. So unpack the tar file, and compile the `libol` package.

```
puppy# ./configure && make && make install
```

■**Tip** If you do not want to install `libol`, you can omit the `make install` command, and when you configure syslog-NG, you need to tell it where to find `libol` using `./configure --with-libol=/path/to/libol`.

Now unpack syslog-NG, enter the syslog-NG directory, and configure the package.

```
puppy# ./configure
```

By default syslog-NG is installed to /usr/local/sbin, but you can override this by entering the following:

```
puppy# ./configure --prefix=/new/directory/here
```

Also by default syslog-NG looks for its conf file in /usr/local/etc/syslog-ng.conf. You can override this also. I recommend using /etc/syslog-ng.

```
puppy# ./configure --sysconfdir=/etc/syslog-ng
```

Then make and install syslog-NG.

```
puppy# make && make install
```

This will create a binary called syslog-ng and install it either to the /usr/local/sbin/ directory or to whatever directory you have specified if you have overridden it with the prefix option.

The contrib Directory

Within the syslog-NG package comes a few other useful items. In the contrib directory is a collection of init scripts for a variety of systems including Red Hat and SuSE. These can be easily adapted to suit your particular distribution. Also in the contrib directory is an awk script called syslog2ng, which converts syslog.conf files to syslog-ng.conf files. See Listing 5-14.

Listing 5-14. *Using the* syslog2ng *Script*

```
puppy# ./syslog2ng < /etc/syslog.conf > syslog-ng.conf
```

This will convert the contents of your syslog.conf file into the file called syslog-ng.conf. This is especially useful if you have done a lot of work customizing your syslog.conf file.

Lastly, in the contrib directory are several sample syslog-ng.conf files, including syslog-ng.conf.RedHat, which provides a syslog-NG configuration that replicates the default syslog.conf file on a Red Hat system. (Note that it assumes you have disabled the klogd daemon and are using syslog-ng for kernel logging as well.) This file should also work on most Linux distributions.[2] Also, among the sample syslog-ng.conf files is syslog-ng.conf.doc, which is an annotated configuration file with the manual entries for each option and function embedded next to that option or function.

Running and Configuring syslog-NG

As mentioned previously, syslog-NG comes with a number of sample init scripts that you should be able to adapt for your system. Use one of these scripts, and set syslog-NG to start when you boot up. As shown in Table 5-2. the syslog-ng daemon has some command-line options.

---

2. I tested it on Mandrake 9.2, SuSE 9, and Debian 3, in addition to Red Hat Enterprise 3, Red Hat 8.0, Red Hat 9.0, and Fedora Core 1, and it logged without issues.

Table 5-2. syslog-ng *Command-Line Options*

Flag	Purpose
-d	Enables debug.
-v	Verbose mode (syslog-ng will not daemonize).
-s	Do not start; just parse the conf file for incorrect syntax.
-f /path/to/conf/file	Tells syslog-ng where the configuration file is located.

The first two flags, -d and -v, are useful to debug the syslog-ng daemon. In the case of the -v flag, syslog-ng will start and output its logging messages to the screen and will not fork into the background. The -d flag adds some debugging messages. The next flag, -s, does not start syslog-NG but merely parses through the syslog-ng.conf file and checks for errors. If it finds any errors, it will dump those to the screen and exit. If it exits without an error, then your syslog-ng.conf has perfect syntax!

But do not start up syslog-NG yet. You need to create or modify a configuration file first. The syslog-ng.conf contains considerably more options than the syslog.conf file, which is representative of the increased functionality and flexibility characteristic of the syslog-NG product. As such, setting up the configuration file can be a little bit daunting initially. I recommend you use the syslog-ng.conf sample file. When it starts, syslog-NG looks for /usr/local/etc/syslog-ng.conf as the default conf file unless you overrode that as part of the ./configure process. I recommend you create your configuration file in /etc/syslog-ng.

Every time you change your syslog-ng.conf file, you need to restart the syslog-ng daemon. Use the provided init script to do this, and use the reload option. For example, on a Red Hat system, enter the following:

```
puppy# /etc/rc.d/init.d/syslog-ng reload
```

Let's start configuring syslog-NG by looking at a simple configuration file. Listing 5-15 shows a sample syslog-ng.conf file that collects messages from the device /dev/log, selects all the messages from the mail facility, and writes them to the console device.

Listing 5-15. *A Sample* syslog-ng.conf *File*

```
options { sync (0); };

source s_sys { unix-dgram ("/dev/log"); };
destination d_console { file("/dev/console"); };
filter f_mail { facility(mail); };

log { source(s_sys); filter(f_mail); destination(d_console); };
```

Listing 5-15 is a functioning (if limited) syslog-NG configuration. It may look intimidating at first, but it is actually a simple configuration model when you break it down. The key line in this example is the last one, the log{} line. The log{} line combines three other types of statements: a source statement to tell syslog-NG where to get the messages from; a filter statement to allow you to select messages from within that source according to criteria, such as their facility or priority; and finally a destination statement to tell syslog-NG where to write the messages to, such as a file or a device. The options{} statement allows you to configure some global options for syslog-NG.

Let's take you through the basics of configuring syslog-NG by running through each of the statement blocks available to you. The syslog-ng.conf file uses five key statement blocks (see Table 5-3).

Table 5-3. syslog-ng.conf *Statement Blocks*

Directive	Purpose
options{}	Global options to be set
source{}	Statements defining where messages are coming from
destination{}	Statements defining where messages are sent or stored
filter{}	Filtering statements
log{}	Statements combining source, destination, and filter statements that do the actual logging

Each statement block contains additional settings separated by semicolons. You can see that I have used all these statements in Listing 5-15.

options{}

These are global options that tell syslog-NG what to do on an overall basis. The options themselves consist of their name and then their value enclosed in parentheses and terminated with a semicolon. As shown in Listing 5-16, these options control functions such as the creation of directories and the use of DNS to resolve hostnames, and they provide control over the process of writing data to the disk.

Listing 5-16. *A Sample* syslog-ng options{} *Statement*

```
options {
sync(0);
time_reopen(10);
use_dns(yes);
use_fqdn(no);
create_dirs(no);
keep_hostname(yes);
chain_hostnames(no);
};
```

Quite a number of options are available to you. In this section I will cover the key options. Probably the most confusing options to new users of syslog-NG are those associated with hostnames. I recommend two key options in this area that every user should put in the syslog-ng.conf file. They are keep_hostname(yes | no) and chain_hostnames(yes | no).

■Tip The syslog-NG documentation also refers to long_hostnames(). This is an alias for chain_hostnames() and is identical in function.

When syslog-NG receives messages, it does not automatically trust that the hostname provided to it by a message is actually the hostname of the system on which the message originated. As a result, syslog-NG tries to resolve the hostname of the system that generated the messages. If the resolved hostname is different, it attempts to rewrite the hostname in the message to the hostname it has resolved. This behavior occurs because by default the keep_hostname() option is set to no. If keep_hostname(yes) is set (as it is in Listing 5-16), then this prevents syslog-NG from rewriting the hostname in the message.

So where does the chain_hostnames() option come into all this? Well, it works in conjunction with keep_hostname(). If keep_hostname() is set to no, then it checks whether chain_hostnames() is set to yes. If chain_hostnames() is set to yes, then syslog-NG appends the name of the host that syslog-NG received the message from to the resolved hostname. So, for example, if the hostname in the message is puppy but the hostname that syslog-NG has resolved the IP address to is puppy2, then the message will change from this:

```
Jul 14 16:29:36 puppy su(pam_unix)[2979]: session closed for user bob
```

to the following:

```
Jul 14 16:29:36 puppy/pupp2 su(pam_unix)[2979]: session closed for user bob
```

If chain_hostnames() is set to no, then syslog-NG simply replaces the hostname with a resolved hostname.

This can be a little confusing, so I will now illustrate it with another example. In Table 5-4 you have a message that has a hostname of server. When syslog-NG resolves this hostname, DNS tells it that the real hostname of the system is server2. The table shows the resulting hostname that will be displayed in the message with all possible combinations of the options.

Table 5-4. chain_hostnames() *and* keep_hostname() *Interaction*

Option Setting	keep_hostname(yes)	keep_hostname(no)
chain_hostnames(yes)	server	server/server2
chain_hostnames(no)	server	server2

■Tip By default chain_hostnames() is set to yes, and keep_hostname() is set to no.

Also related to hostnames are use_dns() and use_fqdn(). The use_dns() option allows you to turn off DNS resolution for syslog-NG. By default it is set to yes. The use_fqdn() option specifies whether syslog-NG will use fully qualified domain names. If use_fqdn() is set to yes, then all hosts will be displayed with their fully qualified domain names; for example, puppy would be puppy.yourdomain.com. By default use_fqdn() is set to no.

You have a whole set of options available that deal with the creation of directories and files (see Table 5-5). They control ownership, permissions, and whether `syslog-ng` will create new directories.

Table 5-5. *File and Directory Options*

Option	Purpose
`owner(`*`userid`*`)`	The owner of any file `syslog-ng` creates
`group(`*`groupid`*`)`	The group of any file `syslog-ng` creates
`perm(`*`permissions`*`)`	The permission of any file `syslog-ng` creates
`create_dirs(yes | no)`	Whether `syslog-ng` is allowed to create directories to store log files
`dir_owner(`*`userid`*`)`	The owner of any directory `syslog-ng` creates
`dir_group(`*`groupid`*`)`	The group of any directory `syslog-ng` creates
`dir_perm(`*`permissions`*`)`	The permission of any directory `syslog-ng` creates

A few additional options could be useful for you. They are `sync(`*`seconds`*`)`, `stats(`*`seconds`*`)`, `time_reopen(`*`seconds`*`)`, and `use_time_recvd()`. The `sync()` option tells syslog-NG how many messages to buffer before it writes to disk. It defaults to 0. The `stats(`*`seconds`*`)` option provides you with regular statistics detailing the number of messages dropped.

■Note Messages are dropped, for example, if syslog-NG reaches the maximum available number of connections on a network source (as defined with the `maxconnections()` option). The `stats` option will record how many messages were dropped.

The *seconds* variable in the option indicates the number of seconds between each stats message being generated. In the `time_reopen(`*`seconds`*`)` option, *seconds* is the amount of time that syslog-NG waits before retrying a dead connection. This currently defaults to 60 seconds, but you may want to reduce this. I have found around ten seconds is a sufficient pause for syslog-NG. The last option you will look at is `use_time_recvd()`. When this option is set to yes, then the time on the message sent is overridden with the time the message is received by syslog-NG on the system. The default for this setting is no. The `use_time_recvd()` option is important to consider when you use the `destination{}` file-expansion macros that I will discuss in the "destination{}" section.

source{}

Your source statements are the key to telling syslog-NG where its message inputs are coming from. You can see an example of a `source{}` statement in Listing 5-17.

Listing 5-17. *A syslog-NG* `source{}` *Statement*

```
source s_sys { unix-stream("/dev/log" max-connections(20)); internal(); };
```

The source{} statement block is much like the options{} statement block in that it contains different possible input sources and is terminated with a semicolon. The major difference is that the first part of each source{} statement block is its name you need to define. You can see that in Listing 5-17 I gave s_sys as the name of the source{} statement. For these purposes, you use a naming convention that allows you to easily identify each source: s_sys for Linux system logs and syslog-NG internal logging, s_tcp for logs that come in over TCP, s_udp for logs that come in over UDP, and s_file for file-based input sources.

Inside the source{} statement you have a number of possible input sources so that one source statement can combine multiple messages sources; for example, the source{} statement in Listing 5-17 receives both internal syslog-NG messages and standard Linux system messages. Table 5-6 describes the sources you are most likely to use.

Table 5-6. *syslog-NG Sources*

Source	Description
unix-stream()	Opens an AF_UNIX socket using SOCK_STEAM semantics (for example, /dev/log) to receive messages
unix-dgram()	Opens an AF_UNIX socket using SOCK_DGAM semantics
tcp()	Opens TCP port 514 to receive messages
udp()	Opens UDP port 514 to receive messages
file()	Opens a specified file and processes it for messages
pipe()	Opens a named pipe

You can use both unix-stream() and unix-dgram() to connect to an AF_UNIX socket, such as /dev/log (which is the source of most Linux system messages). You can also use it to specify a socket file in a chroot jail, as shown in Listing 5-18.

Listing 5-18. *Opening a Socket in a* chroot *Jail*

```
source s_named { unix-stream("/chroot/named/dev/log"); };
```

Listing 5-18 shows syslog-NG opening a log socket for a named daemon inside a chroot jail.

The unix-stream() and unix-dgram() sources are similar but have some important differences. The first source, unix-steam(), opens an AF_UNIX socket using SOCK_STREAM semantics, which are connection orientated and therefore prevent message loss. The second source, unix-dgram(), opens an AF_UNIX socket using SOCK_DGRAM semantics, which are not connection orientated and can result in messages being lost. The unix-dgram() source is also open to DoS attacks because you are unable to restrict the number of connections made to it. With unix-stream() you can use the max-connections() option to limit the maximum number of possible connections to the source.

■**Tip** You can see the max-connections() setting in the first line of Listing 5-17; it is set to 10 by default, but on a busy system you may need to increase that maximum. If you run out of connections, then messages from external systems will be dropped. You can use the stats option, as described in the "options{}" section, to tell you if messages are being dropped.

As such, I recommend you use the unix-stream() source, not the unix-dgram() source. The next types are tcp() and udp() sources.

```
source s_tcp { tcp(ip(192.168.0.1) port(514) max-connections(15)); };
source s_udp { udp(); };
```

These sources both allow syslog-NG to collect messages from external systems. As discussed during the "Syslog" section of this chapter, I do not recommend you use udp() for this purpose. Unlike syslog, however, syslog-NG also supports message send via Transmission Control Protocol (TCP) using the tcp() source. This delivers the same functionality as UDP connections but with the benefit of TCP acknowledgments, which greatly raise the level of reliability. The tcp() connections are also able to be secured by introducing a tool such as Stunnel. Stunnel encapsulates TCP traffic inside a Secure Sockets Layer (SSL) wrapper and secures the connection with public-key encryption. This means attackers are not able to read your log traffic and that you are considerably more protected from any potential DoS attacks because syslog-NG is configured to receive only from those hosts you specify. I will discuss this capability in the "Secure Logging with syslog-NG" section later in the chapter.

The previous tcp() source statements specify 192.168.0.1 as the IP address to which syslog-NG should bind. This IP address is the address of a local interface, not that of the sending system. It also specifies 514 as the port number to run on and 15 as the maximum number of simultaneous connections. If the max-connections() option is not set, then it defaults to 10. This is a safeguard against DoS attacks by preventing an unlimited number of systems from simultaneously connecting to your syslog-NG server and overloading it. I will show how to further secure your TCP connections in the "Secure Logging with syslog-NG" section.

The next type of source is a file() source statement. The file() is used to process special files such as those in /proc.

```
source s_file { file("/proc/kmsg" log_prefix("kernel: ")); };
```

It is also commonly used to collect kernel messages on systems where you have replaced klogd as well as syslogd.

■Tip This will not follow a file like the tail -f command. In the "Testing Logging with logger" section I will explain how you can use logger to feed a growing file to the syslog-NG daemon.

It is easy to replace klogd with syslog-NG. To add kernel logging to syslog-NG, adjust your source{} statement to include file("/proc/kmsg"). A source{} statement used to log most of the default system messages would now look something like this:

```
source s_sys { file("/proc/kmsg" log_prefix("kernel: ")); ➡
unix-stream("/dev/log"); internal(); };
```

The log prefix option ensures all kernel messages are prefixed with "kernel: ". You need to ensure you have stopped the klogd daemon before you enable and start syslog-NG with kernel logging. Otherwise syslog-NG may stop, and all local logging will be disabled.

The last source is the pipe() source. This is used to open a named pipe as an input source.

```
source s_pipe { pipe("/var/programa"); };
```

This allows programs that use named pipes for their logging to be read by syslog-NG. This source can be also used to collect system messages from /proc/kmsg.

```
source s_kern { pipe("/proc/kmsg"); };
```

destination{}

The destination{} statement block contains all the statements to tell syslog-NG where to put its output. This output could be written to a log file, output to a program, or output to a database. Listing 5-19 contains an example of a destination{} statement.

Listing 5-19. *A syslog-NG* destination{} *Statement*

```
destination d_mult { file("/var/log/messages"); usertty("bob"); };
```

The destination{} statement block is constructed like that of the source{} statement block. I have continued in the vein of the naming convention I started in the "source{}" section and prefixed the name of the destination blocks with d_ (for example, d_console).

As with source{} statements, you can combine more than one destination in a single source statement. As you can see in Listing 5-19, the destination d_mult logs both to a file and to a session signed on as the user bob. Various possible destinations for your messages are available.

Probably the most commonly used destination is file(), which logs message data to a file on the system. The next line shows a file destination of /var/log/messages, which will be owned by the root user and group and have its file permissions set to 0644.

```
destination d_mesg { file("/var/log/messages" owner(root) group(root) perm(0644)); };
```

So as you can see, the file() destination statement consists of the name of the file you are logging to and a variety of options that control the ownership and permission of the file itself. These are identical to the file-related permissions you can set at the global options{} level, and the options for each individual destination override any global options specified.

In the next line, you can also see the use of the file-expansion macros:

```
destination d_host { file("/var/log/hosts/$HOST/$FACILITY$YEAR$MONTH$DAY"); };
```

File-expansion macros are useful for including data such as the hostname, facility, and date and time in the filenames of your log files to make them easier to identify and manipulate. Each is placed exactly like a shell script parameter, prefixed with $. Using this example, a cron message on the puppy system on March 1, 2005, would result in the following directory and file structure:

```
/var/log/puppy/cron20050301
```

You can see a list of all possible file-expansion macros in Table 5-7.

Table 5-7. *syslog-NG File-Expansion Macros*

Macro	Description
FACILITY	Name of the facility from which the message is tagged as coming
PRIORITY	Priority of the message
TAG	Priority and facility encoded as a two-digit hexadecimal number
DATE	The date of the message in the form of MMM DD HH:MM:SS
FULLDATE	The date in the form of YYYY MMM DD HH:MM:SS
ISODATE	The date in the form of YYYY-MM-DD HH:MM:SS TZ
YEAR	Year the message was sent in the form YYYY
MONTH	Month the message was sent in the form of MM
DAY	Day of month the message was sent in the form of DD
WEEKDAY	Three-letter name of the day of week the message was sent (for example, Mon)
HOUR	Hour of day the message was sent
MIN	Minute the message was sent
SEC	Second the message was sent
TZOFFSET	Time zone as hour offset from Greenwich mean time (for example, +1200)
TZ	Time zone or name or abbreviation (for example, AEST)
FULLHOST	Name of the source host from where the message originated
HOST	Name of the source host from where the message originated
PROGRAM	Name of the program the message was sent by
MESSAGE	Message contents

The time-expansion macros, such as DATE, can either use the time that the log message was sent or use the time the message was received by syslog-NG. This is controlled by the use_time_recvd() option discussed in the "options{}" section.

Also using the same file-expansion macros you can invoke the template() option, which allows you to write out data in the exact form you want to the destination. The template() option also works with all the possible destination statements, not just file(). Listing 5-20 shows a destination statement modified to include a template.

Listing 5-20. *The* template() *Option*

```
destination d_host { file("/var/log/hosts/$HOST/$FACILITY$YEAR$MONTH$DAY" ➡
template("$HOUR:$MIN:$SEC $TZ $HOST [$LEVEL] $MSG $MSG\n") ➡
template_escape(no) ); };
```

The template_escape(yes | no) option turns on or off the use of quote marks to escape data in your messages. This is useful if the destination of the message is a SQL database, as the escaping prevents the log data being treated by the SQL server as commands.

The pipe() destination allows the use of named pipes as a destination for message data. This is often used to send messages to /dev/console.

```
destination d_cons { pipe("/dev/console"); };
```

Here the destination d_cons sends all messages to the /dev/console device. You will also use the pipe() destination to send messages to the SEC log correlation tool and to a database.

Importantly for a distributed monitoring environment, it is also possible to forward messages to another system using either TCP or UDP with the tcp() and udp() destination{} statements.

```
destination d_monitor { tcp("192.168.1.10" port(514)); };
```

You can see for the third statement of Listing 5-18 where the destination d_monitor is a syslog server located at IP address 192.168.1.10 that listens to TCP traffic on the standard syslog port of 514. As stated elsewhere, I do not recommend using UDP connections for your logging traffic. You will see more of how this is used for secure logging in the "Secure Logging with syslog-NG" section.

The usertty() destination allows you to send messages to the terminal of a specific logged user or all logged users. In the next line, the destination d_root sends messages to terminals logged in as the root user:

```
destination d_root { usertty("root"); };
```

You can also use the wildcard option (*) to send messages to all users.

Finally, the program() destination invokes a program as the destination. You have quite a variety of possible uses for this, including mailing out certain messages or as an alternative method of integrating syslog-NG with log analysis tools such as SEC or Swatch. See Listing 5-21.

Listing 5-21. *Sample* program() *Destination*

```
destination d_mailout { program("/root/scripts/mailout" ➥
template("$HOUR:$MIN:$SEC $HOST $FACILITY $LEVEL $PROGRAM $MSG\n")); };
```

In Listing 5-21 the d_mailout destination sends a message to the script /root/scripts/mailout using a template. Note the \n at the end of the template() line. Because of the use of a template, you have to tell the script that it has reached the end of the line and that the loop must end. With a normal message, syslog-NG includes its own line break.

The mailout script itself is simple (see Listing 5-22).

Listing 5-22. mailout *Script*

```
#!/bin/bash
#  Script to mail out logs

while read line; do
    echo $line | /bin/mail -s "log entry from mail out" pager@yourdomain.com
done
```

■**Caution** Always remember that any time you designate a message to be mailed out, you should ask yourself if you are making yourself vulnerable to a self-inflicted DoS attack if thousands of messages were generated and your mail server was flooded. Either choose only those most critical messages to be mailed out or look at modifying the script you are using to mail out messages to throttle the number of messages being sent out in a particular time period.

Lastly, you also have the destination{} statements unix-stream() and user-dgram() that you can use to send message data to Unix sockets. Neither unix-stream() nor user-dgram() has any additional options.

```
destination d_socket { unix-stream("/tmp/socket"); };
```

filter{}

The filter{} statement blocks contain statements to tell syslog-NG which messages to select. This is much like the facility and priority selector used by the syslog daemon. For example, the following line is a syslog facility and priority selector that would select all messages of the mail facility with a priority of info or higher:

```
mail.info
```

This can be represented by a syslog-NG filter statement block that looks like this:

```
filter f_mail    { facility(mail); priority(info .. emerg) };
```

In the previous line I have selected all messages from the facility mail using the facility() option and with a range of priorities from info to emerg using the priority() option.

But the syslog-NG equivalent is far more powerful than the selectors available to you in the syslog daemon. Selection criteria can range from selecting all those messages from a particular facility, host, or program to regular expressions performed on the message data itself.

The filter{} statement blocks are constructed like the source{} statement block, and each filter must be named. Again, continuing with the naming convention, I generally prefix all my filter statements with f_ (for example, f_kern). In Table 5-8 you can see a complete list of items on which you can filter.

Table 5-8. *Items You Can Filter on in syslog-NG*

Filter	Description
facility()	Matches messages having one of the listed facility code(s)
priority()	Matches messages by priority (or the level() statement)
program()	Matches messages by using a regular expression against the program name field of log messages
host()	Matches messages by using a regular expression against the hostname field of log messages
match()	Tries to match a regular expression to the message itself
filter()	Calls another filter rule and evaluate its value
netmask()	Matches message IP address against an IP subnet mask

The simplest filters are facility and priority filters. With facility and priority filters you can list multiple facilities or priorities in each option separated by commas. For example, in the f_mail filter on the next line, you can see the filter is selecting all mail and daemon facility messages.

```
filter f_mail    { priority(mail,daemon) };
```

You can also list multiple priories in a range separated by .., as you can see in the f_infotoemerg filter on the next line:

```
filter f_infotoemerg { priority(info .. error); };
```

The filter{} statements can also contain multiple types of options combined using Boolean AND/OR/NOT logic. You can see these capabilities in the f_boolean filter statement on the next line where I am selecting all messages of priority info, notice, and error but not those from the mail, authpriv, or cron facilities.

```
filter f_boolean { priority(info .. error) and not (facility(mail) ➡
or facility(authpriv) or facility(cron)); };
```

Another type of filtering is to select messages from a specific host. You can see this in the f_hostpuppy filter on the next line:

```
filter f_hostpuppy { host(puppy); };
```

You can also select messages based on the netmask of the system that generated them. The filter on the next line selects all messages from the network 10.1.20.0/24:

```
filter f_netmask { netmask("10.1.20.0/24") };
```

Another form of filtering you will find useful is to select only those messages from a particular program. The filter on the next line will select only those messages generated by the sshd daemon:

```
filter f_sshd { program("sshd.*") };
```

Finally, you can match messages based on the content of the messages using the match() option. You can use regular expressions to match on the content of a message.

```
filter f_regexp { match("deny"); };
```

Additionally, you can add a not to the front of your match statement to negate a match and not select those messages with a particular content.

```
filter f_regexp2 { not match("STATS: dropped 0")};
```

log{}

As described earlier, after you have defined source{}, destination{}, and filter{} statements, you need to combine these components in the form of log{} statement blocks that actually do the logging. Unlike the other types of statement blocks, they do not need to be named.

For a valid log{} statement, you need to include only a source and a destination statement. The following line logs all the messages from the source s_sys to the destination d_mesg:

```
log { source(s_sys); destination(d_mesg); };
```

But generally your log{} statement blocks will contain a combination of source, destination, and filter statements. You can also combine multiple sources and filters into a log{} statement. As you can see in Listing 5-23, I am selecting messages from two sources, s_sys and s_tcp, and then filtering them with f_mail and sending them to the d_mesg destination.

Listing 5-23. *A syslog-NG* log{} *Statement with Multiple Sources*

```
log { source(s_sys); source(s_tcp); filter(f_mail); destination(d_mesg); };
```

The log{} statement blocks also have some potential flag modifiers (see Table 5-9).

Table 5-9. log{} *Statement Block Flags*

Flag	Description
final	Indicates the processing of log statements ends here. If the messages matches this log{} statement, it will be processed here and discarded.
fallback	Makes a log statement "fall back." This means that only messages not matching any "nonfallback" log statements will be dispatched.
catchall	The source of the message is ignored; only the filters are taken into account when matching messages.

You can add flags to the end of log{} statements like this:

```
log { source(s_sys); destination(d_con); flags(final); };
```

This log statement is modified to show that if the message is from the source s_sys with destination d_con, then log it to that destination and do not match that message against any further log{} statements. This does not necessarily mean the message is logged only once. If it was matched to any log{} listed in your syslog-ng.conf file prior to this one, they will also have logged that message.

Sample syslog-ng.conf File

You have seen what all the possible syslog-NG statement blocks are. Now it is time to combine them into an overall sample configuration. The configuration in Listing 5-24 shows basic host-logging messages on a local system being sent to various destinations. This is a working configuration, and you can further expand on it to enhance its capabilities.

■**Tip** Do not forget syslog-NG comes with an excellent example syslog-ng.conf file, and you can also use the conversion tool, syslog2ng, to create a file from your existing syslog.conf file!

Listing 5-24. *Starter* syslog-ng.conf *File*

```
options {
sync (0);
time_reopen (10);
log_fifo_size (1000);
create_dirs (no);
owner (root);
group (root);
perm (0600);
};
```

```
source s_sys {
pipe ("/proc/kmsg" log_prefix("kernel: "));
unix-dgram ("/dev/log");
internal();
};

filter f_defaultmessages { level(info) and not (facility(mail) ➥
or facility(authpriv) or facility(cron) or facility(local4)); };
filter f_authentication { facility(authpriv) or facility(auth); };
filter f_mail { facility(mail); };
filter f_emerg { level(emerg); };
filter f_bootlog { facility(local7); };
filter f_cron { facility(cron); };

destination d_console { file("/dev/console"); };
destination d_allusers { usertty("*"); };
destination d_defaultmessages { file("/var/log/messages"); };
destination d_authentication { file("/var/log/secure"); };
destination d_mail { file("/var/log/maillog"); };
destination d_bootlog { file("/var/log/boot.log"); };
destination d_cron { file("/var/log/cron"); };

log { source(s_sys); filter(f_defaultmessages); destination(d_defaultmessages); };
log { source(s_sys); filter(f_authentication); destination(d_authentication); };
log { source(s_sys); filter(f_mail); destination(d_mail); };
log { source(s_sys); filter(f_emerg); destination(d_allusers); ➥
destination(d_console); };
log { source(s_sys); filter(f_bootlog); destination(d_bootlog); };
log { source(s_sys); filter(f_cron); destination(d_cron); };
```

To make sure you fully understand what the syslog-ng.conf file is doing, let's step through one of the items being logged here. In the s_sys source statement, you are collecting from the standard logging device, /dev/log.

```
unix-dgram ("/dev/log");
```

Amongst the messages to this device are security-related messages sent to the auth and auth-priv facilities. In the following line, I have defined a filter statement, f_authentication, to pick these up:

```
filter f_authentication { facility(authpriv) or facility(auth); };
```

Next I have defined a destination for the messages, d_authentication. This destination that writes to a file in the /var/log directory is called secure.

```
destination d_authentication { file("/var/log/secure"); };
```

In the global options{} block, I have told syslog-NG using the owner, group, and perm options that this file will be owned by the root user and group and have permissions of 0600 (which allows only the owner to read and write to it).

Lastly, I have defined a `log{}` statement to actually do the logging itself.

```
log { source(s_sys); filter(f_authentication); destination(d_authentication); };
```

The `log{}` statement combines the previous statements to perform the logging function.

With the steps defined here, you should be able to build your own logging statements using the powerful options available to you with syslog-NG.

Logging to a Database with syslog-NG

So why log to a database? If you need to store logs for any length of time, most probably for some statistical purpose or because of the need for an audit trail, you should look at logging to a database, because it will make the task considerably easier. Querying megabytes of text files containing log messages using tools such as grep is cumbersome and prone to error. An SQL database, on the other hand, is designed to be queried via a variety of tools. You can even enable ODBC on your database flavor and query it with third-party tools such as Crystal Reports. This also makes the process of pruning and purging your log entries easier, as you can build SQL queries to perform this task much more simply and with considerably more precision than with file-based log archives.

So if you have the why of it, then how do you do it? I will assume you are using syslog-NG for your logging; however, if you decide to retain `syslogd`, then you can find a link in the "Resources" section to instructions for enabling database logging from `syslogd`.

Note For the backend database I have chosen to use MySQL, but it is also possible to log to PostgreSQL or even Oracle. This section assumes you have MySQL installed and running on your logging system. See the "Resources" section for more information.

The architecture of database logging is simple. syslog-NG logs the messages you want to store to a pipe, and a script reads those entries from the pipe and writes them to the database. I have used d_mysql as the name of the destination in syslog-NG, `mysql.pipe` as the name of the proposed pipe, and `syslog.logs` as the name of the database table. See Figure 5-2.

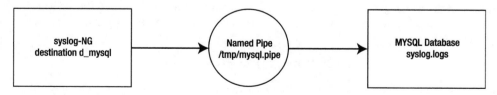

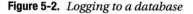

Figure 5-2. *Logging to a database*

So first you need to tell syslog-NG where to send the messages you want to store to a pipe. I will assume you are going to store all messages sent to the s_sys source. Listing 5-25 shows the statements needed to log to the database. You can add these to the configuration file in Listing 5-24 to allow you to test database logging.

Listing 5-25. *syslog-NG Statements to Log to a Database*

```
destination d_mysql { pipe("/tmp/mysql.pipe" template("INSERT INTO logs (host,
facility, priority, level, tag, date, time, program, msg) ➥
VALUES( '$HOST','$FACILITY', '$PRIORITY', '$LEVEL', '$TAG', '$YEAR-$MONTH-$DAY',
'$HOUR:$MIN:$SEC', '$PROGRAM', '$MSG' );\n") template-escape(yes)); };

log { source(s_sys); destination(d_mysql); };
```

■**Tip** You may also what to define a filter statement to select only particular messages you want to keep. For example, you could use the f_authentication filter from Listing 5-24 to log only security-related messages to the database.

Note the use of the template-escape(yes) option to ensure the macros are properly escaped and will be written correctly to the MySQL database.

You then need to create a pipe to store the syslog-NG messages.

```
puppy# mkfifo /tmp/mysql.pipe
```

Now you need to create the MySQL database and a user to connect to it. You can use the syslog.sql script shown in Listing 5-26.

Listing 5-26. *The* syslog.sql *Script*

```
# Table structure for table `log`
CREATE DATABASE syslog;

USE syslog;

CREATE TABLE logs (
host varchar(32) default NULL,
facility varchar(10) default NULL,
priority varchar(10) default NULL,
level varchar(10) default NULL,
tag varchar(10) default NULL,
date date default NULL,
time time default NULL,
program varchar(15) default NULL,
msg text,
seq int(10) unsigned NOT NULL auto_increment,
PRIMARY KEY (seq),
KEY host (host),
KEY seq (seq),
KEY program (program),
KEY time (time),
KEY date (date),
```

```
KEY priority (priority),
KEY facility (facility)
) TYPE=MyISAM;

GRANT ALL PRIVILEGES ON syslog.* TO syslog@localhost identified by 'syslog' ➥
with grant option;
```

This script will create a database called syslog with a table called log accessible by a user called syslog with a password of syslog. You should change the grant privileges, user, and password to suit your environment—the syslog user needs only INSERT privileges to the table.

To run this script, you use the following command:

```
puppy# mysql -u user -p < /path/to/syslog.sql
Enter password:
```

Replace *user* with a MySQL user with the authority to create tables and grant privileges, and replace */path/to/syslog.sql* with the location of the script shown in Listing 5-26. You will be prompted to enter the required password for the user specified with the -u option.

You can check whether the creation of the database is successful by first connecting to the MySQL server as the syslog user and then connecting to the syslog database and querying its tables.

```
puppy# mysql -u syslog -p
Enter password:
mysql> connect syslog;
Current database: syslog
mysql> show tables;
Tables_in_syslog
logs
1 row in set (0.00 sec)
```

If the shows tables command returns a table called logs, then the script has been successful.

You then need a script to read the contents of the mysql.pipe pipe and send them to the database. I provide a suitable script in Listing 5-27.

Listing 5-27. *Script to Read* mysql.pipe

```
# syslog2mysql script#
#!/bin/bash

if [ -e /tmp/mysql.pipe ]; then
        while [ -e /tmp/mysql.pipe ]
                do
                        mysql -u syslog --password=syslog syslog < /tmp/mysql.pipe
        done
else
        mkfifo /tmp/mysql.pipe
fi
```

```
puppy# /etc/rc.d/init.d/syslog-ng restart
```

Second, on the command line, run the script from Listing 5-27 and put it in the background.

```
puppy# /root/syslog2mysql &
```

This script is now monitoring the pipe, `mysql.pipe`, you created in the `/tmp` directory and will redirect any input to that pipe to MySQL.

Tip I recommend you incorporate the starting and stopping of this script into the `syslog-NG init` script to ensure it gets starts and stops when syslog-NG does.

Now send a log message using the `logger` command. If you have added filtering to the `log{}` block defined in Listing 5-25, then you need to ensure whatever log message you send with `logger` is going to be picked up by that filtering statement and sent to MySQL.

```
logger -p auth.info "Test syslog to MySQL messages from facility auth with ➥
priority info"
```

syslog-NG will write the log message to the `mysql.pipe` script, and the `syslog2mysql` script will direct the log message into MySQL. Now if you connect to your MySQL server and query the content of the `logs` table, you should see the log entry you have sent using `logger`. You can do this with the following commands:

```
puppy# mysql -u syslog -p
Enter password:
mysql> connect syslog;
Current database: syslog
mysql> select * from logs
```

Now your syslog-NG should be logging to the MySQL database.

Secure Logging with syslog-NG

I have discussed in a few places the importance of secure logging and protecting your logging system from both DoS attacks and attempts by intruders to read your logging traffic. To achieve this, you will use Stunnel, the Universal SSL Wrapper, which, as mentioned earlier in the chapter, encapsulates TCP packets with SSL. Stunnel uses certificates and public-key encryption to ensure no one can read the TCP traffic.

Tip I have discussed Stunnel in considerably more detail in Chapter 3. This is simply a quick-and-dirty explanation of how to get Stunnel working for syslog-NG tunneling. I also discuss OpenSSL and SSL certificates in that chapter, and you may want to create your certificates differently after reading that chapter.

First, you need to install Stunnel. A prerequisite of Stunnel is OpenSSL, which most Linux distributions install by default. You can get Stunnel from http://www.stunnel.org/ by clicking the Download button in the left menu. Unpack the archive, and change in the resulting directory. The Stunnel install process is simple.

```
puppy# ./configure --prefix=/usr --sysconfdir=/etc
```

The --prefix and --sysconfdir options place the binaries and related files under /usr and the Stunnel configuration files in /etc/stunnel.

Second, make and install like this:

```
puppy# make && make install
```

The make process will prompt you to input some information for the creation of an OpenSSL certificate. Fill in the details for your environment.

Now you need to create some certificates using OpenSSL for both your syslog-NG server and your clients. On your syslog-NG server, go to /usr/share/ssl/certs and create a certificate for your server.

```
puppy# make syslog-ng-servername.pem
```

Tip The certs directory can reside in different places on different distributions. On Red Hat and Mandrake systems it is located in /usr/share/ssl/certs. On Debian it is located in /usr/local/ssl/certs, and on SuSE it is located in /usr/ssl/certs.

Replace the servername variable with the name of your server. Copy this certificate to the /etc/stunnel directory on the system you have designated as the central logging server.

The client certificates are a little different. You need to create a client certificate for each client you want to connect to the syslog-NG server.

```
puppy# make syslog-ng-clientname.pem
```

Your certificates will look something like Listing 5-28.

Listing 5-28. *Your* syslog-ng *Certificates*

```
-----BEGIN RSA PRIVATE KEY-----
MIICXQIBAAKBgQDOX34OBdIzsF+vfbWixN54Xfdo73PaUwb+JjoLeF7bu6qKHlgA
RvLiJaambwNCiRJ8jn6GSLiDwOGaffAuQO3YtSrW/NoOsxH6wHEjvOW8d2tWOkbW
o3fOkAeNKCiqBTNDdDRHWnelY5nXgj3jPXOQsuOQq3TlNGy/Dx5YkbprVQIDAQ
4PRxBezKTsaoecCYOIMCQQCw7bOmpJX+DyqLX43STjHt4s7yKio16IOZR1Srsk68
zlOD7HgjNPW8wQEY6yRK7PI+j5o/LNulOXk7JOfOYQUQ
-----END RSA PRIVATE KEY-----
```

```
-----BEGIN CERTIFICATE-----
MIICoDCCAgmgAwIBAgIBADANBgkqhkiG9w0BAQQFADBFMQswCQYDVQQGE
M7Bfr321osTeeF33aO9z2lMG/iY6C3he27uqih5YAEby4iWmpm8DQokSfI5+hki4
g8Dhmn3wLkDt2LUq1vzaNLMR+sBxI7zlvHdrVjpG1qN3zpAHjSgoqgUzQ3QOR1p3
pWOZ14I94z1zkLLjkKtO5TRsvw8eWJG6a1UCAwEAAaOBnzCBnDAdBgNVHQ4EF
brNsdA==
-----END CERTIFICATE-----
```

As you can see, in each certificate file are two keys. The first is the private key, which is contained within the BEGIN RSA PRIVATE and END RSA PRIVATE KEY text. The second is the certificate, which is contained within the BEGIN CERTIFICATE and END CERTIFICATE text.

To authenticate, your server needs the certificate portion of each of your client certificates. So, copy the newly created client certificate, and remove the private key portion leaving the certificate portion. The file will now look like Listing 5-29.

Listing 5-29. *SSL Certificate*

```
-----BEGIN CERTIFICATE-----
MIICoDCCAgmgAwIBAgIBADANBgkqhkiG9w0BAQQFADBFMQswCQYDVQQGE
M7Bfr321osTeeF33aO9z2lMG/iY6C3he27uqih5YAEby4iWmpm8DQokSfI5+hki4
g8Dhmn3wLkDt2LUq1vzaNLMR+sBxI7zlvHdrVjpG1qN3zpAHjSgoqgUzQ3QOR1p3
pWOZ14I94z1zkLLjkKtO5TRsvw8eWJG6a1UCAwEAAaOBnzCBnDAdBgNVHQ4EF
brNsdA==
-----END CERTIFICATE-----
```

For ease of management I recommend storing all these certificates in a single file; I call mine syslog-ng-clients.pem and simply append the certificate portion of each new client onto the end of the file.

To authenticate on the client end, the client requires a copy of your certificate with the private key and the certificate in it like the original file shown in Listing 5-28. Copy this into the /etc/stunnel directory on the client. You also need the certificate portion of the server certificate. So make a copy of your server certificate. Call it syslog-ng-*servername*.pubcert. From the syslog-ng-*servername*.pubcert file, remove the private key portion file and copy the resulting file to the /etc/stunnel directory on the client

The following example shows the steps taken to add a new client:

1. Create a client certificate like this:

   ```
   puppy# cd /usr/share/ssl/certs/
   puppy# make syslog-ng-clientname.pem
   ```

2. Append the certificate portion of the new client certificate to the syslog-ng-clients.pem file in /etc/stunnel.

3. Copy the /etc/stunnel/syslog-ng-*servername*.pubcert file and the syslog-ng-*client-name*.pem file to the new client.

Now that you have keys on the client and server systems, you need to configure Stunnel to read those keys and set up the connections. You do this by creating and editing `stunnel.conf` files, which you should also locate in `/etc/stunnel` on both the client and server systems.

On the server side, your `stunnel.conf` should look like Listing 5-30.

Listing 5-30. *Server-Side* `stunnel.conf` *Configuration*

```
cert = /etc/stunnel/syslog-ng-servername.pem
pid = /var/run/stunnel.pid
# Some debugging stuff
debug = debug
output = /var/log/stunnel.log
# Service-level configuration
CAfile = /etc/stunnel/syslog-ng-clients.pem
verify = 3
[5140]
accept = 5140
connect = 514
```

■**Tip** I have enabled a fairly high level of logging in Stunnel (which is useful to help diagnose any errors). If you want a lesser amount of logging, then change debug to a higher priority (for example, info).

The `cert` option defines the certificate for the local system (you would replace *servername* with the name of your syslog-NG server), and the `CAfile` option points to the collection of certificates from which this server authorizes connection. The service-level configuration tells Stunnel to accept connections on port 5140 and redirect those connections to port 514 on the local host.

Your `stunnel.conf` should look like Listing 5-31.

Listing 5-31. *Client-Side Configuration*

```
cert = /etc/stunnel/syslog-ng-clientname.pem
pid = /var/run/stunnel.pid
# Some debugging stuff
debug = debug
output = /var/log/stunnel.log
# Service-level configuration
client = yes
CAfile = /etc/stunnel/syslog-ng-servername.pubcert
verify = 3
[5140]
accept = 127.0.0.1:514
connect = syslogserverIP:5140
```

On the client side, the cert file defines the certificate for the local system (you would replace *clientname* with the name of your client system), and the CAfile option points to the certificate of the server (you would replace *servername* with the name of your syslog-NG server) to which you want to connect, in this case syslog-ng-*servername*.pubcert. The additional parameter client is set to yes. This tells Stunnel that this system is a client of a remote Stunnel system. The service-level configuration tells Stunnel to accept connections on IP 127.0.0.1 (localhost) at port 514 and redirect those connections to port 5140 on the syslog-NG server. In Listing 5-31 you would replace *syslogserverIP* with the IP address of your syslog-NG server.

This sets up Stunnel, and now you need to make some changes to allow syslog-NG to receive your Stunnel'ed traffic. On the syslog-NG server, ensure your tcp() source statement in your syslog-ng.conf file looks like Listing 5-32.

Listing 5-32. *Server-Side* syslog-ng.conf *for Stunnel*

```
source s_tcp { tcp(ip("127.0.0.1") port(514)); };
```

This ensures syslog-NG is checking port 514 on localhost or 127.0.0.1 where Stunnel will direct any incoming syslog-NG traffic coming from port 5140.

On the client side, ensure your syslog-ng.conf destination and log statements are also updated, as shown in Listing 5-33.

Listing 5-33. *Client-Side* syslog-ng.conf *for Stunnel*

```
destination d_secure { tcp("127.0.0.1" port(514)); };
log { source(s_sys); destination(d_secure); };
```

This ensures syslog-NG is logging to port 514 on localhost or 127.0.0.1 where Stunnel will redirect that traffic to port 5140 on your syslog-NG server. The log{} statement will log everything from source s_sys to that destination.

■**Tip** If you are using Stunnel for secure logging, you need to ensure the keep_hostname() option is set to yes; otherwise, all the messages will have localhost as their hostname.

Now you are almost ready to go. All you need to do is start Stunnel on both your server and client systems. Starting Stunnel is easy. You do not need any options for the stunnel binary; however, it is probably a good idea to be sure Stunnel is pointing at the right configuration file.

```
puppy# stunnel /path/to/conf/file
```

Now restart syslog-NG on both your server and client systems, and your logging traffic should now be secured from prying eyes.

Testing Logging with logger

Present on all Linux distributions, logger is a useful command-line tool to test your logging configuration. Listing 5-34 demonstrates logger.

Listing 5-34. *Running the* logger *Command*

```
puppy# logger -p mail.info "This is a test message for facility mail and ➡
priority info"
```

Listing 5-34 would write the message "This is a test message for facility mail and priority info" to your syslog or syslog-NG daemon and into whatever destination you have configured for messages with a facility of mail and a priority of info. As you can see, the -p parameter allows you specify a facility and priority combination and then the test message contained in quotation marks.

I often use logger inside bash scripts to generate multiple messages for testing purposes. The script in Listing 5-35 generates a syslog message for every facility and priority combination.

Listing 5-35. *Log Testing* bash *Script*

```
#!/bin/bash
for f in
{auth,authpriv,cron,daemon,kern,lpr,mail,mark,news,syslog,user,uucp,local0,➡
local1,local2,local3,local4,local5,local6,local7}
do
for p in {debug,info,notice,warning,err,crit,alert,emerg}
do
logger -p $f.$p "Test syslog messages from facility $f with priority $p"
done
done
```

You can also use logger to pipe a growing file into syslog or syslog-NG. Try the simple script shown in Listing 5-36.

Listing 5-36. *Piping a Growing File into* syslog

```
#!/bin/bash
tail -f logfile | logger -p facility.priority
```

This script simply runs tail -f on *logfile* (replace this with the name of the file you want to pipe into your choice of syslog daemon) and pipes the result into logger using a facility and priority of your choice. Of course, this script could obviously be greatly expanded in complexity and purpose, but it should give you a start.

Logger works for both syslog and syslog-NG.

Log Analysis and Correlation

Many people think log analysis and correlation are "black" arts—log voodoo. This is not entirely true. It can be a tricky art to master, and you need to be constantly refining that art; however, inherently once you implement a systematic approach to it, then it becomes a simple part of your daily systems' monitoring routine.

The first thing to remember is that analysis and correlation are two very different things. *Analysis* is the study of constituent parts and their interrelationships in making up a whole. It must be said that the best analysis tool available is yourself. System administrators learn the patterns of their machines' operations and can often detect a problem far sooner than automated monitoring or alerting systems have done on the same problem. I have two problems with this model. The first problem is that you cannot be everywhere at once. The second problem is that the growing volume of the data collected by the systems can become overwhelming.

This is where correlation comes in. *Correlation* is best defined as the act of detecting relationships between data. You set up tools to collect your data, filter the "wheat from the chaff," and then correlate that remaining data to put the right pieces of information in front of you so you can provide an accurate analysis. Properly setup and managed tools can sort through the constant stream of data that the daily operations of your systems and any attacks on those systems generate. They can detect the relationships between that data and either put those pieces together into a coherent whole or provide you with the right pieces to allow you to put that analysis together for yourself.

But you have to ensure those tools are the right tools and are configured to look for the right things so you can rely on them to tell you that something is wrong and that you need to intervene. As a result of the importance of those tools to your environment, building and implementing them should be a carefully staged process. I will now cover those stages in brief.

The first stage of building such an automated log monitoring system is to make sure you are collecting the right things and putting them in the right place. Make lists of all your applications, devices, and systems and where they log to. Read carefully through the sections in this chapter discussing `syslog` and syslog-NG, and make sure whatever you set up covers your entire environment. Make sure your logging infrastructure encompasses every piece of data generated that may be vital to protecting your systems.

The second stage is bringing together all that information and working out what you really want to know. Make lists of the critical messages that are important to you and your systems. Throw test attacks and systems failures at your test systems, and record the resulting message traffic; also, port scan your systems and firewalls, even unplugging hardware or deliberately breaking applications in a test environment to record the results. Group those lists into priority listings; some messages you may want to be paged for, others can go via e-mail, and some may trigger automated processes or generate attempts at self-recovery such as restarting a process.

The third stage is implementing your log correlation and analysis, including configuring your correlation tools and designing the required responses. Make sure you carefully document each message, the response to the message, and any special information that relates to this message. Then test them. And test them again. And keep testing them. Your logging environment should not be and almost certainly will never be static. You will always discover something new you want to watch for and respond to. Attackers are constantly finding new ways to penetrate systems that generate different data for your logging systems. Attacks are much like viruses—you need to constantly update your definitions to keep up with them.

So where do you go from here? I will now introduce you to a powerful tool that will help you achieve your logging goals. That tool is called SEC.

SEC is the most powerful open-source log correlation tool available.[3] SEC utilizes Perl regular expressions to find the messages that are important to running your system out of the huge volume of log traffic most Linux systems generate. It can find a single message or match pairs of related messages; for example, it can find matching messages that indicate when a user has logged on and off a system. SEC can also keep count of messages it receives and act only if it receives a number of messages exceeding a threshold that you can define. SEC can also react to the messages it receives by performing actions such as running a shell script. These actions can include the content of the messages. For example, it is possible to run a shell script as a SEC action and use some or all of the message content as a variable to be inputted into that shell script.

■**Note** As a result of SEC's reliance on Perl regular expressions, you need to be reasonably comfortable with using them. The Perl documentation on regular expressions is excellent. Try http://www.perldoc.com/perl5.6.1/pod/perlre.html and http://www.perldoc.com/perl5.8.0/pod/perlretut.html. Also, I have listed several excellent books on regular expressions in this chapter's "Resources" section.

Seeing all this functionality you may think SEC is overkill for your requirements, but the ability to expand your event correlation capabilities far outweighs the cost of implementation. It is my experience that it is critical in your logging environment to avoid having to make compromises in your monitoring that could cause you to be exposed to vulnerabilities or a potentially missing vital messages. The functionality richness of SEC should be able to cover all your current and future event correlation needs.

Because of SEC's complexity, it is impossible to completely cover all its features within this chapter, so I will avoid discussing some of the more advanced features of SEC, most notably contexts. SEC's full implementation and variables could easily occupy a book in their own right. I will get you started with SEC by showing you how to install it, how to get it running, how to point your logs to SEC, and how set up some basic message-matching rules; then I will point you to the resources you will need to fully enable SEC within your own environment.

■**Tip** A good place to start learning more about SEC is the mailing list maintained at the SourceForge site for SEC. You can subscribe to the mailing list and read its archives at http://lists.sourceforge.net/lists/listinfo/simple-evcorr-users. SEC's author Risto Vaarandi is a regular, active, and helpful participant to this list, and the archives of the list contain many useful examples of SEC rules to help you.

---

3. SEC is written by Risto Vaarandi and supported by Vaarandi's employer, The Union Bank of Estonia. It is free to download and uses the GNU General Public License.

Installing and Running SEC

You can download SEC from `http://kodu.neti.ee/~risto/sec/` in the download section. Installing SEC is a simple process. SEC is a Perl script. To use it, you will need at least Perl version 5.005 installed on your system. (But a more recent version such as 5.6 is strongly recommended.) SEC also relies on the modules `Getopt`, `POSIX`, `Fcntl`, and `IO::Handle`, but these modules are included in the Perl base installation. Then unpack the SEC archive. Inside the archive is the engine of the SEC tool, a Perl script called `sec.pl`. Copy the `sec.pl` script to a directory of your choice. For these purposes, I have copied the `sec.pl` file into a directory that I created called `/usr/local/sec`. SEC also comes with a comprehensive man page that you should also install.

You start SEC from the command line by running the `sec.pl` script. Listing 5-37 shows a command line you can use to start SEC.

Listing 5-37. *Sample SEC Startup Options*

```
puppy# /usr/local/sec/sec.pl -input=/var/log/messages ➥
-conf=/usr/local/sec/sec.conf -log=/var/log/sec.log -debug=6 -detach
```

To start SEC, the first option you need is `-input`. Inputs are where you define the source of the messages SEC will be analyzing. You can have multiple input statements on the command line that gather messages from several sources. Listing 5-37 uses one input, `/var/log/messages`.

The next option, `-conf`, tells SEC where to find its configuration file. The configuration file contains all the rules SEC uses to analyze incoming messages. You probably do not have one of these yet, but you can just create an empty file to get started; SEC will start fine just when you use this empty file.

```
puppy# touch /usr/local/sec/sec.conf
```

You can specify more than one configuration file by adding more `-conf` options to the command line. This allows you to have multiple collections of rules for different situations or for different times of the day.

I have also specified some logging for SEC. In Listing 5-37, SEC is logging to the file `/var/log/sec.log` with a debugging level of 6 (the maximum).

The last option, `-detach`, tells SEC to detach and become a daemon.

If you were to run the command in Listing 5-37, it would result in the following being logged to the `sec.log` file in `/var/log`. The last line indicates the start was successful.

```
Fri Mar  5 17:28:09 2004: Simple Event Correlator version 2.2.5
Fri Mar  5 17:28:09 2004: Changing working directory to /
Fri Mar  5 17:28:09 2004: Reading configuration from /usr/local/sec/sec.conf
Fri Mar  5  17:28:09 2004: No valid rules found in configuration ➥
file /usr/local/sec/sec.conf
Fri Mar  5 17:28:09 2004: Daemonization complete
```

SEC is now running as a daemon on the system and awaiting events to process. If you change a rule or add additional rules, you need to restart the SEC process to reload the configuration files.

```
puppy# killall -HUP sec.pl
```

■**Tip** SEC also comes with a file called `sec.startup` that contains an `init` script you can adjust to start SEC automatically when you start your system; this should allow you to easily control reloading and restarting `sec.pl`.

SEC has some additional command-line options to control its behavior and configuration. Table 5-10 covers the important ones.

Table 5-10. *SEC Command-Line Options*

Option	Description
`-input=file pattern[=context]`	The input sources for SEC that can be files, named pipes, or standard input. You can have multiple input statements on your command line. The optional context option will set up a context. Contexts help you to write rules that match events from specific input sources. Note that I do not cover contexts in this chapter.
`-pid=pidfile`	Specifies a file to store the process ID of SEC. You must use this if you want a PID file.
`-quoting and -noquoting`	If quoting is turned on, then all strings provided to external shell commands by SEC will be put inside quotes to escape them. The default is not to quote.
`-tail and -notail`	These tell SEC what to do with files. If `-notail` is set, then SEC will read any input sources and then exit when it reaches the end of the file or source. If `-tail` is set, then SEC will jump to the end of the input source and wait for additional input as if you had issued the `tail -f` command. The default is `-tail`.
`-fromstart and -nofromstart`	These flags are used in combination with `-tail`. When `-fromstart` is enabled, it will force SEC to process input files from start to finish and then go into "tail" mode and wait for additional input. These options obviously have no effect if `-notail` is set. The default option is `-nofromstart`.
`-detach and -nodetach`	If you add `-detach` to the command line, SEC will daemonize. The default is `-nodetach` with SEC running in the controlling terminal.
`-testonly and -notestonly`	If the `-testonly` option is specified, then SEC will exit immediately after parsing the configuration file(s) for any errors. If the configuration file(s) do not contain any errors, then SEC will exit with an exit code of 0 and otherwise with an exit code of 1. The default is `-notestonly`.

You can read about additional SEC options on timeouts in input sources in the SEC man page.

Inputting Messages to SEC

The easiest way to get messages into SEC is to go through a named pipe. I recommend setting up either `syslog` or syslog-NG to point to a named pipe and inputting your messages to SEC through that pipe. First let's create a named pipe. Create a pipe in the `/var/log` directory called `sec`, like so:

```
puppy# mkfifo /var/log/sec
```

When I start SEC, I would now use this named pipe as an input on the starting command line by adding the option `-input /var/log/sec`.

Now you need to define this pipe to the respective logging daemons. For syslog-NG this is an easy process, as shown in Listing 5-38.

Listing 5-38. *syslog-NG Configuration for SEC*

```
destination d_sec { pipe("/var/log/sec"); };
log { source(s_sys); destination(d_sec); };
log { source(s_tcp); destination(d_sec); };
```

As you can see from Listing 5-37, you define a named pipe destination in syslog-NG, in this case `/var/log/sec`, and then log all the sources you want to this pipe. You can add the statements in Listing 5-38 to the sample configuration in Listing 5-24 to get this working immediately. You will need to restart syslog-NG to update the configuration.

■**Tip** If you have an especially busy system or one with performance issues, it may be wise to increase the syslog-NG global option `log_fifo_size` *(num)*; (defined in the `options{}` statement block). This controls the number of lines being held in buffer before they are written to disk. This should help prevent overflows and dropped messages if your pipe is slow to process events.

For `syslogd`, the process of getting messages into SEC requires pointing the facilities and priorities you want to input to SEC to a pipe. See Listing 5-39.

Listing 5-39. `syslogd` *Configuration for SEC*

```
*.info | /var/log/sec
```

This example would send all messages of `info` priority or higher from every facility to the named pipe, `/var/log/sec`.

As SEC can also read from files, you could also log the event messages you want to process with SEC to a file or series of files and use those as input sources. For the purpose of this explanation and for ease of use and configuration, I recommend the named pipe method. This is principally because there is no risk of log data being inputted to SEC twice if you accidentally tell SEC to reprocess a log file (which can happen using the `-fromstart` and `-nofromstart` options). Additionally, if you want to specify that messages go to SEC and to a file or database, you are not required to store the data twice. You keep a copy in a file or database, and the other copy goes into the pipe and directly into SEC without being written to disk and therefore taking up disk space.

Building Your SEC Rules

The SEC configuration file contains a series of rule statements. Each rule statement consists of a series of pairs of keys and values separated by an equals (=) sign. There is one key and value pair per line. You can see an example of a key and value pair on the next line:

```
type=Single
```

For the purposes of this explanation, I will call these *key=value pairs*. You can use the backslash (\) symbol to continue a key=value pair onto the next line. You can specify a comment using the pound (#) symbol. SEC assumes that a blank line or comment is the end of the current rule statement, so only add comments or blank lines at the start or end of a rule statement. Let's look now at an example of a rule statement to better understand how SEC and SEC rules work. See Listing 5-40.

Listing 5-40. *Sample SEC Rule Statement*

```
type=Single
continue=TakeNext
ptype=regexp
pattern=STATS: dropped ([0-9]+)
desc=Dropped $1 messages - go check this out
action=shellcmd /bin/echo '$0' | /bin/mail -s "%s" admin@yourdomain.com
```

Let's discuss this example line by line. The first line indicates the type of SEC rule that is being used. In Listing 5-40 I have used the simplest rule, Single, which simply finds a message and then executes an action.

The second line in Listing 5-40 is optional. The continue line has two potential options, TakeNext and DontCont. The first option, TakeNext, tells SEC that even if the log entry matches this rule, keep searching through the file for other rules that may match the entry. The second option, DontCont, tells SEC that if the log entry matches this rule, then stop here and do not try to match the entry against any additional rules. This means that a log entry will be checked against every single rule in your configuration file until it finds a rule it matches that has a continue setting of DontCont.

This is useful when some messages may be relevant to more than one rule in your configuration file. An example of when you could use this is if a message has more than one implication or purpose. For example, a user login message may be used to record user login statistics, but you may also want to be e-mailed if the root user logs on. You would use one rule to record the user statistics that has a continue option of TakeNext. After processing this rule, the message would be checked against the other rules in the configuration file and would be picked up by the rule that e-mails you if root logged on.

■**Note** If you omit the continue option from the rule statement, SEC defaults to DontCont.

The next two lines in the rules statement allow SEC to match particular events. The first is ptype, or the pattern type. The pattern type tells SEC how to interpret the information on the next line, the pattern itself. You can use the pattern types shown in Table 5-11.

Table 5-11. *SEC Pattern Types*

Pattern Type	Description
RegExp[*number*]	A Perl regular expression.
SubStr[*number*]	A substring.
NRegExp[*number*]	A negated regular expression; the results of the pattern match are negated.
NSubStr[*number*]	A negated substring; the results of the pattern match are negated.

The *number* portion after the pattern type tells SEC to compare the rule against the last *number* of log entries. If you leave *number* blank, then SEC defaults to 1—the last log entry received. Listing 5-40 used a standard regexp pattern type that tells SEC to interpret the pattern line as a Perl regular expression.

The third line in Listing 5-40, pattern, shows the pattern itself. In this example, it is a regular expression. This regular expression would match on any message that consisted of the text STATS: dropped and any number greater than one.

You may notice I have placed part of the regular expression, [0-9]+, in parentheses. In SEC the content of anything in the pattern line that you place in parentheses becomes a variable available to SEC. In this instance, ([0-9]+) becomes the variable $1; any subsequent data enclosed in parentheses would become $2, then $3, and so on. So if the message being tested against this rule was STATS: dropped 123, then the message would be matched and the variable $1 would be assigned a content of 123. Another special variable, $0, is reserved for the content of the log entry or entries the rule is being tested against. In this example, the variable $0 would contain the input line STATS: dropped 123.

The fourth line in Listing 5-40 shows the desc key=value pair. This is a textual description of the event being matched. Inside this description you can use any variables defined in the pattern. Thus, the desc for Listing 5-40 is Dropped $1 messages - go check this out. Using the message data in the previous paragraph, this would result in a description of Dropped 123 messages - go check this out. You will note that I have used the variables, $1, that I defined in the pattern line in the desc line. The final constructed description is also available to you in SEC as the %s variable.

The fifth and last line in Listing 5-40 shows the action key=value pair. This line tells SEC what to do with the resulting match, log entry, and/or variables generated as a result of the match. In the action line, in addition to any variables defined in the pattern (the $0 variable and the %s variable indicating the desc line), you also have access to two other internal variables: %t, the textual time stamp that is equivalent to the result of the date command, and %u, the numeric time stamp that is equivalent to the result of the time command.

Now you have seen your first SEC rule. It just scrapes the surface of what SEC is capable of doing. Let's look at another example to show you what else SEC is capable of doing. Listing 5-41 uses the SingleWithThreshold rule type to identify repeated sshd failed login attempts.

Listing 5-41. *Using the* SingleWithThreshold *Rule Type*

```
type=SingleWithThreshold
ptype=regexp
pattern=(\w+)\s+sshd\[\d+\]\:\s+Failed password for (\w+) from ➥
(\d+.\d+.\d+.\d+) port \d+ \w+\d+
desc=User $2 logging in from IP $3 to system $1 failed to enter the correct password
thresh=3
window=60
action=write /var/log/badpassword.log %s
```

With this rule I am looking to match variations on the following log entry:

```
Mar 12 14:10:01 puppy sshd[738]: Failed password for bob ➥
from 10.0.0.10 port 44328 ssh2
```

The rule type I am using to do this is called SingleWithThreshold. This rule type matches log entries and keeps counts of how many log entries are matched within a particular window of time. The window is specified using the window option and is expressed in seconds. In Listing 5-41 it is set to 60 seconds. The window starts counting when SEC first matches a message against that rule. It then compares the number of matches to a threshold, which you can see defined in Listing 5-41 using the thresh option as three matches. If the number of matches reaches the threshold within the window of time, then the action line is performed. In Listing 5-41 the action I have specified is to write the contents of the desc line to the specified file, /var/log/badpassword.log, using the write action. The write action can write to a file, to a named pipe, or to standard output.

So what other rules types are available to you? Well, SEC has a large collection of possible rules that are capable of complicated event correlation. You can see a list of all the other available rules types in Table 5-12.

Table 5-12. *SEC Rule Types*

Rule Type	Description
SingleWithScript	Matches an event, executes a script, and then, depending on the exit value of the script, executes a further action.
SingleWithSuppress	Matches an event, executes an action immediately, and then ignores any further matching events for *x* seconds.
Pair	Has a paired set of matches. It matches an initial event and executes an action immediately. It ignores any following matching events until it finds the paired event and executes another action.
PairWithWindow	Also has a paired set of matches. When it matches an initial event, it waits for *x* seconds for the paired event to arrive. If the paired event arrives within the given window, then it executes an action. If the paired event does not arrive within the given window, then it executes a different action.
SingleWith2Thresholds	Counts up matching events during *x1* seconds, and if more than the threshold of *t1* events is exceeded, then it executes an action. It then starts to count matching events again, and if the number during *x2* seconds drops below the threshold of *t2*, then it executes another action.

Rule Type	Description
Suppress	Suppresses any matching events. You can use this to exclude any events from being matched by later rules. This is useful for removing high-volume low-informational content messages that would otherwise clog SEC.
Calendar	Executes an action at a specific time.

So how do you use some of these other rules types? Let's look at some additional examples. Specifically, Listing 5-42 shows using the Pair rule type.

Listing 5-42. *Using the* Pair *Rule Type*

```
type=Pair
ptype=regexp
pattern=(\w+\s+\d+\s+\d\d:\d\d:\d\d)\s+(\w+)\s+su\(pam_unix\)➡
(\[\d+\])\:\s+session opened for user root by (\w+)\(\w+\=\d+\)
desc=User $4 has succeeded in an su to root at $1 on system $2. ➡
Do you trust user $4?
action=shellcmd /bin/echo '%s' | /bin/mail -s ➡
"SU Session Open Warning" admin@yourdomain.com
ptype2=regexp
pattern2=(\w+\s+\d+\s+\d\d:\d\d:\d\d)\s+$2\s+su\(pam_unix\)➡
$3\:\s+session closed for user root
desc2=Potentially mischievous user %4 has closed their su session at %1 on system %2
action2=shellcmd /bin/echo '%s' | /bin/mail -s ➡
"SU Session Close Warning" admin@yourdomain.com
```

In this example, I am using Pair to detect whenever somebody used the su command to become root on a system and then monitor the log file for when they closed that su session. So, I will be looking to match variations of the following two log entries:

```
Mar  6 09:42:55 puppy su(pam_unix)[17354]: session opened for user ➡
root by bob(uid=500)
Mar  6 10:38:13 puppy su(pam_unix)[17354]: session closed for user root
```

The rule type I will use for this is Pair, which is designed to detect a matching pair of log entries. You could also use the PairWithWindow rule type, which is designed to find a matching pair of log entries within a particular time window much like the SingleWithThreshold rule type you saw in Listing 5-41. With the Pair rule types you actually define two sets of pattern type and pattern, description, and action items. This is because you are matching two log entries. The second set of items are suffixed with the number 2 and referred to as ptype2 and pattern2, and so on, to differentiate them from the first set. The first set of items are used when the first log entry is matched; for example, the action line is executed when the log entry is matched. The second set of items is used if the second log entry is matched; for example, the action2 line is executed when the second log entry is matched.

For the first set of pattern type and pattern, I have used a regular expression pattern type. Inside the pattern I have also defined a number of elements of the log entry I am seeking to match as variables: the hostname on which the su session took place, the user who used the su command, the time the session opened and closed, and the process ID that issued the su command. You can then see that I have used some of these variables in the desc and action lines. The action I am using in Listing 5-42 is called shellcmd to execute a shell command when a log entry is matched.

The second pattern type will also be a regular expression. In this pattern, how do you know if the log entry indicating the end of the su session is related to the original log entry opening the su session? Well, SEC can use variables from the first pattern line, pattern, and these variables can form part of the regular expression being matched in the second pattern line, pattern2. In the first pattern line I defined the hostname of the system the su session was taking place on as $2 and the process ID of the session as $3. If you refer to those variables in the pattern2 line, then SEC knows you are referring to variables defined in the first pattern line. You use the host name and process ID to match the incoming log entry against the first log entry.

But this raises another question. How does SEC tell the difference between the variables defined in the two pattern lines when you use them in the desc2 line, for example? Well, variables for the first pattern line if you want to use them again in the desc2 or action2 lines are prefixed by %, and variables from the second pattern line are prefixed with $. You can see I have used the $4 variable defined in the first pattern line in the desc2 line by calling it %4.

Another useful rule type is Suppress. Listing 5-43 shows an example of a Suppress rule.

Listing 5-43. *Using the* Suppress *Rule Type*

```
type=Suppress
ptype=regexp
pattern=\w+\s+syslog-ng\[\d+\]\:\s+STATS: dropped \d+
```

Listing 5-43 is designed to suppress the following log entry:

```
Mar 12 01:05:00 puppy syslog-ng[22565]: STATS: dropped 0
```

The Suppress rule type simply consists of the rule type, a pattern type, and a pattern to match. Event suppression is especially useful for stopping SEC processing events you know have no value. You can specify a series of Suppress rules at the start of your configuration file to stop SEC unnecessarily processing unimportant messages. Be careful to be sure you are not suppressing a useful message, and be especially careful not to make your regular expressions too broad and suppress messages you need to see from getting through.

Suppress rules are also a place where you could use the pattern type of Substr. Let's rewrite Listing 5-43 using a substring instead of a regular expression.

```
type=Suppress
ptype=substr
pattern=This message is to be suppressed.
```

To match a log entry to a substring rule, the content of the pattern line must exactly match the content of the log entry. If required in a substring, you can use the backslash constructs \t, \n, \r, and \s to indicate any tabulation, newlines, carriage returns, or space characters.

> ■**Tip** As special characters are indicated with a backslash in Perl, if you need to use a backslash in a substring or regular expression, you must escape it. For instance in Perl, \\ denotes a backslash.

The Suppress rule type is not the only type of rule that allows you to suppress messages. You can also use the SingleWithSuppress rule type. This rule type is designed to match a single log entry, execute an action, and then suppress any other log entries that match the rule for a fixed period defined using the window line. This is designed to allow you to enable message compression. Message compression is useful where multiple instances of a log entry are generated but you need to be notified or have an action performed for only the first matched log entry. You can compress 100 messages to one response or action instead of each of the messages generating 100 individual responses or actions. Listing 5-44 shows an example of the SingleWithSuppress rule type.

Listing 5-44. *Using the* SingleWithSuppress *Rule Type*

```
type=SingleWithSuppress
ptype=RegExp
pattern=(\S+): Table overflow [0-9]+ of [0-9]+ in Table (\S+)
desc=Please check for a table overflow in $2
action=shellcmd notify.sh "%s"
window=600
```

Listing 5-44 uses a regular expression to check for a table overflow message generated by a database. I know this message can be generated hundreds of times in a short period, so I use the SingleWithSuppress rule to match only the first log entry and notify a user about the error message. If additional log entries are matched to this rule within the next 600 seconds (as defined using the window line), then they are suppressed and no action is performed. If the log entry appears again more than 600 seconds after the first log entry was matched, then another action is generated and all further matching log entries would be suppressed for another 600 seconds. This, for example, could be because the original problem has not been fixed and another notification is needed.

Within the last few examples, you have seen only a couple of SEC's possible actions, write and shellcmd. Within SEC additional possible actions are available. Table 5-13 describes some key ones table. These actions you can view in the SEC man page.

Table 5-13. *SEC Actions*

Action	Description
assign %*letter* [*text*]	Assigns the content of *text* to a user-defined %*letter* variable. You can use other % variables in your *text*, like those variables defined in your pattern. If you do not provide any *text*, then the value of the variable %s is used.
event [*time*] [*event text*]	After *time* seconds, a event with the content of [*event text*] is created. SEC treats the [*event text*] string exactly like a log entry and compares it to all rules. If you do not specify any [*event text*], then the value of the %s variable is used. If you specify 0 as [*time*] or omit the value altogether, then it will be created immediately.
logonly	The event description is logged to the SEC log file.
none	Takes no action.
spawn *shellcmd*	This is identical to the *shellcmd* action, but any standard output from *shellcmd* is inputted to SEC as if it were a log entry and matched against the rules. This is done by generating an *event 0* [*output line*] to each line from standard output. Be careful that the *shellcmd* command being spawned does not output a large volume of data or an endless loop, as SEC will process these results first and thus become locked.

You can put more than one action on an action line by separating them with a semicolon. You can see this in the next line:

```
action=shellcmd notify.sh "%s"; write /var/log/output.log %s
```

Here I have combined the shellcmd and write actions.

Listing 5-45 shows one final example, the Calendar rule type. The Calendar rule type is constructed differently than the other rule types are constructed.

Listing 5-45. *Using the* Calendar *Rule Type*

```
type=Calendar
time=1-59 * * * *
desc=This is an important message SEC needs to check
action=shellcmd purge.sh
```

The Calender rule type uses a special line called time. The time line uses the standard crontab format of five fields, separated by whitespace; those fields are minutes, hours, days of the month, months of the year, and weekdays. You can use the Calendar rule type to schedule events or kick off log-related processes. I often use Calendar events to schedule the clearing and management of files I use during the logging process.

These examples should have provided you with the grounding to start writing your own SEC rules. For further information and assistance with writing SEC rules, check the SEC FAQ and the example at http://kodu.neti.ee/~risto/sec/FAQ.html and http://kodu.neti.ee/~risto/sec/examples.html, respectively. Also, as mentioned earlier, the SEC mailing list is an excellent source of assistance and information.

Log Management and Rotation

An important part of managing your logging environment is controlling the volume of your log files and keeping your log files to a manageable size.

■**Tip** If you need to store messages for the long term, I recommend you look at logging to a database. I already discussed earlier in this chapter how to set up logging to a database.

This section will cover the process of automating rotating your logs on a daily, weekly, or monthly basis.

Log rotation can be quite complicated to manually script, so I recommend you use the logrotate tool. Most Linux distributions come with the logrotate tool. Of the common distributions, it is present on all Red Hat variations, Mandrake, Debian, and SuSE, and an e-build exists for it on Gentoo, which can be installed with the following command:

```
puppy# emerge logrotate
```

logrotate is simple to configure and relies on crontab to run on a scheduled basis. The base logrotate configuration is located in /etc/logrotate.conf (see Listing 5-46).

Listing 5-46. `logrotate.conf`

```
#log rotation
weekly
# keep old logs
rotate 4
#create new logs
create
#include .d files
include /etc/logrotate.d
```

This simple file contains the global options that logrotate uses to handle log files. In this example, all logs files rotate weekly, logs are rotated four times before they are deleted, new log files are created, and the logrotate tool checks the logrotate.d directory for any new logrotate files. You can use other options you can use, as shown in Table 5-14. You can delve into the logrotate man file for other options.

Table 5-14. `logrotate.conf` *Options*

Option	Description
daily	Logs are rotated on a daily basis.
weekly	Logs are rotated on a weekly basis.
monthly	Logs are rotated on a monthly basis.
compress	Old log files are compressed with gzip.

(Continues)

Table 5-14. *Continued*

Option	Description
create *mode owner group*	Creates new log files with a mode in octal form of 0700 and the owner and group (the opposite is nocreate).
ifempty	Rotates the log file even if it is empty.
include *directory or filename*	Includes the contents of the listed file and directory to be processed by logrotate.
mail *address*	When a log is rotated out of existence, mail it to *address*.
nomail	Do not mail the last log to any address.
missingok	If the log file is missing, then skip it and move onto the next without issuing an error message.
nomissingok	If the log file is missing, issue an error message (the default behavior).
rotate *count*	Rotate the log files *count* times before they are removed. If *count* is 0, then old log files are removed, not rotated.
size *size[M,k]*	Log files are rotated when they get bigger than the maximum *size*; *M* indicates size in megabytes, and *k* indicates size in kilobytes.
sharedscripts	Pre- and post-scripts can be run for each log file being rotated. If a log file definition consists of a collection of log files (for example, /var/log/samba/*), and *sharedscripts* is set, then the pre/post-scripts are run only once. The opposite is *nosharedscripts*.

Listing 5-46 shows the last command, include, which principally drives logrotate. The logrotate.d directory included in that example stores a collection of files that tell logrotate how to handle your various log files. You can also define additional directories and files and include them in the logrotate.conf file to suit your environment. Most distributions, however, use the logrotate.d directory and come with a number of predefined files in this directory to handle common log rotations such as mail, cron, and syslog messages. I recommend adding your own logrotate files here also. Listing 5-47 shows you one of those files.

Listing 5-47. *Red Hat* syslog logrotate *File*

```
/var/log/messages /var/log/secure /var/log/maillog /var/log/spooler ➥
/var/log/boot.log /var/log/cron
{
daily
rotate 7
sharedscripts
postrotate
      /bin/kill -HUP `cat /var/run/syslog-ng.pid 2> /dev/null` 2> /dev/null || true
endscript
}
```

Inside these files you can override most of the global options in `logrotate.conf` to customize your log rotation for individual files or directories. Listing 5-47 first lists all the files I want to rotate. This could also include directories using the syntax `/path/to/log/files/*`. Then enclosed in { } are any options for this particular set of files. In this example I have overridden the global logging options to rotate these files on a daily basis and keep seven rotations of the log files.

Next you are going to run a script. You can run scripts using the `prerotate` command, which runs the script prior to rotating any logs, or using `postrotate`, which runs the script after rotating the log file(s). Listing 5-47 runs a script that restarts syslog-NG after the log file(s) have been rotated. As the option `sharedscripts` is enabled, the script will be run only once no matter how many individual log files are rotated. The script statement is terminated with the `endscript` option.

So how does `logrotate` run? You can have `cron` run `logrotate` at scheduled times, or you can manually run it on the command line. If running on the command line, `logrotate` defaults to a configuration file of `/etc/logrotate.conf`. You can override this configuration file as you can see on the following line:

```
puppy# logrotate /etc/logrotate2.conf
```

`logrotate` also has several command-line options to use, as shown in Table 5-15.

Table 5-15. `logrotate` *Command-Line Options*

Option	Description
-d	Debug mode in which no changes will be made to log files; it will output the results of what it may have rotated. Implies -v mode also.
-v	Verbose mode.
-f	Forces a log rotation even if not required.

By default on most systems `logrotate` is run on a daily basis by `cron`, and this is the model I recommend you should use. Check your `cron.daily` directory in `/etc` for a `logrotate` script that should contain something like Listing 5-48.

Listing 5-48. `logrotate` cron *Script*

```
#!/bin/sh
/usr/sbin/logrotate /etc/logrotate.conf
EXITVALUE=$?
if [ $EXITVALUE != 0 ]; then
    /usr/bin/logger -t logrotate "ALERT exited abnormally with [$EXITVALUE]"
fi
exit 0
```

Resources

The following are resources you can use.

Mailing Lists

- **syslog-NG**: https://lists.balabit.hu/mailman/listinfo/syslog-ng

- **SEC**: http://lists.sourceforge.net/lists/listinfo/simple-evcorr-users

Sites

- **syslog-NG**: http://www.balabit.com/products/syslog_ng/

- **Regular expressions**: http://www.perldoc.com/perl5.8.0/pod/perlretut.html

    - http://www.perldoc.com/perl5.6.1/pod/perlre.html

    - http://www.weitz.de/regex-coach/

- **SEC**: http://kodu.neti.ee/~risto/sec/

- **Syslog to MySQL**: http://www.frasunek.com/sources/security/sqlsyslogd/

Books

- Friedl, Jeffrey E.F. *Mastering Regular Expressions*, Second Edition. Sebastopol, CA: O'Reilly, 2002.

- Good, Nathan A. *Regular Expression Recipes: A Problem-Solution Approach*. Berkeley, CA: Apress, 2004.

- Stubblebine, Tony. *Regular Expression Pocket Reference*. Sebastopol, CA: O'Reilly, 2003.

CHAPTER 6

■ ■ ■

Using Tools for
Security Testing

So you think you have got world-class security and a hardened site and systems? But do you really? Just because no one has penetrated your systems yet does not mean they are secure or does it mean you should rest on your laurels. If you are serious about security, you need to be constantly updating, refining, and, most important, testing your security and hardened systems. However, this by no means guarantees your security, as new exploits and vulnerabilities are discovered on a daily basis, but it is the best way to become as confident as possible that your systems are secure.

This chapter covers three layers of security testing: the inner security layer, the outer security layer, and the application security layer. I define the inner layer as consisting of the operating system of your systems, including such elements as your kernel security, file security, and user and password security. Outer layer security consists of what is best described as the "crust" of your system. These are your system's network connections, ports, or anything else that connects your systems to an intranet, the Internet, or other systems. The application security layer consists of the security of the applications running on your system. In each chapter where I discuss hardening a particular application, I will provide methods and tools to help you test that particular application for any security holes or vulnerabilities. Additionally, one of the outer layer security tools, Nessus, acts as a security scanner that often highlights potential issues with the applications or versions of applications you have running.

This chapter covers a variety of tools for testing the different layers of your security. Some of these tools need to be installed on your local system (and some should be removed when you are finished with them to prevent them from providing aid to an intruder), and some can be run across your network or from another host. I will take you through installing and running those tools and how to interpret the results of those tools. These tools are by no means the only tools available to you. Also, a variety of other security tools are useful. I will describe some of those in the "Additional Security Tools" section.

Do not take the results of any of these tools as "security gospel." They are fallible. When a particular security tool tells you your systems are secure, it simply means they are secure against all the exploits or vulnerabilities the author of that tool has envisaged or addressed. You need to keep up-to-date with new vulnerabilities, bugs, and exploits and ensure your systems and applications are up-to-date, as discussed in Chapter 1.

> **Tip** As previously mentioned, two good places to start if you want to keep track of vulnerabilities and exploits are the Bugtraq mailing list (`http://www.securityfocus.com/subscribe?listname=1`), the Vulnwatch site (`http://vulnwatch.org/`), and associated mailing lists.

This chapter also covers some methods of detecting a penetration that do not require any tools. Lastly I will cover the worst-case scenario: someone has penetrated your system, and now you need to know how to respond and recover. I will cover some general ideas about how to respond and offer some advice on recovering your systems.

Inner Layer

Your inner layer security consists of the operating-system level of your system, including the various programs, configurations, and settings that make up a well-secured and administered system. The following sections cover three types of applications to assist with your inner layer security. The first type is security-scanning software that can check for operating-system exploits, root kits, weaknesses, and vulnerabilities. The second type is a password cracker that allows you to test the security and strength of your system and users' passwords. The third type of software checks the security-related settings of your system.

Scanning for Exploits and Root Kits

A *root kit* is one variety of hacker tool kit. It can perform a number of functions depending on the flavor of the root kit. The original core of most root kit applications was some kind of network-sniffing tool designed to allow the attacker to find additional usernames and passwords. More recently, these functions have expanded to include capturing passwords using Trojan programs, providing back doors into your system, and masking that your system has been penetrated by purging or filtering logs. Root kits can also contain functionality designed to hide the attacker's logins and any processes they are running.

To install and run a root kit successfully, attackers need root access to your system. Thus, they have totally compromised your system and are now looking to expand their hold on it. Think about a root kit like a crowbar. Your attacker has penetrated your system, probably using a username and password of a low-level user. They seize root access through an exploit and use the root kit to pry open your system further, to grab other usernames and passwords, and to provide themselves with a jumping-off point to attack other systems in your environment.

> **Note** I discuss reducing the risk of an attacker seizing root access in Chapter 1.

Recovery is going to be a long process. Your system has been seriously penetrated by the time your attacker has installed a root kit. Even if he has only cracked open the door slightly, there is still significant risk that he has subverted a variety of your resources. The first thing most attackers do when they penetrate your systems is to secure their foothold, so it will be harder for you to get rid of them. I recommend that if you spot a root kit, then you should pull the plug on that system immediately and isolate it from your network. Then look at the recommendations later in the chapter in the "Detecting and Recovering from a Penetration or Attack" section.

I will cover two tools that are capable of detecting a variety of root kits. These tools are by no means infallible. They are generally not going to pick up root kits that are new or have changed since the tools were released (depending on how they identify root kits). And they are not substitutes for actually knowing what is running on your systems, including activities such as ongoing log analysis and comprehensive systems monitoring. They are after-the-fact tools. They are useful only for telling you what has happened after an attack. Finally, they are capable of generating false positives. Some applications can appear to be acting like a root kit. So, investigate all results carefully before taking drastic action.

Rootkit Hunter

Rootkit Hunter helps you scan your system for signs of a root kit installed and to perform a variety of other checks on related logs, commands, processes, and some configuration settings. You can download Rootkit Hunter at `http://www.rootkit.nl/projects/ rootkit_hunter.html`. It is available in the form of a source download or an RPM.[1] Download it in the form that best suits you.

If you have downloaded it Rootkit Hunter in source form, unpack your source archive, change into the created `rkhunter` directory, and install it using the command in Listing 6-1.

Listing 6-1. *Installing via Source*

```
puppy# ./installer.sh
```

If you have downloaded the RPM, you can install it using the command in Listing 6-2.

Listing 6-2. *Installing via RPM*

```
puppy# rpm -Uvh rkhunter-version.rpm
```

Rootkit Hunter installs a shell script, `rkhunter`, into `/usr/local/bin` and the rest of its files, including Perl scripts and databases, into the directory `/usr/local/rkhunter`.

■**Note** You need Perl installed to run Rootkit Hunter correctly.

---

1. RPM sometimes is incorrectly referred to as the Red Hat Package Manager. It is actually the abbreviation for RPM Package Manager, a command line–driven package management system that you can use to install, uninstall, verify, query, and update software packages. It is not just limited to packages developed by just Red Hat but is commonly used to distribute a variety of software packages.

You can run Rootkit Hunter from the command line or via `cron`. Listing 6-3 shows a sample run of Rootkit Hunter.

Listing 6-3. *Running* rkhunter

```
puppy# rkhunter --checkall --createlogfile
```

Listing 6-3 is running `rkhunter` with `--checkall`, which runs all the Rootkit Hunter tests and, with the option `--createlogfile`, creates a log file called `rkhunter.log` in `/var/log`. You can use a variety of other useful command-lines options (see Table 6-1); I will discuss each of them.

Table 6-1. *Rootkit Hunter Command-Line Options*

Option	Description
--cronjob	Runs as a `cron` job
--help	Shows help
--nocolors	Does not use colors in `rkhunter` output
--report-mode	Cuts down report and is useful when running for `crontab`
--skip-keypress	Runs in batch mode
--versioncheck	Checks for the latest version of Rootkit Hunter

The first option, `--cronjob`, adjusts the output of Rootkit Hunter to be suitable to run as a `cron` job. It is usually run in conjunction with the `--report-mode` option, which cuts down the report to the essentials. The `--cronjob` option does not actually install the `rkhunter` as a `cron` job. You need to add a `crontab` entry, such as in Listing 6-4, which runs the `rkhunter` via `cron` and mails the results of the scan to the user or alias `admin` once a month at 9 p.m.

Listing 6-4. *Rkhunter* crontab *Entry*

```
0 21 1 * * /usr/local/bin/rkhunter --cronjob --report-mode 2>&1 ➥
|/bin/mail -s "Rootkit Hunter report" admin
```

The next option, `--help`, lists all the possible command-line options. You can use the `--nocolors` option for those terminals that do not have color support. I discussed `--report-mode` previously. The next option, `--skip-keypress`, runs Rootkit Hunter in batch mode and removes prompts for key presses. The last option, `--versioncheck`, checks the Rootkit Hunter Web site for a new version and reports if there is a new version and its version number.

So what does Rootkit Hunter report? Well, after some initial self-checks, it checks a list of commonly penetrated binary commands for any sign they have been subverted. Listing 6-5 shows some of the results from this check.

Listing 6-5. *Binary Command Checks*

```
* System tools
  Performing 'known bad' check...
  /bin/cat                                              [ OK ]
  /bin/chmod                                            [ OK ]
  /bin/chown                                            [ OK ]
  /bin/csh                                              [ OK ]
  /bin/date                                             [ OK ]
  /bin/df                                               [ OK ]
```

Then Rootkit Hunter checks for the presence of a variety of root kits and then finally for a number of login back doors, root kit files, and sniffer logs. Check on the screen or the log file if you use the `--createlogfile` option for any positive results.

Chkrootkit

Chkrootkit is another tool for checking for the presence of root kits. It also contains some additional tools to check if interfaces are in promiscuous mode, to check `lastlog` and `wtmp` deletions, and to check for hidden processes. (Although these additional tools run when you run the primary `chkrootkit` script, you can also run them in a stand-alone mode.)

You can get Chkrootkit from `http://www.chkrootkit.org/`. You download a source archive and unpack it to a directory. Enter that directory, and compile Chkrootkit using the command in Listing 6-6.

Listing 6-6. *Compiling* chkrootkit

```
puppy# make sense
```

This will create a shell script called `chkrootkit` in the `chkrootkit-version` directory together with the additional binary tools mentioned in the previous section. You can move these files to a directory of your choice. Listing 6-7 shows how to do this.

Listing 6-7. *Installing* Chkrootkit

```
puppy# rm -f *.c Makefile
puppy# mkdir /usr/local/chkrootkit
puppy# mv * /usr/local/chkrootkit
```

You can run Chkrootkit from the command line or via `cron`, as you can see in Listing 6-8.

Listing 6-8. *Running* Chkrootkit *from the Command Line*

```
puppy# chkrootkit
```

You can run Chkrootkit without any command-line options, and it will perform all available checks by default. You can also use the command-line options in Table 6-2 to alter Chkrootkit's behavior.

Table 6-2. `chkrootkit` *Command-Line Options*

Option	Description
-d	Debug mode
-q	Quiet mode
-x	Expert mode
-n	Skips scanning NFS-mounted directories
-r *directory*	Uses *directory* as the root directory
-p *directory1:directory2*	Alternate paths for the external commands used by `chkrootkit`

The -d option runs Chkrootkit in debug mode, which provides considerable amounts of information about how Chkrootkit performs its checks. The -q option runs Chkrootkit in quiet mode where it will return output only if it finds a root kit or suspicious result. This is useful if you want to run Chkrootkit as a regular `cron` job. The -x option runs Chkrootkit in expert mode. In expert mode Chkrootkit skips any analysis of the strings found in binaries files and leaves any analysis to determine the presence of a Trojan to you. I recommend you pipe the output from expert mode through `more` or into a file that you can then search using a tool such as `grep`. The -n tells Chkrootkit to skip NFS-mounted directories.

The -r option allows you to specify an alternative location as the root directory. This is useful if you have removed the disk or disks from a compromised system and mounted them on another system (for example, an isolated test system). You can specify the root of the mount as the starting point for your Chkrootkit scan.

Chkrootkit uses a variety of commands to perform its checks: `awk`, `cut`, `egrep`, `find`, `head`, `id`, `ls`, `netstat`, `ps`, `strings`, `sed`, and `uname`. Of course, if your system has been penetrated, then an attacker could have subverted these commands, too. This could mean that Chkrootkit has unpredictable results or fails to identify the presence of an intrusion. Chkrootkit uses the -p option to allow you to specify an alternate directory that you can populate with copies of the commands you know are safe (for example, installed from your installation media). You can list multiple directories separated by colons.

When run, Chkrootkit first checks a variety of binaries for the presence of Trojans. Listing 6-9 shows a sample of these results.

Listing 6-9. *Sample* `chkrootkit` *Output*

```
puppy# chkrootkit
ROOTDIR is `/'
Checking `amd'... not found
Checking `basename'... not infected
Checking `biff'... not found
Checking `chfn'... not infected
Checking `chsh'... not infected
Checking `cron'... not infected
Checking `date'... not infected
Checking `du'... not infected
```

Chkrootkit then checks for the presence of log files from sniffer programs and then for the presence of a variety of root kits.

Testing Your Password Security

Chapter 1 talked about controlling the variables associated with your passwords to ensure that your users must use the most secure passwords possible. It also talked about ensuring you use modern password-encryption techniques such as MD5 and shadow passwording. Although this greatly enhances the security of your password, it is not always a guarantee that your passwords are totally impenetrable. Further testing is a good idea to add further reassurance that your passwords are strong and secure. I will show you how to use the password cracker John the Ripper to test the strength of your passwords.

■**Caution** Password cracking can be construed as a serious attack on a system. Do not run password cracking on a system that you do not control or do not explicitly have permission to run password cracking on.

The two most common forms of password cracking are brute-force and dictionary-based cracking. Brute-force cracking requires throwing computing resources at a password you want to crack. Usually a brute-force password-cracking program generates character sequences starting with one character and then incrementing from there and testing those character sequences against the password. This often requires considerable time and resources, and if your passwords are secure, then an attacker is unlikely to break them unless they are prepared to very patient. For example, a random password of eight characters in length and created from the 94 displayable ASCII characters would take a cracker approximately 1,930 years to crack using a typical desktop PC.[2] Of course, the more computing power you can throw at problem, the shorter you can make this time. Thus, password cracking highly lends itself to using parallel processing and using multiple systems to work on cracking passwords simultaneously.

The second form of password cracking relies on inputting a dictionary of potential passwords, encrypting them using the algorithm used by your password encryption, and then testing them against the encrypted password. This sort of cracking assumes users have chosen everyday words or combinations of everyday words as their passwords. This is quite common unless you force your users not to use this style of password. The system administrator's cliché of easily hacked systems with passwords such as sex, *god*, and *love* is still alive and well out there. Given the choice, your users will want to use a password they can easily remember, often containing personal information such as birthdays or pets' names rather than a complex string of characters and symbols.[3] This is simply the most dangerous form of password, and I strongly urge you not to let your users use *any* word that is a dictionary word for a password.

Running a password cracker over your password files on a regular basis is a good way to ensure your users are not choosing weak or easy-to-guess passwords.

Introducing John the Ripper

I use a password cracker called John the Ripper (JTR). A few password crackers are available, including the now venerable Crack.[4] I have chosen to cover JTR because it is regularly

---

2. http://geodsoft.com/howto/password/cracking_passwords.htm#howlong

3. http://zdnet.com.com/2100-11-530187.html?legacy=zdnn

4. http://www.crypticide.com/users/alecm/

updated, fast, and fairly simple to use. The other consideration I am making is that it is a known quantity. Consider this scenario: You decide you would like to test your passwords and go to a search engine and type in *password cracking my Linux root password*. You are directed to a page with a useful-looking piece of software that you then download and install. It turns out to be a Trojan horse program, which at the very least does something malicious with any password files it tests or passwords it cracks if not actually root kits on your system. So you want to make sure you download a safe password cracker.

Download JTR from http://www.openwall.com/john/, preferably verifying it using its MD5 signature.

■Note I used JTR version 1.6.37 for this explanation.

Unpack the archive, and change to the src directory. You have to tell JTR what sort of system you are running. Type **make** to see a list of potential systems. Listing 6-10 shows the possible Linux-based builds you can compile.

Listing 6-10. *Compiling John the Ripper*

```
puppy# make
To build John the Ripper, type:
        make SYSTEM
where SYSTEM can be one of the following:
linux-x86-any-elf        Linux, x86, ELF binaries
linux-x86-mmx-elf        Linux, x86 with MMX, ELF binaries
linux-x86-k6-elf         Linux, AMD K6, ELF binaries
linux-x86-any-a.out      Linux, x86, a.out binaries
linux-alpha              Linux, Alpha
linux-sparc              Linux, SPARC
```

If you have an Intel system, then your best choice is to compile JTR by entering the following:

```
puppy# make linux-x86-any-elf
```

This will create a binary called john in the directory john-*version*/run.

You run JTR from the command line, and Listing 6-11 shows a basic run of JTR.

Listing 6-11. *JTR on the Command Line*

```
puppy# john --wordlist=password.lst passwd
```

Listing 6-11 shows JTR performing a dictionary-based attack using a list of words contained in the file password.lst against passwords contained in a file called passwd. JTR comes with a simple file, password.lst, which is a collection of popular passwords. You will need to need find some additional dictionaries and word lists, including word lists in other languages, especially if you have users who speak English as a second language and may use foreign-language words as passwords. This does not make it any harder for attackers to penetrate their passwords. Attackers also have access to foreign language dictionaries and word lists.

■**Tip** You can find dictionary files in a few places. Try `ftp://ftp.cerias.purdue.edu/pub/dict/` and `ftp://ftp.ox.ac.uk/pub/wordlists/` for a variety of lists, including several foreign-language lists.

Customizing John the Ripper

JTR comes with a number of command-line options you can use to modify its behavior. I will show you the list of the most useful in Table 6-3 and take you through their functions. You can see the others by running the `john` binary without options from the command line.

Table 6-3. *John the Ripper Command-Line Options*

Option	Description
`--wordlist=file` | `--stdin`	Reads in a word list or text from standard in
`--stdout=length`	Outputs passwords to standard out instead of cracking
`--session=name`	Gives this cracking session a name
`--status=name`	Prints the status of a particular session
`--restore=name`	Restores a previous stopped session
`--show`	Shows any passwords JTR has cracked
`--test`	Performs benchmark testing

You saw the first option, `--wordlist`, in Listing 6-11; it allows you to test your passwords against a list of words or a dictionary specified after the = symbol. Or you can add the option `--stdin` to this option and read in a list of words from standard input, which is useful for inputting passwords to be tested programmatically. The second option, `--stdout`, does not actually crack passwords but rather outputs the list of words and combinations of characters that JTR would be testing against your passwords.

The next three options relate to starting, stopping, and restarting JTR. Obviously, some cracking efforts may take a long time. JTR allows you to stop and restart a session later if required. To do this when first starting JTR, add the option `--session=name`, replacing *name* with the name you want for this session. You can then stop that session using Ctrl+C, check the status of that session later, and then, if you want, restart it. Listing 6-12 shows how to stop, check the status of a session, and then restart that session.

Listing 6-12. *Starting, Printing the Status of, and Restarting a Session*

```
puppy# john --session=testsess passwd.1
Loaded 2 password hashes with 2 different salts (FreeBSD MD5 [32/32])
guesses: 0  time: 0:00:00:02 0% (2)  c/s: 1896  trying: ranger
Session aborted
puppy# john --status=testsess
guesses: 0  time: 0:00:00:03 0% (2)  c/s: 1264
puppy# ./john --restore=testsess
```

The following option, --show, prints any passwords that JTR cracked in its last session. The final option, --test, allows you to run benchmarking tests on your system to determine how fast it is capable of cracking particular encryption formats. This is useful for choosing a suitable machine on which to run JTR.

Most systems these days use shadow passwording. JTR comes with a function that allows you to create a file, combining your passwd and shadow files, that JTR can use to attempt to crack your shadow passwords. Listing 6-13 shows how to do this using the unshadow binary in the run directory.

Listing 6-13. *Creating a File for Cracking Shadow Password Files*

```
puppy# unshadow /etc/passwd /etc/shadow > passwd.1
```

This combines the contents of your passwd and shadow files into a file that JTR can attempt to crack.

You can also run JTR using a brute-force method. Listing 6-14 shows JTR running brute force against the passwd.1 file created in Listing 6-13.

Listing 6-14. *Running in Brute-Force Mode*

```
puppy# john passwd.1
```

Be prepared to wait a long time using this method to crack a reasonably secure password!

I cannot tell you how often to run your password-cracking software. I recommend if this is a new procedure to you, or you have recently tightened your password rules, you should be regularly running password-cracking software to ensure all your passwords have been made more secure. JTR also comes with an additional script, mailer (also in the run directory), that you can modify and use to mail to any users that JTR finds with weak passwords. You can also incorporate JTR into a script of your own and disable or expire the passwords of any users JTR finds with weak passwords. After securing your passwords, I recommend you consider adding a JTR dictionary-based scan to the cycle of your regular security checks. Perhaps on a weekly or monthly basis timed in conjunction with your password expiry and automated with a cron job or script.

Automated Security Hardening with Bastille Linux

On a Linux system a number of possible settings can have an impact on security. In this book, I have tried to cover a lot of the basic settings that you need to secure your system and overall how to implement a hardened security configuration methodology. However, a lot of individual settings can be overlooked or are time consuming to modify and secure. I cover an application, Bastille Linux, which will help you secure many of those items.

What Is Bastille Linux?

Bastille Linux (hereafter Bastille) is a Perl-based hardening "script." Bastille can be run in a graphical mode under X or via the console. It is designed to harden or tighten a variety of system security settings. Essentially Bastille takes system administrators through a variety of potential options they can control, tries to educate the administrator about those options and the implications of a variety of settings, and then provides the option (with a clear explanation of the consequences) to change those settings to make them more secure.

Currently Bastille supports a variety of platforms including several Linux flavors: Red Hat, Mandrake, SuSE, Debian, and TurboLinux. Bastille was primarily developed by Jon Lasser and Jay Beale and is available at `http://www.bastille-linux.org/`. It is an open-source application that is freely available under a GPL license.

I will take you through installing and using Bastille Linux. I will not cover every potential security setting that you can manipulate with Bastille because the Bastille team already provides excellent documentation about the various security settings and the implications of changing those settings. I will also take you through how to undo any changes you have made with Bastille.

Installing Bastille Linux

You can get Bastille from the Bastille site at `http://www.bastille-linux.org/`. It requires some additional prerequisites, `perl-TK` (if you want to use the graphical interface) and `perl-Curses` (if you want to use the console-based tool), that you need to install before you can install Bastille. Let's look at installing those first. I will show how to install both to give you the option of either using the graphical application or using the console-based installation. You can install these prerequisites via RPM or download and compile them via CPAN.[5] CPAN is potentially less secure than an RPM whose signature has been verified from a secure source; you need to assess the risk here. Probably the easiest and safest path is to install the RPMs recommended for your version of your distribution and ensure you use their MD5 signature to verify their integrity. Bastille provides a compatibility table for a variety of Linux versions that indicate which are the recommended versions and sources for the required prerequisites. You can find this chart at `http://www.bastille-linux.org/perl-rpm-chart.html`.

■**Note** Also, packages are available for Debian at `http://packages.debian.org/cgi-bin/` `search_packages.pl?searchon=names&version=all&exact=1&keywords=bastille`.

Because so many versions of the prerequisites exist depending on the distribution and version of that distribution you are using, I will cover installing on Red Hat 9 as a baseline; you can adapt this installation to accommodate your specific requirements based on the required combinations of prerequisites. From the compatibility chart, you can see I need to download the following RPMs:

```
http://download.atrpms.net/production/packages/redhat-9-i386/atrpms/➡
perl-Tk-804.027-8.rh9.at.i386.rpm
http://download.atrpms.net/production/packages/redhat-9-i386/atrpms/➡
atrpms-56-1.rh9.at.i386.rpm
http://www.bastille-linux.org/perl-Curses-1.06-219.i586.rpm
```

---

5. Comprehensive Perl Archive Network

Download the RPMs, and install them on your system.

```
puppy# rpm -ivh atrpms* perl-Tk*
Preparing...                 ######################################### [100%]
   1:atrpms                   ######################################### [100%]
   2:perl-Tk                  ######################################### [100%]
puppy# rpm -ivh perl-Curses-1.06-219.i586.rpm
Preparing...                 ######################################### [100%]
   1:perl-Curses              ######################################### [100%]
```

Now download the current version of Bastille, which at the time of writing is
version 2.1.2-01, and install it.

```
puppy# rpm -ivh Bastille-2.1.2-0.1.i386.rpm
Preparing...                 ######################################### [100%]
   1:Bastille                 ######################################### [100%]
```

Bastille is now installed and ready to use.

Running Bastille

Running Bastille is easy. You can run it in interactive or noninteractive (or batch) modes. The
first mode allows you to answer Bastille's configuration questions on the screen interactively.
The second mode allows you to adjust your configuration based on the information contained
in a file. This means you can quickly replicate the security settings of a previous run of Bastille
onto the system, which is useful for replicating security settings across multiple systems. You
need to run Bastille interactively only once, take the configuration file it has created, and then
run Bastille with that configuration file on any other systems. Starting it in interactive mode is
simple; you can see the required command in Listing 6-15. It will generally detect whether it
is able to start in console or graphical mode, or you can override that with a command-line
switch.

Listing 6-15. *Starting Bastille*

```
puppy# bastille
```

Bastille has some additional command-line switches that are useful; I will take you through
those next. Table 6-4 lists all the potential Bastille command-line switches available at the time
of writing.

Table 6-4. *Bastille Linux Command-Line Switches*

Switch	Description
-h	Displays help text for the Bastille command
-c	Uses console mode
-x	Uses the graphical mode
-b	Uses batch mode and a saved configuration file
-l	Lists the configuration file from the last run of Bastille
-r	Reverts Bastille changes

The first option, -h, displays some help text for Bastille's command-line operation. The next two options allow you to specify what mode you would like Bastille to run in: -c for console mode and -x for X-Windows. The next option, -b, tells Bastille to run in batch mode and apply the configuration contained in the /etc/Bastille/config file to the system. As discussed previously, this is useful for ensuring multiple systems have the same security settings.

If you run Bastille using the -b switch, then you need to have a configuration file containing the Bastille run you would like to duplicate in the /etc/Bastille/ directory in a file called config. Listing 6-16 shows the start of a Bastille run using an already existing configuration.

Listing 6-16. *Running Bastille Linux in Batch Mode*

```
puppy# bastille -b
NOTE:    Entering Critical Code Execution.
         Bastille has disabled keyboard interrupts.

NOTE:    Bastille is scanning the system configuration...

Bastille is now locking down your system in accordance with your
answers in the "config" file.  Please be patient as some modules
may take a number of minutes, depending on the speed of your machine.
```

The next option, -l, requests the location of the file containing details of the last interactive run of Bastille performed. Finally, the -r option allows you to revert to your previous configuration. I will cover that option a little further on in this section.

I will show you how to use Bastille running in console mode. To launch Bastille, run the following:

```
puppy# bastille -c
```

If this is the first time you have run Bastille, it will show you its license and disclaimer. To acknowledge the license and disclaimer, type **accept** when prompted, and Bastille will show you a screen explaining how to use the console-based text interface. Bastille uses a simple set of controls. You can use the Tab key to move between menu items and options and Enter to select the required option. Thus, from the explanation screen, you can select the < Next > option using the Tab key and hit Enter to continue through and launch the first of the configuration screens.

Figure 6-1 shows you the first configuration screen.

So what does Bastille do? Well, it runs a variety of modules that allow you to configure system-level security. These modules include such features as the following:

- Securing administration utilities

- Removing setuid from a variety of tools

- Setting password aging

- Setting a default umask

- Protecting GRUB and single-user mode

- Restricting root logons

- Disabling insecure network services

- Restricting use of the compiler

- Configuring firewalling

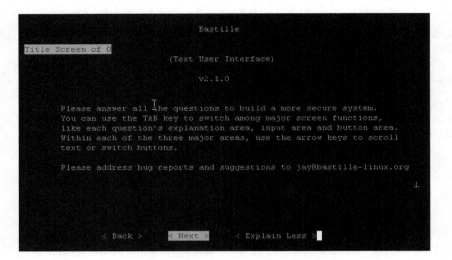

Figure 6-1. *Bastille's text user interface explanation screen*

Bastille explains in some detail what making each change will entail and why it is useful or more secure to change a particular setting; I recommend reading carefully through each section before making any changes.

■Tip After you have run Bastille, you need to reboot your system! This is important, and without it the Bastille hardening process will not be fully active.

You can also undo the changes you have made on your system with Bastille. To do this, run the command shown in Listing 6-17.

Listing 6-17. *Undoing the Bastille Changes*

```
puppy# bastille -r
```

This generally works fine, but a caveat is associated with using this. If you have changed a great deal of your configuration since running Bastille, it may not properly recognize what needs to be undone. In this case, Bastille will terminate with an error rather than try to revert your configuration to what was previously stored.

Bastille Logging

Finally, you can see a log of what Bastille has done. These logs are located in /var/log/Bastille. Two principal logs are generated: action-log and error-log. You should check them both to confirm the actions Bastille has taken and any potential errors generated during the Bastille process. Listing 6-18 shows a sample of the contents of the error-log file.

Listing 6-18. *Bastille Linux* error-log *File*

```
{Mon May 24 10:55:34 2004} ERROR:   open /etc/pam.d/kde failed.
{Mon May 24 10:55:34 2004} # Couldn't prepend line to /etc/pam.d/kde, ➥
since open failed.
{Mon May 24 10:55:34 2004} ERROR:   Unable to open /etc/pam.d/kde as ➥
the swap file etc/pam.d/kde.bastille already exists.  Rename the swap ➥
file to allow Bastille to make desired file modifications.
{Mon May 24 10:55:34 2004} ERROR:   open /etc/pam.d/kde.bastille failed...
{Mon May 24 10:55:34 2004} ERROR:   open /etc/pam.d/kde failed.
{Mon May 24 10:55:34 2004} # Couldn't append line to /etc/pam.d/kde, ➥
since open failed.
```

These are mostly harmless errors indicating that KDE[6] is not installed. But you should review the file for other potential errors that could indicate that part of the hardening process has failed. This has the potential to leave your system exposed without your knowledge.

Outer Layer

Your outer layer security is critical; not only is it the first line of defense for your system, but it is also the layer most commonly targeted by people seeking information about your system. An attacker can tell a lot about your system and the applications running on it from examining that outer "crust," including what ports are open and applications you have running. Indeed, many common applications and daemons routinely respond to queries with their name and version that greatly assists attackers in tailoring exploits and picking the vulnerabilities of your system.

The following sections cover two useful tools, NMAP and Nessus, that will allow you to see what potential attackers see when they scan your system. Both tools perform different functions. The NMAP tool is a powerful network scanner/mapper, and Nessus is a security and vulnerability scanner that will help you find potential exposures in your systems and applications and will offer suggestions for resolving them.

■**Caution** Scanning a system you do not own is not only rude but could readily be construed as an attack in its own right. If you are going to scan hosts and devices across a network or over the Internet, ensure you have carefully selected only those hosts that you either control or have permission to scan. The safest course of action when dealing with hosts you do not personally administer is to get permission in writing from the owner or administrator of those hosts or devices to scan them.

---

6. K Desktop Environment

NMAP

One of the easiest to use and most powerful tools available to you is NMAP, the Network Mapper. NMAP is designed for network exploration and security auditing. It can scan a host or series of hosts using IP packets looking for hosts and devices and the ports, services, and applications running on those hosts and devices. It also uses sophisticated fingerprinting to determine what sort of host or device it is scanning and to detect operating systems and firewalls. NMAP also allows you to save the results of your scan in a variety of forms that are useful for system and security administrators to manipulate. NMAP is a complicated tool; I will cover the key elements that make it so useful. If you want more detailed information on some of NMAP's more sophisticated functions, please use the man pages and resources available on the NMAP Web site. NMAP is open source and comes by default with most distributions of Linux.

■**Tip** If you actually have access to the system you are scanning, it is often much easier to use the netstat -a command to find out what ports are open on that system.

If NMAP is not on your system, you can get it in a number of ways. The easiest way is to check the usual methods you use to update your distributions: apt-get, yum, up2date, emerge, and so on, for an NMAP package in the form used by your distribution. If you cannot find one using this method or want to get the latest version of NMAP, it is available in source form, RPMs, and binaries on the NMAP Web site at http://www.insecure.org/nmap.

If you get the source archive, then compiling NMAP is a simple process. Unpack the archive, and change into the resulting directory. When compiling, you may want to specify some configure variables, such as the location of your OpenSSL installation that is used by NMAP. You can do that by specifying configure flags, as follows:

```
puppy# ./configure --openssl=/path/to/openssl
```

Then make and install NMAP by entering the following:

```
puppy# make && make install
```

By default NMAP will be installed to /usr/local/bin, but you can also override this during the ./configure process using the -prefix option.

NMAP is a command-line tool and comes with a front end that works in X. I will show running NMAP from the command line. You can run NMAP by typing the command in Listing 6-19.

Listing 6-19. *Basic NMAP Scan*

```
puppy# nmap 192.168.0.1
```

This will scan the host 192.168.0.1 (or any other IP address you specify) using a TCP SYN scan. (The example assumes you are logged in as root.) It would return something like Listing 6-20.

Listing 6-20. *NMAP Output*

```
Starting nmap 3.50 ( http://www.insecure.org/nmap/ ) at 2004-03-17 16:20 EST
Interesting ports on host.yourdomain.com (192.168.0.1):
(The 1657 ports scanned but not shown below are in state: closed)
PORT      STATE SERVICE
80/tcp    open  http
8080/tcp  open  http-proxy
Nmap run completed -- 1 IP address (1 host up) scanned in 3.930 seconds
```

This response shows it scanned 192.168.0.1 and found that ports 80 and 8080 were open, probably indicating this system is running a Web server and a proxy server. NMAP also has a lot of additional types of scans, other options that modify your scans, and ways to scan multiple hosts or even whole subnets.

The NMAP command line breaks down into three sections.

```
puppy# nmap [scan type(s)] [options] <host(s) or network list>
```

I will cover each section of the command line separately.

The first section of the NMAP command line is scan types. Each scan type is prefixed with a hyphen (-); for example, you can use -sS for the TCP SYN stealth port scan, which is the default if you run NMAP as root. Several possible scan types address different user requirements. Table 6-5 shows the most common types, and I will go through each of them and explain their purposes. You can use other scan types that you find out about through the NMAP man page.

Table 6-5. *NMAP Scan Types*

Scan Type	Description
-sS	TCP SYN stealth port scan (default for root user)
-sT	TCP connect() port scan (default for normal user)
-sU	UDP port scan
-sP	Ping scan

The three basic types of NMAP scan most useful to you will be the types -sS, -sT, and -sU. The first two are TCP-based based scans, each of which approaches the scanning process quite differently, and the last is UDP based. The first TCP type is -sS, or TCP SYN scanning, also known as *stealth scanning*. In this type of scan, NMAP sends a SYN packet to the target port and requests a connection. The target will respond with a SYN/ACK packet telling NMAP whether the port is open. When NMAP receives that SYN/ACK packet, it sends an RST packet rather than responding with an ACK packet to the target and terminates the connection. The objective is that by not making a full three-way connection to the target, the scan is "stealthy" in nature. These days, however, most IDS[7] systems such as Snort detect SYN scans, and many network devices such as firewalls and packet filters reject SYN packets.

---

7. IDS stands for Intrusion Detection System.

■**Tip** By default I recommend you configure your local firewall (`iptables`, for example) to reject some combinations of packets with certain TCP flags. See Chapter 2 for more details on this.

The second type of TCP scan is `-sT`, or TCP `connect()` scanning. This is a basic form of TCP scan. Here NMAP uses `connect()` to make a connection to a port to determine if the port is open. This is a fast and simple way of scanning, but `connect()`-based scans should be immediately obvious to all good IDS systems because you will see a flurry of `connect()`'s logged to all the listening ports on your target that are then immediately dropped. This will also potentially generate a lot of error messages in some application logs.

The last of the basic scan types is `-sU`, which is a UDP-based scan. UDP scanning is very basic. NMAP sends a zero-byte datagram to a target port and awaits an error response from that port. If NMAP receives an error response, then the port is closed; otherwise NMAP assumes the port is open. This can sometimes be misleading because a lot of firewalls block the error response messages, so occasionally it is hard to present a truly accurate picture of which UDP ports are open. UDP scanning is also slow because, as per RFC 1812,[8] many Linux distributions limit the number of ICMP[9] error messages that are generated at a time, which means you can often wait a long time for all responses to be received if scanning a lot of ports. Many people consider that these two limitations to UDP scanning make it useless as a scanning technique. I do not agree. A lot of Trojan and worm programs lurk on UDP ports; the W32.Blaster worm, for example, utilizes the `tftp` port of 69, or on Linux the various variants of the Apache/`mod_ssl` or Slapper worm utilize UDP ports 1978, 2002, or 4156.[10] It is a good idea to get the best possible picture of what is running on the UDP ports of hosts and devices in your network. The more complete picture you have of the services and applications on your network, the easier it is to recognize and address vulnerabilities and exploits.

Another sometimes useful type of scan is `-sP`, which is "ping-only" scanning. This simply sends an ICMP echo packet to all specified hosts to see if they respond. Any hosts that respond are considered "up." The `-sP` option can also use the `-Px` option (which you can see detailed in the NMAP man page) to change the way it queries target hosts to determine if they are up. This can be useful when ICMP echo packets are disabled on your network, as is common in many places as a result of the variety of worms and viruses that have subverted ICMP traffic.

If you do not specify a scan type on the command line, NMAP uses a different default scan type depending on your level of security. If you are signed on as root, then NMAP will default to the `-sS`, TCP SYN scan type. Any other user will default to the `-sT`, `connect()` scan type.

You can modify each of these scan types with various options. Each option is prefixed by a hyphen, `-`. A large number of possible options for NMAP exist; Table 6-6 lists the most useful options. I will explain in more detail the use of some them after the table.

---

8. Requirements for IP Version 4 Routers (`http://www.faqs.org/rfcs/rfc1812.html`)

9. ICMP is an acronym for Internet Control Message Protocol as defined in RFC 792 (`http://www.faqs.org/rfcs/rfc792.html`).

10. `http://securityresponse.symantec.com/avcenter/venc/data/linux.slapper.worm.html`

Table 6-6. *NMAP Options*

Options	Description
-O	Uses TCP/IP fingerprinting to guess the target's operating system.
-p range	Only scans a range of ports (in other words, -p 21 or -p 1,34, 64-111,139).
-F	Only scans ports listed in the file nmap-services.
-v	Increases NMAP's verbosity. You can use -vv for further details.
-P0	Does not ping hosts; this is useful when ICMP traffic has been disabled.
-T Paranoid|Sneaky|Polite| Normal|Aggressive|Insane	Timing policy. Can also be expressed as T1–T5.
-n/-R	Never does DNS resolution or always resolves.
-S IP_Address	The source IP address of your scan.
-e devicename	The source interface of your scan.
-6	Causes NMAP to scan via IPv6 rather than IPv4.
-oN/-oX/-oG/-oA logfile	Outputs normal, XML, "grepable," or all types of scan logs to logfile.
-iL inputfile	Gets potential targets from a file or uses - for standard input.

One of NMAP's most useful functions is the ability to try to guess what the device you are scanning is based on operating-system fingerprinting.[11] To enable this functionality, use the -O option. If NMAP can find one open and one closed port on the target host, it will try to finger-print the host's operating system and often the version of the operating system. You can see the full list of fingerprints in the file /usr/share/nmap/nmap-os-fingerprints. If NMAP cannot iden-tify the operating system of the target host, it will provide a URL, http://www.insecure.org/cgi-bin/nmap-submit.cgi, which provides instructions on how you can add the fingerprint of that device to NMAP to help improve the operating-system fingerprint database. So be a good open-source citizen and contribute.

The -O option also includes two other functions. These are a TCP uptime option and a TCP Sequence Predictability Classification option. These options try to determine how long a device has been up for and to determine the statistical probability of being able to establish a forged TCP connection to the device. If you use the verbose option -v, NMAP will provide a descrip-tion of the difficulty (for example, "Worthy Challenge" or "Formidable").

■**Tip** You can find more information about operating-system fingerprinting at http://www.insecure.org/nmap/nmap-fingerprinting-article.html.

---

11. The similar tool Xprobe (http://www.sys-security.com/html/projects/X.html) has operating-system fingerprinting as its primary purpose.

The port range option, -p, is useful if you want to scan only some ports. You can specify one port, many ports, or a range of ports. You can also specify a particular protocol by prefixing the port or port range with U: or T:. Listing 6-21 shows UDP port 53 and TCP ports 111 to 164 of the 192.168.0.* network being scanned. If you specify both UDP and TCP ports, you need to select a TCP scan type, such as -sT, and the UDP scan type, -sU.

Listing 6-21. *Scanning a Port Range*

```
puppy# nmap -sT -sU -p U:53,T:111-164 192.168.0.*
```

You can also use the -F option that scans only those ports in the nmap-services file. The file contains the most commonly used ports and means your scan, whilst not being complete, will be considerably faster than if NMAP had to scan all 65,535 ports.

You can get considerable detail from NMAP by using the -v and -vv switches, which increase the amount of information NMAP generates when run. I recommend using at least -v for most NMAP runs.

NMAP is also able to use a variety of ping types to check for the presence of hosts. This is most useful where ICMP (ping) traffic has been disabled on the target hosts or even on the whole network. To perform your scan without NMAP trying to ping the hosts, use the -P0 option as shown in Listing 6-22. You can use a variety of other ping types (including using multiple ping types in combination to increase the chances of being able to ping hosts), and you can see the NMAP man page for these.

Listing 6-22. *Using the -P0 Option*

```
puppy# nmap -sT -P0 -v 192.168.0.1
```

You can also adjust the speed at which NMAP scans your hosts and networks by using different timing policies. You do this using the -Tx option. You have five possible timing policies ranging from -T0 to -T5 (or Paranoid to Insane). Depending on what is selected, NMAP customizes its approach. With the Paranoid timing policy, NMAP serializes all scans and waits at least five minutes between sending packets, which is aimed at avoiding detection by an IDS system, whereas the Insane timing policy is designed for very fast networks and waits only 0.3 seconds for individual probes. By default if you do not specify a timing policy, NMAP uses the -T3 or Normal timing policy, which tries to run as fast as possible without overloading your network or missing any hosts or ports.

■**Caution** Be careful using the -T5 or Insane timing policy, as you can easily lose data, which can result in a very poor scan of your network.

The -S option is useful if NMAP is unable to determine the source address it should be using for the scan. Used in combination with the -e option, it allows you to specify the IP address and interface that NMAP should use to conduct the scan.

The output options (-oX, -oG, -oN, and -oA) allow NMAP to output the results of its scan in a variety of forms. You specify one of the selected output types and then specify the name of a file to store that output. NMAP will automatically create the file; or, if you already have an existing file you want to add to, you can use the -append_output option. The first output type, -oX, will present the results of the NMAP scan in XML format. This is useful for populating monitoring tools such as Nagios or to provide an input source for a script. The second, -oG, presents the scan results in a single line to make it easier to grep the resulting file for the results you want. The -oN option will present the results of a scan in a human-readable form much the same as the results that are displayed on the screen when you run NMAP interactively. The last option, -oA, tells NMAP to output to all three forms. If you specify a filename, then NMAP will create output files: *yourfilename*.grep, *yourfilename*.normal, and *yourfilename*.xml. Listing 6-23 shows an NMAP scan outputting in all output forms.

Listing 6-23. *Outputting a Scan in All Output Types*

```
puppy# nmap -sT -P0 -vv -oA yourfilename 192.168.0.1
```

The last option, -iL, allows you to input target hosts and networks from a file. Specify a filename with a collection of target specifications (which I will describe next) all separated by spaces, tabs, or newlines. You can also specify the hyphen, -, for standard input to allow you to pipe in a target from the command line or a script.

This leads me into the last section of the NMAP command line: target selection. You can specify targets in the form of single IP addresses or hostnames (for example, 192.168.0.1). You can specify a list of IP addresses and hostnames by separating each with a space. If you want to specify an entire network, you can do that in a number of ways. The first is by adding the netmask in the form of /mask; for example, 192.168.0.0/24 will scan the entire 192.168.0.0 Class C network. The second method is to use asterisks (*) to indicate an entire network; for example, 192.168.0.* will scan all the hosts of the 192.168.0.0 network from 1 to 254. You can also specify ranges, with the upper and lower ranges separated by a hyphen (for example, 192.168.0.100-150).

Listing 6-24 shows some typical NMAP scans; I will break down their functionality.

Listing 6-24. *NMAP Scans*

```
puppy# nmap -sT -P0 -v -F 192.168.0.1-64
puppy# nmap -sT -P0 -p 1-1024 -v 192.168.0.*
puppy# nmap -sU -vv -oX xmlscan 192.168.0.1
```

The first scan uses TCP SYN scanning (-sT), does not use ICMP (-P0) to scan the ports contained in the nmap-services (-F) of the target hosts 192.168.0.1 to 192.168.0.64 (192.168.0.1-64), and outputs the data in a verbose form (-v) to standard output.

The second scan shows a port-ranged scan also using a TCP SYN scan with no ICMP pings. The scan will scan the port range of 1–1024 of every host in the 192.168.0.0 network and outputs in a verbose form to standard output.

The last scan is a UDP scan of one host, 192.168.0.1, which will produce very verbose output (-vv) in the form of an XML file called xmlscan (using the -oX output option).

These examples and the preceding explanation should indicate how to use NMAP to find out about open ports on your hosts, on your devices, and across entire networks. NMAP comes with a lot of additional options and capabilities that I recommend you explore using the NMAP man page.

Nessus

Nessus is a security and vulnerability-scanning tool that attempts to scan and determine from the ports open on your hosts if any of your running applications are exploitable. You can run it across remote networks or on a local system. It consists of a client-server model with two components: the server daemon nessusd and the client nessus. The server uses a collection of external plug-ins separate from the core Nessus daemon that allows you to also update or create your own plug-ins without changing the core code of the Nessus package.

■Tip You can create plug-ins in C or using the built-in Nessus Attack Scripting Language (NASL). You can read about NASL at http://www.nessus.org/doc/nasl2_reference.pdf.

Nessus plug-ins are regularly updated by the development and support team, and you can update your collection of plug-ins using a single command.

The scans that Nessus conducts are quick and take place on multiple hosts as simultaneously as possible. Nessus can also output reports in a variety of forms, including HTML, PDF, LaTeX, and plain text. Overall, Nessus is a powerful and extremely useful tool that, if kept up-to-date, will help you determine if any of your systems suffer from vulnerabilities or could be subject to exploits. I will show you how to install and run Nessus in your environment and how to use the results to get the best possible information from Nessus.

■Caution Nessus is a powerful tool, and some of its scans can be dangerous to your systems. Whilst testing for certain exploits, it is possible that some applications or even entire systems can crash. Unless you know precisely what you are testing for, do not run Nessus on a production system without considering the possibility that it could result in a system crash or application outage.

Installing Nessus is actually quite easy. This is because the team behind Nessus provides an automated installation script you can download from a variety of FTP and HTTP servers. But before you do that, you need a couple of prerequisites. The first is the Gimp Toolkit (GTK) version 1.2, and the second is OpenSSL. OpenSSL is not absolutely required, but I strongly urge you to install it—though I hope you would already have it installed. Nessus uses OpenSSL for both securing client-server communications and for testing OpenSSL related services.

Many distributions have GTK installed by default, and a good way of finding out whether it is installed is to try the following command:

```
puppy# gtk-config --version
```

The command should return the version of GTK; for example, on the puppy system, it is 1.2.10. If you have GTK version 1.2 or later, then you can continue with your install of Nessus. If not, you can get GTK from ftp://ftp.gimp.org/pub/gtk/v1.2. You will also need the latest version of the glib libraries, which are also available at the same FTP site. Unpack the archive of the latest version of glib, and configure it by entering the following:

```
puppy# ./configure
```

Then make `glib` by entering the following:

`puppy# make`

Finally, as `root`, install `glib` by entering the following:

`puppy# make install`

Now unpack the GTK archive, and perform the same steps you undertook to install `glib` to install GTK.

Once you have the latest version of GTK and `glib` installed, you are now able to install Nessus. As mentioned earlier, Nessus comes with a shell script that you can download from a variety of sources at `http://www.nessus.org/nessus_2_0.html`. Also available as part of that download is an MD5 file that you can use to verify the script you have downloaded is safe to install.

Download the script, make sure it is owned by the user you intend to install it with, and make sure it possesses execute permissions. Do not use `root` to install Nessus (you will use `root` privileges during the installation), but you should start the install as a normal user. Start the installation process by entering the following:

`Puppy$ sh nessus-installer.sh`

If all your prerequisites are installed, you should see the installation screen in Figure 6-2.

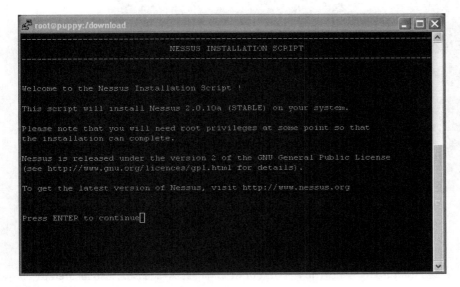

Figure 6-2. *The Nessus installation screen*

Follow the instructions to continue, and Nessus will begin to install. After unpacking itself, Nessus launches a `suid` shell to perform the required `root` install actions. You will need to enter your `root` password at this point to continue with the installation. Nessus next requires the location to install itself; by default it is `/usr/local/`. I recommend you install Nessus to the default location. Nessus will then compile and install itself.

When Nessus is finished compiling and installing itself, it will present a Finished screen that provides some instructions for the remaining additional steps needed to complete your install. The first additional step is to create an SSL certificate to help secure Nessus. Create your certificate using (assuming you installed Nessus into `/usr/local/`), like so:

```
puppy# /usr/local/sbin/nessus-mkcert
```

You will need to be logged in as `root` to create a certificate. Follow the on-screen instructions to create a standard SSL certificate. (See Chapter 3 for more details on SSL certificates.) The `nessus-mkcert` command will create several files, as shown in Figure 6-3.

Note I will not show how to use SSL certificates with Nessus. Instead, I will cover password-based authentication for Nessus. If you want to use SSL authentication, then you can find details at the Nessus Web page at `http://www.nessus.org`.

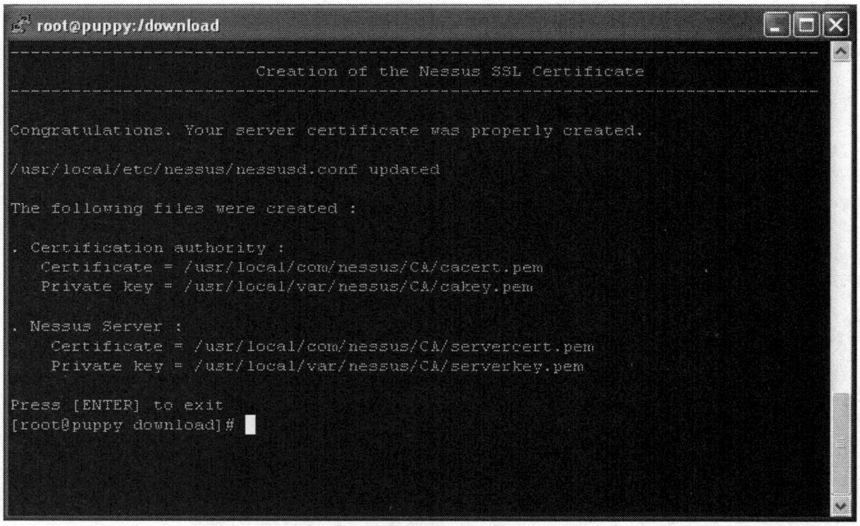

Figure 6-3. *Creating an SSL certificate*

The next step is to create a Nessus user. Nessus requires its own users with logins and passwords to be created to utilize Nessus. The Nessus command `nessus-adduser`, also located in `/usr/local/sbin`, performs this function. You must provide a login name and then tell Nessus whether to use a password or certificate for authentication. I recommend keeping it simple initially and creating a user that is authenticated via password. You enter `pass` at the `Authentication` prompt to do this. You will then be prompted to enter a password.

Nessus also has a user-based rule system that allows you to control what hosts and networks each user is able to scan. These rules consist of the statements `accept`, `deny`, and `default`. The accept and deny rules are both followed by an IP address and netmask. The default statement always comes last and is followed by either accept or deny, which specifies the default response for that particular user. Listing 6-25 shows this.

Listing 6-25. *Basic Nessus* deny default *User Rule*

```
accept 192.168.0.0/24
default deny
```

This rule set would allow the user to scan the 192.168.0.0/24 network, but all other scans would be denied by default. You can reverse this behavior, as shown in Listing 6-26.

Listing 6-26. *Basic Nessus* accept default *User Rule*

```
deny 192.168.0.0/24
default accept
```

In Listing 6-26 the user is specifically excluded from scanning the 192.168.0.0/24 network, but all others are accepted by default.

If you want to allow a user to scan only the system they are located on, then Nessus has a special keyword, client_ip, which is replaced at runtime by the IP address of the system on which you are running Nessus. The user's rule would look like Listing 6-27.

Listing 6-27. *Allow Nessus User Only to Scan Local System*

```
accept client_ip
default deny
```

This would allow that user to scan only the local IP address. All other scan attempts would be denied. You can read about these user rules in more detail in the nessus-adduser man page.

Tip You can also create a user with an empty rule set by pressing Ctrl+D without entering any rules at the rules prompt. That user has no restrictions on what they can and cannot scan.

With a certificate and a Nessus user created, you have completed the base Nessus installation. If you ever want to uninstall Nessus, you can do so with the following command:

```
puppy# /usr/local/sbin/uninstall-nessus
```

Once you have gotten Nessus installed, it is a good idea to ensure the external plug-ins that Nessus uses for its tests are up-to-date. To do so, run the command in Listing 6-28 as the root user to update them.

Listing 6-28. *Updating Your Nessus Plug-Ins*

```
puppy# nessus-update-plugins
```

Running the Nessusd Daemon

The next step in getting your Nessus installation up and running is starting the Nessus daemon that is required for running any scans. The Nessus daemon binary, nessusd, is located by default in /usr/local/sbin/. The simplest way to start nessusd is in the daemon mode, as you can see in Listing 6-29.

Listing 6-29. *Starting* nessusd *As a Daemon*

```
puppy# nessusd -D
```

The -D option in Listing 6-29 detaches the nessusd daemon as a background process. You can also use some additional options to customize the daemon. Table 6-7 shows the most useful of those options.

Table 6-7. nessusd *Options*

Option	Description
-a *address*	Tells nessusd to listen only to connections on the address *address*
-c *config-file*	Uses an alternative configuration file
-d	Makes the server dump its compilation options
-D	Makes the server run in background (daemon mode)
-p *port-number*	Tells the server to listen on the port *port-number* rather than the default port of 1241

The first option, -a, tells nessusd to listen only to requests on the IP address specified after the option; for example, -a 192.1680.1 would accept requests only from the IP address 192.168.0.1.

The default nessusd configuration file is located at /usr/local/etc/nessus/nessusd.conf. Using the -c option you can override this file with one of your choice. Read through the default configuration file for an explanation of the options available in that file.

Another useful option for troubleshooting is -d, which dumps the compilation options and versions of Nessus to the command line. You should see something like Listing 6-30.

Listing 6-30. nessusd -d *Dump*

```
This is Nessus 2.0.10 for Linux 2.4.21-9.EL
compiled with gcc version 3.2.3 20030502 (Red Hat Linux 3.2.3-24)
Current setup :
        Experimental session-saving  : enabled
        Experimental KB saving        : enabled
        Thread manager                : fork
        nasl                          : 2.0.10
        libnessus                     : 2.0.10
        SSL support                   : enabled
        SSL is used for client / server communication
        Running as euid               : 0
```

You should include these details for any requests for support via the Nessus mailing lists at `http://list.nessus.org/` or the Nessus Bugzilla interface at `http://bugs.nessus.org/`.

The last option allows you to specify on which port Nessus will listen for scan requests. By default `nessusd` listens on port 1241, but you can override this on the command line with `-p port-number`. See Listing 6-31.

Listing 6-31. *Running* `nessusd` *on a Different Port*

```
puppy# nessusd -D -p 1300
```

Listing 6-31 detaches `nessusd` as a background process and tells it to listen for scans on port 1300.

Running the Nessus Client

The `nessus` client can be either run as an X11 client based on GTK or run in a batch mode via the command line. It acts as a client interface to the `nessusd` server daemon.

■**Note** Also, a freeware Windows-based client called NessusWX is available for Nessus. You can find it at `http://nessuswx.nessus.org/`. The Windows client is fully featured and replicates the functionality of the Nessus X11 client completely. Because of the ease of use of the interface, many people prefer the NessusWX client. I recommend you try both and choose the one that suits you best.

You can run the Nessus client from the command line by entering the following:

```
puppy# nessus
```

This will start the X11 client by default. If you want to run the batch-mode client or change how the `nessus` client is run, you can add command-line options to the `nessus` client. Table 6-8 lists these options.

Table 6-8. `nessus` *Client Options*

Option	Description
`-c config-file`	Uses another configuration file.
`-n`	No pixmaps. This is handy if you are running Nessus on a remote computer.
`-q host port user password target-file result-file`	Quiet or batch mode.
`-T type`	Save scan data as either `nbe`, `html`, `html_graph`, `text`, `xml`, `old-xml`, `tex`, or `nsr`.
`-V`	Makes batch mode display any status messages to the screen.
`-x`	Does not check SSL certificates.

Running nessus Client in Batch Mode

Most of these options are self-explanatory, but I will go through the batch-mode options because this is a useful way to execute Nessus. The batch mode allows you to run checks from the command line without starting the X11 client. This is useful when running scans from a system that lacks X or when you are using a terminal that is unable to display a graphical environment (a headless server, for example).

You enable batch mode by specifying -q on the nessus command line. To run in this mode, you specify some details after the -q option: a hostname for the nessusd server, a port number, your username and password, a file containing your target selections, and a file for your results. You can also specify a precise output type.

The target file should consist of your target selections in a form Nessus will understand; for example, it should contain a list of IP addresses or an IP address range in the form of *address/netmask* (in other words, 192.168.0.0/24). Put each target on its own line.

You can output the results in a number of forms by using the -T option. Most of the output options will create a file of the type you specify; for example, -T "html" would create an HTML file containing the results of the scan. The only exception to this is the "html_graph" output type, which will create a directory with the same name as the results file you specify that will contain an HTML index file and the Nessus results in a variety of graphs.

■**Tip** If you want to know the progress of your batch scan, then add the -V option to the nessus command line. This option outputs any status messages from the nessusd server to the screen.

So the whole command-line run of a batch scan by the Nessus client could look like Listing 6-32.

Listing 6-32. *Running Nessus in Batch Mode*

```
puppy# nessus -q 192.168.0.1 1241 nessus password targets.file results.file ➥
-T "html_graph" -V
```

Running the Nessus Client in Graphical Mode

If you do not specify batch mode on the command line, Nessus will try to launch the X11 GTK client. The first screen you will see is a setup and login screen from which you need to specify a nessusd server, the port number that nessusd is running on, and a username and password to connect to that server. You can see an example of this screen in Figure 6-4.

■**Tip** By placing your mouse curser over many options and plug-ins in the Nessus client, you will see an explanation of what that option or plug-in does.

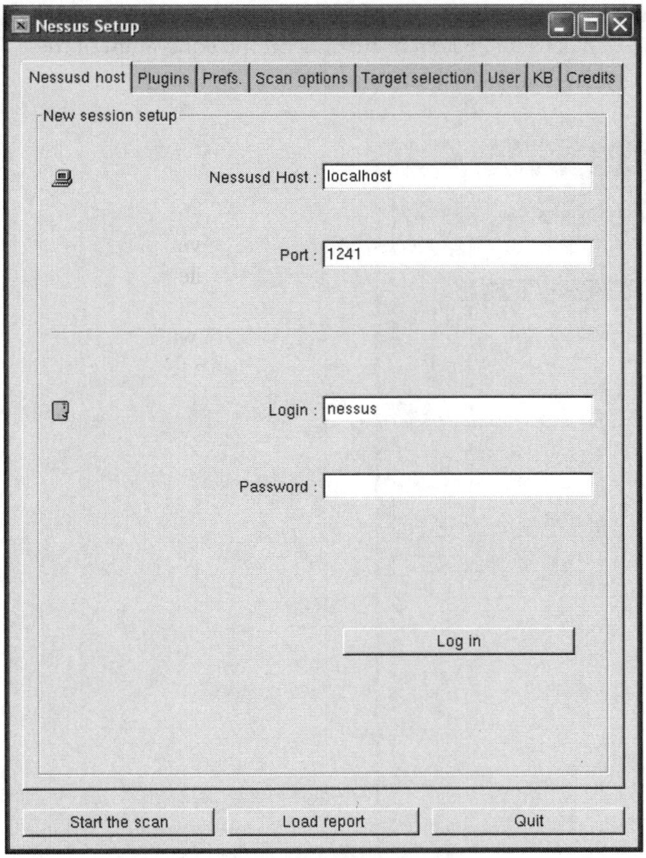

Figure 6-4. *Nessus login and setup session screen*

In Figure 6-4 the session is configured to connect to a Nessus server on localhost using port 1241 with a user of nessus. Put in the details for the nessusd server you want to connect to, and click the Login button. Once you have logged in, the Nessus client will change to the next tab, Plugins, as shown in Figure 6-5. On this screen you can select which attacks and scans you want to run against the target systems.

You will see several options here: Enable All, Enable All but Dangerous Plugins, Disable All, and Upload Plugins. Unless you have a specific attack you are interested in testing against a target, I recommend using the Enable All but Dangerous Plugins option. Then move onto the next tab, Prefs.

The Prefs. tab controls the options and variables for all the plug-ins you have selected to run. Far too many potential options exist to run through each individually, but by browsing through them you should be able to determine the required inputs and potential changes you may like to make. A good example of the sort of options you can specify is the NMAP port scan that Nessus can conduct. You can tell Nessus exactly what sort of scan to conduct; for example, you can specify a TCP SYN scan or a connect() scan or turning on the equivalent of the NMAP -P0 command-line option.

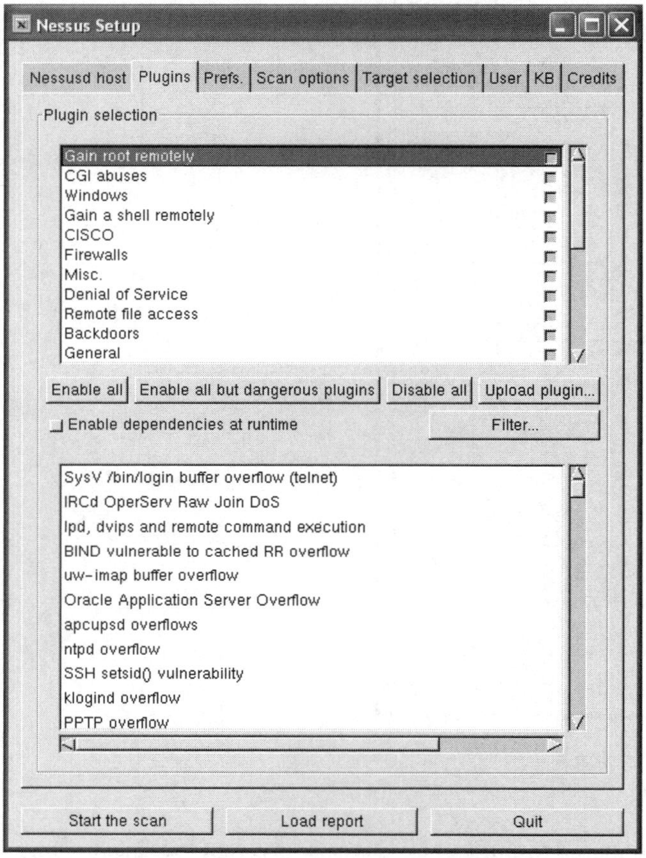

Figure 6-5. *Nessus plug-in screen*

Tip You can find an excellent reference Knowledge Base of most, if not all, of the Nessus X11 client options available at http://www.edgeos.com/nessuskb/.

Select the next tab, Scan Options, to specify the Nessus-specific options for this scan. You can see an example of the Scan Options tab in Figure 6-6. These include the port range you want to scan, which defaults to the setting default (ports 1 to 15000); the number of hosts to test simultaneously; and the number of checks to perform at the same time. One of the more important options here is the Safe Scan option. If selected, this tells Nessus to check only the banners of applications for potential vulnerabilities or exploits rather than actually try to test that vulnerability or exploit. This results in a less accurate scan but reduces the risk that a production application or system will be crashed or disabled as the result of a Nessus scan.

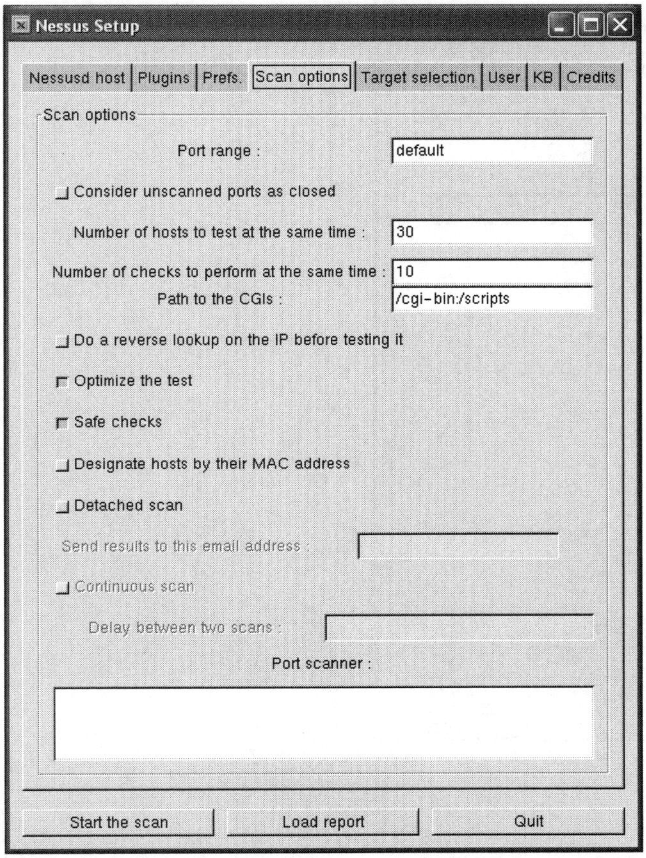

Figure 6-6. *Nessus scan options*

The next tab is Target Selection, where you can specify which hosts Nessus should scan. The first option is a targets line. You can specify targets here in form of a comma-separated list of hosts or in CIDR notation (IP address and netmask). Targets can consist of IP addresses (recommended) or DNS-resolvable hostnames. You can also specify hostnames or IP addresses of virtually hosted services. This allows Nessus to scan an IP address that may host many Web services for several domains and direct Web-based data to a particular name-based virtual host. You can specify this on the target line in the form of IP_Address[Virtual_Domain_Name] (for example, 192.168.0.1[www.yourdomain.com]). Figure 6-7 shows the contents of the Target Selection tab.

You can also tell Nessus to read its target list from a file. This file should take the same form as the target file specified in the command-line batch-mode process with each target host or target network listed on an individual line.

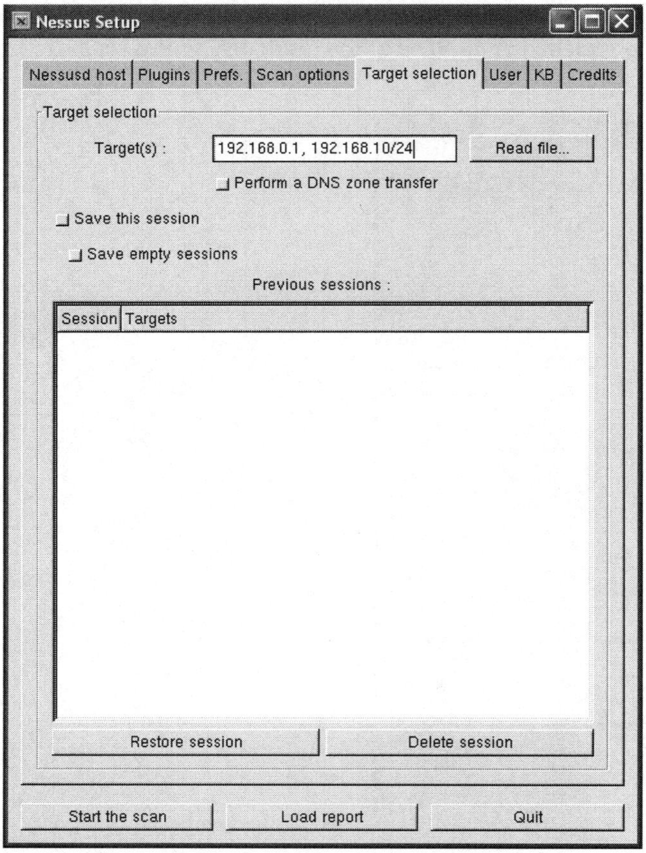

Figure 6-7. *Nessus target selection*

The Target Selection tab also contains records of your previous sessions. If you have scanned targets before and specified that you wanted to save those sessions, they will be displayed in the Previous Sessions box.

Once you have entered your target selection, you should have enough information to start your attack scans. So you can skip the remaining tabs and click the Start the Scan button to begin your scan.

Your attack scans can take a long time to run depending on the number of plug-ins you are testing and the number of hosts or networks you are scanning. The progress screen will show the list of host(s) as they are scanned. When the scan is completed, Nessus will show the Report screen.

From here you can go through all of Nessus's findings. Figure 6-8 shows a Nessus recommendation to upgrade the version of OpenSSH installed on the target host. Nessus provides the exact version of OpenSSH that you need to get to address the issue and even explains how to find out what version you are running. Nessus also usually provides additional links to further information about the issue that will help you decide what action to take.

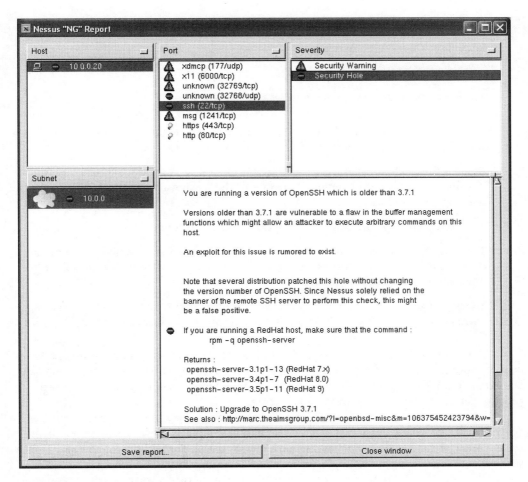

Figure 6-8. *Nessus report screen*

You can save this report in a variety of forms, as discussed earlier, including an HTML page and a collection of graphs that detail the results of the scan.

It is important to remember that Nessus is not always perfect. Not everything that Nessus finds will be an exploit or vulnerability that applies to your system. But all the findings are worth at least investigating. Nessus provides quite detailed explanations of the exploits and vulnerabilities it finds on your systems. They often include potential changes and solutions. To get the full benefit from Nessus and to be able to ensure that all the potential issues Nessus finds are either addressed or determined not relevant, I recommend you study these findings carefully.

Other Methods of Detecting a Penetration

You can look for some additional things that indicate a possible penetration of your system or a compromised system. The following items are all things you should perform regular checks of (in addition to any automated tools such as Chkrootkit that I discussed earlier):

- Log files

- Files, directories, and binaries

- cron and at jobs

- The contents of the /etc/passwd and /etc/group files

The first step, as discussed in Chapter 5, is to make sure you know what is happening on your system by examining your logs. Check the following items especially:

- Base log files including messages, secure, cron, and related operating-system logs for unusual activity or entries. Potentially examine them using a tool such as SEC or Swatch to help filter your logs.

- Any firewall logs you are collecting. See Chapter 2 for further details.

- The wtmp file, which is usually contained in /var/log. This file contains records of the date and time of the last successful login of all users on the system. You can access this information via the last command.

- The utmp file that is contained in /var/run. This file contains information on each user currently logged on. It is what is accessed when you use the w or who command.

Unfortunately, I cannot tell you exactly what to look for, as every system is different; however, I emphasis that as part of securing your system, you should know exactly who and what should be running on your system. It is impossible to secure a system if you do not have a precise picture of what is occurring on your system.

Next you should check for a variety of file-related items. This is mostly based around setting a baseline of what you know is on the system (for example, what setuid files exist on the system and checking against that baseline on a regular basis). The addition of new setuid files without your knowledge, for example, would almost certainly imply something is amiss.

So, you should start with checking for new or changed setuid or setgid root files on your system. These types of files are often not only points of entry and exploited by attackers, but files with these permissions are regularly added by attackers during penetration. The command in Listing 6-33 should show all executable files with setuid and setgid permissions.

■Note I provide much more information about this in Chapter 4.

Listing 6-33. *Finding* setuid *and* setgid *Files*

```
puppy# find / -type f -perm +6000 -ls
```

You should review all the files on your system with these permissions and confirm if they are actually required by setuid or setgid root files. If they are not required, you can remove the permissions with the following command:

```
puppy# chmod -s filename
```

Listing 6-34 shows a command to find all the world-writable files and directories on the system.

Listing 6-34. *Find World-Writable Files and Directories*

```
puppy# find / -perm -2 ! -type l -ls
```

You should also check for any unusually named files. For example, files preceded by a period (.) do not show up when you use the ls command and are a simple way for an attacker to hide a file from a casual inspection. You can use the find command to locate a combination of unusually named files. Listing 6-35 shows find commands that will show all files on your system prefixed by . and .. You can construct other variations of these to find other files.

Listing 6-35. *Finding Unusually Named Files*

```
puppy# find / -name ".*" -print -xdev
puppy# find / -name "..*" -print -xdev
```

Lastly, unowned[12] files and directories may also be an indication of a penetration on your system. Listing 6-36 shows a command to find all the unowned files and directories.

Listing 6-36. *Finding Unowned Files and Directories*

```
puppy# find / -nouser -o -nogroup -ls
```

You should also look at ensuring the integrity of your binaries using a tool such as Tripwire or MD5 or similar checksums. I talk about cryptographic checksums in Chapter 1 and the Tripwire application in Chapter 4.

You should check the contents of the root crontab and at files for any scheduled commands or processes that an attacker may have left behind. You can use the commands in Listing 6-37 to do this.

Listing 6-37. *Checking the Contents of cron and at*

```
puppy# crontab -l
puppy# at -l
```

Lastly, you need to check your /etc/passwd and /etc/group files for any new users you have not created, changes to existing accounts, UID changes (especially those related to UID 0 or root), or accounts without passwords.

Recovering from a Penetration

The first thing you need to come to terms with is that a penetrated system, from a recovery point of view, is generally a lost cause. You can never guarantee you have removed and purged

---

12. Unowned files are those files that are not owned by any user or group.

all the potential malicious exploits left on your system, and you cannot guarantee that you have spotted any potential time bombs or booby traps left by your attacker. You will need to rebuild this system either from a safe set of backups or from safe media. I recommend doing this from safe media and restoring your data carefully from safe backups.

The word *safe* is important here. You may not find out exactly when an attacker penetrated your system. Data and files you have backed up could contain tools, exploits, or other hidden and nasty surprises that come back to haunt your rebuilt system. The worst-case scenario is that you rebuild your system, reinstall your applications, and then restore from your backups, but your attacker has left a binary or a script behind that is now present in your backed-up data that allows them to easily repenetrate your system or has some delayed malicious intent such as damage to your system or deletion of your data.

The following recommendations apply to system recovery after an attack or penetration:

- Isolate the system; remove it from the network, and do not plug it back into your network or any other network that contains production or at-risk systems. If you must plug it back into the network, do so in an isolated, preferably stand-alone network with no connections to the Internet or your local network.

- Check your other systems immediately for signs of attack. Check logs, check logins, and run your collection of scanning tools.

- Change all your secure passwords, including your root passwords and passwords for network devices immediately. Do not use electronic means to disseminate these new passwords.

- Examine your system for the source of the attack, and, if required, involve any relevant law-enforcement agencies.

- Attempt to determine the how the attack was achieved, and ensure you can address the exploit(s) or penetration methods *before* you rebuild your system.

- If you rebuild your system, then confirm you are building from safe and up-to-date media.

- If you rebuild your system, then check that any data you restore to your system is safe and not corrupted, infected, or booby-trapped by your attacker.

But before you rebuild your system, you need to look at that the potential forensic value of that system. If you intend to investigate the nature of the penetration on your system, then you should keep a detailed record of what you do and what you find. This record is useful for your own purposes in tracking the path of the attacker, and it also provides input for any auditors who may become involved in reviewing the attack from a wider security perspective. Additionally, if your organization chooses to involve law enforcement in the aftermath of an attack, this record could eventually form some kind of evidence. The following are a few steps you should take to gather this information:

- Maintain a journal of your actions on the penetrated system.

- Take copies of all major configuration files, including your network configuration, `passwd` and `group` files, and so on.

- Take copies of your log files including any relevant log entries.

- Take snapshots of your running processes, network status, memory states, /proc directory, and disks. Store these securely.

You can use a few basic tools to help you keep a journal of your activities. The first thing to ensure is that you mark all your entries with the system name, the type, and the correct date and time. Prefix all journal entries with the following command:

```
puppy# (date; uname -a)
```

Another useful tool is the script command, which records the contents of an interactive session. You can start script with the following command:

```
puppy# script -a penetration_log.txt
```

The -a option appends data to a previously connected file so you do not overwrite the contents of an existing file. The collection of data will stop when you issue an exit command, log out, or issue Ctrl+D. The script command really works only with commands that write to stdout. If you execute a tool such as ed or vi that clears the screen and opens another screen, this tends to write junk to the script log file.

You should take snapshots of a variety of system configuration files in both hard and soft copy. This includes all the major configuration operating-system files as well as the configuration files of any applications you think may have been penetrated or used to achieve the penetration. You should also take hard and soft copies of any relevant log entries and log files.

Additionally, you need to capture the running state of the system. Start with the running processes on the system. Enter the following:

```
puppy# (ps -aux; ps -auxeww; lsof) > current_procs.txt
```

Then grab the contents of the /proc directory. Enter the following:

```
puppy# tar -cvpf proc_directory.tar /proc/[0-9]*
```

Next, take a snapshot of the network state of the system. Enter the following:

```
puppy# (date; uname -a; netstat -p; netstat -rn; arp -v) > network_status.txt
```

Note I have included the current date and time and the uname information to the start of the records I have generated.

Finally, take a snapshot of the currently active and kernel memory. Listing 6-38 shows the commands to do this.

Listing 6-38. *Snapshot of Currently Active Memory*

```
puppy# dd bs=1024 < /dev/mem > mem
puppy# dd bs=1024 < /dev/kmem > kmem
```

I also recommend taking snapshots of the disk of the suspect system, so you can use them for further forensic work later. You can use the command in Listing 6-39 to take the snapshot. In this example, I am taking a snapshot of the hda1 partition. You need to take snapshots of any additional partitions on the system.

Listing 6-39. *Taking a Disk Snapshot*

```
puppy# dd if=/dev/hda1 bs=1024 > hda1
```

Additional Security Tools

The following sections list (by no means comprehensively) some additional security tools that may be useful to you. These include network scanners and sniffers, traffic-capture tools, network intrusion detection systems, secure kernels, and security-auditing tools.

dsniff

This suite of packet-sniffing tools allows you to monitor traffic on your network for sensitive data. It comes with a number of tools, including its namesake, dsniff, which allows you to sniff network traffic that could potentially contain items such as passwords. It comes with the additional tools filesnarf, mailsnarf, and urlsnarf that specialize in sniffing for filenames, mail passwords, and traffic and HTTP traffic. dsniff requires libnet (http://www.packetfactory.net/projects/libnet/) and libnids (http://www.packetfactory.net/projects/libnids/) for operation. You can find dsniff at http://monkey.org/~dugsong/dsniff/.

Ethereal

Ethereal is a network data-capture tool that can grab data off your network and read in the contents of tcpdump files or read in data from a variety of other sources. You can dissect and analyze a variety of data from a wide selection of protocols and can even edit the contents of captured traffic. Ethereal also comes with an X-based GUI tool that you can use to display data being captured in real time. You can find Ethereal at http://www.ethereal.com/.

Ettercap

The Ettercap suite simulates and sniffs for man-in-the-middle attacks on your network. It is capable of sniffing live connections and performing content filtering on the fly. It can support active and passive dissection of a number of protocols and has built-in fingerprinting capabilities with a large library of fingerprints. You can find Ettercap at http://ettercap.sourceforge.net/.

LIDS

LIDS is a secured kernel designed to replace your existing kernel. It provides file-system protection, provides protection of processes (including hiding processes), introduces access control lists (ACLs) that allow you control access to applications, and contains some network security features and a port scanner detector. LIDS also has a built-in secured alerting system. You can find LIDS at http://www.lids.org/.

Netcat

Netcat is similar in function to nmap but has some useful additional functionality. It is capable of the same network and port scanning as nmap but also allows you to send TCP/IP data. You can use it to open TCP connections, listen on arbitrary TCP and UDP ports, and send TCP and UDP packets. You can find Netcat at `http://netcat.sourceforge.net/`.

SARA

Security Auditor's Research Assistant (SARA) is a security-analysis tool. It is an inheritor of SATAN, the original security analysis tool. SATAN has become outdated and obsolete in recent times, and SARA has overtaken its core functionality. It is able to perform a series of built-in scans or can scan using third-party plug-ins. You can run it in stand-alone and daemon mode. You can find SARA at `http://www-arc.com/sara/`.

Snort

Snort is a packet-sniffing tool and intrusion-detection tool. It is a complex, powerful, and highly configurable tool. It can run in three modes: as a network sniffer reading packets off the network and displaying them, in packet logging mode logging those packets to disk, and in the last mode as a network intrusion detection tool. This allows you to match the packets against a series of rules. Some rules are provided by default, and you can also define your own; for example, as a new virus or worm is discovered, you can define a rule to detect that worm and identify any computers that may be infected. Snort can also perform actions, trigger events, or conduct alerting if it detects packets matching its or your rules. You can find Snort at `http://www.snort.org/`.

tcpdump

One of the more useful tools in your security arsenal, the tcpdump command allows you to dump network traffic in the form of the headers of packets. You can select headers using Boolean expressions, collect packets from a particular interface, and use a variety of other options. You can display the packet headers on the console or log them to a file for later review. Most Linux systems come with the tcpdump command, or you can find it at `http://www.tcpdump.org/`.

Titan

Similar to Bastille Linux in functionality, the Titan package also provides operating-system hardening. Titan runs a series of tests, provides analysis, and corrects deficiencies it detects on your system. It is written in the form of Bourne script and is easily able to be added to and customized. Titan is available at `http://www.fish.com/titan/`.

Resources

The following are some resources you can use.

- **Bastille Linux mailing lists**: `http://www.bastille-linux.org/mail.html`
- **NMAP hacker list**: `http://seclists.org/about/nmap-hackers.txt`
- **Nessus mailing lists**: `http://list.nessus.org/`

Sites

- **Chkrootkit**: http://www.chkrootkit.org/

- **Rootkit Hunter**: http://www.rootkit.nl/

- **John the Ripper**: http://www.openwall.com/john/

- **Bastille Linux**: http://www.bastille-linux.org/

- **NMAP**: http://insecure.org/nmap/

- **Xprobe**: http://sys-security.com/html/projects/X.html

- **Nessus**: http://www.nessus.org

- **Nessus Knowledge Base**: http://www.edgeos.com/nessuskb/

CHAPTER 7

■ ■ ■

Securing Your Mail Server

One of the most vital components in any modern business is e-mail. It has become common for commercial organizations to do a significant part of their communication via e-mail, and end users and management now generally consider an outage of a corporate e-mail system to be a major, if not critical, issue. With the rise of the importance of e-mail, several serious issues have emerged with respect to the stability, functionality, and security of e-mail communication. These include the security of transmitted information, the prevalence of spam, the use of e-mail to disseminate viruses, and the potential for penetrating your Simple Mail Transfer Protocol (SMTP) services either to cause a Denial of Service (DoS) attack or to use as a potential route into your system.

This has not been helped by the fact that (both before and after the rise of popularity of e-mail as a service) the security, integrity, and stability of many of the available mail server applications have had major issues. This is especially true of Unix-based and Linux-based environments where e-mail servers have been frequent targets of attackers; several major vulnerabilities and exploits have been discovered for mail servers running on these platforms. Additionally, many Linux distributions offer pre-installed mail servers and services that are poorly configured and secured or not secured at all.

With the combination of heavy reliance on e-mail functionality and the relatively poor security track record of e-mail servers, system administrators and security officers need to take particular care in selecting, maintaining, and securing their e-mail infrastructures. In this chapter, I will address each of the major threats facing your e-mail server. I will provide practical working configurations that will provide you with some methods of securing the transmission of e-mail, help you reduce spam, and protect your e-mail system and users from viruses. To provide real-world examples of how you can go about doing all this, I will cover principally two mail server applications: Sendmail and Postfix.

More important, what won't I cover? Well, I will not tell you how to configure the base functionality of your e-mail server unless it has some security implications. I will also not explain how to set up and configure complex mail server environments such as virtual addressing or the like. You can get this sort of information from the man pages, FAQs, and associated documentation of the mail server application of your choice.

Which Mail Server to Choose?

An important question is which mail server to choose; unfortunately, not a lot of independent guidance is available to you from a functionality or security standpoint. I will make any recommendations based on the core functionality of a mail server. Whether you choose Sendmail,

Postfix, Qmail, Courier, or one of a number of other variants, the essential function of those mail servers remains similar. I also have no intention of buying into the "my e-mail server is better than your e-mail server" wars that occasionally spring up on Usenet and mailing lists when discussing the relative merits of a particular mail server.

From a security standpoint, however, I do have some opinions and advice that is valuable when selecting a mail server. My recommendation for a mail server is Postfix. Postfix was written by Dr. Wietse Venema, who is one of the authors of the Security Administrator Tool for Analyzing Systems (SATAN); he has a considerable pedigree in the TCP/IP and Unix security worlds.

Postfix was designed with security in mind and contains a variety of security safeguards.

- It has a distributed architecture with smaller programs performing individual functions instead of one monolithic program.

- Almost all these smaller programs can be chrooted.

- Those chrooted functions all run at low privilege.

- You have to penetrate these smaller programs before you have access to local delivery.

- Memory for buffers is allocated dynamically to restrict the risk of buffer overflow attacks.

- No Postfix program uses set-uid.

- Postfix does not trust the content of its own queues.

- Postfix integrates relatively easily with antivirus and antispam tools.

All these in combination mean that Postfix addresses some of the key areas in which Mail Transfer Agents (MTAs) are vulnerable to attack. I recommend you at least look at Postfix as an alternative to your current mail server.

■Note On the functionality front (not as an exercise in one-upmanship but more to articulate that Postfix meets the same functionality standards as alternatives such as Sendmail), Postfix also offers excellent performance in terms of throughput and capacity and is easy to configure.

From a security advice perspective for existing systems, this is not to say I recommend absolutely getting rid of your existing mail server. Obviously, if you have a significant investment in that system or have a technical preference for another variety of MTA, then I recommend you stay with that package and secure it. This is especially true of Sendmail servers. If you ensure you have an up-to-date version of Sendmail (and most of the releases from version 8.11 and beyond have proven to be reasonably secure) and follow some basic steps to secure it, then you should be reasonably confident of a secure MTA.

I believe, though, that the vast numbers of mail servers attached to the Internet mean that attackers have a huge pool of potential targets and thus perceive mail servers as an excellent choice of application to probe and dismember in order to look for exploits and vulnerabilities. So, update your software. Regularly. You should try not to fall too many versions behind the current release of your MTA. Subscribe to the announce mailing list for your MTA. Subscribe to vulnerabilities mailing lists, and watch for posts related to your MTA. Join Usenet news groups. Protect your system with your antivirus and antispam protection. Keep your users up-to-date and informed about potential virus and spam threats.

How Is Your Mail Server at Risk?

So what does security for a mail server mean? Well, in order for your mail server to be considered at least partially secure, you need to address the following issues:

- Reduce the risk of penetration of your system and/or an attacker gaining root via your mail server.

- Reduce the risk of DoS attacks.

- Reduce spam.

- Inhibit the spread of viruses, and protect users from virus infections via e-mail.

- Secure your mail and its transmission.

- Prevent the unauthorized use of relaying whilst allowing authorized users to relay.

- Reduce the risk of forgery of mail messages.

The MTAs I will cover both have some inherent security, but you need to do more to really ensure the security of your MTA. In this chapter, I will take you through addressing the first four issues I listed previously: reducing the risk of penetration of your system, reducing the risk of DoS attacks, providing antispam protection, and providing antivirus protection. In Chapter 8 I will take you through the remaining three issues: securing your mail transmission, preventing relaying, and reducing the risk of mail forgery.

Protecting Your Mail Server

This section covers some ways to protect your MTA from penetration and reduce the risk of an attacker gaining root through your MTA. I will cover a bit about chrooting your MTA, hiding your MTA's identity, disabling some dangerous SMTP commands, protecting your MTA from DoS attacks, and providing some general security.

One of the biggest issues with MTA security is the need for many MTAs to utilize root, utilize setuid, or require quite high privileges to correctly function. Older Sendmail versions are particular culprits of this. Both Postfix and more recent versions of Sendmail, from version 8.12 onward, run without setuid root, which reduces the potential risk of an attacker using your MTA as a conduit to root privileges on your system. This is another reason, if you are running Sendmail, to update to a more recent version.

So how does Sendmail achieve this? Sendmail is split into two operational modes: an MTA function and a Mail Submission Program (MSP) function. How you start Sendmail depends on which function is called. So, effectively now you have two running Sendmail modes: one is an SMTP daemon that performs your MTA functions, and the other is an MSP daemon that handles the submission and queuing of e-mail. To accommodate for this, an additional configuration file has been created, submit.cf, which controls the mail submission functions.

In version 8.12, Sendmail still needs root privileges to perform a few actions, such as binding to port 25, reading .forward files, performing local delivery of mail, and writing e-mail submitted via the command line to the queue directory. The last option is what Sendmail principally had used a setuid root binary for. The new version downgrades the requirements for root privileges by changing the sendmail binary to a setgid binary and writing to a group-writable queue directory. Sendmail still needs to be started as root, but then it drops privileges once it has performed the required root tasks.

This is a fairly simplistic explanation, and I recommend you carefully read the changes articulated in the Sendmail README and SECURITY documents that come with the source distribution to fully understand how the structure and running of Sendmail has changed. You need to consider a few caveats and warnings, though. You can also find these documents on the Sendmail Web site.

■**Note** Both Sendmail and Postfix still use the less dangerous setgid for several functions. Postfix uses setgid as part of the postdrop program for mail submission whilst Sendmail uses it to setgid to a different user and group, called smmsp, as part of the new separate mail submission process.

So how do you further limit the risk to your system from a penetration of your MTA's daemons? Well, one of the possible methods is chrooting. I will cover how both MTAs I am discussing can be chrooted and under what circumstances you may choose to do this.

Sendmail can be highly complicated to completely chroot, and because of its monolithic nature, the benefits derived from chrooting are potentially much more limited. Postfix consists of many small daemons, so you can therefore be selective about which you chroot; however, Sendmail is one binary, which means you have to attempt to chroot all its functions. Since Sendmail requires write access to objects that are almost certainly going to be outside your chroot jail, the value of the jail is negated.

The security changes that have been made to the way Sendmail runs in version 8.12 reduce the risk of a root penetration. This does not mean you should not look at chroot for Sendmail. I still think, though, you may want to run Sendmail chrooted in some important instances, such as if you are running an SMTP gateway, so I will take you through chrooting that type of Sendmail installation in the next section.

Postfix by default is designed to have most of its daemons running chrooted with fixed low privileges. Additionally, adjusting its configuration to enable chroot is simple and quick to achieve. I will cover the configuration of Postfix as a chrooted system in the "Chrooting Postfix" section.

Chrooting a Sendmail SMTP Gateway or Relay

Many enterprises run an SMTP gateway or relay on the "border" of their network, usually housed in a DMZ with a firewall protecting it, to provide front-line mail services on the Internet. The SMTP gateway sends and receives all mail for the enterprise but does no local delivery of mail; rather, it relays it onto other mail servers that handle internal mail. This frontend mail server provides another layer of security for your network and often also performs spam filtering or antivirus functions. See Figure 7-1.

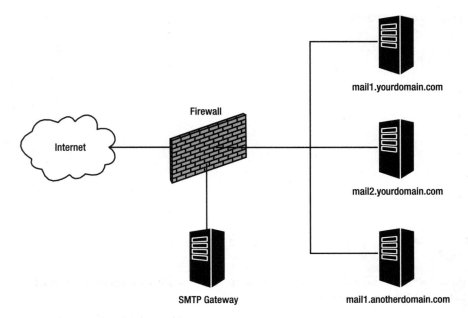

Figure 7-1. *An SMTP gateway or relay server*

As Sendmail is only relaying mail onward (or discarding it in the case of some spam- and virus-infected items), you are able to tightly chroot Sendmail within a jail on the gateway system because it does not need to write mail to local users. As I discussed elsewhere, the chroot jail protects your system from penetrations by locking the hacker into a "jail" where they can access the resources only in that jail and should be unable to take further action to compromise your system. With Sendmail, you achieve this by adding a user that Sendmail will "run as" who has limited privileges.

■Caution The chroot setup for Sendmail is quite complicated; you will need to carefully test that all the potential Sendmail functions you want to use actually work before putting this into production.

The first step in setting up your chroot jail is to create a directory structure. You need to specify a root directory for your chroot jail. I often use /chroot with subdirectories for all the applications chrooted below this directory. In this case, /chroot/sendmail is the Sendmail chroot root directory. Create the directories in Listing 7-1 underneath the /chroot/sendmail directory.

Listing 7-1. chroot *Directory Structure*

```
/dev
/etc
/etc/mail
/lib
/lib/tls
/tmp
/usr
/usr/bin
/usr/sbin
/usr/lib
/usr/lib/sasl2
/var
/var/run
/var/spool
/var/spool/mqueue
```

Next you will want to add a user for Sendmail to run as. I usually call this user sendmail and add it to the mail group. Enter the following:

```
puppy# useradd -u 501 -g mail -s /sbin/nologin -d /dev/null sendmail
```

Then enable the RunAsUser setting in sendmail.mc, and change it to the user you have created to run the Sendmail daemon. The following shows this:

```
define(`confRUN_AS_USER',`sendmail')
```

Re-create your sendmail.cf file to enable this.

Populating the /chroot/sendmail/etc Directory

Now you need to populate these directories with some of the files you will need. You can start with the /chroot/sendmail/etc directory. You need to copy the following:

```
aliases
aliases.db
passwd
group
resolv.conf
host.conf
nsswitch.conf
services
hosts
localtime
```

Once you have copied in your passwd and group files, you should edit these down to just the users and groups you need to run Sendmail. My passwd file contains the following:

```
root:x:0:0:root:/root:/bin/bash
bin:x:1:1:bin:/bin:/sbin/nologin
daemon:x:2:2:daemon:/sbin:/sbin/nologin
mail:x:8:12:mail:/var/spool/mail:/sbin/nologin
mailnull:x:47:47::/var/spool/mqueue:/sbin/nologin
sendmail:x:501:501::/dev/null:/sbin/nologin
```

The group file contains the following:

```
root:x:0:root
bin:x:1:root,bin,daemon
daemon:x:2:root,bin,daemon
mail:x:12:mail,sendmail
mailnull:x:47:
```

Finally, you need to put in your Sendmail configuration files. Simply copy the entire contents of your /etc/mail directory and all subdirectories into the /chroot/sendmail/etc/ directory. As much as I would like to say there is an easier way to do this—mount or links, for example—there is not, and both these methods punch a hole in your chroot jail that could allow an attacker to get out. So you need copy these files from the source directory to the target directory. When you are updating databases and files, ensure that you update the files in the chroot jail.

Populating the /chroot/sendmail/dev Directory

The next directory you will populate is your /chroot/sendmail/dev directory. You need to create some devices in this directory to allow Sendmail to correctly function. These devices, null and random, should duplicate the devices of the same name in the /dev directory. You can do this using the mknod commands shown in Listing 7-2.

Listing 7-2. *Making Devices for Sendmail*

```
puppy# mknod /chroot/sendmail/dev/null c 1 3
puppy# mknod /chroot/sendmail/dev/random c 1 8
```

Now secure your newly created devices. They should both be owned by the root user, with their permissions changed using chmod: null to 0666 and random to 0644.

Also in your /dev directory you need to create a log device to allow the chrooted Sendmail to log to syslog. If you are using syslog, then you need to add the -a switch to the command that starts syslog. For the sample configuration, you would add the following:

```
-a /chroot/sendmail/dev/log
```

If you are using syslog-NG, then add a line similar to the following one to your syslog-ng.conf file in one of your source block statements:

```
unix-stream("/chroot/sendmail/dev/log");
```

■**Tip** See Chapter 5 for more details on how to do this.

Then restart syslog or syslog-NG, a new log device in the dev directory will allow Sendmail to log to your syslog daemon.

Adding the Sendmail Binary and Libraries to the chroot Jail

Next put a copy of your sendmail binary into /chroot/sendmail/usr/sbin. This is the copy of Sendmail that will run when you start your chroot. You should also create symbolic links to this binary for your mailq and newaliases commands. Enter the following:

```
puppy# ln -s /chroot/sendmail/usr/sbin/sendmail /chroot/sendmail/usr/bin/mailq
puppy# ln -s /chroot/sendmail/usr/sbin/sendmail /chroot/sendmail/usr/bin/newaliases
```

Sendmail will also require a variety of libraries to run correctly in the chroot jail. The best way to work this out is to run ldd on the sendmail binary and record the list of libraries shown and to copy them into their respective locations in the chroot jail. Listing 7-3 shows the partial results of the ldd command and the copy of the libraries in their correct locations in the chroot jail.

Listing 7-3. *Adding the Sendmail Libraries*

```
puppy# ldd /usr/sbin/sendmail
libssl.so.4 => /lib/libssl.so.4 (0xb75ab000)
libcrypto.so.4 => /lib/libcrypto.so.4 (0xb74ba000)
libsasl2.so.2 => /usr/lib/libsasl2.so.2 (0xb74a4000)
libdb-4.1.so => /lib/libdb-4.1.so (0xb73e2000)
libpthread.so.0 => /lib/tls/libpthread.so.0 (0xb71b1000)
puppy# cp /lib/libssl.so.4 /chroot/sendmail/lib
puppy# cp /usr/lib/libsasl2.so.2 /chroot/sendmail/usr/lib
puppy# cp /lib/tls/libpthread.so.0 /chroot/sendmail/lib/tls
```

■**Caution** If you see any libraries located in /usr/kerberos/lib in your list of Sendmail libraries, do not copy them into a similar location under the Sendmail chroot; instead, copy them into /chroot/sendmail/ usr/lib. Sendmail seems unable to find them otherwise.

You will also need some other libraries. Listing 7-4 lists these libraries, which are usually contained in /lib.

Listing 7-4. *Additional Libraries Required by Sendmail*

```
libnss_dns.so.2
libresolv.so.2
libnss_files.so.2
```

Copy the libraries from Listing 7-4 to /chroot/sendmail/lib to proceed.

Finally, if you will be using Simple Authentication and Security Layer (SASL), then you need to copy the Sendmail.conf file and all the required SASL mechanisms and plug-ins you intend to support. You do this simply by copying all the files in the /usr/lib/sasl2 directory to /chroot/sendmail/usr/lib/sasl2. If you are using saslauthd, you also need to adjust the location of your saslauthd mux file to within your chroot jail. See Chapter 8 for how to do this.

USING CHROOT

In this and other chapters I have discussed chroot jails. A chroot jail uses the chroot() function to lock a process into its own directory structure. Essentially the chroot() function redefines what the root, or /, directory is for a process. For example, the chroot() function is frequently used for FTP servers to lock local users into their home directories. This way, if user bob signs onto the FTP server, he is placed in his home directory, /home/bob. If he issues the following command:

```
puppy# cd /
```

he will not go to the / directory; rather, he will return to the /home/bob directory, as this has been defined as his root directory. This allows you to control the access your processes have to your file systems.

Because you have no access to resources outside the chroot jail, you need to provide all the resources required by the jailed process or daemon inside the jail. You do this by copying the required files and objects. These include devices, libraries, commands, or files. Hence, an important step in building a chroot jail is creating and populating the directory structure and content of the jail. Throughout this book I have constructed the chroot jails with the bare minimum of resources required for the various processes to function.

Many daemons, such as Postfix or BIND, come with the ability to create their own built-in chroot jails. These processes can be jailed by setting a configuration or command-line option. Other processes require that you build your own custom jail and then execute the chroot command. The chroot command provides a userland interface to the chroot() function. It works by specifying the new root directory of the proposed jail and then executing the required command like so:

```
puppy# chroot /chroot/newroot /usr/sbin/jailed
```

On the previous line, the chroot command changes to the directory /chroot/newroot and then executes the command /usr/sbin/jailed. The jailed daemon will now be able to access only the files and objects in the directory /chroot/newroot and any subdirectories. It will have no other access to the rest of the host's file systems.

It is possible, albeit technically challenging, to break out of a chroot jail. A number of methods exist: buffer overflows, open directory handles in file systems outside the chroot jail, or the injection of code into the kernel. All these methods are made more difficult if the process or daemon inside the chroot jail has dropped privileges. The ideal model for running a chroot jail is with a process that has normal user privileges. For example, this is how the BIND named daemon can be run.

Permissions and Ownership

Before you can start your Sendmail daemon in the chroot jail, you need to ensure some permissions and ownerships are set up correctly. First, the /chroot/sendmail/var/spool/mqueue directory needs to be owned by the user you have specified in the RunAsUser option and chmoded to 0700 (in this case the user sendmail).

```
puppy# chown sendmail /chroot/sendmail/var/spool/mqueue
puppy# chmod 0700 /chroot/sendmail/var/spool/mqueue
```

All files and databases (including alias files, :include: files, statistics files, and databases) must also be readable by that user. Next ensure there are no group-writable files in the chroot jail and that your cf files are secure using the following:

```
puppy# chmod -R go-w /chroot/sendmail
puppy# chmod 0400 /chroot/sendmail/etc/mail/*.cf
```

Finally, because you have chrooted Sendmail and you are running it on an SMTP gateway, you do not need to do local delivery; therefore, your sendmail binary does not need to setgid smmsp or belong to the smmsp group. Change it by entering the following:

```
puppy# chmod g-s /chroot/sendmail/usr/sbin/sendmail
puppy# chgrp root /chroot/sendmail/usr/sbin/sendmail
```

Change any other ownerships and permissions according to the instructions in the Sendmail op.ps file. When you start Sendmail, it should identify any other potential permissions problems—the more recent versions of Sendmail are especially strict about this—and you can correct these as you go.

Starting and Troubleshooting Your Sendmail chroot Jail

Obviously you will also need to configure your Sendmail to relay your mail to its final destination; I recommend setting up some fairly stringent antispam and antivirus rules on any SMTP gateway system. Once this is complete, you can start your chrooted Sendmail. Listing 7-5 shows the required command.

Listing 7-5. *Starting your Chrooted Sendmail*

```
puppy# chroot /chroot/sendmail /usr/sbin/sendmail -bd -q15m
```

This command first specifies the location of the chroot root directory, /chroot/sendmail, and then executes the sendmail binary. The binary it executes is the sendmail you have located in the chroot jail, because /usr/sbin is now relative to the new root directory, not to your existing / root directory.

During your testing phase, I recommend you change your Sendmail logging level in sendmail.cf to the highest level to pick up all the possible error messages whilst you are testing your chroot jail. You need to change the logging setting, LogLevel, to 15. You should change this back to your choice of logging level after you have finished testing. The most common problems with this setup are usually related to permissions. Carefully read your mail logs to determine exactly where the problem is.

Chrooting Postfix

Postfix is remarkably easy to chroot. Or perhaps, better said, most of the Postfix daemons are easy to chroot. Almost all the Postfix daemons can be run in a chroot jail using fixed low privileges with access only to the Postfix queue at /var/spool/postfix. The only daemons that cannot be chrooted are the daemons associated with the local delivery of e-mail.

■Note This assumes you have already installed and configured Postfix and it is running on your system.

You first need to create your chroot jail and populate it with all the files Postfix requires to run. The default place to create your Postfix chroot jail is in /var/spool/postfix.

■**Caution** Always remember any chrooted daemon resolves filenames and directories relative to the root of the chroot jail. In this case, that is /var/spool/postfix. So if it is looking for the file /etc/localtime, then it expects to find it in /var/spool/postfix/etc/localtime.

Create the following subdirectories under this directory:

```
/dev
/etc
/lib
/usr
/usr/lib
/usr/lib/zoneinfo
/var
/var/run
```

You will need some files from elsewhere in the system to allow Postfix to function. Copy the following files into /var/spool/postfix/etc from /etc:

```
/etc/localtime
/etc/host.conf
/etc/resolv.conf
/etc/nsswitch.conf
/etc/services
/etc/hosts
/etc/passwd
```

You also need to add the Postfix required libraries to the /var/spool/postfix/lib directory. You can do this by copying all of the following:

```
puppy# cp /lib/libnss_*.so* /var/spool/postfix/lib
puppy# cp /lib/libresolv.so* /var/spool/postfix/lib
puppy# cp /lib/libdb.so* /var/spool/postfix/lib
```

You also need to copy the file /etc/localtime to /var/spool/postfix/usr/lib/zoneinfo/localtime. You can use the following command for this:

```
puppy# cp /etc/localtime /var/spool/postfix/usr/lib/zoneinfo
```

■**Tip** If you downloaded the Postfix source and installed it that way, then the source package contains some scripts to automate the creation of the required directories and to copy the required files for you. These scripts are located in postfix-*version*/examples/chroot-setup/. An example script called LINUX2 is specifically for Linux. You just need to make the script executable and then run it. It also automatically reloads Postfix.

Also in your /var/spool/postfix/dev directory you need to create a log device to allow the chrooted Postfix to log to syslog. If you are using syslog, then you need to add the -a switch to the command to start syslog. For this configuration, I would use the following:

```
-a /var/spool/postfix/dev/log
```

If you are using syslog-NG, then add a line similar to the following one to your syslog-ng.conf file in one of your source statements:

```
unix-stream("/var/spool/postfix/dev/log");
```

■**Tip** See Chapter 5 for more details on how to do this.

Then restart syslog or syslog-NG, which should create a log device in the dev directory that will allow Postfix to log to your syslog daemon.

Finally, if you are going to be using SASL, then you will need to copy the smtpd.conf file and all the required SASL mechanisms and plug-ins you intend to support. You can do this simply by copying all the files in the /usr/lib/sasl2 directory to /var/spool/postfix/usr/lib/sasl2. If you are using saslauthd, you also need to adjust the location of your saslauthd mux file to within your chroot jail. See Chapter 8 for how to do this.

Now that you have a chroot jail for Postfix, you need to configure Postfix itself to use that jail. The Postfix daemons are controlled by the master.cf file, which is usually located in the /etc/postfix/ or /etc/mail directory. Open this file, and review its contents. The start of the file contains documentation explaining the daemons controlled from this file and their settings. After this documentation you will find a list of daemons that resembles Listing 7-6.

Listing 7-6. *Postfix* master.cf *File*

```
# service    type    private unpriv  chroot  wakeup  maxproc command + args
#                    (yes)   (yes)   (yes)   (never) (100)
smtp         inet    n       -       y       -       -       smtpd
#628         inet    n       -       y       -       -       qmqpd
pickup       fifo    n       -       y       60      1       pickup
cleanup      unix    n       -       y       -       0       cleanup
qmgr         fifo    n       -       y       300     1       qmgr
#qmgr        fifo    n       -       y       300     1       nqmgr
rewrite      unix    -       -       y       -       -       trivial-rewrite
bounce       unix    -       -       y       -       0       bounce
defer        unix    -       -       y       -       0       bounce
flush        unix    n       -       y       1000?   0       flush
proxymap     unix    -       -       y       -       -       proxymap
smtp         unix    -       -       y       -       -       smtp
relay        unix    -       -       y       -       -       smtp
```

```
#          -o smtp_helo_timeout=5 -o smtp_connect_timeout=5
showq    unix  n       -       y       -       -       showq
error    unix  -       -       y       -       -       error
local    unix  -       n       n       -       -       local
virtual  unix  -       n       n       -       -       virtual
lmtp     unix  -       -       y       -       -       lmtp
```

You should see that each daemon is followed by several columns of configuration switches. A hyphen (-) in a column indicates that Postfix will use the default setting for that setting, which is specified in the second commented line beneath the description of what each column does. For example, the default for unpriv is y (for yes).

The most important columns are unpriv and chroot. In the chroot column, make sure all the daemons *except* those that use local or virtual services (check the last column under command to confirm this) are set to y. Then check that all the entries underneath unpriv are set to either - or y again with the same exceptions: the local and virtual services.

Now reload Postfix by entering the following:

```
puppy# postfix reload
```

Check your mail log file (usually /var/log/maillog) for the results of the reload; if it reports that Postfix reloaded without incident, your system is now running Postfix chrooted!

Securing Your SMTP Server

I will now show you some options for securing Sendmail and Postfix, including hiding your banner, disabling some SMTP commands, setting the privacy flags for Sendmail, and using smrsh with Sendmail, amongst other issues. A large portion of the following sections focus on Sendmail rather than Postfix because Postfix provides built-in protection or turns on or off some security-related options by default and does not require you to manually do this. I will identify where any manual intervention for Postfix is required.

Obfuscating the MTA Banner and Version

Your MTA's banner is one of the few occasions when it does not pay to advertise. One of the easiest ways for attackers to customize their assaults on your MTA is by Telneting to port 25 on your system and watching your MTA's banner tell the attackers what application it is and its version. So I will take you through the steps required to change Sendmail and Postfix's banner to something that does not broadcast these details.

Sendmail

Sendmail controls its banner by settings in the sendmail.cf file. If you know Sendmail, you will be aware it is recommended you do not directly edit the sendmail.cf file; rather, you should update the m4 macro file, sendmail.mc, and then re-create the sendmail.cf file. In Listing 7-7 you can see the default Sendmail banner.

Listing 7-7. *Default Sendmail Banner*

```
220 puppy.yourdomain.com ESMTP Sendmail 8.12.11/8.12.10; ➥
Fri, 26 Mar 2004 20:45:50 +1100
```

You can change this by setting the confSMTP_LOGIN_MSG parameter inside the sendmail.mc file. By default it does not appear in most sendmail.mc files, so you will need to add it. Listing 7-8 shows how to do it.

Listing 7-8. *The* sendmail.mc *Parameter That Controls the Sendmail Banner*

```
define(`confSMTP_LOGIN_MSG', `$j')
```

The $j macro represents the fully qualified domain name of your system. Remember, you will need to re-create the sendmail.cf file by issuing an m4 command and restarting sendmail. Enter the following:

```
puppy# m4 /etc/mail/sendmail.mc > /etc/mail/sendmail.cf
puppy# /etc/rc.d/init.d/sendmail restart
```

▬**Note** I am restarting Sendmail on a Red Hat system here using an init script. You should restart using whatever mechanism your distribution provides.

This will produce a banner that looks like Listing 7-9.

Listing 7-9. *A De-identified Sendmail Banner*

```
220 puppy.yourdomain.com ESMTP
```

The word ESMTP[1] is automatically inserted between the first and second words in the banner to encourage other MTAs to speak ESMTP.

Many people happily disable their Sendmail banner and think attackers are now up for a much harder job to determine their software version. But, unfortunately, another SMTP command, HELP, happily spits out your Sendmail version and offers help on the commands you can run on your MTA. It is not easy to disable this. You can remove the content of the HELP command response by adding the contents of Listing 7-10, which specifies you do not want a help file. Add this to your sendmail.mc file.

Listing 7-10. *Hiding Help Contents from Display*

```
define(`HELP_FILE', `')
```

But even if you do hide the content of the HELP command response, it still returns the Sendmail version, as demonstrated in Listing 7-11.

Listing 7-11. *Sendmail Help with Hidden Contents*

```
HELP
502 5.3.0 Sendmail 8.12.11 -- HELP not implemented
```

---

1. The Enhanced Simple Mail Transfer Protocol (ESMTP)

At the time of this writing, the only way for the paranoid (and I fall into this category because I believe *every* trick or edge you can get on potential attackers is good) to disable this behavior is to edit the source code of Sendmail itself. If you really want to do this, then you will find the relevant code in the sendmail subdirectory of your Sendmail source distribution in the file srvrsmtp.c. In this file find the line in Listing 7-12.

Listing 7-12. HELP *Command in* srvrsmtp.c

```
message("502 5.3.0 Sendmail %s -- HELP not implemented",
                    Version);
```

Remove Sendmail %s from the line in Listing 7-12 and recompile. The Sendmail server will now not display the application name or version in the HELP command response. Of course, you would need to repeat this every time you upgrade Sendmail.

■**Caution** If you do not know what you are doing, do not mess with the Sendmail source code, because there is every chance you will break something! Security is good, but your users also need a working MTA.

Postfix

The banner presented by Postfix is easy to configure. It is controlled by the smtpd_banner parameter in the main.cf file. The main.cf file is normally located in /etc/postfix or /etc/mail. Listing 7-13 shows the default banner.

Listing 7-13. *Default Postfix Banner*

```
220 puppy.yourdomain.com ESMTP Postfix
```

You can create this by setting the smtpd_banner parameter in the main.cf file to the following:

```
smtpd_banner = $myhostname ESMTP $mail_name
```

The $myhostname variable expands to the hostname and domain of the system, and the $mail_name variable expands to Postfix. To hide the Postfix server identification from view, change the banner parameter to the following:

```
smtpd_banner = $myhostname ESMTP
```

■**Caution** You must include the $hostname variable. It is a requirement of the RFC. You should also leave ESMTP in the banner, as by default Postfix sends only an EHLO at the start of a connection if ESMTP appears in the banner. You can override this behavior by adding smtp_always_send_ehlo = yes to the main.cf file.

The Postfix MTA does not implement the HELP command.

Disabling Dangerous and Legacy SMTP Commands

One of the first things you need to do is to look at some SMTP commands. SMTP was designed with some useful commands, such as VRFY, that used to make sending e-mail easier. Those commands now represent more of a liability for your SMTP server than a benefit. I will go through all of these "legacy" commands and examine how to deal with them. You can see a list of all the potentially unsafe SMTP commands like this in Table 7-1. Some of these commands may be disabled, may be turned off, or are simply not available in future versions of Sendmail and Postfix, but it is better to be sure you have addressed these commands.

Table 7-1. *SMTP Commands That Are Potentially Insecure*

Command	Purpose	Recommended Setting
VRFY	Verifies the presence of an e-mail address	Disable
EXPN	Expands an e-mail address and shows a list of all the mail-boxes or users who will receive messages when e-mail is sent to this address	Disable
ETRN	Allows dial-up hosts to retrieve only the mail destined for their domain	Disable if not used

Disabling VRFY

VRFY, for example, is a way for a remote SMTP server to verify that a user or e-mail addresses exists and is valid at another SMTP server. For example, if you Telnet to a Sendmail server with VRFY enabled, you should see something like Listing 7-14.

Listing 7-14. *Using the VRFY Command*

```
[john@kitten]$ telnet puppy.yourdomain.com 25
Trying 192.168.0.1...
Connected to puppy.yourdomain.com.
Escape character is '^]'.
220 puppy.yourdomain.com ESMTP
VRFY root
250 2.1.5 root@puppy.yourdomain.com
VRFY jim
```

550 5.1.1 jim... User unknown

This is a Sendmail server, and I have Telneted into it and asked it to check for the presence of some local users. First, I try to VRFY root. Sendmail gives SMTP response code 250 and provides root's e-mail address. In the second attempt I try to VRFY jim. Sendmail reports that jim is an unknown user and returns response code 550.

With the VRFY option enabled only attackers and the harvesters of e-mail addresses for spam purposes are able to do two things—confirm the presences of a username on your system or confirm that an e-mail address will receive mail and is thus of some value as a target for spam.

You can control most of the SMTP command options in Sendmail using this option:

```
define(`confPRIVACY_FLAGS', `flags').
```

In Sendmail to disable VRFY and other SMTP commands, you need to add flags to the confPRIVACY_FLAGS option in sendmail.mc and then rebuild your sendmail.cf. So to disable VRFY in Sendmail, do this:

```
define(`confPRIVACY_FLAGS', `novrfy')
```

Restart Sendmail, and the VRFY command will be disabled. Listing 7-15 shows the results if you try a VRFY with it disabled in Sendmail

Listing 7-15. *Results from Sendmail with* VRFY *Disabled*

```
VRFY jim
252 2.5.2 Cannot VRFY user; try RCPT to attempt delivery (or try finger)
```

In Postfix you need to add the option in Listing 7-16 to the main.cf file and then reload or restart Postfix.

Listing 7-16. *Disabling* VRFY *in Postfix*

```
disable_vrfy_command = yes
```

With this option, Postfix should respond similarly to Listing 7-17.

Listing 7-17. *Results from Postfix with* VRFY *Disabled*

```
VRFY jim
502 VRFY command is disabled
```

Disabling EXPN

EXPN stands for expand and allows someone to Telnet to your MTA and query a name. If that name is an alias for multiple recipients, that EXPN command expands that alias into a list of those users. On a Sendmail server using a .forward file, the EXPN command will also show the real forwarding destination of mail. Or you can issue EXPN for the root user and see who receives mail addressed to the system administrator. As you can imagine, this is dangerous both from a security point of view, as attackers can identify a variety of potential user accounts on your system, and from a spam point of view, as spammers can gather considerable numbers of addresses by expanding aliases.

As with disabling VRFY, you use the same confPRIVACY_FLAGS option for EXPN. In Listing 7-18 you can see the argument for disabling EXPN added to the confPRIVACY_FLAGS option.

Listing 7-18. *Disabling* EXPN *in Sendmail*

```
define(`confPRIVACY_FLAGS', `novrfy,noexpn')
```

Rebuild sendmail.cf, and restart Sendmail. When you issue an EXPN, as shown in Listing 7-19, you should see results.

Listing 7-19. *Results from Sendmail with* EXPN *Disabled*

```
EXPN
502 5.7.0 Sorry, we do not allow this operation
```

In Postfix the EXPN is not implemented by default, and in Listing 7-20 you can see how Postfix will respond to EXPN requests.

Listing 7-20. EXPN *in Postfix*

```
EXPN jim
502 Error: command not implemented
```

Disabling ETRN

Before disabling the ETRN command, you need to put some thought into whether disabling it is the most appropriate choice. The command is a more secure enhancement of the TURN command. It is designed to assist hosts that are not permanently connected to the Internet. The mail for the occasionally connected hosts is accumulated at another SMTP server, and, when the host connects to the Internet, the host sends an ETRN command that instructs the storing SMTP Server to deliver all the stored mail. If the given SMTP server does not have any stored messages, it does not reply to your SMTP server and the SMTP connection times out.

In most cases, ETRN does not pose a significant risk, but at least one exploit has used ETRN for a DoS service attack in the past.[2] If you do not use ETRN for anything, then to err on the side of caution, I recommend you disable it. For Sendmail, simply change your confPRIVACY_FLAGS to Listing 7-21.

Listing 7-21. *Disable* ETRN *in Sendmail*

```
define(`confPRIVACY_FLAGS', `novrfy,noexpn,noetrn')
```

Listing 7-21 now shows all the SMTP commands I have discussed (VRFY, EXPN, and ETRN) in a disabled state.

In Postfix you cannot entirely disable ETRN, but you can reduce the any potential threat by specifying what domains are able to use the ETRN command. Add the option in Listing 7-22 to main.cf, and reload Postfix to enable this.

Listing 7-22. ETRN *in Postfix*

```
smtpd_etrn_restrictions = permit_mynetworks, hash:/etc/postfix/allow_etrn, reject
```

This command tells Postfix to allow ETRN commands from two sources: any networks listed in the main.cf config option $mynetworks, denoting any networks that Postfix trusts for purposes such as relaying, and any domains or IP addresses listed in a Postfix access database called allow_etrn in /etc/postfix. The final statement, reject, tells Postfix to reject any other attempts to use ETRN.

■**Tip** You can create Postfix access databases using the postmap command. You can read about them in the postmap man page or on the Web at http://www.postfix.org/access.5.html.

---

2. http://www.securityfocus.com/bid/904/info/

Some Additional Sendmail Privacy Flags

In addition to the flags I have discussed, Sendmail also has a number of other useful flags for the confPRIVACY_FLAGS option. In Table 7-2 you can see a list of the ones I think are useful and recommend you set to increase the integrity and security of your Sendmail server.

Table 7-2. *Additional Sendmail Privacy Flags*

Flag	Purpose
authwarnings	Inserts a header, X-Authentication-Warnings, into any mail it suspects is not authentic. This is usually on by default in most Sendmail installations.
goaway	Combines the functions of novrfy, noverb, and noexpn and also includes noreceipts, needmailhelo, needvrfyhelo, needexpnhelo, and nobodyreturn.
needmailhelo	A remote server must issue a HELO before sending mail.
nobodyreturn	Does not return the original body of a message when it is bounced.
noreceipts	Disables DSN (SUCCESS return receipts).
noverb	Disables the SMTP VERB command.
restrictexpand	Tells Sendmail to drop privilege when a non-root user runs sendmail -bv to protect ./forward files, aliases, and :include: files from snooping.
restrictmailq	Restricts who can examine the mail queue to root or the queue owner.
restrictqrun	Restrict who can run or process the mail queue using the -q option to root or the queue owner.

I recommend setting your privacy options to the most secure possible. Listing 7-23 shows my recommended setting.

Listing 7-23. *Recommended Sendmail* confPRIVACY_FLAGS *Options*

```
define(`confPRIVACY_FLAGS', `goaway,restrictmailq,restrictqrun')
```

■**Tip** If you are going to restrict access to the mail queue, ensure you turn off read permissions for ordinary users on your logs. You can extract the same information via grepping your logs as you can reading the mail queue.

Sendmail and smrsh

Sendmail also offers users the ability to run programs using the "prog" mailer function. This poses some risks if users are able to execute programs or code that could allow exploits or threaten the integrity of the system. The solution to this issue is the introduction of smrsh, the Sendmail restricted shell. The smrsh shell was designed as a replacement for the standard shell, sh, to prevent people from misusing the Sendmail |program functions by limiting those programs and shell functions that can be executed. If you specify the smrsh shell, then Sendmail can execute only those programs contained in the smrsh directory (by default /usr/adm/sm.bin). It limits the use of shell commands to exec, exit, and echo. The smrsh shell also disables the use of the following characters when executing programs:

```
' < > ; $ ( ) \r  \n
```

You can enable smrsh by adding the feature in Listing 7-24 to your sendmail.mc file.

Listing 7-24. *Enabling SMRSH in Sendmail*

```
FEATURE(`smrsh',`/usr/sbin/smrsh')
```

Ensure the second option /usr/sbin/smrsh is the location of your smrsh binary. Then create your /usr/adm/sm.bin directory to hold your "safe" programs.

■**Tip** Some distributions change the default location for the smrsh programs directory. Use the command strings /path/to/smrsh | grep '^/' to find the directory. One of the directories returned should be the smrsh directory.

You should populate your smrsh "safe" programs directory with only those programs you believe cannot be compromised or used for hacking purposes. So, do not include the perl interpreter, sed, awk, or the like. And do not include shells such as sh or csh, as this defeats the purpose of having a secure shell. I usually include programs such as mail and vacation and, if you use them, programs such as maildrop and procmail. When populating your "safe" programs directory, the easiest method is to simply symbolically link in the required programs.

Writing to Files Safely

Starting with version 8.7, Sendmail also has the ability to control how delivery is made to files, including defining a "safe" directory environment in the form of a limited chroot jail. Ordinarily, Sendmail will write to any file or object it has permission to write to, including ordinary files, directories, and devices. This poses a serious risk if Sendmail were to write over something crucial or if an attacker was able to overwrite something that created a vulnerability or hole in your security.

The SafeFileEnvironment option handles the ability to control how delivery is made to files. Enabling it can achieve two possible outcomes. The first is to restrict delivery to ordinary files only, and the second to create an area to which Sendmail must write its files. Listing 7-25 simply declares the option in sendmail.mc, which restricts delivery to ordinary files only.

Listing 7-25. *Setting* SafeFileEnvironment

```
define(`confSAFE_FILE_ENV', `/')
```

With the SafeFileEnvironment declared as / or root, Sendmail will now to refuse to write to anything except a normal file. This includes banning writes to directory, devices, and, importantly for some systems, symbolic links. The only exception to this is that it is still possible for Sendmail to write to /dev/null. Turning this option on is a good idea as a bare minimum to prevent an inadvertent or malicious write by Sendmail to some critical location.

The second way to use the `SafeFileEnvironment` option is to define a directory or directory tree in which all files that Sendmail wants to write to must be contained. This applies only to delivery to files. This does not include things such as your aliases, include files, maps, or anything written by a delivery agent such as `procmail`. Listing 7-26 shows how you can define a directory.

Listing 7-26. *Setting* `SafeFileEnvironment`

```
define(`confSAFE_FILE_ENV', `/safe')
```

Sendmail will `chroot` into the `/safe` directory before making any writes. But Sendmail also is careful to check that you are not referencing the "safe" directory twice. For example, if your alias file contains the following:

```
jim:     \jim, /safe/home/jim/jim.old
```

and your `SafeFileEnvironment` option is set like Listing 7-26, then Sendmail will strip off the extra `/safe` in your aliases file before writing.

■**Note** The \ in front of `jim` tells Sendmail to write immediately ignoring any other aliasing, including `.forward` files.

This means rather than incorrectly writing to `/safe/safe/home/jim/jim.old`, Sendmail checks for the extra directory and sees that you have included it in both the alias file and the `sendmail.cf` file, removes the extra reference, and actually writes to `/safe/home/jim/jim.old`.

The last thing to consider with the `SafeFileEnvironment` is if you use it in conjunction with the `RunAsUser` option. Turning on the `RunAsUser` option will make all deliveries to files or programs unsafe and thus conflicts with the `SafeFileEnvironment` option. If you use the `RunAsUser` option, then do not enable the `SafeFileEnvironment`.

Limiting the Risk of (Distributed) DoS Attacks

DoS and Distributed Denial of Service (DDoS) attacks are designed to overwhelm your mail server by using multiple, simultaneous requests, e-mails, or commands. Eventually your e-mail server uses too much memory, runs out of disk, or spawns too many processes, or your network is overloaded and your system either becomes ineffective or crashes. There is some good news here. You can prevent some of this behavior with some relatively simple-to-implement changes.

But (and there are a couple of big buts), you must also be careful when setting this up depending on the volume and throughput of your e-mail server. First, you could risk severely crippling the performance of your e-mail server if you restrict it to a certain number of processes/daemons or a certain volume of e-mail. You should watch your system closely, collect performance data and statistics, and set any thresholds at least 50 percent to 100 percent higher than the peak for that service, rate, or process. This reduces the risk of you artificially denying service to your own e-mail server by setting any limits too low.

You need to keep watching and analyzing this also. Do not assume your e-mail server's performance is going to be static. Watch and adjust your thresholds and limits accordingly.[3]

Second, you will probably never be able to fully prevent an all-out DoS attack. There is a good chance your mail server will succumb before you get a chance to protect it. What can help with this (or at least enhance your chances of reducing any potential outage because of a DoS attack) is to ensure that you are protecting your e-mail server from DoS attacks in a multilayered fashion. You should ensure your firewalling is correct and that you have the ability to drop connections to hostile sources quickly and effectively (using a tool such as PortSentry).[4] I cover some of this in more detail in Chapter 2. You should also have early-response warnings set up either by watching performance data and logs or via intrusion detection software such as Snort and alerting via a non-e-mail source!

■**Tip** This is very important to consider. It is all well and good sending incident warnings and alerts via e-mail—until your e-mail server is the target of the attack and you simply are not getting the warnings or they are buried in a sea of other error messages. Look at using SMS or paging as an alternative source of alerts for critical messages related to your e-mail servers and services.

Limiting DoS Attacks with Sendmail

The objective in reducing the risk of DoS and DDoS attacks is to inhibit the overflow of inputs to your Sendmail mail server without inhibiting the normal flow of inputs, where the inputs are the e-mail messages and connections inbound and outbound on your system. You can use a number of settings in Sendmail to help do this. I will divide these settings into rate-control settings and resource settings. Rate-control settings handle the thresholds and levels at which Sendmail conducts itself, including process limits and delays. Table 7-3 shows the rate-control settings. Resource controls are related to the resources available to Sendmail. All these settings are located in your `sendmail.mc` file.

Table 7-3. *Rate-Control Settings to Stop DoS and DDoS Attacks in Sendmail*

Directive	Description
confCONNECTION_RATE_THROTTLE	Limits the number of incoming connection per second per daemon
confMAX_DAEMON_CHILDREN	Limits the number of daemon children Sendmail will spawn

`ConnectionRateThrottle` tells Sendmail how many incoming connections to open per second and per daemon. Remember that this can cause a DoS attack in its own right if set too low for your site. It is set to no limit by default. Sendmail spawns additional daemon children

---

3. You can find some excellent information on tuning Sendmail at
   `http://people.freenet.de/slgig/op_en/tuning.html` and on Postfix at
   `http://www.porcupine.org/postfix-mirror/newdoc/TUNING_README.html`.

4. You can find PortSentry at `http://sourceforge.net/projects/sentrytools/`.

for incoming mail and queue runs. The MaxDaemonChildren setting causes Sendmail to refuse connections if the limit of children is exceeded. This has no effect on outgoing connections. Again, remember this can cause a DoS attack in your site if set too low. It is set to no limit by default.

Additionally, in the upcoming 8.13.0 release of Sendmail, some basic rate-control functionality has been introduced to limit the number of connections from a particular client source. This potentially should significantly reduce the risk of connection-based DoS attacks. The functionality is also available for Sendmail 8.12 in an experimental form. You can find it at http://j-chkmail.ensmp.fr/sm/.

The second category of settings is resource related, including controlling potential attacks based on the size and form of mail messages sent and the minimum free space available on the system in order for Sendmail to receive mail. Table 7-4 shows these directives.

Table 7-4. *Resource-Control Settings to Stop DoS and DDoS Attacks in Sendmail*

Directive	Description
confMAX_HEADERS_LENGTH	Limits the maximum length of all mail headers
confMAX_MIME_HEADER_LENGTH	Limits the maximum length of some MIME headers
confMAX_MESSAGE_LENGTH	Limits the maximum size of a message that Sendmail will receive
confMIN_FREE_BLOCKS	The number of free blocks required to before a mail message is accepted

Listing 7-27 shows the settings for these options for my Sendmail server.

Listing 7-27. *Mail-Based DoS and Overflow Attack Settings for Sendmail*

```
define(`confMAX_HEADERS_LENGTH', `32768')
define(`confMAX_MIME_HEADER_LENGTH', `256/128')
define(`confMAX_MESSAGE_LENGTH', `10485760')
define(`confMIN_FREE_BLOCKS', `250')
```

The first option, MaxHeaderLength, tells Sendmail to limit the maximum header length to 32,768 bytes. By default this is set to 0, which indicates no limit on the header size. The second option, MaxMIMEHeaderLength, is designed to protect your Mail User Agents (MUAs). MaxMIME-HeaderLength is divided into two numbers. The first, before the slash (/), is the maximum size in characters of all those MIME headers belonging to the class {checkMIMETextHeader}. The second number, after the slash (/), is for those headers in that class that take parameters and sets the maximum size in characters of those parameters. The defaults for this are 2048/1024.

The next option, MaxMessageLength, controls the maximum size of an e-mail that Sendmail will accept. In Listing 7-27 I have set this to 10MB but you may want to set this to whatever amount suits your site or organization. I recommend you note that SMTP is *not* a file transfer protocol. If your users need to send huge files, you should encourage them, if not force them, to seek other means and not to resort to e-mail.

■**Note** This also controls the response of the SMTP command SIZE. Smart clients will ask Sendmail first what size messages it will accept and not try to send the message if its size exceeds the threshold. Dumb clients will send the message (which on a dial-up connection, for example, could take a long time) and then realize it has been rejected and stop processing the message. You will need to test your clients to determine what their behavior is.

The last setting, MinFreeBlocks, forces Sendmail to ensure you have a minimum amount of free space before it will accept e-mail. This will stop your spool from filling up and potentially crashing your system. It is set to 100 blocks by default.

Obviously, after changing any of these settings, you need to re-create your sendmail.cf file and restart Sendmail.

Limiting DoS Attacks with Postfix

The objective in reducing the risk of DoS and DDoS attacks is to inhibit the overflow of inputs to your Postfix mail server without inhibiting the normal flow of inputs, where the inputs are the e-mail messages and connections inbound and outbound on your system. You can use a number of settings in Postfix to help you do this. I will divide these settings into rate-control settings and resource settings. Rate-control settings handle the thresholds and levels at which Postfix conducts itself, including process limits and delays. Table 7-5 shows the rate-control settings. Resource controls relate to the resources available to Postfix. Table 7-6 shows these controls. The main.cf file contains all these settings.

Table 7-5. *Rate-Control Settings to Stop DoS and DDoS Attacks in Postfix*

Directive	Default Setting	Description
default_process_limit	100	Controls inbound and outbound delivery rates by limiting the number of concurrent processes
local_destination_concurrency_limit	20	Controls how many messages are delivered simultaneously to a local recipient
smtpd_recipient_limit	1000	Limits the number of recipients the SMTP daemon will take per delivery
smtpd_soft_error_limit	10	Error count
smtpd_hard_error_limit	20	Error count
smtpd_error_sleep_time	1	Pause that Postfix takes between reporting errors in seconds

I will take you through all of the options available to you. The first is default_process_limit, which simply controls the number of possible concurrent Postfix processes and includes SMTP clients and servers as well as local delivery functions. This defaults to 100, which is potentially a substantial number on a smaller system and could easily overload a smaller spec mail server but is probably acceptable for a large mail hub. You can also edit the number of processes available to a specific daemon by editing the `master.cf` file. You need to edit the column `maxproc` to change the maximum number of processes available to that particular daemon. You can also specify 0 for no maximum. This is probably not a good idea, as it defeats the purpose of restricting the number of running processes and leaves you open to a DoS attack.

The `local_destination_concurrency_limit` option controls how many messages are delivered simultaneously to the same local recipient. You should keep this low (or if you want to increase it, do it gradually so you can see the results); otherwise, you could easily allow a DDoS or DoS attack to cripple your system as your mail delivery is overloaded. The default setting of 20 works well for most Postfix systems.

The `smtpd_recipient_limit` option tells Postfix the limit of recipients to take per delivery. It defaults to 1000, which should cover most normal SMTP clients; however, I recommend you lower it to prevent issues with broken client. The limit should also be considered as a potential antispam tool. Messages with large numbers of recipients are often more likely to be spam, Trojans, or viruses than legitimate e-mails. Whilst there is some risk of rejecting mailing list messages by lowering this limit, polite and well-configured mailing list software should divide outgoing mail into multiple mails with small blocks of recipients. This being said, RFC 821 does suggest a minimum of 100 recipients; I recommend not going lower than this.

Postfix also keeps a running tally of errors as messages are sent and received. It tracks two kinds of errors: soft errors and hard errors. Each has its own thresholds, `smtpd_soft_error_limit` and `smtpd_hard_error_limit`, respectively, that can be set. If those thresholds are breached, then there are two possible responses. The first is to pause for the `smtpd_error_sleep_time` period in seconds. The second is to disconnect the connection. Postfix decides what is going to do based on the following rules:

- When the error count is less than `smtpd_soft_error_limit`, it does not pause or sleep between errors.

- When the error count is greater than or equal to `smtpd_soft_error_limit`, then it pauses for the period specified in `smtpd_error_sleep_time`.

- Finally, if the error count is greater than or equal to `smtpd_hard_error_limit`, then the SMTP daemon disconnects the connection.

Listing 7-28 shows the Postfix `smtpd` error-rate controls I generally use, but you would be best served to experiment with different combinations. Be careful of not setting your error limits too low and setting your `smtpd_error_sleep_time` too high in case you slow your system to a halt over minor errors.

Listing 7-28. *Error-Rate Controls in Postfix*

```
smtpd_error_sleep_time = 10
smtpd_soft_error_limit = 10
smtpd_hard_error_limit = 20
```

Recent snapshots of Postfix have included some additional rate-control options. This has consisted of an anvil server that allows Postfix to track connection totals from particular clients. When this is rolled into the main Postfix release, you should be able to introduce client-based limits for simultaneous connections both in terms of number of connections and numbers of connections per time period. If you need this sort of functionality now, then I recommend you look at the snapshots of Postfix—though I stress that they are experimental, and I do not recommend running a production system on one.

Table 7-6. *Resource-Control Settings to Stop DoS and DDoS Attacks in Postfix*

Directive	Default	Description
message_size_limit	10240000	Controls max size in bytes of a Postfix queue file
queue_minfree	No restriction	Controls number of free bytes required in the queue file system to allow incoming mail delivery

The first option controls the size in bytes of any Postfix message queue and therefore any incoming message. You can set this to the limit that bests suits your environment and the policies of your organization. I recommend that you note that SMTP is a mail transfer protocol, *not* a file transfer protocol. If your users need to send huge files, you should encourage them, if not force them, to seek other means and not to resort to e-mail.

The next option is the free space in bytes required in the file system in which your mail queue is contained in order to allow Postfix to accept incoming mail deliveries. I recommend you set this to a multiple of message_size_limit to ensure a single big message does not halt your mail delivery.

You can look other variables to further fine-tune your environment. You can see these at http://www.postfix.org/rate.html and http://www.postfix.org/resource.html.

Obviously, you need to reload Postfix for any changes you have made here to take effect.

Relaying, Spam, and Viruses

Spam, also known as unsolicited commercial e-mail (UCE) or unsolicited bulk e-mail (UBE), and viruses are the major banes of any system administrator's life. The prevalence of both and the scope for potential disaster for your network and users if an infected or spyware e-mail is opened by an unsuspecting user means that anyone who addresses security-hardening issues should also address spam and viruses as threats in their own right.

So I will explain a bit about open relaying and how to ensure you are not an open relay and then launch into a breakdown of some MTA-based methods of significantly reducing the volume of spam that hits your servers. I will also cover adding antivirus scanners to both Sendmail and Postfix.

Relaying

Relaying is the act of an MTA accepting a message from an e-mail client and forwarding that message onto its final destination. Now that sounds like a perfectly reasonable thing for an MTA to do—if not part of an MTA's core functionality. When I talk about relaying being an issue, what I am really talking about is open relaying.

A system can be described as an open relay if its SMTP server is willing to send mail where neither the sender nor the recipient is local to the machine or local trusted network(s). Also, if the SMTP server is willing to send mail if the sender appears to be a local user but is coming from a nontrusted source such as another network.

Caution You may think that if an e-mail is coming from `jim@yourdomain.com`, then the server `mail.yourdomain.com` should relay that message because `jim` is a local user. Unfortunately, "from" e-mail addresses are ludicrously easy to forge, and thus just because a message says it has come from `jim` does not guarantee it actually has.

Spammers use open relays to transmit mail to recipients who have blocked mail from known spammers and also as a means to send e-mail when their ISP blocks mass e-mail. They are also used by spam bots and mail-based viruses to transmit spam or spread themselves to new systems. Open relaying is bad. You will not make yourself or your systems popular if you maintain an open relay, and indeed you may end up blacklisted by a variety of third-party blocking lists or spam prevention systems, which means your user's ability to send e-mail will be seriously compromised.

So why not just not use relaying? Well, unfortunately, if you have remote users, whether they are roaming users or users who work from home, then they are often on networks your system does not recognize as local. They still need to send mail, but you also need some way of authenticating who they actually are. In Chapter 8 I will explain authentication using SMTP AUTH, SASL, and TLS to allow you to do this.

But I have some good news. Most recent releases of all major MTAs (including Microsoft Exchange 2000/2003) come with relaying disabled by default. Both Postfix (pretty much since its first release) and Sendmail (from version 8.9 onward) also both have open relaying disabled by default. This is yet another good reason to keep your software up-to-date. So, you have to explicitly go out of your way to enable open relaying! But, unfortunately, mail servers exist that have open relaying been turned on by accident or as the result of incorrect configuration. I will show you in the next section how to make sure you are not one of those sites.

Testing If You Are an Open Relay

So, you want to find out if you are an open relay? Well, you have a couple of ways to do this. One is to test your own mail server by trying to relay a message through it to another address from an untrusted network, such as a dial-up connection. If the message is sent, then your e-mail server is almost certainly acting as an open relay. If it is not sent and your MTA responds with a message saying relaying is denied, then your MTA is probably not relaying. This is, however, not a 100 percent foolproof method of detecting an open relay, though. Spammers use a lot of tricks to defeat your MTA's relaying restrictions.

The other method you can use to test for an open relay is to use one of the several free open relay test tools. Several are available.

- `http://www.abuse.net/relay.html`

- `http://www.ordb.org/submit/`

- `http://www.rbl.jp/svcheck.php`

If you are not able to use a Web-based test, several Telnet tests are available:

- relay-test.mail-abuse.org

- www.relaycheck.com

- rt.njabl.org 2500

You can access these via Telnet from your command line. Finally, you can download a variety of scripts to do your testing.

- http://www.cymru.com/Tools/mtaprobe.exp (Expect)

- http://www.monkeys.com/mrt/ (Perl)

- http://sorbs.sourceforge.net (Checks incoming servers for open relaying)

Try to test your MTA against a few different test tools. I recommend scheduling periodic testing of your system or including a test of relaying after making configuration changes related to relaying on your MTA.

Relaying in Sendmail

By default, from version 8.9 Sendmail does not allow the relaying of SMTP messages. To confirm this, you can check your sendmail.cf file for the contents of Listing 7-29.

Listing 7-29. *Restricting Relaying in Sendmail*

```
FR-o /etc/mail/relay-domains
```

This forces Sendmail to accept relaying only from the domains listed in the relay-domains file. You can add hosts, domains, IP addresses, and subnets to this file. Listing 7-30 shows you the content of my relay-domains file.

Listing 7-30. *Sendmail* relay-domains *File*

```
yourdomain.com
192.168.0
kitten.anotherdomain.com
```

Listing 7-30 allows relaying from the domain yourdomain.com, the network 192.168.0.0/28, and the host kitten.anotherdomain.com. I recommend you use the relay-domains file for the networks and domains that are local to your system. This is because you need to restart Sendmail to update this file, so you want to make sure it is relatively static. If you want to frequently change your relaying settings, then I recommend you use the access database file. I will discuss how to handle relaying with the access database a little later.

You can further modify the behavior of the relay-domains file (and any RELAY options you specify in your access database also) by adding some options to the sendmail.mc file. Table 7-7 lists those options. I will take you through all these features.

Table 7-7. *Sendmail Relay-Related Configuration Settings*

Option	Description
FEATURE(relay_hosts_only)	Allows relaying from only hosts listed in the relay-domains file
FEATURE(relay_entire_domain)	Allows relaying from any host of all the domains listed in the relay-domains file
FEATURE(relay_based_on_MX)	Allows relaying for any domain that has your host as a mail exchange record

The first feature, relay_hosts_only, changes the behavior of the relay-domains file. By default the relay-domains file allows relaying from *any* host from a domain listed in that file. By adding this feature you must specify each host in that domain that is allowed to relay e-mail. The relay_entire_domain feature does the opposite of the relay_hosts_only and allows relaying from all hosts listed in a domain in the relays-domains file. This is the same as the default behavior for Sendmail. The last option allows you to enable relaying for any domain that is directed at your host; in other words, if the domain anotherdomain.com has a Mail Exchange Record (MX) record of puppy.yourdomain.com, which is your Sendmail host, then relaying for anotherdomain.com will be allowed on that host.

You can also specify relaying using an access database file. The *access db* feature of Sendmail provides for the support for the access database. This feature allows you to maintain a central database that contains a number of rules that tell Sendmail to allow certain functions(for example, relaying), if the criteria in those rules are met. First you need to ensure the *access db* feature is enabled in Sendmail. Look for the following line in your sendmail.mc file:

```
FEATURE(`access_db',`hash -T<TMPF> -o /etc/mail/access.db')
```

■**Tip** This FEATURE is for a hash database and is correct for the Sendmail version 8.12 I am using. If you are using 8.11 or earlier, then the feature would be FEATURE(`access_db',`hash /etc/mail/access.db'). You can see how to enable other database formats in the Sendmail op manual.

If it is not present, add it and re-create sendmail.cf. You may already have an access database located in your /etc/mail directory. This file is created using the Sendmail makemap command, which takes an input of a text file, which I have called access, and creates a map file in a variety of database formats. I have chosen a hash database, but you could use any of one the other database formats. Listing 7-31 shows how this is done.

Listing 7-31. *Creating Your* access.db *File*

```
puppy# makemap hash access.db < access
```

As with your relay-domains file hosts, domains, IP addresses, and subnets can be listed. You list these on the left side of the entry, and you list the required relay response on the right side, separated by whitespace or a tab. Listing 7-32 shows a few examples of *access db*–based relaying.

Listing 7-32. access db *Relaying Sendmail*

```
yourdomain.com        RELAY
evilspamdomain.com        REJECT
anotherevilspammer.com        DISCARD
athirdevilspammer.com        554 Go away you spamming scumbag
```

As you can see, you can have four possible responses. The first is to RELAY the message; the second is to REJECT and refuse connections from this domain; the next is DISCARD, which accepts the message but discards it without processing (the sender will believe it has been received); and the last option is a customized error response. In Listing 7-32 I have used a permanent error code of 554, which is the SMTP error code for transaction failed together with a message indicating how you feel about spammers attempting to relay through your Sendmail server.

I will also cover using the *access db* as part of the "Antispam" section later in this chapter and with SMTP AUTH in Chapter 8.

Relaying in Postfix

Postfix has never allowed the open relaying of e-mail. If you want to change how relaying is handled or enable some form of relaying, you can control this using settings in the main.cf file. The major setting for this is the relay_domains option in the main.cf file. This option, relay_domains, is commented out and disabled by default.

So, will Postfix relay anything by default? Yes, it will, but it allows e-mail to be relayed only from trusted clients. It determines trusted clients to be any user with an IP address that is on the $mynetworks variable list. The $mynetworks option looks like this:

```
mynetworks = 192.168.0.0/28, 127.0.0.0/8
```

This allows relaying for localhost and any users in the local 192.168.0.0/28 subnet.

If you want to enable relaying for some domains or hosts, then you can enable the relay_domains option and add then a comma-separated list of hosts, domains, files, or Postfix lookup tables. Listing 7-33 shows how to set this option.

Listing 7-33. *Postfix's* relay_domains *Option*

```
relay_domains = anotherdomain.com, kitten.yetanotherdomain.com
```

This allows relaying from the trusted clients defined in the $mynetworks variable and from any hosts in the anotherdomain.com domain and the kitten.yetanotherdomain.com host. You can also specify files and lookup tables (created with the postmap command) in this list. If you do not specify any domains of your own when you enable relay_domains, then you will see that Postfix has it set to the variable $mydestination, which would allow relaying only from those hosts and domains specified in the $mydestination variable. Your $mydestination variable will probably contain something like this:

```
mydestination = $myhostname, localhost.$mydomain, $mydomain
```

This would again allow relaying only from the localhost and the local domain picked up by the variable $mydomain.

Postfix also offers control of relaying through the smtpd_recipient_restrictions list. Listing 7-34 shows a typical list.

Listing 7-34. smtpd_recipient_restrictions *in Postfix to Control Relaying*

```
smtpd_recipient_restrictions =
permit_sasl_authenticated,
permit_mynetworks,
check_client_access hash:/etc/postfix/pop-before-smtp,
reject_unauth_destination
```

I will show you how to use of this restriction list in a bit more detail in the "Antispam" section, but Listing 7-34 will allow relaying from any SASL-authenticated (see the discussion of SMTP AUTH in Chapter 8) users, any users who are in the networks defined in the $mynetworks variable, and any users who are in an access map called pop-before-smtpd. It then ends with reject_unauth_destination, which rejects any mail that is not for a relay_domains entry or the local machine. You should always have the reject_unauth_destination option in the smtpd_recipient_restrictions statement. If you fail to have this statement in the restriction list, then Postfix will not function.

Antispam

In this section I will show you the best methods of configuring your MTA to filter as much spam as possible. This section will use the resources of your MTA only. I will not cover adding third-party content filtering software. Though personally I strongly recommend you also investigate the variety of third-party tools available to defeat spam. I will especially highlight the SpamAssassin product available for free and as open source from http://www.spamassassin.org. It is a powerful antispam tool that utilizes Bayesian statistical filtering to help identify tricky spam. (It can also be integrated with tools such as Vipul's Razor and DCC.) It is well maintained, is regularly updated, has an extensive user base, and has good support resources. Most important, it is easy to integrate into both Sendmail and Postfix at a variety of points in the mail delivery process. Commercial products are also available from companies such as GFI (http://www.gfi.com) and Trend Micro (http://www.trendmicro.com) that you can use for the same purpose.

Antispam Settings for Sendmail

Sendmail does not provide a lot of antispam functionality that is easily and simply enabled. It does allow some filtering using the *access db* feature and allows you to enable one or more real-time blackhole lists (RBLs). Most additional spam filtering requires writing rule sets or integrating a product such as SpamAssassin into Sendmail using milter or via procmail.

I will now cover the uses for the *access db* as part of your antispam configuration. I will also cover enabling some RBLs in Sendmail. Finally, I will cover some header checking to reject spam using rule sets. I will not show you how to integrate third-party antispam tools into Sendmail, but a large volume of material is available on the Web that should point you in the right direction to do this.

Using Your access db for Antispam

One of the key features you can enable for Sendmail to process spam is to control the messages based on the connection, MAIL FROM, RCPT TO, or envelope information via an *access db*. I discussed creating an access database in earlier. I also want to enable another two options to expand the functionality of the *access db* feature. Add the following lines to your sendmail.mc file:

```
FEATURE(`blacklist_recipients')
FEATURE(`compat_check')
```

The blacklist_recipients feature allows you to block e-mail directed to specific users on your site. The compat_check feature allows you to create access controls based on envelope-sender and envelope-recipient pairs. Listing 7-35 shows some potential *access db* entries.

Listing 7-35. *Using an* access db *to Control Spam in Sendmail*

```
spamdomain.com      REJECT
203.54.58      REJECT
222.154.19.203      REJECT
Connect:203.43.12.1      REJECT
From:spammer@evildomain.com      DISCARD
To:offers@      ERROR:"550 Go away spammer"
Compat:spammer@dodgydomain.com<@>gooduser@yourdomain.com ERROR:550 ➡
Your dodgy email rejected
From:notaspammer@yetanotherdomain.com      OK
```

I will now go through each entry and explain what is does. The first three lines indicate that Sendmail will reject any message from the domain spamdomain.com, from hosts 203.54.58.0 to 203.54.58.255, and from the host 222.154.19.203. You can gradually build up this list by identifying the senders of spam e-mails and adding them to the database.

The next line blocks connections from the IP address 203.43.12.1. This stops known spam IP addresses from even connecting to your Sendmail server. The next two lines block MAIL FROM and RCPT TO fields. The From: line blocks any e-mail from spammer@evildomain.com, and the To: line blocks any mail addressed to the address offers at any of your local, virtual, or relay domains. (This is indicated by the use of the @ symbol without anything to the right of it.) This line also has a custom rejection error code and message. The remote SMTP server would log the error 550 (a permanent error) and the message "Go away spammer."

The next line uses the compat_check function and matches a sender and recipient pair of addresses. In this case, any e-mail from spammer@dodgydomain.com to gooduser@yourdomain.com will be rejected with the error message "550 Your dodgy email rejected." You can also DISCARD or use the option TEMP: to send a temporary error (you need to add the appropriate 4*xx* error code and message after the colon) rather than rejecting the message with a permanent error.

The last line allows you to whitelist particular addresses, hosts, or domains from being subject to antispam rules. Use this sparingly on sources that you are sure are not spam.

■**Tip** Do not forget to re-create your *access db* file after you have changed it using the makemap command.

When your Sendmail rejects an e-mail because it hits a REJECT statement in your access database, then it sends a standard error response.

```
550 5.7.1 Access Denied
```

You may want to customize this response for your site. You can do this by adding the following line to your sendmail.mc configuration:

```
define(`confREJECT_MSG', `550 Your email has been rejected. See
http://www.yourdomain.com/rejected_email.html')
```

Replace the message with a message of your choice.

Sendmail and RBLs

Sendmail also offers the capability of using RBLs (see the "Blacklists" sidebar) to help filter your incoming e-mail. Sendmail is by default hard-coded to use the RBL list at mail-abuse.org. You can enable this by adding the following line to your sendmail.mc file:

```
FEATURE(dnsbl)
```

You can also add your own RBLs to Sendmail by adding dnsbl feature lines. The next line shows how to add support for the sbl.spamhaus.org RBL to Sendmail:

```
FEATURE(dnsbl,`sbl.spamhaus.org',`"550 Mail rejected by sbl.spamhaus.org"',`t')
```

The feature arguments include the address of the RBL you want to add to Sendmail and an optional error message specifically for that RBL rejection. By adding t as the third argument, you tell Sendmail that in the event of being unable to lookup an RBL it returns a temporary error message and tells the sending site to defer the e-mail. This ensures that a temporary failure at the RBL will not mean a potential spam mail gets past. However, a long outage at an RBL could result in delays in sending mail. Care is needed when setting this argument.

An enhanced version of dnsbl is called enhdnsbl. One of the principal differences is the addition of a further argument, which is the required response code(s) from the RBL. The next line shows an enhanced RBL feature:

```
FEATURE(enhdnsbl,`sbl.spamhaus.org',`"550 Mail from" $&{client_addr} ➥
"rejected by sbl.spamhaus.org"',`t',`127.0.0.2.')
```

■**Note** $&{client_addr} is a macro that inserts the client address from which the message was sent.

The last option present, 127.0.0.2. (note the trailing dot, which you need that for the syntax to be correct), is the response code that Sendmail expects from the RBL in order to reject an e-mail. You can specify more than one response by adding response codes. You can also use rule operators to make up specific response codes. The next two lines show both these capabilities:

```
FEATURE(enhdnsbl,`sbl.spamhaus.org',`"550 Mail from" $&{client_addr} ➥
"rejected by sbl.spamhaus.org"',`t',`127.0.0.2.', `127.0.0.3.', `127.0.0.4.')
FEATURE(enhdnsbl,`bl.spamcop.net',`"550 Mail from" $&{client_addr} ➥
"rejected by bl.spamcop.net"',`t',`127.0.0.$-.')
```

You can see in the first line that the RBL feature will reject e-mail as spam when it receives the response 127.0.0.2., 127.0.0.3., or 127.0.0.4. from the RBL. In the second option I have used the rule operator, $-, which tells the feature to reject any e-mail as spam when the response code matches 127.0.0.*anynumber*. You could also use a class to specify all the possible response codes you want to match against.

Sendmail Header Checks

Using header checks allows you to filter e-mail using Sendmail rule sets. You can filter using normal text or via a regular expression. I will show you how to filter using both methods, focusing on the checking the content of the Subject: line. Using rule sets in Sendmail is a complicated undertaking. I will introduce you to the basics as they relate to my particular requirements to do antispam filtering. I recommend you do further reading on the topic to fully understand the scope and usage of these rule sets.

The first thing to consider is that your rule sets are going to be quite long. You need a lot of code to do filtering using rule sets, and as you add additional items to be checked, this will increase the content of your rule sets. Rather than clutter your sendmail.mc file with a large number of rule sets, I recommend you use the include function to include additional mc files. The next line shows how to include an additional file to your sendmail.mc file:

```
include(`/etc/mail/subject_rulesets.mc')
```

Here I have added another mc file called subject_rulesets.mc located in the /etc/mail directory. I usually divide my different rule sets into separate files and include each of them individually. I have separate files for To:, From:, and other major header fields. This keeps my sendmail.mc file neat and reduces the risk of confusion and errors.

So how do you filter on a particular subject? Listing 7-36 shows header checking, and I will break it down to explain it.

Listing 7-36. *Sample Subject Header Check in Sendmail*

```
HSubject:       $>Check_Subject_Spam

D{SMsg}This email has been rejected as spam
D{Subj001}Test our Internet pharmacy
D{Subj002}Low Interest Rate

SCheck_Subject_Spam
R${Subj001} $*        $#error $: 550 ${SMsg}
RRe: ${Subj001} $*        $#error $: 550 ${SMsg}
R${Subj002} $*        $#error $: 550 ${SMsg}
RRe: ${Subj002} $*        $#error $: 550 ${SMsg}
```

The first line declares the header. It is structured like this:

```
Hheaderfield: $>ruleset
```

where *headerfield:* and *ruleset* are replaced with the relevant header you want to act on; in this case in Listing 7-36 I am using the Subject: header and the name of the rule set that I want to use to process this header field. (You should not include spaces or special characters in your rule set name.) Overall, the line sends the content of the header field, `Subject:`, into the rule set `Check_Subject_Spam` to be processed for matches.

■Tip If you want to include any RFC 2822 comments in the data outputted from the `Subject:` field, then replace the `$>` with `$>+` in the H line.

The next lines declare configuration file macros. The macros are structured like this:

```
D{macroname}macro content
```

The first line declares a macro called `SMsg` with the content of "This email has been rejected as spam." I will use this macro to provide a message that Sendmail will send to the sending SMTP server if the e-mail is rejected because of the `Subject:` content. The next two lines are subject lines that I am testing for in my incoming mail. I have named the first macro `Subj001` and the second `Subj002`. It is important to note that when you test against the subject that it is not a regular expression. The test will try to match the *exact* content of the `Subj001` macro. So the subject "Test our Internet Pharmacy" will be picked up by the rule set, but the subject "Test our Internet Pharmacy!!!" will not be matched. This limits the functionality of this sort of rule set.

The next line declares the start of the particular rule set. The name after the `S` must match the rule set you specified in the `H` line. Following this `S` line are `R` lines that are the actual rules being used. The `R` lines are divided into three sections.

```
RLHS      RHS       comment
```

The `R` line starts the rule. Then you will see the left-and side (LHS) of the rule, the right-hand side (RHS) of the rule, and an optional comment. The LHS of the rule does not need to be separated from the `R` line. But the LHS, RHS, and comments should all be separated by a tab character; otherwise, Sendmail will fail to parse the rule. (You cannot use space characters—the separator must be a tab).

In the case of the `Subject:` checking antispam rule, the LHS content is going to be the macro `${subj001}`. I tell the rule set that it is a macro by prefixing `$` to the front of the macro name (which is still enclosed in brackets). It is then followed by the rule operator `$*`, which is a wildcard operator that tries to match zero or more tokens (in the case the tokens being the content of the `Subject:` header field).

```
R${Subj001} $*       $#error $: 550 ${SMsg}
```

The RHS side starts with the operator `$#`, which indicates an action. When you are testing for a match on your headers, these rule sets can return two possible values: `$#error` and `$#discard`. The first response tells Sendmail to reject the message, and the second tells Sendmail to silently discard it. Following the action returned by the rule is the operator `$:`, which defines the default value to return. So if the `Subject:` field matches the `${subj001}` macro, then Sendmail generates an `$#error` and specifies the value to return to Sendmail, which in this case is: "550 This email has been rejected as spam," which is the content of the first macro I defined as `${SMsg}`.

The second line that matches against the macro `${subj001}` adds `Re:` in front of the macro to match any case where this subject appears with a reply appended to the subject. This pattern is repeated for the next macro `${subj002}` in Listing 7-36.

As you can only match against the exact text in a macro header checking, the previous example has some serious limitations. A small change or variation by a spammer or virus program in the subject line could mean the subject will slip through. To reduce this risk, I will show you how to use regexp maps to perform regular expression matches on your header fields, this time again focusing on the Subject: field. First, you need to check that Sendmail was compiled with regex database maps enabled. Type the following command to check this:

```
puppy# sendmail -bv -d0.4 root | grep 'MAP_REGEX'
```

If you see MAP_REGEX in the Compiled With: options listed, then your Sendmail is compiled with regex enabled.

```
Compiled with: DNSMAP LOG MAP_REGEX MATCHGECOS MILTER MIME7TO8 MIME8TO7
```

If not, then add the following line to your site.config.m4 file and recompile Sendmail using Build -c to enable regex map support:

```
APPENDDEF(`confMAPDEF', `-DMAP_REGEX')
```

Second, you can configure some regular expressions to test your incoming mail against. Listing 7-37 shows a sample regex header check.

Listing 7-37. *Sample Regex Header Check*

```
HSubject:        $>+check_regex
Kregex001 regex -f -a@MATCH ^(Joke|joke|Very.Funny|Great.joke)$

Scheck_regex
R$+     $: $(regex001 $1 $: <OK> $)
R<OK>   $@ OK
R$+     $#error $: 550 Spam rejected with a regular expression
```

As you can see from Listing 7-37, the code is pretty similar to that in Listing 7-36. The H line inputs the content of the Subject: field to the rule set. I have used the $>+ operator instead of the $> operator to capture RFC 822 comment fields in the subject lines. But the major difference is with the specification of a regular expression instead of a pattern.

The next line defines the regular expression. This line starts with a K (which is a configuration line used to match a symbolic name with a particular database map, in this case with a regex map). You define the name of the regex map, regex001, and then define its type, regex. The next item, the -f option, tells the regex map to treat any regular expression as case insensitive and match both uppercase and lowercase examples of the expression. The -a option returns the data @MATCH if the regular expression is matched. Next you have the regular expression itself, which matches any subjects including "Joke," "joke," "Very Funny," and "Great joke." Note the use of periods instead of spaces. You should replace all spaces with periods to ensure the regex functions correctly.

Next you have the actual rule set with its name declared by the S line. The rule set is slightly different in its syntax from Listing 7-37 but achieves the same end. The Subject: line is checked for one of the possible subjects; if it is not found, then the rule set returns OK to Sendmail. If it does match one of the subjects, then it rejects the message with the error "550 Spam rejected with a regular expression." You can create a variety of your own rules to address the requirements of your antispam configuration.

Finally, it is easy to test your new rules. Using the command in Listing 7-38, start Sendmail in Address Test Mode.

Listing 7-38. *Starting Sendmail in Address Test Mode*

```
puppy# sendmail -d21.4 -bt
```

■**Tip** If you want to test your regular expression rule sets, it is basically the same process; start sendmail as `sendmail -d38.2 -bt`, and your regex maps will be automatically initiated.

You will see > on the command line. Enter the name of your rule (for example, `Check_Subject_Spam`) and then the text you are checking for (for example, `Low Interest Rate`). Sendmail will test the rule using the text provided. If you are using Listing 7-36, you should see a response like this one:

```
> Check_Subject_Spam Low Interest Rate
Check_Subject_Sp    input: Low Interest Rate
rewritten as: $# error $: 550 This e-mail has been rejected as spam
Check_Subject_Sp returns: $# error $: 550 This e-mail has been rejected as spam
```

This indicates that the test has been successful; Sendmail has matched the subject and responded with the correct error response.

Antispam Settings for Postfix

The basic idea behind stopping spam with Postfix is to test the message against a variety of restrictions, checks, and filters. If a message successfully navigates through these, then there is a good chance it is not spam. These checks start with a collection of restrictions lists that allow you to block e-mail based on the content of `HELO`, `MAIL FROM`, `RCPT TO`, and other fields. Then you have the ability to specify header and body checks that use regular expressions to filter mail based on their subject or content. Finally, you can integrate tools such as SpamAssassin to provide external content filtering to Postfix. I will show you how to use restriction lists and header and body checks and then provide you with a configuration that should be a good starting point to block spam using Postfix. I will not cover integrating Postfix with third-party content-filtering tools. Quite a few HOWTOs and resources are available on the Postfix site and elsewhere that can explain this.

Postfix processes antispam restrictions, checks, and filters in a particular order. It is important to understand what that order is so as to both design the most efficient antispam structure and ensure you are correctly permitting and restricting the right things. It is no good placing a permit statement in a restriction if Postfix is already going to reject a message because of an earlier processed restriction. So Postfix first processes any restriction lists, then any header or body checks, and then in turn any content filters such as SpamAssassin or ClamAV.

Postfix Restriction List

This section will cover the restriction lists available in Postfix. Postfix also checks these restriction lists in a particular order. Table 7-8 lists all the possible restriction lists, what they do, and displays them in the order in which they are processed.

Table 7-8. *Processing Order of Postfix Restriction Lists*

Restriction	Description
smtpd_client_restrictions	Restrictions on sending e-mail based on the client
smtpd_helo_restrictions	Restrictions on sending e-mail based on the HELO identification string
smtpd_sender_restrictions	Restrictions in sending e-mail based on the sender
smtpd_recipient_restrictions	Restrictions in sending e-mail based on the recipient
smtpd_data_restrictions	Restrictions in sending e-mail based on the content of the SMTP DATA command

Listing 7-39 shows what a restriction list looks like.

Listing 7-39. *Sample Postfix Restriction List*

```
smtpd_recipient_restrictions =
reject_unknown_recipient_domain,
permit_mynetworks,
reject_unauth_destination,
check_sender_access hash:/etc/postfix/access,
permit
```

As you can see from Listing 7-39, each type of restriction is listed in a line after the option and should be separated by either a comma or whitespace. Listing 7-39 is checking the RCPT TO field against recipient data. It first uses reject_unknown_recipient_domain (which rejects if the domain does not have a valid A or MX record). Then it permits all e-mail if the client IP address is listed in $mynetworks. Then it rejects any mail not for the local machine or a domain contained in the relay_domains option using the reject_unauth_destination. (This restriction is mandatory in this restriction list to prevent open relaying.) Finally, it checks the contents of an access map and finally ends with a generic permit statement.

The last permit statement is one of several generic restrictions you can use to specify the default policy in a restriction option. The two simplest options are reject and permit. You also have the options to defer, which informs the client to try again later, and warn_if_reject, which logs a warning instead of rejecting. warn_if_reject is useful for testing new configurations without risking rejecting legitimate mail. You should end each restriction option with either a permit statement or a reject statement. It is not strictly necessary, but it is a neat way of making it clear what the default behavior of the restriction list is.

As you can also see from Listing 7-39, you can specify an access list in the form of a postmap-created map file (in this case, hash:/etc/postfix/access). All the restriction lists are able to check access maps. Listing 7-39 uses the check_sender_access restriction to check the MAIL FROM field. There are also client, HELO, and recipient access checks (check_client_access, check_helo_access, and so on). Listing 7-40 shows the contents of a typical map.

Listing 7-40. *Access Maps for Postfix Restriction Lists*

```
spammer@spamdomain.com     REJECT
anotherdomain.com     OK
morespam.com     DISCARD
confused.uncertain.com     DUNNO
uncertain.com     REJECT
```

The first line shows all e-mail from address spammer@spamdomain.com will be rejected. The second line says that domain anotherdomain.com is OK and should be permitted. The third line tells Postfix that all e-mail from domain morespam.com is to be discarded silently. (The sender will think the message is received.) The fourth line tells Postfix to ignore any messages from the host confused.uncertain.com and thus stop processing that restriction and skip to the next restriction if any. The DUNNO option is useful to provide exceptions to restriction. You can see in Listing 7-40 that messages from confused.uncertain.com would be ignored because they are specified as DUNNO but any other messages from the domain uncertain.com will be rejected.

■**Tip** You can also provide customized error code responses to rejections. Postfix allows you to specify the exact error code response to a remote system. For example, by using the relay_domains_reject_code option (which defaults to error code 554), you can override the error code response Postfix sends when a rejected request is processed. A variety of reject code options exist; you can see them at http://www.postfix.org/uce.html.

Postfix Header and Body Checks

I will now briefly discuss Postfix's header and body checks. These checks occur after your restrictions list checks and before any content filtering. These checks consist of map files that contain entries that are matched against either the headers or the body of e-mail messages. I recommend using the regular expression type of map file to do this, as it allows you do some powerful pattern matching. Listing 7-41 shows a portion of my header checks map.

■**Tip** Regular expression map files are *not* created with postmap. They are simply ASCII files. I use the extension .regexp to identify my files.

Listing 7-41. *Sample Postfix Header Checks Map*

```
/^Subject: Make Money Fast/     REJECT
/^Subject: Need a Home Loan? We Can Help!!/     REJECT
/^Subject: .*Important News On Aging/     REJECT This is a spam message
```

As you can see, I have used the regular expressions (enclosed in / and /) to match a few spam subjects and reject them. In the header checks file, you can test any header that is contained in the e-mail (in Listing 7-41 I have used Subject:), but you could any header field. For body checks it is any text that appears in the body of the message.

If a match occurs, Postfix performs the action specified next to that regular expression. This includes rejecting the message (and optionally adding some text with the rejection as you can in the last line of Listing 7-41); ignoring the message using the IGNORE option, which deletes the matched header from the message; and discarding the message using the DISCARD option. For simplicities sake, I recommend you use header and body checks to REJECT messages only.

You can define both header and body checks to Postfix. Listing 7-42 shows how to define them in your main.cf file.

Listing 7-42. *Defining Header and Body Checks in Postfix*

```
header_checks = regexp:/etc/postfix/header_checks.regexp
body_checks = regexp:/etc/postfix/header_checks.regexp
```

■**Tip** The site at http://www.hispalinux.es/~data/postfix/ contains a good collection of sample header and body checks you can use with Postfix.

A Postfix Antispam Configuration

Now I will try to provide you with a solid basic configuration to defeat spam. I will initially start with some basic options that set the scene for your antispam configuration. Table 7-9 lists these base options and explains their use. I will describe their recommended settings after the table.

■**Note** Many of the options in Table 7-9 complement and interact with the options detailed in the earlier "Limiting DoS Attacks with Postfix" section, and you should implement them in conjunction with those options. Additionally, you should be at least also disabling the VRFY command, as mentioned earlier in this chapter.

Then I will move onto sender, recipient, and data-specific restrictions. I will not the use of header or body checks and content filters such as SpamAssassin.

■**Tip** All the settings I am working with here are located in the main.cf file. You will also need to issue a postfix reload in order for any changes you make to take effect.

Table 7-9. *Basic Antispam Options in Postfix*

Option	Description
`allow_untrusted_routing`	Controls whether sender specified routing will be honored
`smtpd_helo_required`	Specifies whether a `HELO` command is required at the start of an SMTP transaction
`smtpd_delay_reject`	Rejects immediately and does not wait for the `RCPT TO` command
`strict_rfc821_envelopes`	Specifies whether strict RFC 821 rules are applied to `MAIL FROM` and `RCPT TO` addresses

The first option, `allow_untrusted_routing`, tells Postfix whether to trust routing provided by senders, such as `bill%evilspam.com@puppy.yourdomain.com`. You should set this to `no` to prevent people from attempting to spoof your mail server.

The second option, `smtpd_helo_required`, tells Postfix that any SMTP clients must provide a `HELO` (or an `EHLO`) statement at the start of the session or Postfix will not process that session. This is set to `no` by default. This setting addresses the variety of spam bots and clients that do not behave in an RFC-compliant manner and therefore do not send a `HELO` or `EHLO` statement to Postfix. The only problem with enabling this is that there are also a lot of broken clients and badly built e-mail packages that also do not send `HELO` or `EHLO` statements when sending e-mail. This is a judgment call from a setup perspective—I suggest you test it, and see the results. Just remember that if this is set to `no`, then you cannot use the `smtpd_helo_restrictions` option either, because obviously you need a `HELO` before you can test against it.

The third option, `smtpd_delay_reject`, is set to `yes` by default. This tells Postfix to wait until it receives the `RCPT TO` command before processing any rejections. You can set this to `no` to reject mail messages immediately upon determining they are to be rejected. I recommend you do not do this, because there is a risk that some broken clients will suffer unexpected results if you reject before the `RCPT TO` command.

The last option controls whether Postfix will insist that any envelopes are strictly RFC 821 compliant. In reality this means the `MAIL FROM` and `RCPT TO` addresses need to be enclosed in `<>` and not contain any comments or phrases. This should be a good thing. E-mail clients should behave in an RFC-compliant manner. Unfortunately, a number of clients do not deliver with RFC-compliant envelopes. Like the previous three options in this section, this requires some testing before you implement it. I recommend, though, that you turn it on, as I have found it catches more spam than it incorrectly rejects.

Now I will add some restriction lists. I will add two of the restriction lists: `smtpd_recipient_restrictions` and `smtpd_data_restrictions`. Listing 7-43 shows the anti-spam configuration on my Postfix server. I will take you through how it works after the listing.

Listing 7-43. *A Basic Antispam Configuration for Postfix*

```
allow_untrusted_routing = no
smtpd_helo_required = yes
smtpd_delay_reject = yes
strict_rfc821_envelopes = yes
disable_vrfy_command = yes
```

```
smtpd_recipient_restrictions  =
permit_mynetworks,
permit_sasl_authenticated,
reject_unauth_destination,
reject_non_fqdn_sender,
reject_non_fqdn_recipient,
reject_unknown_sender_domain,
reject_unknown_recipient_domain,
reject_invalid_hostname,
reject_unknown_hostname,
reject_multi_recipient_bounce,
reject_rbl_client bl.spamcop.net,
reject_rbl_client sbl.spamhaus.org,
reject_rbl_client relays.ordb.org,
reject_rbl_client opm.blitzed.org,
reject_rhsbl_client bogusmx.rfc-ignorant.org,
reject_rhsbl_client dsn.rfc-ignorant.org,
reject_rhsbl_sender bogusmx.rfc-ignorant.org,
reject_rhsbl_sender dsn.rfc-ignorant.org,
permit

smtpd_data_restrictions =
reject_unauth_pipelining,
permit
```

I have already discussed the first few options earlier, so I will jump straight into the smtpd_recipient_restrictions list. Table 7-10 shows all the restrictions and permissions I have specified here. I will discuss them in more detail after the table together with the RBL-based and RHSBL-based rejections.

Table 7-10. *Restrictions and Permissions in Postfix*

Restriction/Permission	Description
reject_invalid_hostname	Rejects the request when the EHLO or HELO hostname is badly formed
reject_unknown_hostname	Rejects the request when the EHLO or HELO hostname has no A or MX record
reject_non_fqdn_sender	Rejects the request when the MAIL FROM is not a FQDN
reject_non_fqdn_recipient	Rejects the request when the RCPT TO is not a FQDN
reject_unknown_sender_domain	Rejects the request when the sender domain has no A or MX record
reject_unknown_recipient_domain	Rejects the request when the recipient domain has no A or MX record
reject_multi_recipient_bounce	Rejects bounce messages with multiple recipients
reject_unauth_destination	Rejects the message unless the destination is contained in relay_domains or $mydestination
permit_mynetworks	Permits messages from any network defined in $mynetworks
permit_sasl_authenticated	Permits messages from SASL-authenticated users

BLACKLISTS

RBLs and right-hand side blacklist (RHSBLs) are lists of IP addresses (for RBLs) and domain names (for RHS-BLs) that have been marked as being used by spammers, open relays, or systems that are nonconformant to RFC. They could also include other IP addresses or domains that have been marked according to additional criteria or submitted by users, ISPs, or system administrators.

This is the key weakness of blacklists—the data they contain is not always accurate, and you could have e-mail rejected on the basis on incorrect blacklisting. This is especially common with dynamically assigned IP addresses that are often assigned to residential ADSL and cable customers. A spammer uses an address, and it is added to a blacklist and then assigned to someone else. But the address is not removed from the blacklist, and any e-mail sent from the address that is checked against that blacklist is marked as spam.

Another issue with blacklists is that you need to trust the people running the blacklist. You are trusting that a third party is being both dutiful and accurate about the IP addresses and domains being collecting. As anyone who has tried to remove an IP address or domain from a blacklist can tell you, that trust can some-times be misplaced. Some blacklists do not operate in a professional or, what can be worse, a prompt man-ner. This can seriously inconvenience to you and your users if a large volume of false positives are generated because of blacklisting.

If you choose to enable RBLs and RHSBLs, then you should carefully review the blacklists you are select-ing. Check out the blacklist's home page for the frequency of updates and determine its responsiveness by ask-ing questions and investigating it. Many of the MTA mailing lists, such as the Sendmail and Postfix user mailing lists, have people asking about the functionality and stability of various blacklists, so the archives should reveal some further information.

In Listing 7-43 you can see a variety of restriction and permission options. Some of them reject based on information in the HELO/EHLO identification string; others check MAIL FROM or RCPT TO. You may think the HELO/EHLO and MAIL FROM restrictions would have to be checked in the smtpd_helo_restrictions and the smtpd_sender_restrictions lists. But because smtpd_delay_reject is set to yes, Postfix delays until the RCPT TO command before rejecting, which means you can combine a variety of restrictions or permissions from other restriction lists in the smtpd_recipient_restrictions list. This is a much cleaner and more efficient way of doing this and means your antispam configuration is easy to understand and simple to manage.

The first step in the smtpd_recipient_restrictions list is to allow through anything in $mynetworks. It is a waste of processor cycles to test mail from your local network. Then you permit through mail from SASL authenticated users. Next and very importantly you add the reject_unath_destination statement. This statement means that e-mail is rejected from unauthorized locations and ensures your Postfix server is not an open relay.

Next is a series of rejections based on the contents of a variety of fields, including the HELO/EHLO, MAIL FROM, and RCPT TO fields and queries based on the DNS status of senders, recipients, domains, and hosts. Table 7-10 explains all these rejections. Then you have a list of RBLs and RHSBLs, which Postfix checks (see the "Blacklists" sidebar). Finally, you end the restriction list with a permit statement.

Finally, the smtpd_data_restrictions list contains the statement reject_unauth_pipelining. This final restriction list rejects requests from clients that send SMTP commands in a pipeline before knowing whether Postfix supports pipelining. The main offenders in this sort of behavior are usually spam bots.

The contents of Listing 7-43 should provide you with a good basis for your antispam configuration. You can further add access maps customized to your own environment, build a collection of header and body checks, and add the functionality of a SpamAssassin-type product. Also, your antispam configuration should never stay static. Spammers are always adapting and advancing their techniques for defeating antispam measures, so you need to keep updating your own configuration.

Antivirus Scanning Your E-mail Server

A *virus* is loosely defined as a piece of programming or code that is installed on your computer without your knowledge and that has some effect, usually malicious, on your system or data. Viruses are usually coded to replicate themselves via a variety of means. Recently a large spate of virus attacks has occurred via e-mail. An e-mail is sent to the user with an alluring message and an attachment that contains the virus. After a user has executed the script, piece of code, or executable attached to an e-mail, then their system has been infected and the virus spawns an SMTP server and e-mails itself to all the addresses it can find on that system.[5]

This is just one example of virus infection via e-mail. So, protecting your users against e-mail-borne viruses has become absolutely critical. I will take you through installing and configuring an antivirus scanner for your Linux system and integrating it with your MTA. I will cover integration with both Sendmail and Postfix.

Installing ClamAV

I will cover integrating Sendmail and Postfix with an open-source virus-scanning engine. I have chosen to cover ClamAV as that virus-scanning engine. I have chosen ClamAV for a couple of reasons. The first is that it is freely available and well maintained. The second is that its virus definitions are updated as frequently as the commercially available packages.

You can get ClamAV from http://prdownloads.sourceforge.net/clamav. Download the latest stable version, and unpack the archive (I used version 0.70 for this explanation). The first step you need is to create a clamav user and group. Enter the following:

```
puppy# groupadd clamav
puppy# useradd -g clamav -s /sbin/nologin -M clamav
```

I have created a group clamav and a user clamav who cannot login, has no home directory, and belongs to the clamav group. I will also create a directory to hold some ClamAV files. I usually create this under /var/run. I have used clamav as the directory name and set it to be owned by the user clamav and the group clamav. Enter the following:

```
puppy# mkdir /var/run/clamav
puppy# chown clamav:clamav /var/run/clamav
```

Now you need to configure ClamAV. A number of potentially useful configure options are available, but I will cover only a couple. The first is --prefix; by default ClamAV is installed under /usr/local. If you want to move it elsewhere, specify an alternative prefix. A little later I will show how to integrate ClamAV with Sendmail using milter, so if you are using Sendmail, then you want to enable milter support. For this, use the option --enable-milter.

---

5. Examples of this sort of virus include the W32.Beagle, W32.Netsky, W32.Chir worms, as well as a number of others.

So, to install ClamAV, `configure` it, `make`, and then `make install` it. Listing 7-44 shows these commands for a ClamAV installation, which I intend to integrate with Sendmail using `milter`.

Listing 7-44. *Installing ClamAV*

```
puppy# ./configure --enable-milter
puppy# make && make install
```

ClamAV comes with three major components. First, the `clamscan` tool is a command-line virus scanner. Second, the `clamd` daemon has two methods of receiving inputs; the first is via a local socket, and the second is by listening on a particular TCP IP address and port and waiting for items to scan.

Tip You can run `clamd` in only one mode of operation—either local socket or TCP daemon.

Third, the `clamav-milter` program uses the Milter API to provide Sendmail integration. I will cover `clamav-milter` in the next section. Finally, the `freshclam` daemon keeps ClamAV's virus database up-to-date. I will focus on the `clamd` daemon only as it is the easiest and most efficient way for you to integrate a virus scanner into the respective MTAs.

By default all of the binaries I will use are installed into `/usr/local/sbin`, and the first file I will change, ClamAV's configuration file `clamav.conf`, is located in `/usr/local/etc`. Listing 7-45 shows the working `clamav.conf` file. I will take you through all the configuration options you need to configure `clamd`.

Listing 7-45. *The* `clamav.conf` *File*

```
#Example
LogFile /var/log/clamd.log
LogSyslog
LogVerbose
PidFile /var/run/clamav/clamd.pid
#LocalSocket /var/run/clamav/clamd.sock
#FixStaleSocket
#TCPAddr 127.0.0.1
#TCPSocket 3310
User runasuser
ScanMail
ScanArchive
ScanRAR
StreamSaveToDisk
StreamMaxLength 10M
ArchiveMaxFileSize 10M
ArchiveMaxRecursion 5
ArchiveMaxFiles 1000
ArchiveMaxCompressionRatio 200
```

The first option you need to address is to comment out or delete the line labeled Example in your clamav.conf configuration file. Otherwise, ClamAV will ignore the configuration file. Then configure some logging for clamd. Enable LogFile */path/to/your/log/file*; in Listing 7-45 I have used /var/log/clamd.log. If you want to log to syslog, then also enable the line LogSyslog. I also usually enable verbose logging using the line LogVerbose (at least initially while I am getting clamd running). You can always disable it later. I also define the location of a PID[6] file to store the clamd process ID. I have located the PID in the directory I created earlier /var/run/clamav.

Now you come to the first of the possible ways you can configure clamd—as a local socket that receives input and processes them for viruses and then returns them to the inputting program. I will use this method to integrate with Sendmail, so if you are using Sendmail, then choose local socket operation. To use local socket clamd, enable these lines:

```
LocalSocket /var/run/clamav/clamd.sock
FixStaleSocket
```

This creates a local socket in the specified directory. If you want, you can replace /var/run/clamav/clamd.sock with the location where you want to place the clamd local socket. For the sake of consistency, I place it in the /var/run/clamav directory. The option FixStaleSocket ensures clamd cleans up any sockets remaining from an improper shutdown or failure before trying to start a new socket.

The alternative method of configuring clamd is as a TCP daemon. I will use this method to integrate ClamAV with Postfix, so if you are using Postfix, choose TCP daemon operation. To use clamd as a TCP daemon, enable these lines:

```
TCPAddr 127.0.0.1
TCPSocket 3310
```

This binds clamd to localhost on the TCP port 3310. Or you can choose to bind it to another port. By binding it to localhost, you are ensuring you can access the daemon only from the local machine.

The next option, User, tells clamd to run as a particular user. I recommend you specify the clamav user.

The remaining options control what sort of scanning ClamAV conducts. Table 7-11 details all these options and their functions.

Table 7-11. *Additional ClamAV Configuration File Options*

Option	Description
ScanMail	Enables scanning of Microsoft Office document macros.
ScanOLE2	Enables mail scanning.
ScanArchive	Enable scanning of archives.
ScanRAR	Enable the built-in RAR unpacker.
StreamSaveToDisk	Saves the stream to disk before scan to allow archive scanning.
StreamMaxLength 10M	The maximum size of the stream (or message). This should be at least the size of your maximum mail message size. The default is 10MB.

6.   Process ID

Option	Description
ArchiveMaxFileSize 10M	The maximum size of archives files to be scanned. This should be set to at least the size of your maximum mail message size. The default is 10MB.
ArchiveMaxRecursion 5	With this option you may set the recursion level. The default is 5.
ArchiveMaxFiles 1000	Number of files to be scanned within archive. The default is 1000.
ArchiveMaxCompressionRatio 200	Marks potential archive bombs as viruses.
ArchiveDetectEncrypted	Marks encrypted archives as viruses.

These are all fairly self-explanatory; more details are available in the `clamav.conf` file that comes with ClamAV and the ClamAV documentation.

You have now configured `clamd`. You will want to start `clamd` automatically when your system starts (before you start your MTA). A variety of example `init` scripts are available in the ClamAV source distribution in the `contrib/init` directory, which you can use to create your own `init` script.

The last step in configuring ClamAV is to ensure your virus database is kept up-to-date. For this, you use the `freshclam` daemon. This is located in the `/usr/local/bin` directory by default. You can run it from the command line, run it via an `init` script, or run it from `cron` at scheduled intervals. You can also start it as a daemon in its own right—which is how I recommend you run it. It is controlled by a configuration file, `freshclam.conf`, which is located in `/usr/local/etc`. Listing 7-46 shows the `freshclam.conf` file.

Listing 7-46. *The* `freshclam.conf` *File*

```
#Example
DatabaseDirectory /var/lib/clamav
DatabaseOwner clamav
DatabaseMirror database.clamav.net
MaxAttempts 3
UpdateLogFile /var/log/freshclam.log
LogVerbose
NotifyClamd /usr/local/etc/clamav.conf
```

As with the `clamav.conf` file, you first need to delete or comment out the `Example` line. The next line marks the location of the ClamAV virus database. By default this should install to `/var/lib/clamav`. Override this only if you have changed the database's location. Next you specify the owner of the database, which is the user you created previously, `clamav`, and then the location of the download mirror for the ClamAV database. You should not need to change this. The `MaxAttempts` variable sets the maximum number of times `freshclam` should retry to download the virus database if it fails.

I have next specified a logfile located in `/var/log` and called `freshclam.log` to record the details of any update attempts. I initially enabled the option `LogVerbose` to test `freshclam`, but you can take this out once you are sure `freshclam` is working. The last option, `NotifyClamd`, tells the daemon about a new database being downloaded. Just point it to the location of your `clamav.conf` file; by default and here this is `/usr/local/etc/clamav.conf`.

I recommend you run freshclam as a daemon. Listing 7-47 shows the command line you use to start freshclam as a daemon.

Listing 7-47. *Starting* freshclam *As a Daemon*

```
puppy# /usr/local/bin/freshclam -d -c 24
```

The first option, -d, tells freshclam to go into daemon mode. The second option, -c, tells freshclam the frequency of its checks. In this case you have 24 times a day or once an hour. This is probably the most frequently you will need to update your virus database. Any more frequent updates could put an undue load on the database site.

If you want to start freshclam when your system boots, then sample init scripts are available in the ClamAV source distribution in the contrib/init directory.

Your ClamAV setup is now complete, and you can now proceed to integrate your antivirus scanner with your MTA.

Integrating ClamAV with Sendmail

I will use milter, which is the Mail Filtering API that has supported by Sendmail since version 8.10, to integrate ClamAV with Sendmail. This API communicates with Sendmail using sockets and is enabled by defining filters in your sendmail.mc file. The milter functionality comes with Sendmail by default but may not have been compiled into your version of Sendmail. A quick way to check this is to run the following:

```
puppy# sendmail -d0 < /dev/null | grep MILTER
```

If your Sendmail binary supports milter, it should return something like this:

```
Compiled with: DNSMAP LOG MATCHGECOS MILTER MIME7TO8 MIME8TO7
```

If it does not return MILTER in the Compiled with options, you need to enable milter support by adding the following line to your site.config.m4 file. APPENDDEF enables the mail filter interface. Enter the following:

```
APPENDDEF(`confENVDEF', `-DMILTER')
```

Now rebuild Sendmail with the Build -c option.

You also need the libmilter library that comes with Sendmail. In your Sendmail source distribution, change into the libmilter directory and run the following:

```
puppy# ./Build install
```

■Tip If you are using a Red Hat or Mandrake distribution, then you can use the RPM package sendmail-devel. On Debian the package is libmilter-dev.

You should already have clamd configured and running according to the instructions in the "Installing ClamAV" section. You want it to be creating a local socket, which is the first method of setting it up that was described in that section. Now you need to start the `clamav-milter` function running. You can run the daemon from the command line; it comes with a number of options. Table 7-12 details some of those options.

Table 7-12. `clamav-milter` *Command-Line Options*

Option	Description
`-b`	Sends a failure message to the sender (not recommended)
`-D`	Prints debug messages
`-l`	Controls scanning of messages sent from local network
`-o`	Controls scanning of outgoing messages
`--quiet`	Does not send e-mail notifications of virus detection
`--max-children=x`	Restricts the maximum number of processes spawned to filter e-mail

Most of these options are pretty much self-explanatory, but several deserve a special mention. The `-b` option is often turned on in `clamav-milter` configurations. These days this is not a good idea. This is for two reasons. First, more often than not the sender address on a virus infected e-mail is unlikely to be the person who actually sent it. Second, if you are under a serious virus attack, you could create serious performance issues for your MTA by trying to process thousands of outgoing bounce messages in addition to the incoming mail. So do not bother to bounce messages. The other option, `--quiet`, stops `clamav-milter` from sending an e-mail notification of the virus detection to the sender of the e-mail. For the previous reasons this is a good option to have on. Listing 7-48 shows the command line you can use to start `clamav-milter`.

Listing 7-48. *Starting* `clamav-milter` *from the Command Line*

```
puppy# /usr/local/sbin/clamav-milter -ol --quiet ➥
- -max-children=20 local:/var/run/clamav/clamav-milter.sock
```

`local:/var/run/clamav/clamav-milter.sock` defines the socket `milter` will use to communicate with the `clamd` daemon; you need to specify this to Sendmail in the next section. I have put the socket in the same directory as the `clamd` socket specified in the previous section. You should automate the start of your `clamav-milter` daemon when your system starts— make sure it is before you start Sendmail. In the `clamav-milter` directory in the ClamAV source distribution, an `init` script is available for `clamav-milter` that you can customize.

Now you need to tell Sendmail about `clamav-milter`. Add these two lines to your `sendmail.mc` file to define `clamav-milter` as a filter:

```
INPUT_MAIL_FILTER(`clamav', `S=local:/var/run/clamav/clamav-milter.sock, ➥
F=, T=S:4m;R:4m')
define(`confINPUT_MAIL_FILTERS', `clamav')
```

This will define an input mail filter for all incoming mail that will send that mail to the socket `clamav-milter` has created. The delivery agent `F=` option in the first line tells Sendmail how you would like it to handle the `milter` being unavailable. You can make a few possible choices about how Sendmail should handle it if the `milter` is unavailable. By leaving `F=` blank you are specifying mail should keep flowing even if the `milter` is unavailable. This is potentially a very bad idea, because if your `clamav-milter` breaks, then virus-infected e-mail will simply pass straight through Sendmail. You could also set it to `F=T`, which would temporarily reject the message. Or you could even set it to `F=R`, which would reject the message as undeliverable. I recommend you read about the delivery agent options before making a definitive choice as to your response. The `T=` options are all timeouts. For most systems, these defaults should be fine.

Now if you rebuild `sendmail.cf` and restart Sendmail, all your mail will now be filtered through ClamAV. If you initially set the `-D` option in `clamav-milter`, you should be able to track the submission and scanning of all your e-mail via `milter` and ClamAV in your mail logs.

■**Tip** If you do not want to integrate ClamAV and Sendmail using `milter`, you could also look at AMaViS (`http://www.amavis.org/`) or MailScanner. You could also do filtering during the local delivery process using `procmail` or `maildrop`, but I recommend that the earlier you address any virus and spam filtering in the mail process is best.

Integrating ClamAV with Postfix

Integrating ClamAV with Postfix is slightly more complicated than integrating it with Sendmail. You will require an extra component, AMaViS.

■**Caution** Older versions of AMaViS have had security issues. Ensure you are using an up-to-date version of the script and that you add it to your list of products to monitor for security exploits.

AMaViS is a Perl script that processes the mail using your specified antivirus engine (in this case, ClamAV) and then re-injecting it back into Postfix. It is relatively simple to set up, and you can download it at `http://www.amavis.org/download.php3`.

■**Note** You may need some additional Perl CPAN modules to run AMaViS. Check the AMaViS documentation, and use `perl -MCPAN -e shell` to retrieve any modules you require.

Unpack the source archive, and `configure` it. As you are going to integrate it with Postfix, use the next line as your `configure` statement:

```
puppy# ./configure --enable-postfix --with-mailto=virusadmin --with-syslog
```

replacing *virusadmin* with the user you want to have admin notifications of virus detections sent to. Then run `make` and `make install`.

The install process will create an `amavis` user and group. It also creates two directories: `/var/amavis` and `/var/virusmails`. The `/var/virusmails` is the default location for AMaViS to quarantine virus e-mails. By default the AMaViS script itself will be installed into `/usr/sbin`.

You do not need to tell AMaViS anything about your installed ClamAV, because it automatically knows where to look for most packages. You will need to adjust your ClamAV `clamd` daemon so that is it running as a TCP daemon on `localhost` at port 3310 (or whichever port you chose). This is the second way of setting up the `clamd` daemon I showed you earlier. You should also change the user who the `clamd` is running as, using the `User` option in the `clamav.conf` file, to `amavis`. Just remember to also change the ownership of the `/var/run/clamav` directory to allow `clamd` to write its PID file and socket.

Now you need to add some configuration into Postfix. Add the next line into the `main.cf` file, like this:

```
content_filter = amavis:
```

Then add all the lines in Listing 7-49 to the `master.cf` file.

Listing 7-49. *Postfix* `master.cf` *Service Additions for AMaViS*

```
amavis            unix  -  n  n  -  10  pipe user=amavis ➥
argv=/usr/sbin/amavis ${sender} ${recipient}
localhost:10025  inet  n  -  y  -  -    smtpd
        -o content_filter=
        -o local_recipient_maps=
        -o smtpd_helo_restrictions=
        -o smtpd_client_restrictions=
        -o smtpd_sender_restrictions=
        -o smtpd_recipient_restrictions=permit_mynetworks,reject
        -o mynetworks=127.0.0.0/8
```

■**Caution** I have turned on `chroot` for the `localhost` `smtpd` re-injection. If you are not using `chroot`, change the `y` on that line to `n`.

This creates two new services. The first, `amavis`, is a content filter that all incoming mail is piped into for processing by AMaViS, which runs it through the `clamd` daemon to check for viruses. The second is a `localhost` `smtpd` daemon, which sends (re-injects) the mail back to Postfix for further processing.

Finally, reload Postfix, and you should be able to see that AMaViS is now scanning your e-mail for viruses. You can confirm this by checking for a mail header on your e-mails, which should say something like this:

```
X-Virus-Scanned: by AMaViS 0.3.12
```

You should also be able to see the results from this scanning in your mail logs. I recommend you probably tweak your configuration as you go. For example, if you use `procmail` or `maildrop` for local mail delivery, you can customize the handling of any virus e-mail notifications to go into a special folder to allow your users to view them and perhaps identify any false positives.

■**Tip** You could also do this filtering during the local delivery process using `procmail` or `maildrop`, but I recommend that the earlier in your mail process that you address any virus and spam filtering is best.

Resources

The following are resources you can use.

Mailing Lists

- **Sendmail Usenet and mailing list**: `http://www.sendmail.org/usenet.html`

- **Postfix mailing lists**: `http://www.postfix.org/lists.html`

- **ClamAV mailing lists**: `http://www.clamav.net/ml.html#pagestart`

- **AMaViS mailing lists**: `http://sourceforge.net/mail/?group_id=6006`

Sites

- **Sendmail**: `http://www.sendmail.org/`

- **Postfix**: `http://www.postfix.org`

- **ClamAV**: `http://www.clamav.net/`

- **Milter**: `http://www.milter.org/`

- **AMaViS**: `http://www.amavis.org/`

CHAPTER 8

■ ■ ■

Authenticating and Securing Your Mail

In this chapter, I will cover Transport Layer Security (TLS), Simple Authentication and Security Layer (SASL), and SMTP AUTH as tools to further secure and harden your mail server. These tools allow you to secure and encrypt the transmission (though not the content) of your e-mails. They also help ensure that the mail servers and clients that you communicate with are authentic. Probably most important for mail administrators, they provide the ability for roaming and remote users to have an encrypted authenticated connection to their mail server that allows functionality such as relaying. You saw in Chapter 7 how relaying is locked down and the inconvenience this can cause your users. SMTP AUTH using SASL and TLS can allow your users to relay e-mails via your server using authentication whilst you continue to maintain your antispam and antirelaying controls.

I will first take you through setting up TLS and some examples of how to use TLS (though most people will probably use TLS as an encryption layer in conjunction with SASL and SMTP AUTH). Then I will cover Cyrus SASL and SMTP AUTH and how to use them. Finally, I will cover how to implement these tools on both Sendmail and Postfix.

TLS

By default the vast majority of communication on the Internet is both unauthenticated and unencrypted. This means anyone in the right place at the right time with the correct tools can read any of your traffic, including your e-mail traffic. Even potentially more dangerous is the possibility that anyone could alter or delete portions or all of your traffic. With this in mind, Netscape came up with a new protocol called Secure Sockets Layer (SSL), which provides a twofold solution to this. The first part of that solution is to hide your traffic from eavesdropping by encrypting it, and the second part is to provide an authentication mechanism by which the sender and recipient of traffic can be assured that both ends of the transaction are the people they claim to be and that the data being sent has not been altered.

TLS[1] is an extension of the SSL protocol and requires you have OpenSSL installed. TLS uses *public-key encryption* to encrypt mail transactions. Public-key encryption works with two keys; the public key, often called a *certificate*, is available publicly, and the private key is stored on the server and kept secret. So anything that is encrypted using the public key can be decrypted only with the corresponding private key, and vice versa.

---

1. See RFC 2246 (http://www.ietf.org/rfc/rfc2246.txt) for the details of TLS.

■**Note** It is possible to use TLS for encryption without a certificate at all, but I do not recommend this approach. Using a certificate authority (CA) and certificates further enhances the level of security available to you because it adds a layer of authentication in addition to the layer of encryption.

Your Mail Transfer Agent (MTA) can use TLS as part of its initial connection negotiation with a remote client or server. A server or client connecting to your server sends an EHLO request, which your MTA responds to by advertising it has support for the STARTTLS command. The server or client then requests that the server uses TLS by issuing the STARTTLS command.

So what could you use TLS for? Well, TLS is probably most often used in conjunction with SASL and SMTP AUTH to provide encryption for SASL plain-text authentication. Many enterprises also use TLS to encrypt and authenticate the transfer of e-mail traffic from two TLS-enabled hosts each at a different site across the Internet. Or, at the most basic level, many people use a TLS-capable client such as Outlook Express or Eudora to provide encryption and authentication when sending mail directly to a remote server.

TLS has some significant limitations that are especially important to note. What TLS does is to encrypt and authenticate the *transfer* of e-mail from server to server and from client to server, and vice versa. If your e-mail passes through a mail hub that does not have STARTTLS enabled, then it will *not* be secured. It is also not an end-to-end encryption tool. The content of your e-mail messages will remain unencrypted on both the sender and receiver systems— only the transfer is encrypted. If you want to encrypt your e-mail, you need to look at solutions such as S/MIME or PGP-MIME. I will not cover S/MIME or PGP-MIME in any detail, though, because I perceive these as client-based encryption and not therefore directly related to hardening the server end of your e-mail infrastructure. Quite a few resources are available that do discuss e-mail content encryption.[2]

In the next sections, I will take you through creating certificates for using with TLS and your MTA. Then I will show you how to enable TLS in both Sendmail and Postfix and provide examples of how you can use TLS.

Creating Certificates for TLS

TLS uses SSL certificates to authenticate servers and clients for a variety of functions. I discuss SSL in more depth in Chapter 3, but for the purposes of this explanation, I will cover only one type of certificate model. In this model, you are running your own CA and creating X.509 certificates from that CA. The reason I have chosen to look at this model is because it is financially free and does not require you to purchase certificates.

But as I detailed in Chapter 3, some risks come with being your own CA and signing your own certificates; you need to weigh those risks before proceeding, and you need to consult with any partners you intend to authenticate with certificates. However, with mail server authentication, unlike an SSL certificate for a Web page, I usually assume you have only a limited number of partners you are going to authenticate with certificates (almost certainly all clients and systems that you administer); this means it is more likely those partners will accept a private CA rather than a commercial CA.

---

2.   See the "Sites" section for some links.

■Caution By detailing this model, I am not recommending it as the preferred option. If you operate production e-mail systems that use OpenSSL, I recommend you at least examine the option of using a commercial CA.

If you are happy with using your own internal CA, then read about the CA creation process in Chapter 3 to get a better understanding of how this works and then create a CA of your own. When you have created your new CA, you can start to create and sign your own certificates. For this example, I have followed the instructions in Chapter 3 and created a new CA called mailCA.

■Tip I recommend locating your certificates underneath the configuration directory of your MTA. So, Sendmail should look for its certificates in /etc/mail/certs, and Postfix should look in /etc/postfix/certs.

To create your first certificate, you need to create a certificate request that will then be signed by the new CA. I will create the certificate request that is unencrypted and valid for three years together with a private key.

The certificate you create consists of several items, but the most important for the purposes of using TLS for your MTA is the *distinguished name*. This consists of a series of pieces of information you provide during the certificate creation process, including your geographical location, the hostname of the system, and an e-mail address. This information, in conjunction with the validity of the certificate, can be used to create access controls that allow you to enable functionality, such as relaying, for specific hosts that present a valid certificate.

The most important piece of information you need to provide for the certificate's distinguished name is the common name, which for the purposes of TLS is the hostname of your system. If you want this to work with your MTA, then this needs to be the fully qualified domain name (FQDN) of the system the certificate is being created for; so, in Listing 8-1, the common name is puppy.yourdomain.com. To create your first certificate, go to your certs directory. Listing 8-1 shows you how to run the command and what resulting messages you will see.

Listing 8-1. *Creating a Certificate Request*

```
puppy# openssl req -config /etc/mail/certs/mailCA/openssl.cnf -new ➥
-nodes -days 1095 -keyout puppy.yourdomaim.com.key.pem ➥
-out puppy.yourdomaim.com.csr.pem
Generating a 1024 bit RSA private key
.......++++++
..........................++++++
writing new private key to 'puppy.yourdomain.com.key.pem'
-----
You are about to be asked to enter information that will be incorporated
into your certificate request.
What you are about to enter is what is called a Distinguished Name or a DN.
There are quite a few fields but you can leave some blank
```

```
For some fields there will be a default value,
If you enter '.', the field will be left blank.
-----
Country Name (2 letter code) [AU]:
State or Province Name (full name) [New South Wales]:
Locality Name (eg, city) [Sydney]:
Organization Name (eg, company) [puppy.yourdomain.com]:
Organizational Unit Name (eg, section) []:
Common Name (eg, your name or your server's hostname) []:puppy.yourdomain.com
Email Address []:admin@puppy.yourdomain.com
```

■**Caution** I used the -nodes option to create the certificate and private key. This tells OpenSSL to not
secure the certificate with a passphrase. Otherwise, every time the certificate was accessed, it would require
the passphrase. The SMTP server has no scope to enter this passphrase, and a connection would simply hang
while waiting for the passphrase to be entered.

This will create two files: puppy.yourdomain.com.key.pem and puppy.yourdomain.com.csr.pem.
These files consist of a keyfile for your system and a certificate request.

The final stage of your certificate creation is to sign the certificate request using your new
CA. Listing 8-2 shows the resulting messages after you run the command.

Listing 8-2. *Signing Your Certificate Request*

```
puppy# openssl ca -config /etc/mail/certs/mailCA/openssl.cnf ➥
-policy policy_anything -out puppy.yourdomain.com.cert.pem ➥
-infiles puppy.yourdomain.com.csr.pem
Using configuration from /etc/mail/certs/mailCA/mailssl.cnf
Enter pass phrase for /etc/mail/certs/mailCA/private/cakey.pem:
Check that the request matches the signature
Signature ok
Certificate Details:
        Serial Number: 2 (0x2)
        Validity
            Not Before: Apr  2 00:46:41 2004 GMT
            Not After : Apr  2 00:46:41 2007 GMT
        Subject:
            countryName               = AU
            stateOrProvinceName       = New South Wales
            localityName              = Sydney
            organizationName          = puppy.yourdomain.com
            commonName                = puppy.yourdomain.com
            emailAddress              = admin@puppy.yourdomain.com
```

```
    X509v3 extensions:
        X509v3 Basic Constraints:
        CA:FALSE
        Netscape Comment:
        OpenSSL Generated Certificate
        X509v3 Subject Key Identifier:
        EB:62:9D:27:65:3E:AB:55:44:67:8D:A7:09:E5:08:B3:FC:FF:0B:38
        X509v3 Authority Key Identifier:
        keyid:09:6A:E4:42:E8:DD:53:93:9C:49:01:49:D4:B3:BD:20:5F:82:2A:20
DirName:/C=AU/ST=New South Wales/L=Sydney/O=puppy.yourdomain.com/➥
CN=puppy/emailAddress=admin@puppy.yourdomain.com
        serial:00
Certificate is to be certified until Apr  2 00:46:41 2007 GMT (1095 days)
Sign the certificate? [y/n]:y
1 out of 1 certificate requests certified, commit? [y/n]y
Write out database with 1 new entries
Data Base Updated
```

This will output a final file called puppy.yourdomain.com.cert.pem, which is your certificate file. You can now delete the certificate request file, which is puppy.yourdomain.com.csr.pem.

■**Note** You can use whatever naming convention you like for your certificates, keys, and requests. I just use the previous convention because it represents a simple way to identify all your SSL components and to which system they belong.

Finally, as you can see in Listing 8-3, you should change the permissions of the files in your certs directory to ensure they are more secure.

Listing 8-3. *Certificate Permissions*

```
puppy# cd /etc/mail
puppy# chmod 0755 certs
puppy# cd certs
puppy# chmod -R 0400 *
```

Now you have your first set of certificates and can use them to secure your TLS connections.

TLS with Sendmail

The first thing Sendmail needs to run TLS is OpenSSL. You need to ensure the latest version of OpenSSL is installed and that Sendmail has been compiled with SSL support. Listing 8-4 shows the fastest way to check the options with which Sendmail has been compiled.

Listing 8-4. *Determining the Options with Which Sendmail Has Been Compiled*

```
puppy# sendmail -bt -d0.1
```

Sendmail will respond with a list of the options compiled into it similar to the one in Listing 8-5. If you see STARTTLS in that list, then TLS already has been compiled into Sendmail; you can skip to the section "Configuring Sendmail with TLS." Otherwise, see the next section for instructions about how to compile TLS into Sendmail.

Listing 8-5. *Options Compiled into Sendmail*

```
Version 8.12.11
 Compiled with: DNSMAP LOG MATCHGECOS MIME7TO8 MIME8TO7 NAMED_BIND
                NETINET NETUNIX NEWDB PIPELINING SASL SCANF STARTTLS USERDB
                XDEBUG
```

Compiling Sendmail with TLS

Compiling Sendmail with support for TLS is a simple process. Add the lines in Listing 8-6 to site.config.m4.

Listing 8-6. *Sendmail with TLS*

```
APPENDDEF(`conf_sendmail_ENVDEF', `-DSTARTTLS')
APPENDDEF(`conf_sendmail_ENVDEF', `-lssl -lcrypto')
```

On some systems, the SSL libraries and includes are not in the place Sendmail expects. Add the two lines in Listing 8-7 to tell Sendmail where to find the SSL libraries and includes.

Listing 8-7. *Specifing the SSL Libraries and Includes*

```
APPENDDEF(`conf_sendmail_INCDIRS', `-I/path/to/ssl/include')
APPENDDEF(`conf_sendmail_LIBDIRS', `-L/path/to/ssl/lib')
```

■**Tip** On some Red Hat systems, most notably Red Hat 9 and RHEL 3, you may also need to add an include to point Sendmail to the Kerberos includes. Usually they would be located in /usr/include/kerberos, but Red Hat has moved them in recent releases to /usr/kerberos/include.

Compile or recompile Sendmail mail with the Build command from /sendmail-*yourversion*/. Enter the following:

```
puppy# ./Build -c
```

The -c tells the Sendmail compile to include the contents of the site.config.m4 file. Then install the new Sendmail with TLS included by entering the following:

```
puppy# ./Build install
```

Finally, restart Sendmail to make sure you are running the new version.

Configuring Sendmail with TLS

Now that you have your version of Sendmail into which TLS has been compiled in, you need to configure Sendmail to use it. The configuration for STARTTLS is all contained within your sendmail.mc file. You first need to tell Sendmail where to find the certificates you created (see the "Creating Certificates for TLS" section). Add the following lines to your sendmail.mc file:

```
define(`confCACERT_PATH',`/etc/mail/certs/')
define(`confCACERT',`/etc/mail/certs/cacert.pem')
define(`confSERVER_CERT',`/etc/mail/certs/puppy.yourdomain.com.cert.pem')
define(`confSERVER_KEY',`/etc/mail/certs/puppy.yourdomain.com.key.pem')
define(`confCLIENT_CERT',`/etc/mail/certs/puppy.yourdomain.com.cert.pem')
define(`confCLIENT_KEY',`/etc/mail/certs/puppy.yourdomain.com.key.pem')
```

Table 8-1 explains each of these defines.

Table 8-1. STARTTLS-*Related Defines in* sendmail.mc

Define Parameter	Purpose
confCACERT_PATH	The path to the location of your CA certificate
confCACERT	The file containing your CA certificate
confSERVER_CERT	The file containing the server certificate of this server that is used if Sendmail is acting as a server
confSERVER_KEY	The file containing the key of the server certificate
confCLIENT_CERT	The file containing the client certificate of this server that is used if Sendmail is acting as a client
confCLIENT_KEY	The file containing the key of the client certificate

Here I have defined both the same client and server keys. This means the Sendmail server is able to act as both a client and a server for TLS purposes. Now re-create your sendmail.cf file, and restart Sendmail. You should be able to test if STARTTLS is working using Telnet to connect to port 25 on your Sendmail system. Enter the following:

```
puppy# telnet puppy.yourdomain.com 25
```

Issue an EHLO *anotherhostname* to the Sendmail server. This should generate a list of capabilities. If this list includes STARTTLS, then TLS is now enabled for your Sendmail server. Listing 8-8 shows the abbreviated results of this request.

Listing 8-8. *Checking That* STARTTLS *Works*

```
puppy# telnet puppy.yourdomain.com 25
Trying 192.168.0.1...
Connected to puppy (192.168.0.1).
Escape character is '^]'.
220 puppy.yourdomain.com ESMTP
EHLO testbox
250-puppy.yourdomain.com Hello testbox [192.168.0.10], pleased to meet you
250-STARTTLS
```

If STARTTLS does not show up in the list of capabilities, the first place to check is your maillog or equivalent mail-logging file. Sendmail will log its TLS-related errors to syslog. For example, if you leave one of your keys or certificates group-readable, then Sendmail will generate the error, like this:

```
Apr  1 18:41:27 puppy sendmail[2923]: STARTTLS=server: ➡
file /etc/mail/certs/key.pem unsafe: Group readable file
```

Until you change the permissions to a more restrictive choice (I recommend 0400), then Sendmail will not enable TLS.

Using TLS with Specific Hosts

To provide an example of how you can use TLS with Sendmail, I will demonstrate how to force Sendmail to require inbound or outbound connections to specific hosts or domains to use encryption. By default, because only a limited number of MTAs use TLS, most e-mail transfers are clear text. I will assume you need to ensure that connections between specific hosts (for example, if you have two mail servers on different sites connected via the Internet) must send their traffic with encryption. To do this, you need to specifically tell Sendmail about those hosts and that they must use TLS.

How you tell Sendmail involves using the *access db* feature. I discussed the *access db* feature in Chapter 7; refer to that chapter for further information about it and how to enable it. One of the possible rules types is using STARTTLS and certificates to allow certain actions. In this example, I will tell Sendmail to allow a connection to or from my Sendmail server only if the certificate is signed by a trusted CA (for example, the CA created earlier in Chapter 3 or a commercial CA).

Inside your *access db* file (I have used /etc/mail/access), you can specify some rules for connections; these rules are TLS_Clt and TLS_Srv. Let's look at inbound connections first. To insist on encryption from a specific client, you need to add a TLS_Clt rule to your *access db*. The TLS_Clt rule consists of three parts: a *name*, a *requirement*, and a flag determining the nature of the error response from Sendmail if the rule is not met. The name is the hostname or IP address of the client system, and the requirement is the level of encryption required to allow incoming mail. A typical TLS_Clt rule could look like this:

```
TLS_Clt:kitten.yourdomain.com ENCR:128
```

This tells your Sendmail server to allow connections from the host kitten.yourdomain.com only if at least 128-bit encryption is used. If the host kitten.yourdomain.com tries to send mail without at least 128-bit encryption, it will fail, as shown in Listing 8-9, with an error message.

Listing 8-9. TSL_Clt *Encryption Failure*

```
Apr  4 09:51:31 puppy sendmail[18096]: i33NpVcd018096: ➡
--- 403 4.7.0 encryption too weak 0 less than 128
```

I mentioned a flag concerning the nature of Sendmail's error response. By default, if Sendmail receives a message without a suitable level of encryption, it will send back the error code 403. The fact that this error code starts with 4 indicates it is a temporary error and the client sending to Sendmail should try again the next time it processes its ongoing mail. If you want to change this to a permanent error, which would tell the remote client to *not* try to resend the e-mail, then you can prefix your ENCR:*bits* portion of the rule with PERM+. So now your rule would look like the following:

```
TLS_Clt:kitten.yourdomain.com PERM+ENCR:128
```

Any mail that was not suitably encrypted from the specified client will now receive the permanent error 503. What you choose to do here probably depends on the nature of the client to which you are connecting. The default of a temporary error 403 is correct from an RFC perspective, but you may want to address this differently.

Outbound connections are handled in a similar way. These also use your *access db* feature, but they use the rule TLS_Srv. The TLS_Srv and TLS_Clt rules are constructed identically. TLS_Srv consists of a name and requirement with the option to change the error response also available. The following is an access rule telling Sendmail that all mail being sent to the host kitten.yourdomain.com needs to be encrypted to at least 128-bits:

```
TLS_Srv:kitten.yourdomain.net              ENCR:128
```

■**Tip** Do not forget to re-create your *access db* file after you have changed it using the makemap command.

These are just some of the ways you can use TLS in conjunction with Sendmail. One of the other more common uses is to allow or disallow relaying from systems verified with certain certificates. You can find more examples of how to use TLS at the Sendmail site at http://www.sendmail.org.

TLS with Postfix

In this section, I will take you through adding TLS support to Postfix and configuring that support, and I will show an example of forcing Postfix to use TLS to connect to specified hosts and domains.

To use Postfix with TLS, you need OpenSSL. Postfix, as available from the Postfix Web site in source form, does not come with TLS by default. Some distributions contain a version of Postfix with TLS enabled. The fastest way to check for TLS support in Postfix is to use the ldd command to determine what shared libraries are compiled into your smtpd binary (which is the binary that runs the SMTP daemon for Postfix). Listing 8-10 shows how to do this, assuming your smtpd binary is located in /usr/libexec/postfix/ (which it should be by default).

Listing 8-10. *Shared Libraries Compiled into Postfix*

```
puppy# ldd /usr/libexec/postfix/smtpd
libssl.so.2 => /lib/libssl.so.2 (0x40021000)
libcrypto.so.2 => /lib/libcrypto.so.2 (0x40052000)
libdb-4.0.so => /lib/libdb-4.0.so (0x40126000)
libnsl.so.1 => /lib/libnsl.so.1 (0x401ce000)
libresolv.so.2 => /lib/libresolv.so.2 (0x401e4000)
libc.so.6 => /lib/i686/libc.so.6 (0x42000000)
libdl.so.2 => /lib/libdl.so.2 (0x401f6000)
/lib/ld-linux.so.2 => /lib/ld-linux.so.2 (0x40000000)
```

If you can see the `libssl` library in the output from the `ldd` command, then Postfix has been compiled with OpenSSL and therefore TLS support. If you do not see that library, you will either need to compile support into Postfix or find a Postfix package for your release that already contains TLS support.

If you need to find a version of Postfix and you do not want to compile from source, a few options are available depending on your distribution. For Red Hat (a variety of releases), Mandrake, and YellowDog Linux, you can find RPMs with TLS and SASL enabled at `http://postfix.wl0.org/en/`. These RPMs are specifically for Red Hat but should work reasonably well on Mandrake and other RPM-based distributions as well. Debian has a package called `postfix-tls` that contains the functionality for both TLS and SASL, so you can simply `apt-get` this package and add it to the existing `postfix` package. You should keep this up-to-date as part of the stable release. If you use SuSE, Gentoo, Slackware, or other distributions, you will need to install the TLS patch and recompile Postfix. I take you through that in the next section.

Compiling TLS into Postfix

If your distribution does not come with a TLS-enabled Postfix, it is a bit harder than enabling it with Sendmail. This is because Postfix needs a third-party patch to enable TLS. This third-party patch, provided by Lutz Janicke at `http://www.aet.tu-cottbus.de/personen/jaenicke/postfix_tls/`, is kept reasonably up-to-date with the current release of Postfix. I will show you how to integrate that with Postfix in this section.

Note Recent experimental releases of Postfix have included TLS support based on Lutz Janicke's patch. Future production releases of Postfix will include TLS support without the need to apply this patch.

First download the patch from the site mentioned. Second, you will need the Postfix source code. The site lists all the required compatibilities, including what versions of Postfix and OpenSSL you will need depending on the version of the patch you are downloading. Check that you have the correct version of the Postfix source code, check that you have the correct patch version, and check that the version of OpenSSL on your system is also compatible.

Unpack the patch source. It will create a directory such as `pfixtls-0.8.16-2.0.18-0.9.7c`, where `0.8.16` is the version of the Postfix TLS patch, `2.0.18` is the version of Postfix this patch applies to, and `0.9.7c` indicates the version of OpenSSL recommended. You should have at least have version 0.9.6 of OpenSSL installed. Unpack the patch into a directory that also contains the unpacked Postfix source. So, if you did an `ls` of that directory, you see both the Postfix source directory and directory containing the Postfix-TLS patch.

```
drwxr-xr-x   15 1001      wheel      4096 Mar 26 21:54 postfix-2.0.18
drwxr-xr-x    5 11019     11000      4096 Mar 26 21:38 pfixtls-0.8.16-2.0.18-0.9.7c
```

Now you need to patch the Postfix source code. Listing 8-11 shows you how to run the command required to do this. You need to substitute *path/to/patch* and the correct *version* in the command. Then run this command from the directory that contains the subdirectories that contain the patch and the Postfix source code.

Listing 8-11. *Patching the Postfix Code*

```
patch -p0 < /path/to/patch/pfixtls-version/pfixtls.diff
```

This should generate a list of the files being patched and then return you to the command line.

Once the patch is complete, then you need to adjust Postfix's Makefiles to add the OpenSSL header files. Move to the Postfix source directory, and run the command in Listing 8-12, changing the -I to the location of your OpenSSL include files and the -L to the location of your OpenSSL libraries. The locations listed in Listing 8-12 represent the general defaults for an OpenSSL installation. This may differ on your distribution.

Listing 8-12. *Adding OpenSSL to the Postfix* Makefiles

```
make makefiles CCARGS="-DUSE_SSL -I/usr/local/ssl/include" ➥
AUXLIBS="-L/usr/local/ssl/lib -lssl -lcrypto"
```

Then run make and make upgrade if you already have Postfix installed, or run make install for a new install of the Postfix source. Now if you run ldd on the smtpd binary, you should see that libssl is included in the list of libraries. If Postfix is already running, then you will also need to restart it.

Configuring TLS in Postfix

Now that you have TLS compiled into Postfix, you need to enable it. You do this in the main.cf Postfix configuration file, which is usually located in /etc/postfix. You should already have a key, a public certificate, and the CA cert that was generated at the start of the "Creating Certificates for TLS" section. You need to define these and their locations to Postfix.

■**Tip** Do not forget to hash your CA certificate!

You need to define two sets of options: one set for Postfix to act as a TLS server and one set for Postfix to act as a TLS client. For a TLS server, add the following lines in your main.cf file, replacing */path/to/certs* with the path to the location of your certificates (including your CA cert file) and replacing *cert*, *key*, and *CAcert* with the names of your certificate, key, and CA cert files in PEM format, respectively.

```
smtpd_tls_cert_file = /path/to/certs/cert.pem
smtpd_tls_key_file = /path/to/certs/key.pem
smtpd_tls_CAfile = /path/to/certs/CAcert.pem
```

■**Caution** If you are running Postfix chrooted and you have more than one CA certificate, then you need to combine them into one file. Before chrooting itself, the smtpd daemon will read the contents of the file defined by the smtpd_tls_CAfile option and then chroot. This means if all the CA certs are combined in one file, they are available in the chroot jail for Postfix. The same also applies to the smtp_tls_CAfile option in the unusual event you have different CAs for clients.

For a TLS client, add the following lines in your `main.cf` file, again replacing */path/to/certs* with the path to the location of your certificates (including your CA cert file) and replacing *cert*, *key*, and *CAcert* with the names of your certificate, key, and CA cert files in PEM format, respectively.

```
smtp_tls_cert_file = /path/to/certs/cert.pem
smtp_tls_key_file = /path/to/certs/key.pem
smtp_tls_CAfile = /path/to/certs/CAcert.pem
```

You can also add some other options that are useful. The first is logging. Add the following line to `main.cf` to enable logging for Postfix as a TSL server:

```
smtpd_tls_loglevel = 1
```

You can also add the following for Postfix TLS client logging:

```
smtp_tls_loglevel = 1
```

Five logging levels exist and are identical for both the server and client logging options. Table 8-2 details them.

Table 8-2. *TLS Logging levels for Postfix*

Level	Description
0	No logging
1	Startup and certificate information
2	Level 1 plus display levels during negotiation
3	Level 2 plus a HEX and ASCII dump of the negotiation process
4	Level 3 plus a HEX and ASCII dump of the complete STARTTLS transaction

I recommend during normal operations a logging level of 1 or 2. I recommend not using Level 4 unless you absolutely need this information for Postfix TLS client logging, as this will generate a huge volume of data and could considerably slow down your server.

A useful option for server TLS is `smtpd_tls_auth_only`. This stops Postfix from sending AUTH data over an unencrypted channel. This is useful when you are also using SMTP AUTH. If this option is set to yes, then Postfix will send AUTH data only once TLS has been activated via the STARTTLS command. To enable this option, add the following to the `main.cf` file:

```
smtpd_tls_auth_only = yes
```

Finally, you need to add a line explicitly starting TLS to your `main.cf` file. For a Postfix acting as a TLS server, add the following:

```
smtpd_use_tls = yes
```

For Postfix acting as a TLS client, add the following:

```
smtp_use_tls = yes
```

After adding one or both options, you need to reload Postfix.

Now when you Telnet to your Postfix server and issue the EHLO command, you should see STARTTLS as one of the available capabilities of your Postfix server.

```
puppy# telnet puppy.yourdomain.com 25
Trying 192.168.0.1...
Connected to puppy.
Escape character is '^]'.
220 puppy.yourdomain.com
EHLO kitten.yourdomain.com
250-puppy.yourdomain.com
250-STARTTLS
```

You are now ready to use TLS with Postfix!

■**Note** With Postfix-TLS you may want to investigate a few other options. The Postfix-TLS patch also comes with a sample configuration file that details all the options available. This usually located in /etc/postfix/sample-tls.cf.

Using TLS for a Specific Host

As an example of how to use TLS with Postfix, I will take you through the process of enforcing the use of TLS for specific hosts or domains. I will do this by defining a new option, smtp_tls_per_site, in the main.cf file. This option will reference a list of hosts and domains and contain specific instructions that tell Postfix whether to use TLS with that host or domain. Remember to be careful. The host or domain you are sending to must be capable of TLS, and if you specify it must use TLS, then you need to be sure it has TLS capabilities; otherwise, you will not be able to send mail to that host or domain. As most systems on the Internet are not TLS capable, you should reserve this sort of enforcement for hosts and domains with which you were sure you are able to initiate TLS.

To get started, add the following line to your main.cf file:

```
smtp_tls_per_site = hash:/etc/postfix/tls_per_site
```

The hash:/etc/postfix/tls_per_site entry refers to a Postfix hash map created with the postmap command that you will create shortly.

Now you need to specify the hosts and domains that will or will not use TLS. Create a new file called tls_per_site, and add entries for all the hosts and systems you want to define. Each entry should consist of a hostname or domain name followed by a space or tab with each new host or domain on a new line. Listing 8-13 shows you how to do it.

Listing 8-13. *A Sample* tls_per_site *File*

```
puppy.yourdomain.com MUST
yourdomain.com MAY
otherdomain.com NONE
anotherdomain.com MUST_NOPEERMATCH
```

As you can see from Listing 8-13, you can specify four possible options to tell Postfix how to handle potential TLS connections. Table 8-3 details these options.

Table 8-3. *The* smtp_tls_per_site *Options*

Option	Description
NONE	Do not use TLS.
MAY	If available, use TLS; otherwise do not bother.
MUST	Enforces TLS use. E-mail send fails if certificate verify fails.
MUST_NOPEERMATCH	Enforces TLS use and verification of certificate but ignores any difference between the system's FQDN and the certificate's common name.

So, if you had a system you wanted to enforce the use of TLS for any e-mails sent, then you would add it to the tls_per_site file and use the MUST or MUST_NOPEERMATCH option. If you are testing this, I recommend you start with MAY options. This way you can send test e-mails and confirm, using your log files, that a TLS connection is being established and that the certificate is being verified with the specified remote host or domain before attempting to enforce the use of TLS. This limits the risk that you might suffer a mail outage because TLS was not able to be established and e-mail ceased to be sent.

Once you have created your tls_per_site file, then you can create a hash map from that file with the postmap command.

```
puppy# postmap hash:/etc/postfix/tls_per_site
```

This will create the hash map called tls_per_site.db in /etc/postfix. Finally, you then need to reload Postfix to update your configuration.

```
puppy# postfix reload
```

You should now be able to see in your mail logs when Postfix makes a TLS connection. Listing 8-14 shows some of the log entries generated when sending an e-mail from admin@puppy.yourdomain.com to admin@kitten.yourdomain.com, which are both TLS-capable systems and are enforcing TLS.

Listing 8-14. *Postfix TLS Log Entries*

```
Apr  6 18:04:35 puppy postfix/smtp[13437]: ➥
setting up TLS connection to kitten.yourdomain.com
Apr  6 18:04:35 puppy postfix/smtp[13437]: ➥
Verified: subject_CN=kitten.yourdomain.com, issuer=puppy.yourdomain.com
Apr  6 18:04:35 puppy postfix/smtp[13437]: ➥
TLS connection established to puppy.yourdomain.com: TLSv1 with cipher ➥
EDH-RSA-DES-CBC3-SHA (168/168 bits)
Apr  6 18:04:35 puppy postfix/smtp[13437]: 75AB6231E4F: ➥
to=<admin@kitten.yourdomain.com>, relay=kitten.yourdomain.com[192.168.0.2], ➥
delay=0, status=sent (250 2.0.0 i3686BnY019481 Message accepted for delivery)
```

This shows just one of the uses for TLS in Postfix. As you can with Sendmail, you could also use TLS in Postfix to allow relaying from clients using the smtpd_recipient_restrictions options permit_tls_clientcerts and permit_tls_all_clientcerts.

SMTP AUTH Using Cyrus SASL

As mentioned, SMTP does not by default have a mechanism to allow clients to authenticate to servers or to allow servers to authenticate to other servers. Given the increased requirements for security, for remote access to e-mail, and for the prevalence of spam, there was a need to provide an extension to basic SMTP to allow such authentication. This requirement was detailed in RFC 2554, "SMTP Service Extension for Authentication."[3] The functionality contained within RFC 2554 provides administrators with a new SMTP verb, AUTH, to allow remote clients or servers to connect to the resources they require, in the form of a mail server, and for the server to be sure they are who they say they are. This new verb, AUTH, uses the SASL framework to provide that authentication.

I will cover only the basics of SMTP AUTH and SASL and show you how to authenticate using simple mechanisms either using a database map stored on your system or using the saslauthd daemon. SASL comes in a number of different flavors. I will specifically cover the Cyrus SASL libraries, which are widely used on Linux systems for authenticating applications such as mail servers. The SASL libraries themselves are authentication frameworks; they provide the hooks and functions to allow authentication—they do not perform authentication by themselves. To conduct the actual authentication, SASL uses a series of mechanisms that integrate into the SASL framework. Table 8-4 shows these mechanisms.

Table 8-4. *SASL Authentication Mechanisms*

Mechanism	Description
ANONYMOUS	Like an anonymous FTP login. Useless to SMTP servers because it mirrors the behavior of an open relay and should be disabled at all times.
CRAM-MD5	Uses MD5 algorithms for a challenge-response style authentication.
DIGEST-MD5	More advanced form of CRAM-MD5 that offers additional features.
GSSAPI	Uses Kerberos 5 tickets for authentication.
PLAIN	Uses plain-text usernames and passwords.
LOGIN	A nonstandard version of the PLAIN mechanism using the same principles.

SASL also allows you to develop your own mechanisms and use them for authentication. You can choose to use any form of mechanism that suits your environment.

■**Caution** If you want to use LOGIN (used by default if your clients are Outlook derivatives) or PLAIN, then you should combine their use with TLS to ensure your passwords are encrypted before being sent across the network.

As with TLS, some distributions come with Cyrus SASL packages. For example, for Red Hat and Mandrake, you need to install the cyrus-sasl RPM; for Debian you need to apt-get

---

3. http://www.faqs.org/rfcs/rfc2554.html

the package `cyrus-sasl`. Each of these packages Cyrus SASL slightly differently, including dividing SASL functions into multiple packages. You should check with your distribution vendor's documentation or Web site for the exact combination of packages you need in order to install Cyrus SASL using packages. You can also download the most recent Cyrus-SASL source directly from Carnegie Mellon University. I will show you in the next section how to compile that SASL package, but certainly if your system comes with packages for SASL, I recommend trying to use those first.

Compiling Cyrus SASL

If you want to build Cyrus SASL from source, then you need to download the source package from `http://asg.web.cmu.edu/cyrus/download/`. Unpack the source code, and configure the package using the following:

```
puppy# ./configure --enable-login --with-saslauthd
```

Table 8-5 shows some useful options you can use.

Table 8-5. *Cyrus SASL Configuration Options*

Option	Description
--enable-krb4	Enables Kerberos 4 authentication
--enable-login	Enables the usually unsupported LOGIN authentication mechanism
--enable-sql	Enables SQL authentication using auxprop (you must have the MySQL libraries installed)
--with-saslauthd	Adds saslauthd support
--with-pam	Adds PAM support

I recommend you enable the nonstandard LOGIN authentication mechanism because it is the default authentication mechanism used by Outlook-based clients, which are increasingly common for remote users. Also, if you need to enable `saslauthd`, then you also need to add the `with-saslauthd` flag. Then run `make` and `make install`.

By default, the SASL libraries are installed into `/usr/local/lib/sasl2`. Most applications, including Postfix and Sendmail, look for the SASL libraries in `/usr/lib/sasl2`. I recommend you make a symbolic link to the libraries.

```
puppy# ln -s /usr/local/sasl2/lib /usr/lib/sasl2
```

You can also you can use the environment variable `SASL_PATH` to set the location of the libraries.

■Tip Also, if you have chrooted your Sendmail MTA, you will need to copy the contents of your `/usr/local/sasl2` into your `chroot` jail (for example, into `/chroot/sendmail/usr/local/sasl2`). Postfix does not require this.

Configuring SASL saslauthd

The major configuration you need to do for Cyrus SASL is if you intend to use the saslauthd daemon for authentication. The saslauthd daemon provides plain-text authentication for the SASL libraries and replaces the old SASL 1.*x* pwcheck option. The saslauthd daemon uses a named socket to listen for connection requests for authentication.

You can start the daemon from the command line. Listing 8-15 shows the saslauthd daemon being started to do shadow password authentication. You can also start saslauthd using an init script. (Indeed, a number of distributions such as Red Hat come with already installed init scripts for saslauthd.)

Listing 8-15. *Starting* saslauthd *from the Command Line*

```
puppy# /usr/sbin/saslauthd -m /var/run/saslauthd -a shadow
```

The -m flag tells saslauthd where to install its named socket and process ID. The -m flag should point to a directory; in Listing 8-15 it points to the default location for saslauthd, which is /var/run/saslauthd. This directory must exist for saslauthd to start. The -a option tells saslauthd which authentication mechanism to use; in this case, it is saying to perform authentication against your shadow password file. Table 8-6 describes the possible authentication mechanisms you can specify.

Table 8-6. saslauthd -a *Mechanisms*

Mechanism	Description
getpwent	Authenticates using the getpwent library function, usually against the local password file
kerberos4	Authenticates against a local Kerberos 4 realm
kerberos5	Authenticates against a local Kerberos 5 realm
pam	Authenticates using Pluggable Authentication Modules (PAM)
shadow	Authenticates against the local shadow password file
ldap	Authenticates against an LDAP server

A number of other options are available, which you can learn about in the saslauthd man page.

■**Tip** The saslauthd daemon logs to syslog using the auth facility.

SMTP AUTH Using Cyrus SASL for Sendmail

The first version of Sendmail to support SASL was 8.10. I will cover how to add SASL support using the Cyrus SASL libraries from Carnegie Mellon University (in addition to the TLS support you may have already added).

Note I will cover only SASL 2 here! If your system still runs SASL 1.5 or older, then you should upgrade to take advantage of the functionality that SASL 2 offers.

I discussed in the "SMTP AUTH Using Cyrus SASL" section how to get and install the SASL library. Now you need to tell Sendmail those libraries are available and configure Sendmail to activate them. You should first check to see if your version of Sendmail already contains support for SASL. Listing 8-16 shows you how to use the `ldd` command on your `sendmail` binary to do this and gives a selected list of the libraries Sendmail should return if SASL and OpenSSL are supported.

Listing 8-16. *Checking for Cyrus SASL Support in Sendmail*

```
puppy# ldd /usr/sbin/sendmail
libsasl2.so.2 => /usr/lib/libsasl2.so.2 (0xb7474000)
libssl.so.4 => /lib/libssl.so.4 (0xb743f000)
libcrypto.so.4 => /lib/libcrypto.so.4 (0xb734e000)
```

Tip You could also use the `sendmail -d0.1 -bv root` command for this. Check the `compiled with` options for an entry called `SASLv2`.

If you see the entry for `libsasl2` in the list of compiled libraries, then Sendmail already has SASL support; you can skip to the "Configuring Cyrus SASL for Sendmail" section. If the SASL support is not present, then go to the "Compiling Cyrus SASL into Sendmail" section; I will show you how to activate the SASL support.

Compiling Cyrus SASL into Sendmail

To add support to Sendmail, you need to put some additional variables in Sendmail's `site.config.m4` file to allow Sendmail to find the SASL libraries and includes during compilation. Listing 8-17 shows these options.

Listing 8-17. `site.config.m4` *Options for SASL*

```
APPENDDEF(`confENVDEF', `-DSASL=2')
APPENDDEF(`conf_sendmail_LIBS', `-lsasl2')
```

You should now be able to build Sendmail using `Build -c`. (The `-c` option tells Sendmail to include the contents of the `site.config.m4` file.) If this compile fails because it cannot find all the SASL includes and libraries, you may also need to point Sendmail at the SASL includes and libraries. Use the following additional lines in the `site.config.m4` file, replacing */path/to/SASL/includes* and *libraries* with the location of your SASL includes and libraries:

```
APPENDDEF(`confINCDIRS', `-I/path/to/SASL/includes')
APPENDDEF(`confLIBDIRS', `-L/path/to/SASL/libraries')
```

Then try your `Build -c` again. If this completes successfully, then test your Sendmail binary as described in Listing 8-16 to confirm the SASL support has been compiled into Sendmail. Now you need to configure SASL support in Sendmail.

Configuring Cyrus SASL for Sendmail

The first step in configuring SASL is to articulate what authentication method SASL should be using. SASL maintains a separate configuration file for each application with which it works. For Sendmail, you do this by creating a file called `Sendmail.conf` in `/usr/lib/sasl2`. Listing 8-18 shows how you can set up the `Sendmail.conf` file.

Listing 8-18. `Sendmail.conf` *File from* `/usr/lib/sasl2`

```
pwcheck_method: saslauthd
```

In this file you need to specify what method SASL will use to authenticate users. In Listing 8-18 the method is `saslauthd`, which indicates that SASL will use the daemon process `saslauthd` to authenticate. This sort of authentication will use whatever authentication mechanism the `saslauthd` daemon is configured to use. I talked about getting `saslauthd` to run in the "Configuring SASL saslauthd" section earlier.

If you intend to use `saslauthd` and you run Sendmail chrooted, you need to make some modifications to allow the chrooted Sendmail daemon to access SASL. By default, `saslauthd` creates a `mux` file that receives the authentication requests. This `mux` file is usually located in the directory `/var/run/saslauthd` (often together with a PID file). If the file is not created there, you can check with location of the `mux` file by reviewing the command you are using to start `saslauthd`. You can specify the location of the `mux` file using the `-m` option. Or you can run the following command to find it:

```
puppy# netstat -peln | grep saslauthd
unix 2  [ ACC ]    STREAM  LISTENING  256149 7645/saslauthd /var/run/saslauthd/mux
```

The last part of the returned output indicates the location of the `mux` file. As a result of Sendmail being chrooted, it cannot see this file (because it is outside the chroot jail) and therefore refuses to authenticate using SASL. So, you need to move the `mux` and other `saslauthd` files into the `chroot` jail and link it back to its old location via a symbolic link to keep the `saslauthd` daemon happy. The command in Listing 8-19 takes you through the steps needed to do this—making a new directory in your `chroot` environment, moving the required files into the `chroot` jail, and linking (a symbolic link only, which is important to maintain the security of your `chroot` jail) back to the original location. You need to restart `saslauthd` after doing this.

Listing 8-19. *Running* `saslauthd` *in Sendmail* `chroot` *Jail*

```
puppy# mkdir -p /chroot/sendmail/var/run
puppy# mv /var/run/saslauthd /chroot/sendmail/var/run/saslauthd
puppy# ln -s /chroot/sendmail/var/run/saslauthd /var/run/saslauthd
```

If your remote users do not have a local login to the mail system (for example, virtual users), then you can use some other methods to authenticate them. One of the easiest is to create a stand-alone database of usernames and passwords. In this case, you would change your `pwcheck_method` to the following:

```
pwcheck_method: auxprop
```

auxprop stands for *auxiliary property* plug-ins, of which the default is the sasldb type. As it is the default, you do not need to specify anything else other than auxprop, because SASL knows this indicates sasldb. By default with the sasldb plug-in, SASL looks for the file /etc/sasldb2. This may already exist on your system; if it does not, do not panic. When you create your first user, SASL will automatically create the /etc/sasldb2 file if it does not already exist.

To add users to the sasldb2 file, you use the saslpasswd2 command that comes with the SASL package. You will need a username and a domain, which should match the FQDN that is defined in Sendmail. Listing 8-20 shows you how to set up the command.

Listing 8-20. *The* saslpasswd2 *Command*

```
puppy# saslpasswd2 -c -u domain username
```

The -c option tells SASL to create a new user account. The -u option specifies the domain for that user. You should replace the variables *domain* and *username* with the FQDN of the Sendmail server and the required username for the user, respectively. You will be prompted by the saslpasswd2 binary to enter a password for this username. If you have Sendmail located in a chroot jail, then you can use an additional option, -f, to specify the location of the sasldb2 file so you can place it in the jail and have it accessible to Sendmail.

```
puppy# saslpasswd2 -c -f /chroot/sendmail/etc -u domain username.
```

Using the auxprop method, you can also configure Sendmail to authenticate via Lightweight Directory Access Protocol (LDAP) or a variety of SQL-based databases such as MySQL or PostgreSQL. These methods are most useful when setting up virtual domains and virtual users. See the Sendmail Web site for some HOWTOs about how to achieve this authentication.

Finally, it is important to note that if you are using saslauthd or sasldb2 as the authentication method, then you are using the PLAIN or LOGIN mechanism for authentication. These use simple Base64-encoded passwords that can be easily sniffed out and cracked across your network. This is where TLS comes together with SASL to allow encrypted authentication. You should ensure your mail client is configured to attempt an SSL/TLS connection with your mail server as well as configured to do an SMTP AUTH when sending e-mail. You can also ensure your AUTH_OPTIONS flag includes the p parameter, which requires Sendmail to allow SMTP AUTH only if a security layer such as TLS is in place first. If you do not use TLS with SMTP AUTH and SASL, then the level of security offered is minimal; in that case, I recommend you look at alternative methods of authentication.

Using SMTP Server Authentication with Sendmail

To tell Sendmail about the SASL capabilities available to it, you need to define some options in your sendmail.mc file. Add the two lines from Listing 8-21 to your sendmail.mc file.

Listing 8-21. *Enabling SASL in Sendmail*

```
define(`confAUTH_MECHANISMS', `PLAIN LOGIN')
TRUST_AUTH_MECH('LOGIN PLAIN')
```

The first line defines the list of mechanisms that are available to Sendmail to authenticate a connection. In this instance, I have specified only PLAIN and LOGIN. The second line is a class that further refines this list into those mechanisms that allow relaying; again, in this case, they are PLAIN and LOGIN. This class can be a subset of the AUTH_MECHANISMS list or the same list.

You can also define the AUTH_OPTIONS parameter. This allows you to control and tune your Sendmail authentication options. Add this line to your sendmail.mc file:

```
define(`confAUTH_OPTIONS'. `options')
```

options is one of a string of characters that changes the way authentication functions are performed. In Table 8-7 you can see a list of some of the more useful parameters.

Table 8-7. AUTH_OPTION *Options*

Character	Description
a	Provides protection from active attacks during authentication exchange.
y	Does not permit anonymous mechanisms.
d	Does not permit mechanisms that are vulnerable to dictionary attacks (in other words, LOGIN and PLAIN).
p	Does not permit mechanisms that are vulnerable to dictionary attacks (in other words, LOGIN and PLAIN, unless TLS is activated).
A	Fixes from broken MTAs that do not abide by the RFC. This is needed only if you using Sendmail as an SMTP AUTH client.

For example, I recommend you set the AUTH_OPTIONS flags to at least the following:

```
define(`confAUTH_OPTIONS'. `a y p A')
```

The use of the p option means you must have TLS running in Sendmail as well; otherwise, you will be not be able to authenticate with SMTP AUTH.

Re-create your sendmail.cf file with these options configured, and you should now have SMTP AUTH and SASL working. To check this, try the commands in Listing 8-22 to see if your Sendmail server responds to an EHLO with the availability of the AUTH command.

Listing 8-22. *Checking SMTP AUTH Is Available in Sendmail*

```
puppy# telnet puppy.yourdomain.com 25
Trying 192.168.0.1...
Connected to puppy (192.168.0.1).
Escape character is '^]'.
220 puppy.yourdomain.com ESMTP
EHLO kitten
250-puppy.yourdomain.com Hello kitten [192.168.0.2], pleased to meet you
250-AUTH LOGIN PLAIN
250-STARTTLS
```

You can now test SMTP AUTH using the client of your choice. I will show you how it works with Outlook Express in the "Testing SMTP AUTH with Outlook Express" section.

Using SMTP Client Authentication with Sendmail

You can also use SASL in Sendmail to provide SMTP AUTH authentication between servers. In this model, your Sendmail server acts as a client of another MTA. This relies on you having suitable credentials stored on your Sendmail MTA to authenticate you to the remote server. Sendmail can store those credentials either in the `access` database or via the `authinfo` file. I recommend you use the `authinfo` file, as this gives you the ability to separate entries that require higher security from your more general access database, which a number of users might see. To enable `authinfo`, add the following line to your `sendmail.mc` file:

```
FEATURE(`authinfo')
```

This will create an entry in your `sendmail.cf` file when you re-create it using `m4`, which looks like this:

```
Kauthinfo hash /etc/mail/authinfo
```

You need to create this `authinfo` database. Place your authentication entries into a file, call it `authinfo`, and then `makemap` it into a hash database or the database of your choice. The `authinfo` entries follow a simple structure of two columns. The left column contains the `AuthInfo` statement followed by the domain, host, or IP address of the remote server being authenticated to, separated by a colon. The right column contains a list of configuration items, each quoted and separated by a space. Table 8-8 lists them. The two columns are separated by tabs or one or more spaces.

Table 8-8. `authinfo` *Configuration Items*

Item	Description
P : | =	The password for the connection. If it is displayed as P:, the password is in plain text. P= the password is Base64 encoded.
U	Username for authentication.
I	The user allowed to set up the connection.
R	The realm. Usually the FQDN of your system. If it is omitted, Sendmail will use the content of the `$j` macro.
M	A list of the supported mechanisms for this connection, separated by spaces. If you omit this, then Sendmail will use the contents of the `AuthMechanisms` option.

To authenticate, you must have at least a username, `U`, or the authentication identifier, `I`. Listing 8-23 shows some sample entries.

Listing 8-23. *Sample* `authinfo` *Entries*

```
AuthInfo:anotherdomain.com "U:jim" "P:tinker"
AuthInfo:host.overthere.com "U:jim" "P=a1323498fkfg" "M:PLAIN LOGIN"
AuthInfo:192.168.1.100 "U:jim" "P:tailor" "R:puppy.yourdomain.com"
```

Create your `authinfo` database.

```
puppy# makemap hash /etc/mail/authinfo < authinfo
```

Now secure it. It should be owned by the root user and chmoded to 0600. Now restart Sendmail to update your configuration, and you should be able to authenticate using the entries contained in your authinfo database.

■**Caution** Do not ever use the root user or indeed any username or password combination that exists on your client or server system as a login. Always assume that the contents of your authinfo database could be compromised.

SMTP AUTH Using Cyrus SASL for Postfix

To get SMTP AUTH and Cyrus SASL working with Postfix, I will add support for the Cyrus SASL libraries from Carnegie Mellon University (in addition to the TLS support you may have already added).

■**Note** I will cover only SASL 2 here! If your system still runs SASL 1.5 or older, then you should upgrade to take advantage of the functionality that SASL 2 offers. Also, it has been noted that support for earlier versions of SASL will be phased out of the newer versions of Postfix.

I discussed in the "SMTP AUTH Using Cyrus SASL" section how to get and install the SASL library. Now you need to tell Postfix those libraries are available and configure Postfix to activate them. You should check to see if your version of Postfix already contains support for SASL. Listing 8-24 shows you how to use the ldd command on your smtpd binary to do this and gives a selected list of the libraries Postfix should return if SASL and OpenSSL are supported.

Listing 8-24. *Checking for Cyrus SASL Support in Postfix*

```
puppy# ldd /usr/libexec/postfix/smtpd
libsasl2.so.2 => /usr/lib/libsasl2.so.2 (0x40021000)
libssl.so.2 => /lib/libssl.so.2 (0x40035000)
libcrypto.so.2 => /lib/libcrypto.so.2 (0x40065000)
```

If you see the entry for libsasl2 in the list of compiled libraries, then your Postfix already has SASL support; you can skip to the "Configuring Cyrus SASL for Postfix" section. If the SASL support is not present, then go to the "Compiling Cyrus SASL into Postfix" section; I will show you how to activate the SASL support.

Compiling Cyrus SASL into Postfix

To recompile Postfix with support for SASL, you need to change your Makefiles to point to the locations of the SASL includes and libraries. In the TLS section I used the command in Listing 8-12 to add the support for TLS to the Postfix Makefiles. In Listing 8-25 I have taken that `Makefile` update and added support for SASL as well. As with Listing 8-12, the exact location of the OpenSSL and Cyrus SASL includes and libraries may be different, so you will need to adjust Listing 8-25 to match your environment.

Listing 8-25. *Adding SASL and OpenSSL to the Postfix* `Makefiles`

```
make makefiles CCARGS="-DUSE_SASL_AUTH -I/usr/include/sasl ➥
-DHAS_SSL -I/usr/include/openssl" AUXLIBS="-lsasl2 -lssl -lcrypto"
```

Then run `make` and `make upgrade` if you already have Postfix installed, or run `make install` for a new install of the Postfix source. Now if you run `ldd` on the `smtpd` binary, you should see that `libsasl2` is included in the list of libraries. If Postfix is already running, then you will also need to restart it.

Configuring Cyrus SASL for Postfix

The first step in configuring SASL is to articulate what authentication method SASL should be using. SASL maintains a separate configuration file for each application with which it works. For Postfix you do this by creating a file called `smtpd.conf` in `/usr/lib/sasl2`. Listing 8-26 shows a typical file.

Listing 8-26. `smtpd.conf` *File from* `/usr/lib/sasl2`

```
pwcheck_method: saslauthd
```

In this file you need to specify what method SASL will use to authenticate users. In Listing 8-26 the method is `saslauthd`, which indicates that SASL will use the daemon process `saslauthd` to authenticate against your `passwd` file (which is rare these days, as most systems use shadow passwords), against shadow passwords, or via PAM. This sort of authentication uses your existing user and password system to verify users. This implies that the remote users have a login to the mail system that Postfix and SASL are able to authenticate. I earlier discussed in the "Configuring SASL saslauthd" section how to get `saslauthd` running

If you intend to use `saslauthd` and you run Postfix chrooted, you need to make some modifications to allow the chrooted Postfix daemon to access SASL. By default `saslauthd` creates a `mux` file that receives the authentication requests. This `mux` file is usually located in the directory `/var/run/saslauthd` (often with a PID file). If the file is not created there, you can check the location of the `mux` file by reviewing the command you are using to start `saslauthd`. You can specify the location of the `mux` file by using the `-m` option. Or you can run this command to find it:

```
puppy# netstat -peln | grep saslauthd
unix 2  [ ACC ]   STREAM  LISTENING  256149 7645/saslauthd /var/run/saslauthd/mux
```

The last part of the returned output indicates the location of the `mux` file. As a result of Postfix being chrooted, it cannot see this file (because it is outside the chroot jail) and therefore refuses to authenticate using SASL. So, you need to move the `mux` file and other `saslauthd` files into the `chroot` jail and link it back to its old location via a symbolic link to keep the `saslauthd` daemon happy. The command in Listing 8-27 takes you through the steps needed to do this—making a new directory in your `chroot` environment (I have assumed you have installed Postfix in the default `chroot` location, but you can change this to your Postfix chroot location if required), moving the required files into the `chroot` jail, linking (a symbolic link only, which is important for maintaining the security of your `chroot` jail) back to the original location. You need to restart `saslauthd` after doing this.

Listing 8-27. *Running* `saslauthd` *in Postfix* `chroot` *Jail*

```
puppy# mkdir -p /var/spool/postfix/var/run
puppy# mv /var/run/saslauthd /var/spool/postfix/var/run/saslauthd
puppy# ln -s /var/spool/postfix/var/run/saslauthd /var/run/saslauthd
```

If your remote users do not have a local login to the mail system (for example, virtual users), then you can use some other methods to authenticate them. One of the easiest is to create a stand-alone database of usernames and passwords. In this case, you can change your `pwcheck_method` to the following:

```
pwcheck_method: auxprop
```

`auxprop` stands for *auxiliary property* plug-ins, of which the default is the `sasldb` type. As it is the default, you do not need to specify anything else other than `auxprop`, because SASL knows this indicates `sasldb`. By default with the `sasldb` plug-in, SASL looks for the file `/etc/sasldb2`. This may already exist on your system; however, if it does not, do not panic. When you create your first user, SASL will automatically create the `/etc/sasldb2` file if it does not already exist.

To add users to the `sasldb2` file, you use the `saslpasswd2` command that comes with the SASL package. You will need a username and a SASL domain, which for Postfix defaults to the content of the `$myhostname` variable. Listing 8-28 shows how you can set up the command.

Listing 8-28. *The* `saslpasswd2` *Command*

```
puppy# saslpasswd2 -c -u domain username
```

The `-c` option tells SASL to create a new user account. The `-u` option specifies the domain for that user. You would replace the variables *domain* and *username* with the FQDN of the Postfix server and the required username for the user, respectively. You will be prompted by the `saslpasswd2` binary to enter a password for this username.

If you run Postfix in a `chroot` jail, then you need to move your `sasldb2` file in the `chroot` jail or create it in there yourself; otherwise, Postfix will not be able to read the contents of the database. The `saslpasswd2` command allows you to specify where you would like to create the `sasldb2` database using the `-f` option.

```
puppy# saslpasswd2 -f /var/spool/postfix/etc/sasdb2 ➥
-c -u `postconf -h myhostname` admin
```

The command on the previous line will create your `sasldb2` database in the `/var/spool/postfix/etc` directory and add a user called `admin`. I have also added `postconf -h myhostname` as the content of the `-u` option where you would normally specify the domain of the Postfix system. This addition to the command will ensure you get the correct domain in the `-u` option by outputting the correct Postfix value. You also need to adjust the permissions of the `sasldb2` file, as shown in the next line, to allow Postfix to be able to read it:

```
puppy# chmod 0644 /var/spool/postfix/etc/sasldb2
```

Using the auxprop method you can also configure Postfix to authenticate via a MySQL database or via LDAP. These methods are most useful when setting up virtual domains and virtual users. See the Postfix Web site for some HOWTOs about how to achieve this authentication.

Finally, it is important to note that if you are using saslauthd or sasldb2 as the authentication method, then you are using the PLAIN or LOGIN mechanism for authentication. These use simple Base64-encoded passwords that can be easily sniffed out and cracked across your network. This is where TLS comes together with SASL to allow encrypted authentication. You should ensure your mail client is configured to attempt an SSL/TLS connection with your mail server as well as configured to do an SMTP AUTH when sending e-mail. You can also enable the smtpd_tls_auth_only = yes option in your main.cf file, which allows SMTP AUTH to make a connection only if a STARTTLS has been issued first. If you do not use TLS with SMTP AUTH and SASL, then the level of security offered is minimal, and I recommend you look at alternative methods of authentication.

Using SMTP Server Authentication with Postfix

The first step in activating SMTP AUTH with SASL in Postfix is to add some configuration options to the main.cf file. For SASL server functions, all the configuration options start with smtpd_sasl*, and for all the SASL client functions, the configuration options start with smtp_sasl*. Let's activate the SASL server functions. Add the following four lines to your main.cf file:

```
smtpd_sasl_auth_enable = yes
smtpd_sasl_local_domain =
smtpd_sasl_security_options = noanonymous
broken_sasl_auth_clients = yes
```

The first line, smtpd_sasl_auth_enable = yes, simply tells Postfix to turn on support for SASL. The second line, smtpd_sasl_local_domain =, tells SASL what the local domain is. This line can be somewhat confusing for many people. A lot of sources recommend adding the Postfix variable $myhostname (which should be the FQDN of your system) to this line. This was the correct behavior for SASL, but for SASL 2 and Postfix the correct default is to leave this blank. This is something to note if you are upgrading from SASL to SASL 2 as part of this configuration process. The third line, smtpd_sasl_security_options, allows you to control what SASL authentication frameworks Postfix offers. Table 8-9 shows a full list of the options available to you.

Table 8-9. smtpd_security_options *for Postfix*

Option	Description
noanonymous	Disables methods that allow anonymous authentication such as ANON (the default)
noplaintext	Disables methods that use plain-text passwords such as PLAIN and LOGIN
noactive	Disables methods that could be subject to active attacks
nodictionary	Disables methods that could be subject to passive attack

All of these are relatively self-explanatory. But you should note that the nonanoymous option is the default behavior for Postfix. By changing this or adding additional options, you are overriding that default. Thus, I recommend you always leave noanonymous at the end of the list, as shown in the next line:

```
smtpd_sasl_security_options = noactive, noanonymous
```

The previous line is useful if you have users with older e-mail clients. By default, Postfix presents the AUTH command as per the RFC. Some older broken clients (for example, Outlook versions prior to 5 suffer from this problem) expect the command to look like AUTH=. Setting this option to yes tells Postfix to present AUTH both ways and enables these older clients to use SMTP AUTH correctly. I recommend you use it because it has no ill effects for Postfix, and it means if there are any older clients out in your network, SMTP AUTH will work for them.

Now if you restart Postfix, you will be able to Telnet your mail server and see the AUTH statement and any SASL authentication frameworks that are supported.

```
puppy# telnet puppy.yourdomain.com 25
Trying 192.168.0.1...
Connected to puppy.
Escape character is '^]'.
220 puppy.yourdomain.com
EHLO kitten
250-puppy.yourdomain.com
250-STARTTLS
250-AUTH PLAIN LOGIN GSSAPI DIGEST-MD5 CRAM-MD5
```

■**Caution** If you have smtpd_tls_auth_only = yes set in your main.cf file, you will not see the AUTH message presented, because you have not initiated STARTTLS. If you intend to use the smtpd_tls_auth_only option, then I recommend you turn it off during your initial testing.

As you can see, AUTH is available and is advertising the PLAIN, LOGIN, GSSAPI, DIGEST-MD5, and CRAM-MD5 authentication methods.

Now to actually use SASL and SMTP AUTH to authenticate relaying, you need to adjust your smtpd_recipient_restrictions so Postfix uses the results of SMTP AUTH to authenticate users. Find the smtpd_recipient_restrictions option in Postfix. By adding the option permit_sasl_authenticated, you allow any client authenticated with SASL to relay using your mail server. Listing 8-29 shows the restrictions option with SASL authentication permitted.

Listing 8-29. smtpd_recipient_restrictions *in Postfix*

```
smtpd_recipient_restrictions =
    permit_mynetworks,
    permit_sasl_authenticated,
    reject_unauth_destination
```

■**Tip** Always remember to end your restrictions with a rejection, here `reject_unauth_destination`, to ensure that the default behavior is to reject relaying.

Finally, restart Postfix.

Using SMTP Client Authentication with Postfix

You may want to enable server-to-server relaying using SMTP AUTH and SASL. This is handled a bit differently than authorizing client-to-server relaying, because your Postfix server needs to provide a username and password to the remote server to allow it to authenticate your mail server. I provide these usernames and passwords to Postfix in the form of a `postmap`-created password file.

First, enable client-based SMTP AUTH and SASL in Postfix and use the `smtp_sasl_password_maps` option to tell Postfix where to find your password file. Listing 8-30 shows the required commands.

Listing 8-30. *Enabling Client SMTP AUTH*

```
smtp_sasl_auth_enable = yes
smtp_sasl_password_maps = hash:/etc/postfix/sasl_client_passwd
```

Second, create your password file. You will need to specify a *domain* and *username:password* combination. The next line shows a username and password for the `anotherdomain.com` domain to be used when trying to relay through to that domain.

```
anotherdomain.com     admin:secretpassword
```

Then run `postmap` on the file, like so:

```
puppy# postmap /etc/postfix/sasl_client_passwd
```

and reload Postfix. Now if you were to send a message to a user at `anotherdomain.com`, your Postfix system would offer the credentials of `admin` with a password of `secretpassword`.

Testing SMTP AUTH with Outlook Express

To show how to test SMTP AUTH, I will set up an Outlook Express client to use SMTP AUTH to log in with a login name and password and perform a relay. If you do not have Outlook Express, you can use any e-mail client that is capable of authenticating outbound connections. Open Outlook Express, and select Tools ➤ Accounts... to edit the properties of an e-mail account. Click the Servers tab. At the bottom of this tab is an entry under Outgoing Mail Server. Highlight the option for My Server Requires Authentication, and click the Settings... button (see Figure 8-1).

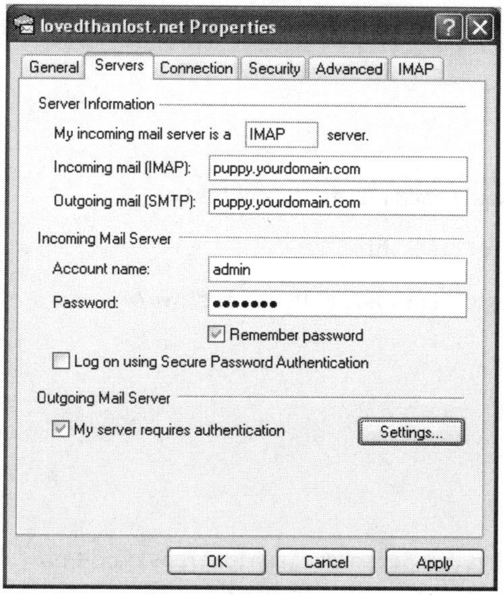

Figure 8-1. *Configuring Outlook Express to use SMTP AUTH*

Inside the Settings tab you have two options. You can tell Outlook to provide the same details it uses to log into your e-mail account (which should be your login name and password for your mail server if you use a local login), or you can specify another login and password, if you are using the `sasldb` authentication option. Click OK; when the dialog box appears, click OK again, and then click Close to shut down the Account Setup tab. Now send a test e-mail to an external e-mail address.

If everything is set up correctly, you should see some resulting messages similar to those in Listing 8-31 in your mail log file. This example shows a successful TLS connection being created from your client and a successful SMTP AUTH authentication using the `LOGIN` method for username `admin`.

Listing 8-31. *Successful SMTP AUTH Authentication in Postfix*

```
Apr  8 14:50:35 puppy postfix/smtpd[30017]: ➥
connect from client.yourdomain.com[192.168.0.50]
Apr  8 14:50:35 puppy postfix/smtpd[30017]: ➥
setting up TLS connection from client.yourdomain.com[192.168.0.50]
Apr  8 14:50:35 puppy postfix/smtpd[30017]: ➥
TLS connection established from client.yourdomain.com[192.168.0.50]: ➥
TLSv1 with cipher RC4-MD5 (128/128 bits)
Apr  8 14:50:35 puppy postfix/smtpd[30017]: ➥
99C9F231E56: client= client.yourdomain.com[192.168.0.50], ➥
sasl_method=LOGIN, sasl_username=admin
```

Resources

The following are resources you can use.

Mailing Lists

- **Sendmail Usenet and mailing list**: http://www.sendmail.org/usenet.html

- **Postfix mailing lists**: http://www.postfix.org/lists.html

- **Postfix TLS mailing list**: http://www.aet.tu-cottbus.de/mailman/listinfo/postfix_tls

Sites

- **Sendmail**: http://www.sendmail.org/

- **Postfix**: http://www.postfix.org

- **Postfix TLS patch**: http://www.aet.tu-cottbus.de/personen/jaenicke/postfix_tls/

- **Postfix TLS RPMs**: http://postfix.wl0.org/en/

- **Cyrus SASL**: http://asg.web.cmu.edu/sasl/

- **S/MIME and PGP-MIME**: http://www.imc.org/smime-pgpmime.html and http://www.ietf.org/html.charters/smime-charter.html

CHAPTER 9

■■■

Hardening Remote Access to E-mail

More and more users expect to be able to access their e-mail remotely, including from home and while traveling. Even more users are best classified as "roving" users who do not regularly return to a home base and need to be able to access their e-mail resources remotely. These users are forced by the nature of their movements to rely on remote access to provide access to vital corporate resources such as e-mail.

To address the requirement for remote access, several protocols were developed to provide remote-access functionality to a variety of resources. This chapter focuses on the protocols that give you remote access to your e-mail resources in the form of messages and message stores. The two key protocols I will cover are the Internet Message Access Protocol (IMAP) and the Post Office Protocol (POP); I will also cover a variety of related offshoots of these protocols. These protocols basically perform the same core function, providing remote access to your e-mail, but they perform that function using different methods.

Naturally, the farther your users are from your internal network (especially as the medium of the Internet is interposed between your remote users and the resources they require), the higher the risk that your data (usernames, passwords, valuable commercial data) could be intercepted, diverted, or altered. Earlier implementations of remote-access protocols and systems assumed that the fabrics and networks those protocols were traveling across were much nicer and friendlier places than the current environment has proven to be. Additionally, opening connections to the Internet for these protocols to operate also puts your system at risk and adds points through which an attacker could attempt to penetrate your system.

I will explain a bit about IMAP and POP. Then I will make some recommendations about particular servers I think are the most secure applications to provide this functionality. I will take you through the risks and potential exploits that running IMAP and POP exposes you to and then take you through installing, configuring, and securing an IMAP server and a POP server. I will also cover the commonly used Fetchmail tool and the security risks associated with using it, as well as how to mitigate some of the risks and harden your Fetchmail installation.

I will not go into a lot of detail about non-security-related configuration and management issues such as performance.

IMAP

IMAP is a protocol for retrieving e-mail messages. The latest version is called IMAP4 and described in RFC 3501.[1] Essentially, it allows a client (such as Pine, mutt, or Outlook) to access messages stores on a remote server as if they were stored locally. This allows users to manipulate messages on that remote server without having to send those messages back and forth.

It is similar in functionality to the other protocol I will cover in this chapter, POP, but has some important differences. IMAP and POP both aim to achieve the same basic objective—allowing remote access to message stores. POP is much more focused on retrieving those messages from the remote message store from a single client, storing those messages on the client, and then deleting the messages from the remote message store. IMAP generally assumes users will retrieve their mail from multiple different systems and thus leaves the messages in place on the remote message store. The following list covers most of the key functionality of IMAP:

- Checking for new messages

- Deleting and permanently removing messages

- Creating, deleting, and renaming mailboxes

- Creating, deleting, and renaming folders in a mailbox

- Searching and selectively retrieving messages and message attributes

- RFC-822 and MIME parsing on the remote server

■**Note** IMAP does not in itself send e-mail. You still need an SMTP server for that. IMAP merely retrieves the messages from your remote message store.

POP

POP is similar to IMAP in nature, designed for the retrieval of messages from remote message stores. It is currently in its third version, POP3, which is described in RFC 1939.[2]

■**Note** When I refer to POP, I am talking about POP3.

POP uses a client (for example, a mail client such as Pine or mutt or a mail retrieval tool such as Fetchmail) to connect to a remote server running POP. The client usually retrieves the messages from the remote message store, stores them locally, and (unlike IMAP) generally

---

1. http://www.faqs.org/rfcs/rfc3501.html

2. Refer to http://www.faqs.org/rfcs/rfc1939.html. You should probably also look at the "POP Extensions" RFC at http://www.faqs.org/rfcs/rfc2449.html.

deletes the remote messages. It was principally designed to allow remote computers without permanent connections to the Internet to use another system as a "post office" and to hold all mail until that remote client could connect and receive its mail. ISPs commonly utilize this system.

■**Note** In fact, most individual ISP users employ POP to retrieve their e-mail. IMAP is considerably less frequently used by ISPs for this function.

POP is also often used to collect e-mail from multiple remote messages stores and to consolidate it to a single central location when a user has multiple e-mail accounts.

■**Note** Like IMAP, POP also does not allow you to send e-mail and instead relies on a SMTP server to perform this function.

Choosing IMAP or POP Servers

Should you choose IMAP or POP? There are really two parts to this question. The first is, should you use IMAP or POP (or should you use both)? Well, that depends on your requirements. As I have talked about previously, POP is a good choice if you have users who are retrieving e-mail from a single location and deleting that e-mail from the remote message store in the process. They maintain local messages stores containing the e-mail they retrieve. For other sites, IMAP is a good choice because it allows you to maintain a central message store where users hold and manipulate their messages. This means they log into that message store from a variety of locations or clients and always have access to their messages. Or you could run both protocols and provide users with the option of having the solution that suits their requirements best. So decide what model suits your organization and then choose a suitable server.

Indeed, a lot of IMAP and POP servers are available from which to choose. IMAP servers include Courier-IMAP, Cyrus IMAP, and UW-IMAP, among others. Also, several open-source POP servers are currently available. Courier-IMAP includes a POP server, as does Cyrus IMAP and UW-IMAP; Qmail includes a POP server; and others include Qpopper, vm-pop3d, GNU pop3d, POPular, and TeaPOP.

■**Note** I provide a list of all the home pages of these IMAP and POP servers in the "Sites" section.

I will choose a package that allows you to use both IMAP and POP, and I will assume you want to enable both IMAP and POP functionality. You can, of course, disable one or more of the protocols if you do not want to use it. This also makes configuring your IMAP and POP server easier because you need to learn how to use only one package. The package I have chosen to cover is Cyrus IMAP. Cyrus IMAP is produced by the same team that developed Cyrus SASL and thus comes with good integration to SASL; it is also easy to integrate with TSL/SSL. It even has a number of additional features that make it an ideal choice for a secure IMAP or POP server. I will discuss those features in the "Cyrus IMAP" section.

This is not to say that whatever you use as your existing IMAP or POP server is not a good solution. But there have been some serious issues with some of the servers available. Of obvious note are the continuing security issues with UW-IMAP and Qpopper, which are both commonly and popularly used packages. If you are running one of these, I recommend at the least you upgrade to the latest version but perhaps also consider looking at alternatives such as Cyrus IMAP. The best idea is to examine the Security Focus Bugtraq mailing list[3] and review any IMAP- or POP-related security exploits and vulnerabilities and the packages they affect. In combination with a careful analysis of your requirements, the functionality offered by particular packages and by examining how they address security-related functionality and issues should give you a good picture of whether a package is secure and suitable for your environment.

How Is Your IMAP or POP Server at Risk?

So in what ways is your IMAP or POP server at risk of attack? Well, there are two major threats here. The first is the risk posed by placing an IMAP and/or POP server on the Internet and the opportunities this offers for an attacker to use that daemon to stage an attack on your system. The second is the privacy and security of your e-mail, passwords, and users as they send and receive data from the remote message store to their clients, especially across the Internet. I will cover both these threats individually and later in this chapter; I will also discuss some ways to mitigate these risks, provide some practical configurations using Cyrus IMAP, and show this risk mitigation in action.

The first area of threat is generally an attacker scanning for an open port, discovering your IMAP or POP server, and attempting to exploit that server and penetrate your system. This is further exacerbated by the large number of exploits that can and have affected IMAP and POP servers. This is a key reason to keep your IMAP or POP server up-to-date with the latest stable version and any available and relevant security patches. You should ensure you are using the most recent stable version of the server and that you regularly check that no new security exposures, exploits, or issues have been discovered.[4]

Additionally, in some cases with some types of services, you can mitigate the risk of having open ports on the Internet by placing that server inside a chroot jail, such as BIND or SMTP. Unfortunately, many IMAP and POP servers are not good candidates for chrooting because of their need to read all users' mbox or Maildir files. Additionally, some IMAP servers insist on running as the root user and not dropping their privileges. The server I have chosen, though, Cyrus IMAP, is able to be chrooted because it stores messages in a central private message store, not in users' home directories. Cyrus IMAP also requires only root to bind to its required IP addresses and ports, and then it drops privileges and by default runs as the cyrus user. I will take you through chrooting Cyrus IMAP in the next section.

---

3. http://www.securityfocus.com/archive/1

4. I discuss the best approach to this in Chapter 1.

The second area of threat is the threat to your users' data, usernames, and passwords. When run out of the box, many IMAP and POP installations perform simple plain-text authentication, usually against a local user in your /etc/passwd file. They also conduct the transmission of those passwords unencrypted between the client and the server. This means that via some fairly simple network-sniffing techniques, attackers can read both the username and password of a user. This results in their ability to access that user's message store or, if the user has a shell login, to log into the system and continue their attack from within your system. You can reduce this threat greatly by using encryption on your IMAP and POP connections using OpenSSL and/or using more sophisticated authentication methods through a framework such as SASL. It is also good to consider whether you would like to create a "sealed" system where no IMAP or POP user has an account with shell access to the system. I will now take you through configuring and running Cyrus IMAP with OpenSSL, cover some authentication methods, and show the best way to create a "sealed" system.

Cyrus IMAP

The Andrews System Group at Carnegie Mellon University produces Cyrus IMAP, which is part of the broader Cyrus Electronic Mail Project that includes close links to its sister project, the Cyrus SASL project. It is designed to be part of a scalable electronic mail infrastructure that can be used by small organizations right up to enterprise-sized deployments. The main home of the Cyrus IMAP project is at http://asg.web.cmu.edu/cyrus/; also, a Cyrus IMAP wiki is available at http://acs-wiki.andrew.cmu.edu/twiki/bin/view/Cyrus/WebHome and is more frequently updated than the project home page.

Several features make Cyrus IMAP an attractive choice as a secure solution for an IMAP and/or POP server. The following list details each of those features; I will go through them to explain why and how they offer security benefits for your IMAP and POP server:

- You do not need to create local user accounts for IMAP/POP users; thus, you can "seal" your system and not allow local logins.

- You can tightly control access to your user's mail using customizable access control lists (ACLs) that utilize the IMAP ACL command.

- You can chroot your Cyrus IMAP server.

- Cyrus IMAP integrates easily with Cyrus SASL for a variety of user authentication methods using the IMAP AUTH command.

- Cyrus IMAP integrates easily with TLS/SSL to allow encrypted communication between your clients and server.

- The package has a limited number of security-related flaws or issues. At the time of publication, Security Focus did not have any Cyrus IMAP vulnerabilities listed.

One of the key factors behind choosing a Cyrus IMAP server is that it overcomes one of the major security flaws I have highlighted—the use of usernames and passwords to authenticate to the message store that can also be used to log into the IMAP/POP server. Whilst under some circumstances, this is not an issue; for example, when you have small volumes of users, or when your IMAP server supports hundreds of users or a large volume of virtual users, it is both a security risk and a large administrative overhead to require that all IMAP/POP users need a valid and unique UID number.

Cyrus IMAP does not need a unique ID (UID) or even a user created on the system to allow access to mailboxes. Rather, Cyrus IMAP allows you to choose the model you would like to implement, including authentication to passwd files, an LDAP server, a MySQL database, PAM authentication, Kerberos 4 or 5 authentication, or a sasldb database file. This is especially useful to create POP/IMAP servers that are "sealed" and allow no user logins at all, which greatly enhances the security of these systems.

Cyrus IMAP also uses ACLs to control access by a user or group of users to the particular mailbox. This allows you to configure some quite complex access models. Cyrus IMAP also provides a comprehensive authentication framework (I have listed some of the possible authentication methods previously) and is easy to integrate with TLS/SSL. This includes the capability, similar to the capability also described in Chapter 8 for Sendmail and Postfix, of allowing only plain-text authentication methods when a session between a client and the server is suitably encrypted using TLS.

Finally, Cyrus IMAP is also a good choice performance-wise. Cyrus IMAP uses a message store database to hold your mail and your message metadata, which provides excellent performance and stability. Using this mail storage format has a caveat: if you have users who sign on and access their e-mail from the command line, then you need to consider that their mail is no longer stored in an mbox- or Maildir-style message store. Rather, it is stored in Cyrus's message store, and the command-line e-mail client needs to access this messages store via IMAP; for instance, the mail command will no longer function. This being said, Cyrus IMAP is designed to run on a "sealed" system where there are no local shell logins except those of administrators. Figure 9-1 illustrates a functional model of a Cyrus IMAP server.

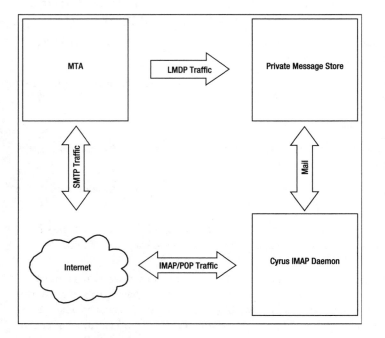

Figure 9-1. *How your Cyrus IMAP server works*

So how does Cyrus IMAP actually work? It is usually integrated with your MTA. You configure your MTA to deliver mail to Cyrus IMAP. (I will show you how to integrate it with both Sendmail and Postfix.) I will be using the Local Mail Transfer Protocol (LMTP)[5] to put e-mail from your MTA into the private message store. In the model, I will show you that the private message store will reside within a chroot jail. When an e-mail client connects to the IMAP or POP daemon, it accesses the Cyrus IMAP message store and retrieves the required message or messages. Figure 9-1 also shows this process.

Installing and Compiling Cyrus IMAP

Installing and compiling Cyrus IMAP can occasionally be a temperamental process, as Cyrus IMAP has a few quirks that I will help you address and that should make your Cyrus IMAP install as smooth as possible.

■**Note** You will also need Cyrus SASL. See Chapter 8 for instructions on how to install and configure Cyrus SASL. You should install Cyrus SASL before you install Cyrus IMAP!

First, you need to download the latest version of Cyrus IMAP from `ftp://ftp.andrew.cmu.edu/pub/cyrus-mail/`.

■**Tip** I used Cyrus IMAP 2.2.3 for this installation.

Second, you need to create a user for Cyrus IMAP and assign the user to a group. Enter the following:

```
puppy# useradd -g mail -s /sbin/nologin -d /dev/null cyrus
```

I have created a user called cyrus who belongs the group mail, who cannot log on, and who has a home directory of /dev/null. You could also create your own cyrus group, but I have chosen to use the mail group rather than clutter the system with additional groups.

Now unpack the source package, and change into the resulting created directory. You need to check whether you have the makedepend command. Use find or locate to check for it; if it does not exist on your system, then you can create it using source from within the Cyrus IMAP source package. Change into the makedepend directory, compile the command, and install it. Listing 9-1 shows the process I undertook to do this.

Listing 9-1. *Installing* makedepend *for Cyrus IMAP*

```
puppy# cd path/to/Cyrus/source/makedepend
puppy# ./configure && make
puppy# cp makedepend /usr/local/bin
```

---

5. `http://www.ietf.org/rfc/rfc2033.txt`

Now to compile Cyrus IMAP, you first need to configure it. Listing 9-2 shows the `configure` statement I used for Cyrus IMAP. I will take you through that statement and, in Table 9-1. some of the other potential `configure` options.

Listing 9-2. *Cyrus IMAP* `configure` *Statement*

```
puppy# ./configure --with-sasl=/usr/lib/sasl2 --with-openssl=/usr/lib/ssl \
--with-auth=unix --disable-sieve
```

The `configure` statement in Listing 9-2 configures Cyrus IMAP and enables SASL support and OpenSSL support. It also specifies the `unix` authorization module, which tells Cyrus IMAP to use Unix-based authorization. I have also disabled `sieve`, which is Cyrus IMAP's mail-filtering language (such as `procmail` for IMAP). Table 9-1 shows some additional configuration options available for Cyrus IMAP.

Table 9-1. *Cyrus IMAP* `configure` *Options*

Option	Description
`--with-cyrus-user=`*user*	Uses *user* as Cyrus IMAP user
`--with-cyrus-group=`*group*	Uses *group* as Cyrus IMAP group
`--with-auth=`*method*	Uses authorization *method* (including `unix`, `krb`, `krb5`, or `pts`)
`--with-openssl=`*/path/to/ssl*	Uses OpenSSL at */path/to/ssl*
`--with-sasl=`*/path/to/sasl*	Uses SASL 2 at */path/to/sasl*
`--with-krb=`*/path/to/krb*	Uses Kerberos at *path/to/krb*
`--with-com_err=`*/path/to/com_err*	Specifies *path* to `com_err` files

The first two options allow you to specify a particular user and group for Cyrus IMAP to use. By default, Cyrus IMAP uses the `cyrus` user and the `mail` group.

The next option controls the authorization module used by Cyrus IMAP. It is important to note I am talking about authorization here, not authentication. Authentication proves you are who you say you are and allows you to connect to Cyrus IMAP. Once connected, authorization determines what rights you have to access the Cyrus IMAP message stores and mailboxes. With Cyrus IMAP, *authorization* refers to controls over permissions and the ACLs. *Authentication* refers to the different ways you can log into Cyrus IMAP. You could also use Kerberos, Kerberos 5, or an external authorization process to perform authorization (using the configure option `krb`, `krb5`, or `pts`, respectively). We have specified `unix` here, which is the most commonly used authorization model. I will cover how to control authorization in the "Cyrus IMAP Access Control and Authorization" section. We cover authentication in the "Cyrus IMAP Authentication with SASL" section.

The next three options all allow you to specify the location of OpenSSL, SASL, and Kerberos, respectively.

■**Note** On Red Hat 8, Red Hat 9, and Enterprise 3 systems, the standard location of the Kerberos includes has been moved, and this causes the Cyrus IMAP compilation to fail. Use the command `CPPFLAGS="-I/ usr/kerberos/include" && export CPPFLAGS` to add the `CPPFLAG` environment flag on these systems to allow Cyrus IMAP to find these additional includes. Add this flag before you make Cyrus IMAP.

The final option allows you to overcome issues with the location of `com_err.h` during compilation. If your `make` fails with an error indicating that it cannot find `com_err.h`, then you can overcome these issues by installing `com_err.h` into the `include` directory of your choice.

Listing 9-3. *Overcoming* `com_err.h` *Compile Errors in Cyrus IMAP*

```
puppy# cd path/to/Cyrus/source/et
puppy# cp com_err.h /usr/local/include
```

If you do not want to install the `com_err.h` include file, then you can also point Cyrus IMAP to the file using a `configure` option. Listing 9-4 shows the previous `configure` statement with the option added.

Listing 9-4. *Specifying the Location of the* `com_err.h` *File Using* `configure`

```
puppy# ./configure --with-sasl=/usr/lib/sasl2 --with-openssl=/usr/lib/ssl \
--with-auth=unix -with-com_err=/path/to/Cyrus/source/et
```

After you have configured Cyrus IMAP, you need to `make` and `install` it. Listing 9-5 shows the relevant commands.

Listing 9-5. *Making and Installing Cyrus IMAP*

```
puppy# make && make install
```

By default Cyrus IMAP installs the Cyrus binaries into `/usr/cyrus`. (You can override this with the `--with-cyrus-prefix` configure option.)

Installing Cyrus IMAP into a chroot Jail

I will take you through the basics of configuring Cyrus IMAP in a `chroot` jail. First, you should create a directory structure to hold the `chroot` jail. I have created a directory called `/chroot/cyrus` in the root directory by entering the following:

```
puppy# mkdir -R /chroot/cyrus
```

Second, you need to create some additional directories under `/chroot/cyrus`. Listing 9-6 shows the directories and directory you need to create.

Listing 9-6. *Cyrus IMAP* `chroot` *Directory Structure*

```
/dev
/etc
/lib
/lib/tls
/tmp
/usr
/usr/cyrus
/usr/cyrus/bin
/usr/lib
/usr/lib/sasl2
```

```
/var
/var/imap
/var/imap/db
/var/imap/log
/var/imap/msg
/var/imap/proc
/var/imap/ptclient
/var/imap/socket
/var/run
/var/spool
/var/spool/imap
/var/spool/imap/stage.
```

■**Note** The trailing full stop, ., in the last directory in Listing 9-6 needs to be there.

Adding Cyrus IMAP Binaries and Libraries to the chroot Jail

Now you need to populate your Cyrus IMAP installation. I will start with the Cyrus IMAP binaries. If you have installed them in the standard location, then copy the binaries into the chroot jail using the following command; otherwise, copy them from wherever you installed them.

```
puppy# cp /usr/cyrus/bin/* /chroot/cyrus/usr/cyrus/bin
```

■**Tip** If you are not using the sieve application, you should not copy the sievec and timsieved binaries.

Next, you need to add the required libraries to the chroot jail. Cyrus Mail will also require a variety of libraries to run correctly in the chroot jail. The best way to work this out is to run ldd on the master and lmtpd binaries. Record the list of libraries shown, and copy them into their respective locations in the chroot jail. Listing 9-7 shows the partial results of running the ldd command on the master binary and a subsequent copy of the required libraries in their correct locations in the chroot jail. You need to perform the same process for the lmtpd binary.

Listing 9-7. *Adding the Cyrus Mail Libraries*

```
puppy# ldd /usr/cyrus/bin/master
libresolv.so.2 => /lib/libresolv.so.2 (0xb75ce000)
libdb-4.1.so => /lib/libdb-4.1.so (0xb750c000)
libssl.so.4 => /lib/libssl.so.4 (0xb74d7000)
libcrypto.so.4 => /lib/libcrypto.so.4 (0xb73e6000)
libcom_err.so.2 => /lib/libcom_err.so.2 (0xb73e4000)
libc.so.6 => /lib/tls/libc.so.6 (0xb72ad000)
libz.so.1 => /usr/lib/libz.so.1 (0xb7207000)
```

```
libpthread.so.0 => /lib/tls/libpthread.so.0 (0xb729c000)
libgssapi_krb5.so.2 => /usr/kerberos/lib/libgssapi_krb5.so.2 (0xb7289000)
puppy# cp /lib/libssl.so.4 /chroot/cyrus/lib
puppy# cp /usr/lib/libz.o.1/chroot/cyrus/usr/lib
puppy# cp /lib/tls/libpthread.so.0 /chroot/cyrus/lib/tls
```

■**Caution** If you see any libraries located in /usr/kerberos/lib in your list of Cyrus Mail libraries, do not copy them into a similar location under the Cyrus Mail chroot; instead, copy them into /chroot/cyrus/usr/lib. Cyrus Mail seems unable to find them otherwise.

You will also need some other libraries. Listing 9-8 lists these libraries, which are usually contained in /lib.

Listing 9-8. *Additional Libraries Required by Cyrus Mail*

```
libnss_files.so.2
libnss_dns.so.2
```

Copy the libraries from Listing 9-8 into /chroot/cyrus/lib to proceed.

If you are using Cyrus SASL (which you almost certainly are), then you should copy the contents of /usr/lib/sasl2 (or /usr/local/lib/sasl2 depending where you have installed the Cyrus SASL libraries) to chroot/cyrus/lib/sasl2.

Populating the /chroot/cyrus/dev Directory

The next directory you will populate is your /chroot/cyrus/dev directory. You need to create some devices in this directory to allow Cyrus IMAP to correctly function. These devices, null and random, should duplicate the devices of the same name in the /dev directory. You can do this using the mknod command. Enter the following:

```
puppy# mknod /chroot/cyrus/dev/null c 1 3
puppy# mknod /chroot/cyrus/dev/random c 1 8
```

Now secure your newly created devices. They should both be owned by root with null being chmoded to 0666 and random to 0644.

Also in your /dev directory, you need to define a log device to allow the chrooted Cyrus IMAP to log to syslog. If you are using syslog, then you need to add an -a switch to the command that starts syslog. For my configuration, I add the following:

-a /chroot/cyrus/dev/log

If you are using syslog-NG, then add a line similar to the following one to your syslog-ng.conf file in one of your source statements:

```
unix-stream("/chroot/cyrus/dev/log");
```

■Tip See Chapter 5 for more details on how to do this.

Then restart `syslog` or `syslog-NG`; a new `log` device in the `dev` directory will allow Cyrus IMAP to log to your `syslog` daemon.

■Tip Cyrus IMAP logs to facility `local6`, so you should be able to create entries that will capture just your Cyrus IMAP log entries.

Populating the /chroot/cyrus/etc Directory

Now you need to copy some files from the `/etc` directory to the `/chroot/cyrus/etc` directory. Copy the following:

```
passwd
group
resolv.conf
host.conf
nsswitch.conf
services
hosts
localtime
```

Once you have copied your `passwd` and `group` files, you should remove all the users and groups that are not required to run Cyrus IMAP. My `passwd` file contains the following:

```
root:x:0:0:root:/root:/bin/bash
bin:x:1:1:bin:/bin:/sbin/nologin
daemon:x:2:2:daemon:/sbin:/sbin/nologin
mail:x:8:12:mail:/var/spool/mail:/sbin/nologin
cyrus:x:503:503::/var/imap:/sbin/nolgin
```

My group file contains the following:

```
root:x:0:root
bin:x:1:root,bin,daemon
daemon:x:2:root,bin,daemon
mail:x:12:mail,cyrus
cyrus:x:503:
```

You should also ensure the `services` file has entries for the IMAP or POP services you want to use. Listing 9-9 shows those entries for POP, IMAP, and IMAPS.

Listing 9-9. *POP and IMAP Services in* /etc/service

```
pop3      110/tcp    pop-3     # POP version 3
pop3      110/udp    pop-3
imap      143/tcp    imap2     # Interim Mail Access Proto v2
imap      143/udp    imap2
imaps     993/tcp              # IMAP over SSL
imaps     993/udp              # IMAP over SSL
pop3s     995/tcp    pop3s     # POP over SSL
pop3s     995/udp    pop3s     # POP over SSL
```

You also need to create the Cyrus IMAP configuration files, imapd.conf, and the master control configuration file. I will cover the imapd.conf file in the "Configuring Cyrus IMAP" section, so for the moment just create an empty file like this:

```
puppy# touch /chroot/cyrus/etc/imapd.conf
```

The source package of Cyrus IMAP contains some sample master daemon control configuration files. These are located in cyrus-imapd-*version*/master/conf in that package. For most configurations, I recommend using the normal.conf file. Copy that file into your /chroot/cyrus/etc directory and then rename it to cyrus.conf.

```
puppy# cp cyrus-imapd-2.2.3/master/conf/normal.conf /chroot/cyrus/etc/cyrus.conf
```

You will find other example master control files in that directory, and you can review the installation documentation to ensure you choose a suitable configuration file. I will talk about editing that configuration to suit your environment in the "Configuring Cyrus IMAP" section.

Permissions and Ownership in the Cyrus IMAP chroot Jail

Now you need to set permissions and ownerships for all your directories. All the directories need to be owned by the Cyrus IMAP user and group. In this case, this is cyrus and mail, respectively. From within the /chroot/cyrus directory, run the following command:

```
puppy# chown -R cyrus:mail *
```

This will recursively change the ownership of all the directories in the chroot jail. Now you need to set the permissions for the directories. Listing 9-10 shows how you set permissions inside your chroot jail from the /chroot/cyrus directory.

Listing 9-10. *Setting Permissions in the Cyrus IMAP* chroot *Jail*

```
puppy# chmod -R 0644 dev/random etc
puppy# chmod -R 0666 dev/null
puppy# chmod -R 0750 dev/log lib tmp usr var/spool var/run
puppy# chmod -R 0755 var/imap
```

Starting and Stopping Cyrus IMAP in the chroot Jail

As Cyrus IMAP is installed in a chroot jail, you need to adjust how you would normally start and stop it. Cyrus IMAP is normally started by running the master daemon, which then spawns additional processes to handle local delivery and incoming connections. Enter the following:

```
puppy# /usr/cyrus/bin/master -d
```

The -d option tells the master daemon to run in the background. Table 9-2 details some additional command-line options for the Cyrus IMAP master daemon.

Table 9-2. *Cyrus IMAP Master Daemon Command-Line Options*

Option	Description
-C *file*	Specifies an alternative imapd.conf file for use by the master process.
-M *file*	Specifies an alternate cyrus.conf file.
-p *pidfile*	Specifies the PID file to use. If not specified, defaults to /var/run/cyrus-master.pid.
-d	Starts in daemon mode.
-D	Does not close standard in, out, and error.

With Cyrus IMAP installed into your chroot jail, you need to start and stop it using the following chroot command:

```
puppy# chroot /chroot/cyrus /usr/cyrus/bin/master -d
```

This starts Cyrus IMAP with the root directory of /chroot/cyrus instead of /. The Cyrus IMAP master binary it starts is located in the /chroot/cyrus/usr/cyrus/bin directory.

For normal operation, I recommend starting Cyrus IMAP using an init script. In Listing 9-11 I have included a basic init script.

Listing 9-11. *Example Cyrus IMAP init Script*

```
#!/bin/bash
# Cyrus IMAP startup script
# Source function library.
. /etc/init.d/functions
prog="/usr/cyrus/bin/master"
opt="-d"
case "$1" in
start)
# Starting Cyrus IMAP Server
chroot /chroot/cyrus/ $prog $opt
;;
stop)
# Stopping Cyrus IMAP Server
killproc $prog
;;
*)
```

```
echo "Usage: $0 {start|stop}"
exit 1
;;
esac
```

■**Tip** Remember that if you are using the `saslauthd` daemon, you need to start that, too.

Configuring Cyrus IMAP

I will now show you how to configure Cyrus IMAP in a basic manner to get it operational using TLS and SASL for encryption and authentication, respectively. I will not go into any detailed Cyrus IMAP configuration. If you need more information, then Cyrus IMAP is well-documented both on the Cyrus IMAP Web site at `http://asg.web.cmu.edu/cyrus/imapd/` and in the extensive man pages that come with the package.

Cyrus IMAP is largely controlled by two files: the `imapd.conf` and `cyrus.conf` files. Both of them are stored in `/etc` or, if using the chrooted configuration described in the previous section, in the `/chroot/cyrus/etc` directory. I will first take you through the `imapd.conf` file and its contents and explain how it impacts the configuration of Cyrus IMAP. Listing 9-12 shows a sample `imapd.conf` file.

Listing 9-12. *Sample* `imapd.conf` *File*

```
configdirectory: /var/imap
partition-default: /var/spool/imap
admins: root bob
sasl_pwcheck_method: saslauthd
```

The first two lines in the `imapd.conf` file control the location of the Cyrus IMAP configuration files and the location of the message store and mailboxes, respectively. If Cyrus IMAP is located in the `chroot` jail, as described in the previous section, then these are subdirectories of `/chroot/cyrus`.

■**Note** You should always remember that any files contained in your `chroot` jail are relative to the root directory (in this case, `/chroot/cyrus`) of the jail, not your root, `/`, directory.

The first line, `configdirectory`, tells Cyrus IMAP where to find its general configuration files. The `partition-default` variable tells Cyrus IMAP where to locate its messages stores and mailboxes. You can specify more than one location for your message stores (for example, spread them over several file systems or disks) if required, but in this example I will just use the one location.

The next two options control two security-related functions. The first, `admins`, allows you to specify one or more users who are able to administer Cyrus IMAP, including functions such as creating or managing mailboxes and using the `cyradm` tool. Separate each user with a space. The last option, `sasl_pwcheck_method`, tells Cyrus IMAP what type of Cyrus SASL authentication to use. Listing 9-12 shows Cyrus IMAP using `saslauthd`, which is the Cyrus SASL authentication daemon. The `saslauthd` daemon is used for authentication for shadow passwords, LDAP, or MySQL. You could also specify `auxprop` or `pwcheck` here, with `auxprop` indicating the use of a Cyrus SASL `sasldb` authentication database and `pwcheck` being used for older versions of Cyrus SASL.

You also need to configure a Cyrus SASL configuration file for Cyrus IMAP. You should call this file `Cyrus.conf`; it is located in `/chroot/cyrus/usr/lib/sasl2/` if you have chrooted Cyrus IMAP or in `/usr/lib/sasl2` or `/usr/local/lib/sasl2` (depending on where you have installed Cyrus SASL). Like you can see in Listing 9-13, you need to add a `pwcheck_method` option to that file.

Listing 9-13. *The* `Cyrus.conf` *File*

```
pwcheck_method:saslauthd
```

The method should match the method you have used in your `imapd.conf` file: `saslauthd`, `auxprop`, and so on.

The four lines in Listing 9-12's `imapd.conf` are enough to get Cyrus IMAP running, so you can add them to your empty `imapd.conf` file in your chroot jail. A few other options are worth mentioning, including those controlling adding TLS to Cyrus IMAP. Table 9-3 shows these options, and I will cover them in more detail after the table. You can read about additional options in the `imapd.conf` man page.

```
puppy# man imapd.conf
```

Table 9-3. `imapd.conf` *File Configuration Variables*

Variable	Description
`allowanonymouslogin:` *yes* | *no*	Allows the use of "anonymous" logins and the Cyrus SASL ANONYMOUS mechanism. This is no by default.
`allowplaintext:` *yes* | *no*	Allows the use of clear-text passwords. This is yes by default.
`servername:` *server_name*	This is the hostname visible in the greeting messages of the POP, IMAP, and LMTP daemons. If not set, then it will default to the result of *gethostname*.
`syslog_prefix:` *string*	A string to be appended to the process name in `syslog` entries.
`temp_path:` *temp_directory*	Location of the temporary directory.
`tls_cert_file:` *filename*	Location of the certificate belonging to the server. Entering **disabled** will disable SSL/TLS.
`tls_key_file:` *filename*	Location of the private key belonging to the server. Entering **disabled** will disable SSL/TLS.
`tls_ca_file:` *filename*	Location of your CA file.
`tls_ca_path:` *path*	Path to the CA certificates. This directory must have the certificate hashes also.

The `allowanonymous` and `allowplaintext` options both relate to the use of SASL authentication mechanisms. The first disables the SASL ANONYMOUS mechanism (which is done by default). You should ensure this remains off, as the ANONYMOUS mechanism provides no security and allows anybody to sign into your Cyrus IMAP. The second controls whether Cyrus IMAP will accept plain-text mechanisms of authentication such as PLAIN or LOGIN. Setting this to no will disable plain-text passwords unless TLS is enabled and running. This ensures that if you use plain-text authentication mechanisms, you can use them only if your connection is encrypted with TLS. I recommend setting this option to no and enabling TLS.

The next three options control additional configuration items in Cyrus IMAP. The servername variable allows you to specify the hostname that Cyrus IMAP will present to incoming IMAP or POP connections. If it is not specified, then this defaults to the result of the gethostname system call. The syslog_prefix variable allows you to append a string to the process field of any Cyrus IMAP syslog entries. The last of these three entries, the temp_path variable, tells Cyrus IMAP what directory to use as its temporary directory. If this is not specified, it defaults to /tmp.

The last four options in Table 9-3 control Cyrus IMAP's use of TLS. The first two entries, tls_cert_file and tls_key_file, specify the location of your server's certificate and keyfile to Cyrus IMAP. You can also specify disabled as the content of either of these options to disable TLS. The next two options, tls_ca_file and tls_ca_path, allow you to specify the location of your CA certificate file and the path that contains your CA files (including your certificate hashes).

■**Note** See Chapter 8 for details of TLS and TLS certificates, and see Chapter 3 for details on OpenSSL.

To enable TLS, you need to add these lines to your `imapd.conf` file. Listing 9-14 shows my `imapd.conf` with TLS enabled and some of the options I have been discussing added.

Listing 9-14. *Enabling TLS with Cyrus IMAP*

```
configdirectory: /var/imap
partition-default: /var/spool/imap
admins: root bob
sasl_pwcheck_method: saslauthd
allowplaintext: no
allowanonymouslogin: no
tls_cert_file: /var/imap/certs/puppy_cert.pem
tls_key_file: /var/imap/certs/puppy_key.pem
tls_ca_file: /var/imap/certs/CA_cert.pem
tls_ca_path: /var/imap/certs/
```

If you have set up Cyrus IMAP in a chroot jail, you need to create, copy, or move your certificates and the directory containing your CA certificate and hashes into the chroot jail. Ensure you use the tightest permissions possible on your keys so they are not vulnerable. I generally set its permissions to 0400. Enter the following:

```
puppy# chmod 0400 puppy_key.pem
```

The next configuration file, `cyrus.conf`, controls the `master` daemon. I have created one from the sample `normal.conf` contained in the Cyrus IMAP source package and copied it into my `chroot` jail as `cyrus.conf`. The `cyrus.conf` file does two important functions for you; it tells Cyrus IMAP which services (IMAP or POP, or both, for example) to start, and it tells Cyrus IMAP the location of the `lmtp` socket your MTA uses to inject mail into Cyrus and then the mailboxes. I will cover these two functions. The `cyrus.conf` man file describes the other options in the `cyrus.conf` file.

```
puppy# man cyrus.conf
```

The functions relating to starting and stopping services and specifying the location of the `lmtp` socket are contained in a block of configuration items called `SERVICES`. This block of configuration items is contained in brackets, { }. The first function the `cryus.conf` file performs is to tell Cyrus IMAP which services to start. As you can see in Listing 9-15, the uncommented items in the first seven lines handle this.

Listing 9-15. *The* `cyrus.conf` *Services*

```
SERVICES {
# add or remove based on preferences
# imap     cmd="imapd"        listen="imap"       prefork=0
imaps      cmd="imapd -s"     listen="imaps"      prefork=0
# pop3     cmd="pop3d"        listen="pop3"       prefork=0
pop3s      cmd="pop3d -s"     listen="pop3s"      prefork=0
# sieve    cmd="timsieved"    listen="sieve"      prefork=0

# these are only necessary if receiving/exporting usenet via NNTP
#  nntp          cmd="nntpd" listen="nntp" prefork=0
#  nntps         cmd="nntpd -s" listen="nntps" prefork=0

# at least one LMTP is required for delivery
#  lmtp          cmd="lmtpd" listen="lmtp" prefork=0

lmtpunix        cmd="lmtpd"      listen="/var/imap/socket/lmtp"       prefork=0

# this is only necessary if using notifications
#  notify        cmd="notifyd" listen="/var/imap/socket/notify" proto="udp" prefork=1
}
```

To stop services from starting when the `master` daemon is started, you need to comment out that particular service. Listing 9-15 shows the following services being started: `imaps` and `pop3s`. The other potential services (`imap`, `pop3`, and `sieve`) are commented out and will not start when the `master` daemon starts.

The next function the `cyrus.conf` file handles for you that I will cover is specifying the location of the `lmtp` socket. The line, starting with `lmtpunix`, in Listing 9-15 tells Cyrus IMAP the location of the `lmtp` socket through which your MTA will inject mail into Cyrus IMAP. In Listing 9-15 this points to /var/imap/socket/lmtp.

Integrating Cyrus IMAP with Sendmail and Postfix

As discussed earlier in the chapter, I will integrate Cyrus IMAP into your MTA using LMTP. LMTP is a fast and efficient method of delivering mail from your MTA to Cyrus IMAP. LMTP is described in RFC 2033.[6] Mail is delivered from your MTA to a local or remote `lmtp` socket on which your Cyrus IMAP server is listening. The mail is received and added to the user's mailbox.

Sendmail

You can start integration with Sendmail by adding some configuration lines to your `sendmail.mc` file. These lines tell Sendmail about Cyrus and specify the location of the `lmtp` socket to your Sendmail configuration. This is made easier by the fact that Sendmail has a custom `Mailer` designed specifically for Cyrus IMAP; I will show how to configure that `Mailer` with a specific location for the `lmtp` socket.

> ■**Tip** You can read more about `Mailers` at the Sendmail site.[7]

Listing 9-16 shows the lines you need to add to your `sendmail.mc` file.

Listing 9-16. *Cyrus IMAP Sendmail Integration*

```
define(`confLOCAL_MAILER', `cyrusv2')dnl
define(`CYRUSV2_MAILER_ARGS', `FILE /chroot/cyrus/var/imap/socket/lmtp')dnl
MAILER(`cyrusv2')dnl
```

You will notice I have defined the location of the `lmtp` socket from the perspective of the root directory of the system, as opposed to inside the `chroot` jail, because Sendmail is running outside the jail and not inside it. After adding these lines, then re-create your `sendmail.cf` file and restart Sendmail. This completes your Cyrus IMAP integration with Sendmail; now Sendmail should be delivering mail into your Cyrus IMAP mailboxes.

Postfix

If instead you use Postfix, you go about the integration a little differently. First, you need to identify the user who Postfix is running as, usually `postfix`. Second, you need to add this user to the `mail` group or to whichever group Cyrus IMAP is running as if you have overridden the default group during the `configure` process. This gives Postfix permission to write to the `lmtp` socket that Cyrus IMAP creates. Listing 9-17 shows the entry I have for the `mail` group.

Listing 9-17. /etc/group *Entry for Postfix and Cyrus IMAP Integration*

```
mail:x:12:mail,cyrus,postfix
```

---

6. http://www.faqs.org/rfcs/rfc2033.html

7. http://www.sendmail.org/m4/mailers.html

Next you need to add a `mailbox_transport` entry to Postfix's `main.cf` file to tell Postfix to write and deliver to Cyrus IMAP the location of the socket. As I did with Sendmail, I will use LMTP because of its excellent performance. You can define the `lmtp` socket created by Cyrus IMAP and indicated in the `cyrus.conf` file to Postfix. In Listing 9.18, you can see the `mailbox_transport`.

Listing 9-18. `main.cf mailbox_transport` *Entry*

```
mailbox_transport = lmtp:unix:/chroot/cyrus/var/imap/socket/lmtp
```

As Postfix is delivering from outside the Cyrus IMAP `chroot` jail, you need to reference the full directory of the socket, not just the directory from the point of view of the root of the `chroot` jail. After you have added this line to the `main.cf` file, then you need to reload Postfix. After this, Postfix should be delivering mail to the indicated socket.

■**Tip** With both Sendmail and Postfix, you can use other methods of integrating with Cyrus IMAP, including using the `deliver` binary that comes with Cyrus IMAP. If you do not want to use LMTP, then see the Cyrus IMAP documentation for other methods.

Cyrus IMAP Authentication with SASL

So, you have compiled, installed, and integrated Cyrus IMAP with your MTA (and installed Cyrus SASL!).

■**Note** I talk about Cyrus SASL in further detail in Chapter 8.

Now you want to use it to connect a client securely over an encrypted connection and retrieve e-mail. I will briefly cover authentication via some simple methods and provide you with the basis for other forms of authentication.

So how does this work? With Cyrus IMAP running, the `master` daemon is bound to your chosen interface and has opened the required ports. The `master` daemon then advertises its capabilities to any clients connecting to it. Amongst those capabilities is the IMAP AUTH command. This lists any authentication mechanisms that Cyrus IMAP is capable of using. These are the authentication mechanisms that Cyrus SASL has provided to Cyrus IMAP; for example, this could be the PLAIN, LOGIN, or GSSAPI mechanism (plain-text login, the Outlook-style LOGIN function, and the Generic Security Services Application Programming Interface that is integrated into Kerberos 5 and allows Kerberos 5 authentication, respectively). The login client provides credentials for one of these authentication mechanisms, and Cyrus IMAP queries the required mechanisms to verify the authenticity of the credentials. For example, a client using Kerberos 5 authentication connects to Cyrus IMAP using the GSSAPI mechanism. Cyrus IMAP queries the Cyrus SASL authentication mechanism and using that configuration queries the required Kerberos 5 server. Figure 9-2 shows this process at work.

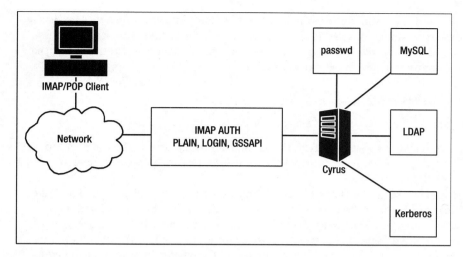

Figure 9-2. *Cyrus IMAP authentication*

■**Note** In Listing 9-14 I have configured Cyrus IMAP to advertise plain-text authentication mechanisms only if I am running TLS for added security. So in Figure 9-2 the IMAP AUTH command would appear only if the STARTTLS command had been initiated first.

So let's go back to Listing 9-14 where I have configured the imapd.conf file to tell Cyrus IMAP how to authenticate itself. In that example, I configured the use of the saslauthd dae-mon to perform the authentication function. You could also have used pwcheck or auxprop as the sasl_pwcheck_method option, which I will talk about later in this section. Before that, I will cover the saslauthd daemon that can be configured to perform a number of different types of authentication. The particular type of authentication used is specified by the -a option when starting saslauthd. Table 9-4 describes some of the saslauthd authentication types.

Table 9-4. saslauthd -a *Mechanisms*

Mechanism	Description
getpwent	Authenticates using the getpwent library function usually against the local password file
kerberos4	Authenticates against a local Kerberos 4 realm
kerberos5	Authenticates against a local Kerberos 5 realm
pam	Authenticates using Pluggable Authentication Modules (PAM)
shadow	Authenticates against the local shadow password file
ldap	Authenticates against an LDAP server

I will cover one of the most commonly used types of authentication: shadow. The shadow authentication mechanisms are designed to allow you to authenticate against a local password file that uses shadow passwording. In Listing 9-19, you can see how to start saslauthd with the shadow authentication mechanism enabled.

Listing 9-19. *Cyrus SASL* saslauthd *with* shadow *Authentication*

```
puppy# /usr/sbin/saslauthd -m /var/run/saslauthd -a shadow
```

The -m option allows you to specify the location of a PID file. The saslauthd daemon will now check the contents of your /etc/shadow file for usernames and passwords passed to Cyrus SASL from Cyrus IMAP.

If you intend to use saslauthd and you have chrooted Cyrus IMAP, you need to make some modifications to allow the chrooted Cyrus IMAP daemon to access saslauthd. By default saslauthd creates a mux file to receive the authentication requests. This mux file is usually located in the directory /var/run/saslauthd (often together with a PID file). If the file is not created there, you can check with location of the mux file by reviewing the command you are using to start saslauthd. You specific the location of the mux file using the -m option. Or you can run the following command to find it:

```
puppy# netstat -peln | grep saslauthd
unix 2  [ ACC ]   STREAM  LISTENING  256149 7645/saslauthd /var/run/saslauthd/mux
```

The last part of the returned output, /var/run/saslauthd/mux, indicates the location of the mux file. As a result of Cyrus IMAP being chrooted, it cannot see this file (because it is outside the chroot jail) and therefore refuses to authenticate using SASL. So you need to move the mux file and other saslauthd files into the chroot jail and link it back to its old location via a symbolic link to keep the saslauthd daemon happy. The command in Listing 9-20 takes you through the steps needed to do this—making a new directory in your chroot environment, moving the required files into the chroot jail, linking (a symbolic link only, which is important to maintain the security of your chroot jail) back to the original location, and changing the ownership of the saslauthd directory.

Listing 9-20. *Running* saslauthd *in Cyrus IMAP* chroot *Jail*

```
puppy# mv /var/run/saslauthd /chroot/cyrus/var/run/saslauthd
puppy# ln -s /chroot/cyrus/var/run/saslauthd /var/run/saslauthd
puppy# chown cyrus:mail /chroot/cyrus/var/run/saslauthd
```

You need to restart saslauthd after doing this.

I have covered using the saslauthd daemon for Cyrus IMAP authentication. You can also use some other mechanisms. I will cover how to use the sasldb mechanism. This is best used for "sealed" systems, as I discussed earlier where the users signing onto the Cyrus IMAP server do not have shell logins. The sasldb file contains usernames and passwords. In this case, change your sasl_pwcheck_method in the imapd.conf to the following:

```
sasl_pwcheck_method: auxprop
```

■**Note** You also need to change the pwcheck_method option in the Cyrus.conf file.

---

auxprop stands for *auxiliary property* plug-ins, of which the default is the sasldb type. As it is the default, you do not need to specify anything else other than auxprop because Cyrus SASL knows this indicates sasldb. By default with the sasldb plug-in, Cyrus SASL looks for the file /etc/sasldb2. This may already exist on your system; however, if it does not, do not panic. When you create your first user, Cyrus SASL will automatically create the /etc/sasldb2 file if it does not already exist.

To add users to the sasldb2 file, you use the saslpasswd2 command that comes with the SASL package. You will need a username and a domain that should match the fully qualified domain name defined in Sendmail. Listing 9-21 shows how to use this command.

Listing 9-21. *The* saslpasswd2 *Command*

```
puppy# saslpasswd2 -c username
```

The -c option tells SASL to create a new user account. You would replace the variable *username* with the required username for the user. You will be prompted by the saslpasswd2 binary to enter a password for this username. If you have Cyrus IMAP located in a chroot jail, then you can use an additional option, -f, to specify the location of the sasldb2 file so you can place it in the jail and have it accessible to Cyrus IMAP.

```
puppy# saslpasswd2 -c -f /chroot/cyrus/etc username
```

You need to ensure Cyrus IMAP can read the sasldb2 file. The sasldb2 file should be owned by the user and group that Cyrus IMAP runs as. In this case, this is the user, cyrus, and the group, mail. You also need to ensure the file is secured against intrusion by restricting its permissions. The most suitable permissions to secure the file are 0400.

```
puppy# chmod 0400 sasldb2
```

Using the auxprop method, you can also configure Cyrus IMAP to authenticate via LDAP or a variety of SQL-based databases such as MySQL or PostgreSQL. These methods are most useful when setting up virtual domains and virtual users. See the Cyrus IMAP Web site's HOW-TOs for information on how to achieve this authentication.

Finally, it is important to note that if you are using saslauthd or sasldb2 as the authentication methods, then you are using the PLAIN or LOGIN mechanisms for authentication. These use simple Base64-encoded passwords that can be easily sniffed out and cracked across your network. This is where TLS comes together with Cyrus SASL to allow encrypted authentication. You should ensure your IMAP/POP client is configured to attempt an SSL/TLS connection by configuring your client to use the SSL-enabled ports (993 for IMAPS and 995 for POP3S) with your Cyrus IMAP server. As I discussed previously, you should ensure you have set the allow-plaintext option to no in the imapd.conf file. This means Cyrus IMAP allows IMAP AUTH only if a security layer such as TLS is in place first. If you do not use TLS with IMAP AUTH and Cyrus SASL, then the level of security offered is minimal, and I recommend you look at alternative methods of authentication.

Cyrus IMAP Access Control and Authorization

I have discussed authenticating and connecting to your Cyrus IMAP server. Cyrus IMAP has an additional layer of security available to you to protect your users' e-mail and mailboxes. This authorization layer allows you to control the access rights to a particular mailbox that you grant to various users. You achieve this using ACLs that are administered with the cyradm tool. The cyradm tool connects you to your Cyrus IMAP server and allows an administrator (who is defined using the admins option in the imapd.conf file) to sign in and manage your Cyrus IMAP site. Listing 9-22 shows you how to start cyradm.

■Note The cyradm binary is a bash script that calls the Perl module Cyrus::IMAP. Sometimes, on some systems, cyradm is unable to find the perl modules it requires. If you get an error message when you run cyradm stating Can't locate Cyrus/IMAP/Shell.pm, then insert the following into the top of the cyradm script: PERL5LIB=/usr/local/lib/perl5/site_perl/5.8.0/i386-linux-thread-multi; export PERL5LIB.

Listing 9-22. *Starting* cyradm *for Cyrus IMAP Administration*

```
puppy# cyradm --user root --port 143 --server puppy
```

This starts the cyradm administration tool and connects to port 143 as the root user of the puppy server.

Now I will show an example of how you can use cyradm. I will create a user and a mailbox for that user and then assign some rights to the user to that mailbox. I will assume you are using Cyrus SASL with the auxprop mechanism using a sasldb file. So first you need to create a user, bob, in the sasldb.

```
puppy# saslpasswd2 -c -f /chroot/cyrus/etc bob
Password:
Again (for verification):
```

When you enter the command, you will be prompted for the new user's password twice.

■Tip Ensure you select passwords for your users that are secure. I discuss approaches to secure passwords in Chapter 1.

Now you need to start cyradm.

```
puppy# cyradm --user root --server puppy
Password:
puppy>
```

Now you need to create a new mailbox. Cyrus IMAP has a default convention for naming mailboxes; it requires that you prefix user's mailboxes with user.*username*. You can use the command createmailbox or its abbreviation, cm, to create the mailbox.

```
puppy> createmailbox user.bob
```

Several other commands are available that you can use on mailboxes, such as commands enabling you to delete and rename the mailbox. Table 9-5 details the some of the commands you can use with cyradm. You can review the cyradm man page for further commands.

Table 9-5. `cyradm` *Commands*

Command	Abbreviation	Description
createmailbox	cm	Creates a mailbox
listmailbox	lm	Lists mailboxes
renamemailbox	renm	Renames a mailbox
deletemailbox	dm	Deletes a mailbox
setaclmailbox	sam	Sets an ACL on a mailbox
listaclmailbox	lam	Lists the ACL on a mailbox
deleteaclmailbox	dam	Deletes an ACL on a mailbox
setquota	sq	Sets quota limits
listquota	lq	Lists quota on root
help		Gets help on commands
quit		Exits cyradm

The new mailbox I have created has some default access rights assigned to it. You can display these default access rights by using the `listaclmailbox` command or its abbreviation, `lam`.

```
puppy> listaclmailbox user.bob
bob lrswipcda
```

You can see that `bob` has a variety of access rights to his mailbox. In fact, as the owner of that mailbox, `bob` has all rights to that mailbox. Now I will explain what those rights means. Table 9-6 lists all the rights and provides an explanation of what each does.

■**Note** The users listed in the `admins` option in the `imapd.conf` file automatically have `l` and `a` rights to the mailbox.

Table 9-6. *Cyrus IMAP ACL Rights*

Letter	Access Right	Description
l	lookup	Sees that the mailbox exists
r	read	Reads the mailbox
s	seen	Modifies the Seen and Recent flags
w	write	Modifies flags and keywords other than Seen and Deleted
i	insert	Inserts new messages into the mailbox
p	post	Sends mail to the submission address for the mailbox
c	create	Creates new submailboxes of the mailbox, or deletes or renames the current mailbox
d	delete	Uses the Deleted flag and expunges deleted mail
a	administer	Changes the ACL on the mailbox

The Cyrus IMAP administrators do not automatically have all the rights to a user's mailbox. I will use this to show you how to grant rights to a mailbox. So now you will see an example of granting rights to a user and using the `setaclmailbox` command or its abbreviation, `sam`, to another user's mailbox.

```
puppy> setaclmailbox user.bob root d
```

In this example, I am giving the `root` user the `d` access right to the mailbox `user.bob`. This gives `root` the right to delete and expunge e-mail from bob's mailbox. You can also use the option `all` to assign all the available access rights for a user to a mailbox.

```
puppy> setaclmailbox user.bob root all
```

You can also delete an ACL from a mailbox using the `deleteaclmailbox` command or its abbreviation, `dam`.

```
puppy> deleteaclmailbox user.bob root
```

This will delete the entire ACL for the `root` user. All access rights granted to the `root` user to the mailbox `user.bob` will be removed.

All the commands used to control ACLs on Cyrus IMAP involve assigning rights to a particular user ID or identifier. You can also two special identifiers: anyone and anonymous. You probably will not (and should not) use the anonymous identifier. It refers to users who have been anonymously authenticated to Cyrus IMAP, and as I have previously mentioned, anonymous authentication is not safe, as it is impossible to verify who the user connecting is. The other special identifier is anyone, which means anyone authenticated can access the mailbox. This is useful for creating public folders.

Testing Cyrus IMAP with imtest/pop3test

Cyrus IMAP comes with two test tools, `imtest` and `pop3test`; the latter is especially useful for testing TLS and Cyrus SASL authentication. I will briefly cover both of them. The `imtest` and `pop3test` tools are usually located in `/usr/local/bin` and cover testing IMAP and POP3, respectively. You can start them from the command line. I will specifically cover the `imtest` command as an example of the two commands; the options and functions of both commands are nearly identical.

```
puppy# imtest servername
```

Without options, `imtest` will try to connect, as the user you are currently logged on as, to the IMAP port 143 and to the particular server indicated by the *servername* variable. You can also try to connect to the SSL-enabled port by adding the `-s` switch to `imtest`.

```
puppy# imtest -s servername
```

This connects to either port 993 (for IMAPS) or port 995 for POP3S (depending on the tool being used) and displays the TLS negotiation and the available capabilities of the server indicated by *servername*. Listing 9-23 shows the messages this command generates on my Cyrus IMAP server.

Listing 9-23. *Using the* imtest -s *Command*

```
puppy# imtest -s puppy
TLS connection established: TLSv1 with cipher AES256-SHA (256/256 bits)
S: * OK puppy Cyrus IMAP4 v2.2.3 server ready
C: C01 CAPABILITY
S: * CAPABILITY IMAP4 IMAP4rev1 ACL QUOTA LITERAL+ MAILBOX-REFERRALS NAMESPACE
UIDPLUS ID NO_ATOMIC_RENAME UNSELECT CHILDREN MULTIAPPEND BINARY SORT
THREAD=ORDEREDSUBJECT THREAD=REFERENCES ANNOTATEMORE IDLE AUTH=PLAIN
AUTH=LOGIN AUTH=DIGEST-MD5 AUTH=CRAM-MD5 SASL-IR
S: C01 OK Completed
C: A01 AUTHENTICATE DIGEST-MD5
S: + bm9uY2U9Ikl3MHZGNHhGY05pbzVXaoN4VU8vSUIORjhwZS9uTldJbTNqMXROdTFrQ1k9
IixyZWFsbT0icHVwcHkiLHFvcD0iYXV0aCIsbWF4YnVmPTQwOTYsY2hhcnNldD11dGYtOCxhb
Gdvcml0aG09bWQ1LXNlc3M=
Please enter your password:
```

You can see that the IMAP AUTH command has displayed the LOGIN and PLAIN mechanisms. If I run this against the non-SSL-enabled IMAP on port 143, you would not see these mechanisms, because the plain-text mechanisms are enabled only with TLS.

Table 9-7 lists a variety of other options you can input as command-line options to imtest.

Table 9-7. imtest/pop3test *Command-Line Options*

Option	Description
-t *keyfile*	Specifies the location of a TLS keyfile that contains the TLS public and private keys. Specify "" to negotiate a TLS encryption layer but not use TLS authentication.
-p *port*	Allows you to specify the port to connect to.
-m *mechanism*	Specifies the particular authentication mechanism to use (for example, PLAIN).
-u *user*	Specifies the username to log in as, which defaults to the current user.
-v	Enables verbose mode.

Listing 9-24 shows the process of logging into my Cyrus IMAP server, puppy, using the PLAIN authentication method on the SSL-enabled port 993 as the user cyrus, with the verbose mode enabled, and using a specific TLS keyfile.

Listing 9-24. *Further* imtest *Options*

```
puppy# imtest -s -a plain -p 993 -u cyrus -t /var/imap/certs/puppy.pem -v puppy
```

Fetchmail

Fetchmail is a popular tool authored by Eric S. Raymond (of open-source fame[8]) to provide remote e-mail retrieval and forwarding functionality using a variety of protocols, including POP3 (and related protocols such as APOP, RPOP, and KPOP) and most flavors of IMAP, ETRN, and ODMR.

■**Note** I briefly discuss ETRN in Chapter 7. ODMR is On-Demand Mail Relay, also known as ATRN, which is best defined as an authenticated version of the SMTP TURN command. It allows SMTP functionality using dynamic IP addresses instead of static IP addresses. See RFC 2645[9] for more details.

As previously mentioned, Fetchmail is a remote mail retrieval and forwarding tool that uses a variety of protocols to retrieve e-mail via TCP/IP links. Fetchmail retrieves mail from remote MTAs and forwards it via SMTP or local delivery such as LMTP to your mailbox or message store. This allows you to gather e-mail from a variety of remote mailboxes and servers and centralize that e-mail at your local server. This also allows the spam filtering, antivirus, or aliasing functionality capabilities of your MTA to be used on these remote messages as they come in. Figure 9-3 shows how this process works.

So why is Fetchmail potentially insecure? Some of the insecurities are related to its use of particular protocols, such as IMAP and POP, to retrieve e-mail. For example, Fetchmail by default runs POP and IMAP unencrypted and transmits your password to the remote system in the clear. This exposes you to the potential risk, which also exists with regular unencrypted IMAP or POP, that with relatively simple network-sniffing tools an attacker could sniff out the username and password you are using to connect. Additionally, if you are using .fetchmailrc, your password is often hard-coded into that file to allow Fetchmail to act as a daemon without requiring you to input your password for each session. Finally, as with any other similar tool, I see the possibility of Fetchmail being used as a conduit for Denial of Service (DoS) attacks.

I will cover installing Fetchmail and then cover some examples of common uses, such as securely retrieving e-mail from a POP and IMAP server using SSL authentication with Fetchmail, encapsulating Fetchmail transactions using ssh, and demonstrating the most secure ways to configure and use Fetchmail. I will also address how to secure your .fetchmailrc file and limit the potential of Fetchmail being used for a DoS attack.

In doing this, I will focus on Fetchmail's use as a mail retrieval tool for POP and IMAP accounts and not cover its use with other protocols such as ETRN or look at using more specialized authenticated protocols such as APOP and KPOP. I am taking this approach because I am attempting to address the practical issues facing most users rather than the more specialized approaches.[10] I will not cover any complex Fetchmail configurations or any of the methods of integrating Fetchmail with your MTA. (I will assume you are injecting the mail into an SMTP server located on your local host.)

---

8. http://www.catb.org/~esr/who-is-ESR.html and http://www.opensource.org/

9. http://www.faqs.org/rfcs/rfc2645.html

10. I recommend if you want to investigate these other protocol and configuration options that you start with the Fetchmail home page, which is referenced in the "Resources" section, and specifically its FAQ section.

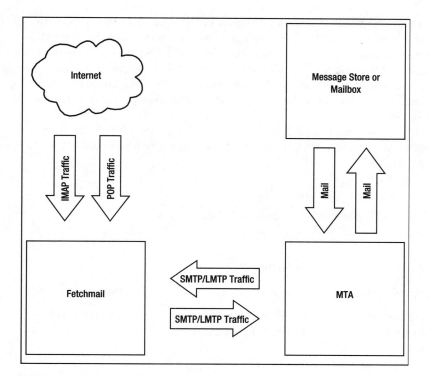

Figure 9-3. *How Fetchmail works*

Installing Fetchmail

You can find Fetchmail at its home page at http://www.catb.org/~esr/fetchmail/. Fetchmail is available from this page in the form of a source package, an RPM, and a source RPM. Additionally, many distributions already come with Fetchmail installed or have a Fetchmail RPM, deb, or package of some kind available. You can check for the presence of Fetchmail on a Red Hat and Mandrake system (or any system that uses the RPM system) using the following command:

```
puppy# rpm -q fetchmail
```

or on a Debian system by entering the following:

```
kitten# dpkg --list fetchmail*
```

If you already have a copy of Fetchmail on your system, then Listing 9-25 shows you how to check what version it is.

Listing 9-25. *Checking the Fetchmail Version*

```
puppy# fetchmail --version
```

At the time of this writing, the current version of Fetchmail was version 6.2.5. Fetchmail is a fairly mature product, and not a great deal of functionality has been added in recent releases; these releases have mostly been focused on addressing maintenance issues.

You can either run the Fetchmail that comes with your distribution or download and install the Fetchmail available from the Fetchmail home page. However, a recent version, Fetchmail 6.2.4, has at least one vulnerability.[11] (However, there have been no known exploits of that vulnerability.) So I recommend you install Fetchmail from the source package and compile it yourself to ensure you have the most secure and up-to-date version of the application. I will show you how to do that next. If you want to use the Fetchmail that comes with your distribution, you can skip to the next section.

If you download Fetchmail from its site, then I recommend you check its GNU Privacy Guard (GPG) signature and checksums to ensure you have an unadulterated copy before you install it (see Listing 9-26).

Note   I talk about GPG and MD5 checksums in more detail in Chapter 1.

Listing 9-26. *Checking the GPG Signature of Fetchmail*

```
puppy# gpg --verify fetchmail-version.tar.gz.asc fetchmail-version.tar.gz
```

You can find the Fetchmail checksums at http://www.catb.org/~esr/fetchmail/checksums. You can use the command in Listing 9-27 to verify those checksums.

Listing 9-27. *Checking the Fetchmail Checksums*

```
puppy# gpg --verify checksums
```

If you have downloaded Fetchmail in the form of an RPM, it is easy to install. Use the command in Listing 9-28 to install the RPM.

Listing 9-28. *Installing Fetchmail via RPM*

```
puppy# rpm -Uvh fetchmail-version.rpm
```

If you want to compile Fetchmail from source, then download the source package and unpack it. Change into the fetchmail-version directory, and configure Fetchmail. You can simply configure Fetchmail using the command in Listing 9-29. Replace the /path/to/ssl with the location of your OpenSSL installation to enable SSL support for Fetchmail. This configuration should cover most purposes for which you want to use Fetchmail.

Listing 9-29. *Configuring Fetchmail*

```
puppy# ./configure --with-ssl=/path/to/ssl
```

---

11. http://www.securityfocus.com/bid/8843

■**Tip** If you are compiling OpenSSL support into Fetchmail, you should note that an issue exists with finding the Kerberos includes on Red Hat systems. Red Hat has relocated the Kerberos includes to `/usr/kerberos/include`. Thus, on these systems, you need to add the following environment variable to the system before you configure Fetchmail: `CFLAGS=-I/usr/kerberos/include; export CFLAG`.

As shown in Table 9-8. Fetchmail also has some additional configuration options that you can use.

Table 9-8. *Fetchmail Configuration Options*

Option	Description
`--prefix=`*`prefix`*	Installs Fetchmail using the directory prefix of *prefix*
`--enable-fallback=`*`procmail`* `|` *`maildrop`* `|` *`sendmail`* `|` *`no`*	Enables Procmail, Sendmail, Maildrop, or no fallback transport
`--enable-RPA`	Compiles support for the RPA protocol
`--enable-NTLM`	Compiles support for NTLM authentication support
`--enable-SDPS`	Compiles support for the SDPS protocol
`--enable-opie`	Supports OTP with the OPIE library
`--enable-inet6`	Supports IPv6 (Requires the `inet6-apps` library)
`--with-kerberos5=`*`dir`*	Compiles Fetchmail with Kerberos 5 support
`--with-kerberos=`*`dir`*	Compiles Fetchmail with Kerberos 4 support
`--with-socks=`*`dir`*	Adds SOCKS firewall support
`--with-socks5=`*`dir`*	Adds SOCKS5 firewall support
`--with-gssapi=`*`dir`*	Adds GSSAPI support to Fetchmail

The first option allows you to change the location prefix of Fetchmail. The second option allows you specify a fallback transport in the event that SMTP is not available. Fetchmail first tries to submit e-mail via SMTP to port 25; then, if a fallback transport is specified, it tries to submit the e-mail using that. You can specify `sendmail`, `procmail`, or `maildrop` as the fallback transport.

The next few options allow you to enable support for other protocols and tools. These include the Remote Passphrase Authentication (RPA) protocol (used by CompuServe), NTML (the Microsoft standard authentication protocol), and Demon Internet's SDPS protocol. The `-enable-opie` option allows you to enable the one-time passwords using the One Time Passwords in Everything library.[12] You can enable IPv6 support (for which you need the `inet6-apps` library) by using the `--enable-inet6` option.

You can enable Kerberos or Kerberos 5 by using the `-enable-kerberos` and `-enable-kerberos5` options. Support for SOCKS and SOCKS5 is also available by using the

---

12. `http://inner.net/opie`

--enable-socks and --enable-socks5 options, respectively. Finally, you can enable the Generic Security Services Application Programming Interface (GSSAPI) by using the option --enable-gssapi.

Once you have configured Fetchmail to your requirements, you need to make and install it by entering the following:

```
puppy# make && make install
```

By default, the Fetchmail binary is installed into /usr/local/bin (unless you have overridden that location using the --prefix configure option).

Configuring and Running Fetchmail

Fetchmail can be run both from the command line and as a daemon. On the command line, you can specify a particular account or system you would like to retrieve mail from via POP or IMAP whilst running in daemon mode. Fetchmail can process multiple accounts for multiple users. Fetchmail draws its configuration from either command-line options or the .fetchmailrc file. Any command-line options override duplicate options specified in the .fetchmailrc file. You can have many .fetchmailrc files (one for each user, for example), each of which can contain multiple potential accounts using different protocols from which to retrieve e-mail. I will primarily cover the basic command-line options and show you some examples of .fetchmailrc configurations that are relevant to using Fetchmail in a secure manner. I will not go into a lot of detail about .fetchmailrc files.

Tip Also, a GUI Fetchmail configuration client called fetchmailconf runs under X-Windows. It requires TCL/TK to operate. It comes with the current releases of Fetchmail, or you can find a Debian version at http://packages.debian.org/stable/mail/fetchmailconf and RPM packages for a variety of distributions at http://rpmfind.net.

I will start by looking at running Fetchmail from the command line. This is often a useful way to test your connection before you commit your configuration to a .fetchmailrc file. Listing 9-30 shows the start of a typical Fetchmail session. I will cover the makeup of that command and explain how to use the options. Then I will cover exactly what the command has done and any potential risks that exist.

Listing 9-30. *Sample Fetchmail Command*

```
puppy# fetchmail -v -p IMAP -u bob kitten.yourdomain.com
Enter password for bob@yourdomain.com:
fetchmail: 6.2.1 querying yourdomain.com (protocol IMAP) at ➥
Thu 27 May 2004 19:45:37 EST: poll started
```

I have executed the fetchmail binary with a few basic options. The first option, -v, enables the verbose mode, which increases the logging level. All logging is done to stdout as Fetchmail runs. The next option, -p, selects the protocol with which you want to connect to the remote system. Table 9-9 shows the list of available protocols.

Table 9-9. *Available Fetchmail Protocols*

Protocol	Description
AUTO	Tests the remote system for IMAP, POP2, and POP3 and then chooses the first acceptable protocol it finds
POP2	Post Office Protocol 2
POP3	Post Office Protocol 3
APOP	POP3 with MD5-challenge authentication
RPOP	POP3 with RPOP authentication
KPOP	POP3 with Kerberos V4 authentication
SDPS	POP3 with Demon Internet's SDPS extensions
IMAP	IMAP2bis, IMAP4, or IMAP4rev1 (detects and selects the correct protocol on the remote system)
ETRN	ETRN
ODMR	On-Demand Mail Relay

In Listing 9-30 I used IMAP to connect to my remote system. The next option, -u, tells you I am trying to retrieve the mail of the user, bob. Finally, I list the name of the remote server I am connecting to, which in this case is kitten.yourdomain.com.

As you can see from Listing 9-30, when you run Fetchmail from the command line, it prompts you for your password. After this it connects to the remote server (in this case via IMAP connecting to port 143 on the remote system) and will attempt to retrieve your mail and then deliver it to port 25 on your local host. This is also probably the safest way to run Fetchmail, as it prompts you for your password when you run it and therefore does not require that you to hard-code a password in a .fetchmailrc file. It is, however, quite inconvenient (if not impossible) to repeatedly have to enter your password, especially if you want to use Fetchmail as a daemon; I will show how to mitigate that risk in the "Automating Fetchmail Securely" section. Additionally, of course, you need to ensure that whatever protocol you are using to connect to the remote system is encrypted; otherwise, your password is traveling across the network in clear text. I will show how to do that now.

Using Fetchmail with OpenSSL

As you can see from Listing 9-29, I have compiled my Fetchmail with OpenSSL. This allows you to use IMAPS and POP3S instead of IMAP and POP3 if the remote server you are connecting to supports these protocols. As you can see from Listing 9-31, it is easy to enable OpenSSL with Fetchmail.

Listing 9-31. *Fetchmail with* SSL-enabled

```
puppy# fetchmail -v -p IMAP -u bob kitten.yourdomain.com --ssl
Enter password for bob@kitten.yourdomain.com:
fetchmail: 6.2.5 querying kitten.yourdomain.com (protocol IMAP) at ➡
Thu 27 May 2004 23:33:50 EST: poll started
fetchmail: Issuer Organization: kitten.yourdomain.com
```

```
fetchmail: Issuer CommonName: kitten.yourdomain.com
fetchmail: Server CommonName: kitten.yourdomain.com
fetchmail: kitten.yourdomain.com key fingerprint: ➥
A3:AE:91:83:91:2C:65:1F:62:6C:1F:F5:B4:FE:3E:70
fetchmail: Warning: server certificate verification: self signed certificate
fetchmail: Issuer Organization: kitten.yourdomain.com
fetchmail: Issuer CommonName: kitten.yourdomain.com
fetchmail: Server CommonName: kitten.yourdomain.com
fetchmail: Warning: server certificate verification: self signed certificate
```

You can see from Listing 9-31 that adding the option --ssl to the command line causes Fetchmail to now connect to kitten.yourdomain.com using SSL. It is thus now not connecting on the IMAP port 143 but rather on the IMAPS port 993. By default if you do not specify a particular port (which you can do with the -P option), Fetchmail tries the ports for the SSL-enabled versions of various protocols (for example, 993 for IMAPS and 995 for POP3S). Table 9-10 shows some additional SSL options you can specify to Fetchmail.

Table 9-10. *Fetchmail OpenSSL-Related Options*

Option	Description
--sslcert *name*	Specifies the filename of the client-side public SSL certificate
--sslkey *name*	Specifies the filename of the client-side private SSL key
--sslcertpath *directory*	Sets the directory Fetchmail uses to look up local certificates
--sslproto *name*	Forces a particular SSL protocol, such as SSL2, SSL3, or TLS1
--sslcertck	Causes Fetchmail to strictly check the server certificate against a set of local trusted certificates
--sslfingerprint	Specifies the fingerprint of the server key (an MD5 hash of the key)

The first three options in Table 9-10 allow you to specify a particular client certificate, a key, and the directory for use when connecting to a remote server. Often you do not need to do this. Many IMAPS and POP3S servers do not require a certificate and enable encryption without it. But if your remote server does require client-based certificates and keys, then you can use these three options to specify them.

The next option, --sslproto, allows you to specify a particular flavor of the SSL protocol with the choice of SSL2, SSL3, and TLS1. The --sslcertck option tells Fetchmail to strictly check the server certificate against the set of local certificates to ensure it is trusted. If the server certificate is not signed by one of the trusted local certificates, then Fetchmail will not connect. This is designed to prevent "man-in-the-middle" attacks and ensure that the remote location you are speaking to is trusted. The location of the trusted local SSL certificates is specified by the --sslcertpath option. The last option, --sslfingerprint, performs a similar function. You can specify the MD5 hash, or fingerprint, of the remote server certificate to Fetchmail, and it will verify that the fingerprint provided matches the remote server certificate fingerprint. If they do not match, Fetchmail will terminate the connection.

Tunneling Fetchmail with SSH

So, in the previous section, I explained what you can do to secure your Fetchmail using SSL-enabled protocols. What do you do if the server to which you are connecting to is not willing or able to run SSL-enabled protocols? Well, you can also tunnel your Fetchmail connection using OpenSSH. This tunneling is achieved by the OpenSSH function known as *port forwarding*. A few prerequisites exist for this. First, you need the OpenSSH package installed on both the local and remote systems. Second, you need access to the ssh command on the local system, and the sshd daemon needs to be running on the remote system.

■**Note** I talk more about OpenSSH and port forwarding in Chapter 3.

You need to start by using ssh to forward a port, such as an IMAP port, on the remote system to a port on your local system. I will choose to forward it to an ephemeral port to allow any user to do this.

■**Tip** I do this because generally only the root user can bind ports lower than 1024.

The command in Listing 9-32 forwards the IMAP port on the remote system, kitten.yourdomain.com, to the local port 10143 and then forks into the background.

Listing 9-32. *Forwarding a Remote IMAP Port Using SSH*

```
puppy# ssh -l bob -f kitten.yourdomain.com -L 10143:kitten.yourdomain.com:143 \
sleep 120
bob@kitten.yourdomain.com's password:
```

Let's break this command down a little. First, you use ssh's -l option to specify the user (for example, bob) to log in as on the remote system. Second, the -f option tells ssh to fork into the background. Then comes the server you are connecting to, kitten.yourdomain.com, and finally the port forwarding itself prefixed by the -L option, which tells ssh to forward to local port 10143 everything from remote port 143 on server kitten.yourdomain.com. Last, you have the sleep 120 command, which, because I have specified the -f option, is executed when ssh forks into the background. As you can see from the next line in Listing 9-32, the remote sshd daemon prompts you for bob's password on the remote system. This is the password for bob's shell account on that system.

■**Caution** Remember that you are still talking to the local port in clear text—before the traffic leaves your system. A network sniffer on your localhost would see your password. This is, of course, a minimal risk and would imply your system is already penetrated, but it does need to be communicated. You have no real way of mitigating this risk, so I recommend that if your systems require the level of the security that makes this an unacceptable risk, then do not use Fetchmail.

Once you have entered your password, your connection should exist for the duration of the `sleep` command, which is 120 seconds in this case. Remember that if Fetchmail has not completed retrieving any e-mail when the connection ends, then it will fail with an error message. So, ensure the `sleep` duration is sufficient time for your Fetchmail session to complete.

■Tip You could also add the `-C` option to the `ssh` command in Listing 9-32. The `-C` option enables SSH compression, which could increase throughput on slower connections.

As shown in Listing 9-33, you can also try to Fetchmail using the port of your local system.

Listing 9-33. *Using Fetchmail over an SSH Tunnel*

```
puppy# fetchmail -v -p IMAP -P 10143 -u bob localhost
```

I have added the option `-P`, which allows you to specify the port number to which you want to connect and changes the target server to `localhost`. Using the `-u` option, you could also specify a different username. For example, you could set it up so that all your users could connect to the remote system using a shell account called bob (which was designed to perform this port forwarding and nothing else) and then log into the resulting SSH-secured and forwarded port using their own POP or IMAP user. Now when using the command in Listing 9-33, you would be prompted for your password—remember this is your POP or IMAP password, not the shell account password you provided earlier. After entering your password, Fetchmail should now retrieve and deliver any e-mail that is waiting for you on the remote system.

So, I have shown two ways to connect to a remote POP- or IMAP-style mail server using an encrypted connection, one with SSL and the other with SSH. But what do you do if you are not able to use SSL-enabled protocols or set up SSH tunneling? Well, the safest thing to do is not use Fetchmail. The risk will always exist with IMAP or POP running without SSL that an attacker will be able to capture your username and password from the network and use it maliciously. Without a way to mitigate that risk, I recommend you do not use Fetchmail!

Automating Fetchmail Securely

You will notice one thing about all the previous commands I have covered: they happen interactively. This works fine if you are using the command line. But many people want to retrieve their e-mail in the background (and indeed most users run Fetchmail in its daemon mode to achieve this). This means you use Fetchmail's other configuration style, the `.fetchmailrc` file. Fetchmail can read this file when launched from the command line or whilst running as a daemon. I will first look at getting Fetchmail running as a daemon. Listing 9-34 shows you how this works, and I will then explain how to use the various options of that command.

Listing 9-34. *Starting Fetchmail As a Daemon*

```
puppy# fetchmail -d 300
```

As you can see, starting Fetchmail as a daemon is simple; you need to use only the `-d` option and a polling interval (in seconds). Fetchmail will run as a daemon in the background and wake up every polling interval to check the remote system for e-mail.

Fetchmail uses the configuration it finds in the home directory of the user who has started Fetchmail, normally stored in the file .fetchmailrc. You can also override options in that file by adding command-line switches to Fetchmail. To give you an idea of what a typical .fetchmail file contains, I will duplicate the command-line configuration for Listing 9-30 and 9-31 in the form of .fetchmailrc files. The first example showed a simple, non-SSL-enabled retrieval of e-mail from an IMAP. Listing 9-35 shows the .fetchmailrc equivalent to the non-SSL-enabled Fetchmail command in Listing 9-30.

Listing 9-35. .fetchmailrc *File*

```
poll kitten.yourdomain.com with proto IMAP
        user "bob"
        pass "yourpassword"
```

This is mostly self-explanatory. As with Listing 9-30, you are polling kitten.yourdomain.com for the user bob's mail, which you want to retrieve via IMAP. In the second example, Listing 9-31 showed this retrieval using SSL-enabled IMAP. Listing 9-36 shows the .fetchmailrc equivalent of the SSL-enabled Fetchmail in Listing 9-31.

Listing 9-36. .fetchmailrc *File #2*

```
poll kitten.yourdomain.com with proto IMAP
        user "bob"
        pass "yourpassword"
   ssl
```

By adding the ssl line to the .fetchmailrc file, you have enabled SSL functionality.

As you can see from both Listings 9-35 and 9-36, your password is contained in the .fetchmailrc file. This poses a risk if someone gets access to your .fetchmailrc file. It is a risk of your mail being intercepted and retrieved by someone else. Additionally, the password you are using to connect to the remote system is also often the password to a shell account on that remote system. That could allow an attacker to use that username and password to penetrate that remote system. So you need to protect your .fetchmailrc file as much as possible. The .fetchmailrc file needs to be owned by the user who is going to launch Fetchmail and have the tightest possible permissions. I recommend you chmod the .fetchmailrc file to 0600. Fetchmail will not start if the .fetchmailrc file is not owned by the user who is starting Fetchmail or if that file has permissions more than 0710. This will restrict who can access your .fetchmailrc file, but it stills means your password is present in that file. If this seems to be an undue risk to you, then I recommend you refrain from using Fetchmail in this way.

Finally, in the previous section, I showed you how to tunnel Fetchmail through an SSH connection. You will remember that starting the ssh port forwarding requires that you enter your shell password on the remote system to make the connection. Obviously, when running in daemon mode, you will not be able to provide this password to Fetchmail. So you need to find an alternative method of authenticating the SSH connection. You have a couple of ways of doing this. In the first example, you need to create an SSH key pair using the ssh-keygen command, as you can see in Listing 9-37, and add the public key to the authorized_keys file on the remote system. I will create the key pair without a passphrase to stop Fetchmail prompting for one.

Listing 9-37. *Generating an SSH Key Pair for Fetchmail*

```
puppy# ssh-keygen -t rsa
Generating public/private rsa key pair.
Enter file in which to save the key (/home/bob/.ssh/id_rsa): ➥
/home/bob/.ssh/fetchmail_rsa
Enter passphrase (empty for no passphrase):
Enter same passphrase again:
Your identification has been saved in /home/bob/.ssh/fetchmail_rsa.
Your public key has been saved in /home/bob/.ssh/fetchmail_rsa.pub.
The key fingerprint is:
b5:33:94:19:32:10:41:38:25:15:c3:7e:d6:af:fa:d5 bob@kitten.yourdomain.com
```

■**Note** I go into more detail on OpenSSH in Chapter 3.

Still, some risks are associated with this. An SSH key pair without a passphrase means anyone who gets hold of your private key has access to any system for which that key is authorized. I recommend using that key pair simply for Fetchmail authorization.

■**Tip** You could also use the functionality of the OpenSSH `ssh-agent` key-caching tool to use keys with passphrases, but the possibility exists that an attacker could extract the private keys from the agent.

Protecting Fetchmail from Denial of Service Attacks

Lastly, I will cover protecting Fetchmail from DoS attacks. The risk exists for both DoS attacks aimed at disrupting your Fetchmail application and at threatening your system through Fetchmail or both.[13] The most obvious way to protect your Fetchmail system is to ensure you are using the latest version of Fetchmail and that you include the Fetchmail application in the list of applications in which you regularly review your Bugtraq or vendor security announcements for potential vulnerabilities. So, as I have often said in this book, update frequently, research carefully, and check for new developments, announcements, exploits, and vulnerabilities.

You can also further reduce the risk to your Fetchmail application by setting a few resource-control settings in your Fetchmail daemon. Table 9-11 shows the command-line switches for resource control in Fetchmail, and I will take you through each of them next.

---

13. Such as this exploit—http://www.securityfocus.com/bid/8843

Table 9-11. *Resource Limit Control Options*

Options	Description	Default
-l *bytes*	Limits the size of messages Fetchmail will retrieve in bytes	0
-w *interval*	Controls the interval between warnings being sent when detecting over-sized messages	0
-B *number*	Limits the number of messages accepted from a given server in a single poll	0

Most of the items in Table 9-11 are self-explanatory. The first option, -l, limits the size of messages that Fetchmail will receive. You can set this in bytes, and it defaults to 0 for no limit. The next option, -w, allows you to specify an interval in seconds (which defaults to 0 or disabled) between warnings being sent for oversized messages to the user who called Fetchmail (or if overridden by the postmaster option to that user). The last option, -B, limits the number of messages Fetchmail will download in a single session.

■**Tip** Your MTA should also be set up to process incoming messages for viruses, spam, or malicious content or attachments.

Resources

The following are resources you can use.

Mailing Lists

- **Security Focus Bugtraq mailing list archives**: http://www.securityfocus.com/archive/1

- **Cyrus IMAP**: http://asg.web.cmu.edu/cyrus/mailing-list.html

- **Fetchmail**: http://lists.ccil.org/mailman/listinfo/fetchmail-friends

Sites

- **IMAP**: http://www.imap.org/

- **IMAP servers**:

    - **Cyrus IMAP**: http://asg.web.cmu.edu/cyrus/imapd/

    - **Courier-IMAP**: http://www.courier-mta.org/imap/

    - **Cyrus wiki**: http://acs-wiki.andrew.cmu.edu/twiki/bin/view/Cyrus/WebHome

- **POP servers**:

  - **GNU pop3d**: http://freshmeat.net/projects/gnupop3d

  - **POPular**: http://www.remote.org/jochen/mail/popular/

  - **Qpopper**: http://www.eudora.com/products/unsupported/qpopper/index.html

  - **TeaPOP**: http://www.toontown.org/teapop/

  - **vm-pop3d**: http://www.reedmedia.net/software/virtualmail-pop3d/

  - **Fetchmail**: http://www.catb.org/~esr/fetchmail/

  - **One Time Passwords in Everything**: http://inner.net/opie

CHAPTER 10

■ ■ ■

Securing an FTP Server

File Transfer Protocol (FTP) is one of the original core protocols of the Internet and was first documented in 1971. It was designed to provide the functionality to exchanges files over the Internet and is specified in RFC 959.[1] It is still currently used for a number of purposes, including running user-authenticated and anonymously authenticated FTP servers to download files and applications. For example, software vendors utilize it to provide updates or patches to clients. It is also used to transfer files between disparate systems; for example, many non-Unix systems also support FTP. One of the most common uses of FTP is by ISPs to provide customers with the ability to upload files to their Web sites.

At first look FTP would seem to fulfill a useful and practical function. Unfortunately, FTP is also inherently insecure. The only security available to most FTP sessions is a username and password combination. By default, FTP transactions are unencrypted, and all traffic is sent in clear text across your network. One example is the transmission of usernames and passwords. This exposes you to a considerable level of risk that is difficult to mitigate with available tools.

Because of the inner workings of FTP, it is not possible to use tools such as Stunnel to secure FTP traffic; I will explain why this is so in the next section. Additionally, many of the available open-source and commercial FTP servers have proven to be highly vulnerable to attack. Many FTP servers are easily compromised and thus can provide a point of access for an attacker to enter your system. Or they have vulnerabilities that could allow Denial of Service (DoS) attacks on your systems. In addition to these potential insecurities, FTP is also vulnerable to so-called man-in-the-middle attacks where your data is intercepted and then either stolen or altered and sent on. For example, this is one of the primary methods hackers use to penetrate and hack Web servers. New material is uploaded to a Web server via FTP. The hacker finds the IP address of the Web server and sets up a sniffer to watch FTP's TCP port 21. The next time you update the site, the attacker grabs your username and password, which are used to upload material of the hacker's choice to the system or to steal any valuable information, such as credit card details, from your site.

Given the weaknesses of FTP, I recommend you not run it at all as a production server on any systems, unless you absolutely require the functionality. Some commercial secure FTP servers are available. But these usually require a client that is compatible with the secure server. If you have a proprietary commercial FTP server running with encryption or enhanced authentication, then generally clients other than the proprietary client designed for that server will not be able to connect or will be able to connect to the server using only standard FTP without any additional security.

---

1. http://www.ietf.org/rfc/rfc0959.txt?number=959

You do have some alternatives to FTP. Indeed, for the process of transferring files between systems, other mechanisms are considerably more secure. These include sftp or scp from the OpenSSH toolkit (as discussed in Chapter 3). If the remote systems are configured correctly, then you can use SSH to upload files to remote systems such as Web servers without requiring an FTP port to be open on them. I recommend you look at these options rather than use FTP.

If you must use FTP, then in this chapter I will try to provide a secure as possible implementation of an FTP server. I will show you how FTP works and how best to firewall it. Additionally, I will take you through installing a secure anonymous FTP server, show you a local user–authenticated FTP server, and cover support for FTP over SSL/TLS. As part of this, I will also demonstrate how to chroot your FTP server and mitigate the risk of DoS attacks.

How Does FTP Work?

FTP has two key components: a client and a server. This chapter will focus on the server component of FTP. FTP is a *stateful* protocol, meaning that connections between clients and servers are created and kept open during an FTP session. Commands that are issued to the FTP server (for example, to upload a file or list files in a directory) are executed consecutively. If a command arrives while another command is being executed, then the new command is queued and will execute when the current command has been completed.

■**Note** FTP is a TCP-only protocol. FTP does not have any UDP elements.

When making an FTP connection, two types of connections are initiated. They are a control connection, also called a *command*, and a data connection. When you connect an FTP client to an FTP server, a single control connection is established by default using the TCP port 21. This connection is used for the authentication process, for sending commands, and for receiving response messages from the remote server. It does not do the actual sending and receiving of information or files. The data connection handles sending and receiving files. A data connection is established only when a file needs to be transferred and is closed at the end of the transfer.

Two types of data connection exist: active mode and passive mode. Active connections use the PORT command and are initiated by the remote server, and the client listens for the connection. Passive connections use the PASV command; the client initiates the connection to the remote server, and the server listens for the data connections. When the client starts a transfer, it tells the server what type of connection it wants to make. In modern FTP clients and servers, the most common connection type is passive connections.

In active mode, the client connects from a random source port in the ephemeral port range (see Chapter 2) to the FTP control port 21. All commands and response codes are sent on this control connection. When you actually want to transfer a file, the remote FTP server will initiate a connection from the FTP data port 20 on the server system back to a destination port in the ephemeral port range on the client. This destination port is negotiated by the port 21 control connection. Often, the destination port used is one port number higher than the source port on the client. Figure 10-1 shows an active mode connection.

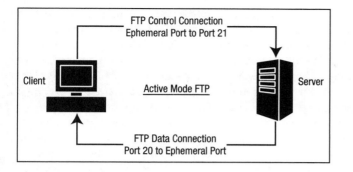

Figure 10-1. *Active mode FTP connection*

Active mode connections often have issues with firewalls. On the server side with an active mode connection, you need to have the TCP ports 20 and 21 open on your firewall. On the client side, you need the range of ephemeral ports open. Often opening these ports is hard to do if your FTP client is behind a firewall. In a secure firewall configuration, these ports should generally be closed. Additionally, because the remote server initiates the connection, many firewalls will drop the connection because they are designed to accept only established connections on specific limited ports. Finally, if you are behind a firewall that uses many-to-one Network Address Translation (NAT), it is often impossible for the firewall to determine which internal IP address initiated the FTP connection. This is caused by the firewall's inability to correlate the control and data connections.

As a result of the issues active mode connections have with firewalls, passive mode connections were introduced. In passive mode, the client initiates both sides of the connection. First, the client initiates the control connection from a random ephemeral port on the client to the destination port of 21 on the remote server. When it needs to make a data connection, the client will issue the PASV command. The server will respond by opening a random ephemeral port on the server and pass this port number back to the client via the control connection. The client will then open a random ephemeral source port on the client and initiate a connection between that port and the destination remote port provided by the FTP server. Figure 10-2 shows a passive mode FTP connection.

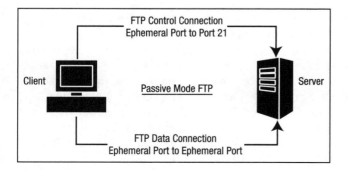

Figure 10-2. *Passive mode FTP connection*

Passive mode connections mitigate the risk of the remote server initiating the connection to the client and being blocked by a firewall. This is because the client initiates both the control and data connections. Thus, firewalls see the outgoing FTP data connection as part of an established connection. You still need to have ephemeral ports open on the server and client side of the connection. But this too can be partially mitigated because many FTP servers allow you to specify the range of ephemeral ports rather than using the entire ephemeral port range. But you still need to open a suitable range to allow your FTP server to function.

Overall, the random ephemeral port selection, for both active and passive connections, is one of the reasons why securing FTP is difficult. To achieve a secure connection, the securing application needs to know which ports to secure. As this port choice is random, the securing application has no means of determining what port needs to be secured.

Firewalling Your FTP Server

Another method exists for further locking down your FTP connections. To do this, you can use iptables with a module called ip_conntrack_ftp. The ip_conntrack_ftp module uses connection state tracking to correlate and track FTP transactions. I first introduced connection state tracking in Chapter 2. Let's look at creating some iptables rules for your FTP server.

I discussed earlier that in order for the FTP server to function, you will need a combination of the port 20, the port 21, and the range of ephemeral ports open on both the client and server. This combination is partially dependant on the connection mode you are running on your FTP server. I will assume you are creating firewall rules for an FTP server running on interface eth0 and bound to IP address 192.168.0.1. I will also assume you want FTP connections only into the system and you do not want to allow outgoing FTP connections.

The first rules you will create are for the FTP server's control connection, which uses TCP port 21. They are identical for active and passive mode FTP, as the control connection is required for both modes.

```
puppy# iptables -A INPUT -i eth0 -p tcp --dport 21 -d 192.168.0.1 -m state \
--state NEW,ESTABLISHED,RELATED -j ACCEPT
puppy# iptables -A OUTPUT -o eth0 -p tcp --sport 21 -s 192.168.0.1 -m state \
--state ESTABLISHED,RELATED -j ACCEPT
```

In the two rules you have just specified, incoming traffic on interface eth0 to IP address 192.168.0.1 and TCP port 21 in the connection state NEW, ESTABLISHED, or RELATED is allowed to enter the host. Outgoing traffic on the same interface, IP address, and port in the connection states ESTABLISHED and RELATED is allowed to exit the host.

The control connection is not the whole story, though. The FTP server also needs the data connection opened in your firewall for the server to correctly function. As I have discussed, this data connection can run in two modes: active and passive. For example, the active mode connection requires a substantial port range to be open. To function correctly, the active mode requires port 20 to be open on the FTP server. Additionally, on the server you need to accept incoming connections from the ephemeral port range on the client host. The passive mode connection requires ports in the ephemeral port range to be open on both the client and the server. Both of these models pose security risks.

To help mitigate this security risk, I will show how to utilize the ip_conntrack_ftp module. This module is an iptables kernel module that extends the functionality of the connection state tracking discussed in Chapter 2. This module is provided with most distributions and with all recent releases of `iptables`.

Load the required module like this:

```
puppy# insmod ip_conntrack_ftp
```

The module may be already loaded on your system, and it will return an error message if this is the case. You need to load the module each time your system restarts. It is recommended you load this module when you start `iptables`.

The `ip_conntrack_ftp` module tracks FTP connections and watches for the use of the `PORT` or `PASV` command on port 21, which indicates that a data connection is being initiated. The module then makes note of and tracks the ports being used by the data connection. This allows `iptables` to correlate and track the control and data connections for a particular FTP transaction. The module allows `iptables` to reference the data connection as a `RELATED` state. Thus, you can use the `RELATED` connection state rather than the `NEW` connection state in your `INPUT` chain. This means ports on your host need to be open only for `RELATED` connections, not `NEW` connections from ephemeral ports. This reduces the risk posed by running an FTP server and allows you to more tightly firewall these connections.

You still need to use a different approach in applying rules for active and passive mode connections to address their different port requirements, but now you can specify a much tighter set of `iptables` rules. Listing 10-1 specifies some rules for active mode data connections.

Listing 10-1. *Rules for Active Mode Connections*

```
puppy# iptables -A INPUT -i eth0 -p tcp --sport 1024: --dport 20 -d 192.168.0.1 \
-m state --state ESTABLISHED,RELATED -j ACCEPT
puppy# iptables -A OUTPUT -o eth0 -p tcp --dport 1024: --sport 20 -s 192.168.0.1 \
-m state --state ESTABLISHED -j ACCEPT
```

The first rule in Listing 10-1 allows incoming traffic from source ports higher than 1024 on interface `eth0` to IP address `192.168.0.1` and port 20 in the `ESTABLISHED` and `RELATED` states. This prevents new connections from being made to this port. The only incoming connections should be the data connection portions of existing FTP connections. This increases the level of security on your host firewall. The second rule allows outgoing traffic in the `ESTABLISHED` and `RELATED` states outbound from the host to destination ports higher than 1024.

Passive mode FTP is similar. Using the `ip_conntrack_ftp` module, you can track the state of the connections and the port numbers used and thus can use the `RELATED` state for your `iptables` rules. Listing 10-2 shows an `INPUT` and `OUTPUT` rule for passive mode connections.

Listing 10-2. *Rules for Passive Mode Connections*

```
puppy# iptables -A INPUT -i eth0 -p tcp --sport 1024: \
--dport 1024:   -d 192.168.0.1 -m state --state ESTABLISHED,RELATED -j ACCEPT
puppy# iptables -A OUTPUT -o eth0 -p tcp --sport 1024: \
--dport 1024:   -s 192.168.0.1 -m state --state ESTABLISHED -j ACCEPT
```

The first rule in Listing 10-2 allows incoming traffic from the ephemeral ports (which you have defined as all ports greater than 1024 in your rules) to interface `eth0` and IP address `192.168.0.1`. The second rule provides the same functionality for outgoing traffic.

Neither Listing 10-1 nor Listing 10-2 is an ideal solution. These rules leave your firewall comparatively quite open compared to the models proposed in Chapter 2. These are the securest possible rules you can create on a host system for an FTP server. This again highlights that there are risks involved in running an FTP server. Some of these risks simply cannot be mitigated.

■Tip When I cover vsftpd, I will refine the range of ephemeral ports that the FTP server can use. This can further limit the range of ports you need to open on your host.

What FTP Server to Use?

Several FTP servers are available, including both commercial and open-source products. I will cover vsftpd, which is an open-source FTP server. The vsftpd package has a reputation for security and is a compact but also fully featured and well-performing application. At the time of writing, vsftpd had only one vulnerability listed at the Security Focus's Bugtraq[2] site as opposed to multiple issues for other FTP server packages such as ProFTPD and WU-FTPD. It is regularly updated and maintained. It is also widely available on most Linux distributions.

The vsftpd daemon has some good security features, including the following:

- Can run as a nonprivileged user with privilege separation

- Supports SSL/TLS FTP transfers

- Can chroot users into their home directories and chroot anonymous FTP access to a particular directory

- Can limit the FTP commands that a user can execute

- Reduces the risk of DoS attacks with bandwidth and connection limits

- Coded to reduce the risk of buffer overflow attacks

The vsftpd FTP server is both secure and high performing. It is used by a number of organizations as a result of this, including Red Hat, Debian, OpenBSD.org, ftp.kernel.org, and ftp.isc.org. If you do not use vsftpd, I recommend you migrate to it, especially if you are using ProFTPD and WU-FTPD, both of which have been subject to several vulnerabilities that are easy to exploit. If you are going to take the risk of using an FTP server, then I recommend you choose the safest and most secure possible server.

Installing vsftpd

Many distributions come with vsftpd, and it should be available through your package management system. On a Debian system it is available as a package, and you can use apt-get to install vsftpd.

---

2. http://www.securityfocus.com/bid

```
kitten# apt-get install vsftpd
```

Or it is available as an RPM for Red Hat and Mandrake. To get the most recent version of vsftpd, you can download the source package from `ftp://vsftpd.beasts.org/users/cevans/`. You can download the source package to ensure you are using the most up-to-date version of the package.

```
puppy# wget ftp://vsftpd.beasts.org/users/cevans/vsftpd-2.0.1.tar.gz
```

After downloading the package, unpack the source package and change into the resulting directory. vsftpd does not use a `configure` script but rather has a file called `builddefs.h` that contains the compilation variables. Listing 10-3 shows the contents of this file.

Listing 10-3. *Initial* builddefs.h

```
#ifndef VSF_BUILDDEFS_H
#define VSF_BUILDDEFS_H

#undef VSF_BUILD_TCPWRAPPERS
#define VSF_BUILD_PAM
#undef VSF_BUILD_SSL

#endif /* VSF_BUILDDEFS_H */
```

You can enable SSL, PAM, and TCP Wrappers in this file. To enable features in vsftpd, you need to change each definition line for the feature you want to enable from the following:

```
#undef VSF_BUILD_SSL
```

to this:

```
#define VSF_BUILD_SSL
```

I will now show how to enable SSL and PAM in vsftpd. Listing 10-4 shows the final builddefs.h file.

Listing 10-4. *Final* builddefs.h

```
#ifndef VSF_BUILDDEFS_H
#define VSF_BUILDDEFS_H

#undef VSF_BUILD_TCPWRAPPERS
#define VSF_BUILD_PAM
#define VSF_BUILD_SSL

#endif /* VSF_BUILDDEFS_H */
```

Now you can make the vsftpd binary.

```
puppy$ make
```

This will create a binary called vsftpd in the package directory. You can then install vsftpd using the following command:

```
puppy# make install
```

vsftpd requires that you create some supporting configuration items. First you need to create a user for the vsftpd binary to run as. This allows the vsftpd binary to drop privileges and run as a normal user, thus providing more security against any compromise of the vsftpd daemon. By default vsftpd runs as the user nobody. This user exists on most systems but may be being used by a number of different daemons. It is safest to create another user. Next, you can use this new user to run the vsftpd daemon. I have chosen to create a user called ftp_nopriv. You can create this user with the command in Listing 10-5.

Listing 10-5. *Creating the* ftp_nopriv *User*

```
puppy# useradd -d /dev/null -s /sbin/nologin ftp_nopriv
```

You also need to create the /usr/share/empty directory.

```
puppy$ mkdir /usr/share/empty
```

This directory may already exist on some systems. It is used by vsftpd as a chroot direc-tory when the daemon does not require file system access. You should ensure that the ftp user cannot write to this directory and that no files are stored in this directory.

If you want to use anonymous FTP, then you need to create a user called ftp. This user needs to have a valid home directory that needs to be owned by the root user and has its per-missions set to 0755. The ftp user's home directory will be the root directory for anonymous FTP access.

```
puppy# mkdir /var/ftp
puppy# useradd -s /sbin/nologin -d /var/ftp ftp
puppy# chown root:root /var/ftp
puppy# chmod 0755 /var/ftp
```

Last, you need to copy the sample configuration file from the vsftpd package into the /etc directory.

```
puppy# cp vsftpd.conf /etc
```

In the next section I will cover how to modify this configuration file.

Configuring vsftpd for Anonymous FTP

The vsftpd.conf file controls the vsftpd daemon. The vsftpd binary has only one command-line option, which allows you to specify the location of the vsftpd.conf configuration file.

```
puppy# vsftpd /etc/vsftpd.conf
```

If the configuration file is not specified on the command line, then vsftpd defaults to the file /etc/vsftpd.conf.

■**Tip** Some Red Hat RPMs install the `vsftpd.conf` file into the directory `/etc/vsftpd/`, and `vsftpd` may look for the configuration file here.

I will now show a sample FTP server configuration and use that to explore the options available in `vsftpd`. Listing 10-6 shows a simple configuration file for a secure stand-alone anonymous FTP server that allows only downloads.

Listing 10-6. *Stand-Alone Anonymous Server*

```
# General Configuration
listen=YES
background=YES
listen_address=192.168.0.1
nopriv_user=ftp_nopriv
xferlog_enable=YES
# Mode and Access rights
anonymous_enable=YES
local_enable=NO
write_enable=NO
cmds_allowed=PASV,RETR,QUIT
# Security
ftpd_banner=Puppy.YourDomain.Net FTP Server
connect_from_port_20=YES
hide_ids=YES
pasv_min_port=50000
pasv_max_port=60000
# DoS
ls_recurse_enable=NO
max_clients=200
max_per_ip=4
```

I will go through each of these options with a particular focus on the security and access control features of the `vsftpd` daemon. Each `vsftpd.conf` option is structured like this:

```
option=value
```

There should be no spaces between the option, the = symbol, and the value. You can add comments to your configuration file by prefixing the comment line with #.

In Listing 10-6 I have divided the configuration into different sections using comments. The first comment-titled section is `General Configuration`, which handles the setup and management of `vsftpd`. I will cover those options first.

General Configuration

The first two options, `listen` and `background`, control how `vsftpd` will be run. Both options have Boolean values, and you can specify either YES or NO as their value. Many `vsftpd.conf` options are Boolean, and you must specify the YES and NO values in uppercase.

The listen option runs vsftpd in stand-alone mode. This means vsftpd is run as a normal daemon rather than through the inetd or xinetd daemon. It defaults to NO. I have enabled vsftpd to run in stand-alone mode by changing this option to YES. The background option tells the vsftpd to fork to the background. It also defaults to NO. I have changed it to YES to have the vsftpd daemon run in the background.

The listen_address option allows you to bind vsftpd to a particular IP address, thus controlling on which interface your FTP server runs. I have specified the IP address of the puppy host, 192.168.0.1.

The nopriv_user option allows you to specify which user the vsftpd daemon will run as. I have specified the ftp_nopriv user that I created as part of the installation process. This causes vsftpd to run as a nonprivileged user and enhances the security of the daemon. This mitigates the risk of an attacker gaining root privileges through the daemon.

The xferlog_enable option enables a log file that records all file uploads and downloads. The log file defaults to /var/log/vsftpd.log, but you can override this with the vsftpd_log_file option.

```
vsftpd_log_file=/var/log/transfer_log.log
```

Also available is the xferlog_std_format option, which allows you to specify that logging should be in the xferlog format. This is the default log format used by WU-FTPD and allows you to also use a variety of statistical tools developed for this application for reporting on vsftpd. You can enable this option like this:

```
xferlog_std_format=YES
```

Alternatively, you can enable the option syslog_enable to log to syslog instead.

```
syslog_enable=YES
```

The syslog_enable option overrides all the other logging options, and if set to YES, then vsftpd will not log to any other specified log files.

Mode and Access Rights

The mode options control what type of FTP server vsftpd will run; for example, it could specify an anonymous FTP server or an FTP server that accepts local user logins. The access rights options control what capabilities are offered to anonymous or local users signed into the FTP server (for example, whether uploads are enabled). In Listing 10-6 I have specified an anonymous FTP server that you can only download files from the server. This is the only type of server I recommend you run.

■**Note** I will demonstrate how to build a local user FTP server with SSL/TLS in the next section.

You can enable anonymous FTP by setting the anonymous_enable option to YES. The anonymous FTP mode is vsftpd's default mode; thus, YES is the default setting for this option. In anonymous FTP mode only the users anonymous and ftp can log onto the FTP server. When either of these users log in, they will be prompted for a password. vsftpd will accept any text as a password when in anonymous mode. It is usually assumed a remote user will enter an e-mail address as this password. You can control this password to some extent using the deny_email_enable and secure_email_list_enable options. The deny_email_enable option allows you to specify a list of passwords (including both e-mail addresses and other passwords) that if used to log in will result in a login failure. You enable this option like this:

```
deny_email_enable=YES
```

By default this list of passwords is stored in the file /etc/vsftpd.banned_emails. You may need to create this file. One of the possible uses of this option is to stop automatic FTP-scanning tools. Many of these tools attempt to log into your server using a default password. You can specify the default passwords these tools use in the /etc/vsftpd.banned_emails file to prevent the tools from logging in.[3] In Listing 10-7 you can see the result of trying to log in with a banned password. For this example I have added the password bob@anotherdomain.com to the /etc/vsftpd.banned_emails file.

Listing 10-7. *Banned Anonymous Passwords*

```
kitten# ftp puppy
Connected to puppy (192.168.0.1).
220 Welcome to Puppy FTP service.
Name (puppy:bob): anonymous
331 Please specify the password.
Password: bob@anotherdomain.com
530 Login incorrect.
Login failed.
```

■**Tip** You can use the banned_email_file option to override the file used by the deny_email_enable option with a different file.

The secure_email_list_enable option allows you to specify a list of passwords that will be accepted for anonymous login. No other passwords will be accepted. This is not overly secure, as these passwords are stored in plain text. These are not as secure as traditional passwords, and you should use this as a low-security restriction only. You can specify this option like this:

```
secure_email_list_enable=YES
```

By default these passwords are specified in the /etc/vsftpd.email_passwords file. You may need to create this file. You can also override this default file using the email_password_file option like this:

```
email_password_file=/etc/accepted_passwords
```

---

3. Grim's Ping (http://grimsping.cjb.net/) is an example of a tool that could be misused for FTP scanning and that can be stopped with this option.

Once the ftp or anonymous user is logged into your anonymous FTP server, the user will have access only to the contents of the home directory of the ftp user. I showed how to create this user and specify their home directory as part of the vsftpd installation process in the "Installing vsftpd" section. In that section I used the /var/ftp directory.

If you want to enable local user mode, which allows local users contained in the /etc/passwd file to log into the FTP server, you should set the local_enable option to YES. I will talk about that option in the "Configuring vsftpd with Local Users" section.

The first of the access rights options, the write_enable option, specifies whether FTP commands that are capable of writing to the file system are enabled. This includes FTP commands such as STOR or DELE.[4] By default this option is set to NO. This means no files can be written to, renamed, or deleted from your system. The vsftpd.conf man file contains a full list of the commands this option disables.

The second access right I have specified, cmds_allowed, controls the FTP commands that you are able to run on your FTP server. This is a powerful tool for locking down your FTP server to a limited number of FTP commands. Listing 10-6 specifies that only the commands PASV, RETR, and QUIT are allowed to run on the server. This means users can only download files and exit the server. With a limited number of FTP commands enabled, you can quite tightly secure your FTP server.

General Security

The general security options control a variety of security-related settings for your FTP server. The first option deals with the use of a banner for your FTP server. Like many services, when you connect to an FTP server, it displays a banner advertising details about the server to which you are connecting. Generally, the default vsftpd banner reveals little information about the server to which you are connecting. You should confirm your banner does not reveal the package or version of your FTP server.

The banner is controlled by two options: the ftpd_banner option and the banner_file option. The ftpd_banner option specifies a line that will be displayed when you connect to the FTP server.

```
ftpd_banner=Welcome to Puppy FTP service.
```

The banner_file option overrides this and allows you to specify a file containing your banner.

```
banner_name=/etc/vsftpd_banner
```

Confirm the details contained in your ftpd_banner. The banner_file option should suitably obfuscate your FTP server package and version or any details that may provide an attacker with information that could aid in an attack.

The next option, connect_from_port_20, tells PORT or active mode connections to use port 20. This is required for some FTP clients. Do not disable this without testing that all your remote clients still function correctly.

The hide_ids option hides the actual owner and group of the objects stored on your FTP server. With this option set to YES, the files will all appear to be owned by the user and group ftp. You can see this in the example in Listing 10-8.

---

4. You can see a list of most FTP commands at http://www.nsftools.com/tips/RawFTP.htm.

Listing 10-8. *Hiding Owners and Groups*

```
ftp> ls
227 Entering Passive Mode (192,168,0,1,63,131)
150 Here comes the directory listing.
drwxr-xr-x    2 ftp       ftp           4096 Oct 04 06:36 pub
-rw-r--r--    1 ftp       ftp             51 Oct 05 15:05 tmp
226 Directory send OK.
```

The next two options, pasv_min_port and pasv_max_port, control the range of the ephemeral ports used by vsftpd. I have specified a lower range of 50000 and an upper range of 60000. This means all passive mode connections will have an ephemeral port assigned from within this port range. This should allow you to tighten your firewall rules down to only this port range rather than the entire ephemeral port range. Listing 10-9 specifies iptables rules, restricting vsftpd to this ephemeral port range.

Listing 10-9. *Rules for Passive Mode Connections*

```
puppy# iptables -A INPUT -i eth0 -p tcp --sport 50000:60000 --dport 50000:60000 \
-d 192.168.0.1 -m state --state ESTABLISHED,RELATED -j ACCEPT
puppy# iptables -A OUTPUT -o eth0 -p tcp --sport 50000:60000 --dport 50000:60000  \
-s 192.168.0.1 -m state --state ESTABLISHED -j ACCEPT
```

You may ask, "Why don't I simply restrict the ephemeral port range to only one or a handful of ports?" The limitation here is that each FTP data connection requires an individual port. You can create a bottleneck on your system by limiting the ephemeral port range to a range that is too small.

Preventing Denial of Service Attacks

The last options from the example anonymous FTP server allow you to specify some limitations to the resources used by the FTP server. These limitations assist in mitigating the risk of DoS attacks against your FTP server. Setting the ls_recurse_enable option to YES allows the use of the ls -R directory-listing command. This can potentially consume a large volume of resources if run from the root directory of a large site. I recommend that if you have a large number of files in multiple directories that you set this option to NO.

The next two options, max_clients and max_per_ip, specify the maximum number of clients and the maximum number of connections from a single IP address, respectively. The max_clients option specifies the maximum number of clients that can be connected simultaneously to your FTP server. Any additional clients that try to connect to the server will get the following error message:

```
Connected to puppy.yourdomain.com
421 There are too many connected users, please try later.
```

The max_per_ip option specifies the maximum number of clients that can connect from a single IP address. Any additional clients will get the following error message:

```
Connected to puppy.yourdomain.com
421 There are too many connections from your internet address.
```

You should tune both of these options while considering the load on your FTP server. Do not cause a self-induced DoS attack on your system by setting these options lower than normal operations require. I recommend setting them to at least a quarter to a third higher than your peak load.

■Tip You can also limit the data volumes transferred to and from your FTP server. See the vsftpd.conf man page for some options that provide this capability.

Configuring vsftpd with Local Users

I have shown you how to create an anonymous FTP server. In this section I will explain how to create an FTP server that your local users can log onto.[5] In doing this I recommend you allow logins only from trusted local networks. You can achieve this by using iptables to limit the source of any FTP connection. Unless you can absolutely avoid it, do not open an FTP server to local user login over the Internet. This is especially true if the data you are hosting on your FTP server is sensitive or valuable. You can mitigate this somewhat by using SSL/TLS for FTP; I will discuss that in the "Adding SSL/TLS Support" section.

Listing 10-10 provides a sample stand-alone configuration for a local user FTP server. This provides the ability for your local users to log on and download files. I have also utilized PAM authentication for this server, and I will demonstrate how to configure that.

Listing 10-10. *Stand-Alone Local User FTP Server*

```
# General Configuration
listen=YES
background=YES
listen_address=192.168.0.1
nopriv_user=ftp_nopriv
xferlog_enable=YES
# Mode and Access rights
anonymous_enable=NO
local_enable=YES
chroot_local_user=YES
write_enable=YES
pam_service_name=vsftpd
# Security
ftpd_banner=Puppy.YourDomain.Net FTP Server
connect_from_port_20=YES
hide_ids=YES
pasv_min_port=50000
pasv_max_port=60000
# DoS
ls_recurse_enable=NO
max_clients=200
max_per_ip=4
```

---

5. Local users are those users contained in the /etc/passwd file on the local machine.

Many of the options in Listing 10-10 are identical to those in Listing 10-6. I will identify the changes in this section and explain how they impact the server configuration. The most obvious modification is in the mode and access rights configuration. Here I have disabled any anonymous access to the server by setting the anonymous_enable option to NO. I have also enabled the option local_enable by setting it to YES. This allows any local user to log into the FTP server.

Tip You can enable anonymous and local user access on the same FTP server if required. You would set the anonymous_enable and local_enable options both to YES.

When local users are signed into the FTP server, they will be placed in their home directory by default. They have access to any files or directories that are available to them as a result of their ownership, permissions, and group membership. For FTP purposes this is quite often a greater level of access than they really require. To reduce this access, I have enabled the chroot_local_user option. This option creates a mini-chroot jail for each of your users. Local users are jailed into their home directories. This prevents them from changing the directory out of their home directory and allows them access only to their home directory and any subdirectories beneath. This prevents them from downloading or uploading files to or from any other directory.

Caution Some small risk is associated with using chroot jails for local users if those local users have upload privileges. See the vsftpd FAQ at ftp://vsftpd.beasts.org/users/cevans/untar/vsftpd-2.0.1/FAQ. If you are restricting access to local users in a trusted network, I think the risk is outweighed by the overall added security of the chroot jail.

If the chroot_local_user option is set to YES, then vsftpd also allows you to not chroot specific users with the chroot_list_enable option, like so:

```
chroot_list_enable=YES
chroot_list_file=/etc/vsftpd.chroot_list
```

You specify the list of users in the file /etc/vsftpd.chroot_list that vsftpd should not chroot. When these non-chroot users log in, they will have access to all file and directories granted to them via their permissions and groups.

Note If chroot_local_user is set to NO and chroot_list_enable is set to YES, then the file specified in the chroot_list_file becomes a list of local users to chroot. All other local users would log on and not be confined to a chroot jail.

I also enabled the write_enable option, setting it to YES. This allows any users logged onto your FTP server to upload files. As the users have been placed in chroot jails in their home directories, they will only be able to upload files to this directory and subdirectories of their home directory.

You can set some additional options to govern file uploads on your FTP server. The first option is `file_open_mode`, which controls the permissions for any uploaded files. By default this is set to `0666`, like so:

```
file_open_mode=0666
```

You can also apply an `umask` (as discussed in Chapter 4) to any uploaded file by specifying the `local_umask` option like this:

```
local_umask=077
```

The default `umask` is `077`. This is quite restrictive and probably the safest option for your FTP server.

■**Caution** Be wary of allowing users to upload executable files to the FTP server. This could be a potential route for an attack. Ensure you set your default upload permissions and `umask` to prevent this.

I have also removed the `cmds_allowed` option, which restricted the commands allowed to be executed on the FTP server. You could reintroduce this with a wider command set on your FTP server if there were specific FTP commands that you did not want your local users to be able to execute.

`vsftpd` can have PAM support compiled into it, as demonstrated during the installation process. This is the best method for authenticating `vsftpd` with your local users. Listing 10-10 specifies the option `pam_server_name`. This allows you to specify the PAM service name that `vsftpd` will use for authentication. The default PAM service name for most Debian systems is `ftp`, and for more recent Red Hat versions it is `vsftpd`. Listing 10-11 shows a sample `vsftpd` PAM service file for a Red Hat system. This file should be located in `/etc/pam.d`.

■**Note** I cover PAM in more detail in Chapter 1.

Listing 10-11. `vsftpd` *PAM Service*

```
#%PAM-1.0
auth      required      pam_listfile.so item=user sense=deny ➥
file=/etc/vsftpd.ftpusers onerr=succeed
auth      required      pam_stack.so service=system-auth
auth      required      pam_shells.so
account   required      pam_stack.so service=system-auth
session   required      pam_stack.so service=system-auth
```

Listing 10-11 will deny login by any user specified in the `/etc/vsftpd.ftpusers` file. You can use this to list any users you explicitly do not want to log in via FTP, such as the `root` user. It will then call the `system-auth` PAM service to provide authentication. All users logging in will thus ultimately be authenticated against the /etc/passwd file, in addition to any further authentication or access control checks the system-auth service is configured to perform.

All other options in Listing 10-10 are the same as those for the anonymous FTP server.

Adding SSL/TLS Support

The more recent versions of vsftpd come with support for SSL/TLS. The first version to do so was vsftpd version 2.0.0. In some cases this support has been backported to the packages available in various distributions. If this support has not been backported, you may be able to compile vsftpd from source or adapt a package that already supports SSL/TLS for your distribution. For example, Red Hat has introduced support to the vsftpd RPM provided with Fedora Core 3. You should be able to use this RPM on some other, earlier versions of Red Hat or potentially on Mandrake systems. So to quickly add SSL/TLS support to vsftpd, you need to ensure vsftpd has support for SSL/TLS, create a certificate, update your vsftpd.conf file with your SSL/TLS configuration, and restart the vsftpd daemon. I will take you through all these steps in this section.

To enable SSL/TLS, you first need to compile it into vsftpd as you did in the "Installing vsftpd" section. You can check if your version of vsftpd is compiled with SSL/TLS using the ldd command.

```
puppy# ldd vsftpd
        libssl.so.4 => /lib/libssl.so.4 (0x4000d000)
        libcrypto.so.4 => /lib/libcrypto.so.4 (0x401ab000)
        libgssapi_krb5.so.2 => /usr/kerberos/lib/libgssapi_krb5.so.2 (0x4029d000)
        libk5crypto.so.3 => /usr/kerberos/lib/libk5crypto.so.3 (0x40311000)
...
```

If your vsftpd binary contains the library libssl.so.*x*, then it has been compiled with SSL/TLS.

You will also need to create a certificate for vsftpd to use. I talk about creating certificates in Chapter 3. Follow the process described in this chapter to create your certificate. Sign it against an existing certificate authority (CA) if you have created a local CA or against a commercial CA if you prefer to do so. If you intend to use this server for customers via the Internet, I recommend you purchase a commercial SSL certificate.

You can also quickly create a certificate using the OpenSSL make process that is provided with the OpenSSL package. This may be a simple option for FTP servers that are accessed only from internal networks. These require SSL encryption, but you may not be overly concerned about needing to prove the authenticity of the FTP server certificate. Listing 10-12 shows how to create such a certificate.

Listing 10-12. *Creating an SSL Certificate*

```
puppy# cd /usr/share/ssl/certs
puppy# make vsftpd.pem
umask 77 ; \
PEM1=`/bin/mktemp /tmp/openssl.XXXXXX` ; \
PEM2=`/bin/mktemp /tmp/openssl.XXXXXX` ; \
```

```
/usr/bin/openssl req -newkey rsa:1024 -keyout $PEM1 -nodes -x509 -days 365 ➥
-out $PEM2 ; \
cat $PEM1 >  vsftpd.pem ; \
echo ""    >> vsftpd.pem ; \
cat $PEM2 >> vsftpd.pem ; \
rm -f $PEM1 $PEM2
Generating a 1024 bit RSA private key
...
```

This will result in a PEM file called vsftpd.pem, which contains a private key and a certificate.

You then need to define your certificate to vsftpd and specify some additional options to control your FTP over SSL/TLS. Listing 10-13 includes the key configuration options you need to set in the vsftpd.conf file.

Listing 10-13. *SSL/TLS Options*

```
# SSL/TLS Options
ssl_enable=YES
rsa_cert_file=/usr/share/ssl/certs/vsftpd.pem
ssl_tlsv1=YES
force_local_data_ssl=YES
force_local_logins_ssl=YES
```

The first option in Listing 10-13, ssl_enable, controls whether SSL/TLS is enabled for your vsftpd server. You must set this option to YES to use SSL/TLS. The next option, rsa_cert_file, allows you to specify the location of your certificate file. I have specified the PEM file I created earlier, /usr/share/ssl/certs/vsftpd.pem.

The ssl_tlsv1 option is one of a series of options that allows you to enable particular versions of SSL. The ssl_tlsv1 option, if set to YES, then enables the use of TLS. You can also enable SSL 2 with the ssl_sslv2 option and SSL 3 with the ssl_sslv3 option. I recommend you use only TLS, as it is generally considered the most secure of the SSL/TLS versions available.

The last two options control when SSL/TLS will be required in the FTP process. When set to YES, the first option, force_local_data_ssl, requires that a SSL/TLS connection be made for all FTP data connections. The second option, force_local_logins_ssl, requires a SSL/TLS connection to be made in order for a user to log in.

Also available is the allow_anon_ssl option. When this option is enabled, it allows the use of SSL/TLS for anonymous connections also.

Once you have updated your vsftpd.conf file, you need to restart the vsftpd daemon for the new setting to take effect.

■**Note** You will need a remote FTP client that supports SSL/TLS to use it with vsftpd. A lot of FTP clients, including the ftp command that comes with most Linux distributions, do not offer SSL/TLS support.

Starting and Stopping vsftpd

You can start and stop vsftpd using the vsftpd binary. The daemon will first check the validity of vsftpd.conf and then, depending on the configuration, will either run in the foreground or fork the process into the background.

```
puppy# vsftpd &
```

To stop vsftpd, simply kill the daemon.

You could also start and stop vsftpd from an init script.[6] I recommend using this approach for ease of operation.

Resources

The following are resources you can use.

Sites

- **vsftpd**: http://vsftpd.beasts.org/

- **vsftpd** HOWTO: http://www.vsftpd.org/

---

6. A Red Hat init script, available at http://freshrpms.net/packages/builds/vsftpd/vsftpd.init, should be easy to adapt to other distributions.

CHAPTER 11
■ ■ ■

Hardening DNS and BIND

Domain Name Services[1] (DNS) is the phone directory of the Internet and private networks. DNS maps the IP addresses of hosts to their names, and vice versa. It provides the ability for applications, tools, and hosts to find and resolve the IP addresses or names of hosts with which they want to communicate. It is one of the most critical Internet and network services utilized by ISPs and organizations. Without DNS, the Internet and your internal network would be unable to function.

A DNS server is, in its simplest form, a database of names and addresses. This DNS database performs two core roles: it tracks the names and addresses of your hosts and provides these names and addresses in response to queries. These names and addresses can describe hosts and networks inside your internal network, on the Internet, or on another network. It can also describe the same host in two different contexts, depending on who asks the question. For example, the host `kitten.yourdomain.com` could have the IP address of `192.168.0.100` on your internal network. Clients of your internal network need to use this address to communicate with this host. On the Internet, however, `kitten.yourdomain.com` may be known by IP address `220.240.52.228`, and clients there need this address instead. Your DNS server determines which IP address for the `kitten.yourdomain.com` host it can provide to a client, depending on whether the query comes from your internal network or the Internet.

This name and address resolution role is critical to how almost all network services and applications function. It is also an extremely useful resource for attackers to control on your network because they can see the contents of your entire network and also use that information to subvert your hosts, stage "man-in-the-middle" attacks, or inflict crippling Denial of Service (DoS) attacks on your environment. In this chapter, I aim to mitigate and minimize the risk of these sorts of compromises and attacks from occurring and prevent an attacker from turning your DNS assets into dangerous liabilities.

In this chapter I will briefly cover some of the potential threats and risks to your DNS servers. Then I will address choosing a suitable DNS server and creating a secure DNS design. I will take you through installing, configuring, and hardening a DNS server and use the BIND DNS server as a model. I will provide an overview of the basic configuration of BIND, which should allow you to set up some simple DNS server configurations. I will also cover TSIG, which allows you to secure transactions between the BIND server and the `rndc` command, which provides an administration interface to your BIND server.

I will not go into a large amount of detail about how DNS functions, unless it relates to securing DNS or DNS servers. To fully appreciate this chapter, you need to have a basic

---

1.   Also known as Domain Name Service, Domain Name Server, or Domain Name System

463

understanding of how DNS works. Additionally, you should understand the relationships between the various DNS infrastructure components, including primary and secondary DNS servers, how record types are used in DNS, and how zone files are constructed. Some excellent information is available, as I have cited in the "Resources" section, that describes the inner workings and design of DNS in much greater depth than is possible here.

■Note I will not cover DNSSEC (as described in RFC 2535).[2] This is principally because I do not believe DNSSEC is mature enough or the RFC itself is final enough. Both the RFC and the current implementation of DNSSEC need a considerable amount of development before they can be readily implemented in a production environment.

Your DNS Server at Risk

Your DNS server is subject to a similar range and type of attacks as most of your other Internet-facing daemons: the exploitation of software vulnerabilities and bugs, DoS attacks, poor configuration, and poor server and infrastructure hardening. Several DNS servers, especially the commonly implemented BIND server, have been subject to a variety of vulnerabilities and compromises in recent years.[3] These have included vulnerabilities such as buffer overflows and other code exposures that could potentially allow attacks or penetrations.

Additionally, DNS server software is often installed but then not regularly updated or properly managed. Many DNS servers operating on the Web are older versions of software or versions with known compromises.[4] Other than configuration changes to add additional zones or hosts, many DNS servers and their configuration are not updated to take advantage of new features or to address security exposures. This has left many DNS systems seriously exposed to potential attacks.

The DNS protocol itself can also be subject to compromises such as improper DNS data updates and to attacks aimed at compromising your DNS data. Many of these attacks are similar in nature or are only subtlety different from each other. Additionally, attacks against your DNS infrastructure are frequently combinations of multiple attack types. For example, many DNS protocol attacks require an attacker to stage a DoS attack against your DNS server prior to another form of attack. Let's look at some of the common types of DNS-specific attacks.

Man-in-the-Middle Attacks

Man-in-the-middle attacks allow an attacker to intercept your DNS traffic or impersonate your DNS server for the purpose of spoofing its input or output or assuming the entire identity of your DNS server. To do this, attackers sniff traffic on your network, detect your DNS packets, and use the information in them to replicate these packets and interpose themselves into the

---

2.   See RFC 2535 at http://www.faqs.org/rfcs/rfc2535.html.

3.   http://www.isc.org/index.pl?/sw/bind/bind-security.php

4.   See a recent survey of DNS server software at http://mydns.bboy.net/survey/.

DNS packet flow. This interposition is easier than it sounds because DNS traffic is generally unsigned, unencrypted UDP packets whose only control is a sequence number. Although the sequence number generally starts from a random point, it is generally simply incremented, which makes it easy to guess the next sequence number. Questions have also been raised about the true randomness of the sequence numbers.[5]

To perform this interposition, the attacker generally initiates a DoS attack against one of the components in your DNS infrastructure; for example, the attackers launch a DoS attack on a secondary DNS server in order to silence it and interpose themselves between the primary and secondary server. An attacker can also simply be in a right position, figuratively "closer" to your DNS server than another component in the DNS traffic flow. For example, an attacker can install a new DNS server on your network and respond to DNS queries before the real DNS server is able to do so. This is often possible if the DNS server being impersonated is on a different network or accessed via the Internet.

Once in this position, the attacker has considerable scope to both gain critical information about the structure and contents of your networks or to insert malicious or bogus information into your environment. For example, by interposing themselves between a primary and secondary DNS server, attackers can acquire details of all the zones for which the DNS servers are responsible. This gives attackers a very detailed picture of your network without requiring them to perform any high-profile activities. These activities, such as scanning or probing your network, potentially have a much higher detection profile than the compromise of your DNS server.

Cache Poisoning

Probably the most dangerous form of DNS-based attack is *cache poisoning*. Cache poisoning occurs when an attacker introduces or substitutes malicious data into the cache of a DNS server. For example, the attacker monitors queries from a DNS server, intercepts the query, and provides a false answer. This could be a bogus IP address for a particular domain, such as providing a new IP address for the domain name of an Internet banking site. This bogus data is now stored in the cache of the DNS server. This bogus data can be used to direct clients that use this poisoned DNS server to the new IP address for that Internet banking site. The attacker situates a forged site, designed to resemble the real Internet banking site, at this new IP address. The user will assume this forged site is the legitimate Internet banking site and provide banking information. The attacker now has this information and can defraud the user.

Denial of Service Attacks

Attackers generally have two reasons why they want to stage a DoS attack on your DNS infrastructure. The first reason is the normal purpose of a DoS attack: to deny service to your organization and users. The second reason is as an adjunct or precursor to another attack and to prevent your DNS server functioning whilst an attacker substitutes bogus information or a bogus name server for the domains and clients for which your DNS server provides services.

Traffic-based DoS attacks are also possible with DNS data. This is because the size of an initial DNS query is quite small but usually results in a reply of a larger size. For example, a DNS

---

5. http://www.securityfocus.com/guest/17905

query asking for the name servers for a domain will require a small volume of data but generally will result in a larger volume of data being generated. An attacker can thus use a DNS server as a traffic multiplier to either deny service to the DNS server itself or target other hosts by directing a large volume of DNS replies toward them.

Data Corruption and Alteration

The contents of your configuration and zone files contain the information that controls your DNS server, in addition to the information it provides to clients in response to queries. One of the ways an attacker can subvert your DNS server is to penetrate your host and change or corrupt this data. This can cause your DNS server to fail, if the data has been corrupted, or it may deliver data that is incorrect or malicious, if the data has been altered.

Other Risks

Finally, I hear you ask, "My DNS server is hardened, is secured, and runs the latest version of DNS software. Am I still at risk?" Unfortunately, one of the reasons DNS is such a vulnerable service is that you are reliant on the security and stability of any DNS servers that are potentially more authoritative than your DNS server or that provide DNS resolution for you. This means if a DNS server that you rely on to provide information for your DNS is compromised, you could receive bogus data from that server. Unfortunately, you cannot do anything to protect yourself from this risk. I hope future developments in RFCs such as DNSSEC can help to somewhat mitigate this risk. In the meantime, you should ensure your own DNS environment is secure and up-to-date.

What DNS Server Should You Choose?

Many DNS servers are available to provide DNS capabilities. But only three major players occupy this space. They are BIND, djbdns, and Microsoft DNS. Obviously, I will not cover Microsoft DNS, as it runs on Windows hosts only. In the Linux (and other *nix and BSD dialects) space, this leaves BIND,[6] provided by Internet Systems Consortium (ISC), and djbdns,[7] written by Daniel. J. Bernstein. The debate between which of these is the better DNS server, both operationally and with respect to security, is both vitriolic and controversial.

The BIND server has the larger market share. Depending on whose figures you believe, it is used by approximately 80 percent of the DNS servers on the Internet.[8] It has also had a difficult past history with a large number of both operational-related and security-related bugs being discovered in various versions of the server software. Some versions of BIND are fundamentally flawed, and running them exposes your organization to an extreme level of risk. More recent versions (from BIND 9 onward) have been somewhat more stable, and the incidence of major security vulnerabilities has decreased. But still a lot of older, easily exploitable versions of BIND are running on the Internet.

---

6. Berkeley Internet Name Domain (http://www.isc.org/index.pl?/sw/bind/)
7. http://cr.yp.to/djbdns.html
8. http://www.isc.org/index.pl?/ops/ds/

Alternatively, djbdns has not had a major security problem. Indeed, Bernstein offers a challenge for anyone to discover one in his code.

■**Note** The djbdns package does have some functional issues. They are described at `http://homepages.tesco.net/~J.deBoynePollard/FGA/djbdns-problems.html`.

But it can also be argued that Bernstein has not fully implemented the total scope of the DNS RFCs and that occasionally djbdns does not have the correct RFC behavior. For example, djbdns does not support TSIG or DNSSEC. These variations result because Bernstein's development approach tends to be based on his interpretation of the RFCs. To his credit, his software does address issues and flaws with the RFCs. Overall, though, this arbitrary and interpretational approach to standards compliance is problematic. Indeed, it has created some problems for djbdns' interoperability with BIND and other DNS servers. Finally, it could also be stated that the djbdns package is limited because it has a single author who controls the code base. The future development of the package depends on that author.

So where does this leave you with regard to choosing a DNS server? Well, it is very much an individual choice. With regard to the core functionality required to run DNS services, both BIND and djbdns offer a full feature set. For many purposes, djbdns is a good choice, such as when running a personal caching server on an individual system with the dnscache application.[9] From a security perspective, you may see some benefits in running djbdns because of its lack of discovered vulnerabilities. For interoperability purposes with other BIND servers, or if you want to use features such as TSIG, you may want to go with a BIND infrastructure.

For the purposes of this chapter, I have chosen to cover securing and hardening the BIND package. I have chosen BIND as a result of its extensive installation base. BIND is the DNS server you are most likely to encounter or to have as a standard for your organization. This is not to say that potentially djbdns is not a better solution. But BIND is distinctly more pervasive. Additionally, in defense of BIND's security, the more recent releases of BIND have been more stable and secure. Finally, the support available for BIND from ISC and other sources also contributed to the decision to cover BIND.

Secure BIND Design

One of the factors in securing your DNS services is designing a secure BIND infrastructure. As with designing a secure network, where you place your BIND servers and what functions those servers will perform is as important as how you build and secure them. I will briefly explain the major concepts in good DNS/BIND design and provide some simple rules that I recommend you follow.

- Do not use a single DNS host as an authoritative name server and a caching server.

- Ensure each DNS host provides only the functionality required. For example, do not provide resolution and caching services on a host that does not require it.

---

9. `http://cr.yp.to/djbdns/run-cache.html`

- Use separate authoritative name servers to answer queries from different sources. For example, queries from the Internet and queries from your internal networks should be answered by separate hosts.

- Always ensure your DNS infrastructure is redundant.

Figure 11-1 illustrates these recommendations for DNS infrastructure.

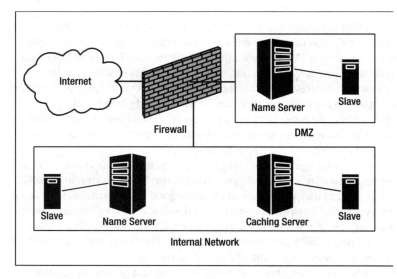

Figure 11-1. *Recommended DNS infrastructure model*

First, let's look at some explanations of the different types of BIND servers and their functions. DNS servers perform two core functions: name server and resolver/caching.[10] Using the name server function, they provide answers to queries about domains they know. This is known as being *authoritative* for these domains. Being authoritative for a domain means you are the principal source of information about that domain, the hosts in it, their IP addresses, and other information. I will refer to this sort of DNS server as a *name server*.

Second, using the resolver/caching function, your DNS servers query other DNS servers for information about domains they do not know. These are domains for which your servers are *nonauthoritative*. This is where you rely on information from other DNS servers to learn about that nonauthoritative domain. This information is stored or cached by BIND for a set period and used to provide answers to DNS lookups by clients. I will refer to this sort of DNS server as a *caching server*.

In the most common implementation model for BIND, single hosts perform both name server and caching functions. So why should you care if a BIND server is authoritative for domains and provides caching and resolution? Well, separating these functions has two

---

10. DNS servers are also capable of forwarding queries to other DNS servers.

principal advantages. The first is that you make your DNS services more resilient from an availability perspective. With a combined name and caching server, you create a single point of failure. For example, if a DoS attack results in the failure of your BIND server, then you will lose both your name server and caching functions. This would stop you from being authoritative for your domains as well as stop you from resolving DNS queries for your clients. With functional separation onto separate hosts, the impact of such a DoS attack is more limited, and you would potentially lose only one function.

The second advantage is that a compromise of your BIND server will allow attackers to take advantage of only one function. If attackers compromise a BIND server that combines both functions, then they now control responses to queries about the domains for which that server is authoritative, and they can influence the results of any DNS queries your clients make or poison the cache of that server. Separating these functions limits the risk of attackers controlling your entire DNS infrastructure with a single attack. So, if you have the resources to provide multiple servers to perform these separate functions, you should look into doing so.

Where you position your BIND servers and what role they play in your DNS infrastructure is also often critical. For example, you only need to place caching servers within your internal network. This is because you will not be providing DNS resolution to external clients. In fact, you should ensure your BIND servers are not providing resolution and caching to external clients to protect them, both from attacks and to prevent external clients using your valuable bandwidth and resources. I recommend you never place a caching DNS server on a bastion host or in a DMZ.

Alternatively, your name servers, which provide resolution for domains you control, generally need to be placed facing both your internal and external networks. This is because you need to provide different DNS answers for external clients and internal clients. You can do this on single name servers using split DNS with `view` statements (which I will demonstrate in the "Views and Zones" section), or you can implement separate name servers, some located in your internal network and some located in a DMZ or in a bastion host protected by a firewall. I recommend you take the separate name server approach and provide different name servers to respond to queries from different clients. This again enhances the availability of your DNS infrastructure and also limits unnecessary connectivity between your higher risk areas, such as a DMZ, and your internal network.

The final element to any secure DNS infrastructure design is redundancy. You should have more than one host providing resolution and caching services to your internal clients. If a caching server fails without a backup, then your clients will not be able to resolve IP addresses and hostnames. This will render most software that requires communication with the network inoperable.

For name servers you also need redundancy. With name servers you should have both primary and secondary name servers (also known as *masters* and *slaves*) configured. What does this mean? Domains (referred to in BIND as *zones*) defined to a BIND name server can be of two major types, masters and slaves. A master zone is the authoritative and primary source of information about that domain. The name server where that master zone is defined is the primary, or master, server for that zone. A slave zone is an exact copy of the master zone, and it is defined on a secondary, or slave, name server. On a regular basis the master zone is transferred from the master server to the slave server. This transfer generally occurs either when the master zone is changed or when a fixed period expires. In your DNS infrastructure you define both your master and slaves as potential name servers for particular domains to your clients. If the master server fails, then the client can use the slave server or servers to answer queries about that domain.

You always need to have secondary or slave name servers to provide redundancy in the event of an attack, a compromise, or an availability issue such as hardware failure. For example, if you have separate name servers, one that performs internal resolution and one that performs external resolution for your domains, then both servers need to have slave servers defined. These slave servers can then take over in the event that the primary master servers are unavailable.

Installing BIND

The first step I will cover is how to install BIND. If you already have a BIND installation, then some of this material may not be relevant to you. But since I recommend you regularly update your BIND version, this process may be useful to gain an understanding of how to do that. Or, if you are running an older BIND version, I recommend you upgrade to the latest available version. You can use these instructions to do that also.

One of the first things you need to know is that three major versions of BIND are in general use as DNS servers. These are versions 4, 8, and 9. Versions 4 and 8 are deprecated and have been the subject of numerous vulnerabilities. However, still a number of version 4 and 8 BIND servers are being utilized. ISC does attempt to ensure security-related patches to address known vulnerabilities that are released for version 4 and 8 releases of BIND. But generally no new development is performed on these versions. If you are running BIND versions 4 and 8, you should upgrade to the latest release of BIND, preferably the latest stable version 9 release. If you do not upgrade, you risk exposing your DNS servers to relatively simple compromises and exploits by attackers. The newer versions of BIND also offer additional functionality and performance improvements.

This chapter will cover BIND version 9 only. BIND 9 has some differing configuration options from previous BIND versions; if upgrading, you will need to review your existing configuration in light of this. In this chapter I will address building a secure BIND server from scratch, and, where possible, I will highlight the areas in which this version of BIND differs from previous releases.

The first step in installing BIND is downloading the latest version of BIND.[11] BIND is also available as a package for those distributions with package management software; for example, it is available as an RPM for Red Hat and a deb package for Debian. I recommend, though, that BIND is a package you compile from source and install, rather than relying on your distribution's version. This is because the latest stable version of BIND is generally the safest version to use. Many distributions provide older versions of BIND or modify BIND to suit their own purposes. This means you get a potential delay between a vulnerability being discovered and a distribution vendor updating its BIND package. Obviously, you should download, compile, and test the latest version of BIND on a test system before upgrading your production environment.

To download BIND, first download ISC's PGP key and import it into your keyring so that you can verify any downloads from ISC.

```
kitten# wget http://www.isc.org/about/openpgp/pgpkey2004.txt
kitten# gpg --import pgpkey2004.txt
gpg: key C3755FF7: public key "Internet Systems Consortium, Inc. ➥
(Signing key, 2004) <pgpkey2004@isc.org>" imported
gpg: Total number processed: 1
gpg:              imported: 1
```

---

11. At the time of writing, the latest stable release is 9.3.0. This chapter is based on this version.

Next, download the latest version of BIND and its associated signature and compare the signature using the PGP key you downloaded to verify the integrity of the package.

```
kitten# wget ftp://ftp.isc.org/isc/bind9/9.3.0/bind-9.3.0.tar.gz
kitten# wget ftp://ftp.isc.org/isc/bind9/9.3.0/bind-9.3.0.tar.gz.asc
kitten#  gpg --verify bind-9.3.0.tar.gz.asc bind-9.3.0.tar.gz
gpg: Signature made Thu 23 Sep 2004 02:03:16 EST using DSA key ID C3755FF7
gpg: Good signature from "Internet Systems Consortium, Inc. ➥
(Signing key, 2004) <pgpkey2004@isc.org>"
gpg: checking the trustdb
gpg: no ultimately trusted keys found
gpg: WARNING: This key is not certified with a trusted signature!
gpg:          There is no indication that the signature belongs to the owner.
Primary key fingerprint: 9254 46B5 D3C8 BB29 E337  379D 6791 2F50 C375 5FF7
```

If you receive the message indicating that a good signature has been found, then the BIND package you have downloaded is authentic.

■**Note** Ignore any messages about no ultimately trusted keys being found. This simply means you do not have the full key chain used by ISC to generate its PGP key.

Now you need to unpack the package file and change into the directory that has been created.

```
kitten# tar -zxf bind-9.3.0.tar.gz
kitten# cd bind-9.3.0
```

Next you need to configure and make BIND. By default BIND will install itself underneath the directory /usr/local. If required, you can override this with the configure option --prefix.

```
kitten# ./configure --prefix=/usr
```

In the previous line, I have specified that BIND should install underneath the directory /usr. Some additional configuration options are also available that you can review with the --help option of the configure script.

```
kitten# ./configure --help
```

Generally, you will not require any of these options for Linux compilation with the exception of the --disable-threads option. BIND is now multithreaded and is better designed to run on multiprocessor systems. Some distributions are running kernels or have modifications that make using threads unwise. If this is the case with your distribution, then you can disable threads support with the --disable-threads configure option, like this:

```
kitten# ./configure --disable-threads
```

You then need to make and install BIND to compile and install the package files into the designated directories.

```
kitten# make && make install
```

Chrooting BIND

The heart of the BIND package is the `named` daemon, which provides the core DNS functionality. To better protect your BIND server, I recommend placing your BIND daemon, `named`, into a `chroot` jail. The `named` daemon is also able to run as a normal user and can drop root user privileges. In combination, these two options provide additional security that can prevent an attacker from compromising your system via the `named` daemon. I will take you through installing BIND into a `chroot` jail and creating a user and group to run the `named` daemon.

■**Note** See Chapter 7 for a description of the `chroot` command.

The first step is to create a directory structure for your `chroot` jail. I have decided to locate my `chroot` jail under the directory `/chroot/named`.

```
kitten# mkdir -p /chroot/named
```

Now you need to add the other directories the jail will require. You need to create the directories in Listing 11-1.

Listing 11-1. `chroot` *Jail Directory Structure Under* `/chroot/named`

```
/dev
/etc
/master
/slave
/var
/var/logs
/var/run
```

■**Note** I created the `/master` and `/slave` directories to hold the zone files for my system. You can create any directory structure you like for your zone files.

Next, you need to populate the jail with some required files. I will start with three device files that the `named` daemon will need to use: random, null, and zero. You can create these with the `mknod` command, and you want to create functional duplicates of the existing device files located `/dev`. You can review the settings of these files like this:

```
kitten# ls -l /dev/zero /dev/null /dev/random
crw-rw-rw-  1 root root 1, 3 Feb 19  2004 /dev/null
crw-r--r--  1 root root 1, 8 Feb 19  2004 /dev/random
crw-rw-rw-  1 root root 1, 5 Feb 19  2004 /dev/zero
```

The new device files need the same minor and major numbers as the existing device files. You can re-create them using the mknod command with the c option. For example, the major and minor numbers for the /dev/null device are 1 and 3, respectively. Listing 11-2 re-creates all the required devices and locates them in the directory /chroot/named/dev.

Listing 11-2. *Creating Jailed Devices*

```
kitten# mknod /chroot/named/dev/null c 1 3
kitten# mknod /chroot/named/dev/random c 1 8
kitten# mknod /chroot/named/dev/zero c 1 5
```

You also want to copy in a time source. I will use the /etc/localtime file and copy it into the /chroot/named/etc/ directory.

```
kitten# cp /etc/localtime /chroot/named/etc/localtime
```

Next, you need to create a user and group to run the named daemon. I have decided to create a user called named and a group of the same name. Listing 11-3 shows how to do this.

Listing 11-3. *Creating a User and Group*

```
kitten# groupadd named
kitten# useradd -g named -d /dev/null -s /sbin/nologin named
```

I have specified a home directory of /dev/null for the named user and a default shell of /sbin/nologin to prevent this user from logging in. The named user will belong to the named group.

I also recommend, for an added level of security, that you lock this user with the passwd -l command, like this:

```
kitten# passwd -l named
Locking password for user named.
passwd: Success
```

Finally, create an empty named.conf file to hold your BIND configuration.

```
kitten# touch /chroot/named/etc/named.conf
```

Permissions in the chroot Jail

So far you have not set permissions for the files and directories in your chroot jail. This is a fairly simple process, but it should be done once you have finished configuring your BIND server and may need to be repeated at regular intervals as you add zones files or change the BIND configuration.

First, you want to set the ownership of the files in your chroot jail. I created a new user and group, both called named, in the previous section. In the next section you will see that the named daemon will run as the named user. Thus, the named user needs access to the files in your chroot jail. The first step in providing this access is setting the ownership of the objects and files in the jail. You can set the ownership like this:

```
kitten# cd /chroot/
kitten# chown -R named:named named
```

Second, you need to change the permissions on the directories. You want the named user to have all permissions to the directory and give the named group read and execute permissions to the directories. You can use the following commands to do this:

```
kitten# cd /chroot/named
kitten# find . -type d -print | xargs chmod 0750
```

The second command finds all directories below the /chroot/named directory and changes their permissions to 0750.

Next, you want to secure your files. Only the named user and group should have permissions to the files in your chroot jail. Everyone else on the system should have no permissions to the files and objects. So, the files need to be readable and writable by the named user, need to be readable by the named group, and need to have no world permissions granted. You can do this using the following commands:

```
kitten# cd /chroot/named
kitten# find . -type f -print | xargs chmod 0640
```

> ■**Caution** As the named group has read permissions to the files in your chroot jail, you should ensure you do not add users to that group, unless absolutely required.

Finally, change the attributes on the localtime file to make it immutable to prevent the time from being changed.

```
kitten# chattr +i /chroot/named/etc/localtime
```

It is especially important to ensure that you carefully secure your configuration and zone files. I recommend using a tool such as Tripwire (see Chapter 4) to monitor these files. Additionally, another potential file to consider making immutable is your named.conf file, which contains your BIND configuration. This can inconvenience the process of administering your BIND server but adds a greater level of assurance that your configuration file cannot be changed for malicious purposes.

```
kitten# chattr +i /chroot/named/etc/named.conf
```

> ■**Tip** You should also update your permissions on a regular basis to ensure they remain correct and that any new files—for example, new zone files—receive the correct ownership and permissions. I generally do this when the named daemon is started and stopped by adding a section resetting permissions to the defaults in my init script.

Starting and Running named

To use BIND, you need to start the named daemon. You can do this by running the named binary. When the named binary is executed without options, it will bind the ports it requires, read in the configuration from the configuration file (which it expects to find in `/etc/named.conf`), and then daemonize.

■**Tip** By default the `named` daemon binary is installed into `/usr/local/sbin`.

You can start the `named` binary on the command line or via an `init` script. Most of the packages available for BIND on various distributions come with an `init` script. If you have installed from source, you can extract one of these `init` scripts from a package and customize it for your own environment. You could also write your own script or get an `init` script from the Web.[12]

■**Tip** I have included a sample `init` script in Appendix B.

Listing 11-4 shows how to start the `named` daemon by running the `named` binary.

Listing 11-4. *Starting* named

```
kitten# named -t /chroot/named -u named
```

In Listing 11-4 the `-t` option specifies the root directory of the `chroot` jail I am using, `/chroot/named`. This is the directory that `named` will change to when it is chrooted. This then becomes the root directory for the `named` daemon. All directories you reference will be relative to this directory rather than the system's normal root directory. For example, the `named` daemon looks for the `random` device in `/dev`. In Listing 11-4, as the daemon is chrooted, the actual directory it will look for the device in is `/chroot/named/dev`.

The `-u` option specifies the user you want to run the `named` daemon; I have specified the user named. In this example, the `named` daemon will start with `root` user privileges and then drop these privileges to run as the `named` user.

■**Note** I show how to create both the `chroot` jail directories and the `named` user in the "Chrooting BIND" section.

Other options are available for the `named` daemon (see Table 11-1).

---

12. For a quick reference for Red Hat systems, see `http://www.vsl.gifu-u.ac.jp/freeman/misc/ initscripts-6.51/sysvinitfiles`. For Debian, see `http://www.debianhelp.org/ modules.php?op=modload&name=News&file=article&sid=3306`.

Table 11-1. named *Command-Line Options*

Option	Description
-4	Uses IPv4 only.
-6	Uses IPv6 only.
-c *file*	Uses *file* as the configuration file. Defaults to /etc/named.conf.
-d *level*	Sets the debug level to *level*.
-f	Runs the daemon in the foreground.
-g	Runs the daemon in the foreground and logs to stderr.
-p *port*	Listens for queries on port *port*. Defaults to port 53.
-v	Reports the version number and exit.

The named daemon generally automatically detects what form of IP networking to utilize, either IPv4 or IPv6. The -4 and -6 options allow you to force which will be used. If you specify the -4 option, then only IPv4 networking will be used, even if IPv6 networking is available. The -6 option dictates that only IPv6 networking will be used, even if IPv4 networking is available. These two options are mutually exclusive and cannot be specified on the command line together.

The -c option allows you to specify the location of the named configuration file. The default file the named daemon expects to find is /etc/named.conf. If you are running the named daemon in a chroot jail, then this location must be relative to the root directory of the jail. For example, if you specified the configuration file named2.conf like this:

```
kitten# named -c /etc/named2.conf -t /chroot/named
```

then the -t option specifies a chroot jail located in /chroot/named, and thus the named2.conf file would have to be located in the /chroot/named/etc/ directory so that the named daemon can locate the correct configuration file.

The -d option specifies the level of logging with which your named daemon will start. You can specify a number between 1 and 99, where 1 is minimal debugging information and 99 is the maximum level of debugging information.

The -f and -g options allow you to launch the named daemon and not to daemonize. The first option, -f, launches named and runs it in the foreground. The second option, -g, does the same but redirects any logging output from the daemon to stderr.

The -p option allows you to override the use of the default port with another port for the named daemon to listen on. By default DNS is principally a UDP-based protocol, and the named daemon listens on UDP port 53. But for some queries the named daemon also uses TCP, and thus it also listens on TCP port 53. The named daemon generally uses TCP connections only for zone transfers and queries that result in large records. Generally, as most clients and others servers expect to find your DNS server listening on port 53, I would not change this option. But it does provide the ability to run a named daemon on another port for testing purposes.

The final option, -v, outputs the named version and exits.

Configuring BIND

The core of BIND's configuration is the named.conf file. It is normally located in the /etc/ directory. It controls all the major BIND configuration options. It is in this file that you define the zones your BIND server knows. This includes any master zones for which your server is authoritative or any zones for which your server is a secondary, or slave, server. It is in this file that you also configure access controls, logging, networking, and other options.

The `named.conf` file contains a number of statement declarations. These statements can define a number of configuration components; Table 11-2 lists the most frequently used statements.

Note This section is a basic introduction to the `named.conf` file and the statements used to configure BIND. I recommend, for more complicated configuration models, that you read more widely on BIND configuration.

Table 11-2. `named.conf` *Statements*

Statement	Description
`acl`	Defines access control lists containing lists of sources that can be defined in access control statements
`controls`	Defines a control statement for the `rndc` command
`key`	Defines a cryptographic key you can use for functions such as TSIG
`logging`	Defines the logging configuration for the BIND server
`options`	Defines the global configuration options for the BIND server
`server`	Defines a server
`view`	Acts as a container for a collections of zones
`zone`	Defines the configuration of a domain

I will cover the `acl`, `logging`, `options`, `view`, and `zone` statements and their various options in this section. I will cover the `server` and `key` statements in the "TSIG" section and the `controls` statement in "The rndc Command" section.

Most statements types in the `named.conf` file are generally constructed like this:

```
statement "name" {
contents-of-statement;
};
```

or like this:

```
statement {
contents-of-statement;
};
```

Some statements are given a name; if so, you should use quotations marks to enclose that name. The quotation marks allow you to use any name, including reserved DNS configuration words, as the name of the statement. Other statements do not require a name, and I will identify them.

Each statement can contain substatements, and these are contained within braces. Each statement must be terminated with a semicolon after the closing brace. Most of the substatements within a statement also need to be terminated with a semicolon.

You can also add comments to your named.conf file by prefixing the comment with any of three commenting syntaxes like this:

```
// This is a comment
/* This is also a comment */
# This is another comment
```

I will go through the key configuration statements in your named.conf file, with a particular emphasis on the security-related features. This should provide you with a good grounding to develop BIND configurations, but it will not be a definitive explanation of exactly how to configure every BIND statement or every configuration option.

Let's start with a sample named.conf file for a caching-only BIND server (see Listing 11-5). This server is not authoritative for any domains but merely provides DNS resolution and caching for clients.

Listing 11-5. *Caching-Only* named.conf *File*

```
acl "trusted" {
192.168.0.0/24;
192.168.1.0/24;
};

logging {
channel "default_syslog" { syslog daemon; severity info; };
category default { default_syslog; };
};

options {
directory "/";
pid-file "/var/run/named.pid";
version "[null]";
allow-query { trusted; };
query-source address * port 53;
};

view "internal" {
match-clients { trusted; };

zone "." {
type hint;
file "/master/db.cache";
};

zone "localhost" {
type master;
file "/master/db.localhost";
notify no;
};
```

```
zone "0.0.127.in-addr.arpa" {
type master;
file "/master/db.127.0.0";
notify no;
};
};
```

Let's now look at each of these statements and see how they combine to make a BIND server configuration.

■**Note** I will also provide several secure named.conf configurations in Appendix B.

Access Control Lists

The first statement I will cover is the acl (access control list) statement. The acl statement allows you to nickname and group lists of IP networks and addresses, other acl statements, or key IDs. These lists can then control access to the BIND server or to individual functions of the server. For example, you can define the IP addresses or networks of all the trusted local clients in an acl. You can then specify that acl as being allowed to recursively query the BIND server. Listing 11-5 defines one acl statement, which looks like this:

```
acl "trusted" {
192.168.0.0/24;
192.168.1.0/24;
};
```

I have called the acl trusted and specified two networks, 192.168.0.0/24 and 192.1.0.0/24, in it. You will note each network has been separated by a semicolon. This is how the named.conf file separates list items.

■**Tip** If you fail to insert a semicolon after a list item, then when you attempt to start the named daemon, a syntax error will result and the daemon will not start. This is one of the most common errors people make in their named.conf files. You should run the named-checkconf command that comes with BIND on your configuration file to confirm its syntax is correct.

The syntax used by the acl statement to match IP addresses, networks, and keys is known as an *address match list* (even though you are matching more than just addresses). It is used by a variety of options in your named.conf file to provide control over who can perform particular functions. For example, the allow-transfer option (which controls who can transfer zones) also uses address match lists. The acl statement allows you to specify these controls in one location rather than having to repeatedly enter lists of IP addresses and networks into every option that requires access control.

For example, I have used the acl in Listing 11-5 to define clients I trust in my internal network. You can refer to the trusted acl in every option where you need to provide access to your trusted network devices. This both reduces the complexity of your named.conf file and reduces the administrative overhead in maintaining the file, as you have to make changes in only one acl rather than in the access controls for multiple options. I recommend placing your acl statements at the top of your named.conf file.

You can list as many matches as you like in each acl statement. The items within each list are processed in sequence. If you include the 192.168.0.0./24 network and then the IP address 192.168.0.100 in an acl like this:

```
acl "sequence" {
192.168.0.0/24;
192.168.0.100;
};
```

then the second 192.168.0.100 IP address entry would have no effect because you have already previously specified the entire 192.168.0.0 network in the acl.

You can also specify four special keywords in acl statements. They are any, none, localhost, and localnets. The any keyword allows access from any source, and none denies access to all sources. The localhost keyboard grants access to all the IP addresses of the local host. The localnets keyword matches all local IP addresses and subnets attached to the local host. You need to be careful with the localhost and localnets keywords if your host is a bastion host and is connected to the Internet on one of its interfaces. For example, you do not want to grant access to inappropriate resources or functionality on your host because you have granted access to an Internet-facing subnet using the localnets keyword.

Additionally, you can also specify a key ID in an acl statement. I discuss TSIG and keys in the "TSIG" section of this chapter.

```
acl "key" {
key_id;
192.168.0.100;
};
```

The key_id must be defined with a key statement if it is to be used in an acl statement.

Finally, you can negate an item in an acl by prefixing it with an exclamation mark, like this:

```
acl "negation" {
! 192.168.0.100;
};
```

The negation acl matches any source except the IP address of 192.168.0.100.

Logging

The next statement in Listing 11-5 is the logging statement. This statement controls what BIND will log, how much it will log, and to where it will log it. Let's dissect the logging statement in Listing 11-5. The logging statement is broken down into channels, categories, and a series of substatements specific to each. Unlike some other statement types, the logging statement does not need to be named.

THE INCLUDE STATEMENT

You can use another statement, include, in the named.conf file. The include statement allows you to include the contents of other files into your named.conf file. It is constructed like so:

```
include "/etc/keys.secret";
```

The previous statement would include the contents of the keys.secret file into the named.conf file at the point where the include statement was placed. Any file you include into the named.conf file needs to have read permissions granted to the user or group that the named daemon is utilizing; otherwise, the daemon will not be able to include it. Additionally, if any sensitive configuration information is contained in included files, you should ensure that the permissions of the files are adequately secure.

Always remember that if your BIND daemon is chrooted, the location of any file you include will be relative to the root of the chroot jail.

Channels

A *channel* is a target destination for your log data; for example, the syslog daemon is a potential logging channel. Each channel consists of a channel name, the destination of the log data, any limits on the message severity to be delivered to the channel, and additional options. You can define as many channels as you like.

Only one channel is defined in Listing 11-5. It is called default_syslog and is one of four built-in channels that are predefined to BIND. (I will discuss the other default channels shortly.) The destination of the default_syslog channel is syslog. The syslog destination also has one option: the facility to which you are going to send the messages. In this case I have defined the daemon facility, but you can specify any of the available syslog facilities.

You are also able to specify the severity of the messages you want to send. In this case I have specified info, which will send all messages of info severity or higher. In combination, these options indicate that the default_syslog channel will send all messages of info severity or higher to the daemon facility of the local syslog daemon.

Tip See Chapter 5 for more detail on syslog facilities and severities.

You can use four possible destinations (including syslog) in BIND logging (see Table 11-3).

Table 11-3. *BIND Logging Destinations*

Destination	Description
file	Logs to a file
null	Discards log entries
stderr	Logs to standard error
syslog	Logs to the syslog daemon

The first destination in Table 11-3 is `file`. This allows BIND logging to a file and comes with a number of additional options. Listing 11-6 defines a typical `file` destination channel.

Listing 11-6. *File Logging Destination*

```
channel "log_file" {
    file "/var/logs/named.log" versions 7 size 1m;
    print-time yes;
    print-category yes;
    print-severity yes;
};
```

I have named the channel `log_file` and specified a destination of `file`. The `file` destination has some additional options. The first option is the actual file you want to log to, in this case `/var/logs/named.log`.

Tip If you were running in a `chroot` jail, the location of this file would be relative to the root directory of the `chroot` jail; for example, it would be `/chroot/named/var/logs/named.log`, not the root directory of the host.

The next two options control the rotation of your log file. The `versions` option specifies how many backup versions of the log file to keep. I have specified 7, which configures BIND to keep the last seven log files. When the log rotates, BIND will create a new file and rename the old file by suffixing a numeric increment to it; for example, `named.log` is renamed to `named.log.0`. When it rotates again, `named.log.0` will be renamed `named.log.1`, `named.log` will be renamed `named.log.0`, and so on. If you specify `versions unlimited`, then BIND will not limit the number of versions. The actual log rotation is controlled by the `size` option. In this case I have specified a logging limit of `10m`, which indicates individual log files of 10MB in size. When this size limit is reached, the log file will be rotated. If the size limit is reached and the `versions` option has not been specified, then BIND will stop logging.

The last three substatements in Listing 11-6 are `print-time`, `print-category`, and `print-severity`. These all output additional logging information and can be used with the `file`, `syslog`, and `stderr` destinations. The `print-time` option prints the current date and time with the message. The `print-category` option prints the category of the messages (see Table 11-5 for details of the categories). Lastly, the `print-severity` option prints the severity of the message (for example, `info` or `debug`).

Another possible destination is `null`. You can define this destination like so:

```
channel "discard" {
    null;
};
```

The `null` destination causes all messages sent to this channel to be discarded.

The last destination is `stderr`. Messages directed to this channel are output to the server's standard error stream. This is designed to be used when `named` is running in foreground (for example, if it has been started with the `-f` option and is used for debugging purposes).

The BIND server comes with four predefined channels (see Table 11-4). You do not need to specify these channels to use them in your `logging` statement, but additionally you cannot redefine new channels with the same name as these predefined channels.

Table 11-4. *Predefined BIND Channels*

Channel	Description
default_debug	Writes debugging messages to the `named.run` according to debugging level
default_stderr	Sends severity info or higher messages to standard error
default_syslog	Sends severity info or higher messages to `syslog`
null	Discards all messages

Most of the channels are self-explanatory, but the `default_debug` channel needs further clarification. The `default_debug` channel is enabled only when you start the `named` daemon with the `-d` debug option; you can see it defined in Listing 11-7.

Listing 11-7. `default_debug` *Channel*

```
channel "default_debug" {
    file "named.run";
    severity dynamic;
};
```

The `severity` setting of `dynamic` indicates that the channel will output messages depending on the level of debug the `named` daemon is started with; for example, if the `-d` option is set to 5, then it outputs debugging level 5 messages. The messages are outputted to a file called `named.run` in the default working directory of the server, usually / or the root directory of your chroot jail. If the `named` daemon is started in the foreground, then the debug output is redirected to standard error rather than the `named.run` file.

You can also output debugging information using the `severity debug` option. To do so, add the required debug level to the `severity debug` option like this:

```
channel "debug_log" {
    file "named_debug.log";
    severity debug 5;
};
```

This channel will, when the `named` daemon is started with the `-d` option, output all level 5 and higher debugging messages.

Categories

Channels are used in conjunction with categories. A category is a particular type of logging data; for example, a category could contain logging entries related to configuration changes. Each category of logging information can be directed to one or more channels. Table 11-5 defines the key categories.

Table 11-5. *Logging Categories*

Category	Description
default	The default category defines the logging options for those categories where no specific configuration has been defined.
general	Any messages that are not defined into a particular category. This is a catchall for these messages.
security	Security-related messages.
config	Configuration messages.
xfer-in	Incoming zone transfer messages.
xfer-out	Outgoing zone transfer messages.
client	Client request processing messages.
network	Network operations messages.
dnssec	DNSSEC and TSIG messages.
lame-servers	Lame server reports.

You can specify one or more channels for each category. Listing 11-5 specified only one category, default, and directed it to the default_syslog channel, like so:

```
category default { default_syslog; };
```

But you can also specify multiple categories and multiple channels, like so:

```
category default { default_syslog; debug_log; log_file; };
category config { default_syslog; default_debug; };
category dnssec { null; };
```

I recommend specifying most of the major categories to your syslog or to a specific log file (or both).

Options

The options statement controls a variety of BIND configuration options (for example, default ports), the location of various directories and files, and default access controls. Like the logging statement, the option statement does not need to be named. The options statement should appear only once in the named.conf file.

The options statement encloses a list of individual options in two possible syntaxes. The first syntax is as follows:

```
option "option value";
```

Here you enclose the option value in quotation marks and terminate it with a semicolon. The second syntax is as follows:

```
option { option value; };
```

In this syntax, the option value is enclosed in braces and terminated with a semicolon. The option itself is also terminated with a semicolon after the closing brace.

Listing 11-8 shows a selection of basic options. Let's walk through each of these and look at related and other options available to use. I will specifically focus on the security and access control options, but I will also cover the options required to run BIND.

Listing 11-8. options *Statement*

```
options {
directory "/";
pid-file "/var/run/named.pid";
version "[null]";
allow-query { trusted; };
query-source address * port 53;
};
```

The first option in Listing 11-8, directory, specifies the default working directory for the named daemon. I have specified / or the root directory. This is either the root directory of the host or, if the named daemon is in a chroot jail, the root directory of the jail. If you have used the directory structure defined in the "Chrooting BIND" section, then the root directory would be /chroot/named/. I also specified the pid-file option, which allows you to define the location of PID file; I have used /var/run/named.pid. Another related option you could use is statistics-file, which allows you to specify a location for the BIND statistics file. You can use this option like so:

```
statistics-file "/var/named.stats";
```

This file is used when the rndc stats command is run, and it stores the statistics generated by this command.

■**Note** See the "The rndc Command" section for more details on using the rndc command.

Hiding the BIND Version

The next option in Listing 11-8 is the version option. This option controls what the BIND server will return when it receives a query for its version. This provides you the ability to obfuscate the BIND version from an attacker by specifying the output to the version query. Whilst this does not gain you a great deal of security, it does at least limit the ability of attackers to easily determine if you have a BIND version that may be vulnerable to a particular attack. In this example, I have specified a version value of [null]. I recommend you always specify this option and never allow the BIND server to return its actual version to queries.

In conjunction with this option, you would generally define a chaos class view and a zone for the pseudo-domain bind. The chaos class specifies zone data for the CHAOSnet protocol, a MIT-developed LAN protocol that was created in the mid-1970s. BIND now uses the chaos class to provide diagnostic information when TXT resource records in that domain are queried. You can define the view and the bind domain using a zone statement as in Listing 11-9.

■**Note** Do not worry too much about the configuration of the view and zone, as I will discuss views and zones in more detail in the "Views and Zones" section.

Listing 11-9. bind *Domain Zone*

```
view "chaosnet" chaos {
match-clients { any; };

zone "bind" chaos {
    type master;
    file "/master/db.bind";
    allow-query { any; };
    allow-transfer { none; };
};
};
```

Listing 11-9 defines a view called chaosnet and a zone called bind. It is defined as a chaos class zone rather than the normal in zone class by specifying chaos after the zone name. The data for the zone is contained in the file db.bind.

You should place the chaosnet view you have created after any other views contained in your named.conf file. I show this in the example files in Appendix B.

I have put the contents of a sample bind domain zone file in Listing 11-10.

Listing 11-10. bind *Domain Zone File*

```
$TTL    1d
@   CH   SOA   kitten.yourdomain.com.   hostmaster.yourdomain.com. (
2004110300 86400 3600 604800 3600 )
CH   NS   kitten.yourdomain.com.
version.bind.   CH   TXT   "[null]"
```

The zone file contains only one record, a TXT record containing the data you want to return when the BIND version is queried. You would need to change the host details in Listing 11-10 to match the name servers in your environment.

To demonstrate the response using the bind domain, I have queried its contents using the dig command in Listing 11-11.

Listing 11-11. *Using Dig to Retrieve the BIND Version*

```
kitten# dig version.bind txt chaos
; <<>> DiG 9.2.3 <<>> version.bind txt chaos
...
;; QUESTION SECTION:
;version.bind.                   CH      TXT
;; ANSWER SECTION:
version.bind.           86400   CH      TXT     "[null]"
;; AUTHORITY SECTION:
bind.                   86400   CH      NS      kitten.yourdomain.com.
...
```

Listing 11-11 shows the dig command and a sample of the output, including the version response of [null].

■**Tip** If you specify only the `version` option without defining the `version` TXT record in the `bind` zone, then BIND will not log attempts to query the version. Only if you have defined the `version.bind` zone will the query be logged. You should define the zone to enable logging of people who query your BIND version. This query is often a precursor to an attack, and logging of this can provide a warning.

Access Controls

One of the key purposes of the `options` statement is to provide global rules for a number of access control options. Access control options allow you to specify which sources are authorized to perform particular functions on your BIND server. For example, the `options` statement in Listing 11-8 contains the access control substatement.

```
allow-query { trusted; };
```

This substatement specifies which hosts or networks can perform ordinary DNS queries using this BIND server. This is important for a couple of reasons. First, it prevents your DNS server from being used for resolution by anyone except the users you want. You want to provide caching and resolution to internal users only. Second, it reduces the risk your BIND server will be used for malicious purposes, for example, as a traffic multiplier in a DoS attack. In Listing 11-8 the `allow-query` access control option is configured to use an `acl` defined earlier: `trusted`. This allows only trusted local clients to query the server. All other query requests from sources not listed in the `trusted` `acl` will be denied. This is the recommended approach for controlling who can query your BIND server.

The access control options use the same address list match syntax as `acl` statements to define the allowed sources. Thus, in each option you can specify individual hosts, networks, `acl` statements, or one of the keywords such as `none` or `localnets` described in the "Access Control Lists" section.

Any options defined in the `options` statement are global rules for the BIND server and specify the server's default behavior. You can override many of these access control options individually within `zone` or `view` statements to allow a greater granularity of access controls. I will cover how to do this in the "Views and Zones" section.

You can use a variety of other access control options (see Table 11-6).

Table 11-6. *Option Statement Access Controls*

Control	Description
allow-notify	Sources allowed to notify a slave server of zone changes. This is relevant only on a slave server.
allow-query	Sources that can perform DNS queries on this server.
allow-recursion	Sources allowed to make recursive queries through this server.
allow-transfer	Sources allowed to receive zone transfers from the server.
blackhole	Sources that the server will not use for queries or query resolution.

Let's look at several of these access controls. I have already discussed the `allow-query` access control, which provides control over who can query the BIND server. The `allow-recursion` control is particularly important. It specifies the sources, if any, that will be allowed to make recursive queries to this BIND server. I will talk more about recursion in the "Notify, Recursion, and Forwarding" section.

The allow-transfer option specifies which hosts are allowed to receive zone transfers from this host. You should limit this to only those hosts that actually need to conduct zone transfers with the server. For example, if this server is authoritative for one or more domains, then I recommend creating an acl containing the IP addresses of any slave servers and limiting the allow-transfer access control to that acl. You can see this in Listing 11-12.

Listing 11-12. *The* allow-transfer *Option*

```
acl "transfer" {
192.168.0.200;
192.168.1.10;
192.168.2.20;
};
...
options {
allow-transfer { transfer; };
};
...
```

In Listing 11-12 I have created an acl called transfer that contains the IP addresses of some hypothetical slave servers. I have then used this acl in the allow-transfer option to allow only these slave servers to receive zone transfers from this server. You can also override the allow-transfer option for an individual view or zone by specifying the option in the view or zone statement.

The last access control option in Table 11-6 is blackhole. The blackhole access control option allows you to specify a list of sources that the server will never accept queries for and, importantly, will never use to resolve a query. Many people define a special acl that contains a variety of IP addresses and networks, such as bogon networks or the IP addresses of attackers, and then uses this acl in the blackhole option to block queries from these addresses.[13] You can see this in Listing 11-13.

Listing 11-13. *The* blackhole *Option*

```
acl "badsource" {
0.0.0.0/8;
1.0.0.0/8;
2.0.0.0/8;
203.28.13.12;
};
...
options {
blackhole { badsource; };
};
...
```

---

13. See Chapter 2 for details of bogon networks and other potential sources to block.

■**Note** See Chapter 2 for some information on IP networks from which you should not accept queries.

You can override all these access controls, except blackhole, by specifying the access control options in individual view or zone statements. This allows you to increase the granularity of your access control by controlling it at the individual view or zone level.

Ports, Addresses, and Firewalling

The next couple of options I will cover control the source IP addresses and ports that your BIND server will use. This can have a significant impact on how you firewall your host and how your network firewalls handle your DNS traffic. By default, when started, BIND will listen on UDP and TCP port 53 on all interfaces attached to your system. When remote clients send their query requests, they originate from ephemeral ports and connect to port 53 on the BIND server.[14] The BIND server sends its replies from port 53 back to the ephemeral port on the client.

■**Note** I describe using iptables to firewall DNS servers in Chapter 2.

Binding to all interfaces on the BIND server is often not an ideal configuration, so you will probably want to limit the interfaces to which BIND is bound. The listen-on option addresses this requirement and allows you to specify the port and IP address on which BIND will listen. Listing 11-14 shows the listen-on option.

Listing 11-14. listen-on *Option*

```
listen-on { 192.168.0.100; };
```

You can also specify multiple IP addresses in your listen-on option to allow BIND to listen on multiple interfaces, like so:

```
listen-on { 192.168.0.101; 203.28.13.12; };
```

By default BIND listens on port 53, but you can also specify a different port using the listen-on option, like so:

```
listen-on port 1053 { 192.168.0.100; };
```

Finally, you can specify more than one listen-on option to provide a greater granularity of control over where BIND listens. You can see this in Listing 11-15.

---

14. For information on ephemeral ports, see Chapter 2.

Listing 11-15. *Multiple* listen-on *Options*

```
listen-on { 192.168.0.100; };
listen-on port 1053 { 10.0.0.100; };
```

Using the configuration in Listing 11-15 configures BIND to listen on IP address 192.168.0.100 on port 53 and also on IP address 10.0.0.100 on port 1053.

You need to also look at the port from which the BIND server sends its own requests and queries. These queries include DNS queries initiated by the BIND server and transfer and DNS NOTIFY queries from slave servers to master servers. In versions prior to BIND 8, the BIND server sent its own queries on port 53. In BIND versions 8 and 9 this behavior has been changed. The BIND server now uses a random ephemeral port as the source port for these queries. You can see this new behavior demonstrated in Figure 11-2.

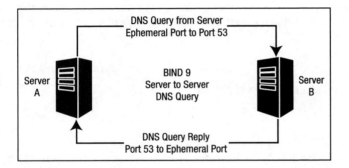

Figure 11-2. *New BIND port usage*

This can create issues for your firewall configuration. This is because generally DNS traffic to and from your BIND servers is firewalled to allow traffic in and out on port 53 only. They do not allow BIND servers to send queries from the ephemeral ports. One potential way of addressing this problem is to open the ephemeral port range on your host and network firewalls. But to most people, opening these ports is not an acceptable option, as it exposes your network and hosts to a greater risk of attack.

You can, however, configure BIND to behave as it did in previous versions. You can achieve this using the query-source, transfer-source, and notify-source option substatements, as you can see in the Listing 11-16.

Listing 11-16. *The Source Substatements*

```
query-source address * port 53;
transfer-source address * port 53;
notify-source address * port 53;
```

These substatements allow you to specify the source IP address and port number for a variety of BIND queries, including zone transfers. The query-source substatement sets the source IP address and port for DNS resolution queries generated by your BIND server. The `transfer-source` substatement controls the source IP address and port used for zone transfers and refresh queries. The `notify-source` substatement defines the source IP address and port used for DNS `NOTIFY` queries.

All these substatements are identical in syntax and have two options: `address`, which allows you to specify the source IP address, and `port`, which allows you to specify the source port. For either you can specify a wildcard using the * symbol. In each substatement in Listing 11-16 I have specified a source `address` of *, which indicates that BIND can send from all local network interfaces. For each substatement I have also specified a source `port` of 53, which indicates that BIND will only send queries from port 53. Setting the source substatements as I have in Listing 11-16 will change its behavior back to that of previous BIND releases where queries are sent from port 53.

■**Caution** The specification of a fixed port applies only to UDP traffic. Any TCP traffic will still use an ephemeral port.

You can also limit the source IP address by specifying a particular IP address, like so:

`query-source address 192.168.0.100 port *;`

I have also specified a wildcard * as the source `port` in the `query-source` substatement. This tells the BIND server to use its new default behavior and to send DNS queries from the ephemeral ports.

You can also use the `transfer-source` and `notify-source` substatements in your zone statements. Using either of these substatements in a `zone` statement will override the values in the `options` statement. This allows you to specify a particular query or transfer query source for an individual zone.[15]

■**Tip** I recommend you revert to the previous behavior for your BIND server, as it makes securing your hosts and networks with firewalls considerably easier.

Notify, Recursion, and Forwarding

You can specify some additional configurations settings in the `options` statement that can be useful when configuring your BIND server. The first option is the `notify` option. This controls whether BIND will send DNS `NOTIFY` messages to slave servers to notify them when zones change.[16] When the zone changes, the master server will send the `NOTIFY` messages to all the name servers, except the master server, listed in each zone. When the slave servers

---

15. See the article at `http://sysadmin.oreilly.com/news/views_0501.html` to learn why this could be useful.

16. See RFC 1996 for details of the DNS NOTIFY function (`http://www.ietf.org/rfc/rfc1996.txt`).

receive the NOTIFY messages, they are prompted to check the master server to ensure they have the most recent version of the zone. If there is an update to the zone, then the slave servers will initiate a zone transfer. The notify option can also be set in individual zone statements to override the value of the option set in the options statement.

The notify option is set to yes by default. You can also specify two other settings for this option: no, which stops the sending of the NOTIFY messages, and explicit, which is used with another option, also-notify. The also-notify option allows you to specify additional servers, other than the name servers defined in your zones, that you can use to receive NOTIFY messages when zones change. You can specify this option in the options statement like this:

```
notify explicit;
also-notify { 192.168.1.10; 192.168.2.10; };
```

You can override the also-notify option in the options statement by placing the option individually in a zone statement. This allows you to specify additional slave servers to be sent NOTIFY messages on an individual zone basis.

This option is further supplemented by the allow-notify access control option. On a slave server this allows you to specify the addresses of all the servers that are authorized to send this slave server NOTIFY messages. You can specify it like this:

```
allow-notify { 192.168.1.100; };
```

The allow-notify option on the previous line configures the server to accept NOTIFY messages with a source address of 192.168.1.100 only.

The next option I will cover is the recursion option. This option controls whether the BIND server will allow recursion. Recursion is the process that occurs when a DNS server receives a query for a domain for which it is not authoritative. To provide an answer to this query, the DNS server must query other DNS servers for the answer. This is called a *recursive query*.

For example, the BIND server kitten.yourdomainc.com is authoritative for the domain yourdomain.com but not for the domain anotherdomain.com. If a client queries the kitten server about the yourdomain.com domain, they will receive an answer because the kitten server is authoritative for that domain. If the client then queries the kitten server about the anotherdomain.com domain and recursion is disabled, then the query will fail. This is because kitten is not authoritative for that domain and, with recursion disabled, is not allowed to ask other DNS servers for an answer. If recursion was enabled, then the kitten server would attempt to provide an answer to the query by querying its cache or other DNS servers.

By default, the recursion option is set to yes like this:

```
recursion yes;
```

The recursion option is linked to the allow-recursion access control option. Using this option you can specify which of your clients is allowed to recursively query the server. Only your trusted internal clients should be allowed to make recursive queries. You do not want to provide answers to recursive queries to external sources. This is to prevent your bandwidth and resources from being used by unauthorized people and to reduce the exposure of your BIND server to a potential attack.

One method of allowing controlled recursion is to define an acl for your trusted hosts or networks and specify this acl in your allow-recursion option. Listing 11-17 demonstrates this method.

Listing 11-17. *Controlling the Recursion Option*

```
acl "trusted" {
192.168.0.0/24;
192.168.1.0/24;
};
...
options {
recursion yes;
allow-recursion { trusted; };
};
...
```

In Listing 11-17 only the `192.168.0.0/24` and the `192.168.1.0/24` networks are able to recursively query the server.

Lastly, I will cover the `forward` and `forwarders` options. These options allow you to configure a BIND server to forward all or some queries to another DNS server for resolution. The `forwarders` options allow you to specify a list of DNS servers for queries to be forwarded to, like this:

```
forwarders { 192.168.1.110; };
```

In the previous line I have configured BIND to forward all queries to the DNS server at `192.168.1.110`. You can also specify forwarding to a particular port on an IP address like this:

```
forwarders { 192.168.0.100 1053; };
```

In the previous line I have configured BIND to forward all queries to the DNS server at IP address `192.168.0.100` and to port 1053.

The `forward` option modifies the behavior of the `forwarders` option. It has two settings, `only` and `first`. When the `forward` option is set to `only`, then the BIND server will forward all queries to the designated forwarders. If set to `first`, then queries will be forwarded; however, if the forwarder is unable to answer the query, then the BIND server will then attempt to answer the query itself. The default setting for this option is `first`.

You can override both of these global options by using them in individual `zone` statements.

■**Note** I recommend you review the BIND Administrator's Reference Manual available at `http://www.bind9.net/Bv9ARM.html` for full details of all the options available in the `options` statement.

Views and Zones

In this section I will briefly cover the `view` and `zone` statements and how they are constructed. This is by no means a definitive explanation of these statements; I recommend you do further research and study to ensure you fully understand how both statement types work and how they can impact your DNS configuration and design.

Views

The view statement is linked to the zone statement and was introduced in BIND version 9. The view statement acts as a container for a series of zone statement and allows you to answer a DNS query differently depending on who is asking. For example, suppose you have a bastion host running BIND and connected to both your internal network and the Internet. Using views, it could provide one answer to a query from your internal network and a different answer to the same query from the Internet.

Why is this useful? Well, it can offer you two advantages. First, it can allow a single BIND host to be simultaneously authoritative for domains internal to your network and external to the Internet. Second, it can allow a single BIND host to perform both server and caching functions.

So, how do views provide these advantages? Let's take the BIND host kitten.yourdomain.com. It is a bastion host connected to the local 192.168.0.0/24 network with an IP address of 192.168.0.100 and also connected to the Internet with an IP address of 203.28.13.12. The kitten.yourdomain.com domain is authoritative for the yourdomain.com domain. From the internal network, if someone queries the hostname puppy.yourdomain.com, you want the BIND server to return the IP address 192.168.0.10. From the Internet, if someone queries the same hostname, you want the BIND server to return its Internet-facing IP address, 203.28.13.13. But before you had views, you could define only one yourdomain.com zone with one zone file in a named.conf file. This meant you could not provide both these answers from a single host, unless you were running two instances of BIND. This configuration required considerable overhead and was highly complicated to administer.

With views you can define a view for each type of query, internal or external. You then match the incoming clients to the appropriate view. You then have two yourdomain.com zones defined, one in each view and each with their own zone files. Clients from the internal network will receive answers from the internal view, and clients querying from the Internet will receive answers from the external view. This combines the functionality of two BIND servers into one server.

You can use the same view functionality to provide two different types of BIND functionality, server and caching, on one host. Using views you can match one set of clients (for example, any external untrusted clients) to a view that resolves queries only for domains for which it is authoritative and does not provide caching or recursion. Another set of clients (for example, your trusted internal clients) can be matched to a view that allows caching and recursive queries but is not authoritative for any domains.

■**Caution** Both internal and external DNS or shared server and caching functions on one host can be useful, especially if your budget for infrastructure is limited, but they are always the best model for your DNS infrastructure. See the discussion in the "Secure BIND Design" section for more details, but I recommend you split your internal and external DNS resolution services and your server and caching functions onto separate hosts. Additionally, you should always ensure you have slave servers to provide redundancy to your master servers.

So, how do you define a view statement? Let's look at Listing 11-18.

Listing 11-18. *A* view *Statement*

```
view "internal" IN {
match-clients { trusted; };
recursion yes;
...
Your zones here.
...
};
```

Views need to be named, and you should place the name in quotation marks to allow the use of any name, including protected BIND configuration words. Listing 11-18 has defined a view called internal. After the name of the view, I have specified its class, IN. This is the Internet class, and it should be used for almost all views. If you do not specify a class, then BIND will default to a class of IN. Finally, the contents of the view are contained within braces, and the last brace needs to be terminated with a semicolon, in line with the standard named.conf configuration statement style.

The view statement has three major sections: the client matching options, the view options, and the zones defined in this view. The client matching option is required for all views, and for this I specify the match-clients substatement. You can see this in Listing 11-18. This substatement allows you to specify the particular clients who can use this view. You must specify this substatement to ensure that the view is matched to particular clients. In the match-clients substatement in Listing 11-18 I have specified an acl, trusted, which was defined in Listing 11-5 earlier in the chapter. This configures BIND to match all the addresses specified in that acl to this view. The match-clients option can also use the normal BIND address matching list parameters such as IP addresses, networks, or keys.

You can also specify an additional client matching substatement, match-destinations. The match-destinations substatement allows you to match clients by the destination to which they have connected. You can also use both of these substatements together to match a client source and destination.

Finally, you can also specify the match-recursive-only substatement, which indicates that only recursive queries from matching clients will be matched to the view. Other types of queries will not be matched to the view.

The order in which you specify your view statements in the named.conf file is also important. BIND will check the client matching criteria from each view in sequence. The first view that matches the selection criteria will be the view BIND will use to resolve queries for that client.

You can also use a number of the same options that you can specify in the options statement in your view statements. If you have set the same option in the options statement and the view statement, then the value in the view statement will override the value in the option statement. The most common option you might use in a view statement is the recursion option. With this option specified in a view statement, you can allow or disallow recursive queries for a particular view. The list of other options you can use with the view statement grows with each release of BIND, but most options can be specified, including the access control options described in the "Access Controls" section.

Inside your view statement you also need to specify all the zones that are to be defined in the view. The default syntax of the zone statement does not change because you have placed the zone in a view.

But if you use views, then you must place all zone statements in the named.conf file into views. If you use views, then you cannot have zones defined outside of view statements, even if you have only one view statement. I recommend that for all BIND servers, including those with only one potential view, that you define a view statement to hold all your zones. You can see how I have done this in the example configurations provided in Appendix B.

Note I discuss zone statements and their structure in the next section.

Let's finish the discussion of zones with an example of how to create a split DNS model using views (see Listing 11-19).

Listing 11-19. *Split DNS Using Views*

```
view "internal" IN {
match-clients { trusted; };
recursion yes;

zone "yourdomain.com" IN {
    type master;
    file "master/db.yourdomain.com.internal";
    };
};

view "external" IN {
match-clients { any; };
recursion no;

zone "yourdomain.com" IN {
    type master;
    file "master/db.yourdomain.com.external";
    };
};
```

Listing 11-19 specifies two views, internal and external. The internal view matches all clients in the trusted acl and allows recursion. It will also answer queries about the youdomain.com domain with information from the db.yourdomain.com.internal zone file in he master directory. The external view matches any client and does not allow recursion. It will also answer queries about the youdomain.com domain with information from the db.yourdomain.com.external zone file in the master directory.

You can see also see the importance of the order of your view statements: all trusted clients would be matched first to the internal view. All other clients will match the external view because you have used the any criteria with the match-clients substatement.

Zones

All BIND servers use zone statements to a varying degree. For example, if your BIND master server is authoritative for any domains, then these are defined in zone statements. On a slave server these domains are defined as slave domains using a zone statement. Even if you are configuring a caching-only BIND server, which has no domains for which it is authoritative, then it is still necessary to define some zone statements, especially the root hints domain that provides your server with the addresses of the DNS root servers.

Tip You will generally always need to define two zone statements: a localhost zone and a reserve mapping of the 127.0.0.1 IP address. This provides DNS resolution to the local system for the loopback address. I have created these zones in the example configurations in Appendix B.

A zone statement defines what the BIND server knows about a domain, including its type, the location of the zone file containing the zone data, and who is allowed to query, transfer, or update the zone, amongst other options.

Let's now look at an example of a simple master zone statement (see Listing 11-20).

Listing 11-20. *A Master Zone Statement*

```
zone "yourdomain.com" IN {
type master;
file "/master/db.yourdomain.com";
```

In Listing 11-20 you can see my zone statement has a name, yourdomain.com, which I have placed in quotation marks. The IN after the zone name indicates that this is an Internet class zone. The Internet class is the normal and default setting for most domains. If you omit a class, then BIND defaults to the IN class.

Inside the zone statement's braces you place the options defining the zone. The first option is type, which indicates the type of zone; in Listing 11-20 I have defined a master zone. Five zones types exist (see Table 11-7).

Table 11-7. *Zone Types*

Type	Description
master	Master copy of the data for a zone.
slave	Replica of a zone. Another server holds the master of this zone.
stub	Abbreviated replica of a zone containing only the NS records. Deprecated in BIND 9.
forward	Allows forwarding for an individual zone.
hint	Specifies the names and IP addresses of the root servers.

Master zones are the master copy of zone data for a domain and provide authoritative answers to queries for that domain. To define a master zone, you must define at least the `type` and `file` options. If either of these is omitted, the zone will not load.

A slave zone is a replica of a master zone. You define a slave zone on a secondary or slave DNS server. The slave server connects to the master server and transfers the zone's data either when prompted by a DNS `NOTIFY` message or on a regular schedule. You define the master DNS servers for each slave zone in the zone definition like this:

```
zone "yourdomain.com" IN {
type slave;
file "/slave/db.yourdomain.com";
masters { 192.168.0.100; };
```

The `masters` option allows you to specify the IP address of DNS server that holds the master zone for a domain. The slave zone will use this IP address to retrieve the zone data. You can specify multiple IP addresses in this option and particular port numbers, as you can see in Listing 11-21.

Listing 11-21. *Multiple Master Servers*

```
masters { 192.168.0.100; 192.168.1.100 1053; };
```

In Listing 11-21 I have specified two master servers, `192.168.0.100` and `192.168.1.100`. I have also configured the slave server to connect to the master server at `192.168.1.100` on port 1053 instead of the normal port 53. To define a functional slave zone, you must define at least the `type`, `file`, and `masters` options. If any of these is omitted, the zone will not load.

A `stub` type zone is like a slave zone but contains only a subset of the data of the master zone. In this case it contains only the `NS`, or name server, records for the zone. Unless you have previously used `stub` zones in BIND 4 or 8, then you will probably not use them with BIND 9, and support is now limited for them.

A `forward` zone allows you to specify the forwarding of DNS queries on an individual domain basis. With a `forward` zone, you can specify a forwarder or forwarders for a particular domain. For example, all queries for the `yetanotherdomain.com` domain could be forwarded to the DNS server `192.168.1.110` like this:

```
zone "yetanotherdomain.com" {
type forward;
forwarders { 192.168.1.110; };
};
```

You can include multiple forwarders in your `forwarders` substatement. Additionally, like the `masters` option, you can specify a particular port on the IP address of the forwarder.

▪Note See the "Notify, Recursion, and Forwarding" section for additional information on forwarding.

The last domain type, `hint`, is used for hint zones that define the initial set of root servers that BIND will use in resolving queries. The root servers provide "seed data" sources to your

THE HINT ZONE

The content of the `hint` zone data file includes the names and IP addresses of the root DNS servers. These addresses change occasionally, so you should ensure you have a regular process to update this file. For example, you could redirect the output of a `dig` command to the hints zone data file like this:

```
kitten# dig @l.root-servers.net . ns > /chroot/named/master/db.hint
```

You can also download this data (if you trust the source) from a variety of FTP servers and Web sites. Many DNS administrators write scripts and automate this process with `cron`.

DNS server to help initiate resolution. These root servers provide an entry point into the DNS "cloud" and point your DNS servers to other DNS servers that may be able to resolve queries.[17] A hint zone is always required for a caching BIND server that resolves recursive queries for clients. It is not required for a BIND server that is simply authoritative for a domain or domains. You can specify a hint zone like this:

```
zone "." {
type hint;
file "db.hint";
};
```

The name for a hint zone is always an ending punctuation mark, and the zone type is `hint`. If you need to define a hint zone, then I recommend you place this `zone` statement before all your other zone statements in the `named.conf` file.

The next option in Listing 11-20 is the `file` option. This option defines the location of the zone file that contains the zone data. Several types of `zone` statements, such as master, slave, and stub, require that a zone file option be defined. I will not discuss the contents of zone files, as this is a much broader topic than the scope of this chapter allows. It is important to remember that if your BIND daemon is in a `chroot` jail, then these files are defined relative to the root directory of the `chroot` jail. I also recommend you distinctly name your zone data files so as to make their contents readily identifiable. I tend to use a naming convention like the following:

`db.domainname.tld.suffix`

replacing `domainname.tld` with the domain name (for example, `yourdomain.com`) and `suffix` with the suffix.

Note For references to information on building zone files, see the "Resources" section at the end of the chapter.

---

17. You will find a brief but comprehensive presentation on root servers at http://www.root-servers.org/presentations/rootops-gac-rio.pdf.

Each zone statement can also contain a number of options, including many of the options that can be defined in the options statement. If you specify an option in the zone statement that is also set in the options statement, then the zone statement option will override the options statement option for that zone.

Table 11-8 lists some of the key options available to the zone statement. I explained almost all these options earlier in the chapter, in a variety of different sections; where I have done this, I have referred to those sections in the table. You can read about the additional options not listed in Table 11-8 in the BIND Administrator Reference Manual.[18]

Table 11-8. *A Selection of Zone Statement Options*

Option	Description
allow-notify	See the description in the "Notify, Recursion, and Forwarding" section.
allow-query	See the description in the "Access Controls" section.
allow-transfer	See the description in the "Access Controls" section.
notify	See the description in the "Notify, Recursion, and Forwarding" section.
also-notify	See the description in the "Notify, Recursion, and Forwarding" section.
masters	Species the master DNS servers for a slave zone.
forward	See the description in the "Notify, Recursion, and Forwarding" section.
forwarders	See the description in the "Notify, Recursion, and Forwarding" section.
transfer-source	See the description in the "Ports, Addresses, and Firewalling" section.
notify-source	See the description in the "Ports, Addresses, and Firewalling" section.
allow-update	Specifies who is allowed to dynamically update master zones.
update-policy	Specifies policy for Dynamic DNS updates.

Note One of the areas I have not covered is the dynamic update of DNS data. This is disabled by default but can be controlled with the allow-update and update-policy access control options. See http://www.bind9.net/Bv9ARM.ch04.html#dynamic_update and http://www.bind9.net/Bv9ARM.ch07.html#dynamic_update_security for more details on dynamic updates.

TSIG

Transaction signatures (TSIG) provide a mechanism for verifying the identity of the DNS servers with which you are communicating.[19] Before TSIG was available, the only method available to determine if information from a particular DNS server was authentic was via IP address verification. Unfortunately, IP addresses are easily spoofed and do not generally provide adequate certainty of a server's identity. TSIG adds cryptographic signatures to DNS

---

18. http://www.nominum.com/content/documents/bind9arm.pdf

19. TSIG is defined by RFC 2845 (http://www.faqs.org/rfcs/rfc2845.html).

transactions to authenticate those transactions. This signature acts as a shared secret between the servers that are communicating. TSIG is most commonly used to authenticate zone transfers between primary and secondary DNS servers but can also be used to secure queries, responses, and dynamic updates.

■**Caution** TSIG will not work for transfers between BIND servers and Microsoft DNS servers. Microsoft DNS supports a variation of GSS-TSIG only, which is a Microsoft-proprietary implementation of secure DNS updates. It uses a different algorithm and is not compatible with TSIG.

TSIG works by signing each DNS transaction between two servers. The transaction is signed by adding a TSIG record to the DNS transaction. The TSIG record is created by hashing the contents of the DNS transaction with a key.[20] This key is identical on both servers and represents the shared secret between the two servers. The sending server hashes the DNS transaction with the key. It then sends the DNS transaction and the TSIG record to the receiving server. The receiving server verifies, using its copy of the key, that the hash is valid. If it is valid, then the receiving server accepts the DNS transaction.

Let's first look at an example of using TSIG. Say you have two servers, kitten.yourdomain.com with the IP address 192.168.0.2 and puppy.yourdomain.com with the IP address 192.168.0.1. You will secure zone transfers between the two servers using TSIG.

The first step in doing this is to create a key that both servers will use. You can do this on either server using the dnssec-keygen command. This command is provided with the BIND distribution and allows you to generate keys for TSIG (and also for DNSSEC, which is where the name of the command comes from), as you can see in Listing 11-22.

Listing 11-22. *The* dnssec-keygen *Command*

```
kitten# dnssec-keygen -a HMAC-MD5 -b 512 -n HOST kitten_puppy.yourdomain.com
```

Let's break down this command. The first option in the command, -a, allows you to specify the algorithm to be used to generate the key. I have specified HMAC-MD5, which is the only algorithm you can use for your TSIG keys. The -b option specifies the length of the key in bits. I have used the highest possible value, 512. I recommend you do the same. The -n option tells the dnssec-keygen command what type of key you want to generate, and I have specified HOST, which is the only appropriate type of key for TSIG transactions. Lastly I have called the key, kitten_puppy.yourdomain.com, making clear its purpose as the shared secret between these two servers. I recommend naming all your keys in a similar manner.

The command in Listing 11-22 created two files: Kkitten_puppy.yourdomain.com.+157+45723.key and Kkitten_puppy.yourdomain.com.+157+45723.private. The filenames are structured like this:

Kname_of_key.+algorithm_number+random_key_id.suffix

They have a key name of kitten_puppy.yourdomain.com and an algorithm number of 157, which indicates the algorithm HMAC-MD5. You can ignore the random key identifier. The

---

20. Much like the digital signatures you looked at in Chapter 8

`Kkitten_puppy.yourdomain.com.+157+45723.private` file contains the key I have created for TSIG. If you examine this file, you can see the key, as shown in Listing 11-23.

Listing 11-23. `dnssec-keygen-`*Created Key*

```
Private-key-format: v1.2
Algorithm: 157 (HMAC_MD5)
Key: faZLpiU7TypWy3kNkp47I9P+GOr1u+aRu2djQN63cv7QGgSDlajn5VrNjlxYhP8enV2RxEwlxxp==
```

The part of the file you require is the key specified after the `Key:` section of this file. The key in Listing 11-23 starts with `faZLp`.

Now you need to define this key to BIND by adding key statements to the `named.conf` files on both the `puppy` and `kitten` systems. Each key is defined using an individual key statement, and you can define multiple keys. The key statement specifies the name of the key being defined and has two required substatements. The first required substatement is the algorithm used by the key. The second required substatement, `secret`, holds the key itself. You can see a key statement in Listing 11-24.

Listing 11-24. *Key Statement*

```
key "kitten_puppy.yourdomain.com" {
algorithm "hmac-md5";
secret ➡
"faZLpiU7TypWy3kNkp47I9P+GOr1u+aRu2djQN63cv7QGgSDlajn5VrNjlxYhP8enV2RxEwlxxp==";
};
```

I have named my key `kitten_puppy.yourdomain.com`. The name of each key statement in your `named.conf` file should be unique. You can see that I have added the actual key I generated to the `secret` option of the key statement. You need to add the key statement to the `named.conf` file on both systems, and you need to ensure the key statements are identical; otherwise, TSIG authentication will not function.

■**Caution** You need to transmit any TSIG keys between systems in a secure manner. You should treat your TSIG keys as if they were PKI private keys and thus use your normal secure key distribution method to distribute the key to other systems. This may involve PGP-encrypted mail, secure fax, or even paper. If attackers acquire your TSIG keys, they can impersonate one of your BIND servers and potentially compromise your DNS environment.

Next you need to tell BIND when to use TSIG to verify transactions. The first part of doing this is to set up `server` statements in your `named.conf` file. These `server` statements allow you to specify options for BIND for each server with which it communicates. You should place your `server` statements after your key statements in the `named.conf` file.

Listing 11-25 provides a `server` statement for the `named.conf` file on the `kitten` system. This defines the `puppy` system (`192.168.0.1`) and the key to the `kitten` server.

Listing 11-25. `kitten` *Server Statement*

```
server 192.168.0.1 {
keys { kitten_puppy.yourdomain.com; };
};
```

In Listing 11-26 you add the `server` statement for the `named.conf` file on the puppy server. This defines the `kitten` system (`192.168.0.2`) and the key to the puppy server.

Listing 11-26. `puppy` *Server Statement*

```
server 192.168.0.2 {
keys { kitten_puppy.yourdomain.com; };
};
```

This now tells BIND that any communications between the servers, `kitten` and `puppy`, will use the `kitten_puppy.yourdomain.com` key.

Finally, you need to restart or reload the BIND configuration on both systems, for example, using the `rndc` command.

```
kitten# rndc reload
```

Listing 11-27 shows an extract from a zone transfer between the `kitten` and `puppy` servers that has been authenticated with the TSIG key `kitten_puppy.yourdomain.com`, which I have defined.

Listing 11-27. *Log of a TSIG-Signed Zone Transfer*

```
26-Oct-2004 22:36:02.489 zone yourdomain.com/IN/internal-in: Transfer started.
26-Oct-2004 22:36:02.514 transfer of 'yourdomain.com /IN' from ➥
192.168.0.1#53: connected using 192.168.0.2#32796
26-Oct-2004 22:36:02.736 zone yourdomain.com /IN/internal-in: ➥
transferred serial 200306073: TSIG 'kitten_puppy.yourdomain.com'
26-Oct-2004 22:36:02.736 transfer of 'yourdomain.com /IN' ➥
from 192.168.0.1#53: end of transfer
```

In Listing 11-27 you can see the transfer has used the TSIG key to transfer the `yourdomain.com` zone.

Tip The time on both servers is crucial to providing authentication. You need to ensure both servers have identical and accurate time; for example, you can use Network Time Protocol (NTP) to provide an identical time source for your servers.[21]

---

21. http://www.ntp.org/

You can also tell BIND to use the TSIG key to authorize individual zone transfers rather than for entire servers. You still need to add key statements defining your keys to the named.conf files on both systems involved. But instead of referring to these keys in a server statement, you refer to them in a zone statement like in Listing 11-28.

Listing 11-28. *Zone Transfers with TSIG*

```
zone "yourdomain.com" in {
type master;
file "master/db.yourdomain.com";
allow-transfer { key kitten_puppy.yourdomain.com; };
};
```

I have specified the key I created in the allow-transfer option and prefixed it with the keyword key to identify it as a key.

Using keys to provide authentication also works with the allow-update and update-policy options used for dynamic DNS.

■**Caution** Your shared keys can be compromised using brute-force methods. You should change your TSIG keys on a regular basis to limit the risk of this occurring.

The rndc Command

Version 9 of BIND introduced a new command called rndc. The rndc command performs a number of administrative functions for BIND servers such as loading changes to the BIND tables or flushing the DNS cache. In previous releases of BIND, you usually had to restart the named daemon to perform these types of function. The rndc command allows your DNS administrators to refresh the zones or flush the cache without the named daemon needing to be restarted.

■**Note** BIND 8 introduced a command, initially in the form of a shell script and then later a binary, called ndc. This command performed similar functions to rndc. The rndc command is a considerably more advanced version of this original command and replaces it in the BIND package.

The rndc command functions by connecting to a control channel. By default this channel usually listens on the localhost address 127.0.0.1 at port 953 and is initiated by the named daemon when it is started. By listening on the IP address 127.0.0.1, the channel will accept connections only from the local host.

You can also configure the channel to listen for remote connections on an external interface. This provides remote DNS administrators the ability to use the rndc command and issues commands to your BIND server. To do this, you need to open port 953 on your host's firewall, and you would need to have a copy of the rndc binary and related configuration file rndc.conf on the remote system.

■**Caution** If you enable remote access to the `rndc` command, you should be careful to grant access only to networks you trust. I recommend you limit connectivity to the local host unless remote access is a critical requirement.

---

rndc.conf

Let's first look at configuring the `rndc` command. The configuration of the `rndc` command is controlled in two places: in the `rndc.conf` configuration file and by `controls` and key statements you need to add to the `named.conf` configuration file.

The `rndc.conf` configuration file contains the configuration options that specify how the `rndc` command connects to the `named` daemon. This file also contains a cryptographic hash, like that used by TSIG (see the "TSIG" section), which authenticates the command to the control channel. The `controls` statement in the `named.conf` file specifies the options to configure the control channel the `rndc` command connects to, and the key statement of the `named.conf` file contains a copy of the cryptographic hash specified in the `rndc.conf` file. Defined in both the `rndc` command's configuration and the BIND server's configuration, the cryptographic hash acts as a shared secret.

By default, the `rndc.conf` file is located in `/etc`. If you have chrooted the `named` daemon, you need to create a symbolic link to the file in the `chroot` jail; for example, using the `chroot` jail created in the "Chrooting BIND" section, you would create the symbolic link in the directory `/chroot/named/etc` (see Listing 11-29).

```
kitten# ln -s /etc/rndc.conf /chroot/named/etc
```

Listing 11-29 shows a typical `rndc.conf` file.

Listing 11-29. `rndc.conf` *File*

```
options {
default-server 127.0.0.1;
default-key "rndc_key";
};

server 127.0.0.1 {
key "rndc_key";
};

key "rndc_key" {
algorithm "hmac-md5";
secret "private-key goes here";
};
```

The `rndc.conf` file can contain three statement types: `options`, `server`, and `key`. These statements use the same syntax as `named.conf` statements, and all must be terminated with semicolons.

The first statement, `options`, specifies any defaults for the `rndc` command. In Listing 11-29 I have specified the `default-server` and `default-key` options. The `default-server` option controls the default server the `rndc` command will try to connect to, in this case 127.0.0.1. The `default-key` option specifies the default key that the `rndc` command will use to make connections. I have specified a key called `rndc_key`, which I will create shortly.

The next statement in Listing 11-29 is a `server` statement. You need to define one `server` statement for each BIND server to which you want to connect. In Listing 11-29 I have specified only one `server` statement. The server can be specified by IP address or hostname. For the `server` statement I have specified the `localhost` IP address `127.0.0.1`. For each `server` statement you also need to specify the key to be used for this server. You can do this using the key substatement. In Listing 11-29 I have defined the key `rndc_key`. You can specify more than one server by adding server options like this:

```
server 127.0.0.1 {
key "rndc_key";
};

server dns1.yourdomain.com {
key "dns1_key";
};
```

In the previous lines I have added another server that the `rndc` command could connect to: `dns1.yourdomain.com`. This server will use the key `dns1_key` to authenticate.

The last statement type, key, defines the key or cryptographic hash you will use to authenticate. Each key is defined using an individual key statement, and you can define multiple keys. The key statement specifies the name of the key being defined and has two required substatements. Listing 11-29 defines a key name of `rndc_key`.

The first required substatement is the algorithm used by the key. In Listing 11-29 I have specified the `hmac-md5` algorithm.[22] The HMAC-MD5 algorithm uses MD5 hashing to make a Base64-encoded version of a password and is currently the only algorithm available to create keys. It is the same algorithm used for TSIG keys. The second required substatement, `secret`, holds the key itself.

Like in TSIG, you can generate keys using the `dnssec-keygen` command that is provided with the BIND package. Listing 11-30 shows how to use the `dnssec-keygen` command to create a key for the `rndc` command.

Listing 11-30. *Creating an* `rndc` *Key*

```
kitten# dnssec-keygen -a HMAC-MD5 -b 512 -n HOST rndc_key
```

Listing 11-30 will create two files: one file with a suffix of `.key` file and one file with a suffix of `.private`. The file with the `.private` suffix contains the key you have created for the `rndc` command. If you examine a typical file, you can see the key (see Listing 11-31).

Listing 11-31. `dnssec-keygen`-*Created Key*

```
Private-key-format: v1.2
Algorithm: 157 (HMAC_MD5)
Key: IoMYJlJoLOKtZnNXxGbcuHB0vY9MME➥
9p1VHJIM7mwnXHjFLyblbf9KGHoLIXR2IGFjbI/MSLYYPYvaHYGxq/wQ==
```

---

22. See http://www.faqs.org/rfcs/rfc2104.html and http://www.faqs.org/rfcs/rfc2085.html for details of HMAC-MD5.

The key is located in the Key: section of this file and consists of a Base64-encoded string of characters. You need to add this key to the secret substatement of the key statement you saw in Listing 11-29, as shown in Listing 11-32.

Listing 11-32. *Key Statement*

```
key "rndc_key" {
algorithm "hmac-md5";
secret
"IoMYJlJoLOKtZnNXxGbcuHBOvY9MME9p1VHJIM7mwnXHjFLyblbf9KGHoLIXR2IGFjbI/MSLYYPYvaHY
Gxq/wQ==";
};
```

This completes the configuration of the rndc.conf file. Like your named.conf file, you do not want people eavesdropping on the rndc.conf file. You should restrict the permissions on this file to 0640 and have it owned by the named user and group.

■**Tip** You should delete the two files created by the dnssec-keygen process. They contain your key, which you do not want to fall into the wrong hands.

Adding rndc Support to named.conf

You now need to add rndc support to the named.conf file so that a control channel is started by the named daemon. You also need to add your key to the named.conf file so that the rndc command can be authenticated to the control channel. You do this using the controls and key statements in the named.conf file (Listing 11-33).

Listing 11-33. named.conf *Key and Controls Statements*

```
key "rndc_key" {
algorithm "hmac-md5";
secret ➡
"IoMYJlJoLOKtZnNXxGbcuHBOvY9MME9p1VHJIM7mwnXHjFLyblbf9KGHoLIXR2IGFjbI/MSLYYPYvaHY
Gxq/wQ==";
};

controls {
inet 127.0.0.1 port 953 allow { 127.0.0.1; } keys { "rndc_key"; };
};
```

First, you add the identical key statement from Listing 11-32 to the named.conf file. You must ensure you have the identical key and that the key name is the same in both the rndc.conf and the named.conf files.

The controls statement declares the control channel to which the rndc command will connect. In Listing 11-33 you can see a typical controls statement. Let's break the statement down. The first part of the statement is the inet option. This option specifies the IP address and port on which the control channel will listen. In Listing 11-33 specifies the loopback address of 127.0.0.1 and the port 953. This means only users on the local system will be able to connect to the control channel, and it will not be open to external connections. If you wanted to open the channel to external connections, you would need to specify an external interface (see Listing 11-34).

Listing 11-34. *Control Channel on an External Interface*

```
controls {
inet 192.168.0.1 port 953 allow { trusted; } keys { "rndc_key"; };
};
```

The allow option specifies who is allowed to connect to the control channel. The option can contain IP addresses, networks, or acl statements that you have already specified. Listing 11-33 allows connections only from the loopback address 127.0.0.1. Listing 11-34 specifies the trusted acl. This acl would need to be defined in your named.conf file.

The last option of the controls statements is the keys option. This specifies which key statement provides the cryptographic signature that is used to authenticate the rndc command to the control channel. Listing 11-33 specifies rndc_key, which I have defined in both the rndc.conf and named.conf files.

Using rndc

Now let's look at the functionality of the rndc command. The rndc command consists of command-line options and server commands and is constructed like this:

```
kitten# rndc options command
```

The options allow you to specify which BIND server to which you want the rndc command to connect. The command-line options are mostly self-explanatory and replicate much of information configured in the rndc.conf file (see Table 11-9).

Table 11-9. rndc *Options*

Options	Description
-c file	Uses file as the configuration file. Defaults to /etc/rndc.conf.
-s server	Connects to the server indicated by server. Defaults to the default-server specified in the rndc.conf file.
-p port	Connects to port. Defaults to 953.
-V	Enables verbose logging.
-y key	Specifies a particular key ID to use. The key ID must be defined in the rndc.conf file.

For example, I use the -c and -s options in Listing 11-35.

Listing 11-35. *Using* rndc *Options*

```
kitten# rndc -c /etc/rndc_other.conf -s puppy.yourdomain.com reload
```

The options in Listing 11-35 point the rndc command to an alternative configuration file, rndc_other.conf, and to a server called puppy.yourdomain.com. I discuss the reload option in a moment.

I will not go into any detail of most of the actual BIND functions that the rndc command can perform, but Table 11-10 lists some of the more useful ones.

Table 11-10. rndc *Commands*

Command	Description
flush [*view*]	Flushes the server cache for a view
halt [*-p*]	Stops the server without saving pending updates
querylog	Toggles query logging on or off
reconfig	Reloads configuration file and any new zones
reload	Reloads configuration file and zones
retransfer zone [*class* [*view*]]	Retransfers a single zone
stats	Writes the server statistics to the statistics file
status	Displays status of the server
stop [*-p*]	Saves any pending updates to master files, and stops the server
trace	Increments the debugging level by one
trace level	Changes the debugging level

Most of these commands are self-explanatory. The most useful and the commands you will most commonly use are reload and reconfig. These allow you to reload your configuration file and zones without having to start and stop the named daemon. Anytime you change your named.conf file or your zone files, you need to perform this function before those changes will take effect, like this:

```
kitten# rndc reload
```

Another useful command is the rndc status command, which provides a summary of the current status of your BIND server. You can see a typical status report in Listing 11-36.

Listing 11-36. rndc *Status Command*

```
number of zones: 15
debug level: 0
xfers running: 2
xfers deferred: 1
soa queries in progress: 1
query logging is ON
recursive clients: 5/1000
tcp clients: 12/100
server is up and running
```

Resources

The following are resources you can use.

Mailing Lists

- **ISC BIND mailing lists**: http://www.isc.org/index.pl?/sw/bind/bind-lists.php

Sites

- **BIND**: http://www.isc.org/index.pl?/sw/bind/

- **BIND 9**: http://www.bind9.net/

- **BIND Administrator Reference Manual**: http://www.nominum.com/content/documents/ bind9arm.pdf

- **BIND FAQ**: http://www.isc.org/sw/bind/FAQ.php

- **djbdns**: http://cr.yp.to/djbdns.html

- **DNSSEC RFC**: http://www.faqs.org/rfcs/rfc2535.html

- **Network Time Protocol**: http://www.ntp.org/

Information About Zone Files

- **An explanation of DNS records**: http://support.algx.net/cst/dns/dns2.html

- **BIND master file format**: http://www.isc.org/index.pl?/sw/bind/docs/ bind8.2_master-file.php

- **BIND 9 zone files**: http://www.bind9.net/Bv9ARM.ch06.html#AEN3755

- **DNS resource records**: http://www.dns.net/dnsrd/rr.html

Books

- Albitz, Paul, and Cricket Liu. *DNS and BIND*, Fourth Edition. Sebastopol, CA: O'Reilly, 2001.

The Bastion Host
Firewall Script

This appendix contains a script to set up firewall rules for a bastion host. I discussed this script and the firewall rules in Chapter 2. Modify the rules and the variables I have specified to suit your firewalling requirements. You can then add these to a script file, make the file executable using the chmod command, and run the script to apply your firewall rules. You will need to modify the script to suit your host. I have included a variables section at the start of the script, and I recommend you configure these to suit your host. This also makes it easier to maintain your rules and settings, as you need to make any required changes in only one place, rather than repeatedly in your script.

You can also find this script in the Downloads section of the Apress Web site (http://www.apress.com).

```
#!/bin/bash
# Bastion Host IPTables Script

# VARIABLES - Change these to match your environment.
# Location of the binaries
IPT="/sbin/iptables"
SYSCTL="/sbin/sysctl"

# Loopback Interface
LOOPBACK="lo"

# Define External Network
EXT_INTER="eth0"
EXT_ADDR="220.240.52.228"

# Define External Servers
EXT_NTP1="clock3.redhat.com"
EXT_NTP2="ntp.public.otago.ac.nz"

# Define Internal Network
INT_INTER="eth1"
INT_ADDR="192.168.0.100"
INT_NET="192.168.0.0/24"
```

```
# Define Internal Servers
INT_SMTP="192.168.0.20"
INT_DNS1="192.168.0.10"
INT_DNS2="192.168.0.11"

# Set Kernel Parameters
$SYSCTL -w net/ipv4/conf/all/accept_redirects="0"
$SYSCTL -w net/ipv4/conf/all/accept_source_route="0"
$SYSCTL -w net/ipv4/conf/all/log_martians="1"
$SYSCTL -w net/ipv4/conf/all/rp_filter="1"
$SYSCTL -w net/ipv4/icmp_echo_ignore_all="0"
$SYSCTL -w net/ipv4/icmp_echo_ignore_broadcasts="1"
$SYSCTL -w net/ipv4/icmp_ignore_bogus_error_responses="0"
$SYSCTL -w net/ipv4/ip_forward="0"
$SYSCTL -w net/ipv4/tcp_syncookies="1"


# Flush all Rules
$IPT -F

#Set Policies
$IPT -P INPUT DROP
$IPT -P OUTPUT DROP
$IPT -P FORWARD DROP

# Delete all User-created Chains
$IPT -X

# Allow access to the Loopback host
$IPT -A INPUT -i $LOOPBACK -j ACCEPT
$IPT -A OUTPUT -o $LOOPBACK -j ACCEPT

# Create ICMP Incoming Chain
$IPT -N ICMP_IN

# Pass ICMP Incoming Traffic to the ICMP Incoming Chain
$IPT -A INPUT -p icmp -j ICMP_IN

# Rules for ICMP Incoming Traffic
$IPT -A ICMP_IN -i $EXT_INTER -p icmp --icmp-type 0 -m state --state ➥
ESTABLISHED,RELATED -j ACCEPT
$IPT -A ICMP_IN -i $EXT_INTER -p icmp --icmp-type 3 -m state --state ➥
ESTABLISHED,RELATED -j ACCEPT
$IPT -A ICMP_IN -i $EXT_INTER -p icmp --icmp-type 11 -m state --state ➥
ESTABLISHED,RELATED -j ACCEPT
$IPT -A ICMP_IN -i $EXT_INTER -p icmp -j LOG --log-prefix ➥
"IPT: ICMP_IN " $IPT -A ICMP_IN -i $EXT_INTER -p icmp -j DROP
```

```
# Create ICMP Outgoing Chain
$IPT -N ICMP_OUT

# Pass ICMP Outgoing Traffic to the ICMP Outgoing Chain
$IPT -A OUTPUT -p icmp -j ICMP_OUT

# Rules for ICMP Outgoing Traffic
$IPT -A ICMP_OUT -o $EXT_INTER -p icmp --icmp-type 8 -m state --state ➥
NEW -j ACCEPT
$IPT -A ICMP_OUT -o $EXT_INTER -p icmp -j LOG --log-prefix "IPT: ICMP_OUT "
$IPT -A ICMP_OUT -o $EXT_INTER -p icmp -j DROP

# Create Bad Sources Chain
$IPT -N BAD_SOURCES

# Pass traffic with bad source addresses to the Bad Sources Chain
$IPT -A INPUT -j BAD_SOURCES

# Rules for traffic with bad source addresses
# Drop incoming traffic allegedly from our own host
$IPT -A BAD_SOURCES -i $INT_INTER -s $INT_ADDR -j DROP
$IPT -A BAD_SOURCES -i $EXT_INTER -s $EXT_ADDR -j DROP

# Drop outgoing traffic not from our own host
$IPT -A BAD_SOURCES -o $INT_INTER -s ! $INT_ADDR -j DROP
$IPT -A BAD_SOURCES -o $EXT_INTER -s ! $EXT_ADDR -j DROP

# Drop traffic from other bad sources
$IPT -A BAD_SOURCES -s 168.254.0.0/16 -j DROP
$IPT -A BAD_SOURCES -i $EXT_INTER -s 10.0.0.0/8 -j DROP
$IPT -A BAD_SOURCES -i $EXT_INTER -s 172.16.0.0/12 -j DROP
$IPT -A BAD_SOURCES -i $EXT_INTER -s 192.168.0.0/16 -j DROP
$IPT -A BAD_SOURCES -i $EXT_INTER -s 192.0.2.0/24 -j DROP
$IPT -A BAD_SOURCES -i $EXT_INTER -s 224.0.0.0/4 -j DROP
$IPT -A BAD_SOURCES -i $EXT_INTER -s 240.0.0.0/5 -j DROP
$IPT -A BAD_SOURCES -i $EXT_INTER -s 248.0.0.0/5 -j DROP
$IPT -A BAD_SOURCES -i $EXT_INTER -s 127.0.0.0/8 -j DROP
$IPT -A BAD_SOURCES -i $EXT_INTER -s 255.255.255.255/32 -j DROP
$IPT -A BAD_SOURCES -i $EXT_INTER -s 0.0.0.0/8 -j DROP

# Create Bad Flags Chain
$IPT -N BAD_FLAGS

# Pass traffic with bad flags to the Bad Flags Chain
$IPT -A INPUT -p tcp -j BAD_FLAGS
```

```
# Rules for traffic with bad flags
$IPT -A BAD_FLAGS -p tcp --tcp-flags SYN,FIN SYN,FIN -j LOG --log-prefix ➡
"IPT: Bad SF Flag "
$IPT -A BAD_FLAGS -p tcp --tcp-flags SYN,FIN SYN,FIN -j DROP
$IPT -A BAD_FLAGS -p tcp --tcp-flags SYN,RST SYN,RST -j LOG --log-prefix ➡
"IPT: Bad SR Flag "
$IPT -A BAD_FLAGS -p tcp --tcp-flags SYN,RST SYN,RST -j DROP
$IPT -A BAD_FLAGS -p tcp --tcp-flags SYN,FIN,PSH SYN,FIN,PSH -j LOG ➡
--log-prefix "IPT: Bad SFP Flag "
$IPT -A BAD_FLAGS -p tcp --tcp-flags SYN,FIN,PSH SYN,FIN,PSH -j DROP
$IPT -A BAD_FLAGS -p tcp --tcp-flags SYN,FIN,RST SYN,FIN,RST -j LOG ➡
--log-prefix "IPT: Bad SFR Flag "
$IPT -A BAD_FLAGS -p tcp --tcp-flags SYN,FIN,RST SYN,FIN,RST -j DROP
$IPT -A BAD_FLAGS -p tcp --tcp-flags SYN,FIN,RST,PSH SYN,FIN,RST,PSH ➡
-j LOG --log-prefix "IPT: Bad SFRP Flag "
$IPT -A BAD_FLAGS -p tcp --tcp-flags SYN,FIN,RST,PSH SYN,FIN,RST,PSH -j DROP
$IPT -A BAD_FLAGS -p tcp --tcp-flags FIN FIN -j LOG --log-prefix ➡
"IPT: Bad F Flag "
$IPT -A BAD_FLAGS -p tcp --tcp-flags FIN FIN -j DROP
$IPT -A BAD_FLAGS -p tcp --tcp-flags ALL NONE -j LOG --log-prefix ➡
"IPT: Null Flag "
$IPT -A BAD_FLAGS -p tcp --tcp-flags ALL NONE -j DROP
$IPT -A BAD_FLAGS -p tcp --tcp-flags ALL ALL -j LOG --log-prefix ➡
"IPT: All Flags "
$IPT -A BAD_FLAGS -p tcp --tcp-flags ALL ALL -j DROP
$IPT -A BAD_FLAGS -p tcp --tcp-flags ALL FIN,URG,PSH -j LOG --log-prefix ➡
"IPT: Nmap:Xmas Flags "
$IPT -A BAD_FLAGS -p tcp --tcp-flags ALL FIN,URG,PSH -j DROP
$IPT -A BAD_FLAGS -p tcp --tcp-flags ALL SYN,RST,ACK,FIN,URG -j LOG ➡
--log-prefix "IPT: Merry Xmas Flags "
$IPT -A BAD_FLAGS -p tcp --tcp-flags ALL SYN,RST,ACK,FIN,URG -j DROP

# Prevent SYN Flooding
$IPT -A INPUT -i $EXT_INTER -p tcp --syn -m limit --limit 5/second -j ACCEPT

# Log and Drop Traffic in the INVALID state
$IPT -A INPUT -m state --state INVALID -j LOG --log-prefix "IPT: INV_STATE "
$IPT -A INPUT -m state --state INVALID -j DROP

# Log and Drop Fragmented Traffic
$IPT -A INPUT -f -j LOG --log-prefix "IPT: Frag "
$IPT -A INPUT -f -j DROP
```

```
# Bastion Host Service Rules
# Internet SMTP Rules
$IPT -A INPUT -i $EXT_INTER -p tcp --dport smtp -m state --state ➥
NEW,ESTABLISHED -j ACCEPT
$IPT -A OUTPUT -o $EXT_INTER -p tcp --sport smtp -m state --state ➥
NEW,ESTABLISHED -j ACCEPT

# Internal Network SMTP Rules
$IPT -A INPUT -i $INT_INTER -p tcp -s $INT_SMTP --sport smtp -m state ➥
--state NEW,ESTABLISHED -j ACCEPT
$IPT -A OUTPUT -o $INT_INTER -p tcp -d $INT_SMTP --dport smtp -m state ➥
--state NEW,ESTABLISHED -j ACCEPT

# Internet DNS Rules
$IPT -A INPUT -i $EXT_INTER -p udp --dport domain -m state ➥
--state NEW,ESTABLISHED -j ACCEPT
$IPT -A INPUT -i $EXT_INTER -p tcp --dport domain -m state ➥
--state NEW,ESTABLISHED -j ACCEPT
$IPT -A OUTPUT -o $EXT_INTER -p udp --sport domain -m state ➥
--state NEW,ESTABLISHED -j ACCEPT
$IPT -A OUTPUT -o $EXT_INTER -p tcp --sport domain -m state ➥
--state NEW,ESTABLISHED -j ACCEPT



# Internal Network Incoming DNS Rules
$IPT -A INPUT -i $INT_INTER -p udp -s $INT_DNS1 --dport domain -m state ➥
--state NEW,ESTABLISHED -j ACCEPT
$IPT -A INPUT -i $INT_INTER -p udp -s $INT_DNS2 --dport domain -m state ➥
--state NEW,ESTABLISHED -j ACCEPT
$IPT -A INPUT -i $INT_INTER -p tcp -s $INT_DNS1 --dport domain -m state ➥
--state NEW,ESTABLISHED -j ACCEPT
$IPT -A INPUT -i $INT_INTER -p tcp -s $INT_DNS2 --dport domain -m state ➥
--state NEW,ESTABLISHED -j ACCEPT

# Internal Network Outgoing DNS Rules
$IPT -A OUTPUT -o $INT_INTER -p udp -d $INT_DNS1 --sport domain -m state ➥
--state NEW,ESTABLISHED -j ACCEPT
$IPT -A OUTPUT -o $INT_INTER -p udp -d $INT_DNS2 --sport domain -m state ➥
--state NEW,ESTABLISHED -j ACCEPT
$IPT -A OUTPUT -o $INT_INTER -p tcp -d $INT_DNS1 --sport domain -m state ➥
--state NEW,ESTABLISHED -j ACCEPT
$IPT -A OUTPUT -o $INT_INTER -p tcp -d $INT_DNS2 --sport domain -m state ➥
--state NEW,ESTABLISHED -j ACCEPT
```

```
# Internet NTP Rules
$IPT -A INPUT -i $EXT_INTER -p udp -s $EXT_NTP1 --dport ntp -m state ➥
--state ESTABLISHED -j ACCEPT
$IPT -A INPUT -i $EXT_INTER -p udp -s $EXT_NTP2 --dport ntp -m state ➥
--state ESTABLISHED -j ACCEPT
$IPT -A OUTPUT -o $EXT_INTER -p udp -d $EXT_NTP1 --sport ntp -m state ➥
--state NEW,ESTABLISHED -j ACCEPT
$IPT -A OUTPUT -o $EXT_INTER -p udp -d $EXT_NTP2 --sport ntp -m state ➥
--state NEW,ESTABLISHED -j ACCEPT

# Internal Network NTP Rules
$IPT -A INPUT -i $INT_INTER -p udp -s $INT_NET --dport ntp -m state ➥
--state NEW,ESTABLISHED -j ACCEPT
$IPT -A OUTPUT -o $INT_INTER -p udp -d $INT_NET --sport ntp -m state ➥
--state ESTABLISHED -j ACCEPT

# Internal Network SSH Rules
$IPT -A INPUT -i $INT_INTER -p tcp -s $INT_NET --dport ssh -m state ➥
--state NEW,ESTABLISHED -j ACCEPT
$IPT -A OUTPUT -o $INT_INTER -p tcp -d $INT_NET --sport ssh -m state ➥
--state ESTABLISHED -j ACCEPT
```

BIND Configuration Files

This Appendix contains a series of secure BIND configuration files demonstrating the different types of BIND configuration files discussed in Chapter 11.

A Caching Server

The `named.conf` file in Listing B-1 is for a caching-only server that is designed to be deployed in your internal network in order to provide recursive DNS resolution to internal clients. It is not authoritative for any domains. You will need to fill in the details of your trusted networks and any IP addresses or networks you would like to block with the `blackhole` option. I would also recommend adding the bad source networks listed in Chapter 2.

I have included extensive logging to the `syslog` daemon, and I have also added a log file, `named_sec.log`, as an additional repository to hold your security-, configuration-, and DNSSEC/TSIG-related logs.[1]

Listing B-1. `named.conf`, *Caching Only*

```
acl "trusted" {
//specify your trusted network here
};

acl "bad_source" {
//specify any sources you wish to blackhole here
};

logging {
channel "default_syslog" { syslog daemon; severity info; };
channel "security_log" {
        file "/var/logs/named_sec.log" versions 32 size 1m;
        severity dynamic;
        print-time yes;
        print-category yes;
        print-severity yes; };
```

---

1. None of the `named.conf` configuration files contain support for `rndc`. See Chapter 11 for details of adding this support.

```
category default { default_syslog; };
category general { default_syslog; };
category xfer-in { default_syslog; };
category xfer-out { default_syslog; };
category client { default_syslog; };
category network { default_syslog; };
category config { default_syslog; security_log; };
category security { default_syslog; security_log; };
category dnssec { default_syslog; security_log; };
};

options {
directory "/";
pid-file "/var/run/named.pid";
version "[null]";
allow-transfer { none; };
blackhole { bad_source; };
query-source address * port 53;
};

view "internal" {
match-clients { trusted; };
recursion yes;

zone "." {
type hint;
file "/master/db.cache";
};

zone "localhost" {
type master;
file "/master/db.localhost";
notify no;
allow-transfer { none; };
};

zone "0.0.127.in-addr.arpa" {
type master;
file "/master/db.127.0.0";
notify no;
allow-transfer { none; };
};
};

view "chaosnet" chaos {
match-clients { any; };
recursion no;
```

```
zone "bind" chaos {
type master;
file "/master/db.bind";
allow-transfer { none; };
};
};
```

An Authoritative Master Name Server

The named.conf file in Listing B-2 is for an authoritative master name server that is designed to be deployed in your DMZ in order to provide answers to DNS queries from external clients. It is authoritative for two domains: yourdomain.com and anotherdomain.com. You will need to replace the zone statements with statements applicable to your domains.

You will need to specify details of any slave servers in the transfer acl statement. I recommend also adding TSIG security for any zone transfers. You will also need to specify any IP addresses or networks you would like to block with the blackhole option. I recommend adding the bad source networks listed in Chapter 2.

I have included extensive logging to the syslog daemon, and I have also added a log file, named_sec.log, as an additional repository to hold your security-, configuration-, and DNSSEC/TSIG-related logs.

Listing B-2. named.conf, *Authoritative Master*

```
acl "transfer" {
//specify your slave servers here
};

acl "bad_source" {
//specify any sources you wish to blackhole here
};

logging {
channel "default_syslog" { syslog daemon; severity info; };
channel "security_log" {
        file "/var/logs/named_sec.log" versions 30 size 1m;
        severity dynamic;
        print-time yes;
        print-category yes;
        print-severity yes; };

category default { default_syslog; };
category general { default_syslog; };
category xfer-in { default_syslog; };
category xfer-out { default_syslog; };
category client { default_syslog; };
category network { default_syslog; };
```

```
category config { default_syslog; security_log; };
category security { default_syslog; security_log; };
category dnssec { default_syslog; security_log; };
};

options {
directory "/";
pid-file "/var/run/named.pid";
version "[null]";
allow-transfer { transfer; };
blackhole { bad_source; };
query-source address * port 53;
};

view "external" IN {
match-clients { any; };
recursion no;

zone "yourdomain.com" {
type master;
file "/master/db.yourdomain.com";
};

zone "anotherdomain.com" {
type master;
file "/master/db.anotherdomain.com";
};
};

view "chaosnet" chaos {
match-clients { any; };
recursion no;

zone "bind" chaos {
type master;
file "/master/db.bind";
allow-transfer { none; };
};
};
```

A Split DNS Name Server

The named.conf file in Listing B-3 is for a split DNS name server that is designed to be deployed in your DMZ in order to provide answers to DNS queries from both internal and external clients for the domains for which it is authoritative. It also allows recursion for your internal clients. It is authoritative for two domains: yourdomain.com and anotherdomain.com. You will need to replace the zone statements with statements applicable to your domains.

You will need to specify details of any slave servers in the transfer acl statement. I recommend also adding TSIG security for any zone transfers. You will also need to specify any IP addresses or networks you would like to block with the blackhole option. I recommend adding the bad source networks listed in Chapter 2.

I have included extensive logging to the syslog daemon, and I have also added a log file, named_sec.log, as an additional repository to hold your security-, configuration-, and DNSSEC/TSIG-related logs.

Listing B-3. named.conf, *Split DNS*

```
acl "trusted" {
//specify your trusted network here
};

acl "transfer" {
//specify your slave servers here
};

acl "bad_source" {
//specify any sources you wish to blackhole here
};

logging {
channel "default_syslog" { syslog daemon; severity info; };
channel "security_log" {
        file "/var/logs/named_sec.log" versions 30 size 1m;
        severity dynamic;
        print-time yes;
        print-category yes;
        print-severity yes; };

category default { default_syslog; };
category general { default_syslog; };
category xfer-in { default_syslog; };
category xfer-out { default_syslog; };
category client { default_syslog; };
category network { default_syslog; };
category config { default_syslog; security_log; };
category security { default_syslog; security_log; };
category dnssec { default_syslog; security_log; };
};

options {
directory "/";
pid-file "/var/run/named.pid";
version "[null]";
recursion no;
allow-recursion { none; };
```

```
allow-transfer { transfer; };
blackhole { bad_source; };
query-source address * port 53;
};

view "internal" IN {
match-clients { trusted; };
recursion yes;

zone "." {
type hint;
file "/master/db.cache";
};

zone "localhost" {
type master;
file "/master/db.localhost";
notify no;
allow-transfer { none; };
};

zone "0.0.127.in-addr.arpa" {
type master;
file "/master/db.127.0.0";
notify no;
allow-transfer { none; };
};

zone "yourdomain.com" {
type master;
file "/master/db.yourdomain.com.internal";
};

zone "anotherdomain.com" {
type master;
file "/master/db.anotherdomain.com.internal";
};
};

view "external" IN {
match-clients { any; };
recursion no;

zone "yourdomain.com" {
type master;
file "/master/db.yourdomain.com.external";
};
```

```
zone "anotherdomain.com" {
type master;
file "/master/db.anotherdomain.com.external";
};
};

view "chaosnet" chaos {
match-clients { any; };
recursion no;

zone "bind" chaos {
type master;
file "/master/db.bind";
allow-transfer { none; };
};
};
```

A Sample Named init Script

Listing B-4 shows a sample named init script.

Listing B-4. *Named* init *Script*

```
#!/bin/sh
# This shell script takes care of starting and stopping named
# chkconfig: 345 55 45
# description: named (BIND) is a Domain Name Server daemon

# Source function library.
. /etc/rc.d/init.d/functions

# Source networking configuration.
. /etc/sysconfig/network

# Check that networking is up.
[ ${NETWORKING} = "no" ] && exit 0
[ -f /usr/local/sbin/named ] || exit 0
[ -f /chroot/named/etc/named.conf ] || exit 0

# See how we were called.
case "$1" in
  start)
        # Start daemons.
        echo -n "Starting named: "
        daemon /usr/local/sbin/named -u named -t /chroot/named
        echo
```

```
            touch /var/lock/subsys/named
            ;;
    stop)
            # Stop daemons.
            echo -n "Shutting down named: "
            killproc named
            rm -f /var/lock/subsys/named
            echo
            ;;
    status)
            status named
            exit $?
            ;;
    restart)
            $0 stop
            $0 start
            exit $?
            ;;
    reload)
            /usr/local/sbin/rndc reload
            exit $?
            ;;
    *)
            echo "Usage: named {start|stop|status|restart|reload}"
            exit 1
esac
exit 0
```

■■■

Checkpoints

This appendix summarizes the checkpoints from each chapter.

Chapter 1

Install only what you need. Use your distribution's minimal installation option. Remove extraneous or unnecessary packages. Confirm that each package on your system is actually required by your system.

Do not install your system when connected to the Internet or an Internet-connected network. Install any required patches and updates offline.

Secure your system's physical security, BIOS, and boot loader. Protect your boot process with passwords. I recommend using the Grub boot loader rather than the LILO boot loader, as Grub has a more robust security model.

Start only the services you need for your system, and secure the functions controlled in the `inittab` file.

Secure your console and virtual terminals. Also ensure your login screen provides the minimum possible information to a user or potential attacker. Defense through obscurity can be a powerful tool. The less information you reveal about your system and its purpose, the better.

Add only those users and groups that you require. Delete any others. Refer to the list of the users and groups I have provided in Chapter 1 to find some of those users who can be removed.

Use MD5 passwords and shadow passwording. Ensure users select secure passwords and configure your passwording environment accordingly. Ensure passwords are scheduled to regularly expire.

Turn on user (and if required process) accounting for your system. Monitor the reports generated by these accounting processes regularly for anomalies.

Use `sudo` rather than `root` to administer your system. Ensure you carefully test your `sudo` configuration before implementing it to ensure it is secure.

Use PAM to secure the authentication processes of your system. PAM offers an easy-to-use, highly configurable framework to control access to your system using a large number of different criteria.

Confirm the integrity of any files you download or install on your system using methods such as MD5 and SHA1 checksums or digital signatures. This includes using the `rpm` command with the `--checksig` option to verify any RPM files.

Review the available kernel hardening options, and install one of the packages or patches to further harden your kernel. I recommend the Openwall patch, but if you want to take kernel security further, then an access control model-based package such as SELinux, whilst requiring more implementation effort, offers a considerable amount of additional security.

Keep up with security updates, and keep informed about newly discovered vulnerabilities using resources such as Security Focus's Vulnerability Database and the CERT advisory mailings.

Chapter 2

Base your firewall on a minimalist design that denies by default and allows by exception. You should build your firewall like building a wall around your host and remove only those bricks you absolutely need to see through.

Use a default policy of `DROP` for your built-in chains. This is in line with the denial by default model I have recommended by allowing only incoming and outgoing traffic you've explicitly authorized.

Model your traffic and design your firewall on paper before you start creating your rules. This should include incoming and outgoing connections, the source, and destination of your traffic, including addresses and ports. You can also include the required connection states for your traffic.

Use connection states to further restrict your allowed incoming and outgoing traffic. If you only require existing connections to enter and leave your host, then you can use states to control this. Only allow new connections in and out of your hosts if they are absolutely required.

Ensure you have a suitable amount of logging in place so that you know what is going on with your firewall. Ensure you have sufficient disk space to hold the required volume of logs.

Set rules to block spoofed addresses, bad flags, bad fragments, and states and to limit the possibility of Denial of Service attacks. These types of attacks change and evolve over time. You should keep updated with new variations and attacks on mailing lists such as the Netfilter list and on the security lists and sites (see Chapter 1).

If you take care to test them, the Patch-O-Matic tool comes with several useful patches and modules that can extend `iptables` functionality. Additionally, review and carefully configure your kernel parameters to best suit the requirements of your environment.

Use a tool such as `tcpdump` to examine the traffic on your host to ensure your firewall is fully functional and allowing or denying the right traffic. Remember you can filter your traffic to display only the traffic on which you want to focus.

Chapter 3

OpenSSL is a widely used and useful open-source version of the SSL protocol that can be used to secure a variety of applications. I recommend developing a solid knowledge of its capabilities and functionality.

If you have unencrypted connections, then you can use Stunnel with OpenSSL to encapsulate and secure them.

Use a VPN tool utilizing IPSec such as Openswan to secure your network connections, securely join two systems, or two subnets together across the Internet.

Do not use clear-text administrations tools such as `rsh` and `telnet`. Replace them with SSH-based tools.

Though you can tunnel X through SSH I recommend you exercise caution in doing this or indeed in running X on a production server system at all.

Chapter 4

Ensure you understand how basic Unix permissions work and grant only the minimum permissions you need to users and applications to maintain functionality.

World permissions are dangerous and potentially allow attackers to misuse files and applications. Review all the objects on your system with world-readable, world-writable, and world-executable permissions and ensure you understand why they have those permissions. If they do not need those permissions, then revoke them!

Sticky bits allow you to better control access to directories where multiple users shared access permissions by allowing users to manage only the files and objects they have created. Investigate the potential of using sticky bits where you have directories in which multiple users shared access permissions.

Amongst the most dangerous permission settings on your system are `setuid` and `setgid` permissions. When set on binaries, these allow any users to adopt the permissions of the object's owner or group when running that binary. These binaries have the potential to be serious vulnerabilities on your system, and you should check that all `setuid` and `setgid` binaries actually require these permissions to function. If they do not, then remove them!

All files and objects on your system should be owned by a user and belong to a group. Any files that do not could potentially be malicious in nature, and you should investigate them and either assign them to a user or group or remove them.

You should regularly scan your system for unowned files and objects with world-permissions set and/or with `setuid` or `setgid` permissions. You can use tools such as sXid or Adeos to do this. Files with these permissions introduced into your system without your approval are often signs of a potential attack or penetration of your system.

Immutable files cannot be changed, deleted, hard-linked to, or renamed even by the root user. They allow you to protect some files—for example, configuration files and some important binaries—from most forms of compromise. You should examine your system for files or binaries that you can make immutable. On some bastion-type systems, you may be able to make most of your configuration files and binaries immutable. Remember, you will need to remove their immutable status to update or upgrade your configuration and binaries.

File encryption provides a useful method of securing your individual files against eavesdropping by an attacker. Use file encryption to secure files that need to be kept private. Always ensure you choose a suitable passphrase to secure your encrypted files to prevent your encrypted files from being compromised.

You can mount your file systems (including removable file systems) with a variety of options, including mounting them read-only, preventing `setuid` and `setgid` permissions from functioning, stopping devices from being interpreted, and disallowing binary execution. These options, especially when used with removable devices such as CD drives, and floppy drives, as well as pluggable devices such as USB drives, reduce the risk of a threat being introduced to your system from these devices. You should examine what file systems you have and how they are mounted.

Like you can encrypt files, you can also create entire encrypted file systems. This allows you to create secure, encrypted file systems for large numbers of files that need to be protected. Or create protected file systems for devices such as laptops to secure sensitive information while in transit.

Monitoring your files and objects for changes is a good way of detecting unauthorized access to your systems. You can use a file integrity scanner such as Tripwire to monitor the characteristics of your files and objects such as size, permissions, ownership, and hash values. Tripwire will alert you via e-mail or through a report of any files or objects on your system that have changed from an established baseline.

Chapter 5

If your logging environment is large, is complicated, or you want to better control your logs and their destinations and filtering, then I recommend you use Syslog-NG.

Constantly refine your logging environment to ensure you have picked up on all the possible sources of information.

Constantly refine your filtering so you are not overwhelmed with irrelevant log data.

Secure the transmission of your logs, as an attacker can gain considerable advantages by reading your logs.

Use correlation and analysis tools to highlight the messages important to you, and use alerting tools to get that information to you.

Design and manage your archiving and rotation of logs to ensure you keep the information you need for the time frame and discard information that is not relevant.

Chapter 6

Remember to keep up-to-date with regular security reviews.

Schedule regular checks of your system for root kits.

Ensure your users have secure passwords, and regularly check the integrity and security of your users' passwords.

For a consistent approach to some base-level security, run a hardening script such as Bastille Linux across your systems.

Use NMAP to scan your systems to confirm that you know and understand all the services and ports that are active on your systems.

Use a tool such as Nessus or SARA to audit your applications and systems for known vulnerabilities.

If you are attempting to investigate a potential penetration, keep detailed records both for your own purposes and in case auditors or law enforcement require evidence of the penetration.

If you recover a system, you should follow the basic rules I have articulated.

Chapter 7

Keep your mail server software up-to-date by regularly checking its site (http:// www.sendmail.org for Sendmail and http://www.postfix.org for Postfix). You should also consider subscribing to any announcement mailing lists available for your mail server.

Keep informed about threats to your mail infrastructure via mailing lists such as BugTraq and via Web sites such as CERT (http://www.cert.org). I also detail a variety of other sites and mailing lists in Chapter 1.

Ensure you have secured your mail server from penetration and DoS attacks by configuring your mail server securely, as described in this chapter. You should also ensure your firewall rules are strong and secure as described in Chapter 2.

Keep on top of new trends in spammer tactics and antispam techniques. You can do this at sites such as http://spam.abuse.net/ and http://www.arachnoid.com/lutusp/ antispam.html.

Regularly tweak your antispam rules and checks to ensure they are doing the job. Ask your users to forward spam that slips through your filters to a central Spam mailbox, and use this spam to tweak your antispam rules. Regularly check the efficiency of any RBLs you have defined against other available RBLs.

Ensure your antivirus software is up-to-date and that your virus definitions are updated regularly.

Chapter 8

Where possible, you should try to always use TLS encryption for your mail transmission.

Handle your TLS keys and passphrases with the same level of security you would treat other system passwords.

If you need relaying, use SMTP AUTH with Cyrus SASL with authenticate your users and ensure only legitimate users are allowed to relay mail through your MTA.

Always try to use SMTP AUTH in conjunction with TLS encryption.

Keep your OpenSSL and Cyrus SASL packages up-to-date to ensure you address any potential vulnerabilities and exploits.

Chapter 9

Choose appropriate remote e-mail access for your site, taking into consideration the purposes, benefits, and disadvantages of the available protocols. I recommend for security, stability and available access controls that you use a server based on IMAP.

Choose a stable and secure server as your platform for remote e-mail access and ensure you periodically update it and apply any relevant security patches.

If you are using a product such as UW-IMAP or Qpopper, which have proven to have a number of security flaws, consider using another application such as Cyrus IMAP.

Consider chrooting your remote e-mail installation to further secure your installations from penetration. I show you how to do this using Cyrus IMAP.

Always ensure you use SSL/TSL-enabled remote access via IMAP or POP, and ensure your clients use SSL/TLS to encrypt any connections. This will protect your e-mail traffic from eavesdropping during its transmission.

Always use a secure authentication method such as those available through Cyrus SASL to authenticate your users against the remote e-mail access server. Also consider using a "sealed" system where the only local shell logins are for system administration use only, and all other users have access to their e-mail stores only.

If you are going to use Fetchmail, then ensure you use TLS to ensure all connections are encrypted. If you cannot use TLS, try to tunnel your connections through OpenSSH. This will help prevent attackers from eavesdropping on your Fetchmail sessions.

Chapter 10

Unless you have a real need to run an FTP server, then I recommend you do not run one. The inherent insecurities in FTP server daemons and the difficulty in securing FTP traffic make FTP an extremely risky proposition as a production service.

If you do choose to run an FTP server, then I recommend the vsftpd FTP server available from http://vsftpd.beasts.org/. It is secure, has good performance, and contains a number of security features including support for SSL/TLS FTP transfers.

Ensure you adequately firewall your FTP server. You should utilize the ip_conntrack_ftp module provided with iptables to enable FTP connection state tracking. This provides you with the ability to limit the types of connections made to your host. Additionally, you should look at limiting the range of ephemeral ports used by your FTP server for its data connections.

If you going to allow local user access to your FTP server, consider limiting the networks able to log into that server. I recommend you allow access only from trusted networks.

I recommend placing your local users in chroot jails. The vsftpd server allows you to chroot your local users into their home directories.

If you are going to allow the uploading of files to your FTP server, ensure you set your umask and default upload permissions carefully to prevent the uploading of files that could be used to compromise your host. For example, restrict the uploading of executable files.

Ensure you set up resource controls on your FTP server to limit the number of incoming connections and the number of connections from an individual IP address. This limits the risk that your FTP server could be subject to a DoS attack. You could also limit the data transfer volumes on your FTP server.

Examine the feasibility of using SSL/TLS for your FTP control and data connections. You will need to utilize FTP clients that support SSL/TLS.0

Chapter 11

One of the key reasons so many BIND servers are the targets of attacks is that a large number of vulnerabilities have been discovered in older versions of BIND. If you are running an older version of BIND, especially a version prior to BIND 8, you should upgrade immediately. You should keep your BIND version up-to-date and regularly monitor the CERT and BIND mailing lists and the ISC Web site for notifications of any vulnerabilities or issues.

When designing your DNS infrastructure, you should provide separate servers for your server and caching functions. This reduces the risk that an attack on one function will affect the other function. The same principle applies to your internal- and external-facing BIND servers. You should place your external BIND servers in a DMZ, protected by a firewall, or a similar network design. These servers should not also provide server or caching functions for your internal network. You should provide other servers, located on your internal network, for the provision of server and caching functions for your internal clients.

Always ensure you have suitable slave servers for all your master servers. For every domain for which you are authoritative, you should ensure you have at least one slave server that will able to resolve that domain in the event the master server is unavailable.

You should place your BIND installation in a `chroot` jail and run it as a nonprivileged user. This will help limit the risk that if an attacker compromises BIND that they will be able to do further damage on your host.

Use access control lists, created with `acl` statements, to centralize the management of whom has access to the functions of your BIND server. This allows you to specify your access controls at one source rather than having to update numerous options in your `named.conf` file.

Ensure you are logging enough information and that you regularly review your logs to check for anomalies. I recommend logging from your BIND daemon be directed to the `syslog` daemon.

Hide your BIND version using the `version` option in your `options` statement. Remember, if you want to log requests for your BIND version, then you need to configure a `bind chaos` class domain in your `named.conf` file.

Only allow trusted sources to perform functions, for example, recursion. Do not open your BIND server to recursive queries or caching functions from external sources. Only allow your internal, trusted networks to perform these functions. The only access external sources should have to your BIND servers is for the external resolution of domains for which your BIND servers are authoritative.

If you use the `rndc` command to control your BIND server, you should preferably allow access only to the local system. The `rndc` command authenticates to the BIND server using a key. You should protect your `rndc.conf` file to ensure an attacker cannot read or write to this file and potentially compromise the key.

Consider using TSIG to secure communications between your DNS servers. Using a key-based hash with your DNS transactions provides a greater level of confidence that you are communicating with the correct and authentic server. Remember you need to protect your TSIG keys by securing the permissions of your configuration files. If attackers compromise your keys, then they can impersonate the server with which you are communicating.

Index